teach®
yourself

latin and english
dictionary
alastair wilson BA

D0595973

For over 60 years, more than 40 million people have learnt over 750 subjects the **teach yourself** way, with impressive results.

be where you want to be
with **teach yourself**

For UK order enquiries: please contact Bookpoint Ltd., 130 Milton Park, Abingdon, Oxon OX14 4SB. Telephone: +44 (0) 1235 827720. Fax: +44 (0) 1235 400454. Lines are open 09.00–18.00, Monday to Saturday, with a 24-hour message answering service. Details about our titles and how to order are available at www.teachyourself.co.uk

For USA order enquiries: please contact McGraw-Hill Customer Services, PO Box 545, Blacklick, OH 43004-0545, USA. Telephone: 1-800-722-4726. Fax: 1-614-755-5645.

For Canada order enquiries: please contact McGraw-Hill Ryerson Ltd., 300 Water St, Whitby, Ontario L1N 9B6, Canada. Telephone: 905 430 5000. Fax: 905 430 5020.

Long renowned as the authoritative source for self-guided learning – with more than 30 million copies sold worldwide – the *Teach Yourself* series includes over 300 titles in the fields of languages, crafts, hobbies, business, computing and education.

British Library Cataloguing in Publication Data: a catalogue record for this title is available from The British Library.

Library of Congress Catalog Card Number: On file

First published in UK 1965 by Hodder Headline Ltd., 338 Euston Road, London NW1 3BH.

First published in US 1992 by Contemporary Books, a Division of the McGraw-Hill Companies, 1 Prudential Plaza, 130 East Randolph Street, Chicago, IL 60601, USA.

This edition published 2003.

The 'Teach Yourself' name is a registered trade mark of Hodder & Stoughton Ltd.

Copyright © 1965, 2003 Hodder & Stoughton

Typeset by Transet Limited, Coventry, England.
Printed in Great Britain for Hodder & Stoughton Educational, a division of Hodder Headline Ltd., 338 Euston Road, London NW1 3BH by Cox & Wyman Ltd., Reading, Berkshire.

Papers used in this book are natural, renewable and recyclable products. They are made from wood grown in sustainable forests. The logging and manufacturing processes conform to the environmental regulations of the country of origin.

Impression number   10 9 8 7 6 5 4 3 2 1
Year   2009 2008 2007 2006 2005 2004 2003

contents

introduction

The chief benefit that a knowledge of Latin confers is the ability to read the works of the Roman authors, particularly those of the Golden and Silver Ages of Latin Literature, i.e. 60 BC–AD 100. This dictionary has been compiled with this in mind, and also with an eye to the 'non-specialist'. To this end, the equivalents in the Latin–English section of the dictionary have been presented in as simple and 'modern' a form as possible, while at the same time the most important distinctions in meaning which each Latin word bears have been indicated. The vocabulary has been based on that commonly used by the authors of the period mentioned above, and a person who is acquainted with Latin grammar and the common forms of the Latin language should be able, with a little help from this dictionary, to read them without much difficulty. *Teach Yourself Latin Grammar*, by Gregory Klyve, may be of assistance to those who are not so acquainted, or whose memory has been dimmed by the passage of time.

In the English–Latin section, the Latin equivalent given is that which represents the best general meaning of the English, and which is used in that sense by a Classical author. Occasionally, however, where no exact Latin equivalent for an English word exists, it has been necessary to give a short circumlocution: in this case the phrase given is always translated into English, e.g. **disinterested** neutri favens (**favouring neither side**). Where several different meanings are borne by the same word, or where ambiguity may occur, care has been taken to differentiate between the various meanings, e.g. **order**, *nn*, (**arrangement**), ordo, *m*; (**in —**), *adj*, dispŏsĭtus; (**command, direction**), iussum, *n*; (**class, rank**), ordo, *m*; (**in — to**), ut.

Where fuller information is required about any of the words given in the dictionary, reference should be made to Lewis and Short's *Latin Dictionary* (Oxford University Press, 1963), available on line via the Perseus Digital Library, at **http://www.perseus.tufts.edu/**, which comprises a magnificent collection of primary and secondary Classical sources.

Advice on learning vocabulary

If you are gifted with a good memory, you will find it particularly easy to learn Latin vocabulary, especially if you try to link in your mind new Latin words and any English derivatives of them which you can think of, e.g. **mare**—sea—marine; **nauta**—ship—nautical. A high proportion of Latin words have quite common English derivatives. If you do this, not only will your interest in both languages grow, but you will begin to form an impression of the debt which our language owes to that of the Romans.

If on the other hand, you are one of those who find it difficult to make words stick, then here is a piece of simple advice – not to be despised because of its simplicity – which might help you to retain words in your memory. To learn a new word it is not only essential to find out and to understand its meaning, but also to see it working in relationship to other words, and to 'meet' it as many times as possible immediately after first acquaintance. It is therefore advisable to re-read the piece in which you originally met the word two or three times after you have learned it, and to make an effort to find the same word again within a day or two of first meeting it, otherwise you may find, on ultimately seeing it again, that it has 'gone'. Above all, try to maintain your interest in learning new vocabulary, for without such an interest no learning of real or lasting nature can take place.

Abbreviations used

( ) Brackets are used to indicate alternative forms.

See *Teach Yourself Latin Grammar*, by Gregory Klyve, for an explanation of the grammar terms used.

a, um   see adj.
abl.   ablative case.
acc.   accusative case.

acis } genitive singular ending of nouns indicating that they
atis } belong to the third declension.
adj.   adjective, **a, um, era, erum** after an adjective indicates
that it declines like a noun of the first or second declensions,
e that it declines like a noun of the third declension.
adv.   adverb. The adverb ending is often given, e.g. **e, iter, nter,
um, o,** and should be attached to the *stem* of the adjective,
e.g. **abditus** (*adj*); **abdite** (*adv*).
ae   genitive singular ending of a noun, indicating that it
belongs to the first declension.
arum   genitive plural ending, indicating that the noun belongs
to the first declension.
auxil.   auxiliary verb.
c.   common gender.
comp.   comparative adjective or adverb.
conj.   conjunction.
cris, cre   nominative feminine and neuter endings, indicating
that an adjective declines like a noun of the third declension.
cl.   clause.
dat.   dative case; also some verbs take a dative case after them.
defect.   a defective verb; i.e. it has not all its parts.
demonst.   demonstrative pronoun.
dep.   see v. dep.
e   see adj.
ei   genitive singular ending of noun, indicating that it belongs
to the fifth declension.
enis } genitive singular endings of nouns indicating that they
etis } belong to the third declension.
exclam.   exclamation.
f.   feminine gender.
f.pl.   feminine plural.
fut.   future.
genit.   genitive case.
i, ii   genitive singular ending of noun, indicating that it belongs
to the second declension.
icis } genitive singular endings of nouns indicating that they
inis } belong to the third declension.
impers.   impersonal verb.
indecl.   indeclinable.
inf.   infinitive.
interj.   interjective.
interr.   interrogative.
irreg.   irregular verb.
is   genitive singular of noun, indicating that it belongs to the
third declension.

iter   see adv.

itis   genitive singular ending of noun, indicating that it belongs to the third declension.

ium   genitive plural ending of noun, indicating that it belongs to the third declension.

m.   masculine gender.

m.pl.   masculine plural.

n.   neuter gender.

nn.   noun.

nter   see adv.

ntis   genitive singular ending of some nouns and adjectives of the third declension.

num   numeral.

n.pl.   neuter plural.

obj.   objective.

onis } genitive singular noun ending, indicating that the noun
oris } belongs to the second declension.

orum   genitive plural ending, indicating that a noun belongs to the second declension.

partic.   participle.

pass.   a passive verb, conjugated in the passive voice only.

perf.   perfect.

pers.   personal.

phr.   phrase.

pl.   plural.

poss.   possessive.

prep.   preposition: the case taken by the preposition is usually indicated.

pres.   present.

pron.   pronoun.

pron. adj.   pronominal adjective; a pronoun which declines and agrees like an adjective.

reflex.   reflexive.

rel.   relative.

semi-dep.   semi-deponent; verbs which are deponent in some of their tenses.

sup(erl).   superlative adjective or adverb.

tis } genitive singular ending of some nouns and adjs. of
tris } the third declension.

um   genitive plural ending of noun, indicating that it belongs to the third declension.

ūs   genitive singular ending of noun, indicating that it belongs to the fourth declension.

v. vb. verb. The conjugation to which a verb belongs is indicated by the figure 1, 2, 3, or 4. In the case of third conjugation verbs, and other verbs whose perfect stem and supine are not regular, these are given with the verb, e.g. **aboleo, evi, itum.** If none of these parts are given, it may be assumed that the verb is regularly conjugated; if some, but not all parts are given, it may be assumed that the ones not given are not in regular use.

v. dep. verb deponent.

v.i. verb intransitive, i.e. a verb which does not have a direct object.

v. impers. verb impersonal.

v.i.t. a verb which can be used intransitively or transitively. The separate uses are indicated by the use of the semi-colon, e.g. **abhorreo,** *v.i.t.*, 2, to shrink back (intransitive); to disagree with (transitive).

voc. vocative case.

v.t. verb transitive, i.e. a verb which has a direct object.

Alphabet

The Latin alphabet contained 23 letters:

A B C D E F G H I K L M N O P Q R S T V X Y Z

Pronunciation

Although there is not complete agreement about the way in which the Romans spoke Latin, this is one method of pronunciation which many people believe to have been used by the Romans.

Vowels

ă (short a) as in 'fat'; ā (long a) as in 'father'.

ĕ (short e) as in 'net'; ē (long e) as in 'they'.

ĭ (short i) as in 'pin'; ī (long i) as in 'police'.

ŏ (short o) as in 'not'; ō (long o) as in 'note'.

ŭ (short u) as 'oo' in 'wood'; ū (long u) as 'oo' in 'mood'.

Diphthongs

Two vowels pronounced together to form one sound are called diphthongs, e.g. ae, au, oe, and are pronounced as follows.

ae, as in 'ai' in 'aisle'.
au, as 'ow' in 'cow'.
oe, as in 'oi' in 'oil'.

Consonants

These are mostly pronounced as in English, but note:

c is always hard, as in 'cat'.
g is always hard, as in 'get'.
i, when it is used as a consonant, is always pronounced as 'y' in 'yellow' e.g. *iam*, 'yam'.
s is always pronounced as in 'son'.
t is always pronounced as in 'top'.
v is pronounced as 'w' in 'wall', e.g. *servi*, pronounced 'serwee'.
th is pronounced as 't' and *ch* as 'k'.

Latin–English dictionary

A

ā, ăb   *prep. with abl,* by (agent);
from (place, time); in, at
(position); since

ăbăcus, i   *m,* sideboard, counting
or gaming board, slab

ăbălīēno   *v.t.* 1, to estrange, make
a legal transfer

ăbăvus, i   *m,* great-great-
grandfather, ancestor

abdīcātĭo, ōnis   *f,* renunciation of
office

abdīco   *v.t.* 1, to resign

abdīco, xi, ctum   *v.t.* 3 to refuse
assent

abdĭtus, a, um   *adj, adv,* ē, hidden,
secret

abdo, didi, dĭtum   *v.t.* 3, to conceal

abdōmĕn, ĭnis   *n,* belly

abdūco, xi, ctum   *v.t.* 3, to lead
away

ăbĕo   *v.i.* 4, to go away

ăberro   *v.i.* 1, to go astray

ăbhinc   *adv,* ago

ăbhorrĕo   *v.i.t.* 2, to shrink back;
disagree with

ăbi   see **ăbĕo**

ăbĭcĭo, iēci, iectum   *v.t.* 3, to
throw away

abiectus, a, um   *adj, adv,* ē,
downcast

ăbīēgnus, a um   *adj,* made of fir

ăbĭēs, ĕtis   *f,* fir

ăbĭgo, ĕre, ēgi, actum   *v.t.* 3, to
drive away

ăbĭtĭo, ōnis   *f,* departure

abiūdico   *v.t.* 1, to deprive by
legal sentence

abiungo, nxi, nctum   *v.t.* 3, to
unyoke

abiūro   *v.t.* 1, to deny on oath

ablātus, a, um   *adj.* from **aufĕro,**
taken away

ablēgātĭo, ōnis   *f,* banishment

ablēgo   *v.t.* 1, to send away

ablŭo, ŭi, ūtum   *v.t.* 3, to wash
away

ablūtĭo, ōnis   *f,* ablution, washing

abnĕgo   *v.t.* 1, to refuse

abnormis, e   *adj,* irregular

abnŭo, ŭi, ūtum   *v.i.t.* 3, to refuse

ăbŏlĕo, ēvi, ĭtum   *v.t.* 2, to destroy

ăbŏlesco, ēvi   *v.i.* 3, to decay

ăbŏlītĭo, ōnis   *f,* abolition

ăbolla, ae   *f,* cloak

ăbōmĭnor   *v.t.* 1, *dep,* to wish
away (being ominous)

ăbŏrīgĭnes, um   *m.pl,* natives

ăbortĭo, ōnis   *f,* miscarriage

ăbortus, ūs   *m,* abortion

abrādo, si, sum   *v.t.* 3, to scrape
off

abrĭpĭo, ŭi, reptum   *v.t.* 3, to drag
away

abrōdo, si, sum   *v.t.* 3, to gnaw
away

abrŏgātĭo, ōnis   *f,* repeal

abrŏgo   *v.t.* 1, to repeal

abrumpo, rūpi, ruptum   *v.t.* 3, to
break off

abruptus, a, um   *adj,* steep

abscēdo, cessi, cessum   *v.i.* 3, to
go away

abscīdo, cīdi, scīsum   *v.t.* 3, to cut
off

abscindo, scĭdi, scissum   *v.t.* 3, to
tear away

abscīsus, a, um   *adj, adv,* ē, steep

abscondĭtus, a, um   *adj, adv,* ē,
hidden

abscondo, di, dĭtum   *v.t.* 3, to
conceal

absens, entis   *adj,* absent

absentĭa, ae   *f,* absence

absĭlĭo   *v.i.* 4, to jump away

absĭmĭlis, e   *adj,* unlike

absinthium, ii   *n,* absinth

absisto, stĭti   *v.i.* 3, to stand aloof

absŏlūtĭo, ōnis   *f,* acquittal

absŏlūtus, a, um   *adj, adv,* ē,
discordant

absolvo, vi. sŏlūtum   *v.t.* 3, to
unfasten, acquit

absŏnus, a, um   *adj, adv,* ē,
discordant

absorbĕo, bŭi, ptum   *v.t.* 2, to
swallow up

absquĕ   *prep. with abl,* without

abstēmĭus, a, um   *adj,* sober

abstergĕo, rsi, rsum   *v.t.* 2, to
wipe off

absterrĕo   *v.t.* 2, to frighten away

abstinens, ntis   *adj, adv,* nter,
temperate

abstĭnentĭa, ae   *f,* self-restraint

abstĭnĕo, ŭi, tentum   *v.i.t.* 2, to abstain from; restrain

abstrăho, xi, ctum   *v.t.* 3, to drag away

abstrūdo, si, sum   *v.t.* 3, to push away

abstrūsus, a, um   *adj, adv,* ē, hidden

absum, esse, abfui (afui)   *v.i. irreg,* to be absent

absūmo, mpsi, mptum   *v.t.* 3, to take away, use up

absurdus, a, um   *adj, adv,* ē, stupid, tuneless

ăbundans, ntis   *adj, adv,* nter, plentiful

ăbundantĭa, ae   *f,* plenty

ăbundo   *v.i.* 1, to overflow

ăbūtor, i, usus sum   *v.* 3, *dep, with abl,* to use up, abuse

āc   *conj,* and

ăcācĭa, ae   *f,* acacia

ăcădēmĭa, ae   *f,* academy

accēdo, cessi, cesssum   *v.i.* 3, to approach

accĕlĕro   *v.i.t.* 1, to hurry; quicken

accendo, ndi, nsum   *v.t.* 3, to set on fire

accensĕo, ŭi, nsum   *v.t.* 2, to add to

accensus, i   *m,* attendant

accentus, ūs   *m,* accentuation

acceptĭo, ōnis   *f,* acceptance

acceptum, i   *n,* receipt

acceptus, a, um   *adj,* agreeable

accessĭo, ōnis   *f,* approach, increase

accessus, ūs   *m,* approach

accīdo, cīdi, cīsum   *v.t.* 3, to cut

accĭdo, cĭdi   *v.i.* 3, to fall upon, happen

accingo, nxi, nctum   *v.t.* 3, to equip, put on

accĭo   *v.t.* 4, to summon

accĭpĭo, cēpi, ceptum   *v.t.* 3, to receive

accĭpĭter, tris   *m,* hawk

accītus, ūs   *m,* summons

acclāmātĭo, ōnis   *f,* shout

acclāmo   *v.t.* 1, to shout at

acclīnis, e   *adj,* leaning on

acclīno   *v.t.* 1, to lean

acclīvis, e   *adj,* uphill

acclīvĭtas, ātis   *f,* ascent

accŏla, ae   *c,* neighbour

accŏlo, cŏlui, cultum   *v.t.* 3, to live near

accommŏdātus, a, um   *adj, adv,* ē, suitable

accommŏdātĭo, ōnis   *f,* compliance

accommŏdo   *v.t.* 1, to adapt

accommŏdus, a, um   *adj,* suitable

accresco, crēvi, crētum   *v.i.* 3, to grow

accrētĭo, ōnis   *f,* increase

accŭbĭtĭo, ōnis   *f,* reclining

accŭbo   *v.i.* 1, to lie near, recline at table

accumbo, cŭbŭi, cŭbĭtum   *v.i.* 3, to lie near, recline at table

accŭmŭlo   *v.t.* 1, to heap up

accūro   *v.t.* 1, to take care of

accūrātus, a, um   *adj, adv,* ē, prepared carefully, precise

accurro, curri, cursum   *v.i.* 3, to run to

accūsātĭo, ōnis   *f,* accusation

accūsātor, ōris   *m,* accuser

accūso   *v.t.* 1, to accuse

ācer, cris, e   *adj, adv,* ĭter, keen

ăcer, ĕris   *n,* maple tree

ăcerbĭtas, ātis   *f,* bitterness

ăcerbo   *v.t.* 1, to embitter

ăcerbus, a, um   *adj,* bitter, keen

ăcernus, a, um   *adj,* made of maple

ăcerra, ae   *f,* incense-box

ăcervo   *v.t.* 1, to heap up

ăcervus, i   *m,* heap

ăcētārĭa, ōrum   *n.pl,* salad

ăcētum, i   *n,* vinegar

ăcīdus, a, um   *adj, adv,* ē, sour

ăcĭes, ēi   *f,* edge, pupil of eye, battle line, keeness

ăcĭnăces, is   *m,* scimitar

ăcĭnus, i   *m* (um, i   *n*), berry

ăcĭpenser, ĕris   *m,* sturgeon

aclys, ўdis   *f,* small javelin

ăcŏnītum, i   *n,* aconite

acquĭesco, ēvi, ĕtum   *v.i.* 3, to rest, aquiesce

acquīro, sīvi, sītum   *v.t.* 3, to procure

ācrĭmōnĭa, ae   *f,* sharpness

ācrĭter *adv*, keenly
acta, ōrum *n.pl* acts, records
actĭo, ōnis *f*, act, legal action
actor, ōris *m*, driver, plaintiff, performer
actŭarĭus, a, um *adj*, swift
actŭārĭus, i *m*, notary
actum, i *n*, deed
actus, a, um see ăgo
actus, ūs *m*, impulse, act (of drama)
ăcūlĕātus, a, um *adj*, prickly
ăcūlĕus, i *m*, sting
ăcūmĕn, ĭnis *n*, point, sting
ăcŭo, ŭi, ūtum *v.t.* 3, to sharpen
ăcus, ūs *f*, needle, pin
ăcūtus, a, um *adj, adv*, ē, sharp
ad *prep. with acc*, to, towards, near (place), about (time), for (purpose)
ădaequo *v.i.t.* 1, to be equal; to make equal
ădaequo *v.i.t.* 1, to be equal; to make equal
ădămas, ntis *m*, steel, diamond
ădămo *v.t.* 1, to love deeply
ădăpĕrĭo, ŭi, rtum *v.t.* 4, to open fully
ădaugĕo, xi, ctum *v.t.* 2, to increase
addīco, xi, ctum *v.t.* 3, to assent, award
addictĭo, ōnis *f*, adjudication
addictus, a, um *adj*, dedicated
addo, dĭdi, dĭtum *v.t.* 3, to add to
addŭbĭto *v.i.t.* 1, to doubt
addūco, xi, ctum *v.t.* 3, to lead to, influence
ădemptĭo, ōnis *f*, seizure
ădĕo *v.i.* 4, to approach, attack
ădĕo *adv*, so much, so long
ădeps, ĭpis *c*, fat
ădeptĭo, ōnis *f*, attainment
ădĕquĭto *v.i.* 1, to gallop up
ădhaerĕo, si, sum *v.i.* 2, to cling to
ădhaeresco, si, sum *v.i.* 3, to cling to
ădhĭbĕo *v.t.* 2, to apply, invite
ădhortātĭo, ōnis *f*, encouragement
ădhortor *v.t.* 1, *dep*, to encourage
ădhuc *adv*, still
adiăcĕo *v.i.* 2, to adjoin
adīcĭo, iēci, iectum *v.t.* 3, to throw to, add to
ădīgo, ēgi, actum *v.t.* 3, to drive to, compel
ădīmo, ēmi, emptum *v.t.* 3, to take away
ădĭpiscor, eptus *v.t.* 3, *dep*, to obtain
ădītus, ūs *m*, approach
adiūdīco *v.t.* 1, to assign
adiūmentum, i *n*, assistance
adiunctĭo, ōnis *f*, union
adiungo, xi, ctum *v.t.* 3, to join to
adiūro *v.t.* 1, to swear, confirm
adiūtor, ōris *m*, helper
adiŭvo, iūvi, iūtum *v.t.* 1, to precipitate
admētĭor, mensus *v.t.* 4, *dep*, to measure out
admĭnĭcŭlum, i *n*, prop
admĭnister, tri *m*, servant
admĭnistrātĭo, ōnis *f*, aid, management, arrangement
admĭnistro *v.t.* 1, to assist, manage
admīrābilis, e *adj, adv*, ĭter, wonderful
admīrātĭo, ōnis *f*, admiration
admīror *v.t.* 1, *dep*, to wonder at
admiscĕo, scŭi, xtum *v.t.* 2, to mix with
admissārĭus, ii *m*, stallion
admissĭo, ōnis *f*, reception
admissum, i *n*, fault
admitto, mīsi, ssum *v.t.* 3, to let in, let go, incur, commit
admixtĭo, ōnis *f*, mixture
admŏdum *adv*, up to the limit, very much, nearly
admŏnĕo *v.t.* 2, to remind
admŏnĭtĭo, ōnis *f*, warning
admŏnĭtus, ūs *m*, suggestion
admordĕo, di, sum *v.t.* 2, to bite at
admōtĭo, ōnis *f*, application
admŏvĕo, mōvi, mōtum *v.t.* 2, to conduct, assault
admurmŭrātĭo, ōnis *f*, murmur
admurmŭro *v.i.* 1, to murmur at
adn- see ann...
ădŏlĕo, ŭi, ultum *v.i.* 3, to grow up
ădŏlescens, ntis *adj*, young
ădŏlescens, ntis *c*, young person
ădŏlescentĭa, ae *f*, youth

ădŏlescentŭlus, i *m*, very young man

ădŏlesco, ēvi, ultum *v.i.* 3, to grow up

ădŏpĕrĭo, ŭi, rtum *v.t.* 4, to cover up

ădoptātĭo, ōnis *f*, adoption

ădoptĭo, ōnis *f*, adoption

ădoptīvus, a, um *adj*, adoptive

ădopto *v.t.* 1, to choose, adopt

ădor, ŏris *n*, grain

ădōrātĭo, ōnis *f*, adoption

ădōrĕa, ae *f*, reward for bravery

ădŏrĭor, ortus *v.t.* 4, *dep*, to attack, undertake

ădorno *v.t.* 1, to equip, decorate

ădōro *v.t.* 1, to worship, entreat

adrādo, si, sum *v.t.* 3, to shave

adsum, esse, adfui *v.i*, *irreg*, to be near

ads… see ass…

ădūlātĭo, ōnis *f*, flattery

ădūlātor, ōris *m*, flatterer

ădūlor *v.t.* 1, *dep*, to flatter

ădulter, ĕri *m*, adulterer

ădultĕra, ae *f*, adulteress

ădultĕrātĭo, ōnis *f*, adulteration

ădultĕrīnus, a, um *adj*, false

ădultĕrĭum, ii *n*, adultery

ădultĕro *v.i.t.* 1, to commit adultery; to falsify, pollute

ădultus, a, um *adj*, grown up

ădumbrātĭo, ōnis *f*, sketch

ădumbro *v.t.* 1, to sketch

ăduncus, a, um *adj*, hooked

ădurgĕo *v.t.* 2, to press

ădūro, ssi, stum *v.t.* 3, to scorch

ădusque *prep. with acc*, right up to

ădusta, ōrum *n.pl*, burns

ădustus, a, um *adj*, burnt

advĕho, xi, ctum *v.t.* 3, to carry to

advĕna, ae *c*, stranger

advĕnĭo, vēni, ventum *v.t.* 4, to reach

advento *v.t.* 1, to approach

adventus, ūs *m*, arrival

adversārĭus, ii *m*, opponent

adversārĭus, a, um *adj*, opposite, opposing

adversor *v.* 1, *dep*, *with dat*, to oppose

adversus, a, um *adj*, opposite; (of winds) contrary

adversus *prep. with acc*, opposite

adversum *adv*, opposite

adverto, ti, sum *v.t.* 3, to direct towards

advespĕrascit, avit *v. impers*, evening approaches

advĭgĭlo *v.i.* 1, to keep watch

advŏcātĭo, ōnis *f*, summons, legal assistance

advŏcātus, i *m*, legal adviser

advŏco *v.t.* 1, to call, summon help

advŏlo *v.i.* 1, to fly towards

advolvo, vi, ūtum *v.t.* 3, to roll, grovel before

ădўtum, i *n*, sanctuary

aedēs, is *f*, temple, house

aedĭcŭla, ae *f*, shrine, niche

aedĭfĭcātor, ōris *m*, builder

aedĭfĭcĭum, ii *n*, building

aedĭfĭcātĭo, ōnis *f*, constructing

aedĭfĭco *v.t.* 1, to build

aedīlĭcĭus, a, um *adj*, of an aedile

aedīlis, is *m*, aedile – Roman magistrate

aedīlĭtas, ātis *f*, aedileship

aedĭtŭus, i *m*, verger

aeger, ra, rum *adj*, ill, sad

aegis, ĭdis *f*, shield

aegrē *adv*, with difficulty, scarcely, amiss, with displeasure

aegresco *v.i.* 3, to fall ill

aegrĭtūdo, ĭnis *f*, illness, grief

aegrŏtātĭo, ōnis *f*, sickness

aegrōto *v.i.* 1, to be ill

aegrōtus, a, um *adj*, ill

aemŭlātĭo, ōnis *f*, rivalry

aemŭlor *v.t.* 1, *dep*, to rival, envy

aemŭlus, a, um *adj*, rivalling

aēnĕus, a, um *adj*, of bronze

aenigma, ătis *n*, riddle

aequābĭlĭs, e *adj*, *adv*, ĭter, similar, uniform

aequābĭlĭtas, ātis *f*, equality

aequaevus, a, um *adj*, of equal age

aequālis, e *adj*, *adv*, ĭter, level, contemporary

aequālĭtas, ātis *f*, uniformity

aequē *adv*, equally, justly

aequĭlĭbrĭum, ii *n*, horizontal position

aequĭnoctĭum, i *n,* equinox
aequĭpăro *v.i.t.* 1, to equal; compare
aequĭtas, ātis *f,* equality, fariness, calmness
aequo *v.i.t.* 1, to equalize; match, raze
aequor, ŏris *n,* even surface, sea
aequum, i *n,* plain, justice
aequus, a, um *adj,* flat, friendly, equal, reasonable
āēr, ris *m,* air
aerārĭa, ae *f,* mine
aerārĭum, i *n,* treasury
aerārĭus, a, um *adj,* of bronze, of the treasury
aerātus, a, um *adj,* bronze covered
aerĕus, a, um *adj,* of bronze
aerĭpes, ĕdis *adj,* bronze-footed
āērĭus, a, um *adj,* lofty
aerūgo, ĭnis *f,* rust, envy
aerumna, ae *f,* suffering
aerumnōsus, a, um *adj,* wretched
aes, aeris *n,* copper, money
aescŭlētum, i *n,* oak-forest
aescŭlĕus, a, um *adj,* oaken
aescŭlus, i *f,* oak
aestas, ātis *f,* summer
aestĭfer, ĕra, ĕrum *adj,* hot, sultry
aestĭmābĭlis, e *adj,* valuable
aestĭmātĭo, ōnis *f,* valuation
aestĭmātor, ōris *m,* valuer
aestĭmo *v.t.* 1, to value, assess
aestīva, ōrum *n.pl,* summer camp
aestīvus, a, um *adj, adv,* ē, summer-like
aestŭārĭum, ii *n,* creek, air-hole
aestŭo *v.i.* 1, to seethe, glow
aestŭōsus, a, um *adj, adv,* ē, sweltering
aestus, ŭs *m,* heat, tide, rage, excitement
aetas, ātis *f,* age, lifetime
aetātŭla, ae *f,* tender age
aeternĭtas, ātis *f,* eternity
aeternus, a, um *adj, adv,* um, everlasting
aether, ĕris *m,* upper air, heaven
aethĕrĭus, a, um *adj,* celestial
Aethĭops, ŏpis *m,* Aethiopian, negro
aethra, ae *f,* upper air

aevum, i *n,* lifetime, generation
affābĭlis, e *adj, adv,* ĭter, courteous
affătim *adv,* enough
affātus *partic. from* **affor**
affectātĭo, ōnis *f,* pretension, whim
affectātus, a, um *adj* far-fetched
affectĭo, ōnis *f,* disposition, whim
affecto *v.t.* 1, to strive after
affectus, ūs *m,* mood, sympathy
affĕro, afferre, attŭli, allātum *v.t, irreg,* to bring to, announce, help, produce, confer
affĭcĭo, affēci, ctum *v.t.* 3, to influence, seize
affigo, xi, xum *v.t.* 3, to fasten to
affingo, nxi, ictum *v.t.* 3, to add to, fabricate
affinis, e *adj,* neighbouring, related
affinĭtas, ātis *f,* kinship
affirmātē *adv,* explicitly
affirmātĭo, ōnis *f,* assertion
affirmo *v.t.* 1, to assert
affixus, a, um *adj,* fastened to
afflātus, ūs *m,* breath, blast
afflicto *v.t.* 1, to trouble, shatter
afflictus, a, um *adj,* damaged, prostrate
affligo, xi, ctum *v.t.* 3, to dash to the ground, damage
afflo *v.t.* 1, to breathe on, inspire
afflŭens, ntis *adj, adv,* nter, rich in
afflŭo, xi, xum *v.i.* 3, to flow towards, flock in
affor *v.t.* 1, to speak to, accost
affulgĕo, ulsi *v.i.* 2, to shine on
affundo, ūdi, ūsum *v.t.* 3, to pour on, in
Āfrĭcus (ventus) S.W. wind
āfui see **absum**
ăgāso, ōnis *m,* groom
ăgĕ! come on!
ăgellus, i *m,* small field
ăgens, ntis *adj,* powerful
ăger, gri *m,* field, territory
agger, ĕris *m,* mound, rampart
aggĕro, ssi stum *v.t.* 3, to convey
aggĕro *v.t.* 1, to heap up
agglŏmĕro *v.t.* 1, to add to
aggrăvo *v.t.* 1, to make heavier or worse

aggrĕdior, grĕssus *v.t.* 3, *dep,* to approach, attack, undertake
aggrĕgo *v.t.* 1, to adhere, join
aggressus see **aggrĕdior**
ăgĭlis, e *adj, adv,* ĭter, active
ăgĭlĭtas, ātis *f,* activity
ăgĭtātĭo, ōnis *f,* quick movement, contemplation
ăgĭtātor, ōris *m,* charioteer
ăgĭtātus, a, um *adj,* driven, dogged
ăgĭto *v.t.* 1, to drive, shake, swing, torment, mock, consider
agmen, ĭnis *n,* marching column
agna, ae *f,* ewe lamb
agnātus, a, um *adj,* related (male line)
agnĭtĭo, ōnis *f,* recognition
agnōmen, ĭnis *n,* surname, additional name
agnosco, nŏvi, ĭtum *v.t.* 3, to recognize, acknowledge
agnus, i *m,* lamb
ăgo, ēgi, actum *v.t.* 3, to drive, steal, bring, do, negotiate, pass (time), act, lead (life)
ăgrārĭus, a, um *adj,* agrarian
ăgrārĭi, ōrum *m.pl,* land reformers
ăgrestis is *m,* peasant
ăgrestis, e *adj,* rural, coarse
agrĭcŏla, ae *m,* farmer, countryman
agrĭcultūra, ae *f,* agriculture
āio *v, defect,* to assert
āla, ae *f,* wing, armpit, porch
ălăcer, cris, e *adj, adv,* ĭter, brisk, vigorous
ălăcrĭtas, ātis *f,* briskness
ălăpa, ae *f,* slap
ălauda, ae *f,* lark
albārĭum, ii *n,* whitewash
albātus, a, um *adj,* clothed in white
albĕo *v.i.* 2, to be white
albesco *v.i.* 3, to become white
album, i *n,* whiteness, register
albus, a, um *adj,* white
alces, is *f,* elk
alcēdo, ĭnis *f,* kingfisher
alcўon, ōnis *f,* kingfisher
alcўonēus, a, um *adj,* halcyon
ālĕa, ae *f,* gambling, a game with dice, chance, hazard

ālĕātor, ōris *m,* gambler
ālĕs, ĭtis *adj,* winged
ālĕs, ĭtis *c,* bird
alga, ae *f,* seaweed
algĕo, si *v.i.* 2, to feel cold
algĭdus, a, um *adj,* cold
algor, ōris *m,* coldness
ălĭā *adv,* in a different way
ălĭās ... ălĭās *adv,* at one time ... at another time, otherwise
ălĭbi *adv,* elsewhere
ălĭcŭbi *adv,* somewhere
ălĭcunde *adv,* from somewhere
ălĭēnātĭo, ōnis *f,* transfer, aversion, delirium
ălĭēnātus, a, um *adj,* alienated
ălĭēnĭgĕna, ae *m,* foreigner
ălĭēno *v.t.* 1, to transfer, estrange
ălĭēnus, a, um *adj,* someone else's, strange, hostile, unsuitable
ălĭēnus, i *m,* stranger
ălĭēnum, i *n,* stranger's property
ālĭger, ĕra, ĕrum *adj,* winged
ălĭi see **ălĭus**
ălĭmentum, i *n,* nourishment
ălĭmōnĭum, ii *n,* nourishment
ălĭō *adv,* to another place
ălĭōqui(n) *adv,* in other respects
ālĭpēs, ĕdis *adj,* wing-footed
ălĭquā *adv,* somehow
ălĭquamdĭu *adv,* for some time
ălĭquando *adv,* at some time
ălĭquantus, a, um *adj, adv,* ō, um, somewhat, some
ălĭqui, qua, quod *pron, adj,* some, any
ălĭquis, quid *pron,* someone, something
ălĭquō *adv,* to some place
ălĭquot *adj,* several
ălĭquŏtĭes *adv,* at different times
ălĭter *adv,* otherwise
ălĭunde *adv,* from elsewhere
ălĭus, a, ud *pron, adj,* other, different
allābor, psus *v.* 3, *dep,* to glide, flow towards
allapsus, ūs *m,* stealthy approach
allātro *v.t.* 1, to bark at
allecto *v.t.* 1, to entice
allēgo *v.t.* 1, to commission
allēgo, ēgi, ectum *v.t.* 3, to elect
allēgŏrĭa, ae *f,* allegory

allěvātǐo, ōnis *f,* raising up
allěvo *v.t.* 1, to lift up, relieve
allícǐo, exi, ectum *v.t.* 3, to attract
allīdo, si, sum *v.t.* 3, to strike
allīgo *v.t.* 1, to bind, fasten
allīno, ēvi, ĭtum *v.t.* 3, to bedaub
allĭum, i *n,* garlic
allŏcūtǐo, ōnis *f,* address
allŏquǐum, ii *n,* exhortation
allŏquor, lŏcūtus *v.t.* 3, *dep,* to speak to, exhort, console
allūdo, si, sum *v.i.t.* 3, to play, joke; sport with
allŭo, ŭi *v.t.* 3, to wash against, bathe
allŭvǐes, ēi *f,* pool
allŭvǐo, ōnis *f,* inundation
almus, a, um *adj,* nourishing, kind
alnus, i *f,* alder
ălo, ŭi, altum *v.t.* 3, to nourish, cherish, encourage
alŏē, ēs *f,* aloe
alpīnus, a, um *adj,* Alpine
alsǐus, a, um *adj,* cold, chilly
alsus, a, um *adj,* cold, chilly
altāre, altāris *n,* high altar
altārǐa, ǐum *n.pl,* high altar
alter, ĕra, ĕrum *adj,* one or the other of two, second
altercātǐo, ōnis *f,* dispute
altercor *v.i.* 1, *dep,* to quarrel
alterno *v.i.t.* 1, to hesitate; alternate
alternus, a, um *adj,* alternate
altĕrŭter, ra, rum *adj,* one or the other, either
altĭlis, e *adj,* fattened, rich
altĭsŏnus, a, um *adj,* high sounding
altĭtūdo, ĭnis *f,* height, depth
altor, ōris *m,* foster-father
altrix, īcis *f,* foster-mother
altum, i *n,* the deep (sea)
altus, a, um *adj,* high, deep, great
ālūcĭnor *v.i.* 1, *dep,* to wander in the mind
ălumna, ae *f,* foster-child
ălumnus, i *m,* foster-child
ălūta, ae *f,* soft leather
alvĕārǐum, ii *n,* beehive
alvĕus, i *m,* salver, channel, canoe

alvus, i *f,* belly, stomach
ămābĭlis, e *adj, adv,* ĭter, lovable, amiable
āmando *v.t.* 1, to remove
ămans, ntis *adj,* fond
ămans, ntis *m,* lover
ămārĭtǐes, ēi *f,* bitterness
ămārus, a, um *adj,* bitter
ămātor, ōris *m,* lover
ămātōrǐum, ii *n,* love-philtre
ămātōrǐus, a, um *adj,* amatory
ambactus, i *m,* vassal
ambāges, is *f,* roundabout way
ambĭgo *v.i.* 3, to waver, go about
ambĭgǔĭtas, ātis *f,* double sense
ambĭgǔum, i *n,* uncertainty
ambĭgǔus, a, um *adj, adv,* ē, doubtful, changeable
ambǐo *v.i.t.* 4, to go round; solicit
ambĭtǐo, ōnis *f,* canvassing
ambĭtǐōsus, a, um *adj, adv,* ē, embracing, fawning
ambĭtus, ūs *m,* going round, circuit, bribery
ambō, ae, ō *adj,* both
ambrŏsǐa, ae *f,* food of the gods
ambrŏsǐus, a, um *adj,* immortal
ambŭlātǐo, ōnis *f,* walk
ambŭlātor, ōris *m,* walker
ambŭlo *v.i.* 1, to walk, lounge
ambūro, ssi, stum *v.t.* 3, to singe
ambustum, i *n,* burn
amellus, i *m,* star-wort
āmens, ntis *adj,* out of one's mind
āmentǐa, ae *f,* madness
āmentum, i *n,* strap
ămĕs, ĭtis *m,* pole, shaft
ămĕthystus, i *f,* amethyst
ămīca, ae *f,* mistress
ămĭcǐo, ŭi, ctum *v.t.* 4, to wrap
ămīcǐtǐa, ae *f,* friendship
ămictus, ūs *m,* cloak
ămīcŭlum, i *n,* cloak
ămīcus, i *m,* friend
ămīcus, a, um *adj, adv,* ē, friendly
āmissǐo, ōnis *f,* loss
ămīta, ae *f,* paternal aunt
āmitto, misi, missum *v.t.* 3, to let go, dismiss, lose
amnis, is *m,* river
ămo *v.t.* 1, to love, like
ămoenĭtas, ātis *f,* pleasantness

ămoenus, a, um   *adj, adv,* ē,
  charming
āmōlĭor   *v.t.* 4, *dep,* to remove,
  refute
ămor, ōris   *m,* love, desire
āmŏvĕo, mōvi, tum   *v.t.* 2, to
  remove
amphĭthĕātrum, i   *n,* amphitheatre
amphŏra, ae   *f,* two-handled jar
amplector, xus   *v.t.* 3, *dep,* to
  embrace
amplexus, ūs   *m,* embrace
amplĭfĭcātĭo, ōnis   *f,* enlargement
amplĭfĭco   *v.t.* 1, to enlarge
amplĭo   *v.t.* 1, to enlarge
amplĭtūdo, ĭnis   *f,* width, size
amplĭus   *comp. adv,* more
amplus, a, um   *adj, adv,* ē, ĭter,
  spacious, great, glorious
ampulla, ae   *f,* bottle
ampŭtātĭo, ōnis   *f,* pruning
ampŭto   *v.t.* 1, to cut away
ămurca, ae   *f,* dregs of oil
ămўlum, i   *n,* starch
ăn   *conj,* or: also used to
  introduce a question
ănăphŏră, ae   *f,* recurrence
ănăs, ătis   *f,* duck
ănătĭcŭla, ăe   *f,* duckling
anceps, cĭpĭtĭs   *adj,* two-headed,
  doubtful
ancīle, is   *n,* oval shield
ancilla, ae   *f,* maidservant
ancŏrāle, is   *n,* cable
ānellus, i   *m,* small ring
anfractus, ūs   *m,* circuitous route,
  digression
angīna, ae   *f,* quinsy
angĭportus, ūs   *m,* alley
ango, xi, ctum   *v.t.* 3, to strangle,
  torment
angor, ōris   *m,* strangling, distress
anguilla, ae   *f,* eel
anguĭnĕus, a, um   *adj,* snaky
anguĭpēs, ĕdis   *adj,* snake-footed
anguĭs, is   *c,* snake
angŭlātus, a, um   *adj,* angular
angŭlāris, e   *adj,* angular
angŭlus, i   *m,* corner
angustĭae, ārum   *f.pl.,* defile,
  straits, difficulties
angustus, a, um   *adj, adv,* ē,
  narrow, difficult

ănhēlĭtus, ūs   *m,* panting, vapour
ănhēlo   *v.i.t.* 1, to pant; exhale
ănhēlus, a, um   *adj,* panting
ănĭcŭla, ae   *f,* little old woman
ănīlis, e   *adj, adv,* ĭter, old
  womanish
ănĭma, ae   *f,* breeze, breath, life,
  soul
ănĭmadversĭo, ōnis   *f,* attention,
  reproof
ănĭmadverto, ti, sum   *v.t.* 3, to pay
  attention to, notice, punish
ănĭmăl, ālis   *n,* animal
ănĭmālis, e   *adj, adv,* ĭter, of air,
  living
ănĭmans, ntis   *adj,* living
ănĭmātus, a, um   *adj,* disposed,
  courageous
ănĭmo   *v.i.t.* 1, to have life; revive,
  give life to
ănĭmōsus, a, um   *adj, adv,* ē, bold
ănĭmōsus, a, um   *adj,* gusty,
  living, spirited
ănĭmus, i   *m,* soul, mind, memory,
  opinion, anger, purpose, courage,
  attitude
annāles, ĭum   *m.pl,* chronicles
annālis, e   *adj,* annual
annĕ   introduces a question
annecto, xŭi, xum   *v.t.* 3, to fasten
  to, add
annītor, nīsus nixus   *v.i.* 3, *dep,* to
  lean against, exert oneself
ănnivversārĭus, a, um   *adj,*
  anniversary
anno   *v.i.* 1, to swim to
annon   *conj,* or not
annōna, ae   *f,* annual produce,
  grain price
annōsus, a, um   *adj,* old
annŏtātĭo, ōnis   *f,* annotation,
  note
annŏto   *v.t.* 1, to note down
annŭa, ōrum   *n.pl,* annuity
annŭmĕro   *v.t.* 1, to pay, include
annŭo, ŭi, ŭtum   *v.i.* 3, to nod,
  assent
annus, i   *m,* year
annŭus, a, um   *adj,* annual, yearly
ănōmălĭa, ae   *f,* anomaly
anquīro, sīvi, sītum   *v.t.* 3, to
  search for
ansa, ae   *f,* handle, opportunity

anser, ĕris *m*, goose

antĕ *prep. with acc*, before, in front of

antĕ (antĕā) *adv*, before

antĕcēdo, ssi, ssum *v.i.t.* 3, to distinguish oneself; precede

antĕcello *v.i.t.* 3, to be outstanding; surpass

antĕcessĭo, ōnis *f*, antecedent

antĕcursor, ōris *m*, advanced guard

antĕ-ĕo *v.i.* 4, to go before, excel

antĕfĕro, ferre, tŭli, lātum *v.t, irreg*, to carry in front, prefer

antĕgrĕdĭor, gressus *v.t.* 3, *dep*, to go in front

antĕhāc *adv*, previously

antĕlūcānus, a, um *adj*, before day-break

antĕmĕrīdĭānus, a, um *adj*, before midday

antĕmitto, mīsi, missum *v.t.* 3, to send on

antenna, ae *f*, sail-yard

antĕpōno, pŏsŭi, ĭtum *v.t.* 3, to place in front

antĕquam *conj*, before

antēris, ĭdis *f*, buttress (pl.)

antes, ĭum *m.pl.* ranks

antĕsignānus, i *m*, in front of the standard, selected soldier

antesto, ĕti *v.i.* 1, to stand before, excel

antestor *v.* 1, *dep*, to call a witness

antĕverto, ti, sum *v.t.* 3, to precede, anticipate

anthrōpŏphăgus, i *m*, cannibal

antīcus, a, um *adj*, foremost

antīcĭpo *v.t.* 1, to anticipate

antīdŏtum, i *n*, remedy

antīpŏdes, um *m.pl*, antipodes

antīquĭtas, ātis *f*, age, olden times

antīqui, ōrum *m.pl*, old writers

antīquus, a, um *adj, adv*, ē, old

antistĕs, ĭtis *m*,   *f*, high priest

antistīta, ae *f*, high priestess

antlīa, ae *f*, pump

antrum, i *n*, cave

ānŭlus, i *m*, ring

ănus, ūs *f*, old woman

anxīĕtas, ātis *f*, anxiety

anxĭus, a, um *adj, adv, ē*, troubled

ăpăgĕ! *interj*, begone

ăper, pri *m*, wild boar

ăpĕrĭo, rŭi, rtum *v.t.* 4, to open, explain

ăpertus, a, um *adj, adv, ē*, open, frank

ăpex, ĭcis *m*, summit, crown

ăpis, is *f*, bee

ăpiscor, aptus *v.t.* 3, *dep*, to reach for, acquire

ăpĭum, ii *n*, parsley

āplustre, is *n*, stern

ăpo, (no perf.) aptum *v.t.* 3, to fasten

ăpŏcha, ae *f*, receipt

ăpŏthēca, ae *f*, store-place

appărātĭo, ōnis *f*, preparation

appărātus, a, um *adj, adv, ē*, ready, elaborate

appărātus, ūs *m*, preparation, apparatus, pomp

appārĕo *v.i.* 2, to appear

appārĭtĭo, ōnis *f*, service

appārĭtor, ōris *m*, public servant

appăro *v.t.* 1, to prepare

appellātĭo, ōnis *f*, calling appeal, title

appellātor, ōris *m*, appellant

appellātus, a, um *adj*, called

appello, ŭli, ulsum *v.t.* 3, to drive towards, land

appello *v.t.* 1, to speak to, appeal to, name

appendix, ĭcis *f*, supplement

appendo, ndi, nsum *v.t.* 3, to weigh

appĕtens, ntis *adj, adv, nter*, eager for

appĕtentĭa, ae *f*, desire

appĕtītĭo, ōnis *f*, desire

appĕtītus, ūs *m*, attack, passion

appĕto, ii, ītum *v.i.t.* 3, to approach; strive after

applĭcātĭo, ōnis *f*, inclination

applĭco *v.t.* 1, to affix, attach, steer

appōno, pŏsŭi, sĭtum *v.t.* 3, to put near, apply, add

apporto *v.t.* 1, to conduct

appŏsĭtus *adj, adv, ē*, bordering, suitable

apprĕhendo, di, sum *v.t.*3, to seize, understand
apprīmus, a, um *adj, adv,* ē, very first
apprŏbātĭo, ōnis *f,* sanction
apprŏbo *v.t.* 1, to approve, make satisfactory
apprŏpĕro *v.i.t.* 1, to hurry; speed up
apprŏpinquātĭo, ōnis *f,* approach
apprŏpinquo *v.i.* 1, to approach
appulsus, ūs *m,* landing, approach
ăprīcātĭo, ōnis *f,* sunning
ăprīcor *v.i.* 1, *dep,* to sun oneself
ăprīcus, a, um *adj,* sunny
Ăprīlis (mensis) April
aptātus, a, um *adj,* suitable
apto *v.t.* 1, to adjust
aptus, a, um *adj, adv,* ē, suitable
ăpŭd *with acc,* at the house of, in the works of, amongst, near
ăqua, ae *f,* water, rain; *pl,* spa
ăquaeductus, ūs *m,* aqueduct
ăquālis, is *c,* wash-basin
ăquārĭus, ii *m,* water-bearer, a sign of the zodiac
ăquātĭcus, a, um *adj,* watery
ăquātĭlis, e *adj,* aquatic
ăquātĭo, ōnis *f,* water-fetching
ăquātor, ōris *m,* water-carrier
ăquĭla, ae *f,* eagle, standard
ăquĭlĭfer, ĕri *m,* standard-bearer
ăquĭlīnus, a, um *adj,* aquiline
ăquĭlo, ōnis *m,* north wind, north
ăquĭlōnāris, e *adj,* northern
ăquor *v.i.* 1, *dep,* to fetch water
ăquōsus, a, um *adj,* moist, rainy
āra, ae *f,* altar
ărānĕa, ae *f,* spider, web
ărānĕus i *m,* spider, web
ărātĭo, ōnis *f,* cultivation
ărātor, ōris *m,* ploughman
ărātrum, i *n,* plough
arbĭter, tri *m,* witness, umpire
arbĭtrātus, ūs *m,* free-will
arbĭtrĭum, ii *n,* verdict, power, inclination
arbĭtror *v.i.* 1, *dep,* to think, decide
arbor, ŏris *f,* tree
arbŏrĕus, a, um *adj,* tree-like
arbustum, i *n,* plantation

arbūtum, i *n,* wild strawberry
arbūtus, i *f,* wild strawberry tree
arca, ae *f,* box, dungeon
arcānus, a, um *adj, adv,* ō, secret
arcĕo *v.t.* 2, to confine, keep off
arcessītus, a, um *adj,* sent for, far-fetched
arcesso, sīvi, sītum *v.t.* 3, to send for
archĭtector *v.t.* 1, *dep,* to design
archĭtectūra, ae *f,* architecture
archĭtectus, i *m,* architect
arcĭtĕnens, ntis *adj,* armed with bow
arctŏs, i *f,* Bear, North Pole
arctūrus, i *m,* chief star in constellation Boötes
arcŭla, ae *f,* small box
arcŭo *v.t.* 1, to bend
arcus, ūs *m,* rainbow, arch
ardĕa, ae *f,* heron
ardens, ntis *adj, adv,* nter, burning, eager
ardĕo, arsi, sum *v.i.* 2, to burn, be eager
ardesco, arsi *v.i* 3, to catch fire
ardor, ōris *m,* blaze, desire
ardŭus, a, um *adj,* high, difficult
ārĕa, ae *f,* open space, threshing-floor
ărēna, ae *f,* sand, arena
ărēnātum, i *n,* mortar, plaster
ărēnōsus, a, um *adj,* sandy
ārens, ntis *adj,* parched
ārĕo *v.i.* 2, to be dry
āresco, ŭi *v.i.* 3, to dry up
argentārĭa, ae *f,* bank, silver-mine
argentārĭus, ii *m,* banker, broker
argentātus, a, um *adj,* silver-plated
argentĕus, a, um *adj,* silver
argentum, i *n,* silver, money
argilla, ae *f,* white clay
argūmentātĭo, ōnis *f,* proof
argūmentor *v.i.* 1, *dep,* to prove
argūmentum, i *n,* proof, content, artistic aim
argŭo, ŭi, ūtum *v.t.* 3, to prove, accuse, convict
argūtĭae, ārum *f.pl,* liveliness
argūtus, a, um *adj, adv,* ē, clear, witty, rattling

ārĭdītas, ātis *f*, dryness
ārĭdum, i *n*, dry land
ārĭdus, a, um *adj*, dry
ărĭēs, tis *m*, ram, battering-ram
ărista, ae *f*, ear of corn
ărithmētĭca, ōrum *n.pl*, arithmetic
arma, ōrum *n.pl*, armour, shield, weapons, army, equipment
armāmenta, ōrum *n.pl*, gear, tackle
armāmentārĭum, ii *n*, arsenal
armāmentum, i *n*, ship's tackle
armārĭum ii *n*, cupboard
armātura, ae *f*, equipment, (light-) armed troops
armātus, a, um *adj*, equipped
armentārĭus, ii *m*, herdsman
armentum, i *n*, plough-animal, herd
armĭfer, ĕra, ĕrum *adj*, warlike, armoured
armĭger, ĕra, ĕrum *adj*, warlike, armoured
armilla, ae *f*, bracelet
armĭpŏtens, ntis *adj*, valiant
armĭsŏnus, a, um *adj*, with clashing armour
armo *v.t.* 1, to arm, equip
armus, i *m*, shoulder, side
ăro, *v.t.* 1, to plough
arquātus, a, um *adj*, bent
arrectus, a, um *adj*, steep
arrēpo, psi, ptum *v.i.* 3, to creep towards
arrha, ae *f*, money given as a pledge
arrīdĕo, si, sum *v.i.* 2, to laugh at, favour
arrĭgo, rexi, rectum *v.t.* 3, to erect, excite
arrĭpĭo, ŭi, reptum *v.t.* 3, to seize, indict
arrŏgans, ntis *pres. partic, adj, adv,* **nter,** haughty
arrŏgantĭa, ae *f*, haughtiness
arrŏgo, *v.t.* 1, to claim, confer
ars, tis *f*, art, skill, theory, habit, stratagem
artē *adv*, closely
arthrītĭcus, a, um *adj*, arthritic
artĭcŭlātim *adv*, piece by piece
artĭcŭlo, *v.t.* 1, to articulate
artĭcŭlus, i *m*, joint, movement

artĭfex, fĭcis *m*, artist, author
artĭfĭciōsus, a, um *adj, adv,* **ē,** skilful
artĭfĭcĭum, ii *n*, trade, skill; *pl*, intrigue
arto *v.t.* 1, to compress
artus, ūs *m*, limb
artus, a, um *adj, adv,* **ē,** confined
ărun, ărus...   see **hărun, hărus...**
arvīna, ae *f*, grease
arvum, i *n*, cultivated land
arvus, a, um *adj*, ploughed
arx, cis *f*, citadel
as, assis *m*, pound weight, coin
ascendo, ndi, nsum *v.i.t.* 3, to climb
ascensus, ūs *m*, ascent
ascĭa, ae *f*, adze
ascĭo *v.t.* 4, to receive
ascisco, īvi, ītum *v.t.* 3, to admit
ascītus, ūs *m*, reception
ascrībo, psi, ptum *v.t.* 3, to insert, enrol, attribute
ascriptīvus, a, um *adj*, supernumerary
ascriptus, a, um *adj*, appointed
ăsella, ae *f*, small ass
ăsellus, i *m*, small ass
ăsĭnus, i *m*, ass, simpleton
aspectābĭlis, e *adj*, visible
aspecto *v.t.* 1, to look at eagerly
aspectus, ūs *m*, look, sight
asper, ĕra, ĕrum *adj, adv,* **ē,** rough, bitter, austere, adverse
aspĕrĭtas, ātis *f*, roughness
aspĕrum, i *n*, rough ground
aspergo, si, sum *v.t.* 3, to scatter, sprinkle, defile
aspergo, ĭnis *f*, sprinkling, spray
aspĕrĭtas, ātis *f*, roughness
aspernātĭo, ōnis *f*, disdain
aspernor *v.t.* 1, *dep*, to despise
aspĕro *v.t.* 1, to roughen, rouse
aspersĭo, ōnis *f*, sprinkling
aspĭcĭo, exi, ectum *v.t.* 3, to look at
aspīrātĭo, ōnis *f*, exhalation
aspīro *v.i.t.* 1, to aspire to; breathe on
aspis, ĭdis *f*, adder
asporto, *v.t.* 1, to carry away
assĕcla, ae *c*, attendant
assectātĭo, ōnis *f*, attendance
assectātor ōris *m*, follower

assector *v.t.* 1, *dep*, to wait upon
assensĭo, ōnis *f*, approval
assensus, ūs *m*, approval
assentātĭo, ōnis *f*, flattery
assentātor, ōris *m*, flatterer
assentĭor, sus *v.* 4, *dep, with dat*, to agree with
assentor *v.* 1, *dep, with dat*, to flatter
assĕquor, sĕcūtus *v.t.* 3, *dep*, to pursue, overtake, comprehend
asser, ĕris *m*, stake
assĕro, rŭi, sertum *v.t.* 3, to claim, set free
assertor, ōris *m*, protector
asservo *v.t.* 1, to keep, guard
assessor, ōris *m*, assessor
assĕvērātĭo, ōnis *f*, assertion
assĕvēro *v.t.* 1, to assert
assĭdĕo, sēdi, sessum *v.i.* 2, to sit by, wait upon, blockade, resemble
assĭdŭĭtas, ātis *f*, constant presence
assĭdŭus, a, um *adj, adv*, ē, constantly present
assignātĭo, ōnis *f*, allotment
assigno *v.t.* 1, to distribute
assĭlĭo, ŭi, sultum *v.i.* 4, to spring upon
assĭmĭlis, e *adj, adv*, ĭter, like
assĭmŭlo *v.i.t.* 1, to resemble, imitate
assĭmŭlātus, a, um *adj*, similar
assisto, astĭti *v.i.* 3, to stand near, aid
assŏlĕo *v.i.* 2, to be in the habit of doing
assŭefăcĭo, fēci, factum *v.t.* 3, to make someone used to
assŭesco, ēvi, ētum *v.i.t.* 3, to become used to; familiarize
assŭētūdo, ĭnis *f*, habit
assŭētus, a, um *adj*, customary
assulto *v.t.* 1, to jump on, attack
assultus, ūs *m*, attack
assūmo, mpse, mptum *v.t.* 3, to take up, adopt
assŭo *v.t.* 3, to sew on
assurgo, surrexi, rectum *v.i.* 3, to rise, stand up
assŭla, ae *f*, splinter, chip
assus, a, um *adj*, roasted; **assa,**

ōrum, *n.pl*, turkish bath
ast see **at**
astĭpŭlātor, ōris *m*, assistant
astĭpŭlor *v.* 1, *dep, with dat*, to bargain with
asto, stĭti *v.i.* 1, to stand near
astrĕpo *v.i.t.* 3, to make a noise; applaud
astringo, nxi, ctum *v.t.* 3, to bind, fasten, cool, limit
astrictus, a, um *adj, adv*, ē, tight, concise
astrŏlŏgĭa, ae *f*, astronomy
astrŏlŏgus, i *m*, astronomer
astrum, i *n*, star, constellation
astrŭo, xi, ctum *v.t.* 3, to build near, add
astŭpĕo *v.i.* 2, to be astonished
astus, ūs *m*, dexterity, craft
astūtĭa, ae *f*, dexterity, slyness
astūtus, a, um *adj, adv*, ē, shrewd, sly
ăsȳlum, i *n*, place of refuge
at *conj*, but, on the other hand
ătăvĭa, ae *f*, ancestor
ătăvus, i *m*, ancestor
āter, tra, trum *adj*, black, deadly
ăthĕŏs, i *m*, atheiest
athlēta, ae *c*, wrestler, athlete
ătŏmus, i *f*, atom
atque *conj*, and, and also
atqui *conj*, but, nevertheless
ātrāmentum, i *n*, ink, varnish
ātrātus, a, um *adj*, in mourning
ātrĭensis, is *m*, house-steward
ātrĭŏlum, i *n*, ante-room
ātrĭum, ii *n*, hall, forecourt
ătrōcĭtas, ātis harshness, cruelty
ătrox, ōcis *adj, adv*, ĭter, horrible, fierce, stern
attactus, ūs *m*, touch
attămen *adv*, but nevertheless
attendo, di, tum *v.t.* 3, to stretch out, give attention to
attentĭo, ōnis *f*, attention
attento *v.t.* 1, to try, attack
attentus, a, um *adj, adv*, ē, engrossed, frugal
attĕnŭo *v.t.* 1, to impair, reduce
attĕro, trīvi, trītum *v.t.* 3, to rub away, exhaust
attĭnĕo, ŭi, tentum *v.i.t.* 2, to strech, concern; retain

attingo, tĭgi, tactum *v.t.* 3, to touch, reach, attack

attollo *v.t.* 3, to raise

attondĕo, di, sum *v.t.* 2, to shear

attŏnĭtus, a, um *adj, adv, ē,* astonished

attŏno, ŭi, ĭtum *v.t.* 1, to stun

attorquĕo *v.t.* 2, to hurl

attrăho, xi, ctum *v.t.* 3, to drag towards, attract

attrecto *v.t.* 1, to handle

attrĭbŭo, ŭi, ŭtum *v.t.* 3, to assign

attrĭbūtum, i *n,* predicate

attrītus, ūs *m,* rubbing against

auceps, ŭpis *c,* bird-catcher, eavesdropper

auctĭo, ōnis *f,* auction, increase

auctĭōnor *v.i.* 1, *dep,* to hold an auction

auctor, ōris *c,* creator, master, witness, supporter, author

auctōrĭtas, ātis *f,* influence, power

auctumnālis, e *adj,* autumnal

auctumnus, a, um *adj,* autumnal

auctumnus, i *m,* autumn

auctus, a, um *adj,* enlarged

auctus, ūs *m,* increase

aucŭpĭum, ii *n,* bird-catching

aucŭpor, v.i.t. 1, *dep,* to go bird-catching; pursue, watch for

audācĭa, ae *f,* boldness, insolence

audax, ācis *adj, adv,* **cter,** bold, rash

audens, ntis *adj, adv,* **nter,** bold

audentĭa, ae *f,* boldness

audĕo, ausus v.i.t. 2 *semi-dep,* to dare

audĭentĭa, ae *f,* hearing, audience

audĭo, v.t. 4, to hear, understand, obey

audītĭo, ōnis *f,* a hearing, report

audītor, ōris *m,* hearer, pupil

audītus, ūs *m,* sense of hearing

aufĕro, ferre, abstŭli, ablātum *v.t, irreg,* to take away, rob, obtain

aufŭgĭo, fūgi, ĭtum *v.i.* 3, to run away

augĕo, xi, ctum v.i.t. 2, to grow; enlarge

augesco v.i. 3, to grow

augur, ŭris *c,* diviner, prophet

augŭrālis, e *adj,* prophetic

augŭrātus, ūs *m,* office of augur

augŭrĭum, ii *n,* omen, augury

augŭrĭus, a, um *adj,* augural

augŭror *v.t.* 1, *dep,* to prophesy, suppose

augustus, a, um *adj, adv, ē,* venerable

aula, ae *f,* palace, court

aulaeum, i *n,* curtain

aulicus, i *m,* courtier

aura, ae *f,* air, soft breeze, sky, publicity, gleam

aurārĭa, ae *f,* gold mine

aurātus, a, um *adj,* gilded

aurĕus, i *m,* gold piece

aurĭcŏmus, a, um *adj,* golden-haired

aurĭcŭla, ae *f,* ear

aurĭfer, ĕra, ĕrum *adj,* gold-producing

aurĭfex, fĭcis *m,* goldsmith

aurīga, ae *c,* charioteer

aurīger, ĕra, ĕrum *adj,* bearing gold

auris, is *f,* ear

aurītus, a, um *adj,* long-eared

aurōra, ae *f,* dawn

aurum, i *n,* gold

ausculto v.i.t. 1, to listen

auspex, ĭcis *c,* diviner

auspĭcātō *adv,* after taking the auspices

auspĭcĭum, ii *n,* divination

auspĭcor v.i.t. 1, *dep,* to take the auspices, begin

auster, tri *m,* south wind

austērus, a, um *adj, adv, ē,* harsh, severe

austrālis, e *adj,* southern

austrīnus, a, um *adj,* southern

ausum, i *n,* bold attempt

aut *conj,* or, **aut … aut,** either … or

autem *conj,* but

autumnālis *adj,* autumnal

autŭmo v.i. 1, to assert

auxĭlĭa, ōrum *n.pl,* auxiliary troops

auxĭlĭāris, e *adj,* helping

auxĭlĭāres, ĭum *m.pl,* auxiliary troops

auxĭlĭor *v.* 1, *dep, with dat.* to help

auxĭlĭum ii   *n,* help
ăvārĭtĭa, ae   *f,* greediness
ăvārus, a, um   *adj, adv,* ē, greedy
ăve! *(pl,* **ăvete)** hail! farewell!
āvĕho, vexi, ctum *v.t.* 3, to carry
  away
āvello, velli, vulsum *v.t.* 3, to tear
  away
ăvēna, ae *f,* oats, shepherd's pipe
ăvĕnācĕus, a, um *adj,* oaten
ăvĕo *v.t.* 2, to long for
ăvĕo *v.i.* 2, to be well
āversor *v.t.* 1, *dep,* to turn away
  from, avoid
āversor, ōris *m,* embezzler
āversus, a, um *adj,* backwards,
  hostile
āverto, ti, sum *v.t.* 3, to push
  aside, steal, estrange
ăvĭa, ae *f,* grandmother
ăvĭārĭum, ii *n,* bird-haunts
ăvĭdĭtas, ātis *f,* eagerness, desire
ăvĭdus, a, um *adj, adv,* ē, greedy
ăvis, is *f,* bird
ăvĭtus, a, um *adj,* ancestral
āvĭum, ii *n,* pathless place
āvĭus, a, um *adj,* pathless
āvŏcātĭo, ōnis *f,* calling away,
  distraction
āvŏco *v.t.* 1, to call away
āvŏlo *v.i.* 1, to fly away
ăvuncŭlus, i *m,* uncle
ăvus, i *m,* grandfather
axis, is *m,* axle, chariot, region

B

bāca, ae *f,* berry
bācātus, a, um *adj,* pearl-set
baccar, ăris *n,* fox-glove
baccha, ae *f,* bacchanal
bacchānālĭa, ĭum *n.pl,* orgies of
  Bacchus
bacchātĭo, ōnis *f,* orgy
bacchor, *v.i.* 1, *dep,* to rave
bācĭfer, ĕra, ĕrum *adj,* berry-
  bearing
băcillum, i *n,* stick
băcŭlum, i *n,* stick, sceptre
bāiŭlo, *v.t.* 1, to carry a load
bāiŭlus, i *m,* porter
bālaena, ae *f,* whale
bălănus, i *f,* acorn

bălătro, ōnis *m,* comedian
bālātus, ūs *m,* bleating
balbus, a, um *adj, adv,* ē,
  stammering
balbūtĭo *v.i.t.* 4, to stammer
ballista, ae *f,* artillery engine
balnĕae, ārum *f.pl,* baths
balnĕātor, ōris *m,* bath-keeper
balnĕum, i *n,* bath
bālo, *v.i.* 1, to bleat
balsămum, i *n,* balm
baltĕus, i *m,* belt, sword-belt
bărāthrum, i *n,* abyss
barba, ae *f,* beard
barbărĭa, ae *f,* foreign country,
  rudeness
barbărus, i *m,* foreigner, stranger
barbărus, a, um *adj, adv,* ē,
  foreign, rude, savage
barbātus, a, um *adj,* bearded
barbĭtos *m, f, (pl,* a), lute,
  lyre
bardus, a, um *adj,* stupid
bāro, ōnis *m,* blockhead
barrus, i *m,* elephant
băsĭlĭca, ae *f,* town-hall
băsĭlĭcus, a, um *adj,* royal
bāsĭo, *v.t.* 1, to kiss
băsis, is *f,* pedestal, base
bāsĭum, ii *n,* kiss
battŭo, ŭi *v.t.* 3, to fence; beat
bĕātĭtas, ātis *f,* happiness
bĕātĭtūdo, ĭnis *f,* happiness
bĕātus, a, um *adj, adv,* ē,
  happy, fortunate
bellans   see **bello**
bellārĭa, ōrum *n.pl,* dessert
bellātor, ōris *m,* warrior
bellātrix, īcis *f,* female-warrior
bellē *adv,* prettily
bellĭcōsus, a, um *adj,* warlike
bellĭcum, i *n,* signal for march
  or attack
bellĭcus, a, um *adj,* military
bellĭger, ĕra, ĕrum *adj,* warlike
bellĭgĕro *v.t.* 1, to wage war
bellis, ĭdis *f,* daisy
bello, *v.i.* 1 (**bellor,** *v.i.* 1, *dep*),
  to make war
bellum, i *n,* war
bellus, a, um *adj,* pretty
bēlŭa, ae *f,* beast
běně *adv,* well, very

běnědīco, xi, ctum *v.i.t.* 3, to praise

běnědictĭo, ōnis *f,* blessing

běněfăcĭo, fēci, factum *v.t.* 3, to do well, oblige

běněfactum, i *n,* good deed

běněficentĭa, ae *f,* kind treatment

běněficĭārĭī, ōrum *m.pl,* privileged soldiers (excused fatigues)

běněficĭum, ii *n,* a kindness

běněfĭcus, a, um *adj,* obliging

běněvŏlentĭa, ae *f,* good will

běněvŏlus, a, um *adj, adv,* ē, well disposed

běnignē *adv,* thank you; no thank you; courteously

běnignus, a, um *adj,* kind, fruitful

běnignĭtas, ātis *f,* kindness

běo, *v.t.* 1, to bless, enrich

bes, bessis *m,* eight ounces

bestĭa, ae *f,* wild beast

bestĭārĭus, ii *m,* wild-beast fighter

bestĭŏla, ae *f,* small animal

bēta, ae *f,* beet

betŭla, ae *f,* birch

biblĭa, ōrum *n.pl,* the Bible

biblĭŏpōla, ae *m,* bookseller

biblĭŏthēca, ae *f,* library

biblĭŏthēcārĭus, ii *m,* librarian

bĭvo, bĭbi, ĭtum *v.t.* 3, to drink

bĭbŭlus, a, um *adj,* given to drink, porous

bĭceps, cĭpĭtis *adj,* two-headed

bĭcŏlōr, ōris *adj,* two-coloured

bĭcornis, e *adj,* two-pronged

bĭdens, ntis *m,* hoe

bīdŭum, ii *n,* space of two days

bĭennĭum, ii *n,* space of two years

bĭfārĭam *adv,* in two ways

bĭfer, ěra, ěrum *adj,* blooming or fruiting twice a year

bĭfīdus, a, um *adj,* cut in two

bĭfŏris, e *adj,* with double opening

bĭformis, e *adj,* two-shaped

bĭfrons, ntis *adj,* two-headed

bĭfurcus, a, um *adj,* two-pronged

bīgae, ārum *f.pl,* pair of horses, two-horsed chariot

bīgātus, a, um *adj,* stamped with a two-horsed chariot (of coins)

bĭĭŭgus, a, um *adj,* yoked two together

bĭlībris, e *adj,* weighing two pounds

bĭlinguis, e *adj,* bilingual

bĭlĭōsus, a, um *adj,* bilious

bĭlis, is *f,* bile

bĭmāris, e *adj,* lying between two seas

bĭmārītus, i *m,* bigamist

bĭmembris, e *adj,* half-man, half-beast

bĭmestris, e, *adj,* two months old

bīmus, a, um *adj,* two years old

bīni, ae, a *adj,* two each, a pair

bĭpartĭo *v.t.* 4, to bisect

bĭpartīto *adv,* in two ways

bĭpědālis, e *adj,* measuring two feet

bĭpennĭfer, ěra, ěrum *adj,* carrying a double-edged axe

bĭpennis, e *adj,* double-edged

bĭpēs, ĕdis *adj,* two-legged

bĭrēmis, e *adj,* two-oared

bĭrēmis, is *f,* a galley with two banks of oars

bis *adv,* twice

bĭsextīlis, e *adj* (of years) leap

bĭsulcus, a, um *adj,* cloven

bĭtūmen, ĭnis *n,* bitumen

bĭvĭum, ii *n,* crossroad

bĭvĭus, a, um *adj,* going in two directions

blaesus, a, um *adj,* stammering

blandīmentum, i *n,* flattery

blandĭor, *v.* 4, *dep, with dat,* to flatter

blandītĭa, ae *f,* flattery

blandus, a, um *adj, adv,* ē, smooth-tongued, enticing

blasphēmo, *v.t.* 1, to revile

blătěro *v.t.* 1, to babble

blătěro, ōnis *m,* gabbler

blatta, ae *f,* cockroach, moth

bŏārĭus, a, um *adj,* of cattle

bōlētus, i *m,* mushroom

bombyx, ȳcis *m,* silk, silk-worm

bŏnĭtas, ātis *f,* excellence

bŏna, ōrum *n.pl,* goods, property

bŏnum, i *n,* goodness, profit

bŏnus, a, um *adj,* good

bŏrěas, ae *m,* north wind

bŏrēus, a, um *adj,* northern

bōs, bŏvis *c,* ox; *pl,* cattle

bŏvārĭus see **boārius**

brācae, ārum *f.pl,* trousers
brācātus, a, um *adj,* wearing trousers, foreign
bracchĭum, ii *n,* forearm, branch, dike
bractĕa, ae, *f,* thin metal plate
branchĭae, ārum *f.pl,* fish gills
brassĭca, ae *f,* cabbage
brĕvī *adv,* in a short time, in a few words
brĕvĭārĭum, ii *n,* summary
brĕvis, e *adj, adv,* ĭter, short, brief
brĕvĭtas, ātis *f,* conciseness, shortness
brūma, ae *f,* shortest day, winter
brūmālis, e *adj,* wintry
brūtus, a, um *adj,* unwieldy, dull
būbo, ōnis *m,* owl
būbulcus, i *m,* ploughman
būbūlus, a, um *adj,* of cattle
bucca, ae *f,* the cheek
buccŭla, ae *f,* small mouth, helmet
būcĭna, ae *f,* trumpet
būcŭla, ae *f,* heifer
būfo, ōnis *m,* toad
bulbus, i *m,* bulb
bulla, ae *f,* bubble, knob, amulet
bullo, *v.i.* 1, to bubble
būmastus, i *f,* grape which grows in large bunches
būris, is *m,* plough-beam
bustum, i *n,* funeral pyre, grave
būtỹrum, i *n,* butter
buxifer, ĕra, ĕrum *adj,* growing box trees
buxum, i *n,* boxwood
buxus, i *f,* box tree
byssus, i *f,* cotton

C

căballus, i *m,* packhorse
cācăbus, i *m,* saucepan
căchinnātĭo, ōnis *f,* guffaw
căchinno, *v.i.* 1, to laugh aloud
căchinnus, i *m,* laughter, jeering
căcūmen, ĭnis *n,* extremity, peak
căcūmĭno *v.t.* 1, to make into a point
cădāver, ĕris *n,* corpse
cădo, cĕcĭdi, cāsum *v.i.* 3, to fall, wane, occur, decay

cādūcĕātor, ōris *m,* herald
cādūcĕum, i *n* (us, i *m*), herald's staff, Mercury's wand
cādūcĭfer, ĕra, ĕrum *adj,* carrying a herald's staff (Mercury)
cādūcus, a, um *adj,* falling, doomed
cădus, i *m,* large jar (for liquids)
caecĭtas, ātis *f,* blindness
caeco *v.t.* 1, to blind
caecus, a, um *adj,* blind, hidden
caedēs, is *f,* slaughter
caedo, cĕcīdi, caesum *v.t.* 3, to cut, strike, slaughter
caelātor, ōris *m,* engraver
caelātūra, ae *f,* carving
caelebs, ĭbis *adj,* unmarried
caelĕs, ĭtis *adj,* heavenly
caelĭtes, um *pl,* gods
caelestĭa, ĭum *n.pl,* the heavenly bodies
caelestis, e *adj,* heavenly
caelestis, is *m,* god
caelĭbātus, ūs *m,* celibacy
caelĭcŏla, ae *m. f,* inhabitant of heaven
caelĭfer, ĕra, ĕrum *adj,* supporting the heavens (Atlas)
caelo *v.t.* 1, to engrave
caelum, i *n,* heaven, climate
caelum, i *n,* chisel
caementum, i *n,* quarry stone
caenum, i *n,* dirt
caepa, ae *f* (e, is *n*), onion
caerĭmōnĭa, ae *f,* religious ceremony, awe
caerŭlĕus(lus), a, um *adj,* dark blue
caesărĭēs, ēi *f,* the hair
caesim *adv,* by cutting
caesĭus, a, um *adj,* green- or grey-eyed
caespĕs, ĭtis *m,* a turf
caestus, ūs *m,* boxing glove
caetra, ae *f,* native shield
călămister, tri *m,* curling-iron; *pl,* flourishes
călămĭtas, ātis *f,* disaster
călămĭtōsus, a, um *adj, adv,* ē, destructive, unhappy
călămus, i *m,* cane, reed-pen
călăthus, i *m,* basket
calcăr, āris *n,* spur, stimulus

calcĕāmentum, i *n*, shoe
calcĕo *v.t.* 1, to shoe
calcĕus, i *m*, shoe
calcĭtrātus, ūs *m*, kicking
calcĭtro *v.i.* 1, to kick, resist
calco *v.t.* 1, to tread on, oppress
calcŭlātor, ōris *m*, accountant
calcŭlus, i *m*, pebble, calculation, vote, piece (chess, draughts)
călĕfăcĭo, fēci, factum *v.t.* 3, to heat, excite
călĕo *v.i.* 2, to be warm, roused
călesco *v.i.* 3, to become warm
călĭdus, a, um *adj*, warm, hot, hot-headed
călĭga, ae *f*, leather boot
călĭgātus, a, um *adj*, weraing soldier's boots
călĭgĭnōsus, a, um *adj*, obscure
călīgo, ĭnis *f*, mist, gloom
călīgo *v.i.* 1, to steam, be dark
călix, ĭcis *m*, cup
calyx see calix
callĕo *v.i.t.* 2, to be callous, insensible; to know by experience
callĭdĭtas, ātis *f*, skill, cunning
callĭdus, a, um *adj, adv*, ē, skilful, sly
callis, is *m*, footpath
callum, i *n*, hard or thick skin
cālo, ōnis *m*, soldier's servant, menial
călor, ōris *m*, heat, ardour
caltha, ae *f*, marigold
călumnĭa, ae *f*, trickery, libel
călumnĭātor, ōris *m*, slanderer
călumnĭor *v.t.* 1, *dep*, to blame or accuse unjustly
calva, ae *f*, scalp
calvārĭa, ae *f*, skull
calvĭtĭum, i *n*, baldness
calvus, a, um *adj*, bald
calx, cis *f*, heel
calx, cis *f*, limestone, chalk
cămēlŏpardălis, is *f*, giraffe
cămēlus, i *m*, camel
cămēna, ae *f*, muse
cămĕra, ae *f*, vault
cămīnus, i *m*, forge, furnace
campester, tris, e *adj*, on level ground
campestre, is *n*, wrestling trunks
campus, i *m*, plain, open country, opportunity, scope

cămŭr, ŭra, ŭrum *adj*, curved inwards
cănālis, is *m*, pipe, groove
cancelli, ōrum *m.pl*, railings
cancer, cri *m*, crab
candēla, ae *f*, candle
candēlābrum, i *n*, candlestick
candens, ntis *adj*, shining white, glowing hot
candĕo *v.i.* 2, to shine, glow
candesco, ŭi *v.i.* 3, to glisten
candĭdātus, i *m*, candidate
candĭdus, a, um *adj, adv*, ē, dazzling white, beautiful, honest
candor, ōris *m*, whiteness, beauty, honesty
cānens, ntis *adj*, grey, white
cānĕo *v.i.* 2, to be white, grey
cānesco *v.i.* 3, to grow white
cănĭcŭla, ae *f*, small dog, Dog-star
cănīnus, a, um *adj*, dog-like
cănis, is *c*, dog, Dog-star
cănistrum, i *n*, open basket
cānĭties (*no genitive*) *f*, grey hair, old age
canna, ae *f*, reed, flute
cannăbis, is *f*, hemp
căno, cĕcĭni, cantum *v.i.t.* 3, to sing, play; prophesy
cănor, ōris *m*, tune
cănōrus, a, um *adj*, melodious
cantērĭus see canthērĭus
cantātor, ōris *m*, singer
canthăris, ĭdis *f*, beetle
canthărus, i *m*, tankard
canthērĭus, ii *m*, mule, rafter
cantĭcum, i *n*, song
cantĭlēna, ae *f*, hackneyed song
canto *v.i.t.* 1, to sing, act; predict
cantor, ōris *m*, singer, actor
cantus, ūs *m*, music, prophecy, singing
cānus, a, um *adj*, white, old
căpācĭtas, ātis *f*, capacity
căpax, ācis *adj*, roomy, capable
căpella, ae *f*, she-goat
căper, pri *m*, goat
căpesso, īvi, ītum *v.t.* 3, to seize, undertake, reach for
căpillāmentum, i *n*, wig
căpillāre, is *n*, hair oil
căpillātus, a, um *adj*, hairy

căpillus, i *m*, the hair
căpĭo, cēpi, captum *v.t.* 3, to
take, capture, tempt, choose,
obtain, undertake, hold, grasp
căpistrum, i *n*, halter
căpĭtālis, e *adj*, of life and death,
criminal, dangerous
capra, ae *f*, she-goat
căprĕa, ae *f*, wild she-goat, roe
căprĕŏlus, i *m*, roebuck, prop
căprĭcornus, i *m*, capricorn
căprĭfĭcus, i *f*, wild fig tree
căprĭgĕnus, a, um *adj*, goat-born
căprīnus, a, um *adj*, of a goat
capsa, ae *f*, box, satchel
captātor, ōris *m*, fortune hunter
captĭo, ōnis *f*, fraud, quibble
captīvĭtas, ātis *f*, captivity
captīvus, a, um *adj* (i *m*),
prisoner
capto *v.t.* 1, to chase, entice
captus, ūs *m*, grasp, capacity
captus, a, um *adj*, taken, disabled
căpŭlus, i *m*, tomb, handle
căpŭt, ĭtis *n*, head, person, chief,
origin, summit, status, paragraph,
chapter
carbăsĕus, a, um *adj*, made of
flax, linen
carbăsus, i *f*, flax, linen
carbo, ōnis *m*, charcoal, coal
carbuncŭlus, i *m*, ruby, carbuncle
carcer, ĕris *m*, prison, jailbird
carchēsĭum, ii *n*, goblet,
masthead
cardĭăcus, a, um *adj*, dyspeptic
cardo, ĭnis *m*, hinge, crisis
cardŭus, i *m*, thistle
cărĕo *v.i.* 2, (*with abl.*) to lack
cārex, ĭcis *f*, reed-grass
cărĭes (*no genitive*) *f*, decay
cārĭca, ae *f*, dried fig
cărīna, ae *f*, hull, keel, boat
cărĭōsus, a, um *adj*, decayed
cărĭtas, ātis *f*, costliness, affection
carmen, ĭnis *n*, song, poem
carnārĭum, ii *n*, larder
carnĭfex, ĭcis *m*, executioner
carnĭfĭcīna, ae *f*, execution,
torment
carnĭfĭco *v.t.* 1, to execute
carnĭvŏrus, a, um *adj*,
carnivorous

carnōsus, a, um *adj*, fleshy
căro, carnis *f*, flesh, meat
carpentum, i *n*, chariot
carpo, psi, ptum *v.t.* 3, to pluck,
graze, slander, weaken, pass over
carptim *adv*, separately
carrus, i *m*, two-wheeled cart
cartīlāgo, ĭnis *f*, cartilage
cārus, a, um *adj, adv*, ē, dear
căsa, ae *f*, cottage, hut
cāsĕus, i *m*, cheese
cāsĭa, ae *f*, cinnamon (tree)
casses, ĭum *m.pl*, hunting-net,
spider's web
cassis, ĭdis *f*, helmet
cassĭda, ae *f*, helmet
cassus, a, um *adj*, empty, vain
castănĕa, ae *f*, chestnut
castē *adv*, purely
castellum, i *n*, stronghold
castīgātĭo, ōnis *f*, punishment
castīgātor, ōris *m*, critic
castīgo *v.t.* 1, to correct, punish
castĭmōnĭa, ae *f*, purity
castītas, ātis *f*, chastity
castor, ŏris *m*, beaver
castra, ōrum *n.pl.*, camp
castrensis, e *adj*, of the camp,
military
castro *v.t.* 1, to castrate
castrum, i *n*, fort
castus, a, um *adj*, pure, virtuous
cāsū *adv*, accidentally
cāsus, ūs *m*, fall, chance, mishap
cătăpulta, ae *f*, catapult
cătaracta, ae *f*, waterfall,
portcullis
cătellus i *m*, (a, ae *f*), puppy
cătēna, ae *f*, chain, fetter
cătēnātus, a, um *adj*, chained
căterva, ae *f*, crowd, company
cătervātim *adv*, by companies
căthēdra, ae *f*, chair
cătillus, i *m*, dish
cătīnus, i *m*, bowl, dish
cătŭlus, i *m*, puppy, young
animal
cătus, a, um *adj, adv*, ē,
intelligent, sly
cauda, ae *f*, tail
caudex, ĭcis *m*, tree trunk, ledger
caulae, ārum *f.pl*, hole, enclosure
caulis, is *m*, stem, cabbage

caupo, ōnis *m,* retailer, innkeeper
caupōna, ae *f,* shop, inn
caupōnor *v.t.* 1, *dep,* to trade
causa, ae *f,* reason, cause,
  motive; *abl.* **causā** for the sake
  of
causĭdĭcus, i *m,* counsel
causor *v.i.t.* 1, *dep,* to make
  excuses; plead
cautē *adv,* cautiously
cautēs, is *f,* crag, rock
cautĭo, ōnis *f,* precaution
cautus, a, um *adj,* safe, cautious
căvĕa, ae *f,* den, coop
căvĕo, cāvi, cautum *v.i.t.* 2, to be
  on one's guard; stipulate
căverna, ae *f,* cave, ship's hold
căvillātĭo, ōnis *f,* jeering
căvillor *v.i.t.* 1, *dep,* to jeer; taunt,
  quibble
căvo *v.t.* 1, to hollow out
căvum, i, *n* (**us, i** *m*), hole
căvus, a, um *adj,* hollow
cēdo, cessi, cessum *v.i.t.* 3, to
  move, yield, happen; befall
cēdo *imperative,* here! say! give!
cĕdrus, i *f,* cedar (wood, tree, oil)
cĕlĕbĕr, ĕbris, ĕbre *adj,* much
  frequented, crowded, famous
cĕlĕbrātĭo, ōnis *f,* crowd, festival
cĕlĕbrātus, a, um *adj,* popular,
  usual, well-known
cĕlĕbrĭtas, ātis *f,* crowd, fame
cĕlĕbro *v.t.* 1, to frequent, use,
  celebrate, praise, proclaim,
  solemnize
cĕlĕr, ĕris, ĕre *adj, adv,* ĭter, swift,
  lively, rash
cĕlĕrĭtas, ātis *f,* speed
cĕlĕro *v.i.t.* 1, to hurry; quicken
cella, ae *f,* store room
cellārĭus, i *m,* butler
cēlo *v.t.* 1, to conceal
cĕlox, ōcis *f,* yacht
celsus, a, um *adj,* high, eminent
cēna, ae *f,* dinner
cēnācŭlum, i *n,* attic, refectory
cēnātĭo, ōnis *f,* dining room
cēnātus, a, um *adj,* having dined
cēno *v.i.t.* 1, to dine; eat
cēnsĕo, ŭi, censum *v.t.* 2, to
  assess, give an opinion
censor, ōris *m,* censor

censōrĭus, a, um *adj,* censorial
censūra, ae *f,* censorship
census, ūs *m,* census, wealth
centaurēum, i *n,* herb (centaury)
centaurus, i *m,* a Centaur
centēni, ae, a *adj* a hundred each
centēsĭmus, a, um *adj,* hundredth
centĭens (centĭes) *adv,* a hundred
  times
centĭmănus, a, um *adj,* hundred-
  handed
cento, ōnis *m,* patchwork
centum, a hundred
centumgĕmĭnus, a, um *adj,* a
  hundredfold
centumpondĭum, ii *n,* weight of a
  hundred pounds
centŭplex, plĭcis *adj* hundredfold
centŭrĭa, ae *f,* division, century
centŭrĭātim *adv,* by hundreds
centŭrĭo, ōnis *m,* centurion
centŭrĭo *v.t.* 1, to divide into
  centuries
cēnŭla, ae *f,* small dinner
cēra, ae *f,* wax, writing tablet
cĕrăsus, i *f,* cherry (tree)
cerdo, ōnis *m,* handicraftsman
cĕrĕbrōsus, a, um *adj,* hot-
  headed
cĕrĕbrum, i *n,* brain,
  understanding
cērĕus, a, um *adj,* of wax
cērĕus, i *m,* wax taper
cervisia, ae *f,* beer
cērintha, ae *f,* wax flower
cerno, crēvi, crētum *v.t.* 3, to
  perceive, decide
cernŭus, a, um *adj,* headfirst
cēro *v.t.* 1, to smear with wax
cerrītus, a, um *adj,* frantic, crazy
certāmen, ĭnis *n,* struggle
certātim *adv,* eagerly
certātĭo, ōnis *f,* contest
certē *adv,* undoubtedly
certĭōrem făcĭo to inform
certō *adv,* certainly
certo *v.i.t.* 1, to struggle; contest
certus, a, um *adj,* certain, fixed
cērussa, ae *f,* white lead
cerva, ae *f,* doe
cervĭcal, ālis *n,* pillow
cervīnus, a, um *adj,* of a deer
cervisia see **cerevisia**

cervix, īcis *f*, neck
cervus, i *m*, deer
cessātĭo, ōnis *f*, loitering
cessātor, ōris *m*, idler
cessātrix, īcis *f*, idler
cesso *v.i.t.* 1, to loiter, cease; fail
cētārĭum, ii *n*, fishpond
cētārĭus, ii *m*, fishmonger
cētĕrōqui *adv*, in other respects
cētĕrum *adv*, otherwise, but yet
cētĕrus, a, um *adj, adv*, um, the rest, remainder
cētus, i *m*, sea monster, whale
ceu *adv*, as, just as
chălybs, ўbis *m*, steel
charta, ae *f*, writing paper
chĕlўdrus, i *m*, water snake
chĕrăgra, ae *f*, gout in the hand
chīrŏgrăphum, i *n*, handwriting
chīrurgĭa, ae *f*, surgery
chīrurgus, i *m*, surgeon
chlămys, ўdis *f*, military cloak
chorda, ae *f*, string of a musical instrument
chŏrēa, ae *f*, dance
chŏrus, i *m*, dance, chorus, group
Christus, i *m*, Christ
Christĭānus, a, um *adj*, Christian
cĭbārĭa, ōrum *n.pl*, food
cĭbārĭus, a, um *adj*, of food
cĭbōrĭum, ii *n*, drinking-cup
cĭbus, i *m*, food
cĭcāda, ae *f*, grasshopper
cĭcātrix, īcis *f*, scar
cĭcer, ĕris *n*, chick pea
cīcĭnus, a, um *adj*, of the cici tree
cĭcōnĭa, ae *f*, stork
cĭcur, ŭris *adj*, tame
cĭcūta, ae *f*, hemlock
cĭĕo, cīvi, cĭtum *v.t.* 2, to rouse, move, summon
cĭlīcĭum, ii *n*, coarse cloth
cīmex, īcis *m*, but
cincinnātus, a, um *adj*, with ringlets
cincinnus, i *m*, lock of hair
cinctus, ūs *m*, girdle
cĭnĕrĕus, a, um *adj*, ash-coloured
cingo, nxi, nctum *v.t.* 3, to enclose, encircle, fasten on, crown, besiege
cingŭla, ae *f*, (um, i *n*), girdle
cĭnis, ĕris *m*, ashes, death

cippus, i *m*, stake
circā *adv, and prep. with acc*, round about
circenses, ĭum *m.pl.*, The Games
circĭnus, i *m*, pair of compasses
circĭter *adv. and prep. with acc*, round about, near
circĭtor, ōris *m*, patrol
circŭĭtĭo, ōnis *f*, patrolling
circŭĭtus, ūs *m*, circuit
circŭlor *v.i.* 1, *dep*, to form a group
circŭlus, i *m*, circle, orbit
circum *adv, and prep. with acc*, around, near
circŭmăgo, ēgi, actum *v.t.* 3, to wheel, drive round, pass (time)
circumcīdo, cīdi, cīsum *v.t.* 3, to cut around, reduce
circumcīsus, a, um *adj*, cut off
circumclūdo, si, sum *v.t.* 3, to shut in, surround
circumdătus, a, um *adj*, surrounded
circumdo, dĕdi, dătum *v.t.* 1, to put around, shut in, surround
circumdūco, xi, ctum *v.t.* 3, to lead around
circŭmĕo, circŭĭtum *v.i.t.* 4, to go around; surround, canvass
circumfĕro, ferre, tŭli, lātum *v.t*, *irreg*, to carry or pass around
circumflecto, xi, xum *v.i.t.* 3, to bend, turn around
circumflŭo, xi, ctum *v.i.t.* 3, to flow round; overflow with
circumfŏrānĕus, a, um *adj*, movable
circumfundo, fūdi, fūsum *v.t.* 3, to pour around, envelop, hem in
circumgrĕdĭor, gressus *v.i.t.* 3, *dep*, to go around
circumĭcĭo, iēci, ctum *v.t.* 3, to throw or set round
circumiectus, a, um *adj*, surrounding
circumlĭgo *v.t.* 1, to tie round
circumlĭno, (*no perf.*) itum *v.t.* 3, to besmear
circummitto, mīsi, missum *v.t.* 3, to send around
circummūnĭo *v.t.* 4, to fortify round

circumplector, xus *v.t.* 3, *dep,* to embrace, surround

circumplīco *v.t.* 1, to wind round

circumrōdo, di *v.t.* 3, to nibble round

circumscrībo, psi, ptum *v.t.* 3, to draw a line round, restrict, deceive

circumscriptĭo, ōnis *f,* circle, outline

circumsĕdĕo, sēdi, sessum *v.t.* 2, to surround, blockade

circumsisto, stĕti *v.t.* 3, to stand around; surround

circumsŏno *v.t.* 1, to resound; fill with sound

circumspecto *v.t.* 1, to look round; survey carefully

circumspectus, a, um *adj,* guarded, considered

circumspectus, ūs *m,* contemplation, spying

circumspĭcĭo, spexi, ctum *v.i.t.* 3, to look around, take care; survey, search for

circumsto stĕti *v.i.t.* 1, to stand around; surround, besiege

circumtextus, a, um *adj,* woven round

circumtŏno, ŭi, *v.t.* 1, to thunder around

circumvādo, si *v.t.* 3, to envelop

circumvallo *v.t.* 1, to surround with a wall, blockade

**circumvector, ** *v.* 1, *dep,* to ride around

circumvĕhor, vectus *v.t.* 3, *dep,* to ride around

circumvĕnĭo, vēni, ventum *v.t.* 4, to surround

circumvŏlĭto, *v.i.t.* 1, to flit; fly around

circumvŏlo, *v.t.* 1, to fly around

circumvolvo, volvi, vŏlūtum *v.t.* 3, to roll around

circus, i *m,* circle, ring

cīris, is *f,* sea bird

cirrus, i *m,* curl

cis *prep. with acc,* on this side of, within

cĭsĭum, ii *n,* two-wheeled vehicle

cista, ae *f,* box, chest

cisterna, ae *f,* cistern

cītātus, a, um *adj,* urged on, quick

cītĕrĭor *comp. adj,* on this side

cĭthăra, ae *f,* guitar, lute

cĭthărista, ae *m,* guitar-player

cĭthăroedus, i *m,* a singing guitar player

cĭto *adv,* soon, quickly

cĭto, *v.t.* 1, to incite, call

cĭtrā *adv, and prep. with acc,* on this side (of)

cĭtrĕus, a, um *adj,* of citrus wood, of the citrus tree

cĭtrō *adv, (with ultro)* to and fro, backwards and forwards

citrus, i *f,* citrus tree

cĭtus, a, um *adj,* swift, quick

cīvĭcus, a, um *adj,* of a citizen, civic, civil

cīvīlis, e *adj, adv,* **īter,** of a citizen, civic, civil

cīvis, is *c,* citizen

cīvĭtas, ātis *f,* citizenship, the state, the citizens

clādes, is *f,* disaster, massacre

clam *adv, and prep. with acc,* secretly; unknown to

clāmĭto *v.i.t.* 1, to call out

clāmo, *v.i.t.* 1, to shout; declare

clāmor, ōris *m,* shout, applause

clāmōsus, a, um *adj,* noisy, bawling

clandestīnus, a, um *adj, adv,* **ō,** secret, hidden, furtive

clangor, ōris *m,* noise, clash

clārĕo *v.i.* 2, to shine, be famous

clāresco, clārŭi *v.i.* 3, to become clear or famous

clārĭtas, ātis *f,* brightness, renown

clārĭtūdo, ĭnis *f,* renown

clārus, a, um *adj, adv,* **e,** clear, bright, plain, famous

classĭārĭi, ōrum *m.pl,* marines

classĭcum, i *n,* battle signal

classis, is *f,* fleet, class or muster of citizens

claudĕo *v.i.* 2, *(no perf),* to limp, be lame

claudĭco *v.i.* 1, to limp, be lame

claudĭcātĭo, ōnis *f,* limping

claudo, si, sum *v.t.* 3, to shut, cut off, enclose, blockade

claudus, a, um *adj,* lame

claustra, ōrum   *n.pl,* lock, bolt, barricade
clausŭla, ae   *f,* conclusion, end
clausum, i   *n,* enclosed space
clāva, ae   *f,* club, cudgel
clāvĭger, ĕra, ĕrum   *adj,* club-armed
clāvĭger, ĕri   *m,* key-bearer
clāvis, is   *f,* key
clāvŭlus, i   *m,* small nail
clāvus, i   *m,* nail, tiller, stripe
clēmens, ntis   *adj, adv,* **nter,** gentle, mild, merciful
clēmentĭa, ae   *f,* mildness, mercy
clĕpo, psi, ptum   *v.t.* 3, to steal
clepsȳdra, ae   *f,* water-clock
clīens, ntis   *c,* retainer, follower
clīentēla, ae   *f,* patronage, train of dependants
clīpĕus, i   *m,* Roman round shield
clītellae, ārum   *f.pl,* saddle bags
clīvōsus, a, um   *adj,* hilly
clīvus, i,   *m,* slope, hill
clŏāca, ae   *f,* sewer, drain
clūnis, is   *m,*   *f,* buttock, haunch
cŏăcervo   *v.t.* 1, to pile together
cŏactor, ōris   *m,* money collector
cŏacum, i   *n,* a thick covering
cŏactus, a, um   *adj, adv,* **ē,** forced
cŏaequo   *v.t.* 1, to level, equalize
cŏagmento   *v.t.* 1, to join together
cŏagŭlo   *v.t.* 1, to coagulate
cŏălesco, ălŭī, ălĭtum   *v.i.* 3, to grow together, combine
cŏargŭo, ŭi   *v.t.* 3, to convict, refute, demonstrate
cŏarto   *v.t.* 1, to compress
coccĭnĕus, a, um   *adj,* scarlet
coccum, i   *n,* scarlet colour
cochlĕa, ae   *f,* snail, spiral
cŏclĕa, ae   *f,* snail, spiral
cŏclĕar, āris   *n,* spoon
coctĭlis, e   *adj,* baked, burned
cŏcus, i   *m,* cook
cōdex, ĭcis   *m,* tree trunk, ledger
cōdĭcilli, ōrum   *m.pl,* notebook
cŏĕmo, ēmi, emptum   *v.t.* 3, to buy up
coenum, i   *n,* dirt
cŏĕo   *v.i.* 4, to assemble, unite, encounter, conspire
(coepĭo) coepi, coeptum   *v.i.t.* 3, *defect,* to begin

coeptum, i   *n,* attempt
coeptus, ūs,   *m,* undertaking
cŏercĕo,   *v.t.* 2, to confine, curb
cŏercĭtĭo, ōnis   *f,* coercion, restraint
coetus, ūs   *m,* meeting, crowd
cōgĭtātĭo, ōnis   *f,* thought, reflection, purpose
cōgĭtātum, i   *n,* idea, thought
cōgĭtātus, a, um   *adj,* thought out
cōgĭto   *v.t.* 1, to consider, think, be disposed towards, plan
cognātĭo, ōnis   *f,* blood relationship, family
cognātus, a, um   *adj,* related by birth; *(as a noun)* blood-relative
cognĭtĭo, ōnis   *f,* study, knowledge, recognition, idea, trial
cognĭtor, ōris   *m,* legal representative
cognĭtus, a, um   *adj,* known, approved
cognōmen, ĭnis   *n,* surname
cognōmĭnis, e   *adj,* of the same name
cognosco, gnōvi, gnĭtum   *v.t.* 3, to learn, understand, inquire
cōgo, cŏēgi, cŏactum   *v.t.* 3, to collect, compel, restrict
cŏhaerens see **cohaerĕo**
cŏhaerĕo, si, sum   *v.i.* 2, to cling together, agree with
cŏhēres, ēdis   *c,* fellow heir
cŏhĭbēo   *v.t.* 2, to hold together, confine, restrain
cŏhŏnesto   *v.t.* 1, to honour
cŏhorresco, horrŭi   *v.i.* 3, to shudder
cŏhors, tis   *f,* company of soldiers (¹/₁₀ of a legion); enclosure
cŏhortālis, e   *adj,* of the poultry farm
cŏhortātĭo, ōnis   *f,* encouragement
cŏhortor   *v.t.* 1, *dep,* to encourage
cŏĭtĭo, ōnis   *f,* meeting, conspiracy
cŏĭtus, ūs   *m,* meeting, crowd, sexual intercourse
cŏlăphus, i   *m,* blow, cuff
collăbĕfacto   *v.t.* 1, to dislodge
collăbĕfīo, fieri, factus   *irreg,* to be overthrown, disabled
collābor, psus   *v.i.* 3, to fall, faint, decay

collăcrĭmo *v.i.t.* 1, to weep; deplore

collactĕus, i *m,* **(a, ae** *f)* foster brother (sister)

collātĭo, ōnis *f,* collection, encounter, comparison

collaudo *v.t.* 1, to praise highly

collēga, ae *m,* partner, colleague

collēgĭum, ii *n,* organization, body of officials

collībet *v. impers,* 2, it is agreeable

collīdo, si, sum *v.t.* 3, to beat or strike together

collĭgo, lēgi, ctum *v.t.* 3, to collect, compress, consider

collĭgo *v.t.* 1, to tie together

collīno, lēvi, lītum *v.t.* 3, to besmear, defile

collīnus, a, um *adj,* hilly

collis, is *m,* hill, high ground

collŏcātĭo, ōnis *f,* setting up, giving in marriage

collŏco *v.t.* 1, to arrange, give in marriage, invest, employ

collŏquĭum, ii *n,* conversation

collŏquor, cūtus *v.i.* 3, *dep,* to hold a conversation, discuss

collūcĕo *v.i,* 2, to shine

collūdo, si, sum *v.i.* 3, to play with, be in collusion with

collum, i *n,* neck, throat

collumna see **columna**

collŭo, lŭi, lūtum *v.t.* 3, to rinse

collūsĭo, ōnis *f,* collusion

collūsor, ōris *m,* playmate

collustro *v.t.* 1, to illumine

collŭvĭo, ōnis *f,* heap of rubbish

collŭvĭes (*no genit.*) *f,* heap of rubbish

cŏlo, ŭi, cultum *v.t.* 3, to cultivate, improve, worship, study

cōlo *v.t.* 1, to filter

cŏlŏcāsĭa, ae *f,* marsh-lily

cōlon, i *n,* colon

cŏlōna, ae *f,* farmer's wife

cŏlōnĭa, ae *f,* Roman outpost, colonial settlement, farm

cŏlōnus, i *m,* farmer, colonist

cŏlor, ōris *m,* colour, dye, beauty

cŏlōrātus, a, um *adj,* coloured

cŏlōro *v.t.* 1, to colour, dye

cŏlossus, i *m,* gigantic statue

cŏlŭber, bri *m,* **(bra, ae,** *f)* snake

cōlum, i *n,* strainer, colander

cŏlumba, ae *f,* **(us, i** *m)* dove

cŏlumbārĭum, ii *n,* dovecot

cŏlumbīnus, a, um *adj,* of a dove, dove-coloured

cŏlŭmella, ae *f,* small pillar

cŏlūmen, ĭnis *n,* summit, prop

cŏlumna, ae *f,* pillar, post

cŏlurnus, a, um *adj,* of hazel

cŏlus, ūs *f,* distaff

cŏma, ae *f,* hair, crest, foliage

cŏmans, ntis *adj,* hairy

cŏmātus, a, um *adj,* long-haired

combĭbo, bĭbi *v.t.* 3, to drink up

combūro, ussi, ustum *v.t.* 3, to burn, consume completely

cŏmĕdo, ēdi, ēsum *v.t.* 3, to eat up, waste

cŏmes, ĭtis *c,* companion, attendant

cŏmētes, ae *m,* comet

cōmĭcus, a, um *adj, adv,* **ē,** comic

cōmĭcus, i *m,* comedian

cōmis, e *adj, adv,* **ĭter,** courteous, obliging

cōmissātĭo, ōnis *f,* drinking party

cōmissātĭo, ōris *m,* reveller

cōmissor *v.i.* 1, *dep,* to have a party

cōmĭtas, ātis *f,* affability

cŏmĭtātus, a, um *adj,* accompanied

cŏmĭtātus, ūs *m,* escort, retinue

cŏmĭtĭa, ōrum *n.pl,* Roman assembly for electing magistrates

cŏmĭtĭālis, e *adj,* of the elections; (*with* **morbus**) epilepsy

cŏmĭtĭum, ii *n,* assembly place for voting

cŏmĭtor *v.t.* 1, *dep,* to accompany

commăcŭlo *v.t.* 1, to stain

commĕātus, ūs *m,* expedition, leave of absence, convoy, supplies

commĕmŏrātĭo, ōnis *f,* mention

commĕmŏro *v.t.* 1, to remember, relate

commendātĭcĭus, a, um *adj,* commendatory

commendātĭo, ōnis *f,* recommendation

commendo *v.t.* 1, to entrust, recommend

commentārĭus, ii *m,* **(ium, ii** *n)* notebook, record

commentātĭo, ōnis *f,* careful study

commentīcĭus, a, um *adj,* thought-out, imaginary, false

commentor *v.i.t.* 1, *dep,* to study

commentor, ōris *m,* inventor

commentum, i *n,* fabrication

commĕo, *v.i.* 1, to come and go, frequent

commercĭum, ii *n,* fabrication

commĕrĕo *v.t.* 2, to deserve fully, be guilty of

commīgro *v.t.* 1, to migrate

commīlĭtĭum, ii *n,* comradeship

commīlĭto, ōnis *m,* comrade

commĭnātĭo, ōnis *f,* threats

commĭniscor, mentus *v.t.* 3, *dep,* to devise, invent

commĭnor *v.t.* 1, *dep,* to threaten

commĭnŭo, ŭi, ūtum *v.t.* 3, to crush, lessen, weaken

commĭnus *adv,* at close quarters

commiscĕo, scŭi, xtum *v.t.* 2, to mix together

commĭsĕror *v.t.* 1, *dep,* to pity

commissĭo, ōnis *f,* opening of the games, prepared speech

commissum, i *n,* offence, secret

commissūra, ae *f,* knot, joint

committo, mīsi, ssum *v.t.* 3, to connect, engage in, begin, entrust, do something wrong, bring together in combat

commŏdātum, i *n,* loan

commŏdē *adv,* appropriately, just in time

commŏdĭtas, ātis *f,* benefit

commŏdo *v.t.* 1, to adjust, lend, be kind to, oblige

commŏdum, i *n,* convenient time or opportunity, advantage

commŏdus, a, um *adj,* suitable, obliging, advantageous

commŏnĕfăcĭo, fēci, factum *v.t.* 3, to remind, impress upon

commŏnĕo *v.t.* 2, to impress upon

commonstro *v.t.* 1, to point out

commŏrātĭo, ōnis *f,* delay

commŏror *v.t.* 1, *dep,* to wait, stay

commōtĭo, ōnis *f,* commotion, excitement

commōtus, a, um *adj,* aroused

commŏvĕo, mōvi, mōtum *v.t.* 2, to shake, move, arouse, disturb

commūnĭcātĭo, ōnis *f,* communication

commūnĭco *v.t.* 1, to share with another, consult, unite, partake

commūnĭo *v.t.* 4, to fortify strongly

commūnĭo, ōnis *f,* partnership

commūnē, is *n,* community, state

commūnis, e *adj, adv,* **īter,** common, general

commūnĭtas, ātis *f,* fellowship

commūtābĭlis, e *adj,* changeable

commūtātĭo, ōnis *f,* change

commūto, *v.t.* 1, to change, exchange

cōmo, mpsi, mptum *v.t.* 3, to arrange, comb, braid, adorn

cōmoedĭa, ae *f,* comedy

cōmoedus, a, um *adj,* comic

cōmoedus, i *m,* comic actor

compactum, i *n,* agreement

compactus, a, um *adj,* thick set

compāges, is *f,* joint, structure

compār, ăris *adj,* equal, like

compār, ăris *m,* companion

compărātĭo, ōnis *f,* comparison, preparation

compărātīvus, a, um *adj,* comparative

compārĕo *v.t.* 2, to be evident

compăro *v.t.* 1, to pair off, compare, make ready, provide

compello, pŭli, pulsum *v.t.* 3, to collect, compel

compello *v.t.* 1, to address, rebuke

compendĭārĭus, a, um *adj,* short

compendĭum, ii *n,* gain, saving, abbreviation

compensātĭo, ōnis *f,* compensation

compenso *v.t.* 1, to make things balance, compensate

compĕrendĭno *v.t.* 1, to remand

compĕrĭo, pĕri, pertum *v.t.* 4, to ascertain

compertus, a, um *adj,* proved

compēs, ĕdis *f,* chain, shackle for the feet

compesco, scŭi *v.t.* 3, to restrain
compĕtītor, ōris *m*, rival
compĕto, īvi, ītum *v.t.* 3, to
correspond, coincide
compīlo *v.t.* 1, to plunder
compingo, pēgi, pactum *v.t.* 3, to
construct, fasten together
compĭtum, i *n*, crossroad
complāno *v.t.* 1, to level
complector, xus *v.t.* 3, *dep*, to
embrace, value, enclose,
understand
complēmentum, i *n*, complement
complĕo, ēvi, ētum *v.t.* 2, to fill
up, supply
complexĭo, ōnis *f*, combination
complexus ūs *m*, embrace, love
complīco *v.t.* 1, to fold up
complōrātĭo, ōnis *f*, lamentation
complōrātus ūs *m*, lamentation
complōro *v.t.* 1, to lament
complūres, a *pl*, *adj*, several
compōno, pŏsŭi, pŏsĭtum *v.t.* 3,
to put together, unite, build,
arrange, compare, put to sleep,
adjust, pretend, agree upon
comporto *v.t.* 1, to bring
together
compŏs, ŏtis *adj, with genit. or
abl*, having control of
compŏsĭtĭo, ōnis *f*, arranging
compŏsĭtus, a, um *adj, adv*, ē,
well-arranged, suitable **ex
compŏsĭto**, by previous
agreement
comprĕhendo, di, sum *v.t.* 3, to
seize, perceive, recount,
understand
comprĕhensĭo, ōnis *f*, arrest
comprĭma, pressi, pressum *v.t.* 3,
to press together, restrain
comprŏbo *v.t.* 1, to approve,
prove
comptus, a, um *adj*, dressed-up
compulsus, a, um *adj*, collected,
driven
compungo, nxi, nctum *v.t.* 3, to
prick, sting
compŭto *v.t.* 1, to calculate
cōnāmen, ĭnis *n*, effort
cōnāta, ōrum *n.pl*, undertaking
cōnātum, i *n*, attempt
cōnātus, ūs *m*, effort, enterprise

concăvus, a, um *adj*, hollow,
arched
concēdo, cessi, ssum *v.t.* 3, to go
away, yield; permit
concĕlēbro *v.t.* 1, to frequent,
celebrate, notify
concentus, ūs *m*, harmony
conceptĭo, ōnis *f*, comprehension,
conception
conceptus, ūs *m*, gathering
concertātĭo, ōnis *f*, dispute
concerto *v.t.* 1, to dispute
concessĭo ōnis *f*, permission
concessu (*abl*), by permission
concessus, a, um *adj*, yielded,
confirmed
concha, ae *f*, shellfish, oyster-
shell, Triton's trumpet
conchўlĭum, ii *n*, shellfish
concĭdo, cĭdī *v.i.* 3, to collapse
concīdo, cīdi, cīsum *v.t.* 3, to cut
up, kill, annihilate
concĭĕo, īvi, ītum *v.t.* 2, to bring
together
concĭlĭābŭlum, i *n*, assembly-place
concĭlĭātĭo, ōnis *f*, union
concĭlĭātor, ōris *m*, promoter
concĭlĭo *v.t.* 1, to unite, win over,
bring about
concĭlĭum, ii *n*, meeting, assembly
concinnĭtas, ātis *f*, elegance
concinnus, a, um *adj, adv*, ē,
well-adjusted, graceful
concĭno, nŭi *v.t.* 3, to harmonize;
celebrate
concĭpĭo, cēpi, ceptum *v.t.* 3, to
take hold of, become pregnant,
understand, formulate, designate
concīsus, a, um *adj, adv*, ē, cut
short
concĭtātĭo, ōnis *f*, quick motion
concĭtātus, a, um *adj, adv*, ē,
swift, roused
concĭto *v.t.* 1, to stir up, rouse
conclāmo *v.t.* 1, to shout out;
call upon
conclāve, is *n*, room
conclūdo, si, sum *v.t.* 3, to
enclose, include, conclude
concoctĭo, ōnis *f*, digestion
concŏlor, ōris *adj*, similar in
colour
concŏquo, xi, ctum *v.t.* 3, to boil

together, digest, put up with
concordĭa, ae *f,* agreement
concordo *v.i.* 1, to agree
concors, cordis *adj, adv,* **ĭter,** of
the same mind
concrēdo, dĭdi, dĭtum *v.t.* 3, to
entrust
concrĕmo *v.t.* 1, to burn up
concrĕpo, ŭi, ĭtum *v.i.t.* 3, to
creak, crack; rattle, clash
concresco, crēvi, tum *v.i.* 3, to
grow together, harden
concrētus, a, um *adj,* hardened
concŭbīna, ae *f,* concubine
concŭbĭus, a, um, *adj, (with* **nox)**
at dead of night
conculco *v.t.* 1, to trample on
concŭpisco, cŭpīvi, ītum *v.t.* 3, to
long for, strive after
concurro, curri, cursum *v.i.* 3, to
rush together, assemble, join
battle
concursātĭo, ōnis *f,* running
together
concursĭo, ōnis *f,* running
together
concurso *v.i.t.* 1, to run, travel
about, skirmish; frequent
concursus, ūs *m,* rush, collision
concŭtĭo, cussi, ssum *v.t.* 3, to
shake, disturb, terrify, examine
condemno *v.t.* 1, to convict
condenso *v.t.* 1, to condense
condensus, a, um *adj,* thick
condĭcĭo, ōnis *f,* agreement,
proposition, terms, alliance, rank,
situation
condīmentum, i *n,* seasoning
condĭo *v.t.* 4, to pickle
condiscĭpŭlus, i *m,* school friend
condisco, dĭdĭci *v.t.* 3, to learn
carefully
condĭtor, ōris *m,* builder, author,
founder
condĭtus, a, um *adj,* fashioned,
composed
condītus, a, um *adj,* savoury
condo, dĭdi, dĭtum *v.t.* 3, to
construct, found, store up, hide,
thrust in
condŏlesco, lŭi *v.i.* 3, to suffer
pain
condōno *v.t.* 1, to present, give

up, surrender, pardon
condūco, xi, ctum *v.i.t.* 3, to be
useful; collect, connect, hire
conductĭo, ōnis *f,* hiring
conductor, ōris *m,* tenant,
contractor
conductum, i *n,* tenement
conductus, a, um *adj,* hired
cōnecto, xŭi, xum *v.t.* 3, to tie
together, involve
confarrĕātĭo, ōnis *f,*
marriage
confectĭo, ōnis *f,* arrangement,
completion
confectus, a, um *adj,* completed,
exhausted
confercĭo, *(no perf.)* **fertum** *v.t.* 4,
to cram, stuff together
confĕro, ferre, tŭli, collātum *v.t,*
irreg, to bring together,
contribute, confer, talk about,
engage, fight, compare,
condense, convey, postpone;
(reflex.) to betake oneself,
go
confertus, a, um *adj, adv,* **ē,**
crowded
confessĭo, ōnis *f,* confession
confessus, a, um *adj,* admitted
confestim *adv,* immediately
confĭcĭo, fēci, fectum *v.t.* 3, to
complete, produce, exhaust, kill
confīdens, ntis *adj, adv,* **nter,**
bold, impudent
confīdentĭa, ae *f,* boldness
confīdo, fīsus sum *v.i.* 3, *semi-*
dep, to feel confident; *with dat,*
to trust
configo, xi, xum *v.t.* 3, to nail,
fasten together, transfix
confingo, nxi, ctum *v.t.* 3, to
fashion, invent
confīnis, e, *adj,* adjoining
confīnĭum, ii *n,* border
confirmātĭo, ōnis *f,*
encouragement, confirming
confirmātus, a, um *adj,* resolute
confirmo, *v.t.* 1, to strengthen,
encourage, prove
confīsus, a, um *adj,* trusting
confĭtĕor, fessus *v.t.* 2, *dep,* to
acknowledge, own
conflăgro *v.i.* 1, to burn

conflicto *v.t.* 1, to strike or dash together, ruin, harass

conflīgo, xi, ctum *v.i.t.* 3, to fight, struggle; strike or dash together

conflo *v.t.* 1, to kindle, cause

conflŭens, ntis *m,* confluence of rivers

conflŭo, xi *v.i.* 3, to flow together, unite, come in crowds

confŏdĭo, fōdi, fossum *v.t.* 3, to dig thoroughly, stab, pierce

conformātĭo, ōnis *f,* shaping

conformo *v.t.* 1, to form, fashion

confrăgōsus, a, um *adj,* broken

confringo, frēgi, fractum *v.t.* 3, to smash up

confŭgĭo, fūgi *v.i.* 3, to run away for help, take refuge

confundo, fūdi, sum *v.t.* 3, to pour together, confuse

confūsĭo, ōnis *f,* blending, disorder

confūsus, a, um *adj, adv,* ē, disorderly

confūto *v.t.* 1, to repress, silence

congĕlo *v.i.t.* 1, to freeze; thicken

congĕmĭno *v.t.* 1, to redouble

congĕmo, ŭi *v.i.t.* 3, to sigh; mourn

congĕrĭes, ēi *f,* heap

congĕro, ssi, stum *v.t.* 3, to bring together, accumulate

congestus, ūs *m,* heap

congĭārĭum, ii *n,* gratuity

congĭus, ii *m,* six-pint measure

conglŏbo *v.t.* 1, to gather, press into a ball

conglūtĭno *v.t.* 1, to glue or cement together, unite

congrĕdĭor, gressus *v.i.* 3, *dep,* to meet, encounter

congrĕgātĭo, ōnis *f,* assembly

congrĕgo *v.t.* 1, to collect into a flock, unite

congressus, ūs *m,* meeting, combat

congrŭens, ntis *adj, adv,* nter, appropriate, proper, consistent

congrŭentĭa, ae *f,* agreement

congrŭo, ŭi *v.t.* 3, to meet, coincide

cōnĭcĭo, iēci, iectum *v.t.* 3, to hurl, infer, drive

conĭecto *v.t.* 1, to hurl, foretell

conĭectūra, ae *f,* inference

conĭectus, ūs *m,* throwing, heap

conĭectus, a, um *adj,* thrown together

cōnĭfer, ĕra, ĕrum *adj,* cone-bearing

cōnītor, nīsus (nixus) *v.i.* 3, *dep,* to strive, struggle towards

cōnīvĕo, nīvi *v.i.* 2, to wink, blink

conĭŭgĭum, ii *n,* union, marriage

conĭunctĭo, ōnis *f,* uniting, junction

conĭunctus, a, um *adj, adv,* ē, near, connected, allied

conĭungo, nxi, nctum *v.t.* 3, to join together, marry

conĭunx, iŭgis *m, f,* husband, wife

conĭūrātĭo, ōnis *f,* conspiracy

conĭūrātus, i *m,* conspirator

conĭūro *v.i.* 1, to conspire, band together

conl... see coll...

connecto see cōnecto

conīvĕo see cōnīvĕo

connūbĭum, ii *n,* marriage

cōnōpĕum, i *n,* gauze net

cōnor *v.t.* 1, *dep,* to try, undertake

conquĕror, questus *v.i.t.* 3, *dep,* to complain (of)

conquĭesco, quĭēvi, quĭētum *v.i.* 3, to rest, pause

conquīro, quīsīvi, sītum *v.t.* 3, to search for

conquīsītĭo, ōnis *f,* search

conquīsītus, a, um *adj,* sought after

consălūto *v.t.* 1, to greet

consānesco, ŭi *v.i.* 3, to heal

consanguĭnĕus, a, um *adj,* related by blood

consanguĭnĭtas, ātis *f,* blood relationship

conscendo, di, sum *v.i.t.* 3, to embark; mount

conscĭentĭa, ae *f,* joint knowledge, moral sense

conscindo, ĭdi, issum *v.t.* 3, to tear in pieces

conscisco, scīvi, ītum *v.t.* 3, to make a joint resolution, decree, inflict

conscĭus, a, um *adj,* sharing knowledge of, (*with* **sibi**) conscious of

conscĭus, i *m,* accomplice

conscrībo, psi, ptum *v.t.* 3, to enroll, enlist, compose

conscriptus, i *m,* senator

consĕco, cŭi, ctum *v.t.* 1, to cut up

consecrātĭo, ōnis *f,* consecration

consecro *v.t.* 1, to dedicate, doom

consector *v.t.* 1, *dep,* to pursue eagerly, imitate

consĕnesco, nŭi *v.i.* 3, to grow old or weak

consensĭo, ōnis *f,* agreement, plot

consensus, ūs *m,* agreement, plot

consentānĕus, a, um *adj,* suited

consentĭo, sensi, sum *v.i.t.* 4, to agree, conspire, resolve; plot

consĕquens, ntis *adj,* according to reason, fit

consĕquor, sĕcūtus *v.t.* 3, *dep,* to follow, pursue, overtake, attain, obtain

consĕro, sēvi, sĭtum (sătum) *v.t.* 3, to plant, sow

consĕro, rŭi, rtum *v.t.* 3, to fasten together

consertus, a, um *adj, adv, ē,* joined, close, serried

conservātĭo, ōnis *f,* maintenance

conservo *v.t.* 1, to maintain, keep safe

conservus, i *m,* fellow slave

consessus, ūs *m,* assembly

consīdĕrātus, a, um *adj, adv, ē,* well-considered, cautious, discreet

consīdĕrātĭo, ōnis *f,* consideration

consīdĕro *v.t.* 1, to examine, contemplate

consīdo, sēdi, sessum *v.i.* 3, to sit down, take up position, subside

consigno *v.t.* 1, to seal, certify

consĭlĭārĭus, ii *m,* adviser

consĭlĭor *v.i.* 1, *dep,* to consult

consĭlĭum, ii *n,* plan, deliberation, policy, advise, assembly, wisdom

consĭmĭlis, e *adj,* quite like

consisto, stĭti, stĭtum *v.i.* 3, to stand, halt, take up position, endure, settle

consōbrīnus, i *m* (**a, ae,** *f*), cousin

consŏcĭātus, a, um *adj,* united

consŏcĭo *v.t.* 1, to share, unite

consōlātĭo, ōnis *f,* comfort

consōlātor, ōris *m,* comforter

consōlor *v.t.* 1, *dep,* to comfort

consŏnans, ntis (*with* **littera**), consonant

consŏno, ŭi *v.i.* 1, to resound, harmonize, agree

consŏnus, a, um *adj, adv, ē,* fit, harmonious

consōpĭo *v.t.* 4, to put to sleep

consors, rtis *adj,* partner

conspectus, ūs *m,* look, sight, view, presence

conspectus, a, um *adj,* distinguished, visible

conspergo, si, sum *v.t.* 3, to sprinkle

conspĭcĭo, spexi, ctum *v.t.* 3, to look at, understand

conspĭcor *v.t.* 1, *dep,* to catch sight of

conspĭcŭus, a, um *adj,* visible, striking

conspīrātĭo, ōnis *f,* agreement, plot

conspīro *v.i.* 1, to agree, plot

consponsor, ōris *m,* joint surety

conspŭo, (*no perf.***), ūtum** *v.t.* 3, to spit on, cover

constans, ntis *adj, adv* **nter,** firm, resolute, consistent

constantĭa, ae *f,* firmness, consistency

constat *v. impers,* it is agreed

consternātĭo, ōnis *f,* dismay

consterno, strāvi, strātum *v.t.* 3, to cover over

consterno *v.t.* 1, to alarm, provoke

constĭtŭo, ŭi, ūtum *v.t.* 3, to put, place, draw up, halt, establish, arrange, determine, decide

constĭtūtĭo, ōnis *f,* arrangement, establishment

constĭtūtum i *n,* agreement

constĭtūtus, a, um *adj,* arranged

consto, stĭti, stātum *v.i.* 1, to agree with, endure, be established, exist, consist of, cost

constrātus, a, um *adj,* covered

constringo, nxi, ctum *v.t.* 3, to tie up, restrain

constrūo, xi, ctum *v.t.* 3, to heap up, build

constūpro *v.t.* 1, to ravish

consŭēfăcĭo, fēci, factum *v.t.* 3, to accustom

consŭesco, sŭēvi, sŭētum *v.i.t.* 3, to be accustomed; train

consŭētūdo, ĭnis *f,* habit, custom, intimacy

consŭētus, a, um *adj,* customary

consŭl, ŭlis *m,* consul (highest Roman magistrate)

consŭlāris, e *adj,* of a consul

consŭlātus, ūs *m,* consulship

consŭlo, ŭi, sultum *v.i.t.* 3, to consider, consult; *with dat,* promote the interests of

consulto *v.i.t.* 1, to deliberate; consult

consultor, ōris *m,* adviser, client

consultum, I *n,* decision, decree

consultus, a, um *adj, adv,* ē, ō, well considered

consummātĭo, ōnis *f,* summing-up, completion

consūmo, mpsi, mptum *v.t.* 3, to use, eat up, consume, waste, destroy

consumptĭo, ōnis *f,* wasting, use

consurgo, surrexi, surrectum *v.i.t.* 3, to stand up, rise

contābŭlātĭo, ōnis *f,* flooring

contăbŭlo *v.t.* 1, to board over

contactus, ūs *m,* touch, contact, contagion

contāgĭo, ōnis *f,* touch, contact, contagion

contāmĭnātus, a, um *adj,* impure

contāmĭno *v.t.* 1, to blend, stain

contĕgo, xi, ctum *v.t.* 3, to cover up, hide

contemnendus, a, um *adj,* contemptible

contemno, mpsi, mptum *v.t.* 3, to despise

contemplātĭo, ōnis *f,* observation

contemplor *v.t.* 1, *dep,* to observe

contemptor, ōris *m,* despiser

contemptus, ūs *m,* contempt

contemptus, a, um *adj,* despicable

contendo, di, tum *v.i.t.* 3, to strive, march, fight, stretch; compare, make a bid for

contentĭo, ōnis *f,* struggle, effort, contrast, dispute

contentus, a, um *adj,* strained

contentus, a, um *adj,* satisfied

contermĭnus, a, um *adj,* bordering on

contĕro, trīvi, trītum *v.t.* 3, to grind, wear away, waste

conterrĕo *v.t.* 2, to frighten

contestor *v.t.* 1, *dep,* to call to witness

contexo, ŭi, xtum *v.i.t.* 3, to weave together; build, compose

contextus, ūs *m,* connection

contĭcesco, tĭcŭi *v.i.* 3, to be silent, cease

contignātĭo, ōnis *f,* wooden floor

contĭgŭus, a, um *adj,* adjoining

contĭnens, ntis *f,* continent

contĭnens, ntis *adj, adv,* nter, moderate, adjacent, unbroken

contĭnentĭa, ae *f,* self-restraint

contĭnĕo, ŭi, tentum *v.t.* 2, to keep together, contain, enclose, restrain

contingo, tĭgi, tactum *v.i.t.* 3, to happen; touch, border on, reach

contĭnŭātĭo, ōnis *f,* succession

contĭnŭō *adv,* immediately

contĭnŭo *v.t.* 1, to connect, to do one thing after another

contĭnŭus, a, um *adj,* unbroken

contĭō, ōnis *f,* meeting, speech

contĭōnātor, ōris *m,* demagogue

contĭōnor *v.* 1, *dep,* to expound

contorquĕo, torsi, tortum *v.t.* 2, to twist, brandish, hurl

contortĭo, ōnis *f,* twisting, intricacy

contortus, a, um *adj, adv,* ē, energetic, complicated

contrā *adv, prep. with acc,* opposite, facing, contrary to

contractĭo, ōnis *f,* contraction

contractus, a, um *adj,* compressed

contrādīco, xi, cutm *v.t.* 3, to reply

contrādictĭo, ōnis *f,* reply

contrăho, xi, ctum *v.t.* 3, to bring

together, shorten, produce, check

contrārĭum, ii *n*, the contrary

contrārĭus, a, um *adj, adv, ē*, opposite, injurious

contrecto *v.t.* 1, to handle, feel

contrĕmisco, mŭi *v.i.t.* 3, to quake; tremble at

contrĭbŭo, ŭi, ūtum *v.t.* 3, to quake; tremble at

contrĭbŭo, ŭi, ūtum *v.t.* 3, to incorporate, unite

contristo *v.t.* 1, to sadden, cloud

contrītus, a, um *adj*, worn out

contrōversĭa, ae *f*, dispute

contrōvērsus, a, um *adj*, questionable

contrŭcīdo *v.t.* 1, to slash

contŭbernālis, is *c*, messmate

contŭbernĭum, ii *n*, companionship

contŭĕor *v.t.* 2, *dep*, to survey

contŭmācĭa, ae *f*, obstinacy

contŭmax, ācis *adj, adv, ĭter*, stubborn, insolent

contŭmēlĭa, ae *f*, insult

contŭmēlĭōsus, a, um *adj*, abusive

contŭmŭlo *v.t.* 1, to bury

contundo, tŭdi, tūsum *v.t.* 3, to grind, crush, subdue

conturbo *v.t.* 1, to confuse

contus, i *m*, pole

contūsum, i *n*, bruise

cōnūbĭum, ĭi, *n*, marriage

cōnus, i *m*, cone, helmet-tip

convălesco, lŭi *v.i.* 3, to regain strength or health

convallis, is *f*, valley

convecto *v.t.* 1, to collect

convĕho, xi, ctum *v.t.* 3, to bring together

convello, velli, vulsum *v.t.* 3, to tear up

convĕnĭens, ntis *adj, adv, nter*, consistent, appropriate

convĕnĭenta, ae *f*, consistency, symmetry

convĕnĭo, vēni, ventum *v.i.t.* 4, to assemble, agree with; meet

convĕnit *impers*, it is agreed, it is right, it suits

conventum, i *n*, agreement

conventus, ūs *m*, meeting, assizes

conversĭo, ōnis *f*, revolution

conversus, a, um *adj*, reversed, turned, transposed

converto, ti, sum *v.i.t.* 3, to turn; change, alter

convexus, a, um *adj*, arched

convīcĭum, ii *n*, outcry, squabbling, abuse

convictor, ōris *m*, close friend

convictus, ūs *m*, intimacy

convinco, vīci, victum *v.t.* 3, to conquer, prove

convīva, ae *c*, guest

convīvĭum, ii *n*, dinner party

convīvor *v.i.* 1, *dep*, to banquet

convŏco *v.t.* 1, to call together

convŏlo, *v.i.* 1, to flock together

convolvo, volvi, vŏlūtum *v.t.* 3, to roll up, interweave

convulsĭo, ōnis *f*, convulsion

convulsus, a, um *adj*, torn-up

cŏŏpĕrĭo, rŭi, rtum *v.t.* 4, to cover up, overwhelm

cŏoptātĭo, ōnis *f*, election

cŏopto *v.t.* 1, to nominate, elect

cŏŏrĭor, ortus *v.i.* 4, *dep*, to arise, break out

cŏphĭnus, i *m*, wicker basket

cōpĭa, ae *f*, abundance, power, supply, opportunity; *pl*, forces

cōpĭōsus, a, um *adj, adv, ē*, well-supplied, eloquent

cōpŭla, ae *f*, thong, grappling iron

cōpŭlo *v.t.* 1, to link, join

cŏquo, xi, ctum *v.t.* 3, to cook, burn, ripen, devise, harass

cŏquus, i *m*, cook

cŏr, cordis *n*, heart, mind

cŏrālĭum, ii *n*, coral

cōram *adv and prep. with abl*, in the presence of, openly

corbis, is *c*, basket

corbīta, ae *f*, merchant ship

cordātus, a, um *adj*, shrewd

cŏrĭārĭus ii, *m*, tanner

cŏrĭum, ii *n*, skin, hide, leather, layer, stratum

cornĕus, a, um *adj*, horny

cornĕus, a, um *adj*, of cornel wood

cornĭcen, ĭnis *m*, horn-player

cornĭcŭla, ae *f*, jackdaw

cornĭcŭlum, i *n*, little horn, feeler

cornĭger, ĕra, ĕrum *adj,* horned
cornĭpēs, ĕdis *adj,* hoofed
cornix, īcis *f,* crow
cornū, ūs *n,* horn, hoof, beak, tributary, promontory, knob, wing of army, bow, trumpet, drinking horn
cornum, i *n,* cornel-cherry
cornus, i *f,* cornel-cherry tree, cornel-wood javelin
cŏrōna, ae *f,* garland, wreath, crown, ring, circle, crowd
cŏrōno *v.t.* 1, to crown, encircle
corpŏrĕus, a, um *adj,* physical
corpŭlentus, a, um *adj,* corpulent
corpus, ŏris *n,* body
correctĭo, ōnis *f,* improvement
corrector, ōris *m,* reformer
corrēpo, psi *v.i.* 3, to creep
corrĭgĭa, ae *f,* shoe lace
corrĭgo, rexi, ctum *v.t.* 3, to put right, improve
corrĭpĭo, pŭi, pertum *v.t.* 3, to snatch, plunder, attack, shorten
corrōbŏro *v.t.* 1, to strengthen
corrūgo *v.t.* 1, to wrinkle
corrumpo, rūpi, ptum *v.t.* 3, to destroy, corrupt, spoil
corrŭo, ŭi *v.i.t.* 3, to collapse; overthrow
corruptēla, ae *f,* corruption
corruptor, ōris *m,* corruptor, seducer
corruptus, a, um *adj, adv,* ē, spoiled, damaged, tainted
cortex, īcis *m,* bark, rind
cortīna, ae *f,* kettle, cauldron
cŏrusco *v.i.t.* 1, to glitter; shake
cŏruscus, a, um *adj,* glittering, vibrating
corvus, i *m,* raven
cŏrȳlus, i *f,* hazel shrub
cŏrymbus, i *m,* cluster of fruit or flowers
cŏrȳtŏs, i *m,* quiver
cōs, cōtis *f,* flintstone
costa, ae *f,* rib, wall
cŏthurnus, i *m,* hunting-boot, buskin (worn by tragic actors)
cottīdĭānus, a, um *adj, adv,* ō, daily, usual
cottīdĭē *adv,* daily
cŏturnix, īcis *f,* quail

coxendix, īcis *f,* hip
crabro, ōnis *m,* hornet
crambē, es *f,* cabbage, kale
crāpŭla, ae *f,* intoxication
crās *adv,* tomorrow
crassĭtūdo, ĭnis *f,* thickness
crassus, a, um *adj, adv,* ē, thick, fat, solid
crastĭnus, a, um *adj,* of tomorrow
crātēr, ĕris *m,* mixing-bowl, basin
crātēra, ae *f,* mixing-bowl, basin
crātĭcŭla, ae *f,* gridiron
crātis, is *f,* wicker-work, hurdle
crĕātĭo, ōnis *f,* appointing
crĕātor, ōris *m,* founder, creator
crĕātrix, īcis *f,* mother
crēber, bra, brum *adj, adv,* ō, think, numerous, repeated
crēbresco, brŭi *v.i.* 3, to become frequent, gain strength
crēdens, ntis *c,* believer
crēdĭbĭlis, e *adj, adv* ĭter, credible, probable
crēdĭtor, ōris *m,* creditor
crēdo, dĭdi, dĭtum *v.t.* 3, to lend, entrust, trust, believe in (*with dat*); suppose
crēdŭlĭtas, ātis *f,* credulity
crēdŭlus, a, um *adj,* ready to believe
crĕmo *v.t.* 1, to burn
crĕo *v.t.* 1, to produce, appoint
crĕpĭda, ae *f,* sandal
crĕpīdo, ĭnis *f,* pedestal, dike
crĕpĭtācŭlum, i *n,* rattle
crĕpĭto *v.i.* 1, to rattle, rustle
crĕpĭtus, ūs *m,* rattling, clashing, cracking
crĕpo, ŭi, ĭtum *v.i.t.* 1, to rattle, creak, jingle; prattle about
crĕpundĭa, ōrum *n.pl,* child's rattle
crĕpuscŭlum, i *n,* twilight, dusk
cresco, crēvi, crētum *v.i.* 3, to arise, grow, appear, thrive
crēta, ae *f,* chalk
crētus, a, um *adj,* arisen, born of
crībro *v.t.* 1, to sift
crībrum, i *n,* sieve
crīmen, ĭnis *n,* accusation, offence
crīmĭnātĭo, ōnis *f,* accusation, calumny

crīmĭnor *v.t.* 1, *dep,* to accuse
crīmĭnōsus, a, um *adj, adv,* ē,
  slanderous, culpable
crīnālis, e *adj,* of the hair
crīnis, is *m,* the hair
crīnītus, a, um *adj,* long-haired
crispo *v.i.t.* 1, to curl; brandish
crispus, a, um *adj,* curled,
  quivering
crista, ae *f,* crest, plume
cristātus, a, um *adj,* crested
crĭtĭcus, i *m,* critic
crŏcĕus, a, um *adj,* of saffron or
  yellow
crōcĭo *v.i.* 4, to croak
crŏcŏdīlus, i *m,* crocodile
crŏcus, i *m* (um, i, *n*), crocus
crŭcĭātus, ūs *m,* torture, pain
crŭcĭo *v.t.* 1, to torture
crūdēlis, e *adj, adv,* ĭter, cruel
crūdēlĭtas, ātis *f,* crulelty
crūdesco, dŭi *v.i.* 3, to get worse
crūdĭtas, ātis *f,* indigestion
crūdus, a, um *adj,* raw, fresh,
  unripe, cruel
crŭento *v.t.* 1, to stain with
  blood
crŭentus, a, um *adj,* bloodstained,
  bloodthirsty
crŭmēna, ae *f,* small purse
crŭor, ōris *m,* blood (from a
  wound), murder
crūs, ūris *n,* leg, shin
crusta, ae *f,* crust, bark, mosaic
crustŭlārĭus, ii *m,* confectioner
crustŭlum, i *n,* confectionery
crustum, i *n,* confectionery
crux, ŭcis *f,* cross
crypta, ae *f,* cloister, vault
crystallum, i *n,* crystal
cŭbĭculārĭus, ii *m,* chamber-
  servant
cŭbĭcŭlum, i *n,* bedroom
cŭbĭcus, a, um *adj,* cubic
cŭbīle, is *n.* bed, lair
cŭbĭtăl, ālis *n,* cushion
cŭbĭtum, i *n,* elbow
cŭbĭtus, i *m,* elbow
cŭbītum see **cŭbo**
cŭbo, ŭi, ĭtum *v.i.* 1, to lie down,
  sleep, lie ill, slant
cŭcullus, i *m,* hood
cŭcūlus, i *m,* cuckoo

cŭcŭmis, ĕris *m,* cucumber
cŭcurbĭta, ae *f,* cup
cūdo *v.t.* 3, to beat, strike, stamp
cūius, a, um *interr. adj,* whose?
cūius *genit. of* qui, quis
culcīta, ae *f,* mattress, cushion
cŭlex, ĭcis *m,* gnat, mosquito
cŭlīna, ae *f,* kitchen, food
cullĕus, i *m,* leather bag
culmen, ĭnis *n,* summit, roof
culmus, i *m,* stem, stalk
culpa, ae *f,* blame, fault,
  weakness
culpābĭlis, e *adj,* culpable
culpandus, a, um *adj,* culpable
culpo *v.t.* 1, to blame
culter, tri *m,* knife, ploughshare
cultor, ōris *m,* cultivator,
  supporter, inhabitant
cultrix, īcis *f,* female inhabitant
cultūra, ae *f,* cultivation, care
cultus, a, um *adj,* cultivated,
  elegant
cultus, ūs, *m,* farming, education,
  culture-pattern, reverence, dress
cŭlullus, i, *m,* drinking-cup
cum *conj,* when, whenever, since,
  although cum ... tum, both ...
  and, not only ... but also
cum *prep. with abl,* together
  with; *it is attached to the abl.
  case of personal prons,* e.g.
  mecum, with me
cumba, ae *f,* small boat
cŭmĕra, ae *f,* box, chest
cŭmīnum, i *n,* cumin (plant)
cumquĕ *adv,* however, whenever
cŭmŭlātus, a, um *adj, adv,* ē, full,
  increased
cŭmŭlo *v.t.* 1, to heap up,
  complete
cŭmŭlus, i *m,* heap, 'last straw'
cūnābŭla, ōrum *n.pl,* cradle
cūnae, ārum *f.pl,* cradle
cunctans, ntis *adj, adv,* nter,
  loitering, sluggish
cunctātĭo, ōnis *f,* delay, doubt
cunctātor, ōris *m,* loiterer,
  cautious person
cunctor *v.i.* 1, *dep,* to hesitate,
  delay
cunctus, a, um *adj,* all together
cūnĕātim *adv,* wedge-shaped

cŭnĕo *v.t.* 1, to fasten with wedges

cŭnĕus, i *m*, wedge, wedge-shaped block of theatre seats or troop formation

cŭnīcŭlum, i *n*, tunnel, mine

cŭnīcŭlus, i *m*, rabbit

cūpa, ae *f*, barrel, cask

cūpēdĭa, ōrum *n.pl*, delicacies

cŭpĭdē *adv*, eagerly

cŭpĭdĭtas, ātis *f*, desire, longing

cŭpīdo, ĭnis *f*, lust, greed

cŭpĭdus, a, um *adj*, eager, longing for, greedy, passionate

cŭpĭens, ntis *adj, adv*, **nter,** eager or longing for

cŭpĭo, īvi, ītum *v.t.* 3, to desire

cŭpressus, i *f*, cypress tree

cūr *adv*, why

cūra, ae *f*, care, attention, management, anxiety

cūrātĭo, ōnis *f*, administration, cure

cūrātor, ōris *m*, manager

cūrātus, a, um *adj*, urgent

curcŭlĭo, ōnis *m*, weevil

cūrĭa, ae *f*, senate house, city ward

cūrĭālis, e *adj*, of the same ward

cūrĭōsus, a, um *adj, adv*, **ē,** careful, inquisitive

cūro *v.t.* 1, to take care of; *with acc. and gerundive,* to see to it that ..., to arrange, command

currĭcŭlum, i *n*, racecourse, chariot, racing, career

curro, cŭcurri, cursum *v.i.* 3, to run

currus, ūs *m*, chariot

cursim *adv*, swiftly

curso *v.i.* 1, to run to and fro

cursor, ōris *m*, runner, courier

cursus, ūs *m*, running, journey, speed, direction

curtus, a, um *adj*, shortened, humble

cŭrūlis, e *adj*, of a chariot; **sella cŭrūlis,** ivory chair of office used by high magistrates

curvāmen, ĭnis *n*, curve

curvo *v.t.* 1, to bend

curvus, a, um *adj*, bent, stooping

cuspis, ĭdis *f*, point, lance, spit, sting

custōdĭa, ae *f*, watch, guard, imprisonment, guard-room

custōdĭo *v.t.* 4, to guard, watch, keep, preserve

custos, ōdis *c*, guardian, gaoler

cŭtis, is *f*, skin, surface

cȳăthus, i *m*, small ladle

cȳcnēus, a, um *adj*, of a swan

cȳcnus, i *m*, swan

cȳlindrus, i *m*, roller, cylinder

cymba, ae *f*, small boat

cymbălum, i *n*, cymbal, bell

cymbĭum, ii *n*, bowl, basin

Cȳnĭcus, i *m*, a Cynic philosopher

cȳpărissus, i *f*, cypress tree

D

dactȳlus, i *m*, dactyl (metrical foot consisting of one long and two short syllables)

daedălus, a, um *adj*, skilful

daemŏnĭum, ii *n*, demon

damma (dāma), ae *f*, deer

damnātĭo, ōnis *f*, condemnation

damnātōrĭus, a, um *adj*, condemnatory

damnātus, a, um *adj*, guilty

damno *v.t.* 1, to condemn

damnōsus, a, um *adj, adv* **ē,** destructive

damnum, i *n*, damage, loss, fine

daps, dăpis *f*, formal banquet

dătĭo, ōnis *f*, distribution

dător, ōris *m*, giver

dē *prep. with abl*, from, down from, about, concerning, on account of

dĕa, ae *f*, goddess

dĕalbo *v.t.* 1, to whitewash

dĕambŭlo *v.i.* 1, to take a walk

dĕarmo *v.t.* 1, to disarm

dēbacchor *v.i.* 1, *dep*, to rage

dēbellātor, ōris *m*, conqueror

dēbello *v.i.t.* 1, to finish a war; subdue

dēbĕo *v.i.t.* 2, to be indebted; owe, (one) ought

dēbĭlis, e *adj*, disabled, weak

dēbĭlĭtas, ātis *f*, weakness

dēbĭlĭtātĭo, ōnis *f*, maiming, enervating

dēbĭlĭto v.t. 1, to cripple, weaken
dēbĭtor, ōris m, debtor
dēbĭtum, i n, debt
dēbĭtus, a, um adj, owed
dēcanto v.i. 1, to sing repeatedly
dēcēdo, ssi, ssum v.i. 3, to go
  away, cease, yield, resign
dēcem indecl. adj, ten
Dĕcember (mensis) December
dĕcempĕda, ae f, measuring rod
  (ten feet long)
dĕcempĕdātor, ōris m, surveyor
dĕcemvĭrālis, e adj, of the
  decemviri
dĕcemvĭrātus, ūs m, the rank of
  decemvir
dĕcemvĭri, ōrum m.pl,
  commission of ten (early rulers
  of Rome)
dĕcens, ntis adj, adv, nter,
  proper, graceful
dĕcentĭa, ae f, comeliness
dēceptus, a, um adj, deceived
dēcerno, crēvi, crētum v.i.t. 3, to
  decide, resolve; fight
dēcerpo, psi, ptum v.t. 3, to
  pluck, gather
dēcertātĭo, ōnis f, struggle
dēcerto v.i.t. 1, to fight it out;
  struggle for
dēcessĭo, ōnis f, departure
dēcessus, ūs m, departure
dĕcet, cŭit v. 2, impers, it is
  becoming or proper
dēcĭdo, cĭdi v.i. 3, to fall down,
  die, perish
dēcĭdo, cĭdi, cīsum v.t. 3, to cut
  off, settle
dĕcĭēs, (dĕcĭens) adv, ten times
dĕcĭma, ae f, tenth part, tithe
dĕcĭmānus, a, um adj, of tithes,
  of the tenth legion; porta
  dĕcĭmāna, main camp gate
dĕcĭmo v.t. 1, to punish every
  tenth man, decimate
dĕcĭmus, a, um adj, tenth
dēcĭpĭo, cēpi, ptum v.t. 3, to
  deceive
dēcīsĭo, ōnis f, decision
dēclāmātĭo ōnis f, practice in
  public speaking
dēclāmātor, ōris m, speech
  expert

dēclāmātōrĭus, a, um adj,
  rhetorical
dēclāmo v.i. 1, to practise
  speaking
dēclāro v.t. 1, to make clear
dēclīnātĭo, ōnis f, avoidance,
  bending
dēclīno v.i.t. 1, to turn aside
dēclīve, is n, slope
dēclīvis, e adj, sloping
  downwards
dēclīvĭtas, ātis f, slope
dēcoctor, ōris m, bankrupt
dēcoctus, a, um adj, boiled,
  refined
dēcŏlor, ōris adj, discoloured
dēcŏlŏro v.t. 1, to discolour
dēcŏquo, xi, ctum v.t. 3, to boil
  down, go bankrupt
dĕcor, ōris m, elegance
dĕcŏro v.t. 1, to adorn
dĕcōrum, I n, decency
dĕcōrus, a, um adj, adv, ē,
  becoming, proper, elegant
dēcrĕpĭtus, a, um adj, decrepit
dēcresco, crēvi, tum v.i. 3, to
  diminish, wane
dēcrētum, i n, decree, decision
dĕcūma, dĕcūmānus see decim...
dēcumbo, cŭbŭi v.i. 3, to lie
  down, lie ill
dĕcŭrĭa, ae f, section of ten
dĕcŭrĭo v.t. 1, to divide into
  sections
decŭrĭo, ōnis m, the head of ten,
  superintendent
dēcurro, cŭcurri, cursum v.i. 3, to
  run down, complete a course,
  manoeuvre, have recourse to
dēcursus, ūs m, descent, course,
  manoeuvre, attack
dĕcus, ŏris n, ornament,
  splendour
dēcussātĭo, ōnis f, intersection
dēcŭtĭo, cussi, ssum v.t. 3, to
  shake off, beat off
dēdĕcet, cŭit v. 2, impers, it is
  unbecoming
dēdĕcŏro v.t. 1, to disgrace
dēdĕcus, ŏris n, disgrace, shame
dēdĭcātĭo, ōnis f, dedication
dēdĭco v.t. 1, to dedicate
dēdignor v.t. 1, dep, to disdain

dēdisco, dĭdĭci *v.t.* 3, to forget
dēdītīcĭus, ii *m*, prisoner-of-war
dēdītĭo, ōnis *f*, surrender
dēdītus, a, um *adj*, addicted to
dēdo, dēdĭdi, dĭtum *v.t.* 3, to give up, surrender, devote
dēdŏcĕo *v.t.* 2, to teach one not to ...
dēdŏlĕo *v.i.* 2, to stop grieving
dēdūco, xi, ctum *v.t.* 3, to bring, lead down, withdraw, conduct, escort, mislead, subtract, launch
dēductĭo, ōnis *f*, diversion, transplanting, inference
dēductus, a, um *adj*, fine-spun
dēerro *v.i.* 1, to go astray
dēfătīgātĭo, ōnis *f*, exhaustion
dēfătīgo *v.t.* 1, to exhaust
dēfectĭo, ōnis *f*, rebellion, failure, eclipse
dēfectus, ūs *m*, rebellion, failure, eclipse
dēfectus, a, um *adj*, worn out
dēfendo, di, sum *v.t.* 3, to repel, defend, support
dēfensĭo, ōnis *f*, defence
dēfensor, ōris *m*, protector
dēfĕro, ferre, tŭli, lātum *v.t, irreg*, to bring down or away, convey, refer, announce, indict, offer
dēfervesco, fervi *v.i.* 3, to cool down
dēfessus, a, um *adj*, weary
dēfĕtiscor, fessus *v.i.* 3, *dep*, to grow tired
dēfĭcĭo, fēci, fectum *v.i.t.* 3, to fail, disappear, revolt; desert
dēfīgo, xi, xum *v.t.* 3, to fasten down, astound
dēfingo, nxi *v.t.* 3, to shape
dēfinĭo *v.t.* 4, to mark off, restrict, define
dēfinītĭo, ōnis *f*, definition
dēfinītus, a, um *adj, adv, ē*, precise
dēfixus, a, um *adj*, fixed
dēflăgrātĭo, ōnis *f*, destruction by fire
dēflăgro *v.i.* 1, to burn out
dēflecto, xi, xum *v.i.t.* 3, to swerve; divert
dēflĕo, ēvi, ētum *v.t.* 2, to deplore
dēflōresco, rŭi *v.i.* 3, to wither

dēflŭo, xi, xum *v.i.* 3, to flow down, vanish
dēfŏdĭo, fōdi, ssum *v.t.* 3, to dig deep, bury
dēfŏre *fut. infinitive* (**dēsum**)
dēformis, e *adj*, deformed, ugly
dēformĭtas, ātis *f*, ugliness
dēformo *v.t.* 1, to shape
dēformo, *v.t.* 1, to disfigure
dēfossus, a, um *adj*, buried
dēfraudo *v.t.* 1, to cheat
dēfrĭco, cŭi, ctum *v.t.* 1, to rub hard
dēfringo, frēgi, fractum *v.t.* 3, to break up, break off
dēfrŭtum, i *n*, syrup
dēfŭgĭo, fūgi *v.i.t.* 3, to escape; avoid
dēfunctus, a, um *adj*, having finished, deceased
dēfundo, fūdi, fūsum *v.t.* 3, to pour out
dēfungor, functus *v.* 3, *dep, with abl*, to bring to an end
dēgĕner, ĕris *adj*, unworthy of one's birth, ignoble
dēgenĕro *v.i.t.* 1, to deteriorate; impair
dēgo, dēgi *v.i.t.* 3, to live; spend
dēgrandĭnat *v. impers*, it is hailing, ceasing to hail
dēgrăvo, *v.t.* 1, to weigh down
dēgrĕdĭor, gressus *v.i.* 3, *dep*, to step down, dismount
dēgusto *v.t.* 1, to taste, graze
dēhinc *adv*, from here, hence, next, afterwards
dēhisco, hīvi *v.i.* 3, to split open, gape
dēhŏnesto *v.t.* 1, to disgrace
dēhortor *v.t.* 1, *dep*, to dissuade
dēĭcĭo, iēci, iectum *v.t.* 3, to throw down, drive out, lower
dēiectus, a, um *adj*, downcast
dēiectus, ūs *m*, descent, felling
dēin *adv*, from there, after that, afterwards
dēindĕ *adv*, from there, after that, afterwards
dēinceps *adv*, in succession
dēlābor, lapsus *v.i.* 3, *dep*, to fall, sink, glide down
dēlasso *v.t.* 1, to tire out

dēlātĭo, ōnis *f,* accusation
dēlator, ōris *m,* informer
dēlectābĭlis, e *adj,* delightful
dēlectātĭo, ōnis *f,* delight, pleasure
dēlecto *v.t.* 1, to allure, charm
dēlectus, a, um *adj,* chosen
dēlectus, ūs *m,* choice, selection, levy
dēlectum hăbere to hold a levy
dēlēgo *v.t.* 1, to dispach, assign, attribute
dēlēnīmentum, i *n,* allurement
dēlēnĭo *v.t.* 4, to soothe, charm
dēlĕo, lēvi, lētum *v.t.* 2, to destroy, finish
dēlībĕrātĭo, ōnis *f,* careful thought
dēlībĕrātus, a, um *adj,* settled
dēlībĕro *v.t.* 1, to consider, consult, resolve
dēlībo *v.t.* 1, to taste, pluck, detract from
dēlībūtus, a, um *adj,* smeared
dēlīcātus, a, um *adj, adv,* e, charming, luxurious
dēlīcĭae, ārum *f.pl,* pleasure, luxury, sweetheart, pet
dēlīctum, i *n,* crime, offence
dēlīgo, lēgi, lectum *v.t.* 3, to pick, choose, gather
dēlīgo *v.t.* 1, to tie down
dēlinquo, līqui, lictum *v.i.* 3, to fail, offend
dēlīrātĭo, ōnis *f,* silliness
dēlīrĭum, ii *n,* delirium
dēlīro *v.i.* 1, to be out of one's mind
dēlīrus, a, um *adj,* crazy
dēlītesco, tŭi *v.i.* 3, to lurk
delphīnus, i *m,* dolphin
dēlūbrum, i *n,* sanctuary
dēlūdo, si, sum *v.t.* 3, to mock
dēmando *v.t.* 1, to entrust
dēmens, ntis *adj, adv,* nter, out of one's mind
dēmensum, i *n,* ration
dēmentĭa, ae *f,* insanity
dēmĕrĕo *v.t.* 2, to deserve, oblige
dēmergo, si, sum *v.t.* 3, to immerse, sink
dēmētĭor, mensus *v.t.* 4, *dep,* to measure off
dēmĕto, messŭi, ssum *v.t.* 3, to

mow, reap, gather
dēmigro *v.i.* 1, to emigrate
dēmĭnŭo, ŭi, ūtum *v.t.* 3, to lessen, infringe
dēmĭnūtĭo, ōnis *f,* decrease
dēmīror *v.t.* 1, *dep,* to wonder
dēmissĭo, ōnis *f,* abasement
dēmissus, a, um *adj, adv,* ē, low-lying, drooping, downcast, shy
dēmitto, mīsi, ssum *v.t.* 3, to send down, lower, descend, enter upon, lose heart
dēmo, mpsi, mptum *v.t.* 3, to take away, remove
dēmōlĭor *v.t.* 4, *dep,* to pull down, destroy
dēmonstrātĭo, ōnls *f,* indication
dēmonstro *v.t.* 1, to point out
dēmŏrĭor, mortŭus *v.i.* 3, *dep,* to die
dēmŏror *v.i.t.* 1, *dep,* to loiter; restrain
dēmŏvĕo, mōvi, mōtum *v.t.* 2, to remove, put aside
dēmum *adv,* at last, not until then, only
dēmūto *v.i.t.* 1, to change
dēnārĭus, ii *m,* small Roman silver coin
dēnăto *v.i.* 1, to swim down
dēnĕgo *v.t.* 1, to deny completely
dēni, ae, a, *adj,* ten each, ten
dēnĭque *adv,* and then, at last, in short
dēnōmĭno *v.t.* 1, to name
dēnormo *v.t.* 1, to disfigure
dēnŏto *v.t.* 1, to mark, point out
dens, ntis *m,* tooth, prong
denso *v.t.* 1, to thicken, close up
densus, a, um *adj,* thick, frequent
dentālĭa, ĭum *n.pl,* plough-beam
dentātus, a, um *adj,* with teeth
dentĭfrĭcĭum, ii *n,* tooth-powder
dentĭo *v.i.* 4, to teethe
dentītĭo, ōnis *f,* teething
dentiscalpĭum, ii *n,* toothpick
dēnūbo, psi, ptum *v.i.* 3, to marry
dēnūdo *v.t.* 1, to lay bare
dēnuntĭātĭo, ōnis *f,* declaration
dēnuntĭo *v.t.* 1, to announce, command, warn
dēnŭō *adv,* anew, again
dĕorsum *adv,* downwards

dēpăciscor see **dēpĕciscor**

dēpasco, pāvi, pastum *v.t.* 3, to feed on, consume

dēpĕciscor, pectus (pactus) *v.t.* 3, *dep,* to bargin for

dēpĕcūlor *v.t.* 1, *dep,* to plunder

dēpello, pŭli, pulsum *v.t.* 3, to drive away, dissuade

dēpendĕo *v.i.* 2, to hang down, depend on

dēpendo, di, sum *v.t.* 3, to spend, pay

dēperdo, dĭdi, dĭtum *v.t.* 3, to destroy, lose

dēpĕrĕo *v.i.* 4, to perish completely, die with love for

dēpingo, pinxi, pictum *v.t.* 3, to paint, portray, sketch

dēplōro *v.i.t.* 1, to lament; deplore

dēpōno, pŏsŭi, pŏsĭtum *v.t.* 3, to put aside, entrust, bet, get rid of

dēpŏpŭlātĭo, ōnis *f,* pillaging

dēpŏpŭlor *v.t.* 1, *dep,* to plunder

dēporto *v.t.* 1, to carry down, carry away, banish, earn

dēposco, pŏposci *v.t.* 3, to demand, challenge

dēpŏsĭtum, i *n,* deposit, trust

dēprāvātĭo, ōnis *f,* corruption

dēprāvo *v.t.* 1, to pervert, corrupt

dēprĕcātĭo, ōnis *f,* pleading, intercession

dēprĕcātor, ōris *m,* pleader

dēprĕcor *v.t.* 1, *dep,* to avert by prayer, beseech, plead for

dēprĕhendo, di, sum *v.t.* 3, to catch, overtake, discover

dēpressus, a, um *adj,* low-lying

dēprĭmo, pressi, pressum *v.t.* 3, to press down, sink, suppress

dēproelĭor *v.i.* 1, *dep,* to battle fiercely

dēprōmo, mpsi, mptum *v.t.* 3, to fetch out

dēprŏpĕro *v.i.t.* 1, to hasten; prepare hastily

dēpugno *v.i.* 1, to fight it out

dēpulsĭo, ōnis *f,* warding off

dēpŭto *v.t.* 1, to prune

dērĕlinquo, līqui, lictum *v.t.* 3, to abandon completely

dērīdĕo, si, sum *v.t.* 2, to mock

dērĭgesco, gŭi *v.i.* 3, to stiffen

dērīpĭo, rĭpŭi, reptum *v.t.* 3, to tear off, pull down

dērīsor, ōris *m,* scoffer

dērīvātĭo, ōnis *f,* turning off

dērīvo *v.t.* 1, to divert water

dērŏgo *v.t.* 1, to remove, restrict

dērōsus, a, um *adj,* nibbled

dēruptus, a, um *adj,* broken, steep

dēsaevĭo *v.i.* 4, to rage

dēscendo, di, sum *v.i.* 3, to go down, come down, go into battle, penetrate, resort to

dēscensus, ūs *m,* descent

dēscisco, īvi, ītum *v.i.* 3, to revolt, desert, degenerate

dēscrībo, psi, ptum *v.t.* 3, to transcribe, describe, define, arrange

dēscripta, ōrum *n.pl,* records

dēscriptĭo, ōnis *f,* sketch, description, arrangement

dēsĕco, cŭi, ctum *v.t.* 1, to cut off

dēsĕro, rŭi, rtum *v.t.* 3, to abandon

dēserta, ōrum *n.pl,* desert

dēsertor, ōris *m,* deserter

dēsertus, a, um *adj,* abandoned

dēservĭo *v.i.* 4, to serve wholeheartedly

dēses, ĭdis *adj,* indolent

dēsĭdĕo, sēdi *v.i.* 2, to sit idle

dēsīdĕrĭum, ii *n,* longing, grief, request

dēsīdĕro *v.t.* 1, to miss, crave for

dēsĭdĭa, ae *f,* idleness

dēsĭdĭōsus, a, um *adj,* lazy

dēsīdo, sēdi *v.i.* 3, to sink down

dēsignātĭo, ōnis *f,* description, arrangement

dēsignātor, ōris *m,* master of ceremonies, undertaker

dēsignātus, a, um *adj,* elect

dēsigno *v.t.* 1, to mark out, indicate, appoint

dēsĭlĭo, sĭlŭi, sultum *v.i.* 4, to jump down

dēsĭno, sĭi, ĭtum *v.i.t.* 3, to cease; put an end to

dēsĭpĭo *v.i.* 3, to be foolish

dēsisto, stĭti, stĭtum *v.i.* 3, to

leave off, halt
dēsōlātus, a, um *adj,* forsaken
dēsōlo *v.t.* 1, to abandon
dēspecto *v.t.* 1, to look down on
dēspectus, ūs *m,* view down on
dēspectus, a, um *adj,* despicable
dēspērātĭo, ōnis *f,* hopelessness
dēspērātus, a, um *adj,* past hope
dēspēro *v.i.t.* 3, to despair; give
   up as lost
dēspĭcĭo, exi, ctum *v.i.t.* 3, to
   look down; despise
dēspŏlĭo *v.t.* 1, to plunder
dēspondĕo, di, nsum *v.t.* 2, to
   promise (in marriage)
dēspūmo *v.t.* 1, to skim off
dēspŭo *v.i.t* 3, to spit; reject
dēstillo *v.i.* 1, to trickle, drip
dēstĭnātĭo, ōnis *f,* purpose
dēstĭnātum, i *n,* aim, intention
dēstĭnātus, a, um *adj,* fixed
dēstĭno *v.t.* 1, to secure, intend
dēstĭtŭo, ŭi, ūtum *v.t.* 3, to place,
   desert
dēstĭtūtus, a, um *adj,* abandoned
dēstringo, nxi, ctum *v.t.* 3, to
   strip off, unsheath, graze
dēstrŭo, xi, ctum *v.t.* 3, to
   demolish
dēsŭesco, sŭēvi, sŭētum *v.i.t.* 3,
   to become unused; cease to use
dēsŭētus, a, um *adj,* disused
dēsultor, ōris *m,* acrobat on
   horseback
dēsum, dĕesse, dēfŭi *v.i,* to be
   lacking, fail, desert
dēsūmo, mpsi, mptum *v.t.* 3, to
   select
dēsŭpĕr *adv,*from above
dēsurgo *v.i.* 3, to rise from
dētĕgo, xi, ctum *v.t.* 3, to expose
dētentus, a, um *adj,* kept back
dētergĕo, si, sum *v.t.* 2, to wipe
   clean
dētĕrĭor, ĭus *adj,* lower, worse
dētĕrĭus *adv,* worse, less
dētermĭno *v.t.* 1, to fix limits
dētĕro, trīvi, trītum *v.t.* 3, to rub
   or wear away, impair
dēterrĕo *v.t.* 2, to discourage
dētestābĭlis, e *adj,* detestable
dētestātĭo, ōnis *f,* cursing
dētestor *v.t.* 1, *dep,* to curse,

loathe, ward off
dētexo, xŭi, xtum *v.t.* 3, to weave,
   finish
dētĭnĕo, tĭnŭi, tentum *v.t.* 2, to
   keep back, delay, lengthen
dētŏno, ŭi *v.i.* 1, to thunder, cease
   thundering
dētorquĕo, si, tum *v.t.* 2, to turn
   aside, distort
dētrăho, xi, ctum *v.t.* 3, to pull
   down, remove, deprecate
dētrecto *v.t.* 1, to reject, detract
   from
dētrīmentum, i *n,* loss, damage,
   defeat
dētrūdo, si, sum *v.t.* 3, to push
   down, dislodge
dētrunco *v.t.* 1, to lop off
dēturbo *v.t.* 1, to throw down
dēūro, ussi, ustum *v.t.* 3, to burn
dĕus, i *m,* god
dēvasto *v.t.* 1, to devestate
dēvĕho, xi, ctum *v.t.* 3, to carry
   down, carry away
dēvĕnĭo, vēni, ventum *v.i.* 4, to
   come down, arrive at
dēversor *v.i.* 1, *dep,* to lodge
dēversor, ōris *m,* lodger
dēversōrĭum, ii *n,* inn
dēverto, ti, sum *v.i.t.* 3, to lodge,
   stay; turn aside
dēvexus, a, um *adj,* sloping down
dēvĭa, ōrum *n.pl,* lonely places
dēvincĭo, nxi, nctum *v.t.* 4, to tie
   up, endear
dēvinco, vīci, ctum *v.t.* 3, to
   conquer completely
dēvinctus see dēvincĭo
dēvīto *v.t.* 1, to avoid
dēvĭus, a, um *adj,* out-of-the-way
dēvŏco *v.t.* 1, to call away
dēvŏlo, *v.i.*1, to fly down
dēvolvo, volvi, vŏlūtum *v.t.* 3, to
   roll down
dēvŏro *v.t.* 1, to gulp down
dēvōtĭo, ōnis *f,* consecration
dēvōtus, a, um *adj,* devoted
dēvŏvĕo, vōvi, vōtum *v.t.* 2, to
   dedicate, doom, devote
dexter, tĕra, tĕrum (tra, trum) *adj,*
   on the right, skilful, suitable
dextĕra (dextra), ae *f,* right hand
dextĕrĭtas, ātis *f,* dexterity

dextrorsum *adv,* on the right
di *pl.* of **děus**
diădēma, ătis *n,* crown, diadem
diăgōnālis, e *adj,* diagonal
diălectĭcus, a, um *adj,* of debate
diălŏgus, i *m,* conversation
diāria, ōrum *n.pl,* rations
dīca, ae *f,* lawsuit
dĭcācĭtas, ātis *f,* wit
dĭcax, ācis *adj,* witty
dĭcĭo, ōnis *f,* dominion, power
dīco *v.t.* 1, to dedicate, devote
dīco, xi, ctum *v.t.* 3, to say, tell, appoint
dicta see **dictum**
dictāta, ōrum *n.pl,* written exercises
dictātĭo, ōnis *f,* dictation
dictātor, ōris *m,* dictator (Roman magistrate appointed in emergencies)
dictātūra, ae *f,* dictatorship
dictĭo, ōnis *f,* speaking, style
dictĭto *v.t.* 1, to repeat, dictate, compose
dicto *v.t.* 1, to declare, dictate
dictum, i *n,* saying, proverb, order
dictus, a, um *adj,* said, told
dīdo, dīdĭdi, dīdĭtum *v.t.* 3, to distribute
dīdūco, xi, ctum *v.t.* 3, to divide, scatter
diēs, diēī *m,f,* day
diffěro, differre, distŭli, dīlātum *v.i.t, irreg,* to differ; scatter, publish, defer
differtus, a, um *adj,* crowded
diffibŭlo *v.t.* 1, to unbuckle
diffĭcĭlis, e *adj, adv,* ē, ĭter, difficult, surly
diffĭcultas, ātis *f,* difficulty, obstinacy
diffĭdens, ntis *adj,* distrustful
diffĭdentĭa, ae *f,* mistrust, despair
diffīdo, fīsus sum *v.i.* 3, *semi-dep, with dative,* to mistrust, despair
diffindo, fĭdi, fĭsum *v.t.* 3, to split, divide
diffingo *v.t.* 3, to re-shape
diffĭtĕor *v.t.* 2, *dep,* to deny
diffluo *v.i.* 3, to flow away
diffŭgĭo, fūgi *v.i.* 3, to disperse

diffundo, fūdi, dūsum *v.t.* 3, to pour out, scatter
diffūsus, a, um *adj, adv,* ē, spread out, wide
dīgěro, gessi, gestum *v.t.* 3, to separate, arrange, interpret
dīgesta, ōrum *n.pl,* digest of writings
dīgĭtus, i *m,* finger, toe, inch
dīglădĭor *v.i.* 1, *dep,* to fight fiercely
dignātĭo, ōnis *f,* reputation
dignĭtas, ātis *f,* worthiness, rank, authority
dignor *v.t.* 1, *dep,* to consider someone worthy
dignus, a, um *adj, adv* ē, *with abl,* worthy, suitable
dīgrĕdĭor, gressus *v.i.* 3, *dep,* to go away
dīgressĭo, ōnis *f,* digression
dīgressus, ūs *m,* departure
dīiūdĭco *v.t.* 1, to decide
diiun... see **disiun...**
dīlābor, lapsus *v.i.* 3, *dep,* to dissolve, scatter, perish
dīlăcĕro *v.t.* 1, to tear apart, or to pieces
dīlănĭo *v.t.* 1, to tear apart, or to pieces
dīlātĭo, ōnis *f,* delay
dīlāto *v.t.* 1, to enlarge
dīlātor, ōris *m,* delayer
dīlātus, a, um *adj,* scattered
dīlectus, a, um *adj,* beloved
dīlĭgens, ntis *adj, adv,* nter, scrupulous, thrifty
dīlĭgentĭa, ae *f,* care, economy
dīlĭgo, lexi, lectum *v.t.* 3, to value highly
dīlūcesco, luxi *v.i.* 3, to grow light, dawn
dīlūcĭdus, a, um *adj,* clear
dīlūcŭlum, i *n,* dawn
dīlŭo, ŭi, ūtum *v.t.* 3, to wash away, dilute, drench, weaken
dīlūtum, i *n,* solution
dīlŭvĭes, ēi *f* (...ĭum, ii, *n*), flood, destruction
dīmētĭor, mensus *v.t.* 4, *dep,* to measure out
dīmĭcātĭo, ōnis *f,* struggle
dīmĭco, *v.i.* 1, to struggle

dīmĭdĭātus, a, um *adj*, halved
dīmĭdĭum, ii *n*, a half
dīmĭdĭus, a, um *adj*, half
dīmissĭo, ōnis *f*, sending out
dīmitto, mīsi, missum *v.t.* 3, to send away, break up, disband, throw away, give up
dīmŏvĕo, mōvi, mōtum *v.t.* 2, to divide, part, remove
dīnŭmĕro *v.t.* 1, to count up
dĭplōma, ātis *n*, official letter of recommendation
dīra, ōrum *n.pl*, curses
dīrectus, a, um *adj, adv*, ē, straight, level
dīreptĭo, ōnis *f*, plundering
dīreptor, ōris *m*, plunderer
dĭrĭgo, rexi, ctum *v.t.* 3, to put in a straight line, arrange
dĭrĭmo, ēmi, emptum *v.t.* 3, to part, divide, interrupt
dĭrĭpĭo, ŭi, reptum *v.t.* 3, to tear apart, plunder
dīrumpo, rūpi, ptum *v.t.* 3, to break in pieces, sever
dīrŭo, ŭi, ŭtum *v.t.* 3, to destroy
dīrus, a, um *adj*, fearful, ill-omened
discēdo, cessi, cessum *v.i.* 3, to depart, abandon, gape, deviate
disceptātĭo, ōnis *f*, discussion
discepto *v.t.* 1, to debate
discerno, crēvi, tum *v.t.* 3, to separate, distinguish between
discerpo, psi, ptum *v.t.* 3, to tear in pieces
discessus, ūs *m*, departure
discĭdĭum, ii *n*, separation
discinctus, a, um *adj*, casually dressed, slovenly
dīscindo, cĭdi, cissum *v.t.* 3, to cut to pieces, divide
discingo, nxi, nctum *v.t.* 3, to take off or undo (clothing)
disciplīna, ae *f*, teaching, knowledge, system, tactics
discĭpŭlus, i *m*, pupil
disclūdo, si, sum *v.t.* 3, to keep apart, separate
disco, dĭdĭci *v.t.* 3, to learn
discŏlor, ōris *adj*, of different colours
discordĭa, ae *f*, disagreement
discordo *v.i.* 1, to differ
discors, dis *adj*, disagreeing
discrĕpantĭa, ae *f*, discrepancy
discrĕpo, ŭi *v.i.* 1, to differ
dīscrībo, scripsi, ptum *v.t.* 3, to distribute
discrīmen, ĭnis *n*, division, distinction, crisis, danger
discrīmĭno *v.t.* 1, to divide
discrŭcĭo *v.t.* 1, to torture
discumbo, cŭbŭi, cŭbĭtum *v.i.* 3, to recline at table
discurro, curri, cursum *v.i.* 3, to run about
discursus, ūs *m*, bustle, activity
discus, i *m*, discus, quoit
discŭtĭo, cussi, ssum *v.t.* 3, to shatter, disperse
dīsertus, a, um *adj, adv*, ē, fluent, clear
dīsĭcĭlo, ĭēcĭ, ctum *v.t.* 3, to scatter, destroy
disiunctus, a, um *adj, adv*, ē, distant, abrupt
disiungo, nxi, nctum *v.t.* 3, to separate, unyoke
dispar, ăris *adj*, unlike, unequal
dispăro *v.t.* 1, to divide
dispello, pŭli, pulsum *v.t.* 3, to drive away, scatter
dispendĭum, ii *n*, expense, cost
dispenso *v.t.* 1, to pay out, distribute, manage
disperdo, dĭdi, dĭtum *v.t.* 3, to spoil, ruin
dispĕrĕo *v.i.* 4, to perish
dispergo, si, sum *v.t.* 3, to scatter about
dispertĭo *v.t.* 4, to distribute
dispĭcĭo, spexi, ctum *v.i.t.* 3, to look around; discern, reflect on
displĭcĕo *v.i.* 2, to displease
dispōno, pŏsŭi, pŏsĭtum *v.t.* 3, to arrange, dispose
dispŏsĭtus, a, um *adj*, arranged
dispungo, xi, ctum *v.t.* 3, to check
dispŭtātĭo, ōnis *f*, debate, dispute
dispŭtātor, ōris *m*, debater
dispŭto *v.i.t* 1, theorize; examine, discuss
dissēmĭno *v.t.* 1, to spread about
dissensĭo, ōnis *f*, disagreement

dissentĭo, si, sum *v.i.* 4, to disagree, differ

dissērēnat *v.impers.* 1, to be clear

dissĕro, rŭi, rtum *v.t.* 3, to discuss, argue

dissĭdĕo, ēdi, essum *v.i.*2, to differ, disagree

dissĭlĭo, ŭi *v.i.* 4 to leap apart, split

dissĭmĭlis, e *adj, adv,* **ĭter,** unlike, different

dissĭmĭlĭtūdo, ĭnis *f,* unlikeness

dissĭmŭlātus, a, um *adj,* disguised

dissĭmŭlo *v.t.* 1, to disguise, hide

dissĭpātĭo, ōnis *f,* scattering, destruction

dissĭpo *v.t.* 1, to scatter, rout

dissŏcĭābĭlis, e *adj,* dividing

dissŏcĭo *v.t.* 1, to estrange

dissŏlūtĭo, ōnis *f,* break-up, destruction

dissŏlūtus, a, um *adj,* loose

dissolvo, solvi, sŏlūtum *v.t.* 3, to unloose, separate, pay, annul, destroy

dissŏnus, a, um *adj,* discordant

dissuādĕo, si, sum *v.t.* 2, to advise against

dissulto *v.i.* 1, to burst apart

distans, ntis *adj,* distant

distendo, di, tum *v.t.* 3, to stretch out, distend, torture

distentus, a, um *adj,* full

distentus, a, um *adj,* busy

distinctĭo, ōnis *f,* difference

distinctus, a, um *adj, adv,* **ē,** separate, clear, adorned

distĭnĕo, tĭnŭi, tentum *v.t.* 2, to keep apart, perplex, hinder

distinguo, nxi, nctum *v.t.* 3, to separate, discriminate, adorn

disto *v.i.*1, to be distant, differ

distorquĕo, rsi, rtum *v.t.* 2, to twist, distort, torture

distortĭo, ōnis *f,* distortion

distortus, a, um *adj,* deformed

distractĭo, ōnis *f,* division

distractus, a, um *adj,* bewildered

distrăho, xi, ctum *v.t.* 3, to pull apart, divide, distract, perplex

distrĭbŭo, ŭi, ūtum *v.t.* 3, to distribute

distrĭbūtē *adv,* methodically

distrĭbūtĭo, ōnis *f,* distribution

districtus, a, um *adj,* busy, strict

distringo, nxi, ctum *v.t.* 3, to stretch tight, distract the attention

disturbo *v.t.* 1, to disturb, demolish, frustrate

dīto *v.t.* 1, to enrich

dĭū *adj,* a long time

dĭurnus, a, um *adj,* daily

dĭurna ōrum *n.pl,* records

dĭūtĭnus, a, um *adj,* long-lasting

dĭūtĭus *comp. adv,* longer

dĭūturnĭtas, ātis *f,* long duration

dĭūturnus, a, um *adj, adv,* **ē,** long-lasting

dīva, ae *f,* goddess

dīvello, velli, vulsum *v.t.* 3, to tear to pieces, destroy

dīvendo, (*no perfect*), **itum** *v.t.* 3, to retail

dīverbĕro *v.t.* 1, to cut

dīversĭtas, ātis *f,* disagreement

dīversus, a, um *adj, adv,* **ē,** opposite, contrary, hostile, separate, different

dīverto, ti, sum *v.i.* 3, to diverge

dīves, ĭtis *adj,* rich

dīvĭdo, vīsi, sum *v.t.* 3, to separate, distribute, destroy

dīvĭdŭus, a, um *adj,* divisible

dīvīnĭtas, ātis *f,* divinity

dīvīnĭtus *adv,* providentially

dīvīno *v.t.* 1, to prophesy

dīvīnus, a, um *adj, adv,* **ē,** divine, prophetic, superhuman

dīvīnus, i *m,* prophet

dīvīsĭo, ōnis *f,* division

dīvīsor, ōris *m,* distributor of bribes to electors

dīvĭtĭae, ārum *f.pl,* wealth

dīvortĭum, ii *n,* separation

dīvulgo *v.t.* 1, to make known

dīvum, i *n,* sky

dīvus, a, um *adj,* divine

dīvus, i *m* (**a, ae** *f*), god, (goddess)

do, dĕdi, dătum *v.t.* 1, to give

dŏcĕo, ŭi, doctum *v.t.* 2, to teach, inform

dŏcĭlis, e *adj,* easily taught

doctor, ōris *m,* teacher

doctrīna, ae *f,* teaching,

education, learning
doctus, a, um   *adj, adv,* **ē,** learned, skilled
dŏcŭmentum, i   *n,* lesson, example
dōdrans, ntis   *m,* three quarters
dogma, ătis   *n,* doctrine, dogma
dŏlābra, ae   *f,* pickaxe
dŏlĕo   *v.i.t.* 2, to suffer pain; grieve, deplore
dōlĭum, ii   *n,* large jar
dŏlo   *v.t.* 1, to chop, beat
dŏlor, ōris   *m,* pain, sorrow
dŏlōsus, a, um   *adj,* deceitful
dŏlus, i   *m,* fraud, trick
dŏmābĭlis, e   *adj,* tamable
dŏmestĭcus, a, um   *adj,* of the home
dŏmestĭci, ōrum   *m.pl,* family, servants, escort
dŏmi   *adv,* at home
dŏmĭcĭlĭum, ii   *n,* dwelling place
dŏmĭna, ae   *f,* mistress, lady
dŏmĭnans, ntis   *adj,* ruling
dŏmĭnātĭo, ōnis   *f,* absolute rule
dŏmĭnātus, ūs   *m,* absolute rule
dŏmĭnĭum, ii   *n,* banquet, property-ownership
dŏmĭnor   *v.i.* 1, *dep,* to reign
dŏmĭnus, i   *m,* master, owner
dŏmĭto   *v.t.* 1, to tame
dŏmĭtor, ōris   *m,* tamer
dŏmĭtus, a, um   *adj,* tamed
dŏmo, ŭi, ĭtum   *v.t.* 1, to tame, conquer
dŏmus, ūs   *f,* house, home
dōnārĭum, ii   *n,* altar, sanctuary
dōnātĭo, ōnis   *f,* donation
dōnātus, a, um   *adj,* presented
dōnĕc   *conj,* while, until
dōno   *v.t.* 1, to present, remit
dōnum, i   *n,* gift, present
dorcas, ădis   *m,* gazelle
dormĭo   *v.i.* 4, to sleep
dormĭto   *v.i.* 1, to fall asleep
dorsum, i   *n,* the back, ridge, ledge
dōs, dōtis   *f,* dowry
dōtālis, e   *adj,* of a dowry
dōtātus, a, um   *adj,* endowed
dōto   *v.t.* 1, to endow
drachma, ae   *f,* small Greek silver coin
drăco, ōnis   *m,* water snake
drŏmas, ădis   *m,* dromedary

drўas, ădis   *f,* wood nymph
dŭbĭē   *adv,* doubtfully
dŭbĭtātĭo, ōnis   *f,* doubt, uncertainity
dŭbĭto   *v.i.t.* 1, to hesitate; doubt
dŭbĭum, ii   *n,* doubt
dŭbĭus, a, um   *adj,* doubtful, dangerous
dŭcēni, ae, a   *adj,* two hundred each
dŭcenti, ae, a   *adj,* two hundred
dūco, xi, ctum   *v.t.* 3, to lead, marry, construct, receive, prolong, consider
ductĭlis, e   *adj,* moveable, malleable
ductor, ōris   *m,* leader
ductus, ūs   *m,* bringing, leadership
dūdum   *adv,* some time ago, formerly
dulcē   *adv,* sweetly
dulcēdo, ĭnis   *f,* sweetness, charm
dulcĭtūdo, ĭnis   *f,* sweetness, charm
dulcis, e   *adj, adv,* **ĭter,** sweet, pleasant, dear
dum   *conj,* while, until, provided that
dūmētum, i   *n,* thicket
dummŏdo   *adv,* as long as
dūmōsus, a, um   *adj,* bushy
dūmus, i   *m,* bramble
dumtaxat   *adv,* in so far as, merely, at least
dŭŏ, ae, ŏ   *adj,* two
dŭŏdĕcĭes   *adv,* twelve times
dŭŏdĕcim   *adj,* twelve
dŭŏdĕcĭmus, a, um   *adj,* twelfth
dŭŏdēni, ae, a   *adj,* twelve each
dŭŏdēvĭcensĭmus, a, um   *adj,* eighteenth
dŭŏdēvīginti   *adj,* eighteen
dŭŏvĭri, ōrum   *m.pl,* board or commission of two men
dŭplex, ĭcis   *adj, adv,* **ĭter,** double, deceitful
dŭplĭco   *v.t.* 1, to double
dŭplus, a, um   *adj,* double
dūra, ōrum   *n.pl,* hardship
dūrābĭlis, e   *adj,* durable
dūrātus, a, um   *adj,* hardened
dūrē   *adv,* roughly
dūresco, rŭi   *v.i.* 3, to harden

dūrĭtĭa, ae *f,* hardness, strictness, austerity

dūro *v.i.t.* 1, to be hard, endure; harden

dūrus, a, um *adj, adv,* ē, ĭter, hard, rough, harsh, stern

dux, dŭcis *m,* leader, commander

dўnastes, ae *m,* chieftain

dўsentĕrĭa, ae *f,* dysentery

dyspnoea, ae *f,* asthma

E

ē *prep. with abl,* out of, from, since

ĕa see is

ĕādem see idem

ĕātĕnus *adv,* so far

ĕvĕnus, i *f,* ebony (tree)

ēbĭbo, bi, bĭtum *v.t.* 3, to drink up, absorb, squander

ēblandĭor *v.t.* 4, *dep,* to obtain by flattery

ēbrĭĕtas, ātis *f,* drunkenness

ēbrĭōsus, a, um *adj,* addicted to drink

ēbrĭus, a, um *adj,* drunk

ēbullĭo *v.t.* 4, to boast about

ĕbŭlum, i *n,* dwarf elder

ĕbŭr, ŏris *n,* ivory

ĕburnĕus, a, ūm *adj,* of ivory

ecce *demonstrative adv,* see!

ĕchīnus, i *m,* hedgehog, sea urchin, rinsing bowl

ēchō, ūs *f,* echo

ecquando *interr. adv,* at any time?

ecqui, ae, od *interr. pron, adj,* any? anyone?

ecquis, id *interr. pron,* anyone? anything?

ĕdācĭtas, ātis *f,* gluttony

ĕdax, ācis *adj,* greedy

ēdentŭlus, a, um *adj,* toothless

ēdīco, xi, ctum *v.t.* 3, to publish, declare

ēdictum, i *n,* proclamation

ēdisco, dĭdĭci *v.t.* 3, to learn by heart, study

ēdissĕro, rŭi, rtum *v.t.* 3, to explain in full

ēdītĭo, ōnis *f,* bringing out, publishing

ēdītus, a, um *adj,* high, raised, brought out

ĕdo, ēdi, ēsum *v.t.* 3, to eat

ēdo, dĭdi, dĭtum *v.t.* 3, to produce, bring out, declare, cause, erect

ēdŏcĕo, cŭi, ctum *v.t.* 2, to teach thoroughly

ēdŏmo, ŭi, ĭtum *v.t.* 1, to subdue

ēdŭcātĭo, ōnis *f,* bringing up, education

ēdŭco, xi, ctum *v.t.* 3, to lead or bring out, summon, educate, erect

ēdŭco *v.t.* 1, to bring up (child)

ĕdūlis, e *adj,* eatable

effātus, a, um *adj,* established

effectĭo, ōnis *f,* doing, performing

effectus, a, um *adj,* completed

effectus, ūs *m,* accomplishment

effēmĭnātus, a, um *adj,* effeminate

effĕrātus, a, um *adj,* wild

effĕro, efferre, extŭli, ēlātum *v.t,* *irreg,* to bring out, bury, declare, raise; *in passive or with* se, to be haughty

effĕro *v.t.* 1, to brutalize

effĕrus, a, um *adj,* savage

effervesco, ferbŭi *v.i.* 3, to boil up, rage

effervo *v.i.* 3, to boil over

effētus, a, um *adj,* exhausted

efficax, ācis *adj,* efficient

effĭcĭens, ntis *adj, adv,* nter, efficient

effĭcĭo, fēci, fectum *v.t.* 3, to bring about, complete, produce

effictus, a, um *adj,* fashioned

effĭges, ēi *f,* portrait, copy

effingo, nxi, ctum *v.t.* 3, to shape, fashion, portray

efflāgĭto *v.t.* 1, to request urgently

efflo *v.t.* 1, to breathe out

efflōresco, rŭi *v.i.* 3, to bloom

efflŭo, xi *v.i.* 3, to flow out, vanish

effŏdĭo, fōdi, fossum *v.t.* 3, to dig out, dig up

effor *v.t.* 1, *dep,* to speak out

effrēnātus, a, um *adj,* unruly

effrēnus, a, um *adj,* unrestrained

effringo, frēgi, fractum *v.t.* 3, to break open, smash

effŭgĭo, fūgi *v.i.t.* 3, to escape;

flee from, avoid
effŭgĭum, ii   *n*, escape
ĕffulgĕo, si   *v.i.* 2, to gleam
effundo, fūdi, fūsum   *v.t.* 3, to
 pour out, let loose, squander; *in
 passive or with reflexive*, to rush
 out
effūsĭo, ōnis   *f*, outpouring,
 profusion
effūsus, a, um   *adj, adv,* ē, poured
 out, spread out, wide, loosened
effūtĭo   *v.t.* 4, to blurt out
ēgĕlĭdus, a, um   *adj*, cool
ĕgens, ntis   *adj*, in want of
ĕgēnus, a, um   *adj*, in want of
ĕgĕo   *v.i.* 2, *with abl*, to be in
 need of
ēgĕro, ssi, stum   *v.t.* 3, to bring
 out
ĕgestas, ātis   *f*, poverty
ĕgŏ   *pers. pron*, I
ĕgŏmet   *pron*, I myself
ēgrĕdĭor, gressus   *v.i.t.* 3, *dep*, to
 go or come out; leave, exceed
ēgrĕgĭus, a, um   *adj, adv,* ē,
 distinguished
ēgressus, ūs   *m*, departure,
 passage
ēheu!   alas!
ēiă!   hey! I say!
ēiăcŭlor   *v.t.* 1, *dep*, to shoot out
ēĭcĭo, iēci, iectum   *v.t.* 3, to drive
 out, expel, wreck; *with reflexive*,
 to rush out
ēiecto   *v.t.* 1, to vomit
ēiūro   *v.t.* 1, to reject on oath,
 abandon
ēius   *genit. of* is, ea, id
ēiusmŏdi   in such a manner
ēlābor, lapsus   *v.i.* 3, *dep*, to slip
 away, escape
ēlăbōrātus, a, um   *adj*, elaborate
ēlăbōro   *v.i.t.* 1, to make an
 effort; take pains with
ēlanguesco, gŭi   *v.i.* 3, to grow
 feeble
ēlātĭo, ōnis   *f*, lifting up, passion
ēlātro   *v.t.* 1, to bark loudly
ēlātus, a, um   *adj*, raised, lofty
ēlectĭo, ōnis   *f*, selection
ēlectrum, i   *n*, amber
ēlectus, a, um   *adj*, selected
ēlĕgans, ntis,   *adj, adv,* nter,

refined, tasteful
ēlĕgantĭa, ae   *f*, refinement
ēlĕgi, ōrum   *m.pl*, elegy
ēlĕgīa, ae   *f*, elegy
ēlĕmentum, i   *n*, element, first
 principle; *pl*, rudiments
ēlĕphantus, I   *m*, elephant, ivory
ēlĕvo   *v.t.* 1, to lift up, weaken,
 disparage
ēlĭcĭo, cŭi, cĭtum   *v.t.* 3, to lure
 out, call out
ēlīdo, si, sum   *v.t.* 3, to knock or
 force out, shatter
ēlīgo, lēgi, ctum   *v.t.* 3, to choose
ēlinguis, e   *adj*, speechless
ēlixus, a, um   *adj*, boiled
ellychnĭum, ii   *n*, lampwick
ēlŏco   *v.t.* 1, to let (a farm)
ēlŏcūtĭo, ōnis   *f*, expression,
 elocution
ēlŏgĭum, ii   *n*, saying, inscription
ēlŏquens, ntis   *adj*, eloquent
ēlŏquentĭa, ae   *f*, eloquence
ēlŏquor, ēlŏcūtus   *v.t.* 3, *dep*, to
 speak out, declare
ēlūcĕo, xi   *v.i.* 2, to shine out
ēluctor   *v.i.t.* 1, *dep*, to struggle
 out; struggle out of
ēlūdo, si, sum   *v.t.* 3, to evade,
 cheat, frustrate
ēlūgĕo, xi   *v.t.* 2, to mourn for
ēlŭo, ŭi, ūtum   *v.t.* 3, to wash off,
 clean
ēlūtus, a, um   *adj*, insipid
ēlŭvĭes *(no genit)*   *f*, inundation
ēlŭvĭo, ōnis   *f*, inundation
ēmancĭpo   *v.t.* 1, to set free,
 transfer, sell
ēmāno   *v.i.*1, to flow out, arise
 from
embŏlĭum ii   *n*, interlude
ēmendātĭo, ōnis   *f*, correction
ēmendātor, ōris   *m*, corrector
ēmendātus, a, um   *adj*, faultless
ēmendo   *v.t.* 1, to correct
ēmentĭor   *v.t.* 4, *dep*, to assert
 falsely
ēmercor   *v.t.* 1, *dep*, to purchase
ēmĕrĕo   *v.t.* 2, (**ēmĕrĕor** *v.t.* 2,
 dep), to deserve, earn, complete
 one's military service
ēmergo, si, sum   *v.i.* 3, to come
 out, escape

ēmĕrĭtus, a, um *adj*, worn out
ēmētĭor, mensus *v.t.* 4, *dep*, to measure out, travel over
ēmĭco, ŭi, ātum *v.i.* 1, to spring out, appear
ēmĭgro *v.i.* 1, to depart
ēmĭnens, ntis *adj*, projecting, distinguished
ēmĭnentĭa, ae *f*, prominence
ēmĭnĕo *v.i.* 2, to stand out, excel
ēmĭnus *adv*, from or at a distance
ēmissārĭum, ii *n*, drain, vent
ēmissārĭus, ii *m*, spy
ēmissĭo, ōnis *f*, sending out, hurling (of missiles)
ēmitto, mīsi, ssum *v.t.* 3, to send out, produce, publish; with **manū**, to set free
ēmo, ēmi, emptum *v.t.* 3, to buy
ēmŏdŭlor *v.t.* 1, *dep*, to sing
ēmollĭo *v.t.* 4, to soften
ēmŏlŭmentum, i *n*, effort, profit
ēmŏrĭor, mortuus *v.i.* 3, *dep*, to die
ēmŏvĕo, mōvi, tum *v.t.* 2, to remove, shake
empīrĭcus, a, um *adj*, empirical
emplastrum, i *n*, plaster
empŏrĭum, ii *n*, market
emptĭo, ōnis *f*, purchase
emptor, ōris *m*, buyer
ēmunctus, a, um *adj*, clean, shrewd
ēmungo, nxi, nctum *v.t.* 3, to wipe the nose
ēmūnĭo *v.t.* 4, to fortify
ēn! see! come!
ēnarro *v.t.* 1, to expound
ēnascor, nātus *v.i.* 3, *dep*, to spring up, be born
ēnăto *v.i.* 1, to swim away
ēnectus, a, um *adj*, killed
ēnĕco, ŭi, ctum *v.t.* 1, to kill, exhaust
ēnervo *v.t.* 1, to weaken
ēnim *conj*, for, indeed
ēnimvēro *conj*, certainly
ēnīsus, a, um *adj*, strenuous
ēnĭtĕo *v.i.* 2, to shine out
ēnĭtesco, tŭi *v.i.* 3, to shine out
ēnītor, nīsus (nixus) *v.i.t.* 3, *dep*, to struggle upwards, climb, strive; give birth to, ascend

ēnixus, a, um *adj, adv*, **ē**, strenuous, earnest
ēno *v.i.* 1, to swim out or away
ēnōdātĭo, ōnis *f*, explanantion
ēnōdis, e *adj*, smooth, clear
ēnōdo *v.t.* 1, to elucidate
ēnormis, e *adj*, enormous, shapeless
ēnormĭtas, ātis *f*, shapelessness
ēnōto *v.t.* 1, to note down
ensĭger, ĕra, ĕrum *adj*, carrying a sword
ensis, is *m*, sword
ēnūclĕātus, a, um *adj, adv*, **ē**, pure, clear, simple
ēnŭmĕrātĭo, ōnis *f*, counting, recapitulation
ēnŭmĕro *v.t.* 1, to count, relate
ēnuntĭo *v.t.* 1, to disclose, declare
ĕo, īre, īvi (ii), ĭtum *v.i, irreg*, to go; *with* **pedibus**, to vote for
ĕō *adv*, to that place, to such an extent, so long, besides
eo ... quo, (*with comparatives*) the more ... the more
ĕōdem *adv*, to the same place, to the same point or purpose
ĕōus, i *m*, (**a, um** *adj*), east
ĕphēbus, i *m*, a youth
ĕphippĭum, ii *n*, saddle
ĕphŏrus, i *m*, Spartan magistrate
ĕpĭcus, a, um *adj*, epic
ĕpiscŏpus, i *m*, bishop
ĕpĭgramma, ătis *n*, inscription
ĕpistŏla, ae *f*, letter
ĕpistŏmĭum, ii *n*, valve
ĕpĭtŏmē (ĕpĭtŏma), ēs *f*, abridgement
ĕpŏs *n*, epic poem
ĕpōto, pōtum *v.t.* 1, to drink up
ĕpŭlae, ārum *f.pl*, food, banquet
ĕpŭlor *v.i.t.* 1, *dep*, to banquet; eat
ĕqua, ae *f*, mare
ĕquārĭa, ae *f*, stud of horses
ĕques, ĭtis *m*, horseman, knight
ĕquester, tris, tre *adj*, of a horseman, of cavalry
ĕquĭdem *adv*, indeed, of course, for my part
ĕquīnus, a, um *adj*, of horses
ĕquĭtātĭo, ōnis *f*, riding on horseback

ĕquĭtātus, ūs *m,* cavalry
ĕquĭto *v.i.* 1, to ride
ĕquŭlĕus, i, *m,* colt, the rack
ĕquus, i *m,* horse
ĕra, ae *f,* lady of the house
ērādīco *v.t.* 1, to root out
ērādo, si, sum *v.t.* 3, to scrape out, abolish
ērectus, a, um *adj,* upright, noble, haughty, resolute
ērēpo, psi *v.i.t.* 3, to creep out; creep over
ergā *prep. with acc,* towards
ergastŭlum, i *n,* detention centre
ergō *adv,* therefore; *prep. following genit,* on account of
ērĭgo, rexi, rectum *v.t.* 3, to raise up, encourage
ērĭlis, e *adj,* of the master, or mistress
ērĭĭo, rĭpŭi, reptum *v.t.* 3, to snatch, take away; *with reflexive,* to escape
ērŏgātĭo, ōnis *f,* paying out
ērŏgo *v.t.* 1, to pay out, squander
errābundus, a, um *adj,* wandering
errātĭcus, a, um *adj,* wandering
errātĭcus, a, um *adj,* rambling
errātum, i *n,* mistake
erro *v.i.* 1, to stray, err
erro, ōnis *m,* wanderer
error, ōris *m,* straying, mistake
ērŭbesco, bŭi *v.i.* 1, to blush, feel ashamed
ērūca, ae *f,* caterpillar
ēructo *v.t.* 1, to belch, emit
ērŭdĭo *v.t.* 4, to polish, instruct
ērŭdītĭo, ōnis *f,* learning
ērŭdītus, a, um *adj, adv, ē,* learned, skilled
ērumpo, rūpi, ptum *v.i.t.* 1, to break out; burst
ērŭo, ŭi, ŭtum *v.t.* 3, to throw out, dig out, destroy, rescue
ēruptĭo, ōnis *f,* break out
ĕrus, i *m,* master of the house
ervum, i *n,* wild pea
esca, ae *f,* food, bait
ēscendo, di, sum *v.i.* 3, to climb
ēscensĭo, ōnis *f,* aascent
escŭlentus, a, um *adj,* eatable
esse see sum

essēdārĭus, i *m,* chariot fighter
essēdum, i *n,* war chariot
ēsŭrĭens, ntis *adj,* hungry
ēsŭrĭo *v.i.t.* 4, to be hungry; long for
ĕt *conj,* and, as
ĕtĕnim *conj,* and indeed
ĕtĭam *conj,* also, even, still
ĕtĭamnum, ĕtĭamnunc *adv,* even then, till now
etsi *conj,* although, even if
eu! well done!
eurīpus, i *m,* canal
eurōus, a, um *adj,* eastern
eurus, i *m,* east wind
ēvādo, si, sum *v.i.t.* 3, to go out, escape; leave behind
ēvăgor *v.i.t.* 1, *dep,* to stray; overstep
ēvălesco, lŭi *v.i.* 3, to grow strong, to be able
ēvānesco, nŭi *v.i.* 3, to vanish
ēvānĭdus, a, um *adj,* vanishing
ēvasto *v.t.* 1, to devastate
ēvĕho, xi, ctum *v.t.* 3, to carry out; *in passive,* to ride or move out
ēvello, velli, vulsum *v.t.* 3, to tear out, eradicate
ēvĕnĭo, vēni, ventum *v.i.* 4, to come out, turn out, result
ēventum, i *n,* occurrence, result, fortune
ēventus, ūs *m,* occurrence, result, fortune
ēventus, ūs *m,* occurrence, result, fortune
ēverbĕro *v.t.* 1, to strike hard
ēverro, verri, versum *v.t.* 3, to sweep out
ēversĭo, ōnis *f,* destruction
ēversor, ōris *m,* destroyer
ēversus, a, um *adj,* overthrown
ēverto, ti, sum *v.t.* 3, to overthrow, ruin
ēvĭdens, ntis *adj,* apparent
ēvĭgĭlo *v.i.t.* 1, to wake up; keep awake, keep watch through
ēvincĭo, nxi, nctum *v.t.* 4, to bind round
ēvinco, vīci, ctum *v.t.* 3, to conquer completely, succeed
ēviscĕro *v.t.* 1, to tear apart

ēvīto *v.t.* 1, to avoid
ēvŏcāti, ōrum *m.pl,* reservists
ēvŏco *v.t.* 1, to call out
ēvŏlo *v.i.* 1, to fly away
ēvolvo, vi, vŏlūtum *v.t.* 3, to unroll (and read a book), disclose
ēvŏmo, ŭi, ĭtum *v.t.* 3, to spit out, vomit
ēvulsĭo, ōnis *f,* pulling out
ex (ē) *prep. with abl,* out of, from, after, since, on account of, according to, made of
exăcerbo *v.t.* 1, to irritate
exactĭo, ōnis *f,* debt or tax collecting, expelling
exactor, ōris *m,* expeller, superintendent, tax collector
exactus, a, um *adj,* accurate
exăcŭo, ŭi, ūtum *v.t.* 3, to sharpen, stimulate
exadversum (...us) *adv and prep. with acc,* opposite
exaedĭfĭco *v.t.* 1, to construct
exaequo *v.t.* 1, to place equal
exaestŭo *v.i.* 1, to seethe
exaggĕro *v.i.* 1, to heap up
exăgĭto *v.t.* 1, to disturb
exalbesco, bŭi *v.i.* 3, to turn pale
exāmen, ĭnis *n,* crowd, swarm
exāmĭno *v.t.* 1, to weigh, test
exănĭmātĭo, ōnis *f,* terror
exănĭmātus, a, um *adj,* out of breath
exănĭmis, e *adj,* lifeless
exănĭmus, a, um *adj,* lifeless
exănĭmo *v.t.* 1, to deprive of breath, kill, terrify
exardesco, arsi, sum *v.i.* 3, to be inflamed
exāresco, rŭi *v.i.* 3, to dry up
exăro *v.t.* 1, to plough, write
exaspĕro *v.t.* 1, to roughen, provoke
exauctōro *v.t.* 1, to discharge honourably or dishonourably from army
exaudĭo *v.t.* 4, to hear, grant
excandesco, dŭi *v.i.* 3, to glow
excēdo, ssi, ssum *v.i.t.* 3, to depart, die; leave, exceed
excellens, ntis *adj, adv,* nter, distinguished, excellent
excello, cellŭi, lsum *v.i.* 3, to be eminent, excel

excelsus, a, um *adj,* distinguished
exceptĭo, ōnis *f,* restriction
excepto *v.t.* 1, to catch
excerno, crēvi, crētum *v.t.* 3, to separate
excerpo, psi, ptum *v.t.* 3, to select
excessus, ūs *m,* departure
excĭdĭum, ii *n,* destruction
excĭdo, cĭdi *v.i.* 3, to fall from, escape, disappear, slip the memory, fail in
excĭdo, cĭdi, cīsum *v.t.* 3, to cut down, destroy
excĭo *v.t.* 4, to call or bring out
excĭpĭo, cēpi, ceptum *v.t.* 3, to take out, make an exception, receive, capture, follow after, overhear, intercept
excĭtātus, a, um *adj,* roused, vigorous
excĭto *v.t.* 1, to rouse up, excite
exclāmātĭo, ōnis *f,* exclamation
exclāmo *v.i.t.* 1, to call out
exclūdo, si, sum *v.t.* 3, to shut out, drive out, remove, hinder, hatch
exclūsĭo, ōnis *f,* exclusion
excōgĭto *v.t.* 1, to think out
excŏlo, cŏlŭi, cultum *v.t.* 3, to cultivate, improve, refine
excŏquo, xi, ctum *v.t.* 3, to boil away, purify
excors, dis *adj,* stupid
excresco, crēvi, crētum *v.i.* 1, to grow up
excrētus, a, um *adj,* full-grown
excrētus, a, um *adj,* separated
excrŭcĭo *v.t.* 1, to torture
excŭbĭae, ārum *f.pl,* watch, guard
excŭbĭtor, ōris *m,* watchman
excŭbo, ŭi, ĭtum *v.i.* 1, to sleep out of doors, keep watch
excūdo, di, sum *v.t.* 3, to hammer out
exculco *v.t.* 1, to trample down
excurro, cŭcurri, cursum *v.i.* 3, to run out, make a sortie, extend
excursĭo, ōnis *f,* attack, invasion, sally
excursus, ūs *m,* attack, invation, sally
excūsābĭlis, e *adj,* excusable

excūsātĭo, ōnis *f,* excuse
excūso *v.t.* 1, to excuse, plead in excuse
excŭtĭo, cussi, cussum *v.t.* 3, to shake off, get rid of, hurl, examine
exĕdo, ēdi, ēsum *v.t.* 3, to eat up
exemplar, āris *n,* copy, model
exemplum, i *n,* copy, model, precedent, warning, example
exemptus, a, um *adj,* removed
exĕo *v.i.t.* 4, to depart, run out (time), die; cross, avoid
exercĕo *v.t.* 2, to keep busy, train, exercise, pester
exercĭtātĭo, ōnis *f,* practice
exercĭtātus, a, um *adj,* trained
exercĭtor, ōris *m,* trainer
exercĭtus, ūs *m,* army
exercĭtus, a, um *adj,* trained, harrassed
exhālātĭo, ōnis *f,* exhalation
exhālo *v.t.* 1, to breathe out
exhaurĭo, si, stum *v.t.* 4, to draw out, exhaust, empty
exhaustus, a, um *adj,* drained, worn out
exhērēdo *v.t.* 1, to disinherit
exhĭbĕo *v.t.* 2, to present, display, procure, cause
exhĭbĭtus, a, um *adj,* produced
exhĭlăro *v.t.* 1, to delight
exhorresco, rŭi *v.i.t.* 3, to tremble; shrink from, dread
exhortor *v.t.* 1, *dep,* to encourage
exiens see **exeo**
exĭgo, ēgi, actum *v.t.* 3, to drive out, enforce, demand, complete, examine, estimate, spend (time)
exĭgŭĭtas, ātis *f,* small size
exĭgŭus, a, um *adj, adv,* ē, small, short
exīlis, e *adj, adv,* ĭter small, thin, feeble, insignificant
exĭlĭum, ii *n,* exile
exĭmĭus, a, um *adj, adv,* ē, unusual, distinguished
exĭmo, ēmis, emptum *v.t.* 3, to take away, free, waste
exĭnānĭo *v.t.* 4, to empty
exindē (exin) *adv,* from there, then, next, accordingly
existĭmātĭo, ōnis *f,* opinion,

reputation, character
existĭmātor, ōris *m,* critic
existĭmo *v.t.* 1, to estimate, think
exĭtĭābĭlis, e *adj,* fatal, deadly
exĭtĭālis, e *adj,* fatal, deadly
exĭtĭōsus, a, um *adj,* destructive
exĭtĭum, ii *n,* destruction
exĭtus, ūs *m,* departure, outlet, conclusion, result, death
exŏlesco, ŏlēvi, lētum *v.i.* 3, to grow up, disappear
exŏnĕro *v.t.* 1, to unload
exoptātus, a, um *adj,* longed for
exopto *v.t.* 1, to long for
exōrābĭlis, e *adj,* easily persuaded
exordĭor, orsus *v.t.* 4, *dep,* to begin, weave
exordĭum, ii *n,* beginning, introduction
exŏrĭor, ortus *v.i.* 4, *dep,* to spring up, arise, appear
exornātĭo, ōnis *f,* decoration
exorno *v.t.* 1, to equip, adorn
exōro *v.t.* 1, to prevail upon
exorsus, a, um *adj,* begun
exortus, ūs *m,* rising
exōsus, a, um *adj,* hating, detested
expăvesco, pāvi *v.i.t.* 3, to be afraid; dread
expect... see **exspect...**
expĕdĭo *v.t.* 4, to set free, prepare, arrange, explain; *impers,* it is expedient
expĕdĭo *v.t.* 4, to set free, prepare, arrange, explain; *impers,* it is expedient
expĕdītĭo, ōnis *f,* campaign
expĕdītē *adv,* promptly
expĕdītus, a, um *adj,* ready
expĕdītus, i *m,* soldier in light-marching order
expello, pŭli, pulsum *v.t.* 3, to drive away
expendo, di, sum *v.t.* 3, to pay out, consider, pay the penalty
expergēfăcĭo, fēci, factum *v.t.* 3, to arouse
expergiscor, perrectus *v.i.* 3, *dep.* to awake
expĕrĭens, ntis *adj,* enterprising
expĕrĭentĭa, ae *f,* experiment, practice

expĕrīmentum, i *n,* proof,
experience

expĕrĭor, pertus *v.t.* 4, *dep,* to
prove, test, try; *perf,* know from
experience

expers, rtis *adj,* devoid of

expertus, a, um *adj,* proved

expĕto, īvi (ii), ītum *v.t.* 3, to long
for, aim at, reach

expĭātĭo, ōnis *f,* atonement

expīlo *v.t.* 1, to plunder

expīlātĭo, ōnis *f,* plundering

expingo, nxi, ctum *v.t.* 3, to paint

expĭo *v.t.* 1, to atone for

expiscor *v.t.* 1, *dep,* to search out

explānātĭo, ōnis *f,* explanation

explāno *v.t.* 1, to explain

explĕo, ēvi, ētum *v.t.* 2, to fill up,
fulfil, finish

explētĭo, ōnis *f,* satisfying

explētus, a, um *adj,* full, complete

explĭcātĭo, ōnis *f,* unfolding,
explanation

explĭcātus, a, um *adj,* spread-out,
plain

explĭco *v.t.* 1, (or … ŭi … ĭtum) to
unfold, spread out, deploy,
arrange, explain

explōdo, si, sum *v.t.* 3, to hiss off
the stage, disapprove

explōrātor, ōris *m,* spy, scout

explōrātus, a, um *adj, adv,* ē,
established, certain

explōro *v.t.* 1, to search out, spy,
test

expŏlĭo *v.t.* 4, to polish

expōno, pŏsŭi, pŏsĭtum *v.t.* 3, to
expose, put on shore, explain

exporto *v.t.* 1, to carry away

exposco, pŏposci *v.t.* 3, to
implore, require

expŏsĭtĭo, ōnis *f,* elucidation

expŏsĭtus, a, um *adj,* accessible

expostŭlātĭo, ōnis *f,* complaint

expostŭlo *v.t.* 1, to demand,
upbraid, complain

expressus, a, um *adj,* clear

exprĭmo, pressi, pressum *v.t.* 3,
to press out, model, extort

exprŏbrātĭo, ōnis *f,* reproach

exprŏbo *v.t.* 1, to reproach

exprōmo, mpsi, mptum *v.t.* 3, to
fetch out, display, explain

expugnātĭo, ōnis *f,* capture by
assault

expugno *v.t.* 1, to storm, capture

expurgo *v.t.* 1, to purify, justify

exquīro, sīvi, sītum *v.t.* 3, to
search out

exquīsītus, a, um *adj, adv,* ē,
choice, excellent

exsanguis, e *adj,* bloodless, weak

exsătĭo *v.t.* 1, to satisfy

exsătŭro *v.t.* 1, to satiate

exscensĭo, ōnis *f,* landing

exscindo, ĭdi, issum *v.t.* 3, to
destroy completely

exscrībo, psi, ptum *v.t.* 3, to write
out, copy

exsĕco, cŭi, ctum *v.t.* 1, to cut
out, cut off

exsĕcrābĭlis, e *adj,* accursed

exsĕcrātĭo, ōnis *f,* curse

exsĕcrātus, a, um *adj,* accursed

exsĕcror *v.i.t.* 1, *dep,* to take an
oath; curse

exsĕcūtĭo, ōnis *f,* execution

exsĕquĭae, ārum *f.pl,* funeral

exsĕquor, sĕcūtus *v.t.* 3, *dep,* to
pursue, follow, carry out,
describe, avenge

exsĕro, rŭi, rtum *v.t.* 3, to put
out, uncover, protrude

exserto *v.t.* 1, to stretch out

exsicco *v.t.* 1, to dry up

exsĭlĭo, ĭlŭi *v.i.* 4, to leap out,
jump up

exsĭlĭum, ii *n,* exile

exsisto, stĭti, stĭtum *v.i.* 3, to
come out, appear, arise, exist

exsolvo, solvī, sŏlūtum *v.t.* 3, to
unloose, free, discharge

exsomnis, e *adj,* sleepless

exsorbĕo *v.t.* 2, to suck up

exsors, rtis *adj,* specially chosen,
deprived of

exspătĭor *v.i.* 1, *dep,* to digress,
launch out

exspectātĭo, ōnis *f,* expectation

exspectātus, a, um *adj,* desired

exspecto *v.t.* 1, to look out for,
wait for, hope for

exspergo (spargo) (*no perf.*),
spersus *v.t.* 3, to scatter

exspīrātĭo, ōnis *f,* breathing out

exspīro *v.i.t.* 1, to rush out,

expire, cease; breathe out
exspŏllo *v.t.* 1, to plunder
exstĭmŭlo *v.t.* 1, to goad on
exstinctor, ōris *m,* destroyer
exstinctus, a, um *adj,* destroyed, extinct
exstinguo, nxi, nctum *v.t.* 3, to quench, kill, destroy
exstirpo *v.t.* 1, to uproot
exsto *v.i.* 1, to project, be conspicuous, exist
exstructĭo, ōnis *f,* structure
exstrŭo, xi, ctum *v.t.* 3, to heap up, build up
exsūdo *v.t.* 1, to toil or sweat at
exsul (exul), ŭlis *c,* an exile
exsŭlo (exulo) *v.i.* 1, to live in exile
exsultans, ntis *adj,* boastful
exsultātĭo, ōnis *f,* rapture
exsultim *adv,* friskingly
exsulto *v.i.* 1, to jump about, run riot, boast
exsŭpĕrābĭlis, e *adj,* surmountable
exsŭpĕro *v.i.t.* 1, to get the upper hand; pass over, exceed
exsurdo *v.t.* 1, to deafen, dull
exsurgo, surrexi *v.i.* 3, to rise, stand up
exsuscĭto *v.t.* 1, to awaken
exta, ōrum *n.pl,* the inwards
extemplō *adv,* immediately
extendo, di, tum *v.t.* 3, to stretch out, enlarge, prolong
extentus, a, um *adj,* extensive
extĕnŭātĭo, ōnis *f,* attenuation
extĕnŭo *v.t.* 1, to diminish, weaken
exter (extĕrus), ĕra, ĕrum *adj,* external, strange, foreign
extergĕo, si, sum *v.t.* 2, to plunder
extĕrĭor, us *comp. adj,* outer
extermĭno *v.t.* 1, to expel
externus, a, um *adj,* external, foreign
extĕro, trīvi, trītum *v.t.* 3, to rub off, wear away
exterrĕo *v.t.* 2, to frighten
extĭmesco, mŭi *v.i.t.* 2, to be afraid; to dread
extollo, sustŭli *v.t.* 3, to raise

extorquĕo, si, sum *v.t.* 2, to wrench away from, extort
extorris, e *adj,* exiled
extrā *adv and prep. with acc.* outside, beyond, except
extrăho, xi, ctum *v.t.* 3, to drag out, release, prolong
extrānĕus, i *m,* stranger
extrăordĭnārĭus, a, um *adj,* extraordinary
extrēma, ōrum *n.pl,* last resort
extrēmĭtas, ātis *f,* extremity
extrēmum, i *n,* the end
extrēmum *adv,* for the last time, finally
extrēmus, a, um *adj,* furthest, the end of, or extremity of
extrīco *v.t.* 1, to disentangle
extrinsĕcus *adv,* from, or on, the outside
extrūdo, si, sum *v.t.* 3, to push out
extundo, tŭdi, tūsum *v.t.* 3, to force out, hammer out
exturbo *v.t.* 1, to drive away
exūbĕro *v.i.* 1, to be abundant
exul see **exsul**
exulcĕro *v.t.* 1, to aggravate
exŭlŭlo *v.i.* 1, to howl
exundo *v.i.* 1, to overflow
exŭo, ŭi, ūtum *v.t.* 3, to strip, deprive of, discard
exūro, ussi, ustum *v.t.* 3, to burn up, consume
exustĭo, ōnis *f,* conflagration
exŭvĭae, ārum *f.pl,* stripped-off clothing or equipment

F

fāba, ae *f,* bean
fābella, ae *f,* short story
fāber, bri *m,* smith, carpenter
fābrĭca, ae *f,* workshop, a trade, a skilled work
fābrĭcatĭo, ōnis *f,* structure
fābrĭcător, ōris *m,* maker
fābrĭcor *v.t.* 1, *dep,* (**fabrĭco** *v.t.* 1), to construct, form
fābrīlis, e *adj,* of a craftsman
fābŭla, ae *f,* story, play
fābŭlor *v.t.* 1, *dep,* to talk, chat
fābŭlōsus, a, um *adj,* legendary

făcesso, cessi, ītum *v.i.t.* 3, to depart; perform, cause
făcētĭae, ārum *f.pl*, witticisms
făcētus, a, um *adj, adv, ē,* courteous, elegant, witty
făcĭes, ēi *f,* face, shape, appearance
făcĭlĭě *adv,* easily
făcĭlis, e *adj,* easy, quick, good-natured
făcĭlĭtas, ātis *f,* ease, affability
făcĭnus, ŏris *n,* deed, crime
făcĭo, fēci, factum *v.i.t.* 3, to do, act, to side with **(cum, ab)**, or against **(contra)**, to be useful; to make, do, produce, assert, pretend, practise (trade)
factĭo, ōnis *f,* faction, party
factĭōsus, a, um *adj,* mutinous
factĭto *v.t.* 1, to keep doing
factum, i *n,* deed
făcultas, ātis *f,* power, opportunity, supply
fācundĭa, ae *f,* eloquence
fācundus, a, um *adj, adv, ē,* eloquent
faecŭla, ae *f,* wine dregs
faenĕrātĭo, ōnis *f,* moneylending
faenĕrātor, ōris *m,* moneylender
faenĕrātōrĭus, a, um *adj,* usurious
faenĕror *v.t.* 1, *dep* **(faenĕro,** *v.t.* 1), to lend on interest
faenīlĭa, ĭum *n.pl,* hayloft
faenum, i *n,* hay
faenus, ŏris *n,* interest, profit
faex, cis *f,* dregs, sediment
fāgĭnĕus (nus), a, um *adj,* of beech
fāgus, i *f,* beech tree
fălārĭca, ae *f,* burning missile
falcātus, a, um *adj,* armed with scythes, curved
falcĭfer, ĕra, ĕrum *adj,* holding a sickle
falco, ōnis *m,* falcon
fallācĭa, ae *f,* trick, deceit
fallax, ācis *adj, adv, ĭter,* deceitful, fallacious
fallo, fĕfelli, falsum *v.t.* 3, to deceive, betray, escape to notice of, appear
falsum, i *n,* falsehood
falsus, a, um *adj, adv, ē, or ō,*

false, counterfeit, deceptive
falx, cis *f,* scythe, hook
fāma, ae *f,* rumour, public opinion, reputation, fame
fămes, is *f,* hunger, famine
fămīlĭa, ae *f,* domestic servants, family property, crowd or set
fămīlĭāris, e *adj, adv, ĭter,* domestic, intimate
fămīlĭāris, is *m,* friend
fămīlĭārĭtas, ātis *f,* friendship
fāmōsus, a, um *adj,* notorious
fămŭla, ae *f,* maid-servant
fămŭlātus, ūs *m,* servitude
fămŭlor *v.i.* 1, *dep,* to serve, wait on
fămŭlus, i *m,* servant
fānātĭcus, a, um *adj,* inspired, frantic
fandus, a, um *adj,* lawful
fānum, i *n,* temple, shrine
fār, farris *n,* grain, corn
farcīmen, ĭnis *n,* sausage
farcĭo, rsi, rtum *v.t.* 4, to cram
fărīna, ae *f,* flour
farrāgo, ĭnis *f,* hotchpotch
fartor, ōris *m,* poultry farmer
fartum, i *n,* stuffing
fartūra, ae *f,* cramming, padding
fās *n, (indeclinable),* divine law, right
fascēs, ĭum *m.pl,* bundle of rods and axes; symbol of magistrates' power of scourging and beheading
fascĭa, ae *f,* band, headband
fascĭcŭlus, i *m,* small bundle
fascĭnātĭo, ōnis *f,* bewiching
fascĭno *v.t.* 1, to charm, enchant
fascĭnum, i *n,* lucky charm
fascĭŏla, ae *f,* small bandage
fascis, is *m,* bundle, pack
fassus, a, um *participle,* having acknowledged
fasti, ōrum *m.pl,* working days, calendar
fastīdĭo *v.i.t.* 4, to be disgusted; to loathe
fastīdĭōsus, a, um *adj, adv, ē,* scornful, squeamish, disagreeable
fastīdĭum, ii *n,* loathing, scorn
fastīgātus, a, um *adj, adv, ē,* sloping

fastīgĭum, ii   *n,* gable, top, bottom, slope
fastīgo   *v.t.* 1, to make jointed
fastus, a, um (dĭes), court-day
fastus, ūs   *m,* arrogance
fātālis, e   *adj, adv,* **ĭter,** destined, deadly
fātĕor, fassus   *v.t.* 2, *dep,* to admit, confess
fātĭdĭcus, a, um   *adj,* prophetic
fātĭfer, ĕra, ĕrum   *adj,* deadly
fātīgātĭo, ōnis   *f,* exhaustion
fātīgātus, a, um   *adj,* exhausted
fātīgo   *v.t.* 1, to weary, harass, torment
fātisco   *v.i.* 3, to fall apart
fātŭĭtas, ātis   *f,* foolishness
fātum, i   *n,* destiny, calamity, prophetic saying
fātŭus, a, um   *adj,* foolish
faucēs, ĭum   *f.pl,* throat, narrow passage
faustus, a, um   *adj, adv,* **ē,** fortunate
fautor, ōris   *m,* supporter
fautrix, īcis   *f,* patroness
făvĕo, fāvi, fautum   *v.i.* 2, *with dat;* to favour, befriend
făvilla, ae   *f,* embers
făvor, ōris   *m,* goodwill, applause
făvōrābĭlis, e   *adj,* popular
făvus, i   *m,* honeycomb
fax, făcis   *f,* torch, stimulus
febrĭcŭlōsus, a, um   *adj* feverish
fēbris, is   *f,* fever
Fēbrŭārĭus (mensis) February
fēbrŭum, i   *n,* atonement
fēcundĭtas, ātis   *f,* fertility
fēcundo   *v.t.* 1, to fertilize
fēcundus, a, um   *adj,* fertile, abundant
fel, fellis   *n,* gall-bladder, poison, bitterness
fēles, is   *f,* cat
fēlīcĭtas, ātis   *f,* happiness
fēlix, īcis   *adj, adv,* **ĭter,** happy, fortunate, abundant
fēmĭna, ae   *f,* woman
fēmĭnĕus, a, um   *adj,* feminine
fĕmur, ŏris (ĭnis)   *n,* thigh
fēn... see **faen...**
fēnestra, ae   *f,* window
fĕra, ae   *f,* wild animal

fērālis, e   *adj,* of the dead
fērax, ācis   *adj,* fertile
fercŭlum, i   *n,* barrow, dish
fērē   *adv,* almost, nearly, usually
fĕrentārĭus, ii   *m,* light-armed soldier
fĕrĕtrum, i   *n,* bier
fērĭae, ārum   *f.pl,* holidays
fērĭātus, a, um   *adj,* on holidays
fērīnus, a, um   *adj,* of wild animals
fērĭo   *v.t.* 4, to strike, kill; *(with* **foedus),** to make treaty
fērĭtas, ātis   *f,* wildness
fermē   *adv,* almost, usually
fermentum, i   *n,* yeast, beer
fĕro, ferre, tŭli, lātum   *v.t, irreg,* to bear, bring, move, produce, plunder, offer, tolerate, show, assert; **fertur, ferunt,** it is said
fĕrōcĭa, ae   *f,* high spirits, ferocity
fĕrōcĭtas, ātis   *f,* high spirits, ferocity
fĕrōcĭter   *adv,* bravely, fiercely
fĕrox, ōcis   *adj,* brave, fierce
ferrāmentum, i   *n,* iron tool
ferrātus, a, um   *adj,* iron-clad
ferrĕus, a, um   *adj,* made of iron
ferrūgĭnĕus, a, um   *adj,* rusty, dark red
ferrūgo, ĭnis   *f,* rust, dark red
ferrum, i   *n,* iron, sword
ferrūmen, ĭnis   *n,* cement, glue, solder
ferrūmĭno   *v.t.* 1, to cement, solder
fertĭlis, e   *adj,* fertile
fertĭlĭtas, ātis   *f,* fertility
fĕrūla, ae   *f,* stalk, rod
fĕrus, a, um   *adj,* wild, cruel
fĕrus, i   *m,* wild animal
fervĕfăcĭo, fēci, factum   *v.t.* 3, to heat, melt
fervens, ntis   *adj, adv,* **nter,** burning, boiling hot
fervĕo, bŭi   *v.i.* 2, to boil, burn, rage, swarm
fervĭdus, a, um   *adj,* burning, impetuous
fervor, ōris   *m,* heat, passion
fessus, a, um   *adj,* tired
festīnans, ntis   *adj, adv,* **nter,** in haste
festīnātĭo, ōnis   *f,* haste

festīno *v.i.t.* 1, to hurry
festīnus, a, um *adj*, quick
festīvītas, ātis *f,* humour
festīvus, a, um *adj, adv,* ē, witty,
  lively, cheerful
festum, i *n*, holiday, banquet
festus, a, um *adj*, festive, gay
fētĕo *v.i.* 2, to stink
fētĭāles, ĭum *m.pl,* college of
  priests concerned with war
  ceremonies
fētĭdus, a, um *adj*, stinking
fētor, ōris *m*, stench
fētūra, ae *f,* bearing of young,
  young brood
fētus, a, um *adj*, pregnant,
  fruitful, newly delivered
fībra, ae *f,* fibre, nerve
fibŭla, ae *f,* brooch, pin
fibŭlo *v.t.* 1, to fasten
fictīlis, e *adj*, made of clay
fictīle, is (ia, īum) *n*, earthern
  pottery
fictor, ōris *m*, designer
fictus, a, um *adj*, imagined
ficus, i or **ūs** *f,* fig tree
fidēlis, e *adj, adv,* ĭter, faithful,
  true, sure
fidēlĭtas, ātis *f,* faithfulness
fidens, ntis *adj, adv,* nter self-
  confident
fidentĭa, ae *f,* confidence
fĭdes, ĕi *f,* trust, faith, confidence,
  honesty, promise
fĭdes, īum *f.pl,* lute, guitar
fĭdīcen, ĭnis *m*, lute-player
fido, fisus sum *v.* 3, *semi-dep.*
  with dat; to trust
fidūcĭa, ae *f,* confidence
fĭdus, a, um *adj*, trustworthy
fĭĕri see **fio**
fīgo, xi, xum *v.t.* 3, to fix, fasten,
  transfix
fĭgŭlāris, e *adj*, of a potter
fĭgŭlus, i *m*, potter
fĭgūra, ae *f,* shape, phantom,
  atom, nature
fĭgūrātus, a, um *adj*, shaped
fĭgūro *v.t.* 1, to shape
fīlĭa, ae *f,* daughter
fīlĭŏla, ae *f,* little daughter
fīlĭŏlus, i *m*, little son
fīlĭus, i *m*, son

fĭlix, ĭcis *f,* hair, fern
fīlum, i *n*, thread, texture
fimbrĭae, ārum *f.pl,* threads,
  fringe
fĭmus, i *m*, manure
findo, fīdi, ssum *v.t.* 3, to split
fines, ĭum *m.pl,* territory
fingo, nxi, ctum *v.t.* 3, to shape,
  adorn, imagine, devise
finĭo *v.t.* 4, to enclose, limit,
  prescribe, end, die
finis, is *m*, boundary, limit, end
finĭtĭmus, a, um *adj*, adjoining
finĭtĭmi, ōrum *m.pl,* neighbours
finĭtor, ōris *m*, surveyor
fio, fĭĕri, factus sum *v, irreg*, to
  become, happen
firmāmen, ĭnis *n*, prop, support
firmāmentum, i *n*, prop, support
firmĭtsas, ātis *f,* strength, firmness
firmĭtūdo, ĭnis *f,* strength, firmness
firmo *v.t.* 1, to strengthen,
  encourage, promise
firmus, a, um *adj, adv,* ē, ĭter,
  strong, stable, constant, true
fiscella, ae *f,* small basket, muzzle
fiscīna, ae *f,* small basket
fiscus, i *m*, purse, imperial
  treasury
fissĭlis, e *adj*, breakable
fissum, i *n*, cleft, chink
fissūra, ae *f,* split, chink
fistūca, ae *f,* rammer
fistŭla, ae *f,* pipe, tube
fistŭlātor, ōris *m*, piper
fisus, a, um *adj*, trusting, relying
  on
flābellum, i *n*, small fan
flābra, ōrum *n.pl,* gusts
flaccĭdus, a, um *adj*, flabby
flăgello *v.t.* 1, to whip
flăgellum, i *n*, whip, thong
flāgĭtātĭo, ōnis *f,* demand
flāgĭtĭōsus, a, um *adj, adv,* ē,
  disgraceful
flāgĭtĭum, ii *n*, disgraceful
  conduct, shame
flāgĭto *v.t.* 1, to demand
flăgrans, ntis *adj*, burning
flăgro *v.i.* 1, to blaze, glow
flăgrum, i *n*, whip
flāmen, ĭnis *m*, priest
flāmen, ĭnis *n*, blast

flāmĭnĭum, ii *n*, priesthood
flamma, ae *f*, flame, blaze
flammĕum, i *n*, bridal veil
flammĕus, a, um *adj*, flaming
flammĭfer, ĕra, ĕrum *adj*, flame-carrying
flammo *v.i.t.* 1, to burn
flātus, ūs *m*, blowing, bluster
flāvens, ntis *adj*, yellow
flāvĕo *v.i.* 2, to be golden, yellow
flāvesco *v.i.* 3, to turn golden
flāvus, a, um *adj*, golden, yellow
flēbĭlis, e *adj, adv*, ĭter, lamentable, tearful
flecto, xi, xum *v.i.t.* 3, to turn; bend, curve, wheel, persuade
flĕo, ēvi, tum *v.i.t.* 2, to weep; mourn
flētus, ūs *m*, weeping
flexĭbĭlis, e *adj*, flexible
flexĭo, ōnis *f*, curve
flexŭōsus, a, um *adj*, crooked
flexus, ūs *m*, bend, turning
flictus, ūs *m*, collision
flō *v.i.t.* 1, to blow
floccus, i *m*, lock of wool
flōrens, ntis *adj*, shining, flourishing
flōrĕo *v.i.* 2, to bloom, flourish
flōresco *v.i.* 3, to come into flower, flourish
flōrĕus, a, um *adj*, made of flowers
flōrĭdus, a, um *adj*, blooming
flōs, ōris *m*, flower, ornament
floscŭlus, i *m*, small flower
fluctŭo *v.i.* 1, to ripple, undulate, hesitate
fluctŭōsus, a, um *adj*, billowy
fluctus, ūs *m*, wave
flŭens, ntis *adj*, lax, fluent
flŭentum, i *n*, stream, flood
flŭĭdus, a, um *adj*, flowing, slack
flŭĭto *v.i.* 1, to flow, float
flūmen, ĭnis *n*, river, flood
flūmĭnĕus, a, um *adj*, of a river
flŭo, xi, xum *v.i.* 3, to flow, wave, vanish
flŭvĭālis, e *adj*, of a river
flŭvĭus, ii *m*, river
fluxĭo, ōnis *f*, flowing
fluxus, a, um *adj*, fluid, slack
fōcāle, is *n*, necktie

fōcŭlus, i *m*, brazier
fŏcus, i *m*, fireplace, home
fŏdĭco *v.t.* 1, to dig, nudge, stab
fŏdĭo, fōdi, fossum *v.i.t.* 3, to dig; dig up, prick, stab
foedĕrātus, a, um *adj*, allied
foedĭtas, ātis *f*, filthiness
foedo *v.t.* 1, to disfigure, disgrace, stain
foedus, a, um *adj, adv*, ē, filthy, shameful
foedus, ĕris *n*, treaty, contract
foet... see **fet...**
fŏlĭum, ii *n*, leaf
follĭcŭlus, i *m*, small bag
follis, is *m*, pair of bellows
fōmentum, *n*, poultice, comfort
fōmes, ĭtis *m*, firewood
fons, ntis *m*, fountain, origin
fontĭcŭlus, i *m*, small fountain
for *v.i.t.* 1, *dep*, to speak; say, predict
fŏrāmen, ĭnis *n*, hole
fŏrās *adv*, out-of-doors
forceps, ĭpis *m, f*, tongs, pincers
fŏrĕ = futurum esse see **esse**
fŏrem = essem see **esse**
fŏrensis, e *adj*, concerning the courts of law
fŏres, um *f.pl*, door, entrance
forfex, ĭcis *f*, scissors (*usually in pl.*)
fŏrĭca, ae *f*, public convenience
fŏrĭcŭlae, ārum *f. pl*, shutters
fŏris, is *f*, door, entrance
fŏris *adv*, outside, from outside
forma, ae *f*, form, shape, beauty
formīca, ae *f*, ant
formīdābĭlis, e *adj*, fearful
formīdo *v.i.t.* 1, to be afraid; fear
formīdo, ĭnis *f*, fear, terror
formīdŭlōsus, a, um *adj, adv*, ē, dreadful, fearful
formo *v.t.* 1, to shape
formōsus, a, um *adj*, beautiful
formŭla, ae *f*, rule, principle, agreement, lawsuit
fornax, ācis *f*, oven
fornix, ĭcis *m*, arch, vault
fors, rtis *f*, chance, luck
fors *adv*, perhaps
forsan *adv*, perhaps
forsĭtan *adv*, perhaps

fortassē   *adv*, perhaps
fortē   *adv*, by chance
fortis, e   *adj, adv*, ĭter, strong, brave
fortĭtūdo, ĭnis   *f*, bravery
fortŭĭtō(ū)   *adv*, by chance
fortŭĭtus, a, um   *adj*, accidental
fortūna, ae   *f*, luck, fate, fortune (good or bad), circumstances, property
fortūnātus, a, um   *adj, adv*, ē, lucky, happy
fortūno   *v.t.* 1, to enrich, bless
fŏrum, i   *n*, marketplace, business
fŏrus, i   *m*, gangway, passage, row of seats
fossa, ae   *f*, ditch
fossĭo, ōnis   *f*, excavation
fossor, ōris   *m*, digger, miner
fŏvĕa, ae   *f*, pit, pitfall
fŏvĕo, fōvi, fōtum   *v.t.* 2, to warm, caress, love
fractūra, ae   *f*, fracture
fractus, a, um   *adj*, weak, feeble
frāga, ōrum   *n.pl*, strawberries
frăgĭlis, e   *adj*, brittle, frail
frăgĭlĭtas, ātis   *f*, frailty
fragmen, ĭnis   *n*, fracture, splinter
fragmentum, i   *n*, fragment
frăgor, ōris   *m*, crash
frăgōsus, a, um   *adj*, rugged, crashing
fragro   *v.i.* 1, to smell
frāgum, i   *n*, strawberry plant
frango, frēgi, fractum   *v.t.* 3, to break, crush, weaken
frāter, tris   *m*, brother
frāternĭtas, ātis   *f*, brotherhood
frāternus, a, um   *adj, adv*, ē, brotherly
frātrĭcīda, ae   *m*, a fratricide
fraudātĭo, ōnis   *f*, deceit
fraudātor, ōris   *m*, deceiver
fraudo   *v.t.* 1, to cheat, defraud
fraudŭlentus, a, um   *adj*, deceitful
fraus, dis   *f*, deceit, crime, mistake, injury
fraxĭnĕus, a, um   *adj*, of ash
fraxĭnus, i   *f*, ash tree
frĕmĭtus, ūs   *m*, murmur, roar
frĕmo, ŭi, ĭtum   *v.i.t.* 3, to roar, murmur, howl; grumble at
frĕmor, ōris   *m*, murmuring

frendĕo, ŭi, frēsum   *v.i.* 2, to gnash the teeth, crush
frēno   *v.t.* 1, to bridle, curb
frēnum, i   *n*, bridle, restraint
frĕquens, ntis   *adj, adv*, nter, usual, repeated, crowded
frĕquentātĭo, ōnis   *f*, frequency
frĕquentĭa, ae   *f*, crowd
frĕquento   *v.t.* 1, to frequent, repeat, crowd, celebrate
frĕtum, i   *n*, channel, strait
frĕtus, a, um   *adj. with abl*, relying on
frĭco, cŭi, ctum   *v.t.* 1, to rub
frictus, a, um   *adj*, rubbed, **(frico)**; roasted **(frigo)**
frīgĕo   *v.i.* 2, to be cold or languid, to be slighted
frīgesco, frixi   *v.i.* 3, to grow cold, become languid
frīgĭdus, a, um   *adj*, cold, stiff, feeble, spiritless
frīgĭda, ae   *f*, cold water
frīgo, xi, ctum   *v.t.* 3, to roast
frīgus, ŏris   *n*, cold, winter
fringilla, ae   *f*, small bird, robin, chaffinch
frondātor, ōris   *m*, pruner
frondĕo   *v.i.* 2, to be in leaf
frondesco, dŭi   *v.i.* 3, to come into leaf
frondĕus, a, um   *adj*, leafy
frondōsus, a, um   *adj*, leafy
frons, dis   *f*, foliage, leaf
frons, ntis   *f*, forehead, front, appearance
fructŭōsus, a, um   *adj*, fruitful, advantageous
fructus, ūs   *m*, enjoyment, fruit, profit
frūgālis, e   *adj, adv*, ĭter, thrifty, careful
frūgālĭtas, ātis   *f*, thrift, worth
frūges, um   *f.pl*, see **frux**
frūgi   *indecl. adj*, worthy, useful
frūgĭfer, ĕra, ĕrum   *adj*, fertile
frūmentārĭus, a, um   *adj*, of corn
frūmentor   *v.i.* 1, *dep*, to fetch corn
frūmentum, i   *n*, corn
frŭor, fructus   *v.* 3, *dep. with abl*, to enjoy
frustrā   *adv*, in vain

frustrātĭo, ōnis *f*, deception, frustration
frustror *v.t.* 1, *dep*, to deceive
frustum, i *n*, piece
frŭtex, ĭcis *m*, bush
frŭtĭcētum, i *n*, thicket
frŭtĭcōsus, a, um *adj*, bushy
frux, frūgis *f*, fruit, crops, value, result
fūcātus, a, um *adj*, painted, counterfeit
fūco *v.t.* 1, to paint, dye
fūcōsus, a, um *adj*, coloured, spurious
fūcus, i *m*, rouge, disguise
fūcus, i *m*, drone
fŭga, ae *f*, flight, exile
fŭgax, ācis *adj*, runaway, swift
fŭgĭens, ntis *adj*, runaway, swift
fŭgĭens, ntis *adj*, fleeing
fŭgĭo, fūgi, fŭgĭtum *v.i.t.* 3, to run away; flee from, avoid
fŭgĭtīvus, a, um *adj*, fugitive
fŭgĭtīvus, i *m*, runaway slave, deserter
fŭgĭto *v.t.* 1, to flee, avoid
fŭgo *v.t.* 1, to rout, chase
fulcĭo, fulsi, fultum *v.t.* 4, to prop up, strenghen
fulcrum, i *n*, foot (of couch)
fulgens, ntis *adj*, shining
fulgĕo, Isi *v.i.* 2, to flash, shine
fulgĭdus, a, um *adj*, flashing, shining
fulgor, ōris *m*, lightning, gleam, splendour
fulgur, ŭris *n*, lightning
fulgŭrat *v. impers*, it lightens
fūlĭca, ae *f*, moorhen
fūlīgo, ĭnis *f*, soot
fūlĭgĭnōsus, a, um *adj*, sooty
fulmen, ĭnis *n*, thunderbolt, lightning
fulmĭnĕus, a, um *adj*, of lightning, destructive, brilliant
fulmĭno *v.i.* 1, to thunder
fultūra, ae *f*, prop, tonic
fulvus, a, um *adj*, deep yellow
fūmĕus, a, um *adj*, smoky
fūmĭdus, a, um *adj*, smoky
fūmĭfer, ĕra, ĕrum *adj*, smoking, steaming
fūmĭfĭcus, a, um *adj*, smoking, steaming
fūmĭgo *v.t.* 1, to smoke out, fumigate
fūmo *v.i.* 1, to smoke
fūmōsus, a, um *adj*, smoky, smoke-dried
fūmus, i *m*, smoke
fūnāle, is *n*, cord, torch
functĭo, ōnis *f*, performing
functus, a, um *partic. adj, with abl*, having completed
funda, ae *f*, sling, missile
fundāmen, ĭnis *n*, foundation
fundāmentum, i *n*, foundation
fundĭtor, ōris *m*, slinger
fundĭtus *adv*, from the bottom, completely
fundo, fūdi, fūsum *v.t.* 3, to pour out, spread out, scatter, overthrow, produce
fundo *v.t.* 1, to found, fix
fundus, i *m*, the bottom, a farm
fundus, i *m*, guarantor
fūnĕbris, e *adj*, of a funeral
fūnĕrĕus, a, um *adj*, of a funeral
fūnĕro *v.t.* 1, to bury, kill
fūnesto *v.t.* 1, to pollute
fūnestus, a, um *adj*, fatal, sad
fungor, functus *v.* 3, *dep, with abl*, to perform, complete
fungus, i *m*, mushroom, fungus
fūnis, is *m*, rope
fūnŭs, ĕris *n*, funeral, death, ruin
fūr, fūris *c*, thief, rogue
fūrax, ācis *adj*, light-fingered
furca, ae *f*, two-pronged fork or pole for punishment
furcĭfer, ĕri *m*, gallows-bird
furcilla, ae *f*, small fork
furcŭla, a *f*, fork-shaped prop, ravine
fŭrens, ntis *adj*, raging
furfur, ŭris *m*, bran
fŭrĭae, ārum *f.pl*, rage, frenzy, avenging Furies
fŭrĭālis, e *adj, adv*, ĭter, raging, wild
fŭrĭbundus, a, um *adj*, raging
fŭrĭo *v.t.* 1, to enrage
fŭrĭōsus, a, um *adj*, raging
furnus, i *m*, oven
fŭro, ŭi *v.i.* 3, to rage, be mad
fūror *v.t.* 1, *dep*, to steal

fŭror, ōris *m*, rage, fury
furtim *adv*, stealthily
furtīvus, a, um *adj*, stolen, secret
furtum, i *n*, theft, trick
furtō *adv*, secretly
fūruncŭlus, i *m*, pilferer, sore, boil
furvus, a, um *adj*, gloomy,
　swarthy
fuscĭna, ae *f*, trident
fusco *v.t.* 1, to blacken, darken
fuscus, a, um *adj*, dark, swarthy
fūsĭlis, e *adj*, fluid, soft
fustis, is *m*, cudgel, club
fūsus, a, um *adj*, spread out, wide
fūsus, i *m*, spindle
futtĭlis (fūtĭlis), e, *adj*, worthless
futtĭlĭtas (fūtĭlitas), ātis *f*,
　worthlessness
fūtūra, ōrum *n.pl*, the future
fūtūrum, i *n*, the future
fūtūrus, a, um *adj*, future

G

gaesum, i *n*, heavy Gallic javelin
galbĭnus, a, um *adj*, greenish-
　yellow
gălĕa, ae *f*, helmet
gălĕo *v.t.* 1, to issue with helmets
gălērum, i *n*, (us, i *m*), hat
galla, ae *f*, oak-apple
gallīna, ae *f*, hen
gallīnārĭŭm, ii *n*, hen-house
gallus, i *m*, cock
gānĕa, ae *f*, eating-house
gānĕo, ōnis *m*, glutton
gannĭo *v.i.* 4, to bark, snarl
gannītus, ūs *m*, chattering
garrĭo *v.t.* 4, to chatter
garrŭlĭtas, ātis *f*, chattering
garrŭlus, a, um *adj*, talkative
gărum (garon), i *n*, fish sauce
gaudĕo, gāvīsus *v.i.t.* 2, *semi-*
　dep, to rejoice
gaudĭum, ii *n*, joy, delight
gausăpa, ae *f*, rough clothing
gāvĭa, ae *f*, seabird
gāza, ae *f*, treasure (of Persia)
gĕlĭdus, a, um *adj*, *adv*, ē, ice-
　cold, frosty
gĕlo *v.i.t.* 1, to freeze
gĕlum, i (gĕlu, ūs) *n*, frost, cold
gĕmellus, a, um *adj*, (us, i *m*),
　twin
gĕmĭno *v.t.* 1, to double, pair
gĕmĭnus, a, um *adj*, twin
gĕmĭni, ōrum *m.pl*, twins
gĕmĭtus, ūs *m*, lamentation
gemma, ae *f*, bud, jewel, goblet,
　signet-ring
gemmārĭus, ii *m*, jeweller
gemmātus, a, um *adj*, set with
　jewels
gemmĕus, a, um *adj*, set with
　jewels
gemmo *v.i.* 1, to come into bud
gĕmo, ŭi, ĭtum *v.i.t.* 3, to groan,
　creak; deplore
gĕna, ae *f*, the cheek
gĕner, ĕri *m*, son-in-law
gĕnĕrālis, e *adj*, of a certain kind,
　general
gĕnĕrātim *adv*, in classes, in
　general
gĕnĕrātor, ōris *m*, breeder
gĕnĕro *v.t.* 1, to create, produce;
　(*passive*) be born
gĕnĕrōsus, a, um *adj*, *adv*, ē, of
　noble birth, generous
gĕnesta, ae *f*, small shrub with
　yellow flowers, broom
gĕnĕtīvus, a, um *adj*, *in*born
gĕnĕtrix, īcis *f*, mother
gĕnĭālis, e *adj*, *adv*, ĭter, bridal,
　cheerful
gĕnĭtālis, e *adj*, of birth, fruitful
gĕnĭtor, ōris *m*, father
gĕnĭus, ii *m*, guardian angel
gens, ntis *f*, clan, race,
　descendant, nation
gentīlĭcĭus, a, um *adj*, of the same
　clan
gentīlis, e *adj*, of the same clan
gentīlis, is *c*, relative
gĕnu, ūs *n*, knee
gĕnŭīnus, a, um *adj*, innate
gĕnŭīnus, a, um *adj*, of the cheek
　or jaw
gĕnus, ĕris *n*, birth, race, kind,
　type, descendant
gĕōgrăphĭa, ae *f*, geography
gĕōmĕtres, ae *m*, mathematician
gĕōmĕtrĭa, ae *f*, geometry
germānĭtas, ātis *f*, brotherhood
germānus, a, um *adj*, own
germānus, i *m*, (a, ae *f*),

brother, (sister)
germen, ĭnis *n*, bud, sprig
germĭno *v.i.* 1, to bud
gĕro, gessi, stum *v.t.* 3, to bear,
wear, bring, produce, behave,
display, carry on, honour
gerrae, ārum *f.pl*, nonsense
gĕrŭlus, i *m*, porter
gestāmen, ĭnis *n*, load
gestātĭo, ōnis *f*, riding, driving
gestĭo *v.i.* 4, to be joyful, desire
passionately
gesto *v.t.* 1, to carry, wear, have
gestus, ūs *m*, posture, gesture
gestus, a, um *adj*, achieved,
carried
gibber, ĕris *m*, hump; *as adj*,
hunchbacked
gibbus, i *m*, hump; *as adj*,
hunchbacked
gĭgantēus, a, um *adj*, of giants
gīgās, ntis *m*, giant
gigno, gĕnŭi, gĕnĭtum *v.t.* 3, to
give birth to; *(passive)* be born
gilvus, a, um *adj*, pale yellow
gingīva, ae *f*, gum
glăber, bra, brum *adj*, bald
glăcĭālis, e *adj*, frozen
glăcĭes, ēi *f*, ice
glăcĭo *v.t.* 1, to freeze
glădĭātor, ōris *m*, gladiator
glădĭātōrĭus, a, um *adj*,
gladiatorial
glădĭus, ii *n*, sword
glaeba (glēba), ae *f*, clod
glans, ndis *f*, acorn, bullet
glārĕa, ae *f*, gravel
glaucus, a, um *adj*, blue-grey
glēba see **glaeba**
glis, glīris *m*, dormouse
glisco, m *v.i.* 3, to swell, grow
glŏbōsus, a, um *adj*, spherical
glŏbus, i *m*, ball, crowd
glŏmĕro *v.t.* 1, to gather into a
heap, crowd together
glŏmus, ĕris *n*, ball of thread
glōrĭa, ae *f*, glory, boasting
glōrĭātĭo, ōnis *f*, boasting
glōrĭor *v.i.t.* 1, *dep*, to boast
glōrĭōsus, a, um *adj, adv*, ē,
famous, conceited
glossārĭum, ii *n*, glossary
glūten, ĭnis *n*, glue

glūtĭnātor, ōris *m*, bookbinder
glūtĭno *v.t.* 1, to glue
gluttĭo *v.t.* 4, to gulp
gnārus, a, um *adj. with genit*,
acquainted with, expert in
gnātus, a, um *adj*, born
gnāv... see **nāv...**
gossypĭum, ii *n*, cotton
grăcĭlis, e *adj*, slender
grăcĭlĭtas, ātis *f*, slenderness
grācŭlus, i *m*, jackdaw
grădātim, *adv*, gradually
grădātĭo, ōnis *f*, gradation, climax
grădĭor, gressus *v.i.* 3, *dep*, to
walk, go, move
grădus, ūs *m*, pace, step, rank,
position, station, stair, plait
graecor *v.i.* 1, *dep*, to live like the
Greeks
grallae, ārum *f.pl*, stilts
grāmen, ĭnis *n*, grass
grāmĭnĕus, a, um *adj*, grassy
grammătĭca, ae *f*, grammar
grammătĭcus, i *m*, grammarian
grānārĭa, ōrum *n.pl*, granary
grānātus, a, um *adj*, with many
seeds
grandaevus, a, um *adj*, old
grandīlŏquus, a, um *adj*, boastful
grandĭnat *v.* 1, *impers*, it is
hailing
grandis, e *adj*, full-grown, large,
old, strong, noble
grando, ĭnis *f*, hail, hailstorm
grānum, i *n*, grain, seed
grānōsus, a, um *adj*, seedy
grassātor, ōris *m*, idler, footpad
grassor *v.i.* 1, *dep*, to hang
about, attack, rage
grātē *adv*, gratefully, willingly
grātes *f.pl*, thanks
grātĭa, ae *f*, esteem, friendship,
charm, beauty, kindness, favour,
gratitude; *in abl*, for the sake of;
grātĭīs (grātīs), as a favour; *pl*,
thanks
grātĭfĭcātĭo, ōnis *f*, doing favours
grātĭfĭcor *v.* 1, *dep*, to do as a
favour, oblige
grātĭōsus, a, um *adj*, popular
grātor *v.i.t.* 1, *dep*, to
congratulate
grātŭītus, a, um *adj*, voluntary

grātŭlātĭo, ōnis *f*, rejoicing
grātŭlor *v.i.t.* 1, *dep*, to
  congratulate
grātus, a, um *adj*, pleasing, grateful
grăvāte *adv*, unwillingly
grăvēdo, ĭnis *f*, cold, catarrh
grăvĕŏlens, ntis *adj*, stinking
grăvesco *v.i.* 3, to grow heavy
grăvĭdus, a, um *adj*, pregnant
grăvis, e *adj, adv, ĭter*, heavy,
  loaded, low, pregnant, severe,
  unpleasant, serious, urgent,
  important
grăvĭtas, ātis *f*, weight, heaviness,
  severity, dignity, urgency
grăvo *v.t.* 1, to load, oppress
grăvor *v.i.t.* 1, *dep*, to be irritated
  or reluctant; not to tolerate
grĕgālis, e *adj*, of the herd,
  gregarious
grĕgārĭus, a, um *adj*, common
  grĕgātim *adv*, in herds
grĕmĭum, ii, *n*, bosom, lap
gressus, ūs *m*, step, way
grex, grĕgis *m*, flock, herd
grūmus, i *m*, hillock
grunnĭo *v.i.* 4, to grunt
grunnītus, ūs *m*, grunt
grus, grŭis *m, f*, crane
grŷllus, i *m*, grasshopper
gryps, gryphis *m*, griffin
gŭbernācŭlum, i *n*, rudder
gŭbernātĭo, ōnis *f*, management
gŭbernātor, ōris *m*, steersman
gŭberno *v.t.* 1, to steer, manage
gŭla, ae *f*, throat, appetite
gŭlōsus, a, um *adj*, gluttonous
gummi *n*, *(indecl.)*, gum
gurges, ĭtis *m*, whirlpool, abyss
gustātĭo, ōnis *f*, taste
gustātus, ūs *m*, sense of taste
gusto *v.t.* 1, to taste
gustus, ūs *m*, tasting, snack
gutta, ae *f*, drop, spot
guttur, ŭris *n*, throat
gutus (guttus), i *m*, flask
gymnăsĭum, ii *m*, gymnasium
gymnĭcus, a, um *adj*, gymnastic
gypsātus, a, um *adj*, covered with
  lime
gypso *v.t.* 1, to plaster
gypsum, i *n*, white line
gŷrus, i *m*, circuit, ring

H

hăbēna, ae *f*, thong, rein
hăbĕo *v.t.* 2, to have, keep, be
  able, render, esteem, use, deal
  with, know; *with* **in animo** to
  intend
hăbĭlis, e *adj*, convenient, expert
hăbĭtābĭlis, e *adj*, habitable
hăbĭtātĭo, ōnis *f*, residence
hăbĭto *v.i.t.* 1, to live; inhabit
hăbĭtus, ūs *m*, condition, bearing,
  state, dress, shape
hāc *adv*, by this way, here
hactĕnus *adv*, up to this point
haec see **hic**
haedus, i *m*, young goat
haemorrhăgĭa, ae *f*, haemorrhage
haerĕo, si, sum *v.i.* 2, to hang,
  cling, hesitate
haesĭtans, ntis *adj*, hesitant
haesĭtantĭa, ae *f*, stammering
haesĭtātĭo, ōnis *f*, embarrassment
haesĭto *v.i.* 1, to hesitate
hālĭtus, ūs *m*, breath, steam
hālo *v.i.t.* 1, to breathe; exhale
hăma, ae *f*, bucket
hāmātus, a, um *adj*, hooked
hāmus, i *m*, hook, fish hook
hăra, ae *f*, coop, pen, sty
hărēna, ae *f*, sand, arena
hărēnārĭus, a, um *adj*, of sand
hărēnōsus, a, um *adj*, sandy
hărĭŏlor *v.i.* 1, *dep*, to foretell
hărĭŏlus, i *m*, prophet
harmŏnĭa, ae *f*, harmony
harpăgo, ōnis *m*, grappling-hook
hărundo, ĭnis *f*, reed, fishing rod,
  shaft, shepherd's pipe
hăruspex, ĭcis *m*, clairvoyant
hasta, ae *f*, spear, lance
hastāti, ōrum *m.pl*, pike-men;
  front line of a Roman army
hastīle, is *n*, spear shaft
haud (haut) *adv*, not at all
haudquāquam *adv*, by no means
haurĭo, si, stum *v.t.* 4, to draw
  up, drink in, drain, exhaust
haustus, ūs *m*, a drink, draught
hav... see **av...**
hĕbĕnus, i *f*, ebony
hĕbĕo *v.i.* 2, to be dull
hĕbes, ĕtis *adj*, blunt, dull

hĕbesco   *v.i.* 3, to grow dull
hĕbĕto   *v.t.* 1, to blunt
hĕdĕra, ae   *f,* ivy
hei   *interj,* ah! alas!
hellŭo, ōnis   *m,* glutton
hellŭor   *v.i.* 1, *dep, with abl,* to
   squander
hem! (em!)   *interj,* ah! indeed!
hēmĭcyclĭum, ii   *n,* semicircle
hēmisphaerĭum, ii   *n,* hemisphere
hĕra, ae   *f,* lady of the house
herba, ae   *f,* grass, plant
herbārĭus, a, um   *adj,* of plants
herbĭdus, a, um   *adj,* grassy
herbōsus, a, um   *adj,* grassy
hercŭle (hercle)! by Hercules!
hĕrĕ   *adv,* yesterday
hērēdĭtārĭus, a, um   *adj, i*inherited
hērēdĭtas, ātis   *f,* inheritance
hēres, ēdis   *c,* heir, heiress
hĕri   *adv,* yesterday
hĕrīlis, e   *adj,* of the master or
   mistress
hernĭa, ae   *f,* rupture
hērōĭcus, a, um   *adj,* heroic
hēros, ōis   *m,* demigod
hĕrus, i   *m,* master of the house
hespĕris, ĭdis   *adj,* western
hespĕrĭus, a, um   *adj,* western
hesternus, a, um   *adj,* yesterday's
heu!   *interj,* oh! alas!
heus!   *interj,* hallo there!
hexămĕtər, tri   *m,* a verse metre
   consisting of six feet
hĭans   see **hĭo**
hĭātus, ūs   *m,* aperture
hīberna, ōrum   *n.pl,* winter
   quarters
hībernācŭla, ōrum   *n.pl,* tents to
   spend winter in
hīberno   *v.i.* 1, to spend the
   winter
hībernus, a, um   *adj,* of winter
hibrĭda, ae   *c,* cross breed
hīc, haec, hōc   *pron,* this
hīc   *adv,* here
hĭĕmālis, e   *adj,* of winter
hĭĕmo   *v.i.t.* 1, to spend the
   winter; freeze
hĭems (hiemps), hĭĕmis   *f,* winter,
   stormy weather
hĭlāris, e   *adj, adv, ē,* cheerful
hĭlărĭtas, ātis   *f,* gaiety

hĭlăro   *v.t.* 1, to cheer up
hillae, ārum   *f.pl,* sausage
hinc   *adv,* from here, hence
hinnĭo   *v.i.* 4, to neigh
hinnītus, ūs   *m,* neighing
hinnŭlĕus, i   *m,* young stag
hĭo   *v.i.* 1, to gape open
hippŏpŏtămus, i   *m,*
   hippopotamus
hircīnus, a, um   *adj,* of a goat
hircus, i   *m,* goat
hirsūtus, a, um   *adj,* shaggy
hirtus, a, um   *adj,* rough, shaggy
hĭrūdo, ĭnis   *f,* leech
hĭrundĭnīnus, a, um   *adj,* of
   swallows
hĭrundo, ĭnis   *f,* a swallow
hisco, —   *v.i.t.* 3, to gape; whisper
hispĭdus, a, um   *adj,* rough,
   shaggy
histŏrĭa, ae   *f,* story, account
histŏrĭcus, a, um   *adj,* historical
histŏrĭcus, i   *m,* historian
histrĭo, ōnis   *m,* actor
hĭulcus, a, um   *adj,* gaping; (of
   speech) badly connected
hoc   see **hic**
hŏdīē   *adv,* today
hŏdĭernus, a, um   *adj,* of today
hŏlus, ĕris   *n,* vegetables
hŏluscŭlum, i   *n,* small vegetable
hŏmĭcīda, ae   *c,* murderer
hŏmĭcīdĭum, ii   *n,* homicide
hŏmo, ĭnis *c,* human being
hŏmullus, i   *m,* puny man
hŏmuncŭlus, i   *m,* puny man
hŏnestas, ātis   *f,* honour, good
   name, integrity
hŏnesto   *v.t.* 1, to honour, adorn
hŏnestum, i   *n,* integrity
hŏnestus, a, um   *adj, adv, ē,*
   respectable, esteemed, eminent
hŏnor (hŏnos), ōris   *m,* esteem,
   public office, reward, charm
hŏnōrārĭus, a, um   *adj,* honorary
hŏnōrātus, a, um   *adj,* respected
hŏnōrĭfĭcus, a, um   *adj, adv, ē,*
   complimentary
hŏnōro   *v.t.* 1, to honour, respect,
   adorn
hŏnos   see **hŏnor**
hŏnus...   see **ŏnus...**
hōra, ae   *f,* hour, time, season

hōrāřĭum, ii *n,* hourglass
hordĕŏlus, i *m,* sty (eye)
hordĕum, i *n,* barley
hŏřĭŏla, ae *f,* fishing boat
hornōtīnus, a, um *adj,* this year's
hornus, a, um *adj,* this year's
hōrŏlŏgĭum, ii *n,* clock
horrendus, a, um *adj,* terrible
horrĕo *v.i.t.* 2, to bristle, tremble;
  dread
horresco, horrŭi *v.i.* 3, to become
  ruffled or frightened
horrĕum, i *n,* barn, warehouse
horrĭbĭlis, e *adj,* terrible
horrĭdŭlus, a, um *adj,* rough
horrĭdus, a, um *adj, adv,* ē, rough,
  bristly, wild, uncouth
horrĭfer, ĕra, ĕrum *adj,* dreadful
horrĭfĭco *v.t.* 1, to ruffle, terrify
horrĭfĭcus, a, um *adj,* terrible
horrĭsŏnus, a, um *adj,* with
  fearful sounds
horror, ōris *m,* bristling,
  trembling, chill, terror
hortāmen, ĭnis *n,* encouragement
hortātĭo, ōnis *f,* encouragement
hortātor, ōris *m,* encourager
hortātus, ūs *m,* encouragement
hortor *v.t.* 1, *dep,* to encourage,
  urge, cheer on
hortŭlus, i *m,* little garden
hortus, i *m,* garden
hospĕs, ĭtis, *m,* (hospĭta, ae *f*),
  host(ess), guest, stranger
hospĭtālis, e *adj,* hospitable
hospĭtĭum, ii *n,* hospitality,
  friendship, lodgings
hostĭa, ae *f,* sacrificial victim
hostĭcus, a, um *adj,* of the enemy
hostīlis, e *adj, adv,* ĭter, hostile
hostis, is *c,* enemy, stranger
hūc *adv,* to this place or point
hui! *interj,* oh!
huius *genitive of* hic
hūiuscĕmŏdi, hūiusmŏdi *pron. adj,*
  (indecl.) of this sort
hūmāna, ōrum *n.pl,* human
  affairs
hūmānē *adv,* like a reasonable
  human being, courteously
hūmānĭtas, ātis *f,* humanity,
  gentleness, refinement
hūmānĭter *adv,* see hūmānē

hūmānus, a, um *adj,* human,
  mortal, humane, gentle, kind
hūmecto *v.t.* 1, to moisten
hūmĕo *v.i.* 2, to be wet
hūmĕrus, i *m,* shoulder, arm
hŭmi *adv,* on or to the ground
hūmĭdus, a, um *adj,* damp, wet
hŭmĭlis, e *adj, adv,* ĭter, low,
  humble, abject
hŭmĭlĭtas, ātis *f,* lowness,
  insignificance, meanness
hŭmo *v.t.* 1, to bury
hūmor, ōris *m,* liquid
hŭmus, i *f,* the ground, region
hўăcinthus(os), i *m,* blue iris
hўaena, ae *f,* hyena
hўălus, i *m,* glass
hybrĭda, ae *c,* crossbreed
hydra, ae *f,* seven-headed water
  snake
hydrĭa, ae *f,* jug
hydrops, ōpis *m,* dropsy
hydrus, i *m,* water snake
hўmen, mĕnis *m,* marriage
hўperbŏlē, es *f,* exaggeration,
  hyperbole
hystrĭx, ĭcis *f,* porcupine

I

ĭambēus, a, um *adj,* iambic
ĭambus, i *m,* iambic foot (two
  syllables, short followed by long)
ĭanthĭnus, a, um *adj,* violet in
  colour
ĭāpyx, iapўgis *m,* West-North-
  West wind
ĭaspis, ĭdis *f,* jasper
ĭbĭ *adv,* there, then
ĭbīdem *adv,* in that same place, at
  that very moment
ĭbis, ĭdis *f,* scared bird, ibis
ĭcĭo (ĭco), ĭci, ictum *v.t.* 3, to hit,
  strike (a bargain)
ictus, ūs *m,* blow, stroke, shot
id *see* is
idcirco *adv,* for that reason
īdem, ĕădem, ĭdem *pron,* the
  same
īdentĭdem *adv,* repeatedly
ĭdĕo *adv,* for that reason
ĭdĭōta, ae *m,* layman
ĭdōnĕus, a, um *adj,* suitable,

capable, sufficient

īdus, ūum *f.pl*, the ides, 13th or 15th day of the month

īdyllīum, ii *n*, idyll

īgītur *adv*, therefore, then

ignārus, a, um *adj*, unaware

ignāvīa, ae *f*, laziness, cowardice

ignāvus, a, um *adj, adv*, ē, lazy, cowardly

ignesco *v.i.* 3, to catch fire

ignĕus, a, um *adj*, burning

ignĭcŭlus, i *m*, spark

ignĭfer, ĕra, ĕrum *adj*, fiery

ignis, is *m*, fire, glow

ignōbĭlis, e *adj*, unknown, obscure

ignōbĭlĭtas, ātis *f*, obscurity

ignōmĭnĭa, ae *f*, disgrace

ignōmĭnĭōsus, a, um *adj*, shameful

ignōrans, ntis *adj*, unaware

ignōrantĭa, ae *f*, ignorance

ignōrātĭo, ōnis *f*, ignorance

ignōro *v.i.t.* 1, to be unaware (of)

ignosco, nōvi, nōtum *v.t.* 3 *(with dat. of person)*, to forgive

ignōtus, a, um *adj*, unknown, of low birth

ii   see **is**

īlex, ĭcis *f*, evergreen, oak

īlīa, ĭum *n.pl*, groin, flank

īlĭcet *adv*, immediately

īlĭco *adv*, immediately

īlignus, a, um *adj*, of oak

illa see **ille**

illăbĕfactus, a, um *adj*, unbroken

illābor, psus *v.i.* 3, *dep*, to slip, glide, fall

illac *adv*, on that side

illăcessītus, a, um *adj*, unprovoked

illăcrĭmābĭlis, e *adj*, unlamented

illăcrĭmo *v.i.* 1, to weep over

illaesus, a, um *adj*, unhurt

illaetābĭlis, e *adj*, gloomy

illăquĕo *v.t.* 1, to ensnare

illātus see **infero**

ille, a, ud *pron, adj*, that, he, she, it

illĕcĕbra, ae *f*, charm, allurement, bait

illĕcĕbrōsus, a, um *adj*, alluring

illĕpĭdus, a, um *adj*, ill-mannered, rude

illex, ĭcis *c*, decoy

illĭbātus, a, um *adj*, unimpaired

illĭbĕrālis, e *adj*, mean

illic *adv*, there, over there

illĭcĭo, lexi, ctum *v.t.* 3, to allure, entice

illĭcĭtus, a, um *adj*, forbidden

illĭco *adv*, there, immediately

illīdo, si, sum *v.t.* 3, to strike, dash, beat

illĭgo *v.t.* 1, to tie, fasten

illinc *adv*, from there

illĭno, lēvi, lĭtum *v.t.* 3, to smear, spread

illittĕrātus, a, um *adj*, illiterate

illīus *genitive of* **ille**

illō *adv*, to that place

illōtus, a, um *adj*, dirty

illūc *adv*, to that place

illūcesco, luxi *v.i.* 3, to grow light, dawn, shine

illud see **ille**

illūdo, si, sum *v.i.t.* 3, to play; mock, ridicule

illūmĭno *v.t.* 1, to light up

illustris, e *adj*, lighted up, distinct, distinguished

illustro *v.t.* 1, to elucidate, make famous

illŭvĭes, ēi *f*, dirt

ĭmāgo, ĭnis *f*, statue, picture, copy, echo, conception

imbēcillĭtas, ātis *f*, weakness

imbēcillus, a, um *adj*, weak

imbellis, e *adj*, unwarlike

imber, bris *m*, rain, shower

imberbis, e *adj*, beardless

imbĭbo, bĭbi *v.t.* 3, to drink in

imbrex, ĭcis *f*, gutter, tile

imbrĭfer, ĕra, ĕrum *adj*, rainy

imbŭo, ŭi, ūtum *v.t.* 3, to soak, infect, instil, train

ĭmĭtābĭlis, e *adj*, easily intimidated

ĭmĭtātio, ōnis *f*, imitation

ĭmĭtātor, ōris *m*, imitator

ĭmĭtātrix, ĭcis *f*, imitator

ĭmĭtor *v.t.* 1, *dep*, to imitate

immădesco, dŭi *v.i.* 3, to become wet

immānĭa, ĭum *n.pl*, horrors

immanis, e *adj, adv*, ē, īter, enormous, frightful, savage

immānĭtas, ātis f, enormity, barbarism, vastness
immansuētus, a, um adj, untamed
immātūrus, a, um adj, untimely, immature
immĕdĭcābĭlis, e adj, incurable
immĕmor, ōris adj, heedless
immĕmŏrātus, a, um adj, unmentioned
immensĭtas, ātis f, immensity
immensum, i n, immensity
immensus, a, um adj, measureless, endless
immĕrens, ntis adj, undeserving, innocent
immergo, si, sum v.t. 3, to dip, plunge, immerse
immĕrĭtus, a, um adj, undeserved
immētātus, a, um adj, unmeasured
immĭgro, v.i. 1, to go into
immĭnĕo v.i. 2, to overhang, overlook, threaten, strive for
immĭnŭo, ŭi, ūtum v.t. 3, to reduce, weaken, destroy
immĭnūtĭo, ōnis f, weakening
immĭnūtus, a, um adj, unabated
immiscĕo, scŭi, xtum v.t. 2, to mix in, blend, unite
immĭsĕrābĭlis, e adj, unpitied
immĭsĕrĭcors, cordis adj, merciless
immissĭo, ōnis f, admission
immītis, e adj, harsh, rough
immitto, mīsi, ssum v.t. 3, to send in, let fly, incite, allow to grow wild
immo adv, on the contrary
immōbĭlis, e adj, immovable
immōbĭlĭtas, ātis f, immobility
immŏdĕrātus, a, um adj, adv, ē, excessive
immŏdĭcus, a, um adj, excessive
immŏlātĭo, ōnis f, sacrifice
immŏlo v.t. 1, to sacrifice, kill
immŏrĭor, mortŭus v.i. 3, dep, to die, die away
immortāles, ĭum m.pl, the gods
immortālis, e adj, immortal
immortālĭtas, ātis f, immortality
immōtus, a, um adj, unmoved
immūgĭo v.i. 4, to roar, resound
immundus, a, um adj, dirty

immūnis, e adj, exempt, idle, devoid of
immūnĭtas, ātis f, exemption
immūnītus, a, um adj, unfortified
immurmŭro v.i. 1, to murmer at
immūtābĭlis, e adj, unchangeable
immūtātĭo, ōnis f, interchange
immūto v.t. 1, to change, alter
impācātus, a, um adj, unsubdued
impar, ăris adj, adv, ĭter, unequal, uneven
impărātus, a, um adj, unprepared
impastus, a, um adj, hungry
impătĭens, ntis adj, impatient
impăvĭdus, a, um adj, fearless
impeccābĭlis, e adj, faultless
impĕdīmenta, ōrum n.pl, luggage
impĕdīmentum, i n, obstacle
impĕdĭo v.t. 4, to hinder, entangle, hamper
impĕdītus, a, um adj, difficult; (soldiers) in full marching-kit
impĕdītĭo, ōnis f, obstruction
impello, pŭli, pulsum v.t. 3, to strike upon, drive on, urge, overthrow
impendens, ntis adj, overhanging
impendĕo v.i.t. 2, to overhang; threaten
impendĭum, ii n, cost, expense
impendo, di, sum v.t. 3, to expend, devote
impĕnĕtrābĭlis, e adj, impenetrable
impensa, ae f, cost, expense
impensus, a, um adj, adv, ē, large, strong, expensive
impĕrātor, ōris m, general
impĕrātŏrĭus, a, um adj, of a general
impĕrātum, i n, order
imperfectus, a, um adj, incomplete
impĕrĭōsus, a, um adj, powerful, mighty, tyrannical
impĕrītĭa, ae f, inexperience
impĕrĭto v.i.t. 1, to command
impĕrītus, a, um adj, with genit, unskilled, or inexperienced in
impĕrĭum, ii n, power, command, control, dominion
impermissus, a, um adj, forbidden

impĕro v.t. 1, *with dat. of person,* to command, impose on, demand, requisition, rule

impertĭo v.t. 4, to share

impervĭus, a, um *adj,* impervious

impĕtĭbĭlis, e *adj,* intolerable

impĕtrābĭlis, e *adj,* attainable

impĕtro v.t. 1, to obtain, get

impĕtus, ūs *m,* attack, impetuosity, impulse

impexus, a, um *adj,* uncombed

impĭĕtas, ātis *f,* lack of respect for duty, disloyalty

impĭger, gra, grum *adj,* energetic

impingo, pēgi, pactum v.t. 3, to thrust, drive, strike (something) against

impĭus, a, um *adj,* undutiful, unpatriotic, disloyal, wicked

implācābĭlis, e *adj,* implacable

implācātus, a, um *adj,* unsatisfied

implăcĭdus, a, um *adj,* rough

implecto, xi, xum v.t. 3, to plait, interweave

implĕo, ēvi, ētum v.t. 2, to fill, complete, fulfil

implīcātĭo, ōnis *f,* entwining, complication

implĭcātus, a, um *adj,* entangled, confused

implĭco v.t. 1, to entangle, involve, grasp, unite

implōrātĭo, ōnis *f,* entreaty

implōro v.t. 1, to implore, beg for

implūmis, e *adj,* unfledged, callow

implŭvĭum, ii *n,* rain-tank in floor of atrium of Roman house

impŏlītus, a, um *adj,* unpolished

impōno, pŏsŭi, pŏsĭtum v.t. 3, to place in or on, impose, assign

importo v.t. 1, to carry in, import, cause

importūnĭtas, ātis *f,* insolence

importūnus, a, um *adj, adv,* ē, inconvenient, unsuitable, troublesome, rude

impŏtens, ntis *adj,* powerless, weak, violent, headstrong

impŏtentĭa, ae *f,* violence

impransus, a, um *adj,* fasting

imprĕcātĭo, ōnis *f,* imprecation, curse

imprĕcor v.t. 1, *dep,* to pray for something for someone

impressĭo, ōnis *f,* imprint, onset

impressus, a, um *adj,* stamped, printed

imprīmīs *adv,* especially

imprĭmo, pressi, ssum v.t. 3, to stamp, imprint, engrave

imprŏbĭtas, ātis *f,* wickedness

imprŏbo v.t. 1, to disapprove

imprŏbus, a, um *adj, adv,* ē, bad, wicked, violent, enormous, shameless

imprōvĭdus, a, um *adj,* not anticipating

imprōvīsus, a, um *adj, adv,* o, unexpected

imprūdens, ntis *adj, adv,* nter, unsuspecting, unaware

imprūdentĭa, ae *f,* lack of foresight

impūbes, is *adj,* youthful

impŭdens, ntis *adj,* shameless

impŭdentĭa, ae *f,* impudence

impŭdīcĭtĭa, ae *f,* shameful behaviour

impŭdīcus, a, um *adj,* shameless, lewd, disgusting

impugno v.t. 1, to attack

impulsor, ōris *m,* instigator

impulsus, ūs *m,* pressure, impulse, suggestion

impūnĕ *adv,* without punishment

impūnĭtas, ātis *f,* impunity

impūnītus, a, um *adj,* unpunished

impūrus, a, um *adj,* filthy

impŭto v.t. 1, to reckon, ascribe, impute

īmus, a, um *adj,* lowest, last

in *prep. with abl,* in, on, within, among; *with acc,* into, towards, till, against

ĭnaccessus, a, um *adj,* inaccessible

ĭnaedĭfĭco v.t. 1, to build on

ĭnaequābĭlis, e *adj,* uneven, unlike

ĭnaequālis, e *adj,* uneven, unlike

ĭnaequālĭtas, ātis *f,* inequality

ĭnaestĭmābĭlis, e *adj,* inestimable

ĭnămābĭlis, e *adj,* hateful

ĭnămāresco v.i. 3, to become bitter

ĭnambŭlo v.i. 1, to walk up and down

ĭnāne, is *n,* emptiness
ĭnănĭmus, a, um *adj,* lifeless
ĭnānis, e *adj, adv,* ĭter, empty,
  useless, vain
ĭnānĭtas, ātis *f,* emptiness
ĭnărātus, a, um *adj,* unploughed
ĭnardesco, arsi *v.i.* 3, to catch
  fire, glow
ĭnassŭētus, a, um *adj,*
  unaccustomed
ĭnaudax, ācis *adj,* timid
ĭnaudĭo *v.t.* 4, to hear
ĭnaudītus, a, um *adj,* unheard of
ĭnaugŭro *v.i.t* 1, to divine omens;
  to consecrate, inaugurate
ĭnaurātus, a, um *adj,* golden
ĭnauro *v.t.* 1, to cover with gold
ĭnauspĭcātus, a, um *adj,* without
  good omens
ĭnausus, a, um *adj,* unattempted
incaedŭus, a, um *adj,* uncut
incălesco, călŭi *v.i.* 3, to grow
  hot, glow
incallĭdus, a, um *adj,* stupid
incandesco, dŭi *v.i.* 3, to grow
  hot, glow
incānesco, nŭi *v.i.* 3, to grow
  grey or white
incanto *v.t.* 1, to chant, bewitch
incānus, a, um *adj,* grey, white
incassum *adv,* in vain
incastĭgātus, a, um *adj,*
  unpunished
incautus, a, um *adj, adv,* ē, rash,
  careless, unexpected
incēdo, cessi, ssum *v.i.* 3, to
  advance, appear, enter
incendĭārĭus, ii *m,* and incendiary
incendĭum, ii *n,* fire, heat
incendo, cendi, censum *v.t.* 3, to
  burn, excite, irritate
incensus, a, um *adj,* unregistered
incensus, a, um *adj,* burning,
  excited
inceptĭo, ōnis *f,* an attempt,
  undertaking
inceptum, i *n,* an attempt,
  undertaking
incertum, i *n,* uncertainity
incertus, a, um *adj,* uncertain,
  hesitating, doubtful
incesso, cessīvi *v.t.* 3, to attack,
  accuse

incessus, ūs *m,* walk, pace,
  approach
incesto *v.t.* 1, to pollute
incestum , i *n,* adultery, incest
incestus, a, um *adj,* impure
incĭdo, cĭdi, cāsum *v.i.* 3, to fall
  into or upon, meet, happen,
  occur
incīdo, cīdi, sum *v.t.* 3, to cut
  into, carve, interrupt
incingo, nxi, nctum *v.t.* 3, to
  encircle
incĭpĭo, cēpi, ceptum *v.i.t.* 3, to
  begin; undertake
incīsĭo, ōnis *f,* an incision
incĭtāmentum, i *n,* incentive
incĭtātĭo, ōnis *f,* instigation,
  energy
incīsūra, ae *f,* cutting, incision
incĭtātus, a, um *adj,* swift
incĭto *v.t.* 1, to urge on, rouse,
  excite, inspire
incĭtus, a, um *adj,* swift
incĭto *v.t.* 1, to urge on, rouse,
  excite, inspire
incĭtus, a, um *adj,* swift
inclāmo *v.i.t.* 1, to cry out; call
  out, to rebuke, abuse
inclēmens, ntis *adj, adv,* nter,
  harsh, severe
inclēmentĭa, ae *f,* harshness
inclīnātĭo, ōnis *f,* leaning,
  tendency
inclīno *v.i.t.* 1, to sink, yield;
  bend, turn, change
inclīnātus, a, um *adj,* bent,
  disposed
inclĭtus, a, um *adj,* famous
inclūdo, si, sum *v.t.* 3, to shut in,
  include, finish
inclūsĭo, ōnis *f,* confinement
inclŭtus, a, um *adj,* famous
incoctus, a, um *adj,* uncooked
incognĭtus, a, um *adj,* unknown
incŏhātus, a, um *adj,* incomplete
incŏho *v.i.t.* 1, to begin;
  undertake
incŏla, ae *c,* inhabitant
incŏlo, lŭi *v.i.t.* 3, to settle;
  inhabit
incŏlŭmis, e *adj,* safe, sound
incŏlŭmĭtas, ātis *f,* safety
incŏmĭtātus, a, um *adj,*

unaccompanied
incommŏdĭtas, ātis *f,* unsuitability
incommŏdo *v.i.* 1, to be annoying
incommŏdum, i *n,* disadvantage
incommŏdus, a, um *adj, adv,* ē, troublesome, unsuitable
incompertus, a, um *adj,* unknown
incompŏsĭtus, a, um *adj,* badly arranged
incomptus, a, um *adj,* unadorned
inconcessus, a, um *adj,* illict
inconcinnus, a, um *adj,* awkward
incondītus, a, um *adj,* irregular, confused, rude
inconsīdĕrātus, a, um *adj, adv,* ē, thoughtless, inconsiderate
inconsōlābĭlis, e *adj,* inconsolable
inconstans, ntis *adj, adv,* nter, inconsistent, fickle
inconstantĭa, ae *f,* inconstancy
inconsultus, a, um *adj, adv,* ē, without advice, indiscreet
inconsumptus, a, um *adj,* unconsumed
incontāmĭnātus, a, um *adj,* uncontaminated
incontĭnens, ntis *adj, adv,* nter, immoderate
incŏquo, xi, ctum *v.t.* 3, to boil, dye
incorruptus, a, um *adj,* unspoiled
incrēbresco, brŭi *v.i.* 3, to increase, become prevalent
incrēdĭbĭlis, e *adj, adv,* ĭter, incredible, unbelievable
incrēdŭlus, a, um *adj,* unbelieving
incrēmentum, i *n,* increase
incrēpo, ŭi, ĭtum *v.i.t.* 1, to rattle, clatter; blare out, rebuke, reprimand
incresco, ēvi *v.i.* 3, to grow
incrŭentus, a, um *adj,* bloodless
incrusto *v.t.* 1, to coat over
incŭbo, ŭi, ĭtum *v.i.* 1, to lie in or on, rest on, fall upon
inculco *v.t.* 1, to trample on, cram in, force on, obtude
incultus, a, um *adj, adv,* ē, uncultivated, unpolished
incumbo, cŭbŭi, ĭtum *v.i.* 3, to lean or lie on, overhang, fall upon, take pains over, influence

incūnābŭla, ōrum *n.pl,* cradle, birthplace, origin, swaddling clothes
incūrĭa, ae *f,* neglect
incūrĭōsus, a, um *adj, adv,* ē, indifferent
incurro, curri, cursum *v.i.t.* 3, to run at, happen; attack
incursĭo, ōnis *f,* raid, attack
incurso *v.i.t* 1, to run to; attack, strike
incursus, ūs *m,* attack
incurvo *v.t.* 1, to bend
invurvus, a, um *adj,* bent
incūs, ūdis *f,* anvil
incūso *v.t.* 1, to accuse, blame
incustōdītus, a, um *adj,* unguarded
incŭtĭo, cussi, cussum *v.t.* 3, to strike upon, hurl, inflict
indāgātĭo, ōnis *f,* investigation
indāgo *v.t.* 1, to track down
indāgo, ĭnis *f,* enclosing
indĕ *adv,* from there, then
indēbĭtus, a, um *adj,* not due
indĕcor, ŏris *adj,* disgraceful
indĕcŏro *v.t.* 1, to disgrace
indĕcōrus, a, um *adj, adv,* ē, unbecoming, unsightly, disgraceful
indēfensus, a, um *adj,* undefended
indēfessus, a, um *adj,* unwearied
indēlēbĭlis, e *adj,* indestructible
indēlībātus, a, um *adj,* untouched
indemnātus, a, um *adj,* unsentenced
indēprensus, a, um *adj,* unnoticed
index, ĭcis *m, f,* forefinger, informer, sign, list
indĭcĭum, ii *n,* information, evidence, proof, indication
indĭco *v.t.* 1, to show, indicate, give evidence
indīco, xi, ctum *v.t.* 3, to announce, appoint, impose
indictus, a, um *adj,* unsaid
indĭdem *adv,* from the same place
indĭes *adv,* from day to day
indiffĕrens, ntis *adj,* indifferent
indĭgĕna, ae *adj,* native
indĭgĕo *v.i.* 2, to need, want
indīgestus, a, um *adj,* confused

indignans, ntis *adj*, enraged
indignātĭo, ōnis *f*, indignation
indignĭtas, ātis *f*, shameful behaviour, unworthiness
indignor *v.t.* 1, *dep*, to be indignant at, scorn
indignus, a, um *adj, adv*, ē, unworthy, shameful, cruel
indĭgus, a, um *adj*, needing
indīlĭgens, ntis *adj, adv*, nter, careless
indīlĭgentĭa, ae *f*, carelessness
indiscrētus, a, um *adj*, unseparated
indĭsertus, a, um *adj*, at a loss for words
indīvĭdŭus, a, um *adj*, indivisible
indo, dĭdi, dĭtum *v.t.* 3, to put or place upon or into, attach
indŏcĭlis, e *adj*, unteachable, untaught
indoctus, a, um *adj*, untaught
indŏles, is *f*, inborn abilities
indŏleso, lŭi *v.i.* 3, to be in pain, to be troubled
indŏmĭtus, a, um *adj*, untamed
indormĭo *v.i.* 4, to fall asleep over
indōtātus, a, um *adj*, without a dowry, poor
indŭbĭto *v.i.* 1, to distrust
indŭbĭus, a, um *adj*, not doubtful
indūco, xi, ctum *v.t.* 3, to lead in, conduct, exhibit, spread over, put on (clothes), induce, resolve, cancel
inductĭo, ōnis *f*, introduction, exhibition, intention
indulgens, ntis *adj, adv*, nter, kind, indulgent, fond
indulgentĭa, ae *f*, indulgence
indulgĕo, si, tum *v.i.t.* 2, *with dat*, to be kind to; permit, grant
indŭo, ŭi, ūtum *v.t.* 3, to put on (garment), assume
indūro *v.t.* 1, to harden
indūsĭum, ii *n*, woman's petticoat
industrĭa, ae *f*, diligence; *with* de *or* ex on purpose
industrĭus, a, um *adj*, diligent
indūtĭae, ārum *f.pl*, truce
indūtus, a, um *adj*, clothed
ĭnēdĭa, ae *f*, fasting
ĭnēlĕgans, ntis *adj, adv*, nter, unrefined
ĭnēluctābĭlis, e *adj*, unavoidable
ĭnemptus, a, um *adj*, unbought
ĭnēnarrābĭlis, e *adj*, indescribable
ĭnĕo *v.i.t.* 4, to begin; enter, calculate, estimate, contrive
ĭneptĭae, ārum *f.pl*, absurdities
ĭneptus, a, um *adj, adv*, ē, improper, inept, foolish
ĭnermis, e *adj*, unarmed
ĭners, rtis *adj*, unskilful, idle, sluggish
ĭnertĭa, ae *f*, ignorance, idleness
ĭnērŭdītus, a, um *adj*, illiterate
ĭnēvītābĭlis, e *adj*, unavoidable
ĭnexcūsābĭlis, e *adj*, inexcusable
ĭnexercĭtātus, a, um *adj*, untrained
ĭnexhaustus, a, um *adj*, inexhaustible
ĭnexōrābĭlis, e *adj*, inexorable
ĭnexpectātus, a, um *adj*, unexpected
ĭnexpertus, a, um *adj*, inexperienced, untried
ĭnexpĭābĭlis, e *adj*, irreconcilable
ĭnexplēbĭlis, e *adj*, insatiable
ĭnexplētus, a, um *adj*, unsatisfied
ĭnexplĭcābĭlis, e *adj*, inexplicable
ĭnexplōrātus, a, um *adj*, unexplored
ĭnexpugnābĭlis, e *adj*, impregnable
ĭnexstinctus, a, um *adj*, imperishable
ĭnextrĭcābĭlis, e *adj*, inextricable
infăbrē *adv*, unskilfully
infăcētus, a, um *adj*, coarse
infāmĭa, ae *f*, disgrace
infāmis, e *adj*, disreputable
infāmo *v.t.* 1, to disgrace
infandus, a, um *adj*, unutterable
infans, ntis *adj*, speechless
infans, ntis *c*, child, baby
infantĭa, ae *f*, speechlessness, infancy
infātŭo *v.t.* 1, to make a fool of
infaustus, a, um *adj*, unfortunate
infector, ōris *m*, dyer
infectus, a, um *adj*, unfinished
infēcundus, a, um *adj*, unfruitful
infēlix, īcis *adj*, unhappy, unfortunate, barren

infensus, a, um   *adj,* enraged
infĕri, ōrum   *m.pl,* the dead
infĕriae, ārum   *f.pl,* sacrifices in honour of the dead
infĕrior, ĭus   *adv,* lower, later, younger, inferior
infĕrĭus   *adv,* lower
infernus, a, um   *adj,* lower, underground
infĕri, ōrum   *m.pl,* inhabitants of the underworld, the dead
infero, inferre, intŭli, illātum   *v.t, irreg,* to bring to or against, attack, produce, inflict
infĕrus, a, um   *adj,* below, lower
infervesco, ferbŭi   *v.i.* 3, to boil
infesto   *v.t.* 1, to attack, molest
infestus, a, um   *adj, adv, ē,* dangerous, hostile, unsafe
inficĭo, fēci, fectum   *v.t.* 3, to stain, dye, taint, corrupt
infidēlis, e   *adj,* untrustworthy
infidēlĭtas, ātis   *f,* treachery
infidus, a, um   *adj,* treacherous
infigo, xi, xum   *v.t.* 3, to fix into, drive in, imprint
infimus, a, um   *adj,* lowest
infindo, fīdi, fissum   *v.t.* 3, to cut into
infinĭtas, ātis   *f,* endlessness
infinītus, a, um   *adj, adv, ē,* unlimited, endless
infirmātĭo, ōnis   *f,* weakening
infirmĭtas, ātis   *f,* weakness
infirmo   *v.t.* 1, to weaken, annul
infirmus, a, um   *adj, adv, ē,* weak
infit   *v, defect,* he (she, it) begins
infitĭas ĕo (ire, ii) to deny
infitĭātĭo, ōnis   *f,* denial
infitĭātor, ōris   *m,* bad debtor
infitĭor   *v.t.* 1, *dep,* to deny
inflammātĭo, ōnis   *f,* inflammation, setting on fire
inflammo   *v.t.* 1, to set on fire
inflātus, ūs   *m,* blast
inflātus, a, um   *adj,* puffed up, haughty, inflated
inflecto, xi, xum   *v.t.* 3, to bend
inflētus, a, um   *adj,* unmourned
inflexĭbĭlis, e   *adj,* inflexible
inflexĭo, ōnis   *f,* bending
infligo, xi, ctum   *v.t.* 3, to strike (something) against

inflo   *v.t.* 1, to blow into
influo, xi, xum   *v.i.* 3, to flow into, crowd in
infŏdĭo, fōdi, fossum   *v.t.* 3, to dig in, bury
informātĭo, ōnis   *f,* outline
informis, e   *adj,* shapeless
informo   *v.t.* 1, to shape, sketch, educate
infortūnātus, a, um   *adj,* unfortunate
infrā   *adv, and prep. with acc,* below, under
infractĭo, ōnis   *f,* breaking
infractus, a, um   *adj,* broken, exhausted
infrĕmo, ŭi   *v.i.* 3, to growl
infrendĕo   *v.i.* 2, to gnash the teeth, threaten
infrēnis, e (us, a, um)   *adj,* unbridled
infrēno   *v.t.* 1, to bridle, curb
infrĕquens, ntis   *adj,* rare, not well filled
infrĕquentĭa, ae   *f,* scantiness
infringo, frēgi, fractum   *v.t.* 3, to break off, crush, weaken
infŭla, ae   *f,* headband, ribbon
infundĭbŭlum, i   *n,* funnel
infundo, fūdi, fūsum   *v.t.* 3, to pour out, lay before, impart
infusco   *v.t.* 1, to darken, stain
infūsus, a, um   *adj,* streaming or falling over
ingĕmĭno   *v.i.t.* 1, to increase; repeat, redouble
ingĕmisco, mŭi   *v.i.* 3, to sigh
ingĕmo, ŭi   *v.i.t.* 3, to groan; lament, mourn
ingĕnĕro   *v.t.* 1, to produce
ingĕnĭōsus, a, um   *adj, adv, ē,* talented, adapted to
ingĕnĭum, ii   *n,* natural disposition, abilities, intelligence
ingens, ntis   *adj,* huge, famous
ingĕnŭĭtas, ātis   *f,* good birth, gentlemanly character
ingĕnŭus, a, um   *adj, adv, ē,* natural, inborn, freeborn, frank, honourable
ingĕnŭus, i   *m,* (**a, ae**   *f*), freeborn man or woman

ingĕro, gessi, gestum *v.t.* 3, to carry, throw or thrust into

ingigno, gĕnŭi, gĕnĭtum *v.t.* 3, to implant, produce

inglōrĭus, a, um *adj,* inglorious

inglŭvĭes, ēi *f,* gizzard, maw

ingrātĭis *adv,* unwillingly

ingrātus, a, um *adj, adv, ē,* unpleasant, ungrateful

ingrăvesco *v.i.* 3, to become heavy or worse

ingrăvo *v.t.* 1, to aggravate

ingrĕdĭor, gressus *v.i.t.* 3, *dep,* to advance; enter, upon

ingressĭo, ōnis *f,* entering, pace

ingressus, ūs *m,* entrance, inroad, commencement

ingrŭo, ŭi *v.i.* 3, to attack

inguen, ĭnis *n,* groin, abdomen

ingurgĭto *v.t.* 1 (*with* se) to gorge, addict one's self to

ĭnhăbĭlis, e *adj,* unwieldy, incapable

ĭnhăbĭtābĭlis, e *adj,* uninhabitable

ĭnhaerĕo, si, sum *v.i.* 2, to cling to, adhere to

ĭnhaeresco, haesi, haesum *v.i.* 3, to cling to, adhere to

ĭnhĭbĕo *v.t.* 2, to restrain

ĭnhĭo *v.i* 1, to gape, gaze

ĭnhŏnestus, a, um *adj,* shameful

ĭnhŏnōrātus, a, um *adj,* unhonoured

ĭnhorrĕo *v.i.* 2, to bristle, shiver

ĭnhorresco *v.i.* 3, to bristle, shiver

ĭnhospĭtālis, e *adj,* inhospitable

ĭnhospĭtus, a, um *adj,* inhospitable

ĭnhūmānĭtas, ātis *f,* barbarity, niggardliness

ĭnhūmānus, a, um *adj, adv, ē, ĭter,* savage, uncivilized, rude

ĭnhūmātus, a, um *adj,* unburied

ĭnĭbi *adv,* there

ĭnĭcĭo, iēci, iectum *v.t.* 3, to throw into, seize, inspire

ĭnĭmīcĭtĭa, ae *f,* enmity

ĭnĭmīco *v.t.* 1, to make into enemies

ĭnĭmīcus, a, um *adj, adv, ē,* unfriendly, hostile

ĭnĭmīcus, i *m,* (a, ae *f*), enemy

ĭnīquĭtas, ātis *f,* unevenness, difficulty, injustice

ĭnīquus, a, um *adj, adv, ē,* uneven, unfair, unfortunate, hostile, disadvantageous

inĭtĭo *v.t.* 1, to initiate

ĭnĭtĭō *adv,* in the beginning

ĭnĭtĭum, ii *n,* beginning, origin; *pl,* first principles, sacred rites

iniūcundus, a, um *adj, adv, ē,* unpleasant

iniungo, nxi, nctum *v.t.* 3, to join on to, inflict, impose

iniūrātus, a, um *adj,* without taking an oath

iniūrĭa, ae *f,* injury, wrong

iniūrĭōsus, a, um *adj,* wrongful

iniussu *adv,* without orders

iniussus, a, um *adj,* of one's accord

iniustĭtĭa, ae *f,* injustice

iniustus, a, um *adj, adv, ē,* unjust, wrongful, harsh

innascor, nātus *v.i.* 3, *dep,* to be born in, grow up in

innăto *v.t.* 1, to swim, float in

innātus, a, um *adj,* innate

innāvĭgābĭlis, e *adj,* unnavigable

innecto, xŭi, xum *v.t.* 3, to tie, fasten, attach, contrive

innītor, nixus (nīsus) *v.* 3, *dep, with dat. or abl,* to lean on

inno *v.i.* 1, to swim, float in

innŏcens, ntis *adj,* harmless, blameless

innŏcentĭa, ae *f,* integrity

innŏcŭus, a, um *adj,* harmless

innoxĭus, a, um *adj,* harmless, innocent, unhurt

innūbus, a, um *adj,* unmarried

innŭmĕrābĭlis, e *adj,* countless

innŭmĕrus, a, um *adj,* countless

innŭo, ŭi, ūtum *v.i* 3, to nod, hint

innuptus, a, um *adj,* unmarried

ĭnobservātus, a, um *adj,* unperceived

ĭnoffensus, a, um *adj,* untouched, uninterrupted

ĭnŏlesco, lēvi, lĭtum *v.i* 3, to grow in, take root

ĭnŏpĭa, ae *f,* lack, need

ĭnŏpīnans, ntis *adj,* unaware

ĭnŏpīnātus, a, um *adj, adv, ē, ō,* unexpected

ĭnŏpīnus, a, um *adj*, unexpected
ĭnopportūnus, a, um *adj*,
 unfitting, inopportune
ĭnops, ŏpis *adj*, helpless, needy
ĭnordĭnātus, a, um *adj*, in disorder
ĭnornātus, a, um *adj*, unadorned
inquam *v, irreg*, I say
inquĭes, ētis *f*, restlessness
inquĭētus, a, um *adj*, restless
inquĭlīnus, i *m*, lodger
inquĭnātus, a, um *adj*, filthy
inquĭno *v.t.* 1, to stain, corrupt
inquīro, sīvi, sītum *v.t.* 3, to
 search for, examine
inquīsītĭo, ōnis *f*, legal
 investigation
insălūbris, e *adj*, unhealthy
insălūtātus, a, um *adj*, without
 saying goodbye
insānābĭlis, e *adj*, incurable
insānĭa, ae *f*, madness, folly
insānĭo *v.i.* 4, to be insane,
 to rage
insānĭtas, ātis *f*, disease
insānus, a, um *adj, adv*, ē, insane,
 frantic, excessive
insătĭābĭlis, e *adj*, insatiable
inscĭens, ntis *adj*, unaware
inscĭentĭa, ae *f*, ignorance,
 inexperience
inscītĭa, ae *f*, ignorance,
 inexperience
inscītus, a, um *adj, adv*, ē,
 ignorant, stupid
inscĭus, a, um *adj*, unaware
inscrībo, psi, ptum *v.t.* 3, to write
 on, attribute
inscriptĭo, ōnis *f*, title
insculpo, psi, ptum *v.t.* 3, to
 engrave
insĕco, cŭi, ctum *v.t.* 1, to cut up
insectātĭo, ōnis *f*, pursuit
insectātor, ōris *m*, pursuer
insector *v.t.* 1, *dep*, to pursue,
 reproach
insectum, i *n*, insect
insĕnesco, nŭi *v.i.* 3, to grow old at
insĕpultus, a, um *adj*, unburied
insĕquor, sĕcūtus *v.i.t.* 3, *dep*, to
 follow; pursue, reproach
insĕro, sēvi, sĭtum *v.t.* 3, to
 implant, ingraft
insĕro, rŭi, rtum *v.t.* 3, to put in,
 introduce
inserto *v.t.* 1, to insert
inservĭo *v.i.* 4, to serve, be
 submissive to, attend to
insĭdĕo, sēdi, sessum *v.i.t.* 2, to
 sit upon, be fixed; occupy,
 inhabit
insĭdĭae, ārum *f.pl*, ambush, plot;
 with ex *or* per, craftily
insĭdĭor *v.* 1, *dep, with dat*, to lie
 in ambush
insĭdĭōsus, a, um *adj, adv*, ē,
 cunning, dangerous
insīdo, sēdi, sessum *v.i.t.* 3, to
 settle on or in; occupy
insigne, is *n*, mark, sign,
 costume, signal, ornament
insignĭo *v.t.* 4, to make
 distinguished
insignis, e *adj*, conspicuous,
 famous, distinguished
insĭlĭo, ŭi *v.i.* 4, to spring upon
insĭmŭlo *v.t.* 1, to accuse
insincērus, a, um *adj*, tainted
insĭnŭo *v.i.t.* 1, to penetrate;
 insinuate
insĭpĭens, ntis *adj*, foolish
insĭpĭentĭa, ae *f*, folly
insisto, stĭti *v.i.t.* 3, to step, stand,
 begin, halt; devote oneself to
insĭtus, a, um *adj*, inborn
insŏlens, ntis *adj, adv*, nter,
 unusual, unaccustomed, haughty
insŏlentĭa, ae *f*, strangeness,
 novelty, affectation, arrogance
insŏlĭtus, a, um *adj*,
 unaccustomed, unusual
insomnĭa, ae *f*, sleeplessness
insomnis, e *adj*, sleepless
insomnĭum, ii *n*, dream
insŏno, ŭi *v.i.* 1, to resound
insons, ntis *adj*, innocent,
 harmless
inspecto *v.t.* 1, to look at
inspērans, ntis *adj*, not hoping
inspērātus, a, um *adj*, unhoped
 for, unexpected
inspergo, si, sum *v.t.* 3, to
 sprinkle
inspĭcĭo, spexi, spectum *v.t.* 3, to
 examine, consider
inspīro *v.t.* 1, to breathe on,
 inspire

instăbĭlis, e *adj,* unsteady, changeable

instans, ntis *adj,* present

instar *n, indecl,* resemblance, appearance, value; *with genit,* as big as, like

instauro *v.t.* 1, to renew

insterno, strāvi, strātum *v.t.* 3, to spread or cover over

instīgo *v.t.* 1, to incite

instillo *v.t.* 1, to instil

instĭmŭlo *v.t.* 1, to spur on

instinctus, ūs *m,* impulse

instinctus, a, um *adj,* incited

instĭtor, ōris *m,* commercial traveller

instĭtŭo, ŭi, ūtum *v.t.* 3, to set up, appoint, undertake, resolve, arrange, train

instĭtūtĭo, ōnis *f,* arrangement, custom, education

instĭtūtum, i *n,* purpose, plan, custom

insto, stĭti, stātum *v.i.* 1, to stand over, harass, impend, urge on, pursue

instructus, a, um *adj,* arranged, provided with

instrūmentum, i *n,* tool, stores

instrŭo, xi, ctum *v.t.* 3, to erect, arrange, provide, teach

insŭāvis, e *adj,* unpleasant

insuesco, ēvi, ētum *v.i.t.* 3, to become accustomed; to accustom

insuētus, a, um *adj,* unaccustomed to, unusual

insŭla, ae *f,* island, block of flats

insŭlānus, i *m,* islander

insulsĭtas, ātis *f,* silliness

insulsus, a, um *adj, adv,* ē, tasteless, silly

insulto *v.i.t.* 1, to jump, leap; to spring at, abuse

insum, inesse, infŭi *v.i, irreg,* to be in, be contained in

insūmo, mpsi, mptum *v.t.* 3, to employ, expend

insŭo, ŭi, ūtum *v.t.* 3, to sew on

insŭper *adv, and prep. with acc,* moreover, besides; above

insŭpĕrābĭlis, e *adj,* insurmountable

insurgo, surrexi, rectum *v.i.* 3, to arise, rise to

insūsurro *v.i.t.* 1, to whisper

intābesco, bŭi *v.i.* 3, to waste away

intactus, a, um *adj,* untouched, unattempted, chaste

intāmĭnātus, a, um *adj,* pure

intectus, a, um *adj,* uncovered

intĕger, gra, grum *adj, adv,* ē, untouched, perfect, blameless, unspoiled, undecided

intĕgo, xi, ctum *v.t.* 3, to cover

intĕgrĭtas, ātis *f,* completeness, uprightness

intĕgro *v.t.* 1, to renew, refresh

intĕgŭmentum, i *n,* covering, disguise

intellēgens, ntis *adj,* understanding

intellĕgentĭa, ae *f,* understanding

intellĕgo, xi, ctum *v.t.* 3, to understand, perceive

intĕmĕrātus, a, um *adj,* pure

intempĕrans, ntis *adj,* extravagant

intempĕrantĭa, ae *f,* extravagance

intempĕrĭes, ēi *f,* inclement weather, violence

intempestīvus, a, um *adj, adv,* ē, untimely, inconvenient

intempestus, a, um *adj,* unseasonable, unhealthy; *(with* nox*)* the dead of night

intendo, di, tum (sum) *v.t.* 3, to stretch or spread out, aim, direct, threaten, concentrate, intend

intentātus, a, um *adj,* untried

intentĭo, ōnis *f,* tension, effort, application

intentus, a, um *adj, adv,* ē, stretched, bent, intent

intĕpesco, pŭi *v.i.* 3, to grow warm

inter *adv, and prep. with acc,* among, between, during

intercēdo, cessi, ssum *v.i.* 3, to go between, intervene, occur

intercessĭo, ōnis *f,* veto, intervention

intercessor, ōris *m,* mediator, surety, user of the veto

intercīdo, di, sum *v.t.* 3, to cut up

intercĭdo, di *v.i.* 3, to happen, fall

down, perish
intercĭpĭo, cēpi, ceptum   *v.t.* 3, to
intercept, seize, steal
interclūdo, si, sum   *v.t.* 3, to
block, cut off, hinder, separate,
blockade
intercurro, curri, cursum   *v.i.* 3, to
run between, intercede
interdīco, dixi, dictum   *v.t.* 3, to
prohibit, banish
interdictum, i   *n,* prohibition
interdīu   *adv,* in the daytime
interdum   *adv,* sometimes
intĕrĕā   *adv,* meanwhile
intĕrĕo, ĭi, ĭtum   *v.i.* 4, to perish,
die, become lost
intĕrest see **intersum**
interfector, ōris   *m,* murderer
interfĭcĭo, fēci, fectum   *v.t.* 3, to
kill, destroy
interflŭo, xi   *v.i.* 3, to flow
between
interfūsus, a, um   *adj,* poured
between, interposed, stained
intĕrim   *adv,* meanwhile
intĕrĭmo, ēmi, emptum   *v.t.* 3, to
take away, destroy, kill
intĕrĭor, ĭus   *comp. adj,* inner
intĕrĭus   *adv,* inside
intĕrĭtus, ūs   *m,* annihilation
interiăcĕo   *v.i.* 2, to lie between
interĭcĭo, iēci, iectum   *v.t.* 3, to put
or throw between
interiectus, a, um   *adj,* interposed
interlābor, lapsus   *v.i.* 3, *dep,* to
glide or flow between
interlĕgo, lēgi, lectum   *v.t.* 3, to
pluck, pick
interlūcĕo, luxi   *v.i.* 2, to shine out,
appear
interlŭo   *v.t.* 3, to flow between
intermĭnātus, a, um   *adj,* endless
intermiscĕo, scŭi, xtum   *v.t.* 2, to
intermix
intermissĭo, ōnis   *f,* interruption,
cessation
intermitto, mīsi, missum   *v.i.t.* 3,
to cease; neglect, omit, stop,
pause, interrupt
intermortŭus, a, um   *adj,* lifeless
internĕcīnus, a, um   *adj,* deadly,
internecine
internĕcĭo, ōnis   *f,* massacre

internecto   *v.t.* 3, to bind up
internosco, nōvi nōtum   *v.t.* 3, to
distinguish between
internuntĭus, ii   *m,* negotiator
internus, a, um   *adj,* internal
interpellātĭo, ōnis   *f,* interruption
interpello   *v.t.* 1, to interrupt
interpŏlo   *v.t.* 1, to furbish
interpōno, pŏsŭi, ĭtum   *v.t.* 3, to
put between, introduce; *with* **se,**
to interfere; *with* **fidem,** to pledge
interpŏsĭtĭo, ōnis   *f,* insertion
interprĕs, ĕtis   *c,* negotiator
interprĕtātĭo, ōnis   *f,* explanation
interprĕtor   *v.t.* 1, *dep,* to explain
interpunctĭo, ōnis   *f,* punctuation
interpungo, nxi, ctum   *v.t.* 3, to
punctuate
interquĭesco, quĭēvi, quĭētum   *v.i.*
3, to rest for a while
interregnum, i   *n,* vacancy in the
kingship or high office
interrex, rēgis   *m,* regent
interrĭtus, a, um   *adj,* fearless
interrŏgātor, ōris   *m,* questioner
interrŏgātum, i   *n,* question
interrŏgo   *v.t.* 1, to inquire
interrumpo, rūpi, ruptum   *v.t.* 3, to
break up, interrupt
intersaepĭo, psi, ptum   *v.t.* 4, to
hedge in, cut off
interscĭndo, scĭdi, scissum   *v.t.* 3,
to tear down, divide
intersĕro, rŭi, rtum   *v.t.* 3, to
interpose
intersum, esse, fŭi   *v.i, irreg,* to lie
between, differ, take part in;
interest, *v, impers,* it concerns, it
is of importance
intertexo, xŭi, xtum   *v.t.* 3, to
intertwine
intervallum, i   *n,* space, pause
intervĕnĭo, vēni, ventum   *v.i.* 4, to
interrupt, happen, prevent
interventus, ūs   *m,* intervention
intervīso, si, sum   *v.t.* 3, to
inspect, visit occasionally
intestābĭlis, e   *adj,* abominable
intestīna, ōrum   *n.pl,* intestines
intestīnus, a, um   *adj,* internal
intexo, xŭi, xtum   *v.t.* 3, to
interlace
intĭmus, a, um   *adj,* inmost

intŏlĕrābĭlis, e *adj,* intolerable
intŏlĕrandus, a, um *adj,* intolerable
intŏlĕrans, ntis *adj, adv,* nter, impatient, intolerable
intŏno, üi *v.i.* 1, to thunder
intonsus, a, um *adj,* unshaven
intorqquĕo, si, sum *v.t.* 2, to twist, sprain, hurl
intrā *adv, and prep. with acc,* on the inside, within
intractābĭlis, e *adj,* unmanageable
intractātus, a, um *adj,* untried
intrĕmo, üi *v.i.* 3, to tremble
intrĕpĭdus, a, um *adj,* fearless
intrō *adv,* within, inside
intro *v.i.t.* 1, to enter
intrōdūco, xi, ctum *v.t.* 3, to lead in, introduce
intrōductĭo, ōnis *f,* introduction
intrōeo *v.i.* 4, to enter
intrōfĕro, ferre, tŭli, lātum *v.t, irreg,* to bring in
intrōgrĕdĭor, gressus *v.i.* 3, *dep,* to enter
intrŏĭtus, ūs *m,* entrance
intrōmitto, mīsi, ssum *v.t.* 3, to send in
introrsum (us) *adv,* within
intrōspĭcĭo, spexi, spectum *v.t.* 3, to look into, examine
intŭĕor *v.t.* 2, *dep,* to look at
intŭmesco, mŭi *v.i.* 3, to swell
intus *adv,* within, inside
intūtus, a, um *adj,* unguarded
ĭnultus, a, um *adj,* unavenged
ĭnumbro *v.t.* 1, to shade
ĭnundātĭo, ōnis *f,* flooding
ĭnundo *v.i.t.* 1, to overflow; flood
ĭnungo, nxi, unctum *v.t.* 3, to anoint
ĭnurbānus, a, um *adj,* rude
ĭnūro, ssi, stum *v.t.* 3, to brand
ĭnūsĭtātus, a, um *adj, adv,* ē, unusual, strange
ĭnūtĭlis, e *adj,* useless
ĭnūtĭlĭtas, ātis *f,* uselessness
invādo, si, sum *v.i.t.* 3, to enter; attack, invade, seize
invălĭdus, a, um *adj,* weak
invĕho, xi, ctum *v.t.* 3, to carry, bring to; *passive or reflex,* to ride, drive, attack (with words)

invĕnĭo, vēni, ventum *v.t.* 4, to find, meet with, devise
inventĭo, ōnis *f,* invention
inventor, ōris *m,* inventor
inventum, i *n,* invention
invĕnustus, a, um *adj,* unattractive
invĕrēcundus, a, um *adj,* immodest
invergo *v.t.* 3, to pour on
inversus, a, um *adj,* inverted, perverted
inverto, ti, sum *v.t.* 3, to turn upside down, exchange
invespĕrascit *v, impers,* evening is approaching
investīgātĭo, ōnis *f,* investigation
investīgo *v.t.* 1, to search for
invĕtĕrasco, rāvi *v.i.* 3, to grow old, become permanent
invĕtĕrātus, a, um *adj,* old-established
invĕtĕro *v.t.* 1, to endure
invĭcem *adv,* alternately
invictus, a, um *adj,* unconquered, invincible
invĭdĕo, vīdi, vīsum *v.t.* 2, *with dat;* to envy, grudge
invĭdĭa, ae *f,* envy, ill will
invĭdĭōsus, a, um *adj, adv,* ē, jealous, enviable
invĭdus, a, um *adj,* envious
invĭgĭlo *v.i.* 1, to be watchful
invĭŏlātus, a, um *adj,* unharmed
invīso, si, sum *v.t.* 3, to visit
invīsus, a, um *adj,* hated
invīsus, a, um *adj,* unseen
invītātĭo, ōnis *f,* challenge, invitation
invīto *v.t.* 1, to invite, challenge, tempt
invītus, a, um *adj,* unwilling
invĭus, a, um *adj,* pathless
invŏcātus, a, um *adj,* uninvited
invŏco *v.t.* 1, to appeal to
invŏlĭto *v.i.* 1, to hover
invŏlo *v.i.t.* 1, to fly at; attack
invŏlūcrum, i *n,* wrapper
invŏlūtus, a, um *adj,* intricate
involvo, volvi, vŏlūtum *v.t.* 3, to roll on, wrap up, envelop
invulnĕrābĭlis, e *adj,* invulnerable
ĭō *interj,* oh! ah! ho!

ipse, a, um (*genit,* **ipsius,** dat, **ipsi),** *emphatic pron,* himself, herself, itself, precisely, just
īra, ae *f,* anger
īrācundīa, ae *f,* rage, temper
īrācundus, a, um *adj,* irritable
īrascor, īrātus *v.* 3, *dep, with dat,* to be angry with
īrātus, a, um *adj,* angry
ire see **ĕo**
īris, ĭdīs *f,* iris
īrōnīa, ae *f,* irony
irpes, ĭcis *m,* harrow
irrĕmĕābĭlis, e *adj,* irretraceable
irrĕpĕrābĭlis, e *adj,* irrecoverable
irrĕpertus, a, um *adj,* undiscovered
irrēpo, psi, ptum *v.i.* 3, to creep in, insinuate oneself
irrĕquiētus, a, um *adj,* restless
irrētĭo *v.t.* 4, to entangle
irrĕtortus, a, um *adj,* not turned back
irrĕvŏcābĭlis, e *adj,* irrevocable
irrīdĕo, si, sum *v.i.t.* 2, to joke, jeer; mock, ridicule
irrĭgātĭo, ōnis *f,* irrigation
irrĭgo *v.t.* 1, to water, refresh
irrĭgŭus, a, um *adj,* well-watered, moistening
irrīsĭo, ōnis *f,* mockery
irrīsus, ūs *m,* mockery
irrīsor, ōris *m,* scoffer
irrītābĭlis, e *adj,* irritable
irrītāmen, ĭnis *n,* incentive
irrītāmentum, i *n,* incentive
irrīto *v.t.* 1, to provoke
irrītus, a, um *adj,* invalid, unsucessful
irrŏgo *v.t.* 1, to propose (against someone), inflict
irrōro *v.t.* 1, to bedew
irrumpo, rūpi, ptum *v.i.t.* 3, to break in; attack, interrupt
irrŭo, ŭi *v.i.* 3, to rush in, seize
irruptus, a, um *adj,* unbroken
īs, ĕa, id *demonst. pron,* he, she, it, that
ischīas, ădis *f,* sciatica
iste, a, ud *demonst. pron,* that
isthmus, i *m,* isthmus
istīc *adv,* there
istinc *adv,* from there

istūc *adv,* to that place
ĭtă *adv,* in such a way, so
ĭtăque *conj,* and so, therefore
ĭtem *adv,* likewise, also
ĭter, ĭtĭnĕris *n,* route, journey, march
ĭtĕrātĭo, ōnis *f,* repetition
ĭtĕro *v.t.* 1, to repeat
ĭtĕrum *adv,* again
ĭtĭdem *adv,* in the same way
ĭtĭo, ōnis *f,* travelling

J (consonantal i)

iăcĕo *v.i.* 2, to lie (recumbent), lie sick
iăcĭo, iēci, iactum *v.t.* 3, to throw, lay down
iactans, ntis *pres. part, adj,* boastful
iactantĭa, ae *f,* ostentation
iactātĭo, ōnis *f,* tossing, bragging
iactātor, ōris *m,* braggart
iacto *v.t.* 1, to throw about, boast
iactūra, ae *f,* throwing overboard, sacrifice
iactus, ūs *m,* throw, shot
iăcŭlātor, ōris *m,* thrower
iăcŭlātrix, īcis *f,* huntress
iăcŭlor *v.t.* 1, *dep,* to hurl
iăcŭlum, i *n,* javelin
iam *adv,* already, now
iamdūdum *adv,* a long time ago
iamprīdem *adv,* for a long time now
iānĭtor, ōris *m,* doorkeeper
iānŭa, ae *f,* door, entrance
lānŭārĭus (mensis) January
iĕcur, ŏris *n,* liver
iēiūnĭtas, ātis *f,* meagreness
iēiūnĭum, ii *n,* fast, hunger
iēiūnus, a, um *adj,* hungry, barren
ientācŭlum, i *n,* breakfast
iento *v.i.* 1, to breakfast
iŏcātĭo, ōnis *f,* joke
iŏcor *v.i.t.* 1, *dep,* to joke
iŏcōsus, a, um *adj,* humorous
iŏcŭlāris, e *adj,* amusing
iŏcŭlātor, ōris *m,* joker
iŏcus, i *m,* joke
iūba, ae *f,* mane, crest

iŭbar, ăris *n,* radiance
iŭbĕo, iussi, iussum *v.t.* 2, to order, tell
iūcundĭtas, ātis *f,* pleasantness
iūcundus, a, um *adj,* pleasant
iūdex, ĭcis *m,* judge
iudicialis, e *adj,* judicial
iudicatio, ōnis *f,* judgement
iūdĭcĭum, ii *n,* trial, verdict, court, discretion, judgement
iūdĭco *v.t.* 1, to judge, decide
iŭgālis, e *adj,* yoked together
iŭgāles *m.pl,* chariot horses
iŭgĕrum, i *n,* acre (approx.)
iŭgis, e *adj,* perpetual
iūglans, dis *f,* walnut
iŭgo *v.t.* 1, to marry, connect
iŭgōsus, a, um *adj,* mountainous
iŭgŭlo *v.t.* 1, to cut the throat
iŭgum, i *n,* yoke, bench, mountain-ridge
lūlĭus (mensis), July
iūmentum, i *n,* pack animal
iuncĕus, a, um *adj,* made of rushes
iuncōsus, a, um *adj,* full of rushes
iunctĭo, ōnis *f,* junction
iunctūra, ae *f,* joint
iuncus, i *m,* bullrush
iungo, nxi, nctum *v.t.* 3, to join
iūnĭor *comp. adj,* from **iŭvĕnis,** younger
iūnĭpĕrus, i *f,* juniper tree
lūnĭus (mensis) June
iūrātor, ōris *m,* commissioner of oaths
iūrātus, a, um *adj,* bound by oath
iurgĭum, ii *n,* quarrel
iurgo *v.i.t.* 1, to quarrel; upbraid
iūris consultus, i *m,* lawyer
iūris dictĭo, ōnis *f,* jurisdiction
iūro *v.i.t.* 1, to take an oath; to swear by
iūs, iūris *n,* law, legal status, right, authority
iūs, iūris *n,* soup
iusiūrandum, i *n,* oath
iussum, i *n,* order
iusta, ōrum *n.pl,* due ceremonies
iustē *adv,* rightly
iustĭtĭa, ae *f,* justice
iustĭtĭum *n,* holiday for lawcourts, public mourning

iusum, i *n,* fairness
iustus, a, um *adj,* fair, lawful
iŭvĕnālis, e *adj,* youthful
iŭvenca, ae *f,* heifer
iŭvencus, i *m,* bullock
iŭvĕnesco, nŭi *v.i.* 3, to reach youth
iŭvĕnīlis, e *adj,* youthful
iŭvĕnis, is *m, f,* young person; (*adj*) young
iŭvĕnor *v.i.* 1, *dep,* to act youthfully
iŭventa, ae *f,* the age of youth
iŭventas, ātis *f,* the age of youth
iŭventus, ūtis *f,* the age of youth
iŭvo, iūvi, iūtum *v.t.* 1, to help, gratify; **iŭvat** (*impers, with acc*), it pleases, it is of use
iuxtā *adv, and prep. with acc,* near
iuxtim *adv, and prep. with acc,* next to

K

Kalendae, ārum *f.pl,* the Kalends, the first day of the month

L

lăbĕfăcĭo, fēci, factum *v.t.* 3, to shake, loosen, overthrow
lăbĕfacto *v.t.* 1, to shake, destroy
lăbellum, i *n,* a lip
lăbellum, i *n,* tub, basin
lābes, is *f,* sinking, downfall
lābes, is *f,* spot, blemish
lābo *v.i.* 1, to totter, waver
lābor, lapsus *v.i.* 3, *dep,* to slip, slide, glide, pass away, be mistaken
lābor, ōris *m,* work, toil, workmanship, distress
lăbŏrĭōsus, a, um *adj, adv,* ē, laborious, industrious
lăbōro *v.i.t.* 1, to strive, be in trouble or difficulty; to make, prepare
lăbrum, i *n,* lip
lābrum, i *n,* tub, basin
lăbўrinthus, i *m,* labyrinth

lac, lactis   *n*, milk
lăcer, ěra, ěrum   *adj*, mangled
lăcerna, ae   *f*, cloak
lăcěātĭo, ōnis   *f*, laceration
lăcēro   *v.t.* 1, to tear, rend,
   censure, destroy
lăcerta, ae   *f* (us, i   *m*), lizard
lăcertōsus, a, um   *adj*, brawny
lăcertus, i   *m*, arm, strength
lăcertus, i   *m*, lizard, newt
lăcesso, īvi, ītum   *v.t.* 3, to
   provoke, attack, irritate, urge
lăcĭnĭa, ae   *f*, edge of garment
lăcrĭma, ae   *f*, tear
lăcrĭmābilis, e   *adj*, mournful
lăcrĭmo *v.i.* 1, to weep
lăcrĭmōsus, a, um   *adj*, tearful
lactens, ntis   *f*, very young
   (unweaned) animal
lactěus, a, um   *adj*, milky
lacto   *v.i.t.* 1, to have milk; suck
lactūca, ae   *f*, lettuce
lăcūna, ae   *f*, ditch, pond, gap
lăcūnar, āris   *n*, ceiling
lăcus, ūs   *m*, lake, tank, tub
laedo, si, sum   *v.t.* 3, to injure,
   offend
laena, ae   *f*, cloak
laetābĭlis, e   *adj*, joyful
laetĭfĭco   *v.t.* 1, to delight
laetĭtĭa, ae   *f*, joyfulness
laetor   *v.i.* 1, *dep*, to rejoice
laetus, a, um   *adj*, *adv*, ē, glad,
   cheerful, willing, pleased,
   prosperous, beautiful
laeva, ae   *f*, the left hand
laevus, a, um   *adj*, on the left side,
   unfortunate, foolish
lăgănum, i   *n*, a cake
lăgēna, ae   *f*, wine jar
lăgōis, ĭdis   *f*, grous
lăgōpūs, ŏdis   *f*, grouse
lăguncŭla, ae   *f*, small bottle
lambo, bi, bĭtum   *v.t.* 3, to lick
lāmentābĭlis, e   *adj*, mournful
lāmentātĭo, ōnis   *f*, mourning
lāmentor   *v.i.t.* 1, *dep*, to weep;
   mourn
lāments, ōrum   *n.pl*, moaning
lāmĭa, ae   *f*, witch, vampire
lāmĭna, ae   *f*, thin metal plate
lampas, ădis   *f*, torch
lāna, ae   *f*, wool

lancěa, ae   *f*, lance, spear
lāněus, a, um   *adj*, woollen
languens, ntis   *adj*, faint, weak
languěo   *v.i.* 2, to be faint or
   listless
languesco, gŭi   *v.i.* 3, to become
   faint or listless
languĭdus, a, um   *adj*, faint, weary,
   sluggish
languor, ōris   *m*, weakness,
   weariness, sluggishness
lănĭātus, ūs   *m*, laceration
lānĭcĭum, ii   *n*, wool
lānĭēna, ae   *f*, butcher's stall
lānĭfĭcus, a, um   *adj*, weaving
lānĭger, ěra, ěrum   *adj*, fleecy
lānĭo   *v.t.* 1, to mutilate
lānista, ae   *m*, fencing master
lānĭus, ii   *m*, butcher
lanterna, ae   *f*, lamp, torch
lānūgo, ĭnis   *f*, down, hair
lanx, ncis   *f*, dish, plate
lăpăthus, i   *f*, sorrel
lăpĭcīda, ae   *m*, quarryman
lăpĭcīdīnae, ārum   *f.pl*, stone
   quarries
lăpĭdātĭo, ōnis   *f*, stoning
lăpĭděus, a, um   *adj*, of stone
lăpĭdōsus, a, um   *adj*, stony
lăpillus, i   *m*, pebble, grain
lăpis, ĭdis   *m*, stone, milestone,
   jewel
lappa, ae   *f*, burr
lapso   *v.i.* 1, to slip, stumble
lapsus, a, um   *adj*, fallen, sinking,
   ruined
lapsus, ūs   *m*, fall, slip, gliding
lăquěar, āris   *n*, ceiling
lăquěātus, a, um   *adj*, panelled
lăquěus, i   *m*, noose, snare
lar, ăris   *m*, guardian deity of a
   house, home
largĭor   *v.t.* 4, *dep*, to lavish, give
largĭtas, ātis   *f*, abundance
largĭtĭo, ōnis   *f*, generous
   distribution, bribery
largĭtor, ōris   *m*, briber, generous
   giver
largus, a, um   *adj*, *adv*, ē, ĭter,
   abundant, lavish, large
lārĭdum (lardum), i   *n*, lard
lārix, ĭcis   *f*, larch
larva, ae   *f*, ghost, mask

lascīvĭa, ae *f*, playfulness
lascīvĭo *v.i.* 4, to frolic
lascīvus, a, um *adj*, playful, licentious
lassĭtūdo, ĭnis *f*, weariness
lasso *v.t.* 1, to tire, fatigue
lassus, a, um *adj*, exhausted
lātē *adv*, far and wide
lătĕbra, ae *f*, hiding-place, subterfuge
lătĕbrōsus, a, um *adj*, full of hiding places, secret
lătens, ntis *adj, adv*, nter, hidden, secret
lătĕo *v.i.* 2, to lie hidden, keep out of sight
lāter, ĕris *m*, brick, tile, ingot
lătĕrīcĭus, a, um *adj*, made of bricks
lātex, ĭcis *m*, liquid
lătĭbŭlum, *n*, hiding-place
Lătīnē *adv*, in Latin
lătĭto *v.i.* 1, to lie hidden
lātĭtūdo, ĭnis *f*, breadth
lātor, ōris *m*, proposer of a law
lātrātor, ōris *m*, a barker
lātrātus, ūs *m*, barking
lātrīna, ae *f*, water-closet
lātro *v.i.t.* 1, to bark; bark at
lātro, ōnis *m*, robber
lătrōcĭnĭum, ii *n*, robbery, fraud, robber-band
lătrōcĭnor *v.i.* 1, *dep*, to practise highway robbery
lătruncŭlus, i *m*, robber
lātus, a, um *adj, adv*, ē, wide
lātus, ĕris *n*, the side, flank, lungs
laudābĭlis, e *adj*, praiseworthy
laudātĭo, ōnis *f*, praises, eulogy
laudātor, ōris *m*, praiser
laudātus, a, um *adj*, praiseworthy
laudo *v.t.* 1, to praise, name
laurĕa, ae *f*, laurel (tree)
laurĕātus, a, um *adj*, crowned with laurel (of victory)
laurĕus, a, um *adj*, of laurel
laurus, i *f*, laurel
laus, dis *f*, praise, merit
lautē *adv*, elegantly
lautĭtĭa, ae *f*, elegance
lautŭmĭae, ārum *f.pl*, stone quarry
lautus, a, um *adj*, elegant, splendid, noble

lăvātĭo, ōnis *f*, ablution, washing
lăvo, lāvi, lautum *v.i.t.* 1 or 3, to wash or wet
laxĭtas, ātis *f*, spaciousness
laxo *v.t.* 1, to enlarge, loosen, relax, relieve, weaken
laxus, a, um *adj*, wide, loose
lĕa, ae *f*, lioness
lĕaena, ae *f*, lioness
lēbes, ētis *m*, copper basin
lectīca, ae *f*, sedan, litter
lectĭo, ōnis *f*, selection, reading aloud
lector, ōris *m*, reader
lectŭlus, i *m*, sofa, couch
lectus, a, um *adj*, chosen, excellent
lectus, i *m*, bed, couch
lectus, ūs *m*, reading
lēgātĭo, ōnis *f*, delegation
lēgātum, i *n*, legacy
lēgātus, i *m*, ambassador, delegate, lieutenant-general
lēges see lex
lēgĭfer, ĕra, ĕrum *adj*, law-giving
lĕgĭo, ōnis *f*, Roman legion (4,000–6,000 soldiers)
lĕgĭōnārĭus, a, um *adj*, of a legion
lēgĭtĭmus, a, um *adj*, legal, legitimate, proper, right
lēgo *v.t.* 1, to send with a commission, appoint as a deputy, leave as a legacy
lĕgo, lēgi, lectum *v.t.* 3, to read, gather, select, steal, pass through, sail by, survey
lĕgūmen, ĭnis *n*, pulse, beans
lembus, i *m*, yacht, cutter
lĕmŭres, um *m.pl*, ghosts, spirits
lēna, ae *f*, bawd
lēnīmen, ĭnis *n*, alleviation, palliative
lēnīmentum, i *n*, alleviation, palliative
lēnĭo *v.t.* 4, to soften, soothe
lēnis, e *adj, adv*, ĭter, soft, smooth, gentle, calm
lēnĭtas, ātis *f*, gentleness
lēno, ōnis *m*, pimp, seducer
lēnōcĭnĭum, ii *n*, pandering, ornamentation
lēnōcĭnor *v.* 1, *dep, with dat*, to flatter, promote

lens, ntis *f*, lentil
lentesco *v.i.* 3, to become soft or sticky
lentīgo, ĭnis *f*, freckle
lentĭtūdo, ĭnis *f*, apathy, sluggishness
lento *v.t.* 1, to bend
lentus, a, um *adj, adv*, ē, slow, flexible, sticky, tedious, calm (of character)
lēnuncŭlus, i *m*, boat
lĕo, ōnis *m*, lion
lĕpĭdus, a, um *adj, adv*, ē, charming, elegant, pleasant
lĕpor (lĕpos), ōris *m*, charm, pleasantness, wit
lĕŏrārĭum, ĭī *n*, warren
leprae, ārum *f.pl*, leprosy
lĕprōsus, a, um *adj*, leprous
lĕpus, ŏris *m*, a hare
lĕpuscŭlus, i *m*, leveret
lētālis, e *adj*, fatal
lēthargĭcus, a, um *adj*, lethargic
lēthargus, i *m*, stupor
lētĭfer, ĕra, ĕrum *adj*, deadly
lētum, i *n*, death
lĕvāmen, ĭnis *n*, consolation, comfort
lĕvāmentum, i *n*, consolation, comfort
lĕvātĭo, ōnis *f*, raising
lĕvis, e *adj, adv*, ĭter, light, mild, light-armed, agile, trivial, unreliable
lēvis, e *adj*, smooth, soft
lĕvĭtas, ātis *f*, inconstancy
lēvĭtas, ātis *f*, smoothness
lēvo *v.t.* 1, to raise, relieve, take away, support, soothe, release
lēvo *v.t.* 1, to smooth
lex, lēgis *f*, law, condition
lībāmen, ĭnis *n*, drink offering
lībāmentum, i *n*, drink offering
lībella, ae *f*, small coin
lībellus, i *m*, small book, pamphlet, diary
lībens, ntis *adj, adv*, nter, with pleasure, willing
līber, ĕra, ĕrum *adj, adv*, nter, free, frank
līber, ĕri *m*, wine
līber, ĕri *m*, child
līber, bri *m*, book, tree bark

lībĕrālis, e *adj, adv*, ĭter, honourable, generous
lībĕrālĭtas, ātis *f*, generosity
lībĕrātĭo, ōnis *f*, release
lībĕrātor, ōris *m*, liberator
lībĕri, ōrum *m.pl*, children
lībĕro *v.t.* 1, to release, free from slavery, acquit
lībertas, ātis *f*, freedom
lībertīnus, i *m*, freedman
lībertīnus, a, um *adj*, of a freedman
lībertus, i *m*, a freedman
lībet, lībŭit, lībĭtum est *v.* 2, *impers*, it is agreeable
lībīdĭnōsus, a, um *adj*, lecherous
lībīdo, ĭnis *f*, desire, passion, whim
lībo *v.t.* 1, to taste, touch, pour out an offering of wine
lībra, ae *f*, Roman pound (12 oz.), pair of scales
lībrāmentum, i *n*, a weight
lībrārĭus, i *m*, secretary
lībrārĭus, a, um *adj*, of books
lībrātus, a, um *adj*, balanced
lībrīlis, e *adj*, weighing a pound
lībro *v.t.* 1, to balance, hurl
lībum, i *n*, pancake
līburna, ae *f*, fast sailing ship
līcenter *adv*, without restraint
līcentĭa, ae *f*, freedom, licence
līcĕo *v.i.* 2, to be for sale, be valued at
līcĕor *v.t.* 2, to be for sale, be valued at
līcĕor *v.t.* 2, *dep*, to bid (for)
līcet, cŭit, cĭtum est *v.* 2, *impers*, it is allowed, one may
līcet *conj*, although
līcĭtus, a, um *adj*, permitted
līcĭtātĭo, ōnis *f*, bidding
līcĭum, ii *n*, a thread
lictor, ōris *m*, official attendant of high magistrates
līen, ēnis *m*, spleen
līgāmen, ĭnis *n*, bandage
līgāmentum, i *n*, ligament
lignārĭus, ii *m*, carpenter, joiner
lignātĭo, ōnis *f*, wood gathering
lignātor, ōris *m*, wood cutter
lignĕus, a, um *adj*, wooden
lignor *v.i.* 1, *dep*, to collect wood

lignum, i *n,* wood
līgo *v.t.* 1, to tie, bind
līgo, ōnis *m,* hoe
līgŭla, ae *f,* small tongue (of land); tongue of a shoe
līgūrĭo *v.t.* 4, to lick, desire
līgustrum, i *n,* a plant, privet
līlĭum, ii *n,* lily
līma, ae *f,* file
līmax, ācis *f,* slug
limbus, i *m,* border, edge
līmen, ĭnis *n,* doorstep, door, lintel
līmĕs, ĭtis *m,* boundary, track
līmo *v.t.* 1, to file, polish, finish
līmōsus, a, um *adj,* slimy, muddy
limpĭdus, a, um *adj,* clear, bright
līmus, a, um *adj,* aslant
līmus, i *m,* slime, mud
līmus, i *m,* apron
līnāmentum, i *n,* linen, lint
līnĕa, ae *f,* thread, string, line, end, goal
līnĕāmentum, i *n,* line, feature
līnĕus, a, um *adj,* linen
lingo, nxi *v.t.* 3, to lick
lingua, ae *f,* tongue, speech, language
līnĭger, ĕra, ĕrum *adj,* clothed in linen
līno, lēvi, lītum *v.t.* 3, to daub, smear over
linquo, līqui *v.t.* 3, to leave
lintĕo, ōnis *m,* linen weaver
linter, tris *f,* boat, tray
lintĕum, i *n,* linen
lintĕus, a, um *adj,* of linen
līnum, i *n,* flax, linen, thread, rope, net
lippĭtūdo, ĭnis *f,* inflammation of the eyes
lippus, a, um *adj,* blear-eyed
līquĕfăcĭo, fēci, factum *v.t.* 3, to melt, dissolve
līquĕfactus, a, um *adj,* molten
līquens, ntis *adj,* liquid
līquĕo, līqui *v.i.* 2, to be clear
līquesco, līcŭi *v.i.* 3, to melt
līquĭdus, a, um *adj,* liquid, flowing, clear
līquo *v.t.* 1, to melt, filter
līquor *v.i.* 3, *dep,* to melt, flow
līquor, ōris *m,* a liquid

līs, tis *f,* dispute, lawsuit
lītĭgĭōsus, a, um *adj,* quarrelsome
lītĭgo *v.i.* 1, to quarrel
līto *v.i.t.* 1, to make a sacrifice with favourable omens; appease
lītŏrĕus, a, um *adj,* of the seashore
littĕra, ae *f,* a letter of the alphabet
littĕrae, ārum *f.pl,* a letter, document, literature, learning
littĕrātus, a, um *adj,* educated
littĕrŭla, ae *f,* small letter, moderate literary knowledge
lītūra, ae *f,* smear, erasure
lītus, ōris *n,* seashore
lītŭus, i *m,* augur's staff, trumpet
līvens, ntis *adj,* bluish
līvĕo *v.i.* 2, to be black and blue
līvĭdus, a, um *adj,* bluish, black and blue, envious
līvor, ōris *m,* leaden colour, envy, malice
lixa, ae *m,* camp-follower
lŏca, ōrum *n.pl,* a region
lŏcātĭo, ōnis *f,* placing, arrangement, lease
lŏco *v.t.* 1, to place, arrange, give in marriage, lease, contract for
lŏcŭlāmentum, i *n,* box
lŏcŭlus, i *m,* satchel, purse
lŏcŭplēs, ētis *adj,* wealthy
lŏcŭplēto *v.t.* 1, to enrich
lŏcus, i *m,* place, position, topic, subject, cause, reason
lŏcusta, ae *f,* locust
lŏcūtĭo, ōnis *f,* speaking, pronunciation, phrase
lōdix, īcis *f,* blanket
lŏgĭca, ōrum *n.pl,* logic
lŏgĭcus, a, um *adj,* logical
lōlīgo, ĭnis *f,* cuttlefish
lōlĭum, ii *n,* darnel
longaevus, a, um *adj,* ancient
longē *adv,* far off, greatly
longinquĭtas, ātis *f,* duration, distance
longinquus, a, um *adj,* distant, strange, prolonged
longĭtūdo, ĭnis *f,* length
longŭrĭus, ii *m,* long pole
longus, a, um *adj,* long, tall, vast, distant, tedious

lŏquācĭtas, ātis *f,* talkativeness
lŏquax, ācis *adj, adv,* **ĭter,**
 talkative, babbling
lŏquēla, ae *f,* speech, discourse
lŏquor, lŏcūtus *v.i.t.* 3, *dep,* to
 speak; tell, mention, declare
lōrīca, ae *f,* breastplate
lōrĭpēs, pĕdis *adj,* bandy-legged
lōrum, i *n,* strap, whip
lōtos (lōtus), i *f,* lotus tree
lūbens, lūbet see **libens, libet**
lūbrĭcus, a, um *adj,* slippery,
 dangerous, deceitful
lŭcellum, i *n,* slight profit
lūcĕo, xi *v.i.* 2, to shine
lūcet *v. impers,* day breaks
lūcerna, ae *f,* lamp
lūcesco *v.i.* 3, to dawn
lūcĭdus, a, um *adj,* bright, clear
lūcĭfer, ĕra, ĕrum *adj,* light-
 bringing
lūcĭfer, ĕri *m,* morning star
lūcĭfŭgus, a, um *adj,* retiring
lŭcrātīvus, a, um *adj,* profitable
lŭcror *v.t.* 1, *dep,* to gain, win
lŭcrum, i *n,* profit, advantage
luctāmen, inis *n,* wrestling,
 struggle
luctātĭo, ōnis *f,* wrestling, struggle
luctātor, ōris *m,* wrestler
luctĭfĭcus, a, um *adj,* woeful
luctor *v.i.* 1, *dep,* to struggle
luctŭōsus, a, um *adj,* sorrowful
luctus, ūs *m,* grief, mourning
 (clothes)
lūcŭbrātĭo, ōnis *f,* night-work
lūcŭlentus, a, um *adj,* bright
lūcus, i *m,* wood, grove
lūdĭbrĭum, ii *n,* mockery, jest,
 laughing-stock
lūdĭbundus, a, um *adj,* playful
lūdĭcer, ĭcra, ĭcrum *adj,* sportive,
 theatrical
lūdĭcrum, i *n,* public show or
 games, a play
lūdĭdĭcātĭo, ōnis *f,* mocking
lūdĭfĭcor *v.i.t.* 1, *dep* **(lūdĭfĭco** *v.t.*
 1**),** to mock, deceive
lūdĭmăgister, tri *m,* schoolmaster
lūdĭus, ii *m,* pantomime-actor
lūdo, si, sum *v.i.t.* 3, to play,
 frolic; mock, deceive
lūdus, i *m,* a play, game, public

games, school, joke
lŭes, is *f,* an epidemic
lūgĕo, xi, ctum *v.i.t.* 2, to mourn
lūgŭbris, e *adj,* lamentable,
 disastrous
lumbus, i *m,* loin
lūmen, ĭnis *n,* light, lamp, gleam,
 life, eye, glory
lūna, ae *f,* moon
lūnāris, e *adj,* lunar
lūnātus, a, um *adj,* crescent-
 shaped
lūno *v.t.* 1, to bend into a
 crescent-shape
lŭo, lŭi *v.t.* 3, to pay a debt or
 penalty, undergo, atone for
lŭpāta, ōrum *n.pl,* horse-bit
lŭpātus, a, um *adj,* jagged
lŭpīnus, a, um *adj,* of the wolf
lŭpīnus, i *m,* lupin (plant)
lŭpus, i *m,* wolf, pike (fish), a
 jagged bit, hook
lūrĭdus, a, um *adj,* lurid, sallow
luscĭnĭa, ae *f,* nightingale
lūsor, ōris *m,* player, mocker
lustrālis, e *adj,* expiatory
lustrātĭo, ōnis *f,* purification by
 sacrifice
lustro *v.t.* 1, to to purify by
 sacrifice, wander over, review
lustrum, i *n,* den, wood
lustrum, i *n,* purificatory sacrifice,
 period of five years
lūsus, ūs *m,* play, sport, game
lūtĕŏlus, a, um *adj,* yellow
lūtĕus, a, um *adj,* golden-yellow
lŭtĕus, a, um *adj,* muddy,
 worthless
lūtra, ae *f,* otter
lŭtŭlentus, a, um *adj,* filthy
lūtum, i *n,* yellow
lŭtum, i *n,* mud, clay
lux, lūcis *f,* light, dawn, day, life,
 brightness, glory
luxŭrĭa, ae *f,* luxuriance,
 extravagance
luxŭrĭo *v.i.* 1, **(luxŭrĭor,** *v.* 1,
 *dep***),** to be overgrown, to have
 in excess, run riot
luxŭrĭōsus, a, um *adj,* luxuriant,
 excessive
luxus, ūs *m,* extravagance, pomp
lychnūcus, i *m,* lamp-stand

lychnus, i *m*, light, lamp
lympha, ae *f*, water
lymphātus, a, um *adj*, frenzied
lyncēus, a, um *adj*, sharp-eyed
lynx, cis *c*, lynx
lȳra, ae *f*, lute, poetry, song
lȳrĭcus, a, um *adj*, of the lute, lyric

M

măcellum, i *n*, food market
măcer, cra, crum *adj*, lean, thin
mācĕrĭa, ae *f*, wall
mācĕro *v.t.* 1, to soften, weaken, torment
māchĭna, ae *f*, engine, machine, battering-ram, trick, plan
māchĭnālis, e *adj*, mechanical
māchĭnātĭo, ōnis *f*, contrivance, machine, trick
māchĭnātor, ōris *m*, engineer, inventor
māchĭnor *v.t.* 1, *dep*, to design, plot
măcĭes, ēi *f*, thinness, poverty
macte or **macti** (*voc. of* **mactus**), good luck! well done!
macto *v.t.* 1, to sacrifice a victim, reward, honour, destroy
mactus, a, um *adj*, worshipped
măcŭla, ae *f*, spot, stain, fault, mesh
măcŭlo *v.t.* 1, to stain, disgrace
măcŭlōsus, a, um *adj*, spotted, dishonoured
mădĕfăcĭo, fēci, factum *v.t.* 3, to soak, drench
mădens, ntis *adj*, moist, drunk
mădĕo *v.i.* 2, to be moist, to drip, to be boiled, softened
mădesco, dŭi *v.i.* 3, to become wet
mădĭdus, a, um *adj*, soaked
maena, ae *f*, small salted fish
maenĭānum, i *n*, balcony
maerens, ntis *adj*, mourning
maerĕo *v.i.t.* 2, to mourn; bewail
maeror, ōris *m*, grief, mourning
maestĭtĭa, ae *f*, sadness
maestus, a, um *adj*, sad
măga, ae *f*, witch
măgālĭa, ĭum *n.pl*, huts

măgĭcus, a, um *adj*, magic
măgis *comp. adv* (**magnus**), more, rather
măgister, tri *m*, master, leader, director, teacher
măgistĕrĭum, ii *n*, president's position
măgistra, ae *f*, mistress
măgistrātus, ūs *m*, magistracy, magistrate
magnănĭmĭtas, ātis *f*, magnanimity
magnănĭmus, a, um *adj*, great-hearted
magnes, ētis *m*, magnet
magnētĭcus, a, um *adj*, magnet
magni see **magnus**
magnĭfĭcentĭa, ae *f*, nobleness, splendour, boasting
magnĭfĭcus, a, um *adj*, *adv*, **ē**, noble, distinguished, sumptuous, bragging
magnĭlŏquentĭa, ae *f*, high-sounding language
magnĭtūdo, ĭnis *f*, size
magnŏpĕrē *adv*, very much
magnus, a, um *adj*, large, great; **magni** or **magno** at a high price
măgus, i *m*, magician
Māius (mensis) May
māiestas, ātis *f*, greatness, grandeur, sovereignty, treason
māior *comp. adj*, larger, greater; **māiōres, um** *m.pl*, ancestors, the Senate; **maior nātu** older
māla, ae *f*, cheekbone, jaw
mălăcĭa, ae *f*, calm at sea
mălagma, ătis *n*, poultice
mălĕ *adv*, badly, exceedingly; often reverses the meaning of an adj: **male sānus** deranged
mălĕdīcens, ntis *adj*, abusive
mălĕdīco, xi, ctum *v.i.* 3, to abuse, slander
mălĕdictĭo, ōnis *f*, abuse
mălĕdictum, i *n*, abusive word
mălĕdīcus, a, um *adj*, abusive
mălĕfĭcĭum, ii *n*, wrongdoing
mălĕfĭcus, a, um *adj*, evil-doing
mălĕsuādus, a, um *adj*, persuading towards wrong
mălĕvŏlens, ntis *adj*, spiteful
mălĕvŏlentĭa, ae *f*, malice

mălĕvŏlus, a, um   *adj*, spiteful
mălignus, a, um   *adj*, malicious
mălītĭa, ae   *f*, malice
mălītĭōsus, a, um   *adj*, wicked
mallĕus, i   *m*, hammer
mālo, malle, mālŭi   *v.t*, *irreg*, to prefer
mălŏbăthrum, i   *n*, a costly ointment
mālum, i   *n*, apple, fruit
mălum, i   *n*, evil, misfortune
mălus, a, um   *adj*, bad, harmful
mālus, i   *m*, mast
malva, ae   *f*, the mallow
mamma, ae   *f*, breast, teat
manceps, cĭpis   *m*, contractor
mancĭpĭum, ii   *n*, legal purchase, right of ownership, slave
mancĭpo   *v.t*. 1, to sell, transfer
mancus, a, um   *adj*, maimed
mandātum, i   *n*, order, commission
mandātus, ūs   *m*, order, commission
mando   *v.t*. 1, to order, commission, commit
mandūco   *v.t*. 1, to chew
māne   *n*, *indecl*, morning;   *adv*, in the morning
mănĕo, nsi, nsum   *v.i.t*. 2, to stay, remain, continue; await
mānes, ĭum   *m.pl*, deified ghosts of the dead
mănĭcae, ārum   *f.pl*, glove, gauntlet, handcuff
mănĭfestus, a, um   *adj*, *adv*, ō, clear, apparent
mănĭpŭlāris, e   *adj*, belonging to a company (a soldier)
mănĭpŭlus, i   *m*, handful, bundle, company of soldiers
mannus, i   *m*, coach-horse, pony
māno   *v.i.t*. 1, to flow, trickle; pour out
mansĭo, ōnis   *f*, a stay, inn
mansŭĕfăcĭo, fēci, factum   *v.t*. 3, to tame, civilize
mansŭesco, sŭēvi, sŭētum   *v.i*. 3, to grow tame or gentle
mansŭētus, a, um   *adj*, gentle
mansŭētūdo, ĭnis   *f*, gentleness
mansūrus, a, um   *adj*, lasting

mantēle, is   *n*, towel, cloth
mantĭca, ae   *f*, suitcase
mănūbĭae, ārum   *f.pl*, money from the sale of booty
mănūbrĭum, ii   *n*, handle
mănūmissĭo, ōnis   *f*, the freeing of a slave
mănūmitto, mīsi, missum   *v.t*. 3, to set free a slave
mănus, ūs   *f*, hand, bravery, combat, violence, grappling-iron, armed band
măpālĭa, ĭum   *n.pl*, African huts
mappa, ae   *f*, towel, napkin
marcĕo   *v.i*. 2, to be weak
marcesco   *v.i*. 3, to wither
marcĭdus, a, um   *adj*, decayed
măre, is   *n*, the sea
marga, ae   *f*, marl
margărīta, ae   *f*, pearl
margo, ĭnis   *m*, *f*, edge, border
mărīnus, a, um   *adj*, of the sea
mărīta, ae   *f*, wife
mărītālis, e   *adj*, matrimonial
mărītĭmus, a, um   *adj*, of the sea
mărītus, a, um   *adj*, matrimonial
mărītus, i   *m*, husband
marmor, ŏris   *n*, marble, statue; *in pl*, surface of the sea
marmŏrĕus, a, um   *adj*, of marble
martĭālis, e   *adj*, sacred to Mars
Martĭus (mensis) March
martyr, ўris   *c*, martyr
martўrĭum, ii   *n*, martyrdom
mās, măris   *adj*, male
mascŭlus, a, um   *adj*, male, bold
massa, ae   *f*, lump, mass
mătellĭo, ōnis   *m*, pot
māter, tris   *f*, mother
māterfămĭlĭas, mātrisfămĭlĭas   *f*, mistress of the house
mătĕrĭa, ae   *f*, timber, materials, topic, opportunity
mătĕris, is   *f*, Celtic javelin
māternus, a, um   *adj*, maternal
mātertĕra, ae   *f*, maternal aunt
măthēmătĭca, ae   *f*, mathematics
măthēmătĭcus, a, um   *adj*, mathematical
mātrĭcīda, ae   *c*, murderer of his (her) mother
mātrĭmōnĭum, ii   *n*, marriage
mātrōna, ae   *f*, married woman

mātrōnālis, e *adj,* of a married woman
mātūrē *adv,* at the proper time, soon, quickly
mātūresco, rŭi *v.i.* 3, to ripen
mātūrĭtas, ātis *f,* ripeness
mātūro *v.i.t.* 1, to ripen, hurry; bring to maturity
mātūrus, a, um *adj,* mature, ripe, early
mātūtīnus, a, um *adj,* of the morning
maxilla, ae *f,* jawbone, jaw
maxĭmē *adv,* expecially, very
maxĭmus, a, um *sup. adj,* very large or great
māxŏnŏmus, i *m,* dish
me *acc. or abl. of* ĕgŏ
mĕātus, ūs *m,* motion, course
mĕdĕor *v.* 2, *dep, with dat,* to heal, remedy, amend
mĕdĭastīnus, i *m,* drudge
mĕdĭca, ae *f,* a kind of clover
mĕdĭcābĭlis, e *adj,* curable
mĕdĭcāmen, ĭnis *n,* remedy, drug
mĕdĭcāmentum, i *n,* remedy, drug
mĕdĭcāmentārĭus, a, um *adj,* of drugs
mĕdĭcīna, ae *f,* the art of medicine, remedy
mĕdĭco *v.t.* 1, to heal, sprinkle, dye
medĭcor *v.t.* 1, *dep,* to heal
mĕdĭcus, a, um *adj,* healing
mĕdĭcus, i *m,* doctor, surgeon
mĕdimnum, i *n,* bushel
mĕdĭŏcris, e *adj, adv,* ĭter, ordinary, insignificant
mĕdĭŏcrĭtas, ātis *f,* a middle state, insignificance
mĕdĭtātĭo, ōnis *f,* contemplation, preparation
medĭtātus, a, um *adj,* considered
mĕdĭterrānĕus, a, um *adj,* inland
mĕdĭtor *v.i.t.* 1, *dep,* to consider, muse; study, intend, practise
mĕdĭum, ii *n,* middle, the public
mĕdĭus, a, um *adj,* middle, neutral
mĕdĭus, i *m,* mediator
mĕdulla, ae *f,* kernel, marrow
mēio *v.i.* 3, to urinate
mĕl, mellis *n,* honey

mĕlanchŏlĭcus, a, um *adj,* melancholic
mēles, is *f,* badger
mĕlĭmēla, ōrum *n.pl,* honey apples
mĕlĭor, us *comp. adj,* better
mĕlissphyllum, i *n,* balm
mĕlĭus *comp. adv,* better
mellĭfer, ĕra, ĕrum *adj,* honey producing
mellĭfĭco *v.t.* 1, to make honey
mellītus, a, um *adj,* of honey
mēlo, ōnis *m,* melon
mēlos, i *n,* tune, song
membrāna, ae *f,* skin, parchment
membrātim *adv,* piece by piece
membrum, i *n,* limb, division
mĕmmĭni, isse *v.i, defective,* to remember
mĕmor, ŏris *adj,* remembering, mindful
mĕmŏrābĭlis, e *adj,* memorable
mĕmŏrandus, a, um *adj,* memorable
mĕmŏrātus, a, um *adj,* renowned
mĕmŏrĭa, ae *f,* memory, posterity, historical account, tradition
mĕmŏro *v.t.* 1, to mention
menda, ae *f,* defect
mendācĭum, ii *n,* a lie
mendax, ācis *adj,* lying, false
mendīcĭtas, ātis *f,* poverty
mendīco *v.i.* 1, to beg
mendīcus, a, um *adj,* needy
mendīcus, i *m,* beggar
mendōsus, a, um *adj, adv,* ē, faulty, false
mendum, i *n,* blunder, defect, mistake
mens, ntis *f,* mind, intellect, understanding, intention, courage
mensa, ae *f,* table, course; sĕcunda mensa dessert
mensārĭus, ii *m,* banker
mensis, is *m,* month
mensor, ōris *m,* valuer, surveyor
menstrŭus, a, um *adj,* monthly
mensūra, ae *f,* measurement, quantity
mensus, a, um *adj,* measured off
menta, ae *f,* mint
mentĭo, ōnis *f,* recollection,

mention
mentǐor *v.i.t.* 4, *dep,* to lie, cheat; counterfeit, imitate
mentītus, a, um *adj,* counterfeit
mentum, i *n,* chin
měo *v.i.* 1, to go
měrācus, a, um *adj,* unmixed
mercātor, ōris *m,* wholesaler
mercātūra, ae *f,* trade
mercātus, ūs *m,* trade, market
mercēdǔla, ae *f,* small wages
mercēnārǐus, a, um *adj,* hired
merces, ēdis *f,* pay, wages, rent, interest, reward
merces *(pl)* see **merx**
mercor *v.t.* 1; *dep,* to buy
měrens, ntis *adj,* deserving
měrěo *v.t.* (**měrěor** *v. dep*) 2, to deserve, earn; *with* **stǐpendǐa,** to serve as a soldier
měrětrīcǐus, a, um *adj,* of prostitutes
měrětrix, trīcis *f,* prostitute
merges, ǐtis *f,* sheaf
mergo, si, sum *v.t.* 3, to immerse
mergus, i *m,* seabird (diver)
měrīdǐānus, a, um *adj,* of midday
měrīdǐes, ēi *m,* midday, south
měrǐtōrǐus, a, um *adj,* bringing in money
měrǐtum, i *n,* reward, benefit, fault, blame
měrǐtus, a, um *adj, adv,* **ē,** deserved, deserving
měrops, ǒpis *m,* bee-eating bird
merso *v.t.* 1, to immerse, drown
měrǔla, ae *f,* blackbird
měrum, i *n,* pure wine
měrus, a, um *adj,* pure, only, genuine
merx, cis *f,* goods, commodities
messis, is *f,* harvest, crops
messor, ōris *m,* harvester
mēta, ae *f,* winning-post, end, cone
mětallǐcus, a, um *adj,* metallic
mětallǐcus, i *m,* miner
mětallum, i *n,* mine, metal
mětātor, ōris *m,* surveyor
mētǐor, mensus *v.t.* 4, *dep,* to measure, distribute, traverse, estimate, value
měto, ssǔi, ssum *v.t.* 3, to mow,

gather, cut down
mētor *v.t.* 1, *dep,* to measure, mark out, traverse
mětrǐcus, a, um *adj,* metrical
mětǔendus, a, um *adj,* formidable
mětǔo, ǔi, ūtum *v.i.t.* 3, to be afraid; to fear
mětus, ūs *m,* fear, awe
měus, a, um *adj,* my, mine: **měi, ōrum** *m.pl,* my relatives
mīca, ae *f,* crumb
mǐco, ǔi *v.i.* 1, to tremble, sparkle
mǐgrātǐo, ōnis *f,* migration
mǐgro *v.i.* 1, to depart, change
mīlěs, ǐtis *c,* soldier, army
mīlia see **mille**
mīlǐārǐum, ii *n,* milestone
mīlǐtāris, e *adj,* military
mīlǐtāris, is *m,* soldier
mīlǐtǐa, ae *f,* military service, warfare
mīlǐto *v.i.* 1, to serve as a soldier
mǐlǐum, ii *n,* millet
mille *(pl,* **mīlia,** *with genit.*) a thousand; **mille passus,** or **passuum,** a mile
millēsǐmus, a, um *adj,* the thousandth
millǐes (millǐens) *adv,* a thousand times
milǔīnus, a, um *adj,* kite-like
milǔus, i *m,* kite, gurnard
mīmǐcus, a, um *adj,* farcical
mīmus, i *m,* mime, mimic actor
mǐna, ae *f,* Greek silver coinage
mǐnae, ārum *f.pl,* threats
mǐnax, ācis *adj, adv,* **ǐter,** threatening, projecting
mǐnǐmē *sup. adv,* very little
mǐnǐmus, a, um *sup. adj,* very small
mǐnister, tri *m,* **mǐnistra, ae** *f,* servant, assistant
mǐnistěrǐum, ii *n,* service, occupation
mǐnistrātor, ōris *m,* servant
mǐnistro *v.t.* 1, to wait upon, serve, manage
mǐnǐtor *v.i.t.* 1, *dep,* to threaten
mǐnǐum, ii red-lead
mǐnor *v.i.t.* 1, *dep,* to threaten
mǐnor, us *comp. adj,* smaller
mǐnǔo, ǔi, ūtum *v.i.t.* 3, to ebb; to reduce, weaken, chop up

mĭnus *comp. adv,* less

mĭnuscŭlus, a, um *adj,* rather small

mĭnūtal, ālis *n,* mincemeat

mĭnūtātim *adv,* little by little

mĭnūtus, a, um *adj, adv,* ē, small

mīrābĭlis, e *adj, adv,* īter, wonderful, strange

mīrācŭlum, i *n,* a wonder, marvel

mīrandus, a, um *adj,* wonderful

mīrātĭo, ōnis *f,* surprise

mīrātor, ōris *m,* admirer

mīrĭfĭcus, a, um *adj, adv,* ē, marvellous, extraordinary

mīror *v.i.t.* 1, *dep,* to be amazed; to marvel at, admire

mīrus, a, um *adj, adv,* ē, marbellous, extraordinary

miscĕo, scŭi, xtum *v.t.* 2, to mix, unite, disturb

mĭsellus, a, um *adj,* wretched

mĭser, ĕra, ĕrum *adj, adv,* ē, wretched, pitiable, worthless

mĭsĕrābĭlis, e *adj, adv,* īter, pitiable, sad

mĭsĕrandus, a, um *adj,* pitiable

mĭsĕrātĭo, ōnis *f,* pity

mĭsĕrĕor *v.* 2, *dep, with genit,* to pity

mĭsĕret (me, te, etc.) *v.* 2, *impers,* it distresses (me), I pity, am sorry for

mĭsĕresco *v.i.* 3, to feel pity

mĭsĕrĭa, ae *f,* misfortune, wretchedness

mĭsĕrĭcordĭa, ae *f,* pity

mĭsĕrĭcors, dis *adj,* merciful

mĭsĕror *v.t.* 1, *dep,* to lament, pity

missĭle, is *n,* missile, javelin

missĭlis, e *adj,* that is thrown

missĭo, ōnis *f,* throwing, discharge, release

missus, ūs *m,* dispatching, throwing, shot

mĭtella, ae *f,* turban, bandage

mĭtesco *v.i.* 3, to grow mild or soft or ripe

mītĭgātĭo, ōnis *f,* mitigation

mītĭgo *v.t.* 1, to make soft or ripe, to tame, soothe

mītis, e *adj,* mild, ripe, calm

mītra, ae *f,* headband

mitto, mīsi, missum *v.t.* 3, to send, announce, cease, release, throw, escort

mītŭlus, i *m,* sea mussel

mixtūta, ae *f,* mixture

mixtus, a, um *adj,* mixed

mōbĭlis, e *adj, adv,* īter, movable, agile, flexible, fickle

mōbĭlĭtas, ātis *f,* speed, inconstancy

mŏdĕrāmen, ĭnis *n,* rudder, management

mŏdĕrātĭo, ōnis *f,* moderation, restraint

mŏdĕrātor, ōris *m,* manager

mŏdĕrātus, a, um *adj, adv,* ē, moderate

mŏdĕror *v.t.* 1, *dep,* to restrain, govern

mŏdestĭa, ae *f,* moderation, discretion, modesty

mŏdestus, a, um *adj, adv,* ē, modest, gentle

mŏdĭcus, a, um *adj, adv,* ē, modest, ordinary

mŏdĭfĭcātus, a, um *adj,* measured

mŏdĭus, ii *m,* peck, measure

mŏdŏ *adv,* only, but, just, lately; non mŏdŏ not only; mŏdŏ … mŏdŏ at one time … at another time

mŏdŭlātor, ōris *m,* musician

mŏdŭlor *v.t.* 1, *dep,* to sing, play

mŏdŭlātus, a, um *adj,* sung, played

mŏdŭlus, i *m,* a small measure

mŏdus, i *m,* measure, quantity, rhythm, limit, restriction, end, method, way

moechus, i *m,* adulterer

moenĭa, ĭum *n.pl,* ramparts

mŏla, ae *f,* millstone, grain mixed with salt to be sprinkeld on sacrificial animals

mŏlāris, is *m,* millstone

mōles, is *f,* mass, bulk, dam, pier, power, difficulty

mŏlestĭa, ae *f,* trouble, affectation

mŏlestus, a, um *adj, adv,* ē, troublesome, affected

mōlīmen, ĭnis *n,* undertaking, attempt

mōlīmentum, i *n,* undertaking,

attempt

mōlīor *v.i.t.* 4, to strive, depart; to rouse, construct, attempt

mŏlītor, ōris *m*, miller

mōlītor, ōris *m*, contriver

mollesco *v.i.* 3, to grow soft

mollīo *v.t.* 4, to soften, restrain

mollis, e *adj, adv,* **īter** soft, supple, tender, effeminate

mollītĭa, ae *f*, softness, weakness

mollītĭes, ēi *f*, softness, weakness

mollītūdo, ĭnis *f*, softness, weakness

mŏlo, ŭi, ĭtum *v.t.* 3, to grind

mōmentum, i *n*, movement, motion, moment, instant, cause, influence, importance

mŏnăcha, ae *f*, nun

mŏnastērĭum, ii *n*, monastery

mŏnēdŭla, ae *f*, jackdaw

mŏnĕo *v.t.* 2, to warn, advise, remind, instruct, tell

mŏnēta, ae *f*, the mint, coin

mŏnētālis, e *adj*, of the mint

mŏnīle, is *n*, necklace, collar

mŏnītĭo, ōnis *f*, warning

mŏnītor, ōris *m*, adviser, instructor

mŏnītum, i *n*, advice

mŏnītus, ūs *m*, warning, omen

mŏnŏcĕros, ōtis *m*, unicorn

mŏnŏpōlĭum, ii *n*, monopoly

mons, ntis *m*, mountain

monstrātĭo, ōnis *f*, showing, pointing out

monstrātor, ōris *m*, teacher

monstro *v.t.* 1, to show, tell

monstrum, i *n*, omen, monster

monstrŭōsus, a, um *adj*, strange, monstrous

montānus, a, um *adj*, of a mountain, mountainous

montĭcŏla, ae *c*, mountain-dweller

montĭvăgus, a, um *adj*, wandering in the mountains

montŭōsus, a, um *adj*, mountainous

mŏnŭmentum, i *n*, monument, memorial, written record

mŏra, ae *f*, delay, hindrance

mōrālis, e *adj*, moral

mōrātus, a, um *adj*, mannered;

mŏrātus *partic. from* **mŏror,** having delayed

morbĭdus, a, um *adj*, diseased

morbus, i *m*, illness, disease

mordax, ācis *adj*, biting, stinging

mordĕo, mŏmordi, morsum *v.t.* 2, to bite, clasp, sting

mordīcus, a, um *adj*, by biting

mōres see mos

mŏrētum, i *n*, salad

mŏrībundus, a, um *adj*, dying

mŏrĭens, ntis *adj*, dying

mŏrĭor, mortŭus *v.i.* 3, *dep*, to die

mŏror *v.i.t.* 1, *dep*, to delay

mōrōsĭtas, ātis *f*, fretfulness

mōrōsus, a, um *adj*, fretful, fastidious

mors, mortis *f*, death

morsus, ūs *m*, bite, pungency

mortālis, e *adj*, mortal, human, temporary

mortālis, is *c*, human being

mortālĭtas, ātis *f*, mortality

mortārĭum, ii *n*, a mortar

mortĭfer, ĕra, ĕrum *adj*, fatal

mortŭus, a, um *adj*, dead

mortŭus, i *m*, dead person

mōrum, i *n*, blackberry

mōrus, i *f*, blackberry-bush

mos, mōris *m*, custom, manner, habit, fashion; *in pl*, character

mōtăcilla, ae *f*, wagtail

mōtĭo, ōnis *f*, motion

mōto *v.t.* 1, to move about

mōtus, ūs *m*, motion, movement, impulse, emotion, rebellion

mŏvĕo, mōvi, mōtum *v.t.* 2, to move, stir, excite, cause

mox *adv*, soon, immediately

mūcĭdus, a, um *adj*, musty

mūcor, ōris *m*, mouldiness

mūcōsus, a, um *adj*, mucous

mūcro, ōnis *m*, sword's point

mūgil, is *m*, mullet

mūgĭnor *v.i.* 1, *dep*, to hesitate

mūgĭo *v.i.* 4, to low, bellow, groan, crash

mūgītus, ūs *m*, bellowing, roaring

mūla, ae *f*, she-mule

mulcĕo, si, sum *v.t.* 2, to stroke, soothe

mulco *v.t.* 1, to maltreat

mulctra, ae *f*, milk-bucket

mulctrārĭum, ii *n*, milk-bucket

mulgĕo, si, sum *v.t.* 2, to milk

mŭlĭĕbris, e *adj, adv*, **ĭter**, female, effeminate

mŭlĭer, ĕris *f*, woman, wife

mŭlĭercŭla, ae *f*, girl

mūlĭo, ōnis *m*, mule-driver

mullus, i *m*, mullet

mulsum, i *n*, honey-wine

multa, ae *f*, penalty, fine

multātĭo, ōnis *f*, penalty, fine

multi see **multus**

multĭfārĭam *adv*, on many sides

multĭplex, ĭcis *adj*, with many windings, numerous, many

multĭplĭcātĭo, ōnis *f*, multiplication

multĭplĭco *v.t.* 1, to multiply

multĭtūdo, ĭnis *f*, crowd, great number

multō *adv*, a great deal

multo *v.t.* 1, to punish

multum *adv*, very much, greatly

multus, a, um *adj*, much; *pl*, many

mūlus, i *m*, mule

mundĭtĭa, ae *f*, cleanliness, neatness

mundĭtĭes, ēi *f*, cleanliness, neatness

mundo *v.t.* 1, to cleanse

mundus, a, um *adj*, clean, elegant

mundus, i *m*, world, universe, ornaments

mūnĕro *v.t.* 1 (**mūnĕror**, *v.t.* 1, *dep*.), to reward, honour

mūnĭa, ōrum *n.pl*, duties

mūnĭceps, cĭpis *c*, citizen

mūnĭcĭpālis, e, *adj*, municipal

mūnĭcĭpĭum, ii *n*, self-governing town

mūnĭfĭcentĭa, ae *f*, generosity

mūnĭfĭcus, a, um *adj, adv*, **ē**, generous

mūnīmen, ĭnis *n*, rampart, protection

mūnīmentum, i *n*, rampart, protection

mūnĭo *v.t.* 4, to fortify, secure, make a way

mūnītĭo, ōnis *f*, fortification

mūnītor, ōris *m*, engineer

mūnītus, a, um *adj*, fortified

mūnus, ĕris *n*, service, duty, employment, post, tax, gift, public show

mūnuscŭlum, i *n*, small present

mūrālis, e *adj*, of a wall

mūrex, ĭcis *m*, purple fish, purple dye, pointed rock

mŭrĭa, ae *f*, brine, pickle

murmur, ŭris *n*, murmur, crash

murmŭro *v.i.* 1, to murmur, roar

murra, ae *f*, myrrh (tree)

murrĕus, a, um *adj*, perfumed with myrrh

mūrus, i *m*, wall, defence

mūs, mūris *c*, mouse

mūsa, ae *f*, goddess of the arts

musca, ae *f*, a fly

muscĭpŭlum, i *n*, mousetrap

muscōsus, a, um *adj*, mossy

muscŭlus, i *m*, little mouse, mussel, muscle, military shed

muscus, i *m*, moss

mūsēum, i *n*, museum

mūsĭca, ae *f*, music

mūsĭcus, a, um *adj*, musical

mūsĭcus, i *m*, musician

musso *v.i.* 1, to mutter, be silent, be in doubt

mustēla, ae *f*, weasel

mustum, i *n*, new wine

mūtābĭlis, e *adj*, changeable

mūtābĭlĭtas, ātis *f*, changeableness

mūtātĭo, ōnis *f*, alteration

mŭtĭlo *v.t.* 1, to cut off, maim

mŭtĭlus, a, um *adj*, maimed

mūto *v.i.t.* 1, to alter, change

mŭtŭlus, i *m*, bracket

mūtŭō *adv*, in turns

mūtŭor *v.t.* 1, *dep*, to borrow

mūtus, a, um *adj*, dumb, mute

mūtŭum, i *n*, loan

mūtŭus, a, um *adj*, borrowed, mutual

mўrīca, ae *f*; **mўrīce, es** *f*, a shrub, tamarisk

myrr... see **murr...**

myrtētum, i *n*, myrtle grove

myrtĕus, a, um *adj*, of myrtle

myrtum, i *n*, myrtle berry

myrtus, i *f*, myrtle tree

mysta (es), ae *f*, priest of Ceres' mysteries

mystērĭum, ii *n*, secret rites

mystĭcus, a, um *adj*, mystical

N

naevus, i *m*, wart, mole
Nāïās, ădis *f*, water-nymph
nam *conj*, for
namque *conj*, for indeed
nanciscor, nactus *v.t.* 3, *dep*, to
  obtain, meet with, find
nānus, i *m*, dwarf
nāpus, i *m*, turnip
narcissus, i *m*, narcissus
nardus, i *f*, perfumed balm
nāris, is *f*, nostril; *pl*, nose
narrātĭo, ōnis *f*, narrative
narrātor, ōris *m*, narrator
narro *v.t.* 1, to tell, relate
narthēcĭum, ii *n*, medicine chest
nascor, nātus *v.i.* 3, *dep*, to be
  born, rise, proceed
nasturtĭum, ii *n*, cress
nāsus, i *m*, nose
nāsūtus, a, um *adj*, large-nosed
nāta, ae *f*, daughter
nātālīcĭus, a, um *adj*, birthday
nātālis, e *adj*, of birth
nātālis, is *m*, birthday
nătantes, um *f.pl*, fish
nătātĭo, ōnis *f*, swimming
nătātor, ōris *m*, swimmer
nātĭo, ōnis *f*, race, nation
nătis, is, *f*, buttock
nātīvus, a, um *adj*, created,
  inborn, natural
năto *v.i.* 1, to swim, float, waver
nătrix, īcis *f*, water snake
nātūra, ae *f*, nature
nātūrālis, e *adj, adv*, ĭter, by birth,
  natural
nātus, ūs *m*, birth
nātus, i *m*, son
nātus, a, um *adj*, born, aged
nauarchus, i *m*, ship's master
naufrăgĭum, ii *n*, shipwreck
naufrăgus, a, um *adj*,
  shipwrecked
naumăchĭa, ae *f*, mock sea fight
nausĕa, ae *f*, seasickness
nausĕābundus, a, um *adj*, seasick
nausĕo *v.i.* 1, to be seasick
nauta, ae *m*, sailor
nautĭcus, a, um *adj*, nautical
nāvālĭa, ĭum *n.pl*, dockyard
nāvāle, is *n*, dockyard

nāvālis, e *adj*, naval
nāvĭcŭla, ae *f*, boat
nāvĭcŭlārĭus, ii *m*, shipowner
nāvĭfrăgus, a, um *adj*, ship
  wrecking
nāvĭgābĭlis, e *adj*, navigable
nāvĭgātĭo, ōnis *f*, sailing
nāvĭger, ĕra, ĕrum *adj*, navigable
nāvĭgĭa, ōrum *n.pl*, ships,
  shipping
nāvĭgĭum, ii *n*, ship, boat
nāvĭgo *v.i.t.* 1, to sail; navigate
nāvis, is *f*, ship; nāvis longa,
  warship
nāvīta, ae *m*, (nauta), sailor
nāvīter *adv*, completely
nāvo *v.t.* 1, to do vigorously
nāvus, a, um *adj*, hard-working
nē *conj*, lest; nē ... quidem, not
  even ...
-nĕ attached to the first word of
  a sentence to form a question
nē *interj*, indeed, truly
nĕbŭla, ae *f*, mist, fog, smoke
nĕbŭlo, ōnis *m*, rascal, wretch
nĕbŭlōsus, a, um *adj*, misty
nĕc *adv*, not; *conj*, and not; nĕc
  ... nĕc, neither ... nor
necdum *conj*, not yet
nĕcessārĭus, a, um *adj, adv*, ō,
  unavoidable, necessary, related
nĕcessārĭus, ii *m*, relative
nĕcesse *indecl. adj*, unavoidable
nĕcessĭtas, ātis *f*, necessity,
  compulsion, destiny
nĕcessĭtūdo, ĭnis *f*, necessity,
  relationship
necnĕ *adv*, or not
nec-non and also
nĕco *v.t.* 1, to kill
nĕcŏpīnans, ntis *adj*, unaware
nĕcŏpīnātus, a, um *adj, adv*, ō,
  unexpected
nĕcŏpīnus, a, um *adj*, unexpected
nectar, ăris *n*, the drink of the
  gods
nectārĕus, a, um *adj*, of nectar
necto, xŭi, xum *v.t.* 3, to tie,
  fasten together
nĕcŭbi *adv*, so that nowhere
nēdum *conj*, still less
nĕfandus, a, um *adj*, abominable,
  heinous, wrong

nĕfārĭus 90

nĕfārĭus, a, um *adj,* heinous, wrong

nĕfas *n, indecl,* wrong, sin

nefastus, a, um *adj, with* **dies,** a day on which neither trials nor public meetings could be held, wicked, unlucky

nĕgātĭo, ōnis *f,* denial

nĕgĭto *v.t.* 1, to persist in denying

neglectus, a, um *adj,* despised

neglĕgens (neglĭgens), ntis *adj,* careless, indifferent

neglĕgentĭa, ae *f,* carelessness

neglĕgo, xi, ctum *v.t.* 3, to neglect, slight, despise

nĕgo *v.i.t.* 1, to say no (not); refuse

nĕgōtĭātĭo, ōnis *f,* wholesale business, banking

nĕgōtĭātor, ōris *m,* wholesaler, banker

nĕgōtĭor *v.i.* 1, *dep,* to carry on business, trade or banking

nĕgōtĭōsus, a, um *adj,* busy

nĕgōtĭum, ii *n,* business, occupation, difficulty

nēmo, ĭnis *m, f,* nobody

nĕmŏrālis, e *adj,* woody

nĕmŏrōsus, a, um *adj,* woody

nempĕ *conj,* certainly

nĕmus, ŏris *n,* wood, grove

nēnĭa, ae *f,* funeral hymn, sad song, popular song

nĕo, nēvi, nētum *v.t.* 2, to spin

nĕpa, ae *f,* scorpion

nĕpos, ōtis *m, f,* grandson (...daughter), descendant, spendthrift

neptis, is *f,* granddaughter

nēquam *indecl. adj, adv* **nēquĭter,** worthless, bad

nēquăquam *adv,* not at all

nĕque *adv,* not; *conj,* and not; **nĕque ... nĕque,** neither ... nor

nĕquĕo, īvi (ĭi), ĭtum *v.i.* 4, to be unable

nēquīquam *adv,* in vain

nēquĭtĭa, ae *f,* worthlessness, idleness, extravagance

nervōsus, a, um *adj, adv,* **ē,** sinewy, energetic

nervus, i *m,* sinew, string of musical instrument or bow

nescĭo *v.t.* 4, not to know, to be unable

nescĭus, a, um *adj,* unaware

neu *adv,* and so that ... not

neuter, tra, trum *adj,* neither the one nor the other

neutĭquam *adv,* not at all

neutrō *adv,* neither way

nēve *adv,* and so that ... not

nex, nĕcis *f,* death, slaughter

nexĭlis, e *adj,* tied together

nexum, i *n,* slavery for debt, obligation

nexus, ūs *m,* tying together

nī *conj,* unless

nictātĭo, ōnis *f,* winking

nicto *v.i.* 1, to wink, blink

nīdor, ōris *m,* steam, smell

nīdŭlus, i *m,* little nest

nīdus, i *m,* nest, home; *in pl,* nestlings

nĭger, gra, grum *adj,* black, dark, ill-omened, funereal

nigrans, ntis *adj,* black

nigresco, grŭi *v.i.* 3, to grow dark

nĭhil (nīl) *n, indecl,* nothing

nĭhĭli of no value

nĭhĭlōmĭnus *adj,* nevertheless

nĭhĭlum, i *n,* nothing

nīl *n, indecl,* nothing

nimbĭfer, ĕra, ĕrum *adj,* stormy, rainy

nimbōsus, a, um *adj,* stormy, rainy

nimbus, i *m,* heavy rain, rain-cloud, cloud

nīmīrum *adv,* without doubt

nĭmis *adv,* too much

nĭmĭum *adv,* too much

nĭmĭum, ii *n,* excess

nĭmĭus, a, um *adj,* excessive

ningit *v.i.* 3, *impers,* it is snowing

nĭsĭ *conj,* if not, unless

nīsus, ūs *m,* pressure, effort, labour of childbirth

nītēdŭla, ae *f,* dormouse

nĭtens, ntis *adj,* bright, shining, sleek, beautiful

nĭtĕo *v.i.* 2, to shine, to look handsome, thrive

nĭtĕsco, tŭi *v.i.* 3, to shine

nĭtĭdus, a, um *adj,* shining, sleek, handsome, refined

nŏvus

nītor, nīsus (nixus) *v.i.* 3, *dep,* to lean, press forward, fly, make an effort, argue

nītor, ōris *m,* brightness, splendour, beauty, elegance

nītrum, i *n,* soda

nĭvālis, e *adj,* snowy, cold

nĭvĕus, a, um *adj,* snowy, white

nĭvōsus, a, um *adj,* snowy

nix, nĭvis *f,* snow

nixor *v.i.* 1, *dep,* to strive

nixus, ūs *m,* pressure, effort, labour of childbirth

no *v.i.* 1, to swim

nōbĭlis, e *adj,* famous, noble

nōvĭlĭtas, ātis *f,* fame, noble birth

nōbĭlĭto *v.t.* 1, to make famous

nōbis *dat. or abl. of* **nos**

nŏcens, ntis *adj,* wicked, bad, harmful, injurious

nŏcĕo *v.i.* 2, *with dat,* to harm

nocte *adv,* at night

noctĭlūca, ae *f,* moon

noctĭvăgus, a, um *adj,* wandering at night

noctu *adv,* at night

noctŭa, ae *f,* night owl

nocturnus, a, um *adj,* nocturnal

nōdo *v.t.* 1, to tie in a knot

mōdōsus, a, um *adj,* knotty, difficult

nōdus, i *m,* knot, knob, band, obligation, difficulty

nōli, nōlĭte *imper,* do not …

nōlo, nolle, nōlŭi *v, irreg,* to be unwilling

nōmen, ĭnis *n,* name, debt, fame, repute, excuse, reason

nōmenclātor, ōris *m,* slave who reminded his master of the names of the people he met

nōmĭnātim *adj,* by name

nōmĭnātĭo, ōnis *f,* nomination

nōmĭnātus, a, um *adj,* renowned

nōmĭno *v.t.* 1, to name, make famous

nŏmisma, ătis *n,* a coin

nōn *adv,* not

nōnae, ārum *f.pl,* the Nones; 5th or 7th day of the month

nōnāgēni, ae *adj,* ninety each

nōnāgēsĭmus, a, um *adj,* ninetieth

nōnāgĭes *adv,* ninety times

nōnāgintā *indecl. adj,* ninety

nondum *adv,* not yet

nongenti, ae, a *adj,* nine hundred

nonnĕ *adv,* used to introduce a question expecting the answer 'yes'

nonnēmo, ĭnis *m,* someone

nonnĭhil *n,* something

nonnĭsi *adv,* only

nonnullus, a, um *adj,* several

nonnumquam *adv,* sometimes

nōnus, a, um *adj,* ninth

norma, ae *f,* rule, pattern, standard

nōs *pron, pl.* of **ĕgŏ,** we, us

noscĭto *v.t.* 1, to know, observe

nosco, nōvi, nōtum *v.t.* 3, to get to know, know, recognize, acknowledge

noster, tra, trum *adj,* our, ours

nostras, ātis *adj,* of our country

nŏta, ae *f,* mark, sign, brand

nŏtābĭlis, e *adj,* noteworthy

nŏtātĭo, ōnis *f,* branding, observation

nŏthus, a, um *adj,* illegitimate, counterfeit

nōtĭo, ōnis *f,* investigation

nōtĭtĭa, ae *f,* fame, knowledge

nōto *v.t.* 1, to mark, write, indicate, brand, reprimand

nōtus, a, um *adj,* well-known

nŏtus, i *m,* the south wind

nŏvācŭla, ae *f,* razor

nŏvālis, is *f,* fallow land

nŏvellus, a, um *adj,* young, new

nŏvem *indecl. adj,* nine

Nŏvember (mensis) November

nŏvendĭālis, e *adj,* lasting nine days

nŏvēnus, a, um *adj,* nine each

nŏverca, ae *f,* stepmother

nŏvīcĭus, a, um *adj,* new

nŏvĭens *adv,* nine times

nŏvĭes *adv,* nine times

nŏvissĭmus, a, um *adj,* last; in *m.pl, or* **nŏvissĭmum agmen** rear ranks

nŏvĭtas, ātis *f,* novelty, unusualness

nŏvo *v.t.* 1, to renew, refresh, change

nŏvus, a, um *adj,* new, recent, fresh; **nŏvus hŏmo** an upstart; **nŏvae res** revolution

nox, noctis *f,* night

noxa, ae   *f,* injury, harm fault, crime

noxĭa, ae   *f,* injury, harm, fault, crime

noxĭus, a, um   *adj,* harmful, guilty

nūbes, is   *f,* cloud

nūbĭfer, ĕra, ĕrum   *adj,* cloud-capped, cloud-bringing

nūbĭla, ōrum   *n.pl,* the clouds

nūbĭlis, e   *adj,* marriageable

nūbĭlus, a, um   *adj,* overcast

nūbo, psi, ptum   *v.i.t.* 3, *with dat,* to marry

nŭclĕus, i   *m,* nut, kernel

nūdĭus   *with a number* **(tertĭus)** (three) days ago

nūdo   *v.t.* 1, to strip, expose

nūdus, a, um   *adj,* naked, destitute of, poor, simple

nūgae, ārum   *f.pl,* jokes, nonsense, trifles

nūgātor, ōris   *m,* silly person

nūgātōrĭus, a, um   *adj,* trifling

nūgor   *v.i.* 1, *dep,* to play the fool

nullus, a, um   *adj,* none, no

nullus, ĭus   *m,* no-one

num   *adv,* used to introduce a question expecting answer 'no'; whether

nūmen, ĭnis   *n,* divine will, divine power, divinity

nŭmĕrābĭlis, e   *adj,* able to be counted

nŭmĕrātor, ōris   *m,* counter

nŭmĕrātum, i   *n,* ready money

nŭmĕro   *v.t.* 1, to count, pay out, number

nŭmĕrō   *adv,* in number, just

nŭmĕrōsus, a, um   *adj, adv,* ē, numerous, rhythmic

nŭmĕrus, i   *m,* number, band (of soldiers), class, category, sequence, rhythm, poetic metre

nummārĭus, a, um   *adj,* of money

nummātus, a, um   *adj,* rich

nummus, i   *m,* money, a Roman silver coin, farthing

numquam   *adv,* never

numquid   *interr. adv,* is there anything…?

nunc   *adv,* now, at present

nuncia, nuncius …   see nunt…

nuncŭpo   *v.t.* 1, to call, name

nundĭnae, ārum   *f.pl,* ninth day, market-day

nundĭnātĭo, ōnis   *f,* trading

nundĭnor   *v.i.t.* 1, *dep,* to trade; buy, sell

nunquam   *adv,* never

nuntĭātĭo, ōnis   *f,* announcement

nuntĭo   *v.t.* 1, to announce, tell

nuntĭus, i   *m,* messenger, message

nūper   *adv,* lately, recently

nupta, ae   *f,* wife, bride

nuptĭae, ārum   *f.pl,* marriage

nuptĭālis, e   *adj,* of marriage

nuptus, a, um   *adj,* married

nŭrus, ūs   *f,* daughter-in-law, young wife

nusquam   *adv,* nowhere

nūto   *v.i.* 1, to nod, waver

nūtrīcĭus, a, um   *adj,* foster-father

nūtrīco   *v.t.* 1, to nurse, rear

nūtrīcula, ae   *f,* nurse

nūtrīmen, ĭnis   *n,* nourishment

nūtrīmentum, i   *n,* nourishment

nūtrĭo   *v.t.* 4, to feed, bring up, support

nūtrix, īcis   *f,* nurse

nūtus, ūs   *m,* nod, command

nux, nŭcis   *f,* nut

nympha, ae   *f,* bride, nymph (demi-goddess inhabiting woods, trees, fountains, etc.)

O

ŏb   *prep. with acc,* on account of, in front of

ŏbaerātus, a, um   *adj,* involved in debt

ŏbambŭlo   *v.i.* 1, to walk about

obdo, dĭdi, dĭtum   *v.t.* 3, to shut, place, expose

obdormĭo   *v.i.* 4, to fall asleep

obdormisco   *v.i.* 3, to fall asleep

obdūco, xi, ctum   *v.t.* 3, to lead forward, bring forward, cover over, swallow

obdūresco, rŭi   *v.i.* 3, to become hardened

obdūro   *v.i.* 1, to persist

ŏbēdĭens, ntis   *adj,* obedient

ŏbēdĭentĭa, ae   *f,* obedience

ŏbēdĭo   *v.i.* 4, to obey, be subject to

ŏbĕliscus, i   *m*, obelisk

ŏbĕo   *v.i.t.* 4, to go to meet, die, set (constellations); to go to, reach, travel over, visit, undertake, perform

ŏbĕquĭto   *v.i.* 1, to ride towards

ŏbēsĭtas, ātis   *f*, fatness

ŏbēsus, a, um   *adj*, fat, dull

ōbex, ĭcis   *m, f*, bolt, barrier

obiăcĕo   *v.i.* 2, to lie opposite

ōbĭcĭo, iēci, iectum   *v.t.* 3, to throw forward, expose, oppose, taunt, reproach

obiectātĭo, ōnis   *f*, reproach

obiecto   *v.t.* 1, to place against, expose, reproach, accuse

obiectus, ūs   *m*, opposing, putting in the way

obiectus, a, um   *adj*, lying opposite

ŏbĭtus, ūs   *m*, setting, downfall

obiurgātĭo, ōnis   *f*, rebuke

obiurgātor, ōris   *m*, blamer

obirgātōrĭus, a, um   *adj*, reproachful

obiurgo   *v.t.* 1, to blame, rebuke

oblectāmen, ĭnis   *n*, pleasure, delight

oblectāmentum, i   *n*, pleasure, delight

oblecto   *v.t.* 1, to amuse, please

oblĭgātĭo, ōnis   *f*, obligation

oblĭgo   *v.t.* 1, to bind, put under obligation, render liable

oblĭmo   *v.t.* 1, to cover with mud, squander

oblĭno, lēvi, lĭtum   *v.t.* 3, to besmear, defile

oblīquo   *v.t.* 1, to bend aside

oblīquus, a, um   *adj, adv*, ē, slanting, sideways

oblīvĭo, ōnis   *f*, oblivion

oblīvĭōsus, a, um   *adj*, forgetful, producing forgetfulness

oblīviscor, oblītus   *v.* 3, *dep, with genit*, to forget

oblīvĭum, ii   *n*, oblivion

oblōquor, lŏcūtus   *v.i.* 3, *dep*, to contradict, accompany a song

obluctor   *v.i.* 1, *dep*, to struggle against

obmūtesco, tŭi   *v.i.* 3, to become speechless

obnītor, xus   *v.i.* 3, to become speechless

obnītor, xus   *v.i.* 3, *dep*, to push or struggle against

obnixus, a, um   *adj*, resolute

obnoxĭus, a, um   *adj*, resolute

obnoxĭus, a, um   *adj*, liable to, submissive, indebted

obnūbo, psi, ptum   *v.t.* 3, to veil

obnuntĭātĭo, ōnis   *f*, announcement of bad omens

obnuntĭo   *v.t.* 1, to announce bad omens

ŏboedĭens, oboedĭo   see obēd...

ŏbŏrĭor, ortus   *v.i.* 4, *dep*, to arise, appear

obrēpo, psi, ptum   *v.t.* 3, to creep up to, surprise

obrĭgesco, gŭi   *v.i.* 3, to stiffen

obrŏgo   *v.t.* 1, to invalidate

obrŭo, ŭi, ŭtum   *v.t.* 3, to overwhelm, bury, hide

obsaepĭo, psi, ptum   *v.t.* 4, to fence in

obscēnĭtas, ātis   *f*, obscenity, foulness

obscēnus, a, um   *adj*, ominous, filthy, obscene

obscūrĭtas, ātis   *f*, uncertainty, lowness

obscūro   *v.t.* 1, to darken, hide

obscūrus, a, um   *adj, adv*, ē, dark, shady, indistinct, ignoble, humble, reserved

obsĕcrātĭo, ōnis   *f*, appeal

obsĕcro   *v.t.* 1, to implore

obsĕcundo   *v.t.* 1, to humour, obey

obsēp...   see obsaep...

obsĕquens, ntis   *adj*, amenable

obsĕquĭum, ii   *n*, compliance, obedience

obsĕquor, sĕcūtus   *v.* 3, *dep, with dat*, to comply with, submit to, humour

obsĕro   *v.t.* 1, to fasten

obsĕro, sēvi, sĭtum   *v.t.* 3, to sow, plant

observans, ntis   *adj*, attentive

observantĭa, ae   *f*, attention, respect

observātĭo, ōnis   *f*, care, observation

observo *v.t.* 1, to watch, take note of, respect, comply with

obses, ĭdis *m, f,* hostage

obsessĭo, ōnis *f,* blockade

obsessor, ōris *m,* besieger

obsĭdĕo, sēdi, sessum *v.t.* 2, to besiege, hem in, frequent

obsĭdĭo, ōnis *f,* siege

obsīdo *v.t.* 3, to besiege

obsignātor, ōris *m,* witness

obsigno *v.t.* 1, to seal up

obsisto, stĭti, stĭtum *v.i.* 3, to resist, oppose

obsĭtus, a, um *adj,* covered over

obsŏlesco, lēvi, lētum *v.i.* 3, to wear out, decay

obsŏlētus, a, um *adj,* worn out, low, mean

obsōnĭum, ii *n,* eatables

obsōnātor, ōris *m,* caterer

obsōno *v.t.* 1, (**obsōnor** *v.i.* 1, *dep*), to cater

obsorbĕo *v.t.* 2, to swallow

obstĕtrix, īcis *f,* midwife

obstĭnātĭo, ōnis *f,* firmness, obstinacy

obstĭnātus, a, um *adj, adv, ē,* determined, resolute, stubborn

obstĭpesco, pŭi *v.i.* 3, to be amazed

obstīpus, a, um *adj,* bent

obsto, stĭti, ātum *v.i.* 1, *with dat,* to obstruct, withstand

obstrĕpo, ŭi, ĭtum *v.i.* 3, to roar at, resound

obstringo, nxi, ctum *v.t.* 3, to tie up, put under obligation

obstrŭo, xi, ctum *v.t.* 3, to build up, barricade, impede

obstŭpĕfăcĭo, fēci, factum *v.t.* 3, to astonish

obstŭpesco, pŭi *v.i.* 3, to be stupified, amazed

obsum, obesse, obfŭi *v.i, irreg,* to hinder, injure

obsŭo, ŭi, ūtum *v.t.* 3, to sew up

obsurdesco, dŭi *v.i.* 3, to grow deaf

obtĕgo, xi, ctum *v.t.* 3, to cover up

obtempĕro *v.t.* 1, *with dat,* to comply with

obtendo, di, tum *v.t.* 3, to spread before, hide

obtentus, ūs *m,* outspreading

obtĕro, trīvi, trītum *v.t.* 3, to crush to pieces

obtestātĭo, ōnis *f,* appeal

obtestor *v.t.* 1, *dep,* to call as a witness, implore

obtexo, xŭi *v.t.* 3, to cover up

obtĭcesco, tĭcŭi *v.i.* 3, to be struck dumb

obtĭnĕo, nŭi, tentum *v.i.t.* 2, to prevail, continue; keep, hold, gain, obtain

obtingo, tĭgi *v.i.* 3, to befall

obtorpesco, pŭi *v.i.* 3, to become stiff

obtorquĕo, si, tum *v.t.* 2, to twist, wrench

obtrectātĭo, ōnis *f,* disparagement

obtrectātor, ōris *m,* slander

obtrecto *v.i.t.* 1, to disparge

obtrunco *v.t.* 1, to trim, kill

obtundo, tŭdi, tūsum *v.t.* 3, to blunt, weaken, deafen, annoy

obtūrācŭlum, i *n,* stopper

obtūrāmentum, i *n,* stopper

obturbo *v.t.* 1, to disturb

obtūro *v.t.* 1, to close

obtūsus, a, um *adj,* blunt, dull

obtūtus, ūs *m,* gaze, stare

ŏbumbro *v.t.* 1, to overshadow

ŏbuncus, a, um *adj,* hooked

ŏbustus, a, um *adj,* hardened in fire

obvĕnĭo, vēni, ventum *v.i.* 4, to meet, befall one, happen

obversor *v.i.* 1, *dep,* to move to and fro, hover

obversus, a, um *adj,* directed towards

obverto, ti, sum *v.t.* 3, to turn downwards

obvĭam *adv, with verbs of motion,* towards, against

obvĭus, a, um *adj,* in the way, so as to meet, courteous, exposed

obvolvo, volvi, vŏlūtum *v.t.* 3, to wrap round, cover

occaeco *v.t.* 1, to blind, hide

occāsĭo, ōnis *f,* opportunity

occāsus, ūs *m,* setting (of sun, etc.) downfall, ruin

occĭdens, ntis *m,* the west

occĭdentālis, e *adj*, west
occīdĭo, ōnis *f*, massacre
occīdo, cīdi, cīsum *v.t*. 3, to strike
  down, crush, kill
occĭdo, cĭdi, cāsum *v.i*. 3, to fall,
  perish, set (of sun, etc.)
occĭdŭus, a, um *adj*, setting,
  western
occīsĭo, ōnis *f*, slaughter
occlūdo, si, sum *v.t*. 3, to close
occo *v.t*. 1, to harrow
occŭbo *v.i*. 1, to lie down, rest
occŭlo, lŭi, ltum *v.t*. 3, to hide
occultātĭo, ōnis *f*, concealment
occulto *v.t*. 1, to hide
occultus, a, um *adj, adv*, ē,
  hidden, secret
occumbo, cŭbŭi, cŭbĭtum *v.i*. 3,
  to die
occŭpātĭo, ōnis *f*, employment
occŭpātus, a, um *adj*, busy
occŭpo *v.t*. 1, to seize, occupy,
  attack, anticipate, fill
occurro, curri, cursum *v.i*. 3, to
  meet
occursātĭo, ōnis *f*, greeting
occurso *v.i*. 1, to meet, attack
occursus, ūs *m*, meeting
ōcĕănus, i *m*, ocean
ŏcellus, i *m*, small eye, darling
ōchra, ae *f*, ochre
ōcĭor, ĭus *comp. adj*, swifter
ōcĭus *adv*, more quickly
ŏcrĕa, ae *f*, leg-shield, greave
octāvus, a, um *adj*, eighth
octĭens (octĭes) *adv*, eight times
octingenti, ae, a *pl. adj*, eight
  hundred
octŏ *indecl. adj*, eight
Octōber (mensis) October
octōgēsĭmus, a, um *adj*, eightieth
octōginta *indecl. adj*, eighty
octōgōnum, i *n*, octagon
octōni, ae, a *pl. adj*, eight each
octōphŏron, i *m*, sedan carried by
  eight men
ŏcŭlārĭus, a, um *adj*, of the eyes
ŏcŭlus, i *m*, eye, bud
ōdi, ōdisse *v.t, defect*, to hate
ŏdĭōsus, a, um *adj, adv*, ē,
  hateful, troublesome
ŏdĭum, ii *n*, odour, smell
ŏdor, ōris *m*, odour, smell

ŏdōrātĭo, ōnis *f*, smell
ŏdōrātus, ūs *m*, smelling
ŏdōrātus, a, um *adj*, scented
ŏdōrĭfer, ĕra, ĕrum *adj*, fragrant
ŏdōro *v.t*. 1, to perfume
ŏdōror *v.t*. 1, *dep*, to smell out,
  investigate
ŏdōrus, a, um *adj*, fragrant
oestrus, i *m*, gad fly
offa, ae *f*, morsel
offendo, di, sum *v.i.t*. 3, to make
  a mistake; strike against, meet
  with, find, offend
offensa, ae *f*, hatred, crime
offensĭo, ōnis *f*, stumbling,
  dislike, displeasure
offensus, a, um *adj*, offensive,
  offended
offĕro, offerre, obtŭli, oblātum *v.t*,
  irreg, to offer, show, cause, bring
officīna, ae *f*, workshop
officĭo, fēci, fectum *v.i*. 3, to
  obstruct, hinder
officĭōsus, a, um *adj, adv*, ē,
  obliging, courteous
officĭum, ii *n*, kindness, duty,
  employment, office
offirmātus, a, um *adj*, firm
offulgĕo, si *v.i*. 2, to shine on,
  appear
offundo, fūdi, fūsum *v.t*. 3, to
  pour out, spread over
ŏhē *interj*, ho there!
ŏlĕa, ae *f*, olive
ŏlĕācĕus, a, um *adj*, oily
ŏlĕārĭus, a, um *adj*, of oil; (...i
  m), oil-seller
ŏlĕaster, stri *m*, wild olive tree
ŏlens, ntis *adj*, fragrant, rank
ŏlĕo, ŭi *v.i.t*. 2, to smell of
ŏlĕum, i *n*, olive oil
olfăcĭo, fēci, factum *v.t*. 3, to
  smell
ŏlīdus, a, um *adj*, stinking
ōlim *adv*, once upon a time, once,
  sometime in the future
ŏlītor, ōris *m*, market gardener
ŏlīva, ae *f*, olive tree, olive branch
ŏlīvētum, i *n*, olive grove
ŏlīvĭfer, ĕra, ĕrum *adj*, olive
  growing
ŏlīvum, i *n*, oil
olla, ae *f*, pot, jar

ŏlor, ōris *m,* swan
ŏlōrīnus, a, um *adj,* of swans
ŏlus, ĕris *n,* vegetables
ōmāsum, i *n,* tripe
ōmen, ĭnis *n,* omen, sign
ōmĭnor *v.t.* 1, *dep,* to forbode
ŏmitto, mīsi, missum *v.t.* 3, to put
  aside, give up, leave out
omnĭgĕnus, a, um *adj,* of all
  kinds
omnīno *adv,* altogether, entirely
omnĭpārens, ntis *adj,* all-
  producing
omnĭpŏtens, ntis *adj,* almighty
omnes, ĭum *c, pl,* all men
omnĭa, ĭum *n.pl,* all things
omnis, e *adj,* all, every
omnĭvăgus, a, um *adj,* wandering
  everywhere
ŏnăger (grus), i *m,* wild as
ŏnĕrārĭa, ae *f,* merchant ship
ŏnĕrārĭus, a, um *adj,* of, or for,
  freight
ŏnĕro *v.t.* 1, to load, oppress
ŏnĕrōsus, a, um *adj,* burdensome
ŏnŭs, ĕris *n,* load, burden
ŏnustus, a, um *adj,* loaded, full
ŏnyx, ychis *m, f,* yellow marble
ŏpāco *v.t.* 1, to cover, shade
ŏpācus, a, um *adj,* shady
ŏpālus, i *m,* opal
ŏpem (*no nomin.*) *f,* power,
  wealth, help
ŏpĕra, ae *f,* exertion, effort; *in pl,*
  workmen
ŏpĕram do to give careful
  attention to
ŏpĕrārĭus, a, um *adj,* of labour
ŏpĕrārĭus, ii *m,* labourer
ŏpercŭlum, i *n,* lid, cover
ŏpĕrĭo, ŭi, ŏpertum *v.t.* 4, to
  cover, hide
ŏpĕror *v.i.* 1, *dep,* to work,
  labour, perform a sacrifice
ŏpĕrōsus, a, um *adj, adv,* ē,
  painstaking, busy, troublesome
ŏpertus, a, um *adj,* hidden
ŏpes, um *f.pl,* wealth, resource
ŏpĭfer, ĕra, ĕrum *adj,* helping
ŏpĭfex, ĭcis *c,* craftsman
ŏpīmus, a, um *adj,* fat, rich,
  fertile; **spŏlĭa ŏpima** arms won by
  a general in single combat with

  opposing general
ŏpīnābĭlis, e *adj,* imaginary
ŏpīnātĭo, ōnis *f,* supposition
ŏpīnātus, a, um *adj,* imagined
ŏpīnĭo, ōnis *f,* supposition, belief,
  reputation, rumour
ŏpīnor *v.i.t.* 1, *dep,* to suppose
ŏpīpărē *adv,* sumptuously
ŏpĭtŭlor *v.i.* 1, *dep,* to help
ŏpĭum, ii *n,* opium
ŏportet *v.* 2, *impers, with acc.* of
  person it is necessary
oppĕrĭor, pertus *v.i.t.* 4, *dep,* to
  wait; wait for
oppĕto, īvi, ītum *v.t.* 3, to
  encounter (especially death)
oppĭdāni, ōrum *m.pl,*
  townspeople
oppĭdānus, a, um *adj,* provincial
oppĭdŭlum, i *n,* small town
oppĭdum, i *n,* town
oppignĕro *v.t.* 1, to pledge
oppīlo *v.t.* 1, to shut, stop
opplĕo, ēvi, ētum *v.t.* 2, to fill up
oppōno, pŏsŭi, sĭtum *v.t.* 3, to
  place opposite, oppose, offer,
  expose, object
opportūnĭtas, ātis *f,* convenience,
  advantage
opportūnus, a, um *adj, adv,* ē,
  suitable, convenient
oppŏsĭtĭo, ōnis *f,* opposition
oppŏsĭtus, a, um *adj,* opposite
opprĭmo, pressi, ssum *v.t.* 3, to
  supress, close, surprise, hide
opprŏbrĭum, i *n,* scandal, taunt
oppugnātĭo, ōnis *f,* attack, siege
oppugnātor, ōris *m,* attacker
oppugno *v.t.* 1, to attack
ops, ŏpis *f,* power, aid
optābĭlis, e *adj,* desirable
optātĭo, ōnis *f,* wish
optātum, i *n,* wish
optātus, a, um *adj, adv,* ō,
  desired, pleasant
optĭmas, ātis *adj,* aristocratic
optĭmātes, um *c, pl,* the
  aristocratic party
optĭmus, a, um *adj, adv,* ē, best
optĭo, ōnis *f,* choice
optĭo, ōnis *m,* assistant
opto *v.t.* 1, to choose, desire
ŏpŭlens, ntis *adj,* rich

ŏpŭlentĭa, ae f, wealth
ŏpŭlentus, a, um adj, rich
ŏpus, ĕris n, work, task; ŏpus est
there is need (a necessity)
ŏpuscŭlum, i n, a small work
ōra, ae f, border, sea coast,
region
ōrācŭlum, i n, oracle
ōrātĭo, ōnis f, speech, language,
eloquence
ōrātĭuncŭla, ae f, brief speech
ōrātor, ōris m, speaker, orator,
ambassador
ōrātōrĭus, a, um adj, oratorical
orbĭcŭlātus, a, um adj, circular
orbis, is m, circle; orbis terrarum
the world
orbĭta, ae f, track, rut
orbĭtas, ātis f, bereavement
orbo v.t. 1, to bereave, deprive
orbus, a, um adj, bereaved,
destitute
orca, ae f, large tub
orchas, ādis f, olive
orchēstra, ae f, a place at the
front of the theatre
orchis, is f, orchid
Orcus, i m, death, the Lower
World
ordĭnārĭus, a, um adj, regular,
usual, orderly
ordĭnātim adv, in proper order
ordĭnātus, a, um adj, orderly,
regulated
ordĭne adv, in order
ordĭno v.t. 1, to arrange
ordĭor, orsus v.i.t 4, dep, to
begin, undertake
ordo, ĭnis m, row, rank, band or
company of soldiers, series, class
of society
Òrēăs, ādis f, mountain-nymph
orgĭa, ōrum n.pl, revels in honour
of Bacchus
ŏrĭchalcum, i n, copper ore
ŏrĭens, ntis m, the east
ŏrīgo, ĭnis f, beginning, origin,
family, ancestor
ŏrĭor, ortus v.i. 4, dep, to arise,
appear, originate
ŏrĭundus, a, um adj, descended or
sprung from
ornāmentum, i n, equipment,

decoration
ornātus, a, um adj, adv, ē,
equipped, decorated
ornātus, ūs m, equipment, dress,
ornament
orno v.t. 1, to equip, adorn,
praise
ornus, i f, mountain ash
ōro v.t. 1, to plead, beg, pray
orsa, ōrum n.pl, undertaking,
speech
orsus, ūs m, undertaking
ortus, ūs m, rising (of sun, etc.),
beginning, source
ŏrȳsa, ae f, rice
ōs, ōris n, mouth, face, opening
ŏs, ossis n, bone
oscen, ĭnis m, singing bird from
whose notes omens were taken
oscillātĭo, ōnis f, swinging
oscillum, i n, small mask
oscĭtātĭo, ōnis f, yawning
oscĭto v.i. 1, to gape, yawn
oscŭlor v.i.t. 1, dep, to kiss
oscŭlum, i n, mouth, kiss
ossĕus, a, um adj, made of bone
ossĭfrăgus, i m, sea eagle
ostendo, di, sum v.t. 3, to show,
make known
ostentātĭo, ōnis f, display
ostento v.t. 1, to show, display
ostentum, i n, prodigy
ostĭārĭum, ii n, door tax
ostĭātim adv, from door to door
ostĭum, ii n, door, entrance
ostrĕa, ae f, oyster
ostrĕārĭum, ii n, oyster-bed
ostrum, i n, purple, purple
coverings or dress
ōtĭor v.i. 1, dep, to be on holiday
ōtĭōsus, a, um adj, adv, ē, at
leisure, unemployed, quiet
ōtĭum, ii n, leisure, peace
ŏvans, ntis adj, triumphant
ōvātus, a, um adj, oval
ŏvillus, a, um adj, of sheep
ŏvīlis, e adj, of sheep
ŏvīle, is n, sheepfold
ŏvis, is f, sheep
ŏvo v.i. 1, to exult
ōvum, i n, egg

P

păbo, ōnis *m*, wheelbarrow
pābŭlātĭo, ōnis *f*, collection of
fodder
pābŭlātor, ōris *m*, forager
pābŭlor *v.i.* 1, *dep*, to look for
fodder
pābŭlum, i *n*, food, fodder
pācālis, e *adj*, peaceful
pācātus, a, um *adj*, peaceful
pācĭfer, ĕra, ĕrum *adj*, peace-
bringing
pācĭfĭcātĭo, ōnis *f*, pacification
pācĭfĭco *v.t.* 1, to make peace
pācĭfĭcus, a, um *adj*, peaceable
păciscor, pactus *v.i.t.* 3, *dep*, to
make a bargain; barter
pāco *v.t.* 1, to subdue, pacify
pactĭo, ōnis *f*, an agreement
pactum, i *n*, an agreement
pactus, a, um *adj*, agreed
paean, ānis *m*, hymn to Apollo
paedăgōgus, i *m*, slave who took
chidren to school, and looked
after them at home
paedor, ōris *m*, filth
paelex, ĭcis *f*, concubine
paenĕ *adv*, almost, nearly
paeninsŭla, ae *f*, peninsula
paenĭtens, ntis *adj*, repentant
paenĭtentĭa, ae *f*, penitence
paenĭtet *v.* 2, *impers, with acc.* o
f person, it grieves
paenŭla, ae *f*, cloak
paenultĭmus, a, um *adj*,
penultimate
paetus, a, um *adj*, with a slight
cast in the eye
pāgānus, a, um *adj*, rural
pāgānus, i *m*, country-dweller
pāgĭna, ae *f*, page, leaf, book
pāgus, i *m*, village, district
pāla, ae *f*, spade
pălaestra, ae *f*, wrestling ground
or school, wrestling, rhetorical
exercise
pălam *adv*, openly; *prep. with*
*abl, i*n the presence of
pălētĭum, ii *n*, palace
pălātum, i *n*, palate
pălĕa, ae *f*, chaff
pălĭūrus, i *m*, Christ's thorn
(plant)
palla, ae *f*, stole, robe
pallens, ntis *adj*, pale
pallĕo *v.i.* 2, to be pale
pallesco, pallŭi *v.i.* 3, to turn pale
pallĭātus, a, um *adj*, cloaked like
Greeks
pallĭdus, a, um *adj*, pale
pallĭŏlum, i *n*, hood
pallĭum, ii *n*, coverlet, cloak
pallor, ōris *m*, paleness
palma, ae *f*, palm, hand, oar-
blade, palm tree, broom, palm
wreath, prize, glory
palmāris, e *adj*, excellent, worthy
of the palm
palmātus, a, um *adj*, marked with
the hand, decorated with palm
palmĕs, ĭtis *m*, wine shoot
palmētum, i *n*, palm grove
palmĭfer, ĕra, ĕrum *adj*, palm-
bearing
palmōsus, a, um *adj*, with many
palm trees
palmŭla, ae *f*, oar-blade
palmus, i *m*, palm of hand, span
pālor *v.i.* 1, *dep*, to wander
palpĕbra, ae *f*, eyelid
palpĭtātĭo, ōnis *f*, palpitation
palpĭto *v.i.* 1, to throb, pant
palpo *v.t.* 1, to stroke, carress
pălūdāmentum, i *n*, military
cloak, general's cloak
pălūdātus, a, um *adj*, dressed in
general's cloak
pălūdōsus, a, um *adj*, marshy
pălumbes, is *m, f*, wood-pigeon
pālus, i *m*, stake
pālus, ūdis *f*, marsh
pāluster, tris, tre *adj*, marshy
pampĭnĕus, a, um *adj*, full of vine
leaves
pampĭnus, i *m, f*, vine shoot, vine
leaf
pănăcēa, ae *f*, a herb which
healed all diseases
panchrestus, a, um *adj*, good for
anything
pando, di, nsum *v.t.* 3, to unfold,
open out, spread out, publish
pandus, a, um *adj*, curved
pango, pĕpĭgi, pactum *v.t.* 3, to
fasten, settle, agree upon

pānis, is *m*, bread
pannōsus, a, um *adj*, tattered
pannus, i *m*, garment, rags
panthēra, ae *f*, panther
pantŏmīmus, i *m*, ballet dancer
păpāver, ĕris *n*, poppy
pāpĭlĭo, ōnis *m*, butterfly
păpilla, ae *f*, breast, nipple
păpŭla, ae *f*, pimple
păpўrĭfer, ĕra, ĕrum *adj*, papyrus
  producing
păpўrus, i *m*, *f*, paper
pār, păris *adj*, equal, suitable
pār, păris *m*, companion
părābĭlis, e *adj*, easily procured
părăbŏla *f*, parable, comparison
părallēlus, a, um *adj*, parallel
părălўsis, is *f*, paralysis, palsy
părăsītus, i *m*, parasite
părātus, a, um *adj*, prepared
părātus, ūs *m*, preparation
parco, pĕperci, parsum *v.i.* 3,
  with dat, to spare, desist
parcus, a, um *adj*, *adv*, ē, thrifty,
  sparing, scanty
pārens, ntis *adj*, obedient
pārens, ntis *m*, *f*, parent,
  ancestor, founder
părentālĭa, ĭum *n.pl*, festival in
  honour of dead relations
părentālis, e *adj*, parental
părento *v.t.* 1, to honour dead
  relatives, avenge a relative's death
  by killing
pārĕo *v.i.* 2, *with dat*, to obey, to
  appear
părĭēs, ĕtis *m*, wall
părĭĕtĭnae, ārum *f.pl*, ruins
părīlis, e *adj*, equal
părĭo, pĕpĕri, partum *v.t.* 3, to
  bring forth, produce, acquire
părĭter, *adv*, equally, at the same
  time
parma, ae *f*, small round shield
parmŭla, ae *f*, small round shield
păro *v.t.* 1, to prepare, intend,
  obtain
părŏchus, i *m*, caterer
păroecĭa, ae *f*, parish
parra, ae *f*, owl
parrĭcīda, ae *c*, murderer of a
  parent of relative, assassin
parrĭcīdĭum, ii *n*, murder of a

parent, or relative, treason
pars, partis *f*, part, party, faction,
  part in a play; *in pl*, duty, office;
  in utramque partem on both
  sides; pro parte to the best of
  one's ability
parsĭmōnĭa, ae *f*, thrift
partĭceps, cĭpis *adj*, *with genit*,
  sharing; (*as noun*) sharer
partĭcĭpo *v.t.* 1, to give a share of
partĭcŭla, ae *f*, small part
partim *adv*, partly
partĭo *v.t.* 4, to share, divide
partĭor *v.t.* 4, *dep*, to share,
  divide
partītĭo, ōnis *f*, division
partītus, a, um *adj*, divided
partŭrĭo *v.i.t.* 4, to be pregnant of
  in labour; produce
pārtus, ūs *m*, birth, confinement,
  offspring
părum *adv*, too little
părumper *adv*, for a short time
parvĭtas, ātis *f*, smallness
parvŭlus, a, um *adj*, slight
parvus, a, um *adj*, small, petty,
  short; parvi, of little value
pasco, pāvi, pastum *v.i.t.* 3, to
  feed; pasture, nourish
pascor, pastus *v.i.* 3, *dep*, to
  graze, feast
pascŭum, i *n*, pasture
pascŭus, a, um *adj*, for grazing
passer, ĕris *m*, sparrow, turbot
passim *adv*, in all directions
passum, i *n*, raisin wine
passus, a, um *adj*, spread out,
  dried
passus, a, um *partic. adj*, having
  suffered
passus, ūs *m*, step, pace
pastillus, i *m*, lozenge to dispel
  bad breath
pastor, ōris *m*, shepherd
pastōrālis, e *adj*, of shepherds,
  pastoral
pastōrīcĭus, a, um *adj*, of
  shepherds, pastoral
pastōrĭus, a, um *adj*, of
  shepherds, pastoral
pastus, ūs *m*, pasture, food
pătĕfăcĭo, fēci, factum *v.t.* 3, to
  throw open, disclose

pătĕfactĭo, ōnis *f*, opening up
pătella, ae *f*, plate
pătens, ntis *adj*, open
pătĕo *v.i.* 2, to be open, to
  extend, to be evident
păter, tris *m*, father; *in pl*,
  forefathers, senators
pătĕra, ae *f*, saucer, bowl
păterfămĭlĭas, patrisfămĭlĭas *m*,
  master of the house
păternus, a, um *adj*, of a father
pătesco, pătŭi *v.i.* 3, to be
  opened, to extend, be evident
pătĭbĭlis, e *adj*, endurable
pătĭbŭlum, i *n*, fork-shaped yoke
  or gibbet
pătĭens, ntis *adj, adv*, nter,
  suffering, patient, hard
pătĭentĭa, ae *f*, endurance
pătĭna, ae *f*, pan, dish
pătĭor, passus *v.t.* 3, *dep*, to
  suffer, bear, allow
pătrĭa, ae *f*, fatherland
pătrĭarcha, ae *m*, patriarch
pătrĭcĭus, a, um *adj*, noble
pătrĭcĭus, i *m*, member of the
  Roman nobility
pătrĭmōnĭum, ii *n*, inherited estate
pătrītus, a, um *adj*, of one's father
  or ancestor
pătrĭus, a, um *adj*, of a father,
  hereditary, established, native
pătro *v.t.* 1, to perform, finish
pătrōcĭnĭum, ii *n*, defence
pătrōna, ae *f*, patroness
pătrōnus, i *m*, protector, patron,
  counsel
pătrŭēlis, is *c*, cousin
pătrŭus, i *m*, uncle
pătrŭus, a, um *adj*, of an uncle
pătŭlus, a, um *adj*, open wide
pauci, ae, a *pl. adj*, few
paucĭtas, ātis *f*, small number
paucŭlus, a, um *adj*, very few
paucus, a, um *adj*, few, little
paulātim *adv*, gradually
paulisper *adv*, for a short time
paulō *adv*, a little, somewhat
paulŭlum *adv*, a little, somewhat
paulum *adv*, a little, somewhat
pauper, ĕris *adj*, poor, meagre
pauper, ĕris *c*, a poor man
paupĕrĭes, ēi *f*, poverty

paupertas, ātis *f*, poverty
paupĕro *v.t.* 1, to impoverish
pausa, ae *f*, stop, end
păvĕfăcĭo, fēci, factum *v.t.* 3, to
  alarm
păvĕo, păvi *v.i.t.* 2, to be afraid;
  dread
păvesco *v.i.* 3, to become
  alarmed
păvĭdus, a, um *adj*, terrified
păvīmentum, i *n*, pavement
păvĭo *v.t.* 4, to beat, strike
păvĭto *v.i.t.* 1, to tremble (at)
pāvo, ōnis *m*, peacock
păvor, ōris *m*, anxiety, dread
pax, pācis *f*, peace, grace, favour,
  tranquillity; *in abl*, by permission
peccans, ntis *c*, offender
peccātor, ōris *m*, sinner
peccātum, i *n*, fault, mistake
pecco *v.i.t.* 1, to make a mistake;
  to miss
pecten, ĭnis *m*, comb, reed, rake,
  a plectrum to strike the strings of
  the lyre
pecto, pexi, xum *v.t.* 3, to comb
pectŏrālis, e *adj*, pectoral
pectus, ōris *n*, breast, heart, soul,
  mind
pĕcŭārĭus, a, um *adj*, of cattle
pĕcŭārĭus, ii *m*, cattle-breeder
pĕcūlātor, ōris *m*, embezzler
pĕcūlātus, ūs *m*, embezzlement
pĕcūlĭāris, e *adj*, one's own,
  special
pĕcūlĭum, ii *n*, property, savings
pĕcūnĭa, ae *f*, money
pĕcūnĭārĭus, a, um *adj*, pecuniary
pĕcūnĭōsus, a, um *adj*, rich
pĕcus, ŏris *n*, cattle, herd
pĕcus, ŭdis *f*, an animal, beast
pĕdālis, e *adj*, a foot in length or
  thickness
pĕdes, ĭtis *m*, infantryman
pĕdes see **pes**
pĕdester, tris, tre *adj*, on foot,
  prosaic, plain
pĕdĕtemptim *adv*, gradually
pĕdĭca, ae *f*, shackle, snare
pĕdĭcŭlōsus, a, um *adj*, lousy
pĕdĭcŭlus, i *m*, louse
pĕdĭsĕquus, i *m*, footman
pĕdĭtātus, ūs *m*, infantry

pědum, i *n*, shepherd's crook
pēiěro *v.i.* 1, to swear falsely
pēior *comp. adj*, worse
pēius *comp. adv*, worse
pělăgus, i *n*, open sea
pellax, ācis *adj*, seductive
pellex, īcis *f*, concubine
pellīcĭo, lexi, lectum *v.t.* 3, to allure, coax
pellīcŭla, ae *f*, small skin
pellis, is *f*, skin, leather, tent
pellītus, a, um *adj*, clothed in skins
pello, pēpŭli, pulsum *v.t.* 3, to strike, push, drive out, rout, affect, impress
pellūcĕo, xi *v.i.* 2, to shine through, be transparent
pellucīdus, a, um *adj*, transparent
pělōris, īdis *f*, mussel
pelta, ae *f*, small shield
pelvis, is *f*, basin
pěnārĭus, a, um *adj*, for provisions
pěnātes, ĭum *m.pl*, guardian deities of the home, home
pendĕo, pěpendi *v.i.* 2, to hang, float, loiter, depend upon, be interrupted, be in suspense
pendo, pěpendi, pensum *v.t.* 3, to weigh or pay out, ponder
pendŭlus, a, um *adj*, hanging, uncertain
pěnēs *prep. with acc*, in the power of
pěnětrābĭlis, e *adj*, penetrable, penetrating
pěnětrālĭa, ĭum *n.pl*, inner places or rooms
pěnětrālis, e *adj*, inner
pěnětro *v.i.t.* 1, to enter; penetrate
pēnĭcillum, i *n*, painter's brush, pencil
pēnĭcŭlāmentum, i *n*, train of a dress
pēnĭcŭlus, i *m*, brush
pēnis, is *m*, tail, penis
pěnītus *adv*, inwardly, deep within, entirely
penna, ae *f*, feather, wing
pennātus, a, um *adj*, winged
pennĭger, ěra, ěrum *adj*, winged
pensĭlis, e *adj*, hanging

pensĭo, ōnis *f*, payment
pensĭto *v.t.* 1, to pay, weigh, ponder
penso *v.t.* 1, to weigh out, repay, consider
pensum, i *n*, a task
pēnūrĭa, ae *f*, need, want
pěnus, ūs (*or* ĭ), *m, f*, store of food
pěpo, ŏnis *m*, pumpkin
per *prep. with acc*, through, during, by means of, on account of
per... in compound words usually adds intensity: very ...
pěractĭo, ōnis *f*, completion
pěrăgo, ēgi, actum *v.t.* 3, to complete, relate, transfix
pěrăgro *v.t.* 1, to travel over
pěrambŭlo *v.t.* 1, to go through
pěrăro *v.t.* 1, to plough through
perbrěvis, e *adj*, very short
perca, ae *f*, perch (fish)
percělěbro *v.t.* 1, to say frequently
percello, cŭli, culsum *v.t.* 3, to upset, destroy, dishearten
percensĕo *v.t.* 2, to reckon up
perceptĭo, ōnis *f*, perception
percĭpĭo, cēpi, ceptum *v.t.* 3, to gather, perceive, understand
percontātĭo, ōnis *f*, inquiry
percontor *v.i.t.* 1, *dep*, to investigate
percŏquo, xi, ctum *v.t.* 3, to boil, cook, heat
percrēbesco, bŭi *v.i.* 3, to become prevalent
percrěpo, ŭi, ĭtum *v.i.* 1, to resound, ring
perculsus, a, um *adj*, upset
percurro, curri, cursum *v.i.t.* 3, to run; pass over, mention
percussĭo, ōnis *f*, beating
percussor, ōris *m*, assassin
percŭtĭo, cussi, cussum *v.t.* 3, to thrust through, kill, strike, astound
perdisco, dĭdĭci *v.t.* 3, to learn thoroughly
perdĭtor, ōris *m*, destroyer
perdĭtus, a, um *adj, adv*, ē, ruined, desperate, corrupt

perdix, īcis *c,* partridge
perdo, dīdi, dītum *v.t.* 3, to destroy, waste, lose
perdŏcĕo *v.t.* 2, to teach thoroughly
perdŏmo, üi, ĭtum *v.t.* 1, to subdue completely
perdūco, xi, ctum *v.t.* 3, to conduct, bedaub, prolong, induce
perductor, ōris *m,* pimp
perdŭellĭo, ōnis *f,* treason
perdŭellis, is *m,* public enemy
pĕrĕdo, ēdi, sum *v.t.* 3, to eat up
pĕrĕgrē *adv,* abroad
pĕrĕgrīnātĭo, ōnis *f,* travel abroad
pĕrĕgrīnātor, ōris *m,* traveller
pĕrĕgrīnor *v.i.* 1, *dep,* to live or travel abroad
pĕrĕgrīnus, a, um *adj,* foreign
pĕrĕgrīnus, i *m,* foreigner
pĕrendĭē *adv,* on the day after tomorrow
pĕrennis, e *adj,* everlasting
pĕrenno *v.i.* 1, to last, endure
pĕrĕo, ĭi, ĭtum *v.i.* 4, *irreg,* to pass away, disappear, die, to be ruined or wasted
pĕrĕquĭto *v.i.* 1, to ride about
pĕrerro *v.t.* 1, to wander through
perfectĭo, ōnis *f,* completion
perfectus, a, um *adj, adv, ē,* complete, perfect
perfĕro, ferre, tŭli, lātum *v.t, irreg,* to bring or bear through, convey, announce, complete, suffer
perfĭcĭo, fēci, fectum *v.t.* 3, complete, finish
perfĭdĭa, ae *f,* treachery
perfĭdĭōsus, a, um *adj* treacherous
perfĭdus, a, um *adj,* treacherous
perflo *v.t.* 1, to blow through
perflŭo, xi *v.i.* 3, to flow through
perfŏdĭo, fōdi, fossum *v.t.* 3, to dig through
perfŏro *v.t.* 1, to bore through
perfrĭco, cŭi, cātum *v.t.* 1, to rub all over, put on a bold front
perfringo, frēgi, fractum *v.t.* 3, to shatter, infringe
perfrŭor, fructus *v.* 3, *dep, with abl,* to enjoy thoroughly
perfŭga, ae *m,* deserter
perfŭgĭo, fūgi *v.i.* 3, to flee for

refuge, desert
perfūgĭum, ii *n,* shelter
perfundo, fūdi, fūsum *v.t.* 3, to pour over, besprinkle
perfungor, functus *v.* 3, *dep, with abl,* to fulfil, discharge
perfūro, — *v.i.* 3, to rage
pergo, perrexi, perrectum *v.i.t.* 3, to proceed, go; continue
pĕrhĭbĕo, ŭi, ĭtum *v.t.* 2, to extend, assert, name
pĕrhorresco, rŭi *v.i.t.* 3, to tremble; shudder at
pĕrīclītor *v.i.t.* 1, *dep,* to try, be in danger; test, endanger
pĕrīcŭlōsus, a, um *adj, adv, ē,* dangerous
pĕrīcŭlum, i *n,* danger, proof, attempt
pĕrīmo, ēmi, emptum *v.t.* 3, to anihilate, prevent
pĕrinde *adv,* just as, equally
pĕrĭŏdus, i *f,* complete sentence
pĕrītĭa, ae *f,* experience, skill
pĕrītus, a, um *adj, adv, ē, with genit,* skilled, expert
periŭrĭum, ii *n,* perjury
periūro see **pēĭĕro**
periūrus, a, um *adj,* perjured, lying
perlābor, lapsus *v.i.* 3, *dep,* to glide through
perlectĭo, ōnis *f,* reading through
perlĕgo, lēgi, lectum *v.t.* 3, to survey, examine, read through
perlūcĕo, xi *v.i.* 2, to shine through, be transparent
perlŭo, ŭi, ūtum *v.t.* 3, to wash
perlūcĭdus, a, um *adj,* transparent
perlustro *v.t.* 1, to wander through
permănĕo, nsi, nsum *v.i.* 2, to flow through, penetrate
permansĭo, ōnis *f,* persisting
permĕo *v.t.* 1, to cross, penetrate
permētĭor, mensus *v.t.* 4, *dep,* to measure out, travel over
permiscĕo, scŭi, xtum *v.t.* 2, to mix together
permissĭo, ōnis *f,* permission, surrender
permissū *abl,* by permission
permitto, mīsi, missum *v.t.* 3, to

let loose, commit, entrust; allow (*with dat*)

permōtĭo, ōnis *f*, excitement

permŏvĕo, mōvi, mōtum *v.t.* 2, to stir up, rouse

permulcĕo, mulsi, mulsum *v.t.* 2, to stroke, charm, flatter

permultus, a, um *adj*, *adv*, ō, or um, very much

permūtātĭo, ōnis *f*, exchange

permūto *v.t.* 1, to change

perna, ae *f*, leg of pork

pernĕgo *v.t.* 1, to deny flatly

pernĭcĭes, ēi *f*, disaster

pernĭcĭōsus, a, um *adj*, *adv*, ē, destructive

pernĭcītas, ātis *f*, agility

pernix, īcis *adj*, agile

pernocto *v.i.* 1, to stay all night

pernox, ctis *adj*, night-long

pēro, ōnis *m*, rawhide boot

pĕrōsus, a, um *adj*, detesting, detested

pĕrōro *v.t.* 1, to wind up a speech

perpendĭcŭlum, i *n*, plumb line

perpendo, pendi, pensum *v.t.* 3, to ponder, consider

perpĕram *adv*, untruly

perpĕtĭor, pessus *v.i.t.* 3, *dep*, to suffer; endure

perpĕtŭĭtas, ātis *f*, continuity

perpĕtŭus, a, um *adj*, *adv*, ō, perpetual, entire, continuous

perplexus, a, um *adj*, intricate

perpŏlĭo *v.t.* 4, to perfect

perprĭmo, pressi, ssum *v.t.* 3, to press hard

perpurgo *v.t.* 1, to clean up

perquam *adv*, very much

perquīro, sīvi, sītum *v.t.* 3, to make a careful search for

perrārō *adv*, very rarely

perrumpo, rūpi, ruptum *v.i.t.* 3, to break through

perscrībo, psi, ptum *v.t.* 3, to write in full

perscriptĭo, ōnis *f*, written entry or note

perscrūtor *v.t.* 1, *dep*, to examine

persĕco, cui, ctum *v.t.* 1, to cut up

persentĭo, si, sum *v.t.* 4, to perceive plainly, feel deeply

persĕquor, sĕcūtus *v.t.* 3, *dep*, to pursue, overtake, revenge

persĕvērantĭa, ae *f*, constancy

persĕvēro *v.i.t.* 1, to persevere; persist in

persīdo, sēdi, sessum *v.i.* 3, to penetrate

persisto, stĭti *v.i.* 3, to persist

persolvo, solvi, sŏlūtum *v.t.* 3, to pay out, give

persōna, ae *f*, mask, character, part, person

parsōnātus, a, um *adj*, fictitious

persŏno, ŭi, ĭtum *v.i.t.* 1, to resound; fill with sound

perspectus, a, um *adj*, well known

perspĭcācĭtas, ātis *f*, perspicacity

perspĭcax, ācis *adj*, astute

perspĭvĭo, spexi, spectum *v.t.* 3, to look at, examine, perceive

perspĭcŭĭtas, ātis *f*, clearness, perspicuity

perspĭcŭus, a, um *adj*, *adv*, ē, clear, evident

persto, stĭti, stātum *v.i.* 1, to endure, continue, persist

perstringo, nxi, ctum *v.t.* 3, to graze, blunt, stun, blame, allude to, slight

persuādĕo, si, sum *v.t.* 2, *with dat*, to persuade

persuāsĭo, ōnis *f*, conviction

persuāsus, a, um *adj*, settled; **persuāsum hăbēre** to be convinced

pertento *v.t.* 1, to consider

pertĕrĕbro *v.t.* 1, to bore through

perterrĕo *v.t.* 2, to frighten thoroughly

pertĭca, ae *f*, pole, rod

pertĭmesco, mŭi *v.i.t.* 3, to be very afraid; to fear greatly

pertĭnācĭa, ae *f*, obstinancy

pertĭnax, ācis *adj*, firm, constant, stubborn

perttĭnĕo *v.i.* 2, to extend, pertain, concern, be applicable

pertracto *v.t.* 1, to touch

pertundo, tŭdi, tūsum *v.t.* 3, to make a hole through

perturbātĭo, ōnis *f*, confusion

perturbātus, a, um *adj*, disturbed

perturbo *v.t.* 1, to disturb

pĕrungo, nxi, nctum *v.t.* 3, to besmear

pĕrūro, ssi, stum *v.t.* 3, to burn up, rub sore, nip

pervādo, si, sum *v.i.* 3, to spread through, pervade

pervăgātus, a, um *adj,* well-known

pervăgor *v.i.t.* 1, *dep,* to wonder through; pervade

pervĕho, xi, ctum *v.t.* 3, to carry through

pervello, velli *v.t.* 3, to pull, disparage

pervĕnĭo, vēnis, ventum *v.i.* 4, to reach, arrive at

perversĭtas, ātis *f,* obstinacy

perversus, a, um *adj,* askew, perverse

perverto, ti, sum *v.t.* 3, to overturn, destroy, corrupt

pervestīgo *v.t.* 1, to investigate

pervĭcācĭa, ae *f,* obstinacy

pervĭcax, ācis *adj, adv, ĭter,* stubborn, wilful

pervĭdĕo, vīdi, vīsum *v.t.* 2, to view, survey

pervĭgĭl, is *adj,* ever-watchful

pervĭgĭlātĭo, ōnis *f,* vigil

pervĭgĭlo *v.i.* 1, to remain awake all night

pervinco, vīci, victum *v.t.* 3, to gain victory over

pervĭus, a, um *adj,* able to be crossed or passed

pervŏlĭto *v.i.* 1, to flit about

pervŏlo *v.i.* 1, to fly about or through or to

pervŏlo, velle, vŏlŭi *v.i, irreg,* to wish greatly

pervulgo *v.t.* 1, to spread about

pēs, pĕdis *m,* foot; rope attached to a sail, sheet

pessĭmē *adv,* very badly

pessĭmus, a, um *adj,* very bad

pessŭlus, i *m,* latch

pessum *adv,* to the ground; **pessum ire,** to go to ruin

pestĭfer, era, ĕrum *adj,* destructive, harmful

pestĭlens, ntis *adj,* unhealthy

persĭlentĭa, ae *f,* infectious disease

pestis, is *f,* disease, ruin

pĕtăsātus, a, um *adj,* dressed for a journey

pĕtăsus, i *m,* travelling-hat

pĕtītĭo, ōnis *f,* blow, candidature for office

pĕtītor, ōris *m,* candidate, plaintiff

pĕto, īvi, ītum *v.t.* 3, to make for, seek, aim at, request

pĕtōrĭtum, i *n,* four-wheeled carriage

petŭlans, ntis *adj,* impudent

petŭlantĭa, ae *f,* impudence

pexus, a, um *adj,* new

phălanx, ngis *f,* military formation

phălĕrae, ārum *f.pl,* military decoration

phărĕtra, ae *f,* quiver

phărĕtrātus, a, um *adj,* wearing a quiver

pharmăcŏpōla, ae *m,* quack

phărus, i *f,* lighthouse

phăsēlus, i *m, f,* kidney bean, light boat, yacht

phengītes, ae *m,* selenite, mica

phĭlŏlŏgĭa, ae *f,* love of learning

phĭlŏlŏgus, m, man of learning

phĭlŏmēla, ae *f,* nightingale

phĭlŏsŏphĭa, ae *f,* philosophy

phĭlŏsŏphor *v.i.* 1, *dep,* to study philosophy

phĭlŏsŏphus, i *m,* philosopher

phĭlȳra, ae *f,* bark of the linden tree

phīmus, i *m,* dice-box

phōca, ae *f,* seal, sea-dog

phoenix, īcis *m,* bird which was said to live 500 years

phthĭsis, is *f,* phthisis

phȳlarchus, i *m,* chief, prince

phȳsĭca, ōrum *n.pl,* physics

phȳsĭcus, i *m,* naturalist

phȳsĭŏlŏgĭa, ae *f,* physiology

pĭācŭlāris, e *adj,* expiatory

pĭācŭlum, i *n,* sacrificial offering of atonement, victim, sin, crime

pīca, ae *f,* magpie

pĭcĕa, ae *f,* pitch-pine

pĭcĕus, a, um *adj,* pitch-black

pictor, ōris *m,* painter

pictūra, ae *f,* painting, picture

pictūrātus, a, um *adj,* embroidered

pictus, a, um *adj,* painted, decorated

pīcus, i *m,* woodpecker

pīĕtas, ātis *f,* sense of duty, loyalty, mercy

pĭger, gra, grum *adj,* lazy, sluggish

pĭget (me, te) *v.* 2, *impers, it* annoys or displeases (me, you)

pigmentum, i *n,* paint, pigment

pignĕro *v.t.* 1, to pledge, pawn

pignĕror *v.t.* 1, *dep,* to take possession of

pignus, ŏris (ĕris) *n,* security, mortgage, pledge, bet

pĭgrĭtĭa, ae *f,* laziness, indolence

pĭgrĭtĭes, ēi *f,* laziness, indolence

pīla, ae *f,* pillar, pier

pĭla, ae *f,* ball

pīlātus, a, um *adj,* armed with javelins

pīlentum, i *n,* carriage

pillĕātus, a, um *adj,* wearing a felt cap, *see below*

pillĕus, i *m* (pillĕum, i, *n*), felt cap, worn by Romans at festivals, and by freed slaves

pĭlōsus, a, um *adj,* hairy

pĭlŭla, ae *f,* pill

pīlum, i *n,* the heavy javelin of the Roman infantry

pĭlus, i *m,* a hair, the hair

pĭlus, i *m,* (*with* prīmus), senior centurion, senior division of trĭārĭi- men who fought in the 3rd rank

pīnētum, i *n,* a wood of pines

pīnĕus, a, um *adj,* of pinewood

pingo, nxi, ctum *v.t.* 3, to paint, decorate

pinguesco *v.i.* 3, to grow fat or fertile

pingue, is *n,* fat

pinguis, e *adj,* rich, fertile, plump, dull, stupid

pinguĭtūdo, ĭnis *f,* plumpness, richness

pīnĭfer, ĕra, ĕrum *adj,* pine-bearing

pīnĭger, ĕra, ĕrum *adj,* pine-bearing

pinna, ae *f,* feather, wing

pinnātus, a, um *adj,* winged

pinnĭger, ĕra, ĕrum *adj,* winged

pīnus, ūs (or i) *f,* pine tree

pĭo *v.t.* 1, to appease, atone for

pīpātus, ūs *m,* chirping

pĭper, ĕris *n,* pepper

pīpĭlo *v.i.* 1, to chirp

pīpĭo *v.i.* 4, to chirp

pīrāta, ae *m,* pirate

pīrātĭcus, a, um *adj,* of pirates

pĭrum, i *n,* pear

pĭrus, i *f,* pear tree

piscātor, ōris *m,* fisherman

piscātōrĭus, a, um *adj,* of fishing or fishermen

piscātus, ūs *m,* fishing

piscīna, ae *f,* fish pond

piscis, is *m,* a fish

piscor *v.i.* 1, *dep,* to fish

piscōsus, a, um *adj,* full of fish

pistor, ōris *m,* miller, baker

pistrīnum, i *n,* mill

pistris, is (pistrix, īcis) *f,* sea-monster

pĭsum, i *n,* pea

pītŭīta, ae *f,* phlegm

pīī, ōrum *m.pl,* the departed

pĭus, a, um *adj, adv,* ē, dutiful, loyal, kind, affectionate

pix, pĭcis *f,* pitch

plācābĭlis, e *adj,* easily pacified, mild

plācātus, a, um *adj, adv,* ē, calmed, still

plăcens, ntis *adj,* pleasing

plăcenta, ae *f,* cake

plăcĕo *v.i.* 2, *with dat,* to please, to be welcome

plăcĭdus, a, um *adj, adv,* ē, quiet, calm, peaceful

plăcĭtus, a, um *adj,* agreeable

plāco *v.t.* 1, to reconcile, soothe

plāga, ae *f,* wound, blow

plăga, ae *f,* region

plăga, ae *f,* hunting-net

plăgĭārĭus, ii *m,* oppressor

plăgōsus, a, um *adj,* fond of flogging

plăgŭla, ae *f,* curtain

planctus, ūs *m,* lamentation

plango, nxi, nctum *v.t.* 3, to beat, strike, lament

plangor, ōris *m*, lamentation
plānĭtĭes, ēi *f*, plain
planta, ae *f*, shoot, twig
plantārĭa, ĭum *n.pl*, young trees
plantārĭum, ii *n*, plantation
plānum, i *n*, plain
plānus, a, um *adj, adv*, ē, flat, level, clear
plănus, i *m*, imposter, cheat
plătănus, i *f*, plane tree
plătēa, ae *f*, street
plauso, si, sum *v.i.t.* 3, to applaud; strike, beat
plausĭbĭlis, e *adj*, acceptable
plaustrum, i *n*, cart, waggon
plausus, ūs *m*, applause
plēbēcŭla, ae *f*, the mob
plēbēĭus, a, um *adj*, vulgar
plēbĭcŏla, ae *c*, demagogue
plebs (plēbes), is *f*, the common people
plecto *v.t.* 3, to punish
plectrum, i *n*, quill with which to strike a stringed instrument
plēnĭtūdo, ĭnis *f*, fulness
plēnus, a, um *adj, adv*, ē, full, laden, complete, plentiful
plērīque, aeque, ăque *adj*, most, very many
plērumque *adv*, for the most part
plerētis, ĭdis *f*, pleurisy
plĭco *v.t.* 1, to fold up
plinthus, i *m, f*, plinth
plōrātus, ūs *m*, weeping
plōro *v.i.t.* 1, to weep; bewail
plostellum, i *n*, small cart
plŭit *v. impers*, it rains
plūma, ae *f*, feather, down
plumbĕus, a, um *adj*, made of lead, heavy
plumbum, i *n*, lead, bullet
plūmeus, a, um *adj*, downy, soft
plūrālis, e *adj*, plural
plūres, es, a *comp. adj*, more
plūrĭmum *adv*, very much
plūrĭmus, a, um *adj*, very much
plūs, plūris *n*, more
plūs *adv*, more
pluscŭlum, i *n*, somewhat more
plŭtĕus, i *m*, shed, parapet, shelf
plŭvĭa, ae *f*, rain
plŭvĭālis, e *adj*, rainy
plŭvĭus, a, um *adj*, rainy

pōcŭlum, i *n*, cup, beaker
pŏdăgra, ae *f*, gout
pŏdĭa, ae *f*, sail-rope
pŏdĭum, ii *n*, height, balcony
pŏēma, ătis *n*, poem
poena, ae *f*, punishment, penalty
poenālis, e *adj*, penal
pŏēsis, is *f*, poetry
pŏēta, ae *m*, poet
pŏētĭcus, a, um *adj*, poetical
poi! *interj*, indeed!
pŏlĭo *v.t.* 4, to polish, improve
pŏlītĭcus, a, um *adj*, political
pŏlītus, a, um *adj, adv*, ē, polished, refined
pollens, ntis *adj*, powerful
pollĕo *v.i.* 2, to be powerful, to prevail
pollex, ĭcis *m*, thumb
pŏllĭcĕor *v.i.t.* 2, *dep*, to promise
pollĭcĭtātĭo, ōnis *f*, promise
pollĭcĭtum, i *n*, promise
pollinctor, ōris *m*, undertaker
pollŭo, ŭi, ūtum *v.t.* 3, to pollute, contaminate
pŏlus, i *m*, pole, north-pole
pŏlўpus, i *m*, polypus
pōmārĭum, ii *n*, orchard
pōmārĭus, ii *m*, fruiterer
pōmĕrīdĭnus, a, um *adj*, in the afternoon
pōmĭfer, ĕra, ĕrum *adj*, fruit-bearing
pōmoerĭum, ii *n*, open space inside and outside city walls
pompa, ae *f*, procession, retinue, pomp
pōmum, i *n*, fruit
pōmus, i *f*, fruit tree
pondĕro *v.t.* 1, to consider
pondĕrōsus, a, um *adj*, ponderous
pondo *adv*, by weight
pondus, ĕris *n*, weight, mass, influence, authority
pōne *adv. and prep. with acc*, behind, after
pōno, pŏsŭi, pŏsĭtum *v.t.* 3, to put, place, set, plant, wager, invest, spend, lay aside, appoint, calm, allege, propose
pons, ntis *m*, bridge
pontĭcŭlus, i *m*, drawbridge

pontĭfex, ĭcis *m*, high-priest
pontĭfĭcĭus, a, um *adj*, of a high-
  priest
pontus, i *m*, the sea
pŏpa, ae *m*, priest's assistant
pŏpīna, ae *f*, restaurant
poplĕs, ĭtis *m*, knee
pŏpŭlāris, e *adj, adv*, ĭter, of the
  people, popular, democratic
pŏpŭlāris *c*, fellow-countryman
pŏpŭlāres, ĭum *m.pl*, the people's
  party
pŏpŭlātĭo, ōnis *f*, devastation
pŏpŭlātor, ōris *m*, plunderer
pōpŭlĕus, a, um *adj*, of poplars
pŏpŭlo *v.t.* 1, to plunder,
  devastate
pŏpŭlor *v.t.* 1, *dep*, to plunder,
  devastate
pŏpŭlus, i *m*, the people
pōpŭlus, i *f*, poplar tree
porcīna, ae *f*, pork
porcŭlus, i *m*, young pig; (*with
  mărīnus*) porpoise
porcus, i *m*, pig
porrectĭo, ōnis *f*, extension
porrectus, a, um *adj*, extended
porrĭcĭo, ēci, ctum *v.t.* 3, to offer
  to the gods
porrĭgo, rexi, rectum *v.t.* 3, to
  stretch out, offer
porrīgo, ĭnis *f*, dandruff
porro *adv*, forwards, next,
  moreover
porrum, i *n*, leek
porta, ae *f*, gate, door
portendo, di, tum *v.t.* 3, to foretell
portentum, i *n*, omen, monster
portĭcus, ūs *f*, colonnade
portĭo *in phrase*, **pro prortĭōne** in
  proportion
portĭtor, ōris *m*, customs officer
portĭtor, ōris *m*, boatman
porto *v.t.* 1, to carry, bring
portōrĭum, ii *n*, customs duty
portŭōsus, a, um *adj*, with many
  harbours
portus, ūs *m*, harbour, refuge
posco, pŏposci *v.t.* 3, to demand
pŏsĭtĭo, ōnis *f*, placing, situation
pŏsĭtus, a, um *adj*, situated
pŏsĭtus, ūs *m*, arrangement,
  disposition

possessĭo, ōnis *f*, seizure,
  occupation
possessor, ōris *m*, possessor
possĭdĕo, sēdi, sessum *v.t.* 2, to
  be master of, possess
possĭdo, sēdi, sessum *v.t.* 3, to
  take possession of, occupy
possum, posse, pŏtŭi *v.i. irreg*, to
  be able, to have power
post *adv, and prep. with acc*,
  behind, backwards, after
postĕā *adv*, afterwards
postĕāquam *conj*, after
postĕri, ōrum *m.pl*, posterity
postĕrĭor, ĭus *comp. adj*, next,
  worse
postĕrĭtas, ātis *f*, posterity
postĕrĭus *adv*, later
postĕrus, a, um *adj*, next
postgĕnĭti, ōrum *m.pl*, posterity
posthăbĕo *v.t.* 2, to postpone,
  neglect
posthāc *adv*, in future
postīcum, i *n*, back door
postis, is *m*, door-post
postmŏdo *adv*, afterwards
postpōno, pŏsŭi, pŏsĭtum *v.t.* 3,
  to postpone, neglect
postquam *conj*, after, when
postrēmo *adv*, at last
postrēmus, a, um *adj*, the last
postrīdĭē *adv*, on the next day
postŭlāta, ōrum *n.pl*, demand,
  request
postŭlātĭo, ōnis *f*, demands,
  requests
postŭlo *v.t.* 1, to demand,
  prosecute, accuse
postŭmus, a, um *adj*, last-born,
  posthumous
pōtātĭo, ōnis *f*, drinking
pōtātor, ōris *m*, drinker
pŏtens, ntis *adj*, powerful, master
  of (*with genit*)
pŏtentātus, ūs *m*, power, rule
pŏtentĭa, ae *f*, power, authority
pŏtestas, ātis *f*, power,
  dominion, control, value, force,
  ability, permission, opportunity
pōtĭo, ōnis *f*, a drink
pŏtĭor *v.* 4, *dep, with abl*, to
  obtain, hold, possess
pŏtĭor, ĭus *comp. adj*, preferable

pŏtis, e *adj*, possible
pŏtĭus *adv*, preferably
pōto *v.i.t.* 1, to drink
pōtor, ōris *m*, drinker
pōtus, a, um *adj*, intoxicated, drained
pōtus, ūs *m*, a drink
prae *adv, and prep. with abl*, before, in comparison with
prae se ferre (gĕrere) to reveal
praeăcŭo, ŭi, ūtum *v.t.* 3, to sharpen
praeăcūtus, a, um *adj*, pointed
praebĕo *v.t.* 2, to offer, give, show
praevăvĕo, cāvi, cautum *v.i.t.* 2, to be on one's guard; prevent
praecēdo, cessi, cessum *v.i.t.* 3, to lead the way; precede
praecellens, ntis *adj*, excellent
praecelsus, a, um *adj*, very high
praeceps, cĭpĭtis *adj*, headlong
praeceps, cĭpĭtis *n*, precipice, danger
praeceptor, ōris *m*, teacher
praeceptum, i *n*, rule, maxim, order, command
praecerpo, psi, ptum *v.t.* 3, to gather before time
praecīdo, cīdi, cīsum *v.t.* 3, to cut off, cut short
praecingo, nxi, nctum *v.t.* 3, to encircle, gird
praecĭno, nŭi, centum *v.i.t.* 3, to sing before; predict
praecĭpĭo, cēpi, ceptum *v.t.* 3, to receive in advance, anticipate, advise, teach
praecĭpĭto *v.i.t* 1, to rush down; throw headlong
praecĭpŭus, a, um *adj, adv, ē*, particular, especial, excellent
praeclārus, a, um *adj, adv, ē*, splendid, excellent
praeclūdo, si, sum *v.t.* 3, to close
praeco, ōnis *m*, herald
praecōnĭum, ii *n*, office of herald, proclamation
praecōnĭus, a, um *adj*, of a herald
praecordĭa, ōrum *n.pl*, midriff, heart
praecox, ŏcis *adj*, premature
praecurro, cŭcurri, cursum *v.i.t.*

3, to run in front; excel
praecursor, ōris *m*, scout, spy
praecŭtĭo, cussi, cussum *v.t.* 3, to brandish in front
praeda, ae *f*, plunder, prey
praedātor, ōris *m*, plunderer
praedātōrĭus, a, um *adj*, predatory
praedĭātor, ōris *m*, estate agent
praedĭcātĭo, ōnis *f*, proclamation, commendation
praedĭco *v.t.* 1, to proclaim, declare, praise
praedīco, xi, ctum *v.t.* 3, to predict, advise, command
praedictĭo, ōnis *f*, prediction
praedictum, i *n*, prediction
praedisco *v.t.* 3, to learn beforehand
praedĭtus, a, um *adj*, provided with
praedĭum, ii *n*, farm, estate
praedīvěs, ĭtis *adj*, very rich
praedo, ōnis *m*, robber
praedor *v.i.t.* 1, *dep*, to plunder
praedūco, xi, ctum *v.t.* 3, to make or put in front
praedulcis, e *adj*, very sweet
praedūrus, a, um *adj*, very hard
praeĕo, ĭi, ĭtum *v.i.t.* 4, to lead the way; recite, dictate
praefātĭo, ōnis *f*, preface
praefectūra, ae *f*, superintendence
praefectus, i *m*, director, commander, governor
praefĕro, ferre, tŭli, lātum *v.t*, *irreg*, to carry in front, offer, prefer, show
praefĭcĭo, fēci, fectum *v.t.* 3, to put in command
praefidens, ntis *adj*, overconfident
praefigo, xi, xum *v.t.* 3, to fix in front
praefĭnĭo *v.t.* 3, to fix, appoint
praeflŭo *v.i.* 3, to flow past
praefŏdĭo, fōdi *v.t.* 3, to dig in front
praefor, fātus *v.i.t.* 1, *dep*, to say in advance
praefringo, frēgi, fractum *v.t.* 3, to break off
praefulgĕo, si *v.i.* 2, to glitter

praegestĭo *v.i.* 4, to desire greatly
praegnans, ntis *adj,* pregnant
praegrăvis, e *adj,* very heavy
praegrĕdĭor, gressus *v.i.t.* 3, *dep,* to go in advance
praeiŭdĭcātus, a, um *adj,* preconceived
praeiŭdĭcĭum, ii *n,* precedent (at law)
praeiŭdĭco *v.t.* 1, to pre-judge
praelābor, lapsus *v.i.t.* 3, *dep,* to glide or flow along or past
praelambo *v.t.* 3, to taste in advance
praelūcĕo, xi *v.i.* 2, to carry a light in front
praemandāta, ōrum *n.pl,* warrant of arrest
praemĕdĭtātĭo, ōnĭs *f,* premeditation
praemĕdĭtor *v.t.* 1, *dep,* to premeditate
praemitto, mīsi, missum *v.t.* 3, to send in advance
praemĭum, ii *n,* booty, reward
praemŏnĕo *v.t.* 2, to forewarn
praemūnĭo *v.t.* 4, to fortify
praenăto *v.i.* 1, to flow past
praenĭtĕo *v.i.* 2, to outshine
praenōmen, ĭnis *n,* first (Christian) name
praenosco *v.t.* 3, to learn in advance
praenuntĭo *v.t.* 1, to predict
praenuntĭus, a, um *adj,* foreboding
praenuntĭus, i *m,* foreteller
praeoccŭpo *v.t.* 1, to seize in advance
praeopto *v.t.* 1, to prefer
praepărātĭo, ōnis *f,* preparation
praepăro *v.t.* 1, to prepare
praepĕdĭo *v.t.* 4, to bind, obstruct
praependĕo *v.i.* 2, to hang down in front
praepes, ĕtis *adj,* swift
praepes, ĕtis *c,* bird
praepinguis, e *adj,* very fat
praepōno, pŏsŭi, pŏsĭtum *v.t.* 3, to put first, put in command, prefer
praepŏsĭtĭo, ōnis *f,* preference
praepŏsĭtus, i *m,* chief, head
praepostĕrus, a, um *adj,* preposterous
praepŏtens, ntis *adj,* very powerful
praeprŏpĕrus, a, um *adj,* sudden, precipitate
praerĭpĭo, rĭpŭi, reptum *v.t.* 3, to snatch away
praerōdo, rōsum *v.t.* 3, to nibble
praerŏgātīva, ae *f,* the Roman tribe to which the first vote was allotted
praerumpo, rūpi, ruptum *v.t.* 3, to break off
praeruptus, a, um *adj,* steep
praes, dis *m,* security, bail
praesaepe, is *n,* stable, pen
praesaepĭo, psi, ptum *v.t.* 4, to barricade
praesāgĭo *v.t.* 4, to have a presentiment or premonition
praesāgĭum, ii *n,* a foreboding
praesāgus, a, um *adj,* foretelling
praescisco *v.t.* 3, to learn in advance
praescĭus, a, um *adj,* knowing in advance
praescrībo, psi, ptum *v.t.* 3, to order, appoint, prescribe
praescriptĭo, ōnis *f,* excuse, order, law
praescriptum, i *n,* order, law
praesens, ntis *adj,* present, prompt, powerful, resolute, helping
praesensĭo, ōnis *f,* foreboding
praesentĭa, ae *f,* presence
praesentĭa, ĭum *n.pl,* present circumstances
praesentĭo, si, sum *v.t.* 4, to have a premonition
praesēpe see **praesaepe**
praesertim *adv,* especially
pareses, ĭdis *adj,* guarding
praeses, ĭdis *c,* guardian, chief
praesĭdĕo, sēdi *v.i.t.* 2, to guard, direct, superintend
praesĭdĭum, ii *n,* garrison, fortification, camp
praesignis, e *adj,* excellent, distinguished
praestābĭlis, e *adj,* excellent, distinguished

praestans, ntis *adj*, excellent, distinguished
praestantĭa, ae *f*, excellence
praestat *v*. 1, *impers*, it is preferable
praestĭgĭae, ārum *f.pl*, juggling tricks
praestĭtŭo, ŭi, ūtum *v.t*. 3, to appoint in advance
praesto *adv*, ready, present
praesto, stĭti, stĭtum *v.i.t*. 1, to be superior; surpass, vouch for, perform, fulfil, show, give, offer
praestringo, nxi, ctum *v.t*. 3, to tie up, graze, blunt
praestrŭo, xi, ctum *v.t*. 3, to build or block up
praesum praeesse, praefŭi *v.i, irreg, with dat*, to be in command of
praesūmo, mpsi, mptum *v.t*. 3, to anticipate, imagine in advance
praetento, di, tum *v.t*. 3, to hold out, pretend
praetento *v.t*. 1, to examine in advance
praeter *adv, and prep. with acc*, past, beyond, beside, except, unless
praetĕrĕā *adv*, besides, henceforth
praetĕrĕo, ĭi, ĭtum *v.i.t*. 4, to pass by; go past, omit, neglect
praeterflŭo, xi, ctum *v.i*. 3, to flow past
praetergrĕdĭor, gressus *v.i.t*. 3, *dep*, to pass beyond
praetĕrĭtus, a, um *adj*, past, gone
praeterlābor, lapsus *v.i.t*. 3, *dep*, to glide or flow past
praetermissĭo, ōnis *f*, omission
praetermitto, mīsi, missum *v.t*. 3, to let pass, omit, neglect
praeterquam *adv*, besides, except
praetervĕhor, vectus *v.i.t*. 3, *dep*, to sail, ride or drive past
praetervŏlo *v.i.t*. 1, to escape; fly past
praetexo, xŭi, xtum *v.t*. 3, to edge, border, pretend
praetexta, ae *f*, purple-edged toga worn by Roman magistrates and children

praetexta, ae *f*, a tragedy
praetextātus, a, um *adj*, wearing the toga praetexta
praetextus, a, um *adj*, wearing the toga praetexta
praetor, ōris *m*, chief, head, Roman magistrate concerned with administration of justice
praetōrĭum, ii *n*, general's tent, governor's residence
praetōrĭus, a, um *adj*, of the praetor or general
praetūra, ae *f*, praetorship
praeūro, ussi, ustum *v.t*. 3, to burn at the end
praeustus, a, um *adj*, burnt, frostbitten
praevălĕo *v.i*. 2, to be superior
praevălĭdus, a, um *adj*, very strong
praevĕhor, ctus *v.i.t*. 3, *dep*, to ride, fly or flow in front
praevĕnĭo, vēni, ventum *v.i.t*. 4, to come before; outstrip
praeverto, ti *v.t*. 3, to outstrip, anticipate, prevent
praevertor, sus *v.i.t*. 3, *dep*, to concentrate one's attention (on)
praevĭdĕo, vīdi, vīsum *v.t*. 2, to anticipate, see in advance
praevĭus, a, um *adj*, leading the way
prandĕo, di, sum *v.i.t*. 2, to breakfast, lunch (on)
prandĭum, ii *n*, breakfast, luncheon
pransus, a, um *adj*, having breakfasted
prātensis, e *adj*, growing in meadows
prātŭlum, i *n*, small meadow
prātum, i *n*, meadow
prāvĭtas, ātis *f*, deformity, depravity
prāvus, a, um *adj, adv*, ē, wrong, bad, deformed
prĕcārĭus, a, um *adj, adv*, ō, obtained by prayer
prĕcātĭo, ōnis *f*, prayer
prĕcīae, ārum *f.pl*, grapevine
prĕcor *v.i.t*. 1, *dep*, to pray, beg
prĕhendo, di, sum *v.t*. 3, to seize, detain, take by surprise

prĕhenso *v.t.* 1, to grasp, detain

prēlum, i *n,* wine-press

prĕmo, ssi, ssum *v.t.* 3, to press, grasp, cover, close, pursue closely, load, overwhelm, plant, prune, check, repress

prendo see **prĕhendo**

prensus, a, um *adj,* grasped

presso *v.t.* 1, to press

pressus, ūs *m,* pressure

pressus, a, um *adj,* subdued, compact

prĕtĭōsus, a, um *adj, adv, ē,* valuable, costly

prĕtĭum, ii *n,* price, value, money, wages, reward

prex, prĕcis *f,* prayer, request

prīdem *adv,* long ago

prīdĭē *adv,* on the day before

prīmaevus, a, um *adj,* youthful

prīmārĭus, a, um *adj,* of the first rank, chief

prīmĭgĕnus, a, um *adj,* primitive

prīmĭpīlus see **pilus**

prīmĭtĭae, ārum *f.pl,* first fruits

prīmō *adv,* at first

prīmordĭa, ōrum *n.pl,* origin

prīmōris, e *adj,* first, front end

prīmōres, um *m.pl,* nobles

prīmum *adv,* at first; **cum prīmum** as soon as; **quam prīmum** as soon as possible

prīmus, a, um *adj,* first, chief

princeps, cĭpis *adj,* first, chief

princeps, cĭpis *m,* chief, originator

princĭpālis, e *adj,* original, primitive, principal

princĭpālis, is *m,* overseer

princĭpātus, ūs *m,* the first place, command, rule

princĭpĭo *adv,* in the beginning

princĭpĭum, ii *n,* origin; *in pl,* principles, elements

prĭor, ĭus *comp. adj,* previous, former

prĭōres, um *m.pl,* ancestors

priscus, a, um *adj,* ancient

prisma, ătis *n,* prism

pristīnus, a, um *adj,* primitive

prĭus *comp. adv,* previously

prĭusquam *conj,* before

prīvātim *adv,* privately

prīvātĭo, ōnis *f,* taking-away

prīvātus, a, um *adj,* private

prīvātus, i *m,* private citizen

prīvigna, ae *f,* step-daughter

prīvignus, i *m,* step-son

prīvĭlēgĭum, ii *n,* bill or law concerned with an individual

prīvo *v.t.* 1, to deprive, release

prīvus, a, um *adj,* one's own

prō *prep. with abl,* before, in front of, on behalf of, instead of, just as, on account of, according to, in relation to

prō! (prōh!) *interj,* Ah! Alas!

prŏăvus, i *m,* great-grandfather

prŏbābĭlis, e *adj, adv, īter,* likely, pleasing

prŏbābĭlĭtas, ātis *f,* probability

prŏbātĭo, ōnis *f,* trial, proving

prŏbātus, a, um *adj,* tried, good

prŏbĭtae, ātis *f,* honesty

prŏbo *v.t.* 1, to try, test, approve of, recommend, prove

prŏboscis, ĭdis *f,* elephant's trunk

prŏbrōsus, a, um *adj,* shameful

prŏbrum, i *n,* disgraceful deed, lechery, disgrace, abuse

prŏbus, a, um *adj, adv, ē,* good, honest, virtuous

prŏcācĭtas, ātis *f,* impudence

prŏcax, ācis *adj,* impudent

prŏcēdo, cessi, cessum *v.i.* 3, to go forward, advance, turn out, prosper

prŏcella, ae *f,* storm, violence

prŏcellōsus, a, um *adj,* tempestuous

prŏcer, ĕris *m,* chief, prince

prŏcērĭtas, ātis *f,* height

prŏcērus, a, um *adj,* tall

prŏcessus, ūs *m,* advance

prŏcĭdo, di *v.i.* 3, to fall flat

prŏcinctus, ūs *m,* readiness for battle

prŏclāmo *v.t.* 1, to cry out

prŏclīno *v.t.* 1, to bend forwards

prŏclīve, is *n,* slope, descent

prŏclīvis, e *adj,* sloping downhill, liable, willing

prŏconsul, is *m,* provincial govenor

prŏcrastino *v.t.* 1, to defer

prōcrĕātĭo, ōnis *f,* procreation

prōcrĕātor, ōris *m*, creator
prōcrĕo *v.t.* 1, to produce
prōcŭbo *v.i.* 1, to lie stretched-out
prōcūdo, di, sum *v.t.* 3, to forge
prŏcul *adv*, in the distance
prōculo *v.t.* 1, to trample on
prōcumbo, cŭbŭi, cŭbĭtum *v.i.* 3, to lean or fall forwards, sink
prōcūrātĭo, ōnis *f*, administration
prōcūrātor, ōris *m*, manager, agent
prōcūro *v.t.* 1, to look after
prōcurro, curri, cursum *v.i.* 3, to run forward, project
prŏcus, i *m*, suitor
prōdĕo, ĭi, ĭtum *v.i.* 3, to come forward, appear
prōdesse see prōsum
prōdĭgĭōsus, a, um *adj*, strange, marvellous
prōdĭgĭum, ii *n*, omen, monster
prōdĭgus, a, um *adj*, wasteful
prōdĭtĭo, ōnis *f*, treachery
prōdĭtor, ōris *m*, traitor
prōdo, dĭdi, dĭtum *v.t.* 3, to bring out, relate, betray, bequeath
prōdūco, xi, ctum *v.t.* 3, to lead forward, prolong, produce, promote
prōductus, a, um *adj, adv, ē*, prolonged
proelĭor *v.i.* 1, *dep*, to join battle
proelĭum, ii *n*, battle
prŏfāno *v.t.* 1, to desecrate
prŏfānus, a, um *adj*, wicked, common
prŏfectĭo, ōnis *f*, departure
prŏfectō *adv*, certainly
prŏfectus, ūs *m*, advance
prŏfectus, a, um *adj*, having advanced
prŏfĕro, ferre, tŭli, lātum *v.t, irreg*, to bring out, extend, defer, reveal, mention; *with* gradum, to proceed; *with* signa, to march forward
prŏfessor ōris *m*, teacher, professor
prŏfessĭo, ōnis *f*, declaration
prŏfessus, a, um *adj*, avowed
prŏfestus, a, um *adj*, working (days)

prŏfĭcĭo, fēci, fectum *v.i.t.* 3, to progress; perform, help
prŏfĭciscor, prŏfectus *v.i.* 3, *dep*, to set out, originate
prŏfĭtĕor, fessus *v.i.* 2, *dep*, to declare, acknowledge, promise
prōflīgātus, a, um *adj*, wretched, dissolute
prōflīgo *v.t.* 1, to overthrow
prōflo *v.t.* 1, to blow out
prōflŭo, xi, xum *v.i.* 3, to flow out, proceed
prōflŭens, ntis *adj*, fluent
prōflŭvĭum, ii *n*, flowing out
prŏfor *v.t.* 1, *dep*, to speak, say
prŏfŭgĭo, fūgi *v.i.t.* 3, to escape; flee from
prŏfŭgus, a, um *adj*, fugitive
prŏfŭgus, i *m*, fugitive, exile
prŏfundo, fūdi, fūsum *v.t.* 3, to pour out, utter, squander
prŏfundum, i *n*, the deep, the sea, an abyss
prŏfundus, a, um *adj*, deep
prŏfūsĭo, ōnis *f*, outpouring, prodigal use
prŏfūsus, a, um *adj*, extravagant
prōgĕnĕro *v.t.* 1, to beget
prōgĕnĭes, ēi *f*, family, offspring
prōgigno, gĕnŭi, gĕnĭtum *v.t.* 3, to produce
prōgnātus, a, um *adj*, born
prōgnātus, i *m*, descendant
prōgrĕdĭor, gressus *v.i.* 3, *dep*, to advance, proceed
prōgressĭo, ōnis *f*, growth
prōgressus, ūs *m*, advance
proh! see prō!
prŏhĭbĕo *v.t.* 2, to prevent, prohibit, defend
prōiectus, a, um *adj*, projecting
prōĭcĭo, iēci, iectum *v.t.* 3, to throw forward, extend, expel, yield, disdain
prŏin or prŏindē *adv*, in the same way, equally, accordingly, therefore
prōlābor, lapsus *v.i.* 3, *dep*, to slip or slide forward, fall
prōlātĭo, ōnis *f*, postponement, mentioning
prōlāto *v.t.* 1, to postpone
prōles, is *f*, offspring, child

prōlētārĭus, ii   *m*, citizen of lowest class

prōlixus, a, um   *adj, adv*, ē, stretched out, fortunate

prōlŏgus, i   *m*, prologue

prōlūdo, si, sum   *v.i.* 3, to practise in advance

prōlŭo, lŭi, lūtum   *v.t.* 3, to wash away, moisten

prōlūsĭo, ōnis   *f*, prelude

prōlŭvĭes, ēi   *f*, overflow

prōmĕrĕo   *v.t.* 2, to deserve, merit

prōmĕrĕor   *v.t.* 2, *dep*, to deserve, merit

prōmĭnens, ntis   *adj*, prominent

prōmĭnĕo   *v.i.* 2, to project

prōmiscŭus, a, um   *adj*, common, indiscriminate

prōmissĭo, ōnis   *f*, promise

prōmissum, i   *n*, promise

prōmissus, a, um   *adj*, hanging

prōmitto, mīsi, missum   *v.t.* 3, to promise, assure

prōmo, mpsi, mptum   *v.t.* 3, to bring out, produce, tell

prōmontūrĭum, ii   *n*, headland

prōmŏvĕo, mōvi, mōtum   *v.t.* 2, to move forward, extend

promptus, a, um   *adj*, ready, quick

promptus, ūs   *m*, only in phrase; in promptu, in public; in promptu esse, to be at hand

prōmulgo   *v.t.* 1, to publish

prōmus, i   *m*, butler

prōmūtŭus, a, um   *adj*, loaned

prōnĕpos, ōtis   *m*, great-grandson

prōnōmen, ĭnis   *n*, pronoun

prōnŭba, ae   *f*, bridesmaid

prōnuntĭātĭo, ōnis   *f*, proclamation

prōnuntĭo   *v.t.* 1, to announce

prōnus, a, um   *adj*, leaning or bending forward, disposed; setting, sinking (of stars, etc.)

prŏoemĭum, ii   *n*, preface

prŏpāgātĭo, ōnis   *f*, extension

prŏpāgo   *v.t.* 1, to generate, extend

prŏpāto, ĭnis   *f*, shoot (of plant), offspring, child

prōpălam   *adv*, openly

prōpătŭlus, a, um   *adj*, uncovered

prŏpe   *adv, and prep. with acc*, near, nearly

prŏpĕdĭem   *adv*, soon

prŏpello, pŭli, pulsum   *v.t.* 3, to push or drive forward

prŏpĕmŏdum   *adv*, almost

prŏpendĕo, di, sum   *v.i.* 2, to be inclined or disposed

prōpensus, a, um   *adj*, inclined, disposed

prŏpĕro   *v.i.t.* 1, to hurry

prŏpĕrus, a, um   *adj, adv*, ē, quick, hurrying

prōpexus, a, um   *adj*, combed forward

prōpīno   *v.t.* 1, to drink a toast

prŏpinquĭtas, ātis   *f*, nearness, relationship

prŏpinquo   *v.i.t.* 1, to approach; hasten

prŏpinquus, a, um   *adj*, near

prŏpinquus, i   *m*, relative

prŏpĭor, ĭus   *comp. adj*, nearer

prŏpĭtĭus, a, um   *adj*, kind, favourable

prŏpĭus   *comp. adv*, nearer

prōpōno, pŏsŭi, pŏsĭtum   *v.t.* 3, to but forward, state, display, offer

prōpŏsĭtĭo, ōnis   *f*, representation, theme

prōpŏsĭtum, i   *n*, plan, purpose

prŏprĭĕtas, ātis   *f*, peculiarity

prŏprĭus, a, um   *adj, adv*, ē, special, particular, its (his, her) own

propter   *prep. with acc*, on account of, near; *adv*, nearby

proptĕrĕā   *adv*, for that reason

prŏpugnācŭlum, i   *n*, rampart

prŏpugnātĭo, ōnis   *f*, defence

prŏpugnātor, ōris   *m*, defender

prŏpugno   *v.i.t.* 1, to make sorties; defend

prōpulso   *v.t.* 1, to ward off

prōra, ae   *f*, prow, ship

prōrēpo, psi, ptum   *v.i.* 3, to creep out, crawl forward

prōrĭpĭo, pŭi, reptum   *v.t.* 3, to drag forward; *with* se, to rush

prōrŏgātĭo, ōnis   *f*, prolonging

prōrŏgo   *v.t.* 1, to prolong, defer

prorsus (prorsum)   *adv*, certainly, utterly

prōrumpo, rūpi, ruptum   *v.i.t.* 3, to rush forward; send forward

prōrŭo, rŭi, rŭtum *v.i.t.* 3, to rush forward; overthrow

proscaenĭum ii *n,* stage

prōscindo, scĭdi, scissum *v.t.* 3, to tear up, plough

prōscrībo, psi, ptum *v.t.* 3, to publish, confiscate, outlaw

prōscriptĭo, ōnis *f,* confiscation, outlawing

prōscriptus, i *m,* outlaw

prōsēmĭno *v.t.* 1, to sow

prōsĕquor, sĕcūtus *v.t.* 3, *dep,* to accompany, follow, pursue, bestow, proceed with

prōsĭlĭo, ŭi *v.i.* 4, to leap up

prospecto *v.t.* 1, to look at, expect, await

prospectus, ūs *m,* view, sight

prospĕrus, a, um *adj, adv, ē,* favourable, fortunate

prospĕrĭtas, ātis *f,* prosperity

prospĕro *v.t.* 1, to make (something) successful

prōspĭcĭo, spexi, spectum *v.i.t* 3, to look out; discern, overlook, forsee

prōsterno, strāvi, strātum *v.t.* 3, to overthrow, prostrate

prōsŭbĭgo *v.t.* 3, to dig up

prōsum, prōdesse, prōfŭi *v.i, irreg, with dat,* to be useful

prōtectum, i *n,* eaves

prōtĕgo, xi, ctum *v.t.* 3, to cover, protect

prōtēlum, i *n,* team of oxen

prōtendo, di, sum (tum) *v.t.* 3, to stretch out, extend

prōtĕro, trīvi, trītum *v.t.* 3, to trample down, crush, destroy

prōterrĕo *v.t.* 2, to terrify

prōtervĭtas, ātis *f,* impudence

prōtervus, a, um *adj, adv, ē,* forward, impudent, violent

prōtĭnus *adv,* straightforwards, continuously, immediately

prōtrăho, xi, ctum *v.t.* 3, to drag forward, reveal

prōtrūdo, si, sum *v.t.* 3, to push out

prōturbo *v.t.* 1, to repel

prout *adv,* just as

prōvectus, a, um *adj,* advanced (of time)

prōvĕho, xi, ctum *v.t.* 3, to carry forward, advance, promote

prōvĕnĭo, vēni, ventum *v.i.* 4, to be born, thrive, occur, turn out (well or badly)

prōventus, ūs *m,* produce, result

prōverbĭum, ii *n,* proverb

prōvĭdens, ntis *adj,* prudent

prōvĭdentĭa, ae *f,* foresight

prōvĭdĕo, vīdi, vīsum *v.i.t.* 2, to make preparations; forsee, provide for

prōvĭdus, a, um *adj,* prudent

prōvincĭa, ae *f,* province, duty, sphere of duty

prōvincĭālis, e *adj,* provincial

prōvŏcātĭo, ōnis *f,* appeal

prōvŏco *v.i.t.* 1, to appeal; call out, challenge, rouse

prōvŏlo *v.i.* 1, to fly out

prōvolvo, volvi, vŏlūtum *v.t.* 3, to roll forward

proxĭmē *adv,* nearest, next

proxĭmĭtas, ātis *f,* proximity

proxĭmus, a, um *adj,* nearest, next, previous

prūdens, ntis *adj, adv, nter,* experienced, wise, sensible

prūdentĭa, ae *f,* experience, skill, discretion

prūīna, ae *f,* frost, snow

prūīnōsus, a, um *adj,* frosty

prūna, ae *f,* burning coal

prūnum, i *n,* plum

prūnus, i *f,* plum tree

prūrĭo *v.i.* 4, to itch

prūrītus, ūs *m,* itching

psallo, i *v.i.* 3, to play on an instrument

psalmus, i *m,* a psalm

psittăcus, i *m,* parrot

ptīsăna, ae *f,* pearl barley

pūbens, ntis *adj,* flourishing

pūbertas, ātis *f,* puberty, manhood

pūbes (pūber), ĕris *adj,* adult

pūbes, is *f,* young men

pūbesco, bŭi *v.i.* 3, to grow up, ripen

pūblĭcānus, i *m,* tax collector

pūblĭcātĭo, ōnis *f,* confiscation

pūblĭco *v.t.* 1, to confiscate

pūblĭcum, i   *n*, a public place
pūblĭcus, a, um   *adj, adv*, ē, of the
  state, public, general
pŭdendus, a, um   *adj*, disgraceful
pŭdens, ntis   *adj, adv*, nter,
  modest
pŭdet   *v*. 2, *impers*, it brings
  shame
pŭdībundus, a, um   *adj*, modest
pŭdīcĭtĭa, ae   *f*, modesty, virtue
pŭdīcus, a, um   *adj*, modest, pure
pŭdor, ōris   *m*, a sense of decency,
  shyness
pŭella, ae   *f*, girl, sweetheart,
  young wife
pŭellāris, e   *adj*, girlish
pŭer, ĕri   *m*, boy
pŭĕrīlis, e   *adj*, youthful
pŭĕrĭtĭa (pŭertĭa), ae   *f*, childhood,
  youth
pŭgil, īlis   *m*, boxer
pŭgillāres, īum   *m.pl*. writing
  tablets
pŭgĭo, ōnis   *m*, dagger
pugna, ae   *f*, fight, battle
pugnātor, ōris   *m*, fighter
pugnax, ācis   *adj*, warlike,
  quarrelsome
pugno   *v.i*. 1, to fight, disagree,
  struggle
pugnus, i   *m*, fist
pulcher, chra, chrum   *adj, adv*, ē,
  beautiful, handsome, glorious
pulchrĭtūdo, ĭnis   *f*, beauty
pūlex, ĭcis   *m*, flea
pullārĭus, ii   *m*, chicken-keeper
pullŭlo   *v.i*. 1, to sprout
pullus, i   *m*, young animal,
  chicken
pullus, a, um   *adj*, dark, black
pulmentārĭum, ii   *n*, sauce
pulmentum, i   *n*, sauce
pulmo, ōnis   *m*, lung
pulpĭtum, i   *n*, platform
puls, pultis   *f*, porridge
pulsātĭo, ōnis   *f*, beating
pulso   *v.t*. 1, to beat, push, touch,
  disturb
pulsus, ūs   *m*, push, blow,
  beating
pulvĕrĕus, a, um   *adj*, dusty
pulvĕrŭlentus, a, um   *adj*, dusty
pulvīnar, āris   *n*, couch

pulvīnus, i   *m*, cushion
pulvis, ĕris   *m*, dust
pūmex, ĭcis   *m*, pumice stone
pūmĭlĭo, ōnis   *m*, dwarf
punctim   *adv*, with the point
punctum, i   *n*, point, vote,
  moment
pungo, pŭpŭgi, punctum   *v.t*. 3, to
  prick, sting, vex, annoy
pūnĭcĕus, a, um   *adj*, red
pūnĭo   *v.t*. (pūnĭor   *v.t, dep*.) 4,
  to punish
pūpa, ae   *f*, doll
pūpilla, ae   *f*, orphan, ward
pūpillus, i   *m*, orphan, ward
puppis, is   *f*, ship's stern
pūpŭla, ae   *f*, pupil of the eye
purgāmen, ĭnis   *n*, refuse, filth
purgāmentum, i   *n*, refuse,
  filth
purgātĭo, ōnis   *f*, cleansing
purgo   *v.t*. 1, to clean, purify,
  excuse, justify, atone for
purpŭra, ae   *f*, purple, purple
  clothes
puprŭrĕus, a, um   *adj*, purple,
  clothed in purple, brilliant
pūrum, i   *n*, clear sky
pūrus, a, um   *adj, adv*, ē, pure,
  clean, plain
pūs, pūris   *n*, pus
pŭsillus, a, um   *adj*, little, petty
pūsĭo, ōnis   *m*, urchin
pustŭla, ae   *f*, pimple
pŭtāmen, ĭnis   *f*, peel, shell
pŭtĕal, ālis   *n*, fence of a well
pūtĕo   *v.i*. 2, to stink
pŭter (pŭtris), tris, tre   *adj*,
  decaying, rotten
pūtesco, pūtŭi   *v.i*. 3, to rot
pŭtĕus, i   *m*, well, pit
pūtĭdus, a, um   *adj*, rotten,
  disgusting
pŭto   *v.t*. 1, to think, prune
pŭtresco   *v.i*. 3, to decay
pŭtrĭdus, a, um   *adj*, rotten
pȳra, ae   *f*, funeral pyre
pȳrămis, ĭdis   *f*, pyramid
pȳrum, i   *n*, pear
pȳrus, i   *f*, pear tree
pȳthon, ōnis   *m*, python
pyxis, ĭdis   *f*, box

Q

quā *adv*, where, in which direction, how; **qua ... qua,** partly...partly

quācumque *adv*, wheresoever

quădra, ae *f*, square, dining table

quădrāgĕni, ae, a *adj*, forty each

quădrāgēsĭmus, a, um *adj*, fortieth

quădrāgĭes *adv*, forty times

quădrāginta *adv*, forty

quădrans, ntis *m*, a quarter

quădrātum, i *n*, square

quădrātus, a, um *adj*, square

quădrĭdŭum, ii *n*, period of four days

quădrĭfāriam *adv*, into four parts

quădrĭfĭdus, a, um *adj*, split into four

quădrīgae, ārum *f.pl*, four-horse team or chariot

quădrīiŭgis, e *adj*, yoked in a four-horse team

quădrīiŭgus, a, um *adj*, yoked in a four-horse team

quădrĭlātĕrus, a, um *adj*, quadrilateral

quădrīmus, a, um *adj*, four years old

quădringēnārĭus, a, um *adj*, of four hundred each

quădringenti, ae, a *adj*, four hundred

quădringentĭes *adv*, four hundred times

quădro *v.i.t.* 1, to be square, agree; make square, complete

quădrum, i *n*, square

quădrŭpēdans, ntis *adj*, galloping

quădrŭpēs, ĕdis *adj*, galloping, going on four feet

quădrŭplex, ĭcis *adj*, quadruple

quădrŭplum, i *n*, fourfold amount

quaero, sīvi, sītum *v.t.* 3, to search for, acquire, inquire

quaesītĭo, ōnis *f*, investigation

quaesītor, ōris *m*, investigator

quaesītum, i *n*, question

quaesītus, a, um *adj*, far-fetched

quaeso, īvi *v.t.* 3, to beseech, seek

quaestĭo, ōnis *f*, investigation, trial, case, question, problem

quaestor, ōris *m*, Roman magistrate in charge of public revenues

quaestōrĭus, a, um *adj*, of a quaestor

quaestŭōsus, a, um *adj*, profitable

quaestūra, ae *f*, quaestorship

quaestus, ūs *m*, gain, profit, employment

quālis, e *adj*, of what kind

quāliscumque, quālĕcumque *adj*, of whatever kind

quālĭtas, ātis *f*, state, condition

quālum, i *n*, basket, hamper

quam *adv*, how; *with comparatives*, than

quamdĭu *adv*, as long as, until

quamlībet *adv*, as much as you wish

quămobrem *adv*, why, wherefore

quamprīmum *adv*, as soon as possible

quamquam *conj*, although

quamvīs *conj*, although; *adv*, very

quando *adv*, when?, some time; *conj*, since, because

quandōcumque *adv*, whenever

quandōque *adv*, whenever, at some time or other

quandōquĭdem *adv*, since

quanti? at what price?

quantō *adv*, by as much as

quantŏpĕrē *adv*, how much

quantŭlus, a, um *adj*, how small

quantŭluscumque *adj*, however small

quantum *adv*, as much as

quantus, a, um *adj*, how great

quantuscumque *adj*, however big

quantusvis, quantăvis, quantumvis *adj*, as big as you like

quāpropter *adv*, wherefore

quārē *adv*, wherefore, why

quartānus, a, um *adj*, occurring on the fourth day

quartum *adv*, for the fourth time

quartō *adv*, for the fourth time

quartus, a, um *adj*, fourth

quăsĭ *adv*, as if, just as

quăsillum, i *n*, small basket

quassātĭo, ōnis *f*, shaking

quasso *v.t.* 1, to shake, shatter

quātĕnus *adv*, to what extent, how long, since

quăter *adv*, four times

quătemi, ae, a *pl. adj*, four each

quătĭo (*no perf.*), quassum *v.t.* 3, to shake, shatter, excite

quattŭor *indecl. adj*, four

quattŭordĕcim *adj*, fourteen

quĕ *conj*, add

quĕmadmŏdum *adv*, how

quĕo, ĭi, ĭtum *v.i.* 4, to be able

quercētum, i *n*, oak forest

quercus, ūs *f*, oak tree

quĕrēla, ae *f*, complaint

quĕrĭbundus, a, um *adj*, complaining

quĕrĭmōnĭa, ae *f*, complaint

quernus, a, um *adj*, of oak

quĕror, questus *v.i.t.* 3, *dep*, to complain

quĕrŭlus, a, um *adj*, full of complaints, cooing, chirping

questus, ūs *m*, complaint

qui, quae, quod *rel. pron*, who, which, what

quī *adv*, how, wherewith

quĭă *conj*, because

quicquid *pron*, whatever

quīcumque, quaecumque, quodcumque *pron*, whoever, whatever

quid *interr. pron*, what? why?

quīdam, quaedam, quoddam *pron*, a certain somebody or something

quĭdem *adv*, indeed; ne ... quidem, not even ...

quidni why not?

quĭes, ētis *f*, rest, quiet

quĭescens, ntis *adj*, quiescent

quĭesco, ēvi, ētum *v.i.* 3, to rest, keep quiet, sleep

quĭētus, a, um *adj*, calm

quīlĭbet, quaelĭbet, quodlĭbet *pron*, anyone or anything you like

quīn *conj*, that not, but that, indeed, why not

quīnam, quaenam, quodnam *pron*, who, what, which

quincunx, ncis *m*, five-twelfths, trees planted in oblique lines

qindĕcĭes *adv*, fifteen times

quīndĕcim *indecl. adj*, fifteen

quingēni, ae, a *pl. adj*, five hundred each

quingenti, ae, a *pl. adj*, five hundred

quingentĭes *adv*, five hundred times

quīni, ae, a *pl. adj*, five each

quinquāgēni, ae, a *pl. adj*, fifty each

quinquāgēsĭmus, a, um *adj*, fiftieth

quinquāginta *indecl. adj*, fifty

quinquātrĭa, ōrum *n.pl*, festival of Minerva (19th–23rd March)

quinquĕ *indec. adj*, five

quinquennālis, e *adj*, quinquennial

quinquennis, e *adj*, every fifth year

quiquennĭum, ii *n*, period of five years

quinquĕrēmis *adj*, ship with five banks of oars

quinquĭens *adv*, five times

Quintīlis (menis) July

quintus, a, um *adj*, fifth

quippe *adv*, certainly; *conj*, in as much as

quis, quid *interr pron*, who? which? what? *indef. pron*, anyone, anything

quisnam, quaenam, quidnam *interr. pron*, who? which?

quispĭam, quaepĭam, quodpĭam *indef. pron*, anybody, anything

quisquam, quaequam, quicquam *indef. pron*, anyone, anything

quisque, quaeque, quodque *indef. pron*, each, every, everybody, everything

quisquĭlĭae, ārum *f.pl*, rubbish

quisquis, quaeque, quodquod *indef. pron*, whoever, whatever

quīvis, quaevis, quodvis *indef. pron*, anyone or anything you please

quō *adv. and conj*, wherefore, where to, whither, so that

quŏad *adv*, as long as, until, as, far as

quōcircă *conj*, wherefore

quōcumque *adv,* to whatever place
quod *conj,* because
quod *neuter* of qui
quōdammŏdo in a certain manner
quōmĭnus *conj,* that ... not
quōmŏdŏ *adv,* how
quondam *adv,* once, at times
quŏnĭam *adv,* since, because
quōquam *adv,* to any place
quŏque *conj,* also, too
quōquō *adv,* to whatever place
quorsum (quorsus) *adv,* to what place, to what purpose
quŏt *indecl. adj,* how many
quŏtannis *adv,* every year
quŏtīdīānus, a, um *adj,* daily
quŏtīdĭe *adv,* daily
quŏtĭes (quŏtĭens) *adv,* how often
quŏtĭescumquĕ *adv,* however often
quotquŏt *adv,* however many
quŏtus, a, um *adj,* how many
quŏusquē *adv,* how long
quum see cum

R

răbĭdus, a, um *adj,* raving mad
răbĭes (em, e) *f,* madness, anger
răbĭōsus, a, um *adj,* raging
răbŭla, ae *f,* argumentative lawyer
răcēmĭfer, ĕra, ĕrum *adj,* clustering
răcēmux, i *m,* bunch, cluster
rādīcĭtus *adv,* by the roots
rădĭans, ntis *adj,* shining
rădĭātĭo, ōnis *f,* shining
rădĭo *v.i.* 1, to shine
rădĭus, ii *m,* rod, spoke, radius, shuttle, ray
rādix, īcis *f,* root, radish, source
rādo, si, sum *v.t.* 3, to scrape, shave
raeda, ae *f,* carriage
raedārĭus, i *m,* coachman
raia, ae *f,* ray (fish)
rāmālĭa, ĭum *n.pl,* brushwood
rāmōsus, a, um *adj,* branching
rāmus, i *m,* branch
rāna, ae *f,* frog

rancĭdus, a, um *adj,* rancid
rānuncŭlus, i *m,* tadpole
răpācĭtas, ātis *f,* rapacity
răpax, ācis *adj,* grasping
răphănus, i *m,* radish
răpĭdus, a, um *adj, adv,* ē, swift, violent, tearing
răpīna, ae *f,* robbery, plunder
răpĭo, ŭi, raptum *v.t.* 3, to seize, snatch, drag away
raptim *adv,* hurriedly
raptĭo, ōnis *f,* abduction
rapto *v.t.* 1, to snatch, drag away, plunder
raptor, ōris *m,* robber
raptum, i *n,* plunder
raptus, ūs *m,* robbery, rape
răpŭlum, i *n,* turnip
rāpum, i *n,* turnip
rāresco *v.i.* 3, to grow thin, open out
rārĭtas, ātis *f,* looseness, rarity, infrequency
rārus, a, um *adj, adv,* ē, ō, loose, loose in texture, thin, scattered, straggling, few, remarkable, rare
rāsĭlis, e *adj,* polished
rastellus, i *m,* hoe, rake
rastrum i *n,* rake, hoe
rătĭo, ōnis *f,* account, calculation, business affairs, relationship, concern for, consideration, conduct, plan, reason, motive, reckoning, order, law, theory, system, way, manner
rătĭōcĭnor *v.i.t.* 1, *dep,* to calculate
rătĭōnālis, e *adj,* rational, theoretical
rătis, is *f,* raft
rătus, a, um *adj,* established; (*partic.*) having thought; pro rătā, proportionally
raucus, a, um *adj,* hoarse
rāvus, a, um *adj,* grey, tawny
rē, rēvērā *adv,* really
rĕapse *adv* (re ipsa) in fact
rĕbellĭo, ōnis *f,* revolt
rĕbellis, e *adj,* rebellious
rĕbello *v.i.* 1, to rebel, rebuff
rĕboo *v.i.* 1, to re-echo
rĕcalcĭtro *v.i.* 1, to kick back
rĕcalfăcĭo, fēci *v.t.* 3, to warm

rĕcandesco, dŭi   *v.i.* 3, to grow white or hot

rĕcanto (*no perf.*)   *v.t.* 1, to retract

rĕcēdo, cessi, cessum   *v.i.* 3, to retreat, withdraw

rĕcens, ntis   *adj,* fresh, new

rĕcens   *adv,* newly, recently

rĕcensĕo, ŭi, ītum   *v.t.* 2, to count, rekon, survey, review

rĕcensĭo, ōnis   *f,* review

rĕceptācŭlum, i   *n,* shelter

rĕcepto   *v.t.* 1, to recover

rĕceptor, ōris   *m,* receiver

rĕceptus, ūs   *m,* retreat

rĕcessus, ūs   *m,* retreat, recess

rĕcĭdīvus, a, um   *adj,* recurring

rĕcĭdo, cĭdi, cāsum   *v.i.* 3, to fall back, recoil, return

rĕcīdo, cīdi, cīsum   *v.t.* 3, to cut down, cut off, cut short

rĕcingo (*no perf.*) cinctum   *v.t.* 3, to loosen

rĕcĭno   *v.i.* 3, to re-echo

rĕcĭpĕro (rĕcŭpĕro)   *v.t.* 1, to regain

rĕcĭpĭo, cēpi, ceptum   *v.t.* 3, to take back, regain, receive, give an assurance; *with* sē to retreat, recover oneself

rĕcĭprŏco   *v.i.t.* 1, to move backwards

rĕcĭprŏcus, a, um   *adj,* receding

recĭtātĭo, ōnis   *f,* reading aloud

rĕcĭtātor, ōris   *m,* reader

rĕcĭto   *v.t.* 1, to read aloud

rĕclāmātĭo, ōnis   *f,* remonstrance

rĕclāmo   *v.i.t.* 1, to resound; contradict loudly, remonstrate

rĕclīno   *v.t.* 1, to lean back

rĕclūdo, si, sum   *v.t.* 3, to reveal

rĕcognĭgĭo, ōnis   *f,* review

rĕcognosco, gnōvi, gnĭtum   *v.t.* 3, to recollect, investigate

rĕcŏlo, cŏlŭi, cultum   *v.t.* 3, to cultivate again, renew

rĕconcĭlĭātĭo, ōnis   *f,* re-establishment, reconciliation

rĕconcĭlĭo   *v.t.* 1, to restore, reconcile

rĕcondĭtus, a, um   *adj,* hidden

rĕcondo, dĭdi, dĭtum   *v.t.* 3, to put away, hide

rĕcŏquo, xi, ctum   *v.t.* 3, to cook again, forge again

rĕcordātĭo, ōnis   *f,* recollection

rĕcordor   *v.i.t.* 1, *dep,* to think over, remember

rĕcrĕātĭo, ōnis   *f,* recovery

rĕcrĕo   *v.t.* 1, to revive, reproduce

rĕcresco, crēvi, crētum   *v.i.* 3, to grow again

rectā   *adv,* straightforwards

rector, ōris   *m,* master, leader, helmsman

rectum, i   *n,* virtue

rectus, a, um   *adj, adv,* ē, straight, upright, correct

rĕcŭbans, ntis   *adj,* recumbent

rĕcŭbo   *v.i.* 1, to lie back

rĕcumbo, cŭbŭi   *v.i.* 3, to lie down

rĕcŭpĕrātĭo, ōnis   *f,* recovery

rĕcŭpĕro   *v.t.* 1, to recover, regain

rĕcurro, curri   *v.i.* 3, to run back, return

rĕcurso   *v.i.* 1, to return

rĕcursus, ūs   *m,* return, retreat

rĕcurvo   *v.t.* 1, to bend back

rĕcurvus, a, um   *adj,* bent

rĕcūsātĭo, ōnis   *f,* refusal

rĕcūso   *v.t.* 1, to refuse

rĕcussus, a, um   *adj,* roused

rĕdargŭo, ŭi   *v.t.* 3, to contradict

reddo, dĭdi, dĭtum   *v.t.* 3, to give back, deliver, pay, produce, render, translate, recite, repeat, resemble

rĕdemptĭo, ōnis   *f,* buying back

rĕdemptor, ōris   *m,* contractor

rĕdĕo, ĭi, ĭtum   *v.i.* 4, to go back, return, be reduced to

rĕdīgo, ēgi, actum   *v.t.* 3, to bring back, restore, collect, reduce to

rĕdĭmīcŭlum, i   *n,* necklace

rĕdmĭo   *v.t.* 4, to encircle

rĕdĭmo, ēmi, emptum   *v.t.* 3, to repurchase, ransom, release, hire, obtain

rĕdintĕgro   *v.t.* 1, to restore

rĕdĭtus, ūs   *m,* return

rĕdŏlĕo   *v.i.t.* 2, to smell; smell of

rĕdōno   *v.t.* 1, to restore

rĕdūco, xi, ctum   *v.t.* 3, to bring back, restore

rĕductus, a, um   *adj,* remote

rĕdundantĭa, ae   *f,* redundancy

rĕdundo

rĕdundo *v.i.* 1, to overflow, abound in

rĕdus, dŭcis *adj,* brought back

rĕfello, felli *v.t.* 3, to refute

rĕfercĭo, si, tum *v.t.* 4, to cram

rĕfĕro, fĕrre, rettŭli, rĕlātum *v.t, irreg,* to bring back, restore, repay, report, reply, propose, record, reckon, refer, resemble; *with* **pedem,** to retreat

rēfert *v. impers,* it is of importance, it matters

rĕfertus, a, um *adj,* filled

rĕfĭcĭo, fēci, fectum *v.t.* 3, to re-make, repair, refresh

rĕfīgo, xi, xum *v.t.* 3, to unfix

rĕfingo *v.t.* 3, to renew

rĕflecto, xi, xum *v.i.t.* 3, to turn back; bend back

rĕflo *v.i.* 1, to blow back

rĕflŭo *v.i.* 3, to flow back

rĕformīdo (*no perf.*) *v.t.* 1, to dread, avoid

rĕfrāgor *v.i.* 1, *dep,* to resist

rĕfrēno *v.t.* 1, to curb, check

rĕfrīco, ŭi *v.t.* 1, to scratch open

rēfrīgĕro *v.t.* 1, to cool

rĕfrīgesco, frixi *v.i.* 3, to grow cool, grow stale

rĕfringo, frēgi, fractum *v.t.* 3, to break open, break off

rĕfŭgĭo, fūgi *v.i.t.* 3, to run away, escape; flee from, avoid

rĕfulgĕo, si *v.i.* 2, to shine

rĕfundo, fūdi, fūsum *v.t.* 3, to pour out, cause to overflow

rĕfūtandus *gerundive,* see **rĕfūto**

rĕfūto *v.t.* 1, to repress, refute

rēgālis, e *adj,* royal, splendid

rēgĭa, ae *f,* palace, court

rēgīfĭcus, a, um *adj,* royal

rēgigno *v.t.* 3, to reproduce

rēgĭmen, ĭnis *n,* guidance

rēgīna, ae *f,* queen

rēgĭo, ōnis *f,* district, region, direction, boundary; **ē rēgĭōne —** in a straight line

rēgĭus, a, um *adj, adv,* **ē,** royal, magnificent

regnātor, ōris *m,* ruler

regno *v.i.t.* 1, to reign; rule

regnum, i *n,* kingdom, sovereignty, dominion

rēgo, xi, ctum *v.t.* 3, to rule, guide, direct

rĕgrĕdĭor, gressus *v.i.* 3, *dep,* to return, retreat

rĕgressus, ūs *m,* return, retreat

rēgŭla, ae *f,* wooden ruler, model, pattern

rēgŭlus, i *m,* prince

rēĭcĭo, iēci, iectum *v.t.* 3, to throw back, repel, reject, postpone

rēiectĭo, ōnis *f,* rejection

rĕlābor, lapsus *v.i.* 3, *dep,* to slide or sink back

rĕlanguesco, gŭi *v.i.* 3, to grow faint, relax

relātĭo, ōnis *f,* proposition

rĕlaxo *v.t.* 1, to loosen, ease

rĕlēgātĭo, ōnis *f,* banishment

rĕlēgo *v.t.* 1, to send away, banish

rĕlĕgo, lēgi, lectum *v.t.* 3, to gather together, travel over again, read over again

rĕlĕvo *v.t.* 1, to lift up, lighten, comfort, refresh

rĕlictĭo, ōnis *f,* abandonment

rĕlictus, a, um *adj,* left

rĕlĭgĭo, ōnis *f,* piety, religion, religious scruple, good faith, conscientiousness, sanctity

rĕlĭgĭōsus, a, um *adj,* devout, scrupulous, precise, sacred

rĕlĭgo *v.t.* 1, to bind, fasten

rĕlīno, lēvi *v.t.* 3, to unseal

rĕlinquo, rĕlīqui, lictum *v.t.* 3, to leave, leave behind, abandon, surrender

rĕlĭquĭae, ārum *f.pl,* remains

rĕlĭquum, i *n,* remainder

rĕlĭquus, a, um *adj,* remaining

rĕlūcĕo, xi *v.i.* 2, to shine

rĕluctor *v.i.* 1, *dep,* to resist

rĕmănĕo, nsi *v.i.* 2, to stay behind, endure

rĕmĕdĭum, ii *n,* cure, relief

rĕmĕo *v.i.* 1, to return

rĕmētĭor, mensus *v.t.* 4, *dep,* to remeasure

rēmex, ĭgis *m,* oarsman

rēmĭgĭum, ii *n,* rowing, oars, rowers

rēmĭgo *v.i.* 1, to row

rĕmīgro *v.i.* 1, to return
rĕmĭniscor *v.*3, *dep, with genit,*
to remember
rĕmiscĕo (*no perf.*) mixtum *v.t.*
2, to mix up
rĕmissĭo, ōnis *f,* relaxation
rĕmissus, a, um *adj, adv,* ē, loose,
gentle, cheerful
rĕmitto, mīsi, missum *v.i.t.* 3, to
decrease; send back, send out,
yield, loosen, slacken, grant,
surrender, give up; *with infin,* to
cease
rĕmollesco *v.i.* 3, to grow soft
rĕmordĕo (*no perf.*), morsum
v.t. 2, to torment
rĕmŏror *v.i.t.* 1, *dep,* to loiter;
obstruct
rĕmōtus, a, um *adj,* distant
rĕmŏvĕo, mōvi, mōtum *v.t.* 2, to
remove, withdraw, set aside
rĕmūgĭo *v.i.* 4, to resound
rĕmulcum, i *n,* tow rope
rĕmūnĕrātĭo, ōnis *f,* reward
rĕmūnĕror *v.t.* 1, *dep,* to reward
rĕmurmŭro *v.i.t.* 1, to murmur
back
rēmus, i *m,* oar
rĕnascor, nātus *v.i.* 3, *dep,* to be
born again, spring up again
rēnes, um *m.pl,* kidneys
rĕnīdĕo *v.i.* 2, to glisten
rĕnŏvātĭo, ōnis *f,* revewal
rĕnŏvo *v.t.* 1, to renew, restore,
refresh, repeat
rĕnuntĭātĭo, ōnis *f,* announcement
rĕnuntĭo *v.t.* 1, to report,
announce, refuse, renounce
rĕnŭo, ŭi *v.i.t.* 3, to refuse
rĕor, rātus *v.t.* 2, *dep,* to suppose,
think, believe
rĕpāgŭla, ōrum *n.pl,* bolts, bars
rĕpărābĭlis, e *adj,* able to be
repaired
rĕpăro *v.t.* 1, to recover, repair,
restore, refresh
rĕpello, pŭli, pulsum *v.t.* 3, to
drive back, reject
rĕpendo, di, sum *v.t.* 3, to weigh
out in return, repay
rĕpens, ntis *adj, adv,* ē, sudden
rĕpentīnus, a, um *adj, adv,* ō,
sudden, unexpected

rĕpercussus, ūs *m,* reflection
rĕpercŭtĭo, cussi, cussum *v.t.* 3,
to drive back, reflect
rĕpĕrĭo, repperi, rĕpertum *v.t.* 4,
to find, discover
rĕpertor, ōris *m,* discoverer
rĕpĕto, ĭi, ītum *v.t.* 3, to attack
again, re-visit, fetch back,
resume, recollect, demand back
rĕpĕtundae, ārum *f.pl,* (*with* res),
extortion
rĕplĕo, ēvi, ētum *v.t.* 2, to fill up,
complete
rĕplētus, a, um *adj,* full
rēpo, psi, ptum *v.i.* 3, to creep
rĕpōno, pŏsŭi, pŏsĭtum *v.t.* 3, to
replace, preserve, put away
rĕporto *v.t.* 1, to bring back,
carry back, obtain
rĕposco *v.t.* 3, to demand back
rĕpraesentātĭo, ōnis *f,*
representation
rĕpraesento *v.t.* 1, to display, do
immediately
rĕprĕhendo, di, sum *v.t.* 3, to
blame, rebuke, convict
rĕprĕhensĭo, ōnis *f,* blame
rĕprĭmo, pressi, ssum *v.t.* 3, to
keep back, check, restrain
rĕpŭdĭātĭo, ōnis *f,* refusal,
renunciation
rĕpŭdĭo *v.t.* 1, to divorce, reject,
scorn
rĕpugnans, ntis *adj,*
contradictory, irreconcilable
rĕpugnantĭa, ae *f,* opposition,
inconsistency
rĕpungo *v.i.* 1, to resist, disagree
with
rĕpulsa, ae *f,* refusal, rejection
rĕpurgo *v.t.* 1, to clean
rĕpŭto *v.t.* 1, to ponder,
reckon
rĕquĭes, ētis *f,* rest, relaxation
rĕquĭesco, ēvi, etum *v.i.* 3, to rest
rĕquīro, sīvi, sītum *v.t.* 3, to
search for, enquire, need, notice
to be missing
rēs, rĕi *f,* thing, matter, affair,
reality, fact, property, profit,
advantage, business, affair,
lawsuit; rēs nŏvae, rērum
nŏvārum *f.pl,* revolution;

respublĭca, rēĭpublĭcae *f,* the State, statesmanship

rēscindo, scĭdi, ssum *v.t.* 3, to cut down, break down, abolish

rēscisco, īvi, ītum *v.t.* 3, to learn, ascertain

rēscrībo, psi, ptum *v.t.* 3, to write back, reply, repay

rěsěco, ŭi, ctum *v.t.* 1, to cut off, curtail

rěsěro *v.t.* 1, to unlock, open

rěservo *v.t.* 1, to save up, keep

rěsěs, īdis *adj,* inactive

rěsĭděo, sēdi *v.i.* 2, to remain, linger, sit

rěsīdo, sēdi *v.i.* 3, to settle

rěsĭdŭus, a, um *adj,* remaining

rěsigno *v.t.* 1, to unseal, open

rěsĭlĭo, ŭi *v.i.* 4, to recoil

rēsīna, ae *f,* resin

rěsĭpĭo *v.t.* 3, to taste of

rěsĭpisco, īvi *v.i.* 3, to revive

rěsisto, stĭti *v.i.* 3, to stop, remain; *with dat,* to resist

rěsolvo, solvi, sŏlūtum *v.t.* 3, to untie, release, open, relax, annul, abolish

rěsŏno *v.i.t.* 1, to resound; re-echo with

rěsŏnus, a, um *adj,* resounding

rěsorběo *v.t.* 2, to re-swallow

respecto *v.t.* 1, to look at, respect

respectus, ūs *m,* looking back, retreat, refuge, respect

rěspergo, si, sum *v.t.* 3, to besprinkle

rēspĭcĭo, spexi, spectum *v.i.t.* 3, to look back, give attention; look at, regard, respect

rēspīrātĭo, ōnis *f,* breathing

rēspīro *v.i.t.* 1, to revive; breathe out, breathe

rěsplenděo *v.i.* 2, to shine

rěsponděo, di, sum *v.t.* 2, to reply, give advice, agree, correspond, answer one's hopes

rēsponso *v.t.* 1, to reply, resist

rēsponsum, i *n,* answer

respublĭca see **rēs**

rěspŭo, ŭi *v.t.* 3, to spit out, expel, reject

rēstinguo, nxi, nctum *v.t.* 3, to quench, extinguish

restis, is *f,* rope

rēstĭtŭo, ŭi, ūtum *v.t.* 3, to replace, rebuild, renew, give back, restore

rēstĭtūtĭo, ōnis *f,* restoration

rēsto, stĭti *v.i.* 1, to remain

rēstrictus, a, um *adj,* bound

rēstringo, nxi, ctum *v.t.* 3, to bind, restrain

rěsulto (*no perf.*) *v.i.* 1, to jump back, resound

rěsūmo, mpsi, mptum *v.t.* 3, to resume, take back, recover

rěsŭpīnus, a, um *adj,* lying on one's back

rěsurgo, surrexi, surrectum *v.i.* 3, to rise, reappear

rěsurrectĭo, ōnis *f,* resurrection

rěsuscĭto *v.t.* 1, to revive

rětardo *v.i.t.* 1, to delay

rēte, is *n,* net, snare

rětěgo, xi, ctum *v.t.* 3, to uncover, reveal

rětendo, di, tum *v.t.* 3, to slacken

rětento *v.t.* 1, to keep back

rětento *v.t.* 1, to try again

rětexo, ŭi, xtum *v.t.* 3, to unravel, cancel

rětĭcěo *v.i.t.* 2, to be silent; conceal

rētĭcŭlātus, a, um *adj,* net-like

rētĭcŭlum, i *n,* small net

rětĭnācŭlum, i *n,* rope, cable

rětĭnens, ntis *adj,* tenacious

rětĭněo, ŭi, tentum *v.t.* 2, to hold back, restrain, maintain

rětorquěo, si, tum *v.t.* 2, to twist back, drive back

rětracto *v.t.* 1, to handle or undertake again, reconsider, refuse

rětrăho, xi, ctum *v.t.* 3, to draw back, call back, remove

rětrĭbŭo, ŭi, ūtum *v.t.* 3, to repay

rětrō *adv,* backwards, formerly, back, behind, on the other hand

rětrorsum(s) *adv,* backwards

rětundo, tŭdi, tūsum *v.t.* 3, to blunt, dull, weaken

rětūsus, a, um *adj,* blunt, dull

rěus, i *m* (**rěa, ae,** *f*), defendant, criminal, culprit rĕvălesco, lŭi　*v.i.* 3, to grow well again

rĕvĕho, xi, ctum　*v.t.* 3, to bring back; *in passive,* to return

rĕvello, velli, vulsum　*v.t.* 3, to pull out, tear away

rĕvĕnĭo, vēni, ventum　*v.i.* 4, to return

rēvērā　*adv,* really

rĕvĕrens, ntis　*adj,* reverent

rĕvĕrentĭa, ae　*f,* respect

rĕvĕrĕor　*v.t.* 2, *dep,* to revere

rĕverto, ti　*v.i.* 3, to return

rĕvertor, versus　*v.i.* 3, *dep,* to return

rĕvincendus　*gerundive,* see revinco

rĕvincĭo, nxi, nctum　*v.t.* 4, to bind, fasten

rĕvinco, vīci, victum　*v.t.* 3, to conquer, convict

rĕvĭresco, rŭi　*v.i.* 3, to grow green again

rĕvīso　*v.i.t.* 3, to revisit

rĕvīvisco, vixi　*v.i.* 3, to revive

rĕvŏcābĭlis, e　*adj,* able, to be recalled

rĕvŏcāmen, ĭnis　*n,* recall

rĕvŏcātĭo, ōnis　*f,* recalling

rĕvŏco　*v.t.* 1, to recall, restrain, refer

rĕvŏlo　*v.i.* 1, to fly back

rĕvolvo, volvi, vŏlūtum　*v.t.* 3, to unroll, repeat

rĕvŏmo, ŭi　*v.t.* 3, to vomit up

rex, rēgis　*m,* king

rhēda, ae　*f,* carriage

rhētor, ŏris　*m,* teacher of oratory

rhētŏrĭca, ae　*f,* rhetoric

rhētŏrĭcus, a, um　*adj,* rhetorical

rhīnŏcĕros, ōtis　*m,* rhinoceros

rhombus, i　*m,* magic circle, turbot

rhonchus, i　*m,* snore, sneer

rīca, ae　*f,* veil

rīcīnĭum, ii　*n,* small veil

rictus, ūs　*m,* gaping mouth

rīdĕo, si, sum　*v.i.t.* 2, to laugh, smile; laugh at, ridicule

rīdĭcŭlum, i　*n,* joke

rīdĭcŭlus, a, um　*adj, adv,* ē, amusing, absurd

rĭgĕo　*v.i.* 2, to be stiff

rĭgesco, gŭi　*v.i.* 3, to stiffen

rĭgĭdus, a, um　*adj,* stiff, stern

rĭgo　*v.t.* 1, to wet, water

rĭgor, ōris　*m,* stiffness, hardness, chilliness, severity

rĭgŭus, a, um　*adj,* irrigating

rīma, ae　*f,* crack, chink

rīmor　*v.t.* 1, *dep,* to tear up, explore, examine

rīmōsus, a, um　*adj,* leaky

rīpa, ae　*f,* river back

rīsus, ūs　*m,* laughter

rītĕ　*adv,* rightly, properly

rītus, ūs　*m,* religious ceremony, custom, way; rītu *with genit,* in the manner of

rīvālis, is　*m,* rival

rīvŭlus, i　*m,* brook

rīvus, i　*m,* brook, stream

rixa, ae　*f,* quarrel

rixor　*v.i.* 1, *dep,* to quarrel

rōbīgĭnōsus, a, um　*adj,* rusty

rōbīgo, ĭnis　*f,* rust, mould

rōbŏro　*v.t.* 1, to strengthen

rōbur, ŏris　*n,* oak, strength, power, vigour, force

rōbustus, a, um　*adj,* oaken, firm, strong, robust

rōdo, si, sum　*v.t.* 3, to gnaw, corrode, slander

rŏgātĭo, ōnis　*f,* proposed law or bill, request

rŏgātor, ōris　*m,* polling-clerk

rŏgo　*v.t.* 1, to ask; *with* legem, to propose (law), beg

rŏgus, i　*m,* funeral pile

rōro　*v.i.t.* 1, to drop, drip, trickle; wet, besprinkle

rōs, rōris　*m,* dew, moisture

rŏsa, ae　*f,* rose

rŏsārĭum, ii　*n,* rose garden

roscĭdus, a, um　*adj,* dewy

rŏsētum, i　*n,* rosebed

rŏsĕus, a, um　*adj,* of roses, rose-coloured

rostra, ōrum　*n.pl,* speaker's platform

rostrātus, a, um　*adj,* with beaks

rostrum, i　*n,* beak, snout

rŏta, ae　*f,* wheel, chariot

rŏto　*v.i.t.* 1, to revolve; swing round, whirl around

rŏtundĭtas, ātis　*f,* rotundity

rŏtundo　*v.t.* 1, to round off

rŏtundus, a, um *adj*, round, polished
rŭbĕfăcĭo, fēci, factum *v.t.* 3, to redden
rŭbens, ntis *adj*, red
rŭbĕo *v.i.* 2, to be red, blush
rŭber, bra, brum *adj*, red
rŭbesco, bŭi *v.i.* 3, to grow red
rŭbēta, ae *f*, toad
rŭbēta, ōrum *n.pl*, brambles
rŭbĭcundus, a, um *adj*, red
rūbīgo... see **rōbīgo...**
rŭbor, ōris *m*, redness, blush, bashfulness
rŭbrīca, ae *f*, red-chalk
rŭbus, i *m*, bramble bush
ructo *v.i.t.* 1, to belch
ructor *v.* 1, *dep*, to belch
ructus, ūs *m*, belching
rŭdens, ntis *m*, rope, rigging
rŭdīmentum, i *n*, first try
rŭdis, e *adj*, rough, raw, wild, awkward, inexperienced
rŭdis, is *f*, stick, wooden sword
rŭdo, īvi, ītum *v.i.* 3, to bellow
rŭdus, ĕris *n*, broken stones, rubbish
rūfus, a, um *adj*, red
rūga, ae *f*, wrinkle
rūgōsus, a, um *adj*, shrivelled
rŭīna, ae *f*, downfall, ruin
rŭīnōsus, a, um *adj*, in ruins
rūmĭno *v.t.* 1, to chew over
rūmor, ōris *m*, rumour, general opinion, reputation
rumpo, rūpi, ruptum *v.t.* 3, to break, burst, destroy, interrupt
runcīna, ae *f*, plane
runcīno *v.t.* 1, to plane
runco *v.t.* 1, to weed
rŭo, ŭi, ŭtum *v.i.t.* 3, to fall, rush, hurry; hurl down, throw up
rūpes, is *f*, rock
rūrĭcŏla, ae *adj*, rural
rursus (rursum) *adv*, again, on the contrary, backwards
rūs, rūris *n*, countryside
rustĭcānus, a, um *adj*, rustic
rustĭcĭtas, ātis *f*, behaviour of country-people
rustĭcor *v.i.* 1, *dep*, to live in the country
rustĭcus, a, um *adj*, rural

rustĭcus, i *m*, countryman
rūta, ae *f*, bitter herb, rue
rŭtĭlo *v.i.* 1, to be red
rŭtĭlus, a, um *adj*, red

S

sabbăta, ōrum *n.pl*, sabbath
săbīnum, i *n*, Sabine wine
săbŭlum, i *n*, gravel
săburra, ae *f*, sand, ballast
sacchăron, i *n*, sugar
saccŭlus, i *m*, small bag
saccus, i *m*, bag
săcellum, i *n*, chapel
săcer, cra, crum *adj*, sacred, venerable, accursed
săcerdos, dōtis *c*, priest
săcerdōtālis, e *adj*, priestly
săcerdōtĭum, ii *n*, priesthood
săcra, ōrum *n.pl*, worship, religion
săcrāmentum, i *n*, oath
săcrārĭum, ii *n*, sanctuary
săcrātus, a, um *adj*, sacred
săcrĭfĭcĭum, ii *n*, sacrifice
săcrĭfĭco *v.i.t.* 1, to sacrifice
săcrĭfĭcus, a, um *adj*, sacrificial
săcrĭlĕgus, a, um *adj*, temple robbing, sacrilegious
săcro *v.t.* 1, to consecrate, condemn, doom
săcrōsanctus, a, um *adj*, sacred, inviolable
săcrum, i *n*, sacred thing, religious act, religion
saecŭlum, i *n*, age, generation, century
saepe *adv*, often
saepes, is *f*, hedge, fence
saepīmentum, i *n*, fencing
saepĭo, psi, ptum *v.t.* 4, to fence in, surround
saeptum, i *n*, fence, pen
saeta, ae *f*, hair, bristle
saetĭger, ĕra, ĕrum *adj*, bristly
saetōsus, a, um *adj*, bristly
saevĭo *v.i.* 4, to rage
saevĭtĭa, ae *f*, savageness
saevus, a, um *adj*, savage, violent, furious, cruel
sāga, ae *f*, fortune-teller
săgācĭtas, ātis *f*, shrewdness

săgax, ācis   adj, adv, ĭter, keen, shrewd, acute
săgīno   v.t. 1, to fatten
săgitta, ae   f, arrow
săgittārĭus, ii   m, archer
săgŭlum, i   n, military cloak
săgum, i   n, military cloak
sal, sălis   m, salt, sea, wit, sarcasm
sălăco, ōnis   m, braggart
sălārĭum, ii   n, pension, salary (salt money)
sălax, ācis   adj, lecherous
sălĕbra, ae   f, roughness
sălĭāris, e   adj, splendid
sălictum, i   n, willow-grove
sălignus, a, um   adj, of willow
Sălĭi, ōrum   m.pl, priests of Mars
sălīnae, ārum   f.pl, salt-works
sălīnum, I   n, saltcellar
sălĭo, ŭi, saltum   v.i. 4, to jump
sălīva, ae   f, saliva
sălix, ĭcis   f, willow tree
salmo, ōnis   m, salmon
salsāmentum, i   n, brine
salsus, a, um   adj, adv, ē, salted, witty
saltātĭo, ōnis   f, dancing
saltātor, ōris   m, dancer
saltātrix, īcis   f, dancing-girl
saltātus, ūs   m, dancing
saltem   adv, at least
salto   v.i.t. 1, to dance
saltus, ūs   m, leap, bound
saltus, ūs   m, woodland, mountain pass
sălūbris, e   adj, adv, ĭter, health-giving, beneficial
sălūbrĭtas, ātis   f, wholesomeness
sălum, i   n, sea
sălūs, ūtis   f, welfare, safety
sălūtāris, e   adj, adv, ĭter, beneficial, wholesome
sălūtātĭo, ōnis   f, greeting
sălūtātor, ōris   m, visitor
sălūtĭfer, ĕra, ĕrum   adj, healing
sălūto   v.t. 1, to greet
salvē, salvēte, salvēto   v. imperative, how are you? welcome!
salvĭa, ae   f, sage (herb)
salvus, a, um   adj, safe, well; with noun in abl, e.g. salvā lege
without violating the law
sambūcus, i   f, elder tree
sānābĭlis, e   adj, curable
sānātĭo, ōnis   f, cure
sancĭo, xi, ctum   v.t. 4, to appoint, establish, ratify
sanctĭfĭcātĭo, ōnis   f, sanctification
sanctĭo, ōnis   f, establishing
sanctĭtas, ātis   f, sacredness, purity
sanctus, a, um   adj, adv, ē, sacred, inviolable, good
sandix, īcis   f, scarlet
sānē   adv, certainly, very
sanguĭnārĭus, a, um   adj, bloody, blood-thirsty
sanguĭnĕus, a, um   adj, bloody
sanguĭnŏlentus, a, um   adj, bloody
sanguis, ĭnis   m, blood, bloodshed, race, stock
sānĭes, em, e   f, bad blood
sānĭtas, ātis   f, health, good sense, discretion
sannĭo, ōnis   m, buffoon
sāno   v.t. 1, to cure, restore
sānus, a, um   adj, healthy, rational, discreet
sāpĭdus, a, um   adj, tasty
săpĭens, ntis   adj, adv, nter, wise, sensible
săpĭens, ntis   m, wise man
săpĭentĭa, ae   f, discretion, philosophy
săpĭo, īvi   v.i.t. 3, to be wise, discreet; to taste of savour of
sāpo, ōnis   m, soap
săpor, ōris   m, flavour, taste
sapphīrus, i   f, sapphire
sarcĭna, ae   f, pack, load
sarcĭo, si, tum   v.t. 4, to patch
sarcŏphăgus, i   m, sarcophagus
sarcŭlum, i   n, light hoe
sarda, ae   f, sardine
sarīsa, ae   f, Macedonian lance
sarmentum, i   n, brushwood
sarrācum, i   n, cart
sarrānus, a, um   adj, Tyrian
sarrĭo   v.t. 4, to hoe
sartāto, ĭnis   f, frying pan
sartus, a, um   adj, repaired
săta, ōrum   n.pl, crops
sătelles, ĭtis   c, attendant; in pl, escort

sătĭas, ātis *f,* abundance, disgust
sătĭĕtas, ātis *f,* abundance, disgust
sătĭo *v.t.* 1, to satisfy, glut
sătĭo, ōnis *f,* sowing
sătĭrĭcus, a, um *adj,* satirical
sătis (săt) *adv, or indecl. adj,* enough
sătisdătĭo, ōnis *f,* giving bail
sătisfăcĭo, fēci, factum *v.t.* 3, to satisfy, make amends
sătisfactĭo, ōnis *f,* excuse, reparation
sătĭus *comp. adv,* better
sător, ōris *m,* sower, creator
sătrăpes, is *m,* viceroy, satrap
sătur, ŭra, ŭrum *adj,* full, fertile
sătŭra, ae *f,* food made of various ingredients, satire
Sāturnālĭa, ōrum *n.pl,* festival in honour of Saturn (Dec. 17th)
sătŭro *v.t.* 1, to fill, glut
sătus, ūs *m,* planting
sătus, a, um *adj,* sprung from
sătўrus, i *m,* forest god
saucĭo *v.t.* 1, to wound
saucĭus, a, um *adj,* wounded
saxĕus, a, um *adj,* rocky
saxĭfĭcus, a, um *adj,* petrifiying
saxōsus, a, um *adj,* rocky
saxum, i *n,* rock
scăbellum, i *n,* stool
scăber, bra, brum *adj,* rough, scabby
scăbĭes, em, e *f,* roughness, scab, itch
scăbo, scābi *v.t.* 3, to scratch
scaena, ae *f,* stage, scene
scaenĭcus, a, um *adj,* theatrical
scaenĭcus, i *m,* actor
scăla, ae *f,* ladder, stairs
scalmus, i *m,* rowlock
scalpo, psi, ptum *v.t.* 3, to carve
scalpellum, i *n,* lancet
scalprum, i *n,* chisel
scalptor, ōris *m,* engraver
scalptūra, ae *f,* engraving
scamnum, i *n,* bench
scando *v.i.t.* 3, to rise; climb
scăpha, ae *f,* small boat
scăpŭlae, ārum *f.pl,* shoulder blades
scărăbaeus, i *m,* beetle

scărus, i *m,* sea fish (scar)
scătĕbra, ae *f,* spring water
scătĕo *v.i.* 2, to bubble, swarm with
scaurus, a, um *adj,* with swollen ankles
scĕlĕrātus, a, um *adj,* wicked
scĕlĕro *v.t.* 1, to contaminate
scĕlestus, a, um *adj,* wicked
scĕlus, ĕris *n,* crime, scoundrel
scēna see **scaena**
scēnĭcus see **scaenĭcus**
sceptrum, i *n,* sceptre; *in pl,* dominion, authority
schĕda, ae *f,* sheet of paper
schŏla, ae *f,* lecture, school
scĭens, ntis *adj, adv,* **nter,** knowing (*i.e.* purposely), expert in
scĭentĭa, ae *f,* knowledge
scīlĭcet *adv,* certainly, of course, namely
scĭlla, ae *f,* sea-onion, prawn
scindo, scĭdi, scissum *v.t.* 3, to split
scintilla, ae *f,* spark
scintillans, ntis *adj,* sparkling
scintillo *v.i.* 1, to sparkle
scĭo *v.t.* 4, to know, understand
scīpĭo, ōnis *m,* staff
scirpĕus, a, um *adj,* of rushes
sciscĭtor *v.t.* 1, *dep,* to enquire
scisco, scīvi, scītum *v.t.* 3, to approve, appoint, decree
scissūra, ae *f,* tearing, rending
scītor *v.t.* 1, *dep,* to enquire
scītum, i *n,* decree, statute
scītus, a, um *adj, adv,* **ē,** shrewd, sensible, witty
scĭūrus, i *m,* squirrel
scŏbīna, ae *f,* rasp, file
scŏbis, is *f,* sawdust
scomber, bri *m,* mackerel
scōpae, ārum *f.pl,* broom
scŏpŭlōsus, a, um *adj,* rocky
scŏpŭlus, i *m,* rock, cliff
scŏpus, i *m,* target
scorpĭo, ōnis *m,* scorpion, missile launcher
scortum, i *n,* prostitute
scrība, ae *m,* clerk
scrībo, psi, ptum *v.t.* 3, to write, draw, compose, describe, enroll

scrīnĭum, ii   *n*, letter-case
scriptĭo, ōnis   *f*, writing
scriptor, ōris   *m*, secretary, author
scriptum, i   *n*, book, writing
scriptūra, ae   *f*, composition
scriptus, a, um   *adj*, written
scrŏbis, is   *m*, ditch
scrūpĕus, a, um   *adj*, rugged
scrūpŭlus, i   *m*, anxiety,
  embarrassment
scrūta, ōrum   *n.pl*, frippery
scrūtātĭo, ōnis   *f*, scrutiny
scrūtor   *v.t.* 1, *dep*, to examine
sculpo, psi, ptum   *v.t.* 3, to carve
sculpōnĕae, ārum   *f.pl*, clogs
sculptor, ōris   *m*, sculptor
sculptūra, ae   *f*, sculpture
scurra, ae   *m*, clown, dandy
scurrīlis, e   *adj*, jeering
scūtātus, a, um   *adj*, armed with
  oblong shields
scūtella, ae   *f*, salver
scūtĭca, ae   *f*, whip
scūtŭla, ae   *f*, wooden roller
scūtum, i   *n*, oblong shield
scўphus, i   *m*, goblet
sē   *acc. or abl. of reflexive pron*,
  herself, itself etc.
sēbum, i   *n*, suet
sĕcāle, is   *n*, rye
sēcēdo, cessi, cessum   *v.i.* 3, to
  go away, withdraw
sēcerno, crēvi, crētum   *v.t.* 3, to
  separate, part
sēcessĭo, ōnis   *f*, withdrawal
sēcessus, ūs   *m*, solitude
sēcĭus (sĕquĭus) *comp. adv*,
  differently
sēclūdo, si, sum   *v.t.* 3, to
  separate, shut off
sēclūsus, a, um   *adj*, remote
sĕco, ŭi, ctum   *v.t.* 1, to cut,
  wound, separate
sēcrētum, i   *n*, solitude
sēcrētus, a, um   *adj, adv*, ō,
  separate, remote, secret
secta, ae   *f*, way, method, sect
sectātor, ōris   *m*, follower
sectĭo, ōnis   *f*, sale by auction
sector, ōris   *m*, cutthroat, bidder
  at an auction
sector   *v.t.* 1, *dep*, to pursue
sectūra, ae   *f*, mine

sēcul...   see **saecul**
sĕcundārĭus, a, um   *adj*,
  secondary, second-rate
sĕcundo   *v.t.* 1, to favour
sĕcundum   *prep. with acc*,
  after, behind, by, next to,
  according to
sĕcundus, a, um   *adj*, following,
  second, favourable
sĕcūrĭger, ĕra, ĕrum   *adj*, armed
  with a battle-axe
sĕcūris, is   *f*, axe, hatchet
sĕcūrĭtas, ātis   *f*, freedom from
  care
sĕcūrus, a, um   *adj*, carefree,
  tranquil
sĕcus   *adv*, differently
sĕd   *conj*, but
sēdātĭo, ōnis   *f*, a calming
sēdātus, a, um   *adj*, calm
sēdĕcim   *indecl. adj*, sixteen
sĕdentārĭus, a, um   *adj*, sedentary
sĕdĕo, sēdi, sessum   *v.i.* 2, to sit,
  remain, settle, be settled
sēdes, is   *f*, seat, residence,
  temple, bottom, foundation
sēdīle, is   *n*, seat
sēdītĭo, ōnis   *f*, mutiny
sēdītĭōsus, a, um   *adj, adv*, ē,
  mutinous, rebellious
sēdo   *v.t.* 1, to calm, check
sēdūco, xi, ctum   *v.t.* 3, to lead
  aside, separate
sēdūlĭtas, ātis   *f*, zeal
sēdūlō   *adv*, diligently, on
  purpose
sēdŭlus, a, um   *adj*, industrious
sĕges, ĕtis   *f*, cornfield, crop
segmenta, ōrum   *n.pl*, trimmings
segmentum, i   *n*, piece
segnis, e   *adj, adv*, ĭter, lazy
segnĭtĭa, ae   *f*, inactivity, slowness
sēgrĕgo   *v.t.* 1, to separate
sēiungo, nxi, ntum   *v.t.* 3, to
  separate, divide
sēlīgo, lēgi, lectum   *v.t.* 3, to select
sella, ae   *f*, seat, chair
sĕmĕl   *adv*, once
sēmen, ĭtis   *n*, seed, cutting, graft,
  offspring, instigator
sēmentis, is   *f*, sowing
sēmestris, e   *adj*, half-yearly
sēmēsus, a, um   *adj*, half-eaten

sēmǐǎnǐmǐs, e   *adj,* half-dead
sēmǐdĕus, a, um   *adj,* half-divine
sēmǐfer, ĕra, ĕrum   *adj,* half-man,
  half-beast
sēmǐhŏmo, ǐnis   *m,* half-human
sēmǐhōra, ae   *f,* half-hour
sēmǐnārǐum, ii   *n,* nursery
sēmǐnātor, ōris   *m,* author
sēmǐnĕcis, is   *adj,* half-dead
sēmǐno   *v.t.* 1, to produce
sēmǐplēnus, a, um   *adj,* half-full
sēmǐrūtus, a, um   *adj,* half-ruined
sēmis, issis   *m,* (coin of very low
  value)
sēmǐsomnus, a, um   *adj,* half-
  asleep
sēmǐta, ae   *f,* footpath
sēmǐustus, a, um   *adj,* half-burned
sēmǐvir, vǐri   *m,* half-man; *as adj,*
  effeminate
sēmǐvīvus, a, um   *adj,* half-alive
sēmōtus, a, um   *adj,* remote
sēmŏvĕo, mōvi, mōtum   *v.t.* 2, to
  remove, separate
semper   *adv,* always
sempǐternus, a, um   *adj,*
  everlasting
sēmustŭlo   *v.t.* 1, to half burn
sĕnātor, ōris   *m,* senator
sĕnātōrǐus, a, um   *adj,* senatorial
sĕnātus, ūs   *m,* the Senate
sĕnecta, ae   *f,* old age
sĕnectus, ūtis   *f,* old age
sĕnesco, nŭi   *v.i.* 3, to grow old
sĕnex, sĕnis   *m,* old man
sēni, ae, a   *pl. adj,* six each
sĕnīlis, e   *adj,* old (of people)
sĕnǐor, ōris   *c,* elderly person
sĕnǐum, ii   *n,* old age, decay,
  trouble
sensīlis, e   *adj,* sensitive
sensim   *adv,* slowly, gently
sensus, ūs   *m,* perception,
  disposition, good taste, sense,
  understanding, meaning
sententǐa, ae   *f,* opinion, decision,
  meaning, sentence, axiom; **ex**
  mĕā sententǐā   to my liking
sententǐōsus, a, um   *adj,*
  sententious
sentīna, ae   *f,* bilge-water, dregs,
  ship's hold
sentǐo, si, sum   *v.t.* 4, to feel,

perceive, endure, suppose
sentis, is   *m,* thorn, bramble
sentus, a, um   *adj,* rough
sĕorsum   *adv,* separately
sēpǎrātim   *adv,* separately
sēpǎrātǐo, ōnis   *f,* separation
sēpǎrātus, a, um   *adj,* separate
sēpǎro   *v.t.* 1, to separate
sĕpĕlǐo, līvi, pultum   *v.t.* 4, to
  bury, overwhelm
sēpǐa, ae   *f,* cuttle fish
sēpǐo   see **saepǐo**
sēpōno, pŏsǔi, pŏsǐtum   *v.t.* 3, to
  put aside, select
septem   *indecl. adj,* seven
September (mensis)   September
septemgĕmǐnus, a, um   *adj,* seven-
  fold
septemplex, ǐcis   *adj,* seven-fold
septendĕcim   *indecl. adj,*
  seventeen
septēni, ae, a   *pl. adj,* seven each
septentrǐōnālis, um   *m.pl,* the
  Great Bear, the North
septǐes   *adv,* seven times
septǐmus, a, um   *adv,* seventh
septingenti, ae, a   *pl. adj,* seven
  hundred
septŭāgēsǐmus, a, um   *adj,*
  seventieth
septŭāginta   *indecl. adj,* seventy
septum   see **saeptum**
sĕpulcrum, i   *n,* grave, tomb
sĕpultūra, ae   *f,* burial
sĕquax, ācis   *adj,* pursuing
sĕquens, ntis   *adj,* following
sĕquester, tris   *m,* agent
sĕquor, sĕcūtus   *v.i.t.* 3, *dep,* to
  follow, attend, pursue
sĕra, ae   *f,* bolt, bar
sĕrēnǐtas, ātis   *f,* fair weather
sĕrēno   *v.t.* 1, to brighten
sĕrēnum, i   *n,* fair weather
sĕrēnus, a, um   *adj,* clear, fair,
  cheerful, glad
sērǐa, ōrum   *n.pl,* serious matters
sērǐcus, a, um   *adj,* silken
sērǐes, em, e   *f,* row, series
sērǐus, a, um   *adj,* serious
sermo, ōnis   *m,* talk,
  conversation, common talk
sĕro, sēvi, sǎtum   *v.t.* 3, to sow,
  plant, cause

sĕro, ŭi, sertum   *v.t.* 3, to plait, join, connect, compose
sērŏ   *adv,* late
serpens, ntis   *f,* snake
serpo, psi, ptum   *v.i.* 3, to crawl
serpyllum, i   *n,* thyme
serra, ae   *f,* saw
serrŭla, ae   *f,* small saw
serta, ōrum   *n.pl,* garlands
sĕrum, i   *n,* whey
sērus, a, um   *adj,* late
serva, ae   *f,* maid-servant
servātor, ōris   *m,* saviour
servīlis, e   *adj, adv,* ĭter, of a slave, servile
servĭo   *v.i.* 4, to be a servant, to be of use to
servītĭum, ii   *n,* slavery, slaves
servĭtus, ūtis   *f,* slavery, slaves
servo   *v.t.* 1, to save, protect, preserve, keep, keep watch
servus, a, um   *adj,* servile
servus, i   *m,* slave, servant
sescēni, ae, a   *pl. adj,* six hundred each
sescenti, ae, a   *pl. adj,* six hundred
sescentĭes   *adv,* six hundred times
sesquĭpĕdālis, e   *adj,* one foot and a half long
sessĭo, ōnis   *f,* sitting, session
sestertĭum 1,000 sestertii
sestertĭus, ii   *m,* small silver coin (worth about 1 p.)
sēt... see saet...
seu   *conj,* whether, or
sĕvērĭtas, ātis   *f,* sternness
sĕvērus, a, um   *adj, adv,* ē, stern, serious, harsh, gloomy
sēvŏco   *v.t.* 1, to call aside
sex   *indecl. adj,* six
sexāgēnārĭus, i   *m,* sexagenarian
sexāgēni, ae, a   *pl. adj,* sixty each
sexāgēsĭmus, a, um   *adj,* sixtieth
sexāgĭes   *adv,* sixty times
sexāginta   *indecl. adj,* sixty
sexennĭum, ii   *n,* six years
sextans, ntis   *m,* a sixth part
sextārĭus, ii   *m,* a pint
Sextīlis (mensis)   August
sextus, a, um   *adj,* sixth
sexus, ūs   *m,* sex

sī   *conj,* if
sĭbi   *dat. of reflexive pron,* to himself, herself, itself, etc.
sībĭlo   *v.i.t.* 1, to hiss; hiss at
sībĭlus, i   *m,* hissing
sĭbylla, ae   *f,* prophetess
sīc   *adv,* so, in this way
sīca, ae   *f,* dagger
sīcārĭus, ii   *m,* assassin
siccĭtas, ātis   *f,* dryness, firmness
sicco   *v.t.* 1, to dry up, drain
siccum, i   *n,* dry land
siccus, a, um   *adj,* dry, firm, tough, thirsty, sober
sīcŭbī   *adv,* if anywhere
sīcut (sīcŭti)   *adv,* just as
sīdĕrĕus, a, um   *adj,* starry
sīdo, di   *v.i.* 3, to sit down, settle, sink
sīdus, ĕris   *n,* star, sky, constellation, season, weather
sĭgilla, ōrum   *n.pl,* little figures or images
sĭgillātus, a, um   *adj,* figured
signĭfer, ĕri   *m,* standard-bearer
signĭfĭcātĭo, ōnis   *f,* sign, mark
signĭfĭco   *v.t.* 1, to show, notify
signĭfĭcans, antis   *adj,* significant
signo   *v.t.* 1, to mark out, seal, indicate
signum, i   *n,* mark, sign, military standard, watchword, statue, constellation, symptom
sĭlens, ntis   *adj,* still, quiet
sĭlentĭum, ii   *n,* stillness, quietness
sĭlĕo   *v.i.t.* 2, to be silent; to keep quiet about
sĭlesco   *v.i.* 3, to grow quiet
sĭlex, ĭcis   *m,* flint-stone
sĭlus, a, um   *adj,* snub-nosed
silva, ae   *f,* wood, forest, grove, abundance
silvestrĭa, ĭum   *n.pl,* woodlands
silvestris, e   *adj,* woody, rural
silvĭcŏla, ae   *adj,* living in woods
sīmĭa, ae   *f,* ape
sĭmĭlis, e   *adj, adv,* ĭter, similar, like
sĭmĭlĭtūdo, ĭnis   *f,* resemblance
sīmĭus, ii   *m,* ape
simplex, ĭcis   *adj, adv,* ĭter, unmixed, simple, frank
simplĭcĭtas, ātis   *f,* honesty

sĭmul *adv*, at once, together, at the same time, as soon as

sĭmŭlac *conj*, as soon as

sĭmŭlatque *conj*, as soon as

sĭmŭlācrum, i *n*, portrait, statue, phantom

sĭmŭlātĭo, ōnis *f*, pretence

sĭmŭlātor, ōris *m*, pretender

sĭmŭlātus, a, um *adj*, feigned

sĭmŭlo *v.t*. 1, to imitate, pretend

sĭmultas, ātis *f*, animosity

sīmus, a, um *adj*, snub-nosed

sīn *conj*, but if

sĭnāpi, is *n*, mustard

sincērĭtas, ātis *f*, cleanness, purity, entirety, sincerity

sincērus, a, um *adj, adv*, ē, clean, pure, genuine, entire, sincere

sĭně *prep. with abl*, without

singillātim *adv*, one by one

singŭlāris, e *adj*, single, solitary, unique, remarkable

singŭlātim see **singillātim**

singŭli, ae, a *pl. adj*, one each

singultim *adv*, with sobs

singultĭo *v.i*. 4, to hiccup

singulto (*no perf.*) *v.i*. 1, to sob

sinultus, ūs *m*, sobbing

sĭnister, tra, trum *adj*, left, awkward, wrong, unlucky, lucky

sĭnistra, ae *f*, left hand

sĭnistrorsus *adv*, to the left

sĭno, sīvi, sĭtum *v.t*. 3, to allow

sĭnum, i *n*, drinking-cup

sĭnŭo *v.t*. 1, to bend, curve

sĭnŭōsus, a, um *adj*, curved

sĭnus, ūs *m*, curve, fold, bosom, lap, hiding-place, bay

sĭpho, ōnis *m*, siphon, syringe

sīquandō *adv*, if ever

sīquĭdem *adv*, if indeed

sīquis *pron*, if any

sīrēn, ēnis *f*, siren

sisto, stĭti, stătum *v.i.t* 3, to stand still, resist, hold out; put, place, bring, check, establish

sīstrum, i *n*, rattle

sĭtĭens, ntis *adj, adv*, **nter**, thirsty

sĭtĭo *v.i.t*. 4, to thirst; long for

sĭtis, is *f*, thirst, drought

sĭtŭla, ae *f*, bucket

sĭtus, a, um *adj*, situated

sĭtus, ūs *m*, position, site, rust, mould, inactivity

sīve *conj*, whether, or

smăragdus, i *c*, emerald

sŏbŏles, is *f*, sprout, twig, offspring

sōbrĭĕtas, ātis *f*, sobriety, temperance

sōbrīnus, i *m*, cousin

sōbrĭus, a, um *adj, adv*, ē, sober, moderate, sensible

soccus, i *m*, slipper

sŏcer, ĕri *m*, father-in-law

sŏcĭālis, e *adj*, allied

sŏcĭĕtas, ātis *f*, fellowship, partnership, alliance

sŏcĭo *v.t*. 1, to unite

sŏcĭus, ii *m*, companion, ally

sŏcĭus, a, um *adj*, allied

sōcordĭa, ae *f*, laziness, folly

sōcors, cordis *adj*, lazy, careless, stupid

socrus, ūs *f*, mother-in-law

sŏdālĭcĭum, ii *n*, secret society

sŏdālis, is *c*, companion

sŏdālĭtas, ātis *f*, friendship

sōdes if you wish

sōl, sōlis *m*, sun, sunshine

sōlācĭum, ii *n*, comfort, solace

sōlāmen, ĭnis *n*, consolation

sōlārĭum, ii *n*, sundial

sōlātĭum see **sōlācĭum**

soldūrĭi, ōrum *m.pl*, retainers of a chieftain

sŏlĕa, ae *f*, sandal, sole (fish)

sŏlĕātus, a, um *adj*, wearing sandals

sŏlĕo, sŏlĭtus *v.i*. 2, *semi-dep*, to be accustomed

sŏlĭdĭtas, ātis *f*, solidity

sŏlĭdo *v.t*. 1, to strengthen

sŏlĭdum, i *n*, a solid, solidity

sŏlĭdus, a, um *adj*, compact, complete, genuine, real

sōlĭtārĭus, a, um *adj*, alone

sōlĭtūdo, ĭnis *f*, loneliness, desert

sōlĭtus, a, um *adj*, usual

sŏlĭum, ii *n*, seat, throne

sollemnis, e *adj*, established, appointed, usual, religious

sollemne, is *n*, religious ceremony, sacrifice

sollers, tis *adj*, skilled

sollertĭa, ae *f*, skill, ingenuity

sollĭcĭtātĭo, ōnis f, instigation
sollĭcĭto v.t. 1, to stir up, molest, instigate
sollĭcĭtūdo, ĭnis f, anxiety
sollĭcĭtus, a, um adj, troubled
sōlor v.t. 1, dep, to comfort, relieve
solstĭtĭālis, e adj, of summer
solstĭtĭum, ii n, summer time
sŏlum, i n, bottom, base, floor, sole, soil, ground, country, place
sōlum adv, only
sōlus, a, um adj, alone, only, lonely, deserted
sŏlūtĭo, ōnis f, unloosing, payment, explanation
sŏlūtus, a, um adj, adv, ē, free, loose, independent
solvendum see solvo
solvo, solvi, sŏlūtum v.t. 3, to set free, dissolve, release, open up, pay, perform, fulfil, acquit; with ancŏram to sail
somnĭcŭlūsus, a, um adj, drowsy
somnĭfer, ĕra, ĕrum adj, sleep-bringing
somnĭfĭcus, a, um adj sleep-bringing
somnĭo v.t. 1, to dream
somnĭum, ii n, dream
somnus, i m, sleep
sŏnĭpēs, pĕdis adj, noisy-footed
sŏnĭtus, ūs m, noise, sound
sŏno, ŭi, ĭtum v.i.t. 1, to resound; call out, utter
sŏnor, ōris m, noise, sound
sŏnōrus, a, um adj, resounding
sons, ntis adj, guilty
sŏnus, i m, noise, sound
sŏphistes, ae m, philosopher
sōpĭo v.t. 4, to lull to sleep
sōpor, ōris m, sleep
sōpōrĭfer, ĕra, ĕrum adj, sleep-bringing
sōpōro v.t. 1, to heat, stupefy
sōpōrus, a, um adj, sleep-bringing
sorbĕo v.t. 2, to suck in
sordĕo v.i. 2, to be dirty, to be despised
sordes, is f, dirt, mourning dress, meanness
sordĭdātus, a, um adj, shabbily dressed (in mourning)

sordĭdĭus, a, um adj, adv, ē, dirty, despicable, mean
sŏror, ōris f, sister
sŏrōrĭus, a, um adj, of a sister
sors, tis f, chance, lot, drawing of lots, prophesy, fortune, share, destiny
sortĭor v.i.t. 4, dep, to draw lots; to appoint by lot, obtain by lot, choose
sortĭtĭo, ōnis f, drawing of lots
sortītō adv, by lot
sortītus, a, um adj, drawn by lot
sospĕs, ĭtis adj, safe, lucky
spādix, īcis adj, nut-brown
spargo, si, sum v.t. 3, to sprinkle, scatter, spread
spărus, i m, hunting spear
spasmus, i m, spasm
spătĭor v.i. 1, dep, to walk about
spătĭōsus, a, um adj, spacious
spătĭum, ii n, space, room, distance, walk, track, interval
spĕcĭes, ēi f, sight, view, shape, appearance, pretence, display, beauty
spĕcĭmen, ĭnis n, mark, sign, pattern
spĕcĭōsus, a, um adj, handsome, plausible
spectābĭlis, e adj, visible, remarkable
spectācŭlum, i n, show, spectacle
spectātĭo, ōnis f, sight
spectātor, ōris m, onlooker
spectātus, a, um adj, tested, respected
speco v.t. 1, to watch, face, examine, consider, refer
spectrum, i n, image
spĕcŭla, ae f, look-out point
spēcŭla, ae f, slight hope
spĕcŭlātor, ōris m, spy, scout
spĕcŭlor v.t. 1, dep, to watch, observe, explore
spĕcŭlum, i n, mirror
spēcus, ūs m, cave, pit
spēlunca, ae f, cave, den
sperno, sprēvi, sprētum v.t. 3, to despise, scorn
spēro v.t. 1, to hope, expect
spes, spēi f, hope
sphaera, ae f, sphere

spīca, ae *f,* ear (of corn)
spīcĕus, a, um *adj,* made of ears of corn
spīcŭlum, i *n,* point, dart
spīna, ae *f,* thorn, spine, difficulties
spīnētum, i *n,* thorn-hedge
spīnōsus, a, um *adj,* thorny
spīnus, i *f,* sloe-tree
spīra, ae *f,* coil, twist
spīrābĭlis, e *adj,* breathable
spīrācŭlum, i *n,* air-hole
spīrāmentum, i *n,* air-hole
spīrĭtus, ūs *m,* breath, breeze, pride, arrogance, soul
spīro *v.i.t.* 1, to breathe, blow, live; exhale
spisso *v.t.* 1, to condense
spissus, a, um *adj,* thick, dense
splendĕo *v.i.* 2, to shine
splendesco *v.i.* 3, to become bright
splendĭdus, a, um *adj, adv,* ē, shining, magnificent, noble
splendor, ōris *m,* brilliance, excellence
spŏlīa see spŏlĭum
spŏlīātĭo, ōnis *f,* plundering
spŏlīo *v.t.* 1, to plunder, rob
spŏlīum, ii *n,* skin (of an animal); *in pl,* booty, spoils
sponda, ae *f,* couch, sofa
spondĕo, spŏpondi, sponsum *v.t.* 2, to promise, pledge, betroth, warrant
spongĭa, ae *f,* sponge
spongĭōsus, a, um *adj,* spongy
sponsa, ae *f,* bride
sponsālĭa, ĭum *n.pl,* betrothal
sponsĭo, ōnis *f,* promise, guarantee, security
sponsor, ōris *m,* surety
sponsum, i *n,* covenant
sponsus, a, um *adj,* promised
sponsus, i *m,* bridegroom
spontē (*abl.*) *f, with* mĕā, sŭā, *etc.,* voluntarily
sportella, ae *f,* fruit basket
sportŭla, ae *f,* little basket
spūma, ae *f,* froth, foam
spūmĕus, a, um *adj,* foaming
spūmĭfer, ĕra, ĕrum *adj,* foaming
spūmĭger, ĕra, ĕrum *adj,* foaming

spūmo *v.i.*1, to foam, froth
spūmōsus, a, um *adj,* foaming
spŭo, ŭi, ūtum *v.i.t.* 3, to spit
spūtum, i *n,* spit
spurcus, a, um *adj,* dirty
squālĕo *v.i.* 2, to be stiff or rough, to be neglected, filthy
squālĭdus, a, um *adj,* stiff, dirty, neglected
squālor, ōris *m,* filthiness
squāma, ae *f,* scale (of fish)
squāmĕus, a, um *adj,* scaly
squāmĭger, ĕra, ĕrum *adj,* scaly
squāmōsus, a, um *adj,* scaly
stăbĭlĭo *v.t.* 4, to fix
stăbĭlis, e *adj,* firm, steadfast
stăbĭlĭtas, ātis *f,* firmness
stăbŭlo *v.i.* (**stăbŭlor,** *v.i. dep,*) 1, to have a home, resting-place
stăbŭlum, i *n,* stable, hut
stădĭum, ii *n,* stade (distance of 200 yds./metres approx.), racecourse
stagnans, ntis *adj,* stagnant
stagno *v.i.* 1, to stagnate
stagnum, i *n,* pool, pond
stălagmĭum, i *n,* pendant
stāmen, ĭnis *n,* thread
stătārĭus, a, um *adj,* firm, calm,
stătim *adv,* immediately
stătĭo, ōnis *f,* post, station, outposts, sentries
stătīva, ōrum *n.pl,* permanent camp
stătīvus, a, um *adj,* stationary
stător, ōris *m,* messenger
stătŭa, ae *f,* statue
stătŭo, ŭi, ūtum *v.t.* 3, to set up, place, build, establish, settle, decide
stătūra, ae *f,* stature
stătus, ūs *m,* posture, position, condition, state, circumstance
stătus, a, um *adj,* fixed
stella, ae *f,* star
stellātus, a, um *adj,* starry
stellĭger, ĕra, ĕrum *adj,* starry
stellĭo, ōnis *n,* newt
stemma, ătis *n,* garland, pedigree
stercus, ŏris *n,* manure
stĕrĭlis, e *adj,* barren
stĕrĭlĭtas, ātis *f,* sterility
sternax, ācis *adj,* bucking (horse)

sterno, strāvi, strātum   *v.t.* 3, to
  scatter, extend, smooth, arrange,
  cover, overthrow, pave
sternūmentum, i   *n*, sneezing
sternŭo, ŭi   *v.i.t.* 3, to sneeze
sterto, ŭi   *v.i.* 3, to snore
stigma, ătis   *n*, brand
stillĭcĭdĭum, ii   *n*, dripping rain-
  water
stillo   *v.i.t.* 1, to drip; distil
stĭlus, i   *m*, pen, style
stĭmŭlo   *v.t.* 1, to torment, incite
stĭmŭlus, i   *m*, goad, sting,
  incentive
stĭpātor, ōris   *m*, attendant
stĭpendĭārĭus, a, um   *adj*, tribute
  paying
stĭpendĭum, ii   *n*, tax, dues, pay,
  military service campaign
stĭpes, ĭtis   *m*, log, post
stĭpo   *v.t.* 1, to compress,
  surround, accompany
stips, stĭpis   *f*, donation
stĭpŭla, ae   *f*, stalk, stem
stĭpŭlātĭo, ōnis   *f*, agreement
stĭpŭlor   *v.i.t.* 1, *dep,* to bargain;
  demand
stīria, ae   *f*, icicle
stirps, pis   *f*, root, stem, plant,
  race, family
stīva, ae   *f*, plough-handle
sto, stĕti, stătum   *v.i.* 1, to stand,
  remain, endure, persist, cost
stōĭcus, a, um   *adj*, stoic
stŏla, ae   *f*, gown, robe
stŏlĭdus, a, um   *adj*, dull, stupid
stŏmăchor   *v.i.* 1, *dep,* to be
  angry
stŏmăchōsus, a, um   *adj*, irritable
stŏmăchus, i   *m*, gullet, stomach,
  taste, distaste
stŏrĕa, ae   *f*, straw mat
strābo, ōnis   *m*, one who squints
strāges, is   *f*, destruction,
  massacre, slaughter
strāgŭlum, i   *n*, rug
strāgŭlus, a, um   *adj*, covering
strāmen, ĭnis   *n*, straw
strāmentum, i   *n*, straw
strāmĭnĕus, a, um   *adj*, of straw
strangŭlo   *v.t.* 1, to strangle
strătēgēma, ătis   *n*, stratagem
strātum, i   *n*, blanket, quilt,

pillow, bed
strātus, a, um   *adj*, stretched out
strēnŭus, a, um   *adj, adv,* ē, brisk,
  quick, vigorous
strĕpĭto   *v.i.* 1, to rattle
strĕpĭtus, ūs   *m*, din
strĕpo, ŭi   *v.i.* 3, to rattle, rumble,
  roar
strictim   *adv,* briefly
strictūra, ae   *f*, iron bar
strictus, a, um   *adj*, tight
strīdĕo, si (strīdo, di 3)   *v.i.* 2, to
  creak, hiss, rattle
strīdor, ōris   *m*, creaking, hissing
strīdŭlus, a, um   *adj*, creaking,
  hissing
strĭgĭlis, is   *f*, scraper used by
  bathers for cleaning the skin
stringo, nxi, ctum   *v.t.* 3, to draw
  tight, graze, strip off, draw
  (sword)
stringor, ōris   *m*, touch, shock
strix, strĭgis   *f*, screech owl
structor, ōris   *m*, builder
structūra, ae   *f*, construction
strŭes, is   *f*, heap, pile
strŭo, xi, ctum   *v.t.* 3, to pile up,
  build, contrive
strūthĭŏcămēlus, i   *m*, ostrich
stŭdĕo   *v.i.t.* 2, *with dat,* to be
  eager about, strive; pursue,
  favour
stŭdĭōsus, a, um   *adj, adv,* ē,
  eager, anxious, friendly
stŭdĭum, ii   *n*, eagerness,
  endeavour, affection, devotion,
  study
stultĭtĭa, ae   *f*, foolishness
stultus, a, um   *adj, adv,* ē, foolish
stūpa, ae   *f*, flax, tow
stŭpĕfăcĭo, fēci, factum   *v.t.* 3, to
  stun, daze
stŭpĕfactus, a, um   *adj*, stunned
stŭpĕo   *v.i.t.* 2, to be stunned,
  amazed; be astonished at
stŭpĕus, a, um   *adj*, made of tow
stŭpĭdus, a, um   *adj*, amazed
stŭpor, ōris   *m*, astonishment,
  stupidity
stupp...   see stūp...
stŭpro   *v.t.* 1, to ravish
stŭprum, i   *n*, disgrace, lewdness
sturnus, i   *m*, starling

suādĕo, si, sum *v.i.t.* 2, *with dat,* to urge, persuade, recommend

suāsĭo, ōnis *f,* recommendation

suāsor, ōris *m,* adviser

suāvĭlŏquens, ntis *adj,* pleasant speaking

suāvĭor *v.t.* 1, *dep,* to kiss

suāvis, e *adj, adv,* **ĭter,** agreeable, pleasant

suāvĭtas, ātis *f,* pleasantness

suāvĭum, ii *n,* kiss

sub *prep. with acc. and abl,* under, beneath, near, during, towards, just after

sŭbactĭo, ōnis *f,* preparation

sŭbausculto *v.t.* 1, to eavesdrop

subcentŭrĭo, ōnis *m,* subaltern

subdītīvus, a, um *adj,* counterfeit

subdo, dĭdi, dĭtum *v.t.* 3, to place under, subdue

subdŏlus, a, um *adj,* crafty

subdūco, xi, ctum *v.t.* 3, to pull up, haul up, remove, calculate, balance (accounts)

sŭbĕo *v.i.t.* 4, to come up to, spring up, occur; enter, submit to, suffer, incur

sūber, ĕris *n,* cork tree

subflāvus, a, um *adj,* yellowish

sūbĭcĭo, iēci, iectum *v.t.* 3, to throw or place under or near, counterfeit, subject, affix, prompt

subiectĭo, ōnis *f,* placing under, forging

subiecto *v.t.* 1, to throw up

subiectus, a, um *adj,* lying near, subject

sŭbĭgo, ēgi, actum *v.t.* 3, to bring up, plough, conquer, subdue, compel, rub down

sŭbinde *adv,* immediately, now and then

sŭbĭtō *adv,* suddenly

sŭbĭtus, a, um *adj,* sudden

subiungo, nxi, nctum *v.t.* 3, to subordinate, subdue

sublābor, lapsus *v.i.* 3, *dep,* to glide away

sublātus, a, um *adj,* proud

sublĕgo, lēgi, lectum *v.t.* 3, to gather up, kidnap

sublĕvo *v.t.* 1, to lift up, support, alleviate

sublīca, ae *f,* stake, palisade

sublīgo *v.t.* 1, to tie on

sublīme *adv,* aloft, on high

sublīmis, e *adj,* high, eminent

sublūcĕo *v.i.* 2, to glimmer

sublŭo (*no perf.*) **lūtum** *v.t.* 3, to flow along, wash

sublustris, e *adj,* glimmering

subm... see **summ...**

subnecto, xŭi, xum *v.t.* 3, to tie on underneath

subnixus, a, um *adj,* propped up

sŭbŏles, is *f,* offspring, race

sŭborno *v.t.* 1, to equip, fit out, instigate

subr... see **surr...**

subscrībo, psi, ptum *v.t.* 3, to write underneath, note down

subscriptĭo, ōnis *f,* anything written underneath

subsĕco, ŭi, ctum *v.t.* 1, to clip

subsellĭum, ii *n,* seat, law court

subsĕquor, sĕcūtus *v.i.t.* 3, *dep,* to follow, ensue; follow closely, imitate

subsĭcīvus, a, um *adj,* remaining

subsĭdĭārĭus, a, um *adj,* reserve

subsĭdĭum, ii *n,* reserve-ranks, assistance, aid, protection

subsīdo, sēdi, sessum *v.i.t.* 3, to settle down, lie in ambush; waylay

subsisto, stĭti *v.i.* 3, to stop, halt, remain, withstand

subsortĭor *v.t.* 4, *dep,* to choose as a substitute

substerno, strāvi, strātum *v.t.* 3, to spread underneath, cover

substĭtŭo, ŭi, ūtum *v.t.* 3, to put under, substitute

substringo, nxi, ctum *v.t.* 3, to tie; **aurem** prick up the ear

substructĭo, ōnis *f,* foundation

substrŭo, xi, ctum *v.t.* 3, to lay foundations

subsum, esse *v, irreg,* to be under or near, to be at hand

subtēmen, ĭnis *n,* texture, weft

subter *adv. and prep. with abl,* beneath, below

subterfŭgĭo, fūgi *v.t.* 3, to avoid

subterlābens, ntis *adj,* gliding under

subterlābor *v.i.* 3, *dep,* to glide under
subterrānĕus, a, um *adj,* underground
subtexo, ŭi, xtum *v.t.* 3, to veil
subtīlis, e *adj, adv,* ĭter, slender, delicate, precise
subtīlĭtas, ātis *f,* exactness, subtlety
subtrăho, xi, ctum *v.t.* 3, to remove stealthily, carry off
sŭbūcŭla, ae *f,* shirt
sŭbulcus, i *m,* pig-keeper
sŭburbānus, a, um *adj,* suburban
sŭburbĭum, ii *n,* suburb
subvectĭo, ōnis *f,* conveyance
subvecto *v.t.* 1, to convey
subvĕho, xi, ctum *v.t.* 3, to convey
subvĕnĭo, vēni, ventum *v.i.* 4, *with dat,* to help, aid, occur to the mind
subverto, ti, sum *v.t.* 3, to overthrow
subvŏlo *v.i.* 1, to fly up
subvolvo *v.t.* 3, to roll up
succēdo, cessi, cessum *v.i.t.* 3, to go under, advance, enter; ascend, follow after, succeed
succendo, di, sum *v.t.* 3, to kindle
succensĕo, ŭi, sum *v.t.* 2, to be angry
successĭo, ōnis *f,* succession
successor, ōris *m,* successor
successus, ūs *m,* advance, success
succĭdo, di *v.i.* 3, to sink
succĭdo, di, sum *v.t.* 3, to cut down
succingo, nxi, nctum *v.t.* 3, to surround, girdle, tuck up
succlāmo *v.t.* 1, to shout out
succumbo, cŭbŭi, cŭbĭtum *v.i.* 3, to surrender
succurro, curri, cursum *v.i.* 3, *with dat,* to help, aid, occur
sūcĭnum, i *n,* amber
sūcōsus, a, um *adj,* juicy
suctus, ūs *m,* sucking
sūcus, i *m,* energy, life
sūdārĭum, i *n,* handkerchief
sŭdis, is *f,* stake, pile
sūdo *v.i.t.* 1, to sweat, toil; exude

sūdor, ōris *m,* sweat, toil
sūdum, i *n,* clear weather
sūdus, a, um *adj,* clear, bright
sŭesco, sŭēvi, sŭētum *v.i.t.* 3, to be accustomed
sŭētus, a, um *adj,* accustomed
suffĕro, ferre, sustŭli, sublātum *v,* *irreg,* to undergo, suffer
sufficĭo, fēci, fectum *v.i.t.* 3, to be sufficient; impregnate, supply, substitute, elect
suffīgo, xi, xum *v.t.* 3, to fix
suffīmentum, i *n,* incense
suffĭo *v.t.* 4, to perfume
sufflāmen, ĭnis *n,* drag-chain
sufflātus, a, um *adj,* puffed up
sufflo *v.t.* 1, to inflate
suffōco *v.t.* 1, to strangle
suffŏdĭo, fōdi, fossum *v.t.* 3, to pierce underneath
suffrāgātĭo, ōnis *f,* support
suffrāgātor, ōris *m,* supporter
suffrāgĭum, ii *n,* vote, ballot
suffrāgor *v.i.* 1, *dep, with dat,* to vote for, support
suffundo, fūdi, fūsum *v.t.* 3, to spread over, tinge
suffulcĭo, fulsi, fultum *v.t.* 4, to prop up
suffūsus, a, um *adj,* spread over
suggĕro, gessi, gestum *v.t.* 3, to carry up, supply
suggestum, i *n,* platform
suggestus, ūs *m,* platform
sūgo, xi, ctum *v.t.* 3, to suck
sŭi *genit. of reflexive pron,* of himself, herself, itself etc.
sulco *v.t.* 1, to plough
sulcus, i *m,* furrow, ditch
sulfur, ŭris *n,* sulphur
sulfūrāta, ōrum *n.pl,* matches
sulfūrĕus, a, um *adj,* sulphurous
sum, esse, fŭi *v, irreg,* to be, exist, happen
summa, ae *f,* top, chief, point, perfection, amount, sum
summātim *adv,* briefly
summē *adv,* extremely
summergo, si, sum *v.t.* 3, to submerge, overwhelm
summĭnistro *v.t.* 1, to supply
summissus, a, um *adj, adv,* ē, gentle, soft, low, mean

summitto, mīsi, missum *v.t.* 3, to send up, produce, rear, raise, lower, submit, supply, send

summŏvĕo, mōvi, mōtum *v.t.* 2, to drive away, remove

summus, a, um *adj,* highest, topmost

sūmo, mpsi, mptum *v.t.* 3, to take hold of, assume, inflict, choose, claim, suppose, spend, use, buy

sumptĭo, ōnis *f,* assumption

sumptŭōsus, a, um *adj, adv,* ē, expensive, lavish

sumptus, ūs *m,* expense

sŭo, sŭi, sūtum *v.t.* 3, to sew

sŭpellex, lectīlis *f,* furniture

sŭper *adv, and prep. with acc. and abl,* above, over, on, besides, concerning

sŭpĕrābĭlis, e *adj,* able to be overcome

sŭperbĭa, ae *f,* pride, arrogance

sŭperbĭo, *v.i.* 4, to be proud

sŭperbus, a, um *adj, adv,* ē, proud, haughty, delicate, squeamish, magnificent

sŭpercĭlĭum, ii *n,* eyebrow, ridge, summit, arrogance

sŭpercresco, crēvi *v.i.* 3, to grow up

sŭpĕrēmĭnĕo *v.t.* 2, to overtop

sŭperfĭcĭes, ēi *f,* top, surface

sŭperfundo, fūdi, fūsum *v.t.* 3, to pour over

sŭpĕri, ōrum *m.pl,* the gods

sŭpĕrimmĭnĕo *v.i.* 2, to overhang

sŭpĕrimpōno (no perf.) posĭtum *v.t.* 3, to place upon

sŭpĕrĭnĭcĭo (no perf.), iectum *v.t.* 3, to throw over or upon

sŭpĕrĭăcĭo, iēci, iectum *v.t.* 3, to throw over, overflow

sŭpĕrĭor, ĭus *comp. adj,* higher, previous, former, superior

sŭperlātĭo, ōnis *f,* exaggeraton, hyperbole

sŭpernus, a, um *adj, adv,* ē, upper, on high ground

sŭpĕro *v.i.t.* 1, to have the upper hand, remain; ascend, outstrip, conquer

sŭpersĕdĕo, sēdi, sessum *v.i.t.* 2, with *abl,* to refrain (from)

sŭperstĕs, ĭtis *adj,* surviving

sŭperstĭtĭo, ōnis *f,* excessive fear of the gods

sŭperstĭtĭōsus, a, um *adj,* superstitious

sŭpersto *v.i.t.* 1, to stand over

sŭpersum, esse, fŭi *v.i, irreg,* to remain, survive

sŭpĕrus, a, um *adj,* upper, higher

sŭpervăcānĕus, a, um *adj,* unnecessary

sŭpervăcŭus, a, um *adj,* unnecessary

sŭpervĕnĭo, vēni, ventum *v.i.t.* 4, to come up, arrive; fall upon

sŭpervŏlo *v.i.t.* 1, to fly over

sŭpīno *v.t.* 1, to bend backwards

sŭpīnus, a, um *adj,* lying on the back, sloping

suppĕdĭto *v.i.t.* 1, to be enough, plenty; to supply

suppĕto, īvi, ītum *v.i.* 3, to be at hand, to be enough

supplanto *v.t.* 1, to trip up

supplēmentum, i *n,* reinforcements

suppleo, ēvi, ētum *v.t.* 2, to complete, fill up

supplex, ĭcis *c,* suppliant

supplex, ĭcis *adj,* beseeching

supplĭcātĭo, ōnis *f,* public thanksgiving

supplĭcĭum, ii *n,* punishment

supplĭco *v.i.* 1, to implore

supplōdo, si *v.i.t.* 3, to stamp

suppōno, pŏsŭi, pŏsĭtum *v.t.* 3, to put under, substitute

supporto *v.t.* 1, to convey

supprĭmo, pressi, pressum *v.t.* 3, to sink, suppress

suppūro *v.i.* 1, to suppurate

sŭprā *adv, and prep. with acc,* above, over, beyond, before

sŭprēmus, a, um *adj,* highest, last

sūra, ae *f,* calf of the leg

surcŭlus, i *m,* shoot, twig

surdĭtas, ātis *f,* deafness

surdus, a, um *adj,* deaf

surgo, surrexi, rectum *v.i.t.* 3, to rise, stand up; raise

surrēgŭlus, i *m,* subordinate ruler

surrēmĭgo *v.i.* 1, to row along

surrēpo, psi, ptum   *v.i.t.* 3, to creep under
surrīdĕo, si, sum   *v.i.* 2, to smile
surrĭpĭo, ŭi, reptum   *v.t.* 3, to snatch away, steal
surrŏgo   *v.t.* 1, to substitute
surrŭo, ŭi, ŭtum   *v.t.* 3, to undermine, overthrow
sursum   *adv,* upwards, on high
sūs, sŭis   *c,* pig
susceptĭo, ōnis   *f,* undertaking
suscĭpĭo, cēpi, ceptum   *v.t.* 3, to undertake, acknowledge, undergo
suscĭto   *v.t.* 1, to raise, arouse
suspectus, a, um   *adj,* mistrusted
suspectus, ūs   *m,* height
suspendĭum, ii   *n,* hanging
suspendo, di, sum   *v.t.* 3, to hang up, lift up, keep in suspense, interrupt
suspensus, a, um   *adj,* raised, hesitating
suspĭcĭo, spexi, ctum   *v.i.t.* 3, to look up; admire, suspect
suspĭcĭo, ōnis   *f,* suspicion
suspĭcĭōsus, a, um   *adj, adv,* ē, suspicious
suspĭcor   *v.t.* 1, *dep,* to suspect, suppose
suspīrītus, ūs   *m,* sigh
suspīrĭum, ii   *n,* sigh
suspīro   *v.i.t.* 1, to sigh; long for
sustento   *v.t.* 1, to support, maintain, endure
sustĭnĕo, ŭi, tentum   *v.t.* 2, to support, restrain, withstand, maintain
sūsurro   *v.i.t.* 1, to hum; mutter
sūsurrus, i   *m,* humming
sūsurrus, a, um   *adj,* whispering
sūta, ōrum   *n.pl,* joints
sūtĭlis, e   *adj,* sewed together
sūtor, ōris   *m,* cobbler
sūtōrĭus, a, um   *adj,* of a cobbler
sūtūra, ae   *f,* seam
sŭus, a, um   *adj,* his, hers, its, their
sўcŏmŏrus, i   *f,* sycamore
sўcŏphanta, ae   *m,* sycophant, cheat
syllăba, ae   *f,* syllable
syllăbātim   *adv,* by syllables
symphōnĭa, ae   *f,* harmony
symphōnĭăcus, i   *m,* chorister

sўnăgōga, ae   *f,* synagogue
syngrăpha, ae   *f,* promissory note
syngrăphus, i   *m,* passport
syntaxis, is   *f,* syntax

T

tăbānus, i   *m,* gadfly
tăbella, ae   *f,* small board or table, writing-tablet, letter, ballot paper, small picture
tăbellārĭus, ii   *m,* letter-bearer
tābĕo   *v.i.* 2, to melt away
tăberna, ae   *f,* hut, shop, inn
tăbernācŭlum, i   *n,* tent
tăbernārĭus, ii   *m,* shopkeeper
tābes, is   *f,* wasting-away, disease
tābesco, bŭi   *v.i.* 3, to melt away
tābĭdus, a, um   *adj,* decaying
tābŭla, ae   *f,* plank, writing-tablet, letter, account book, picture, painting, map, table
tăbŭlārĭa, ae   *f,* record office
tăbŭlārĭum, ii   *n,* archives
tăbŭlārĭus, ii   *m,* registrar
tăbŭlātum, i   *n,* floor, storey
tābum, i   *n,* pus, matter, infectious disease
tăcĕo   *v.i.t.* 2, to be silent; to be silent about
tăcĭturnĭtas, ātis   *f,* silence
tăcĭturnus, a, um   *adj,* silent
tăcĭtus, a, um   *adj, adv,* ē, secret, silent
tactus, ūs   *m,* touch, feel, influence
taeda, ae   *f,* pine tree, torch
taedet, taedŭit   *v.* 2, *impers, with acc. of person,* it offends, disgusts, wearies
taedĭum, ii   *n,* weariness, disgust
taenĭa, ae   *f,* hair ribbon
taeter, tra, trum   *adj,* hideous
taetrĭcus, a, um   *adj,* harsh
tālāris, e   *adj,* ankle-length
tālĕa, ae   *f,* stick, stake
tălentum, i   *n,* sum of money (app. £400-£500); weight (¹/₂ cwt.)
tālĭo, ōnis   *f,* similar punishment, reprisal
tālis, e   *adj,* of such a kind
talpa, ae   *f,* mole
tālus, i   *m,* ankle bone, heel, die

(marked on four sides)

tam *adv,* so, as, equally

tamdīū *adv,* so long

tămen *adv,* nevertheless, however, still

tămetsi *conj,* although

tamquam *adv,* as much as, just as, as if, for example

tandem *adv,* at length

tango, tĕtĭgi, tactum *v.t.* 3, to touch, taste, reach, strike, affect, impress, mention

tanquam see **tamquam**

tantisper *adv,* so long, meanwhile

tantŏpĕre *adv,* so greatly

tantŭlus, a, um *adj,* so little

tantum *adv,* so much, only

tantummŏdo *adv,* only, merely

tantundem *adv,* just as much

tantus, a, um *adj,* so great; **tanti esse** to be worth so much; **tantō** by so much

tăpēte, is *n,* tapestry

tardĭtas, ātis *f,* slowness

tardo *v.i.t.* 1, to delay; hinder

tardus, a, um *adj, adv,* ē, slow

tăta, ae *m,* dad, daddy

taurĕus, a, um *adj,* of a bull

taurīnus, a, um *adj,* of a bull

taurus, i *m,* bull, ox

taxus, i *f,* yew tree

tē *acc. or abl. of* **tū**

tector, ōris *m,* plasterer

tectōrĭum, ii *n,* plaster

tectum, i *n,* roof, house

tectus, a, um *adj, adv,* ō, covered, hidden, secret

tĕges, ĕtis *f,* mat

tĕgĭmen, ĭnis *n,* cover

tĕgo, xi, ctum *v.t.* 3, to cover, hide, protect

tĕgŭla, ae *f,* tile

tĕgŭmen see **tĕgĭmen**

tĕgŭmentum, i *n,* cover

tēla, ae *f,* web, warp, loom

tellūs, ūris *f,* earth, globe, land, region

tēlum, i *n,* weapon, javelin

tĕmĕrārĭus, a, um *adj,* rash

tĕmĕrē *adv,* by chance, rashly

tĕmĕrĭtas, ātis *f,* rashness

tĕmĕro *v.t.* 1, to defile, disgrace

tēmētum, i *n,* wine

temno *v.t.* 3, to despise

tēmo, ōnis *m,* pole, beam

tempĕrans, ntis *adj,* moderate

tempĕrantĭa, ae *f,* moderation

tempĕrātĭo, ōnis *f,* symmetry, temperament

tempĕrātus, a, um *adj,* moderate

tempĕrĭes, ēi *f,* mildness

tempĕro *v.i.t.* 1, to abstain, be moderate, be indulgent; mix properly, regulate, govern

tempestas, ātis *f,* time, period, weather, storm

tempestīvus, a, um *adj, adv,* ē, suitable, timely, early

templum, i *n,* temple, open space

tempto see **tento**

tempus, ŏris *n,* time, opportunity; **tempŏra** times, temples (of the head); **ad tempus** (*adv. phr.*) at the right time, for the time being

tēmŭlentus, a, um *adj,* drunk

tĕnācĭtas, ātis *f,* tenacity

tĕnax, ācis *adj,* holding tight, firm, stingy

tendo, tĕtendi, tentum *v.i.t.* 3, to aim, go, march, stretch, strive, encamp; stretch, extend

tĕnĕbrae, ārum *f.pl,* darkness

tĕnĕbrĭcōsus, a, um *adj,* dark, gloomy

tĕnĕbrōsus, a, um *adj,* dark, gloomy

tĕnĕo, ŭi, tentum *v.i.t.* 2, to hold a position, sail, continue; hold, have, keep, restrain, uphold, maintain, control, comprehend, include

tĕner, ĕra, ĕrum *adj,* tender

tĕnor, ōris *m,* course, career

tensa, ae *f,* triumphal chariot

tentāmentum, i *n,* attempt

tentātĭo, ōnis *f,* trial, attempt

tentātor, ōris *m,* tempter

tento (tempto) *v.t.* 1, to handle, attack, attempt, tempt, excite

tentōrĭum, ii *n,* tent

tentus, a, um *adj,* extended

tĕnŭis, e *adj, adv,* ĭter, thin, fine, meagre, poor, subtle

tĕnŭĭtas, ātis *f,* slenderness,

poverty
tĕnŭo   *v.t.* 1, to make thin, reduce, weaken, degrade
tĕnus   *prep. with abl*, as far as, according to
tĕpĕfăcĭo, fēci, factum   *v.t.* 3, to warm
tĕpĕo   *v.i.* 2, to be warm
tĕpesco, pŭi   *v.i.* 3, to grow warm
tĕpĭdus, a, um   *adj*, warmth
tĕr   *adv*, three times
tĕrĕbinthus, i   *f*, terebinth tree
tĕrĕbra, ae   *f*, tool
tĕrĕbor   *v.t.* 1, to bore through
tĕrĕs, ĕtis   *adj*, rounded, smooth, polished
tergĕmĭnus, a, um   *adj*, triple
tergĕo, si, sum   *v.t.* 2, to clean, polish
tergĭbersātĭo, ōnis   *f*, backsliding
tergĭversor   *v.i.* 1, *dep*, to shuffle, refuse
tergo, si, sum   see **tergĕo**
tergum, i   *n*, back, rear, skin; **a tergo** (*adv. phr.*)   at the rear
termĭnālĭa, ĭum   *n.pl*, festival of Terminus (God of boundaries)
termĭnātĭo, ōnis   *f*, fixing
termĭno   *v.t.* 1, to limit, fix, define, determine, end
termĭnus, i   *m*, boundary, end
terni, ae, a   *pl. adj*, three each
tĕro, trīvi, trītum   *v.t.* 3, to rub, grind, smooth, polish, wear out, spend or waste time
terra, ae   *f*, earth, land, ground, region
terrēnus, a, um   *adj*, made of earth, terrestrial
terrĕo   *v.t.* 2, to frighten
terrestris, e   *adj*, of earth or land
terrĕus, a, um   *adj*, of earth or land
terrĭbĭlis, e   *adj*, dreadful
terrĭcŭla, ōrum   *n.pl*, scarecrow bugbear
terrĭfĭco   *v.t.* 1, to terrify
terrĭfĭcus, a, um   *adj*, frightful
terrĭgĕna, ae   *c*, earthborn
terrĭto   *v.t.* 1, to terrify
terror, ōris   *m*, terror, dread
tertĭus, a, um   *adj, adv*, **ō**, third
tĕruncĭus, ii   *m*, trifling sum

tessellātus, a, um   *adj*, tesselated, mosaic
tessĕra, ae   *f*, stone or wooden cube, die, watchword, ticket
testa, ae   *f*, jug, broken piece of pottery, shell-fish
testāmentum, i   *n*, will, testament
testātor, ōris   *m*, testator
testātus, a, um   *adj*, manifest
testĭfĭcātĭo, ōnis   *f*, evidence
testĭfĭcor   *v.t.* 1, *dep*, to give evidence, demonstrate
testĭmōnĭum, ii   *n*, evidence
testis, is   *c*, witness
testor   *v.t.* 1, *dep*, to call a witness, prove, declare
testu(m), i   *n*, lid, earthen pot
testūdĭnĕus, a, um   *adj*, of a tortoise
testūdo, ĭnis   *f*, tortoise, lute, military shelter
tĕtănus, i   *m*, tetanus
tēter, tra, trum   *adj*, hideous
tĕtrarches, ae   *m*, petty princeling
tĕtrĭcus, a, um   *adj*, harsh
texo, ŭi, xtum   *v.t.* 3, to weave, build, devise
textĭle, is   *n*, fabric
textĭlis, e   *adj*, woven
textor, ōris   *m*, weaver
textum, i   *n*, web, fabric
textus, ūs   *m*, texture
thălămus, i   *m*, apartment, bedroom, marriage
thĕātrālis, e   *adj*, theatrical
thĕātrum, i   *n*, theatre
thēca, ae   *f*, envelope
thĕŏlŏgĭa, ae   *f*, theology
thĕŏlŏgus, i   *m*, theologian
thĕōrēma, ătis   *n*, theorem
thermae, ārum   *f.pl*, warm baths
thēsaurus, i   *m*, store, hoard, treasure, treasure house
thĭăsus, i   *m*, dance in honour of Bacchus
thŏlus, i   *m*, dome
thōrax, ācis   *m*, breastplate
thunnus, i   *m*, tunny fish
thūs, thūris   *n*, incense
thymbra, ae   *f*, savory (plant)
thỹmum, I   *n*, thyme
thyrsus, i   *m*, stem of plant, staff carried by Bacchus

tĭāra, ae *f,* tiara
tībĭa, ae *f,* flute
tībĭāle, is *n,* stocking
tībīcen, ĭnis *m,* flute-player
tībīcĭna, ae *f,* flute-player
tībīcĭnĭum, ii *n,* flute-playing
tignum, i *n,* timber, log
tĭgris, is (ĭdis) *c,* tiger
tĭlĭa, ae *f,* linden or lime tree
tĭmĕo *v.i.t.* 2, to fear
tĭmĭdĭtas, ātis *f,* cowardice
tĭmĭdus, a, um *adj, adv,* ē, afraid,
   cowardly
tĭmor, ōris *m,* fear, alarm, object
   of fear
tĭnĕa, ae *f,* moth, bookworm
tingo, nxi, nctum *v.t.* 3, to
   moisten, dye
tinnĭo *v.i.t.* 4, to ring; tinkle
tinnītus, ūs *m,* ringing
tinnŭlus, a, um *adj,* tinkling
tintinnābŭlum, i *n,* bell
tīro, ōnis *m,* recruit, novice
tīrōcĭnĭum, ii *n,* first campaign,
   inexperience
tītillātĭo, ōnis *f,* tickling
tītillo *v.t.* 1, to tickle
tītŭbo *v.i.* 1, to stagger, hesitate,
   be perplexed
tītŭlus, i *m,* title, placard, notice,
   honour, glory
tōfus, i *m,* tufa (rock)
tŏga, ae *f,* toga the long outer
   garment of the Romans
tŏgātus, a, um *adj,* wearing the toga
tŏlĕrābĭlis, e *adj,* endurable
tŏlĕrantĭa, ae *f,* tolerance
tŏlĕro *v.t.* 1, to bear, endure
tollēno, ōnis *m,* a swing-beam
tollo, sustŭli, sublātum *v.t.* 3, to
   lift, raise, remove, destroy,
   educate, acknowledge
tŏnans, ntis *m,* god of thunder
tondĕo, tŏtondi, tonsum *v.t.* 2, to
   shave, crop, prune, graze
tŏnĭtrus, ūs *m,* thunder
tŏnĭtrŭum, i *n,* thunder
tŏno, ŭi *v.i.t.* 1, to thunder;
   thunder out
tonsa, ae *f,* oar
tonsillae, ārum *f.pl,* tonsils
tonsor, ōris *m,* barber
tonsōrĭus, a, um *adj,* of shaving

tonsūra, ae *f,* shearing
tŏpĭārĭus, ii *m,* landscape
   gardener
tŏreuma, ătis *n,* embossed work
tormentum, i *n,* missile, rope,
   missile-launcher, instrument of
   torture, rack, pain
tormĭna, um *n.pl,* the gripes
torno *v.t.* 1, to round off
tornus, i *m,* lathe
tŏrōsus, a, um *adj,* muscular
torpĕfăcĭo, fēci, factum *v.t.* 3, to
   numb
torpens, ntis *adj,* numb
torpĕo *v.i.* 2, to be stiff, numb,
   sluggish, listless
torpesco, pŭi *v.i.* 3, to become
   stiff or listless
torpor, ōris *m,* numbness
torquātus, a, um *adj,* wearing a
   collar
torquĕo, torsi, sum *v.t.* 2, to
   twist, bend, wield, hurl, rack,
   torture
torquis (torques), is *m, f,* collar,
   necklace, wreath
torrens, ntis *adj,* burning
torrens, ntis *m,* torrent
torrĕo, ŭi, tostum *v.t.* 2, to dry,
   bake, scorch, burn
torrĭdus, a, um *adj,* parched
torris, is *m,* firebrand
tortĭlis, e *adj,* twined
tortor, ōris *m,* torturer
tortŭōsus, a, um *adj,* winding,
   complicated
tortus, a, um *adj,* twisted
tortus, ūs *m,* twisting
tŏrus, i *m,* muscle, knot, cushion,
   sofa, bed
torvus, a, um *adj,* wild, grim
tŏt *indecl. adj,* so many
tŏtĭdem *indecl. adj,* just as many
tŏtĭens (tŏtĭes) *adv,* so often
tōtum, i *n,* whole
tōtus, a, um *adj,* the whole
trăbālis, e *adj,* of a beam
trăbĕa, ae *f,* robe of state
trabs, trăbis *f,* beam, timber, tree,
   ship
tractābĭlis, e *adj,* manageable,
   pliant, flexible
tractātĭo, ōnis *f,* handling,

treatment
tractātus, ūs   *m,* handling,
treatment
tractim   *adv,* little by little
tracto   *v.t.* 1, to handle, manage,
practise, discuss, drag
tractus, ūs   *m,* dragging, track,
district, course, progress
trādītĭo, ōnis   *f,* surrender
trādo, dĭdi, dĭtum   *v.t.* 3, to hand
over, commit, bequeath, relate
trādūco, xi, ctum   *v.t.* 3, to bring
over, degrade, spend (time)
trāductĭo, ōnis   *f,* transferring
trăgĭcus, a, um   *adj,* tragic,
fearful, grand
trăgoedĭa, ae   *f,* tragedy
trăgoedus, i   *m,* tragic actor
trāgŭla, ae   *f,* javelin, dart
trăhĕa, ae   *f,* sledge
trăho, xi, ctum   *v.t.* 3, to drag,
extract, inhale, quaff, drag away,
plunder, spin, influence, delay,
protract
trāĭcĭo, iēci, iectum   *v.t.* 3, to
throw across, transport, transfix
trāiectĭo, ōnis   *f,* crossing over,
passage
trāiectus, ūs   *m,* crossing
trāmĕs, ĭtis *m,* footpath, way
trāno   *v.t.* 1, to swim across
tranquillĭtas, ātis   *f,* calmness
tranquillo   *v.t.* 1, to calm
tranquillum, i   *n,* a calm
tranquillus, a, um *adj, adv,* ē, calm,
placid, serene
trans   *prep. with acc,* across,
beyond, on the further side of
transăbĕo   *v.t.* 4, to transfix
transădĭgo, ēgi, actum   *v.t.* 3, to
thrust through
transalpīnus, a, um   *adj,* beyond
the Alps
transcendo, si, sum   *v.i.t.* 3, to
climb over, surmount; exceed
transcrībo, psi, ptum   *v.t.* 3, to
transcribe, forge, transfer
transcurro, curri, cursum   *v.i.t.* 3,
to run across; pass through
transĕo   *v.i.t.* 4, to go over or
across, pass by, surpass
transfĕro, ferre, tŭli, lātum   *v.t,*
irreg, to bring across, carry

along, transfer, translate
transfīgo, xi, xum   *v.t.* 3, to pierce
through
transfŏdĭo, fōdi, fossum   *v.t.* 3, to
pierce through
transformo   *v.t.* 1, to transform
transfŭga, ae   *c,* deserter
transfŭgĭo, fūgi   *v.t.* 3, to desert
transfundo, fūdi, fūsum   *v.t.* 3, to
transfer
transgrĕdĭor, gressus   *v.i.t.* 3,
dep, to pass or climb over,
across
transgressĭo, ōnis   *f,* passage
transĭgo, ēgi, actum   *v.t.* 3, to
complete, transact, settle (a
difference)
transĭlĭo, ŭi   *v.i.t.* 4, to leap across
transĭtĭo, ōnis   *f,* going over,
passage
transĭtus, ūs   *m,* going over,
passage
translātīcĭus, a, um   *adj,* handed
down
translātĭo, ōnis   *f,* transferring
translātus, a, um   *adj,* transferred,
copied, figurative
translūcĕo   *v.i.* 2, to shine
through
transmărīnus, a, um   *adj,* across
to sea
transmĭgro   *v.i.* 1, to migrate
transmissus, ūs   *m,* transferring
transmitto, mīsi, missum   *v.i.t.* 3,
to go across; send across,
transfer, hand over
transmūto   *v.t.* 1, to change
transnăto   *v.i.* 1, to swim over
transpădānus, a, um   *adj,* beyond
the river Po
transporto   *v.t.* 1, to carry across
transtrum, i   *n,* rowing-bench
transvĕho, xi, ctum   *v.t.* 3, to
carry over
transverbĕro   *v.t.* 1, to transfix
transversārĭus, a, um   *adj,*
crosswise
transversus, a, um   *adj,* crosswise
transvŏlo   *v.i.t.* 1, to fly across
trĕcēni, ae, a   *pl. adj,* three
hundred each
trecentensĭmus, a, um   *adj,* three
hundredth

trĕcenti, ae, a *pl, adj,* three hundred

trĕdĕcim *indecl. adj,* thirteen

trĕmĕbundus, a, um *adj,* trembling

trĕmĕfăcĭo, fēci, factum *v.t.* 3, to cause to tremble

trĕmendus, a, um *adj,* dreadful

trĕmesco *v.i.t.* 3, to tremble; tremble at

trĕmo, ŭi *v.i.t.* 3, to tremble; tremble at

trĕmor, ōris *m,* shuddering

trĕmŭlus, a, um *adj,* trembling

trĕpĭdans, ntis *adj,* trembling

trĕpĭdātĭo, ōnis *f,* confusion

trĕpĭdo *v.i.t.* 1, to be alarmed; tremble at

trĕpĭdus, a, um *adj,* alarmed

trēs, trĭa *adj,* three

trĭangŭlum, i *n,* triangle

trĭangŭlus, a, um *adj,* triangular

trĭārĭi, ōrum *m.pl,* veteran soldiers who fought in the third rank

trĭbŭārĭus, a, um *adj,* of a tribe

trĭbŭlis, e *adj,* of the same tribe

trĭbŭlum, i *n,* threshing-platform

trĭbŭlus, i *m,* thistle

trĭbūnal, ālis *n,* platform, judgement seat

trĭbūnātŭs, ūs *m,* position of tribune

trĭbūnĭcĭus, a, um *adj,* of a tribune

trĭbūnus, i *m,* tribune; 1. army officer; 2. magistrate to defend to defend the rights of the people

trĭbŭo, ŭi, ūtum *v.t.* 3, to allot, give, attribute

trĭbus, ūs *f,* tribe

trĭbus see **trēs**

trĭbūtim *adv,* by tribes

trĭbūtum, i *n,* tribute, tax

trīcae, ārum *f. pl,* tricks

trīcēni, ae, a *pl. adj,* thirty each

trīceps, cĭpĭtis *adj,* three-headed

trīcēsĭmus, a, um *adj,* thirtieth

trīcĭes *adv,* thirty times

trĭclīnĭum, i *n,* dining-couch, dining-room

trĭcorpor, ŏris *adj,* three-bodied

trĭdens, ntis *adj,* three-pronged; as *nn,* trident

trĭdŭum, i *n,* three days

trĭennĭum, i *n,* three years

trĭens, ntis *m,* a third part

trĭĕtērĭca, ōrum *n.pl,* festival of Bacchus

trĭfaux, cis *adj,* with three throats

trĭdĭdus, a, um *adj,* three-forked

trĭfŏlĭum, i *n,* shamrock

trĭformis, e *adj,* three-fold

trĭgĕmĭnus, a, um *adj,* triple

trĭgēsĭmus, a, um *adj,* thirtieth

trĭginta *indecl. adj,* thirty

trĭgōn, ōnis *m,* ball

trĭlībris, e *adj,* weighing three pounds

trĭlinguis, e *adj,* three-tongued

trĭlix, īcis *adj,* with three thongs

trĭmestris, e *adj,* of three months

trĭmus, a, um *adj,* three years old

trīni, ae, a *pl. adj,* three each

trĭnōdis, e *adj,* three-knotted

trĭōnes, um *m.pl,* constellation of the Great and Lesser Bear

trĭpertītus, a, um *adj, adv, ō,* threefold

trĭpēs, ĕdis *adj,* three-footed

trĭplex, ĭcis *adj,* triple

trĭplĭco *v.t.* 1, to treble

trĭpŭdĭum, ii *n,* religious dance, favourable omen

trĭpūs, ŏdis *m,* tripod

trĭquĕtrus, a, um *adj,* triangular

trĭrēmis, e *adj,* with three banks of oars

tristis, e *adj,* sad, gloomy, harsh, disagreeable

tristĭtĭa, ae *f,* sadness, gloominess, harshness

trĭsulcus, a, um *adj,* three-forked

trītĭcĕus, a, um *adj,* of wheat

trītĭcum, i *n,* wheat

trītūra, ae *f,* threshing (of grain)

trītus, a, um *adj,* beaten, common, worn, familiar

trĭumphālis, e *adj,* triumphal

trĭumpho *v.i.t.* 1, to celebrate a triumph; triumph over

trĭumphus, i *m,* triumphal procession after a victory

trĭumvīrātŭs, ūs *m,* triumvirate

trĭumvĭri, ōrum *m.pl,* board of three men

trĭvĭum, ii *n,* crossroad

trŏchaeus, i   *m*, metrical foot
trochlĕa, ae   *f*, pulley
trŏchus, i   *m*, hoop
trŏpaeum, i   *n*, trophy, victory
trŏpĭcus, a, um   *adj*, tropical
trŭcīdātĭo, ōnis   *f*, butchery
trŭcīdo   *v.t.* 1, to slaughter
trŭcŭlentus, a, um   *adj*, harsh
trŭdis, is   *f*, pole, pike
trūdo, si, sum   *v.t.* 3, to push,
   drive, put out
trulla, ae   *f*, ladle
truncātus, a, um   *adj*, maimed
trunco   *v.t.* 1, to maim, cut off
truncus, a, um   *adj*, maimed
truncus, i   *m*, trunk, stem
trŭtĭna, ae   *f*, pair of scales
trux, ŭcis   *adj*, harsh, stern
tū   *pron*, you (singular)
tŭba, ae   *f*, trumpet
tŭber, ĕris   *n*, swelling, tumour
tŭbĭcen, ĭnis   *m*, trumpeter
tŭbŭlātus, a, um   *adj*, tubular
tŭbŭlus, i   *m*, tube
tŭĕor   *v.t.* 2, *dep*, to look at, gaze
   at, consider, guard, maintain,
   support
tŭgŭrĭum, i   *n*, cottage
tŭli   see fero
tum   *adv, and conj*, then
tŭmĕfăcio, fēci, factum   *v.t.* 3, to
   cause to swell
tŭmĕo   *v.i.* 2, to swell, be puffed up
tŭmesco, mui   *v.i.* 3, to become
   swollen, be puffed up
tŭmĭdus, a, um   *adj*, swollen,
   excited, enraged
tŭmor, ōris   *m*, swelling,
   commotion
tŭmŭlo   *v.t.* 1, to bury
tŭmultŭārĭus, a, um   *adj*, hurried,
   hurriedly raised (troops)
tŭmultŭor   *v.i.* 1, *dep*, to be
   confused
tŭmultŭōsus, a, um   *adj, adv*, ē,
   restless, confused, turbulent
tŭmultus, ūs   *m*, uproar, tempest,
   rebellion
tŭmŭlus, i   *m*, hill, mound
tunc   *adv*, then
tundo, tŭtŭdi, tunsum (tusum)   *v.t.*
   3, to beat, strike, pound
tŭnĭca, ae   *f*, tunic, husk

tŭnĭcātus, a, um   *adj*, dressed in a
   tunic
tŭnĭcopallĭum, i   *n*, short cloak
tūrārĭus, ii   *m*, a dealer
turba, ae   *f*, hubbub, uproar,
   crowd, band, quarrel, confusion
turbātor, ōris   *m*, disturber
turbātus, a, um   *adj*, disturbed
turbĭdus, a, um   *adj, adv*, ē,
   confused, troubled, violent
turbo   *v.t.* 1, to confuse, disturb,
   make thick
turbo, ĭnis   *m*, hurricane, spinning
   top, revolution
turbŭlentus, a, um   *adj, adv*, nter,
   restless, boisterous, troublesome
turdus, i   *m*, thrush
tūrĕus, a, um   *adj*, of incense
turgĕo, rsi   *v.i.* 2, to swell
turgesco   *v.i.* 3, to swell up
turgĭdŭlus, a, um   *adj*, swollen
turgĭdus, a, um   *adj*, swollen
tūrĭbŭlum, i   *n*, incense-vessel
tūrĭcrĕmus, a, um   *adj*, for
   burning incense
tūrĭfer, ĕra, ĕrum   *adj*, incense-
   producing
turma, ae   *f*, cavalry troop, crowd
turmālis, e   *adj*, of a squadron
turmātim   *adv*, by squadrons
turpis, e   *adj, adv*, ĭter, filthy,
   ugly, disgraceful, scandalous
turpĭtūdo, ĭnis   *f*, disgrace,
   baseness
turbo   *v.t.* 1, to pollute, soil
turrĭger, ĕra, ĕrum   *adj*, turreted
turris, is   *f*, tower
turrītus, a, um   *adj*, turreted
turtur, ŭris   *m*, turtle-dove
tūs, tūris   *n*, incense
tussĭo   *v.i.* 4, to cough
tussis, is   *f*, cough
tūtāmen, ĭnis   *n*, defence
tūtēla, ae   *f*, safeguard, defence,
   position of guardian, object
   under guardianship
tūtō   *adv*, safely
tūtor ōris   *m*, guardian
tūtor   *v.t.* 1, *dep*, to guard, watch
tūtus, a, um   *adj*, safe, prudent
tŭus, a, um   *adj*, your(s)
tympănum, i   *n*, tambourine, door
   panel

tyrannĭcus, a, um *adj,* tyrannical

tyrannis, ĭdis *f,* despotic rule

tyrannus, i *m,* sovereign, ruler, despot

U

ūber, ĕris *n,* teat, udder, breast

ūber, ĕris *adj,* fertile, rich

ūbertas, ātis *f,* fertility, richness

ŭbĭ *adv,* where, when, as soon as

ŭbĭcumque *adv,* wherever

ŭbīque *adv,* everywhere, anywhere

ŭbĭvīs *adv,* everywhere, anywhere

ūdus, a, um *adj,* moist, wet

ulcĕrātĭo, ōnis *f,* ulceration

ulcĕro *v.t.* 1, to make sore

ulcĕrōsus, a, um *adj,* ulcerous

ulciscor, ultus *v.t.* 3, *dep,* to avenge, punish, take vengeance on

ulcus, ĕris *n,* sore, ulcer

ulex, ĭcis *m,* furze

ūlīgĭnōsus, a, um *adj,* moist, marshy

ūlīgo, ĭnis *f,* moisture

ullus, a, um *adj,* (*genit,* **ullīus,** *dat,* **ulli**) any

ulmĕus, a, um *adj,* of elm

ulmus, i *f,* elm tree

ulna, ae *f,* elbow, arm, ell

ultĕrĭor, ĭus *comp. adj,* beyond, on the farther side

ultĕrĭus *comp. adv,* beyond, farther

ultĭmus, a, um *sup. adj,* farthest, extreme, last

ultĭo, ōnis *f,* revenge

ultor, ōris *m,* avenger

ultrā *adv, and prep. with acc,* beyond, past, farther, besides

ultrix, īcis *adj,* avenging

ultrō *adv,* on the other side, moreover, spontaneously

ŭlŭla, ae *f,* screech owl

ŭlŭlātus, ūs *m,* wailing

ŭlŭlo *v.i.t.* 1, to howl; cry out to

ulva, ae *f,* sedge

umbella, ae *f,* parasol

umbĭlīcus, i *m,* navel, centre, end of rod on which Roman books were rolled

umbo, ōnis *m,* shield, knob

umbra, ae *f,* shadow, shade, ghost, trace, shelter

umbrācŭlum, i *n,* shady spot, school

umbrātĭlis, e *adj,* private, retired

umbrĭfer, ĕra, ĕrum *adj,* shady

umbro *v.t.* 1, to shade, cover

umbrōsus, a, um *adj,* shady

ūmecto *v.t.* 1, to moisten

ūmĕo *v.i.* 2, to be damp

ūmĕrus, i *m,* shoulder, arm

ūmesco *v.i.* 3, to grow wet

ūmĭdus, a, um *adj,* wet, damp

ūmor, ōris *m,* moisture, liquid

umquam *adv,* ever

ūnā *adv,* at the same time, in the same place, together

ūnănĭmus, a, um *adj,* of one mind

ūnănĭmĭtas, ātis *f,* unanimity

uncĭa, ae *f,* a twelfth, ounce

unctĭo, ōnis *f,* anointing

unctus, a, um *adj,* oiled, rich, luxurious

uncus, i *m,* hook

uncus, a, um *adj,* hooked

unda, ae *f,* wave, tide

undĕ *adv,* from where, whence

undĕ ... (with number) one from ... e.g. **undēvigint i** (one from 20) 19

undĕcĭes *adv,* eleven times

undĕcĭm *indecl. adj,* eleven

undĕcĭmus, a, um *adj,* eleventh

undēni, ae, a *pl. adj,* eleven each

undĭquĕ *adv,* from all sides, everywhere

undo *v.i.* 1, to surge, undulate

undōsus, a, um *adj,* billowy

ungo (unguo), unxi, unctum *v.t.* 3, to besmear, oil

unguen, ĭnis *n,* ointment

unguentārĭus, ii *m,* perfume seller

unguentum, i *n,* ointment, perfume

unguis, is *m,* finger or toe nail

ungŭla, ae *f,* hoof, claw

ungo (3) see **ungo**

ūnĭcŏlor, ōris *adj,* of one colour

ūnĭcus, a, um *adj, adv,* **ē,** only, single, singular, unique

ūnĭo, ōnis *m, f,* unity

ūnĭversĭtas, ātis *f,* universe
ūnĭversum, i *n,* whole world
ūnĭversus, a, um *adj, adv, ē,*
  entire, all together
unquam *adv,* ever
ūnus, a, um *adj,* one only
ūnusquisque *pron.* each
ūpĭlĭo, ōnis *m,* shepherd
urbānĭtas, ātis *f,* city life,
  elegance, courtesy, refinement
urbānus, a, um *adj, adv, ē,* of the
  city, refined, elegant, courteous,
  humorous
urbs, urbis *f,* city
urcĕus, i *m,* water jug
urgĕo, ursi *v.t.* 2, to press, push,
  oppress, urge, crowd
ūrīna, ae *f,* urine
ūrīnātor, ōris *m,* diver
urna, ae *f,* water-jar, urn (for
  voting tablets or ashes of the
  dead)
ūro, ussi, ustum *v.t.* 3, to burn,
  destroy by fire, scorch, nip with
  cold
ursa, ae *f,* she-bear
ursus, i *m,* bear
urtīca, ae *f,* nettle
ūrus, i *m,* wild fox
ūsĭtātus, a, um *adj,* usual
uspĭam *adv,* anywhere,
  somewhere
usquam *adv,* anywhere
usquĕ *adv,* all the way, all the
  time, as far as, until
ustor, ōris *m,* corpse-burner
ūsūra, ae *f,* money-lending,
  interest
ūsurpātĭo, ōnis *f,* using, use
ūsurpo *v.t.* 1, to use, practise,
  exercise, acquire
ūsus, ūs *m,* using, use, practice,
  custom, habit, familiarity,
  advantage
ut (ūti) *conj,* so that, that, in
  order to, to; *adv,* now as, when,
  as soon as, where
utcumquĕ (utcunquĕ) *adv,* in
  whatever way, however,
  whenever
ūter, tris *m,* bottle, bag
ūter, tra, trum *interr. pron,* which
  of the two

ūtercumquĕ, utrăcumque,
  utrumcumque *pron,* whichever
  of the two
ūterlībet, utrălībet, utrumlībet
  pron, which of the two you
  please
ūterque, utrăque, utrumque *pron,*
  each of the two, both
ūtĕrus, i *m,* womb, belly
ūtervīs, utrăvīs, utrumvīs *pron,*
  which of the two you please
ŭti see **ut**
ūti see **ūtor**
ūtĭlis, e *adj, adv,* ĭter, useful,
  suitable, advantageous
ūtĭlĭtas, ātis *f,* usefulness,
  advantage
ŭtĭnam *adv,* if only ! would that!
ūtĭquĕ *adv,* at any rate, at least,
  certainly
ūtor, ūsus *v.* 3, *dep, with abl,* to
  use, practise, be familiar with
utpŏtĕ *adv,* namely, as, since
ŭtrimquĕ *adv,* on both sides
ŭtrŏbīquĕ (ŭtrŭbīquĕ) *adv,* on
  both sides
ŭtrōquĕ *adv,* in both directions
ŭtrum *adv, used to form an
  alternative question,* is it this …
  or that?
ūva, ae *f,* grape, cluster
ūbĭdus, a, um *adj,* moist, damp
uxor, ōris *f,* wife
uxōrĭus, a, um *adj,* of a wife

V

văcans, ntis *adj,* unoccupied
văcātĭo, ōnis *f,* exemption
vacca, ae *f,* cow
vaccīnĭum, ii *n,* whortleberry
văcillātĭo, ōnis *f,* vacillation
văcillo *v.i.* 1, to stagger, sway,
  hesitate
văco *v.i.* 1, to be empty, free
  from, have leisure (for)
văcŭĕfăcĭo, fēci, factum *v.t.* 3, to
  empty, clear
văcŭĭtas, ātis *f,* exemption
văcŭus, a, um *adj,* empty, free,
  without, unoccupied, worthless
vădīmōnĭum, i *n,* bail, security
vādo *v.i.* 3, to go, walk, rush

vădor *v.t.* 1, *dep*, to bind over by bail

vădōsus, a, um *adj*, shallow

vădum, i *n*, a shallow ford (*often in pl.*)

vae *interj*, ah! alas!

văfer, fra, frum *adj*, sly

văgātĭo, ōnis *f*, wandering

vāgīna, ae *f*, sheath, scabbard

vāgĭo, *v.i.* 4, to cry, bawl

vāgītus, ūs *m*, crying, bawling

văgor *v.i.* 1, *dep*, to wander, roam

văgus, a, um *adj*, wandering, roaming, uncertain, vague

valdē *adv*, energetically, very much, very

văle *imperative* (*pl*, vălēte), farewell!

vălens, ntis *adj*, powerful, strong, healthy

vălĕo *v.i.* 2, to be strong, vigorous or healthy, to have power or influence, to be capable or effective, be worth

vălesco *v.i.* 3, to grow strong

vălētūdĭnārĭum, ii *n*, hospital

vălētūdĭnārĭus, i *m*, invalid

vălētūdo, ĭnis *f*, health (good or bad)

vălĭdus, a, um *adj*, strong, powerful, healthy

valles (vallis), is *f*, valley

vallo *v.t.* 1, to fortify with rampart, protect

vallum, i *n*, rampart, palisade

vallus, i *m*, stake, palisade

valvae, ārum *f.pl*, folding doors

vānesco *v.i.* 3, to disappear

vānĭtas, ātis *f*, emptiness, uselessness, vanity

vannus, i *f*, fan

vānus, a, um *adj*, empty, groundless, false, deceptive

văpĭdus, a, um *adj*, spoiled, flat

văpor, ōris *m*, steam, vapour

văpōro *v.t.* 1, to fumigate, warm

vappa, ae *f*, flat wine; *m*, a good-for-nothing

vāpŭlo *v.i.* 1, to be flogged

vārĭco *v.i.* 1, to straddle

vărĭcōsus, a, um *adj*, varicose

vărĭētas, ātis *f*, variety

vārĭo *v.i.t.* 1, to vary; diversify, change

vārĭus, a, um *adj, adv*, ē, variegated, changing, varying

vărix, ĭcis *m, f*, varicose vein

vārus, a, um *adj*, knock-kneed

văs, vădis *m*, bail, security

vās, vāsis *n*, dish, utensil, military equipment

vāsārĭum, ii *n*, expense account

vascŭlārĭus, ii *m*, metal worker

vastātĭo, ōnis *f*, devastation

vastātor, ōris *m*, destroyer

vastĭtas, ātis *f*, desert, destruction, ruin

vasto *v.t.* 1, to devastate, destroy, leave vacant

vastus, a, um *adj*, deserted, desolate, rough, devastated, enormous, vast

vātes, is *c*, forecaster, poet

vātĭcĭnātĭo, ōnis *f*, prediction

vātĭcĭnātor, ōris *m*, prophet

vātĭcĭnor *v.i.t.* 1, *dep*, to predict

vātĭus, a, um *adj*, bow-legged

vĕ *conj*, or

vēcordĭa, ae *f*, folly, madness

vēcors, dis *adj*, foolish, mad

vectĭgal, ālis *n*, tax, income

vectĭgālis, e *adj* tax paying

vectis, is *m*, pole, bar, lever

vecto *v.t.* 1, to convey

vector, ōris *m*, carrier, traveller, passenger

vectōrĭus, a, um *adj*, for carrying

vectūra, ae *f*, transportation, fare

vectus, a, um *adj*, conveyed, carried

vĕgĕtus, a, um *adj*, lively

vēgrandis, e *adj*, small

vĕhĕmens, ntis *adj, adv*, nter, violent, powerful, strong

vĕhĭcŭlum, i *n*, vehicle

vĕho, si, ctum *v.t.* 3, to convey; *in passive, or with reflexive pron*, to ride, sail, go

vĕl *conj*, either, or, indeed

vēlāmen, ĭnis *n*, cover, garment

vēlāmentum, i *n*, olive branch

vēles, ĭtis *m*, light-armed soldier

vēlĭfer, ĕra, ĕrum *adj*, carrying sails

vēlĭfĭcātĭo, ōnis *f*, sailing

vēlīfĭcor   *v.i.* 1, *dep,* to sail, gain, procure

vēlīvŏlus, a, um   *adj,* sail-winged; (**măre**) dotted with ships

vellīco   *v.t.* 1, to nip, taunt

vello, vulsi, vulsum   *v.t.* 3, to tear out, pluck off

vellus, ĕris   *n,* fleece, hide

vēlo   *v.t.* 1, to cover, wrap up

vēlōcĭtas, ātis   *f,* speed

vēlox, ōcis   *adj, adv,* īter, swift, fast, fleet

vēlum, i   *n,* sail, covering

vēlut   *adj,* just as, like

vēna, ae   *f,* vein, disposition

vēnābŭlum, i   *n,* hunting spear

vēnālīcĭum, ii   *n,* slave-dealing

vēnālīcĭus, ii   *m,* slave-dealer

vēnālis, e   *adj,* for sale, able to be bribed, corrupt

vēnālis, is   *m,* slave for sale

vēnātĭcus, a, um   *adj,* of hunting

vēnātĭo, ōnis   *f,* hunting, a, hunt, combat of wild beasts

vēnātor, ōris   *m,* hunter

vēnātrix, īcis   *f,* huntress

vēnātus, ūs   *m,* hunting

vendĭbĭlis, e   *adj,* saleable

vendĭtātĭo, ōnis   *f,* boasting

vendĭtĭo, ōnis   *f,* sale

vendĭto   *v.t.* 1, to try to sell

vendĭtor, ōris   *m,* salesman

vendo, dĭdi, dĭtum   *v.t.* 3, to sell, betray, praise

vĕnēfĭca, ae   *f,* witch

vĕnēfĭcĭum, ii   *n,* poisoning, magic

vĕnēfĭcus, a, um   *adj,* poisonous, magic

vĕnēfĭcus, i   *m,* poisoner, sorcerer

vĕnēnātus, a, um   *adj,* poisonous

vĕnēnĭfer, ĕra, ĕrum   *adj,* poisonous

vĕnēno   *v.t.* 1, to poison, dye

vĕnēnum, i   *n,* poison, magic charm, drug

vēnĕo, ii, ītum   *v.i.* 4, to be sold

vĕnĕrābĭlis, e   *adj,* worthy of respect

vĕnĕrābundus, a, um   *adj,* devout

vĕnĕrātĭo, ōnis   *f,* great respect

vĕnĕrĕus, a, um   *adj,* venereal

vĕnĕror   *v.t.* 1, *dep,* to worship, revere, honour, entreat

vĕnĭa, ae   *f,* indulgence, mercy, permission, pardon

vĕnĭo, vēni, ventum   *v.i.* 4, to come

vēnor   *v.i.t.* 1, *dep,* to hunt

venter, tris   *m,* belly

ventĭlo   *v.t.* 1, to wave, fan

ventĭto   *v.i.* 1, to keep coming

ventōsus, a, um   *adj,* windy, swift, light, changeable, vain

ventrĭcŭlus, i   *m,* ventricle

ventūrus   *fut. partic. from* **vĕnĭo**

ventus, i   *m,* wind

vēnūcŭla (uva)   a preserving grape

vēnundo, dĕdi, dătum   *v.t.* 1, to sell

vĕnus, ūs   *m,* (**vēnum, i,**   *n*) sale

vĕnustas, ātis   *f,* charm, beauty

vĕnustus, a, um   *adj, adv,* ē, charming, graceful, beautiful

vĕprēcŭla, ae   *f,* small thorn-bush

vĕpres, is   *m,* thorn-bush

vēr, vēris   *n,* spring

vēra   see **vērus**

vērācĭtas, ātis   *f,* veracity

vērax, ācis   *adj,* true

verbēna, ae   *f,* foliage, branches

verber, ĕris   *n,* lash, whip, flogging, blow

verbĕrātĭo, ōnis   *f,* punishment

verbĕro   *v.t.* 1, to whip, strike

verbōsus, a, um   *adj,* effusive

verbum, i   *n,* word, language, conversation; **verba dare** to deceive

vērē   *adj,* really, truly

vĕrēcundĭa, ae   *f,* shyness

vĕrēcundor   *v.i.* 1, *dep,* to be shy

vĕrēcundus, a, um   *adj, adv,* ē, shy, modest

vĕrendus, a, um   *adj,* venerable, terrible

vĕrĕor   *v.i.t.* 2, *dep,* to fear, respect

verto   *v.i.* 3, to turn, bend, lie, be situated

vērĭdĭcus, a, um   *adj,* truthful

vērĭsĭmĭlis, e   *adj,* probable

vērĭtas, ātis   *f,* truth, reality

vermĭcŭlus, i   *m,* worm, grub

vermĭnōsus, a, um   *adj,* worm-eaten

vermis, is   *m,* worm

verna, ae *c,* slave born in his master's house

vernācŭlus, a, um *adj,* domestic

vernīlĭter *adj,* slavishly

verno *v.i.* 1, to flourish, bloom

vernus, a, um *adj,* of spring

vērō *adj,* in fact, certainly, but indeed, however

verres, is, *m,* pig

verro, verri, versum *v.t.* 3, to sweep, brush, impel, take away

verrūca, ae *f,* wart, blemish

versātĭlis, e *adj,* movable

versĭcŏlor, ŏris *adj,* of different colours

versĭcŭlus, i *m,* single line of verse (or prose)

verso *v.t.* 1, to turn, twist, whirl, consider

versor *v.i.* 1, *dep,* to live, stay, be situated, be engaged on

versūra, ae *f,* borrowing, loan

versus *adv,* towards

versus, ūs *m,* row, line, verse

versūtus, a, um *adj, adv,* ē, clever, shrewd, cunning, sly

vertĕbra, ae *f,* vertebra

vertex, ĭcis *m,* whirlpool, whirlwind, flame, crown of the head, summit, peak

vertĭcōsus, a, um *adj,* eddying

vertīgĭnōsus, a, um *adj,* suffering from giddiness

vertīgo, ĭnis *f,* dizziness

vēro see **vērus**

verto, ti, sum *v.i.t.* 3, to turn, change; turn, change, alter overthrow, translate

vĕru, ūs *n,* roasting-spit, javelin

vĕrūcŭlum, i *n,* skewer, small javelin

vērum *adv,* but, yet, still

vērum, i *n,* truth, reality, fact

vērumtămen *conj,* nevertheless

vērus, a, um *adj, adv,* ō, ē, true, real, proper, right

vĕrūtum, i *n,* javelin

vĕrūtus, a, um *adj,* armed with a javelin

vervex, ēcis *m,* wether, sheep

vēsānĭa, ae *f,* insanity

vēsănus, a, um *adj,* mad, fierce

vescor *v.i.t.* 3, *dep. with abl,* to feed on

vescus, a, um *adj,* thin, weak

vēsīca, ae *f,* bladder

vespa, ae *f,* wasp

vesper, ĕris (ĕri) *m,* evening, the West

vespĕra, ae *f,* evening, the West

vespĕrasco, āvi *v.i.* 3, to draw towards evening

vespertīnus, a, um *adj,* of evening, western

vespillo, ōnis *m,* undertaker

vesta, ae *f,* fire

vestālis, e *adj,* of the Vesta, the Goddess of Fire, Hearth, Home

vestālis, is *f,* priestess of Vesta

vester, tra, trum *adj,* your

vestiārĭum, i *n,* wardrobe

vestībŭlum, i *n,* entrance hall

vestīgĭum, i *n,* footstep, track, sole of foot, mark, moment, instant; ē, **vestīgĭo** instantly

vestīgo *v.t.* 1, to search out, investigate

vestīmentum, i *n,* clothing

vestĭo *v.t.* 4, to clothe, cover

vestis, is *f,* clothing, clothes, carpet, curtain

vestītus, ūs *m,* clothes, dresss

vĕtĕrānus, a, um *adj,* old, veteran

vĕtĕrānus, i *m,* veteran soldier

vĕtĕrātor, ōris *m,* crafty, wily or sly person

vĕtĕrātōrĭus, a, um *adj,* sly

vĕtĕres, um *m.pl,* ancestors

vĕtĕrīnārĭus, a, um *adj,* veterinary

vĕternus, i *m,* sluggishness

vĕtĭtum, i *n,* something forbidden, prohibition

vĕtĭtus, a, um *adj,* forbidden

vĕto, ŭi, ĭtum *v.t.* 1, to forbid

vĕtŭlus, a, um *adj,* old

vĕtus, ĕris *adj,* old, former

vĕtustas, ātis *f,* old age, antiquity, posterity

vĕtustus, a, um *adj,* old

vexātĭo, ōnis *f,* distress

vexillārĭus, i *m,* standard-bearer

vexillum, i *n,* standard, ensign

vexo *v.t.* 1, to shake, injure, molest, harrass, torment

vĭa, ae *f,* road, street, way, method

vĭātĭcum, i   *n*, travelling expenses, soldier's savings
vĭātor, ōris   *m*, traveller
vībex, īcis   *f*, weal
vĭbro   *v.i.t* 1, to quiver; brandish, shake
vĭcārĭus, i   *m*, deputy
vīcēni, ae, a   *pl. adj*, twenty each
vīcēsĭmus (vīcensĭmus), a, um   *adj*, twentieth
vĭcĭa, ae   *f*, vetch
vīcĭes (vīcĭens)   *adv*, twenty times
vīcīnĭa, ae   *f*, neighbourhood
vīcīnus, a, um   *adj*, neighbouring, similar
vīcīnus, a, um   *adj*, neighbouring, similar
vīcīnus, i   *m*, neighbour
vĭcis (*genitive*), vĭcem, vĭce   change, alternation, recompense, lot, misfortune, position, duty; in vĭcem, per vĭces   alternately; vĭcem, vĭce, instead of
vĭcĭssim   *adv*, in turn
vĭcĭssĭtūdo, ĭnis   *f*, change
victīma, ae   *f*, victim for sacrifice
victor, ōris   *m*, conqueror
victōrĭa, ae   *f*, victory
victrix, īcis   *f*, female conqueror
vitrix, īcis   *adj*, victorious
victus, ūs   *m*, nutriment, diet
vīcus, i   *m*, street, village
vīdēlīcet   *adv*, obviously
vĭdĕo, vīdi, vīsum   *v.t.* 2, to see, perceive, understand, consider, take care, see to it
vĭdĕor, vēsus   *v.* 2, *dep*, to seem; *impers*, it seems right or good
vĭdŭa, ae   *f*, widow
vĭdŭĭtas, ātis   *f*, bereavement
vĭdŭlus, i   *m*, valise
vĭdŭo   *v.t.* 1, to deprive
vĭdŭus, a, um   *adj*, robbed, widowed
vĭētus, a, um   *adj*, withered
vĭgĕo   *v.i.* 2, to flourish, thrive
vĭgesco, gŭi   *v.i.* 3, to flourish, thrive
vĭgil, īlis   *adj*, alert, watching
vĭgil, īlis   *m*, watchman
vĭgĭlans, ntis   *adj, adv*, nter, watchful, careful
vĭgĭlantĭa, ae   *f*, watchfulness

vĭgĭlĭa, ae   *f*, wakefulness, vigilance, guard, watch
vĭgĭlo   *v.i.t.* 1, to keep awake, be vigilant; spend (time) in watching
vīginti   *indecl. adj*, twenty
vīgor, ōris   *m*, liveliness
vīlīco   *v.i.t.* 1, to superintend
vīlīcus (villicus), i   *m*, superintendent
vīlis, e   *adj*, cheap, mean
vīlĭtas, ātis   *f*, cheapness
villa, ae   *f*, country house
villātĭcus, a, um   *adj*, of a villa
villicus   see vīlicus
villōsus, a, um   *adj*, hairy, shaggy
villŭla, ae   *f*, small villa
villus, i   *m*, tuft of hair
vīmen, ĭnis   *n*, pliant branch
Vīmĭnālis (collis)   the Viminal, one of the seven hills of Rome
vīmĭnĕus, a, um   *adj*, of wickerwork
vīnārĭum, ii   *n*, wine bottle
vīnārĭus, a, um   *adj*, of wine
vīnārĭus, i   *m*, vintner
vincĭo, nxi, nctum   *v.t.* 4, to bind, tie, surround
vinco, vīci, victum   *v.i.t.* 3, to prevail; conquer, overcome, prove conclusively
vincŭlum (vinclum), i   *n*, cord, bond fetter; *pl*, prison
vindēmĭa, ae   *f*, grape-gathering, wine
vindēmĭātor, ōris   *m*, grape-gatherer
vindex, īcis   *c*, claimant, defender, liberator, avenger
vindĭcĭae, ārum   *f.pl*, legal claim
vindĭco   *v.t.* 1, to claim, appropriate, set free, protect, avenge
vindicta, ae   *f*, rod used ot set free a slave
vīnĕa, ae   *f*, vineyard, protective shed for soldiers
vīnētum, i   *n*, vineyard
vīnītor, ōris   *m*, vine-pruner
vīnŏlentĭa, ae   *f*, wine-drinking
vīnŏlentus, a, um   *adj*, drunk
vīnōsus, a, um   *adj*, drunken
vīnum, i   *n*, wine
vĭŏla, ae   *f*, violet

vĭŏlābĭlĭs, e   *adj,* able to be injured or harmed

vĭŏlārĭum, ii   *n,* bed of violets

vĭŏlātĭo, ōnis   *f,* violation, profanation

vĭŏlātor, ōris   *m,* injurer

vĭŏlens, ntis   *adj, adv,* **nter,** impetuous, furious

vĭŏlentĭa, ae   *f,* ferocity

vĭŏlentus, a, um   *adj,* violent, impetuous

vĭŏlo   *v.t.* 1, to injure, outrage, break

vīpĕra, ae   *f,* viper

vīpĕrĕus, a, um   *adj,* of a viper or snake

vīpĕrĭnus, a, um   *adj,* of a viper or snake

vĭr, vĭri   *m,* man, husband

vĭrāgo, ĭnis   *f,* female soldier, heroine

vĭrectum, i   *n,* glade, turf

vĭrĕo   *v.i.* 2, to be green, flourish

vīres   see **vis**

vĭresco   *v.i.* 3, to become green, flourish

vĭrētum, i   *n,* glade, turf

virga, ae   *f,* twig, rod

virgātus, a, um   *adj,* striped

virgĕus, a, um   *adj,* made of rods

virgĭnālis, e   *adj,* girl-like

virgĭnĕus, a, um   *adj,* of a virgin

virgĭnĭtas, ātis   *f,* virginity

virgo, ĭnis   *f,* virgin girl

virgŭla, ae   *f,* small twig

virgultum, i   *n,* shrubbery

virgultus, a, um   *adj,* bushy

vĭrĭdārĭum, ii   *n,* park

vĭrĭdis, e   *adj,* green, fresh, young, blooming

vĭrĭdĭtas, ātis   *f,* greenness, freshness

vĭrĭdo   *v.i.t.* 1, to be green; make green

vĭrīlis, e   *adj,* male, manly, full-grown, vigorous

vĭrītim   *adj,* individually

vĭrōsus, a, um   *adj,* stinking

virtūs, ūtis   *f,* courage, manhood, military skill, goodness, moral perfection

vīrus, i   *n,* slime, poison, virus

vīs   (*no genit*), **vim, vi**   *f,* force,

power, violence, quantity, meaning; **vīres, ĭum**   *pl,* strength, power

viscātus, a, um   *adj,* sprinkled with lime

viscĕra, um   *n.pl,* innards, flesh, bowels

viscum, i   *n,* mistletoe, birdlime

vīsĭo, ōnis   *f,* idea, notion

vīsĭto   *v.t.* 1, to visit

vīso, si, sum   *v.t.* 3, to survey, visit

vīsum, i   *n,* appearance, sight

vīsus, ūs   *m,* look, sight, appearance

vīta, ae   *f,* life

vītābĭlis, e   *adj,* to be avoided

vītālis, e   *adj,* of life, vital

vītātĭo, ōnis   *f,* avoidance

vītellus, i   *m,* small calf, egg yolk

vītĕus, a, um   *adj,* of the vine

vĭtĭo   *v.t.* 1, to spoil, mar, infect

vĭtĭōsĭtas, ātis   *f,* vice

vĭtĭōsus, a, um   *adj, adv,* **ē,** faulty, defective, wicked

vītis, is   *f,* vine, vine branch

vītĭsātor, ōris   *m,* vine planter

vĭtĭum, ii   *n,* fault, defect, blemish, error, crime

vīto   *v.t.* 1, to avoid

vĭtrĕus, a, um   *adj,* made of glass, transparent, shining

vĭtrĭcus, i   *m,* step-father

vĭtrum, i   *n,* glass, woad

vitta, ae   *f,* hair-ribbon

vittātus, a, um   *adj,* bound with a hair-ribbon

vĭtŭlīnus, a, um   *adj,* of a calf

vĭtŭlus, i   *m* (**vĭtŭla, ae,**   *f*) calf

vĭtŭpĕrātĭo, ōnis   *f,* blame, censure

vĭtŭpĕro   *v.t.* 1, to blame, censure

vīvārĭum, ii   *n,* fishpond, game reserve

vīvācĭtas, ātis   *f,* vigour or length of life

vīvax, ācis   *adj,* long-lived

vīvĭdus, a, um   *adj,* lively, animated

vīvo, xi, ctum   *v.i.* 3, to live

vīvus, a, um   *adj,* alive, fresh, natural, life-like

vix   *adv,* scarcely, barely

vixdum   *adv,* scarcely then

vŏcābŭlum, i   *n*, name
vōcālis, e   *adj*, vocal
vŏcātu   *abl*, at the bidding
vōcĭfĕrātĭo, ōnis   *f*, outcry
vōcĭfĕror   *v.i.t.* 1, *dep*, to cry out
vŏcĭto   *v.i.t.* 1, to call out; name
vŏco   *v.i.t.* 1, to call; summon,
   urge, challenge, arouse, name
vōcŭla, ae   *f*, feeble voice
vŏlantes, ĭum   *c, pl*, birds
vŏlātĭcus, a, um   *adj*, flighty,
   fleeting
vŏlātĭlis, e   *adj*, flying, swift
vŏlātus, ūs   *m*, flight
vŏlens, ntis   *adj*, willing,
   favourable
volg... see vulg...
vŏlĭto   *v.i.* 1, to fly about, flit,
   flutter
vŏlo, velle, vŏlŭi   *v.i.t, irreg*, to
   wish, mean
vŏlo   *v.i.* 1, to fly
volp... see vulp...
volsella, ae   *f*, tweezers
volt... see vult...
vŏlūbĭlis, e   *adj*, turning, spinning,
   changeable
vŏlūbĭlĭtas, ātis   *f*, whirling
   motion, fluency
vŏlūcer, cris, cre   *adj*, flying,
   swift, transient
vŏlūmen, ĭnis   *n*, book, roll, fold
vŏluntārĭus, a, um   *adj*, voluntary;
   (of soldiers) volunteers
vŏluntas, ātis   *f*, wish, choice,
   will, affection, good-will
vŏluptārĭus, a, um   *adj*, sensual
vŏluptas, ātis   *f*, pleasure, delight
vŏlūto   *v.i.t.* 1, to roll, twist,
   writhe about; ponder, consider
volva (vulva), ae   *f*, womb
volvo, volvi, vŏlūtum   *v.t.* 3, to
   roll, unroll, turn, ponder,
   consider
vōmer, ĕris   *m*, ploughshare
vŏmĭca, ae   *f*, abscess, boil
vŏmĭtĭo, ōnis   *f*, vomiting
vŏmo, ŭi, ĭtum   *v.i.t.* 3, to vomit;
   throw up, pour out
vŏrāgo, ĭnis   *f*, abyss, whirlpool

vŏrax, ācis   *adj*, greedy,
   destructive
vŏro   *v.t.* 1, to devour, destroy
vortex   see vertes
vos   *pron, pl*, you (*plural*)
vōtīvis, a, um   *adj*, concerning a
   promise or vow
vōtum, i   *n*, promise, vow,
   offering, wish, longing
vŏvĕo, vōvi, vōtum   *v.t.* 2, to
   promise, vow, dedicate
vox, vōcis   *f*, voice, sound, speech,
   saying, proverb
vulgāris, e   *adj*, general, ordinary,
   common
vulgātor, ōris   *m*, a gossip
vulgātus, a, um   *adj*, ordinary,
   notorious
vulgo   *v.t.* 1, to divulge, spread
   about
vulgō   *v.t.* 1, to divulge, spread
   about
vulgō   *adv*, everywhere, openly
vulgus, i   *n*, the public, crowd,
   rabble
vulnĕrātus, a, um   *adj*, wounded
vulnĕro   *v.t.* 1, to wound, hurt
vulnĭfĭcus, a, um   *adj*, wounding
vulnus, ĕris   *n*, wound, blow
vulpēcŭla, ae   *f*, small fox
vulpes, is   *f*, fox
vulsus, a, um   *adj*, hairless,
   effeminate
vultur, ŭris   *m*, vulture
vultŭrĭus, ii   *m*, vulture
vultus, ūs   *m*, expression, look,
   features, aspect, face

X

xĭphĭas, ae   *m*, swordfish
xystus, i   *m*, (systum, i   *n*), open
   colonnade

Z

zĕphўrus, i   *m*, west wind
zōdĭācus, i   *m*, zodiac
zōna, ae   *f*, belt, girdle, zone

English–Latin dictionary

A

a, an (*indefinite article*), no equivalent in Latin

abandon *v.t*, rĕlinquo (3), dēsĕro (3)

abandoned dērĕlictus, dēsertus; **(person)**, perdĭtus

abandonment rĕlictĭo, *f*

abase *v.t*, dēprĭmo (3)

abasement hŭmĭlĭtas *f*, dēmĭssĭo, *f*

abash *v.t*, confundo (3), pertubo (1)

abashed pŭdōre confūsus **(perplexed with shame)**

abate *v.t*, immĭnŭo (3), rĕmitto (3)

abatement dēcessus *m*, dēcessĭo, *f*, dēmĭnūtĭo, *f*

abbot pontĭfex *m*, **(high priest)**, săcerdos, *c*

abbreviate *v.t*, immĭnŭo (3), contrăho (3)

abbreviation compendĭum *n*, contractĭo, *f*

abdicate *v.i*, se abdĭcare (1. *reflex*)

abdication abdĭcātĭo, *f*

abdomen venter, *m*, abdōmen, *n*

abduction raptus, *m*, raptĭo, *f*

abet *v.i*, adsum (*irreg. with dat. of person*), adiŭvo (1)

abettor mĭnister *m*, adiŭtor, *m*

abeyance (to be in —) *v.i*, iăcĕo (2)

abhor ăbhorrĕo (2) (*with acc. or ab and abl*), ōdi. (*v. defect*)

abhorrence ōdĭum, *n*

abide *v.i*, mănĕo (2), hăbĭto (1)

abide *v.t*, **(wait for)**, exspecto (1)

abiding *adj*, **(lasting)**, mansūrus

ability (mental —), ingĕnĭum, *n*; **(power)**, pŏtestas, *f*

abject abiectus, hŭmĭlis

abjectness hŭmĭlĭtas, *f*

abjure *v.t*, abiūro (1), ēiūro (1)

ablaze *adj*, flăgrans

able *use* possum **(be able)**, pŏtens

able (to be —) *v.i*, possum (*irreg*)

able-bodied vălĭdus

ablution lăvātĭo, *f*, ablūtĭo, *f*

ably *adv*, ingĕnĭōsē

abnegation nĕgātĭo, *f*, mŏdĕrātĭo, *f*

abnormal abnormis, ĭnūsĭtātus

aboard in năve; **(to go —)**, *v.i*, năvem conscendo (3); **(to put —)**, *v.t*, in năvem impōno (3)

abode dŏmus, *f*, dŏmĭcĭlĭum, *n*, sēdes, *f*, hăbĭtātĭo, *f*

abolish *v.t*, tollo (3), ăbŏlĕo (2), dissolvo (3)

abolition dissŏlūtĭo, *f*, ăbŏlĭtĭo, *f*

abominable infandus, dētestābĭlis

abominate *v.t*, ōdī (*defect*), ăbhorrĕo (2)

abomination (hatred) ōdĭum, *n*; **(crime)**, flāgĭtĭum, *n*

aborigines indĭgĕnae, *m.pl*

abortion ăbortus, *m*, ăbortĭo, *f*

abortive (unsuccessful) irrĭtus

abound (in) *v.i*, ăbundo (1), sŭpĕro (1), circumflŭo (3), suppĕdĭto (1)

abounding ăbundans, afflŭens, fēcundus

about *prep*, circā, circum, ăd, sŭb (*with acc*), dē (*with abl*); **(of time)**, circĭter (*with acc*)

about *adv*, **(nearly)**, circĭter, fermē, fĕrē

above *prep*, sŭper, sŭprā (*with acc*); **(more than)**, amplĭus

above *adv*, sŭprā, insŭper; **(from above)**, dēsŭper, sŭpernē

abrasion attrītus, *m*

abreast *adv*, părĭter

abridge *v.t*, contrăho (3)

abridgement ĕpĭtŏmē, *f*, ĕpĭtŏma, *f*

abroad *adv*, **(in a foreign country)**, pĕrĕgrē

abroad (to be —) *v.i*, pĕrĕgrīnor (1. *dep*)

abrogate *v.t*, abrŏgo (1); rescindo (3)

abrogation abrŏgātĭo, *f*

abrupt (sudden) sŭbĭtus; **(steep)**, praeruptus

abruptly *adv*, sŭbĭto, praerupte

abscess vŏmĭca, *f*

abscond *v.i*, lătĕo (2)

absence absentĭa, *f*

absent absens

absent (to be—) *v.i*, absum (*irreg*)

absinth absinthĭum, *n*

absolute absŏlūtus

absolute power tӯrannis, *f,*
impĕrĭum, *n,* dŏmĭnātĭo, *f*
absolutely (completely) *adv,*
prorsum, prorsus
absolve *v.t,* absolvo (3), lībĕro
(1)
absorb *v.t,* bĭbo (3), haurĭo (4),
absorbĕo (2)
absorbent *adj,* bĭbŭlus
abstain *v.i,* abstĭnĕo (2)
abstemious tempĕrātus
abstinence abstĭnentĭa, *f*
abstinent abstĭnens, mŏdĕrātus
abstract *nn,* ĕpĭtŏme, *f*
abstract *adj,* abstractus
abstract *v.t,* abstrăho (3)
abstruse rĕcondĭtus, obscūrus
absurd ĭneptus, absurdus
absurdity ĭneptĭa, *f,* insulsĭtas, *f*
absurdly *adv,* ĭneptē, absurdē
abundance cōpĭa, *f,* ăbundantĭa,
f
abundant largus, fēcundus
abuse *nn,* (insult), contūmelia
abuse *v.t,* mălĕdīco (3); (misuse),
ăbūtor (*v. dep*)
abusive contūmēlĭōsus
abut *v.i,* adiăcĕo (2)
abutting adiunctus
abyss gurges, *m,* vŏrāgo, *f*
acacia ăcācĭa, *f*
academic ăcădēmĭcus
academy ăcădēmĭa, *f*
accede *v.i,* consentĭo (4)
accelerate *v.t,* accĕlĕro (1)
accent vox, *f*
accentuate *v.t,* ăcŭo (3)
accentuation accentus, *m*
accept *v.t,* accĭpĭo (3), rĕcĭpĭo (3)
acceptability suāvĭtas, *f,* făcĭlĭtas,
f
acceptable grātus
acceptance acceptĭo, *f*
access (approach) ădĭtus, *m,*
accessus, *m*
accessible făcĭlis; (to be —), *v.i,*
pătĕo (3)
accession (— to the throne)
ĭnĭtĭum (*n*) regni (beginning of
reign); *or use phr. with* incipio (to
begin) *and* regno (to reign)
accessory (of crime) *adj,*
conscĭus; (helper), auctor, *m*

accident cāsus, *m*
accidental fortŭītus
accidentally *adv,* cāsū, fortē
acclaim *v.t,* clāmo (1)
acclamation clāmor, *m*
acclimatized assŭētus
accommodate *v.t,* accommŏdo
(1)
accommodating obsĕquens
accommodation (lodging)
hospĭtĭum, *n;* (loan), commŏdum,
n
accompaniment (musical) cantus,
m
accompany *v.t,* prōsĕquor (3
dep), cŏmĭtor (1 *dep*); (— in
singing), oblŏquor (3 *dep*
accomplice *adj,* conscĭus,
partĭceps
accomplish *v.t,* conficĭo (3)
accomplished (learned) ērŭdītus
accomplishment (completion)
confectĭo, *f*
accord (of my (your) own —) mĕā
(tŭā) spontĕ, ultrō
accord *v.t,* concēdo (3); *v.i,*
consentĭo (4)
accordance (in — with) *prep,* ex,
dē, prō (*with abl*)
according to *as above*
accordingly *adv,* ĭtăque
accost *v.t,* compello (1);
allŏquor (3 *dep*)
account *nn,* rătĭo, *f;* (statement),
mĕmŏrĭa, *f*
on account of *prep,* propter, ŏb
(*with acc*)
to render account for rătĭonem
reddo (3)
accountant calcŭlātor, *m,* scrība,
m
account-book tăbŭlae, *f.pl*
accoutre *v.t,* orno (1); armo (1)
accoutrements arma, *n.pl*
accredit *v.t,* (establish),
confirmio (1)
accrue *v.i,* accēdo (3)
accumulate *v.t,* cŭmŭlo (1),
cŏăcervo (1); *v.i,* cresco (3)
accumluation (bringing together)
collātĭo, *f*
accuracy (exactness) subtīlĭtas, *f;*
(carefulness), cūra, *f*

accurate **(exact)** subtīlĭs, vērus;
(careful), dīlĭgens
accursed exsĕcrābĭlĭs
accusation crīmen, *n,* accūsātĭo, *f*
accuse *v.t,* accūso (1); arcesso
(3), nōmen dēfĕro (*v. irreg*)
accused person rĕus, *m*
accuser accūsātor, *m,* dēlātor, *m*
accustom *v.t,* assŭēfacĭo (3)
to be accustomed *v.i,* sŏlĕo (2)
to become accustomed *v.i,*
assŭesco (3)
accustomed assŭētus, sŏlĭtus
ache *v.i,* dŏlĕo (2)
ache *nn,* dŏlor, *m*
achieve *v.t.* confĭcĭo (3), perfĭcĭo
(3)
achievement res gesta, *f,* făcĭnus,
n
acid *adj,* ăcerbus, ăcĭdus
acknowledge *v.t,* **(confess),**
confĭtĕor (2 *dep*), agnosco (3);
(accept), tollo (3)
acknowledgement confessĭo, *f*
acme summa, *f*
aconite ăcŏnītum, *n*
acorn glans, *f*
acquaint *v.t,* certĭōrem făcĭo (3)
(*with acc. of person, and* dē *with*
abl)
to become acquainted with *v.t,*
nosco (3), cognosco (3)
acquaintance **(knowledge of)**
scĭentĭa, *f;* **(with a person),**
consŭētūdo, *f;* **(a person),** nōtus,
m
acquiesce *v.i,* acquĭesco (3)
acquire *v.t,* acquīro (3)
acquirement **(obtaining)** ădeptĭo, *f*
acquit *v.t,* absolvo (3), lībĕro (1)
acquittal absŏlūtĭo, *f,* lībĕrātĭo, *f*
acre iūgĕrum, *n*
acrid asper, ācer
acrimonious ăcerbus, asper,
ămārus
acrimony ăcerbĭtas, *f*
across *prep,* trans (*with acc*)
act *v.i,* ăgo (3), gĕro (3)
act *v.t,* **(a part in a play),** ăgo (3)
act *nn,*factum, *n;* **(law)** lex, *f*
action **(carrying out)** actĭo, *f,*
actus, *m,* **(at law)** līs, *f,* **(battle),**
proelĭum, *n*

active impĭger, ălăcer
actively impĭgrē
activity **(energy)** industrĭa, *f;*
(agility, mobility) ăgĭlĭtas, *f*
actor actor, *m*
actual vērus
actually *adv,* rē vērā
actuary actŭārĭus, *m*
actuate *v.t,* mŏvĕo (2), impello
(3)
acumen ăcūmen, *n*
acute ācer, ăcūtus
acuteness ăcĭes, *f,* ăcūmen, *n*
adage dictum, *n*
adapt *v.t,* accomŏdo (1),
compōno (3)
adapted accommŏdātus, aptus
add *v.t,* addo (3), adĭcĭo (3)
adder vīpĕra, *f*
addict *v.t,* dēdo (3) (*with dat*)
addicted dedĭtus
addition **(numerical)** *use verb*
addo (3); **(increase)** accessĭo, *f*
additional **(more, new, fresh)**
nŏvus
address *v.t,* **(a letter),** inscrībo
(3); **(person)** allŏquor (3 *dep*)
address *nn,* **(letter),** inscriptĭo, *f;*
(speaking) allŏquĭum, *n*
adduce *v.t,* prōdūco (3), prōfĕro
(*v. irreg*)
adept prītus
adequacy *use* sătĭs **(enough)**
(*with nn. in genit*)
adequate sătĭs (*with genit*)
adhere *v.i,* **(cling)** haerĕo (2)
adherent clĭens, *m,* sectātor, *m*
adhesive tĕnax
adjacency vīcīnĭtas, *f*
adjacent fīnĭtĭmus, vīcīnus,
contermĭnus
adjoin *v.i,* adiăcĕo (2)
adjoin *v.t,* adiungo (3)
adjoining coniunctus, contĭgŭus
adjourn *v.t,* differo (*v. irreg*)
adjournment dīlātĭo, *f*
adjudge **(adjudicate)** *v.t,* adiūdĭco
adjudication addictĭo, *f*
adjure *v.t,* obtestor (1 *dep*),
obsĕcro (1)
adjust *v.t,* apto (1), compōno (3)
adjustment compŏsĭtĭo, *f*
adjutant optĭo, *m*

administer　*v.t,* admĭnistro (1)
administration　admĭnistrātĭo, *f,*
　prōcūrātĭo, *f*
administrator　procūrātor, *m*
admirable　mīrābĭlis
admirably　*adv,* praeclārē
admiral　praefectus (*m*) classis
admiration　admīrātĭo, *f*
admire　*v.t,* admīror (1 *dep*),
　mīror (1 *dep*)
admirer　laudātor, *m*
admissible, (letting in)　ădĭtus,
　m; (acknowledgement) confessĭo, *f*
admit　*v.t,* (let in) admitto (3);
　(grant) dō (1), concēdo (3);
　(confess) confĭtĕor (2 *dep*)
admonish　*v.t,* mŏnĕo (2)
admonition　admŏnĭtĭo, *f*
adolescence　ădŏlescentĭa, *f*
adolescent　ădŏlescens, *c*
adopt　*v.t,* (person), ădopto (1);
　(custom) ascisco (3)
adoption　ădoptĭo, *f*
adorable　cŏlendus
adoration　cultus, *m,* ădōrātĭo, *f*
adore　*v.t,* cŏlo (3), ădōro (1)
adorn　*v.t,* orno (1)
adorned　ornātus
adornment (as an act)　exornātĭo,
　f; (a decoration) ornāmentum, *n*
adrift　*adj,* in mărī iactātus (driven
　about on the sea)
adroit　callĭdus, sollers
adroitness　dextĕrĭtas, *f*
adulation　ădūlātĭo, *f*
adult　*adj,* ădultus
adulterate　*v.t,* vĭtĭo (1)
adulteration　adultĕrātĭo, *f*
adulterer(-ess)　ădulter, *m,* (-era, *f*)
adultery　ădultĕrĭum, *n*
advance　*nn,* prōgressus, *m*
advance　*v.i,* prōcēdo (3),
　prōgrĕdĭor (3 *dep*), incēdo (3),
　pĕdem inférro (*irreg*)
advance　*v.t,* inféro (*irreg*),
　prōmŏvĕo (2)
in advance　*adv,* prae,
　compounded with vb: e.g. send
　in advance, praemitto (3)
advance-guard　prīmum agmen, *n*
advantage　commŏdum, *n*
to be advantageous　*v.i,* prōsum
　(*irreg*), ūsui esse (*irreg*) (*with dat*)

advantageous　ūtĭlis
advantageously　*adv,* ūtĭlĭter
advent　adventus, *m*
adventure　făcĭnus, *n*
adventurous　audax
adventurously　*adv,* audacter
adversary　hostis, *c*
adverse　adversus
adversity　res adversae, *f.pl*
advert to　*v.t,* attingo (3)
advertise　*v.t,* prōscrībo (3),
　prōnuntĭo (1)
advertisement　prōscriptĭo, *f*
advice　consĭlĭum, *n*
advisable (advantageous)　ūtĭlis
advise　*v.t,* mŏnĕo (2), suādĕo
　(2), censĕo (2)
advisedly　*adv,* consultō
adviser　suāsor, *m,* auctor, *m*
advocate　*nn,* patrōnus, *m*
advocate　*v.t,* suādĕo (2)
adze　ascĭa, *f*
aedile　aedĭlis, *m*
aedileship　aedĭlĭtas, *f*
aerial　*adj,* (of the air), āĕrĭus
afar　*adv,* prŏcŭl
affability　cōmĭtas, *f*
affable　cōmis
affably　*adv,* cōmĭter
affair　rēs, *f,* nĕgōtĭum, *n*
affect　*v.t,* afficĭo (3); (the
　feelings) mŏvĕo (2)
affectation (show)　sĭmŭlātĭo, *f*
affected　pūtĭdus
affection (love)　ămor, *m*
affectionate　ămans
affiance　*v.t,* spondĕo (2)
affianced　sponsus
affidavit　testĭmōnĭum, *n*
affiliate　*v.t,* cŏ-opto (1)
affinity　cognātĭo, *f*
affirm　*v.t,* affirmo (1)
affix　*v.t,* affigo (3)
afflict　*v.t,* afficĭo (3)
afflicted (with grief)　mĭser
affliction (with grief etc)　mĭsĕrĭa,
　f; (a bad thing), mălum, *n*
affluence　dīvĭtĭae, *f.pl*
affluent　dīves
afford　*v.t.* (give), praebĕo (2);
　otherwise use phr. with satis
　pecuniae habere ut… (to have
　enough money to …)

affright *v.t,* terrĕo (2)

affront contŭmēlĭa, *f*

affront *v.t,* contŭmēlĭam facio (3) (*with dat*)

afire *adj,* flăgrans

afloat (*use phr. with* in aquā **(on the water)**

afoot *adv,* pĕdĭbus

afore *adv,* sŭprā

aformentioned sŭprā scriptus

aforesaid sŭprā scriptus

afraid tĭmĭdus

afraid (to be—) *v.i. and v.t,* tĭmĕo (2), vĕrĕor (2 *dep*), mĕtŭo (3)

afresh *adv,* rursus

aft *nn,* puppis, *f*

after *prep,* post (*with acc*)

after *conj,* postquam

after *adv,* post, postĕa

after all (nevertheless) *adv,* tămen

afternoon *adv,* post mĕrīdĭem

afternoon *adj,* pōmĕrīdĭānus

afterwards *adv,* post, postĕa

again *adv,* ĭtĕrum, rursus

again and again *adv,* ĭdentĭdem

against *prep,* contra, in (*with acc*)

agape *adj,* hĭans

age aetas, *f,* aevum, *n,* **(old—)** sĕnectus, *f*

aged (old) sĕnex

aged (three) years nātus (tres) annos

agency (doing, action) ŏpĕra, *f*

agent actor, *m*

aggrandize *v.t,* amplĭfico (1)

aggrandizement amplĭficătĭo, *f*

aggravate *v.t,* grăvo (1); **(annoy)** aspĕro (1); **(increase)** augĕo (2)

aggregate *nn,* summa, *f*

aggression incursĭo, *f*

aggressive hostĭlis

aggressor *use phr.* suā sponte bellum infĕrre (*irreg*), **(inflict war of one's own accord)**

aggrieve *v.t. use* afficĭo (3) **(affect)**

aghast stŭpĕfactus

agile ăgĭlis

agility ăgĭlĭtas, *f*

agitate *v.t,* ăgĭto (1), commŏvĕo (2)

agitated sollĭcĭtus

agitation (violent movement) ăgĭtătĭo, *f*; **(of the mind),** commōtĭo, *f*

agitator (political) turbātor, *m*

ago *adv,* ăbhinc (*with acc*) e.g. **two years—** ăbhinc duos annos

agonize *v.t,* crŭcĭo (1)

agony dŏlor, *m*

agrarian ăgrārĭus

agree with *v.i,* consentĭo (4) (*with* cum *and abl*); *v.t.* compōno (3); **(it is—by all)** constat inter omnes

agreeable grātus

agreeableness dulcēdo, *f*

agreed upon (it is—) constat, convĕnit, *v. impers*

agreeing congrŭens, convĕnĭens

agreement (the—itself) pactum, *n;* **(of opinions, etc)** consensĭo, *f*

agricultural rustĭcus

agriculture agrĭcultūra, *f*

agriculturist agrĭcŏla, *m*

aground (to run—) *use phr.* in vădo haerĕo (2) **(stick fast in a shallow place)**

ague horror, *m*

ah! (alas!) eheu!

ahead *adv, use* prae, pro, *compounded with verbs,* e.g. **send ahead,** praemitto (3)

aid auxĭlĭum, *n,* subsĭdĭum, *n*

aid *v.t,* adiŭvo (1), subvĕnĭo (4) (*with dat*)

ail *v.i,* aegresco (3)

ailing aeger, aegrōtus

aim *v.t.* **(point a weapon, etc.)** dīrĭgo (3); **(to aim at)** pĕto (3)

aim *nn,* **(purpose)** finis, *m;* **(throwing)** coniectus, *m*

air āēr, *m;* **(manner)** spĕcĭes, *f*

air *v.t,* ventĭlo (1)

air-hoe spīrācŭlum, *n*

airy āērĭus

akin *adj,* **(similar)** fīnĭtĭmus

alabaster ălăbastrītes ae, *m*

alacrity ălăcrĭtas, *f*

alarm (fear) păvor, *m,* trĕpĭdātio, *f;* **(confusion)** tŭmultus, *m*

alarm *v.t,* perturbo (1), terrĕo (2)

alarmed trĕpĭdus

alas! heu!

alcove angŭlus, *m* **(corner)**
alder alnus, *f*
alderman măgistrātus, *m*
ale cerevisia, *f*
ale-house caupona, *f*
alert ălăcer
alertness ălăcrĭtas, *f*
alien (*adj and nn*) **(foreign)**,
  pĕrĕgrīnus
alienate *v.t*, ălīēno (1)
alienation ălĭēnātĭo, *f*
alight *v.i*, dēsĭlĭo (4)
alike *adj*, sĭmĭlis
alike *adv*, sĭmĭlĭter
alive vīvus
alive (to be —) vivo (3)
all *adj*, **(every)** omnis; **(the whole)**
  tōtus; (*with superlative*, e.g. **all**
  the best people) optĭmus
  quisque; **(at all, in all)** *adv*,
  omnīno
all-powerful omnĭpŏtens
allay *v.t*, sēdo (1)
allegation affirmātĭo, *f*
allege *v.t*. **(assert)** argŭo (3),
  affĕro (*irreg*)
allegiance fĭdes, *f*, offĭcĭum, *n*
allegory allēgŏrĭa, *f*
alleviate *v.t*, lĕvo (1)
alleviation, (as an act) lĕvātĭo, *f*;
  (something which brings—)
  lĕvāmen, *n*
alley angĭportus, *m*
alliance sŏcĭĕtas, *f*, foedus, *n*; **(to**
  make an—) foedus făcĭo (3)
allied (states) foedĕrātus
allot *v.t*, distrĭbŭo (3), assigno (1)
allotment (of land) ăger
  assignātus, *m*
allow *v.t*. **(permit)**, pătĭor (3 *dep*),
  sĭno (3), concēdo (3); *or use*
  impers. vb. lĭcet (*with dat. of*
  person allowed)
allowable *use* fās, (*indecl. nn*)
  (right)
allowance (to make —) ignosco
  (3), rĕmitto (3)
allude to *v.t*, signĭfĭco (1)
allure *v.t*, allĭcĭo (3)
allurement blandĭtĭa, *f*, illĕcĕbra
alluring blandus
allusion signĭfĭcātĭo, *f*
alluvium allŭvĭo, *f*

ally *nn*, sŏcīus, *m*
ally *v.t*, **(unite)**, iungo (3); **(—**
  oneself) se coniungere (*with dat*)
almanack fasti, *m.pl*
almighty omnĭpŏtens
almond ămygdălum, *n*; **(tree)**,
  ămygdăla, *f*
almost *adv*, paenĕ, prŏpĕ, fĕrē,
  fermē
alms stips, *f*
aloe ălŏē, *f*
aloft *adv*, sublīmĕ; *adj*, sublīmis
alone *adj*, sōlus
alone *adv*, sōlum
along *prep*, sĕcundum, praeter
  (*with acc*)
aloof *adv*, prŏcŭl; **(to stand —**
  from), discēdo (3)
aloud *adv*, magnā vōcē
alphabet *use* litterae *f.pl* **(letters)**
already *adv*, iam
also *adv*, ĕtiam, quŏque, ĭtem;
  (likewise), necnōn
altar āra, *f*
alter *v.t*, mūto (1), verto (3),
  corrĭgo (3)
alter *v.i*, mūtor (1 *dep*)
alteration mūtātĭo, *f*
altercation rixa, *f*
alternate *v.t*, alterno (1)
alternate *adj*, alternus
alternately *adv*, invĭcem
alternation vĭcissĭtūdo, *f*
alternative *use phr. with* ălĭus
  mŏdus **(other way)**
although *conj*, quamquam
  (*indicating fact*); quamvīs
  (*indicating a supposition*); etsi,
  tametsi
altitude altĭtūdo, *f*
altogether *adv*, omnīno
always *adv*, semper
amalgamate *v.t*, iungo (3),
  miscĕo (2)
amalgamation coniunctĭo, *f*
amass *v.t*, cŏăcervo (1), cŭmŭlo
  (1)
amatory ămātōrĭus
amaze *v.t*, obstŭpĕfăcĭo (3)
amazed stŭpĭdus, stŭpĕfactus
amazement stŭpor, *m*
amazing mīrus
amazingly *adv*, mīris mŏdis

amazon vĭrāgo, *f*
ambassador lēgātus, *m*
amber sŭcĭnum, *n*
ambiguity ambāges, *f.pl*
ambiguous ambĭgŭus, anceps
ambiguously *adv*, per ambāges
ambition glōrĭa, *f*, ambĭtĭo, *f*
ambitious *use phr.* cŭpĭdus
 glōrĭae **(keen on glory)**
amble *v.i*, lēnĭter ambŭlo (1)
 (walk quietly)
ambrosia ambrŏsĭa, *f*
ambrosial ambrŏsĭus
ambush insĭdĭae *(f.pl)* ; **(to**
 ambush) insĭdĭor (1 *dep*)
ameliorate *v.t*, mĕlĭōrem făcĭo (3)
amen! fiat! **(let it be)**
amenable obēdĭens
amend *v.t*, ēmendo (1), corrĭgo
 (3)
amendment **(correction)**
 ēmendātĭo, *f*
amends *use* expĭo (1) **(to make**
 —s)
amenity ămoenĭtas, *f*
amethyst ămĕthystus, *f*
amiability suāvĭtas, *f*
amiable suāvis
amiably *adv*, suāvĭter
amicable ămīcus
amid(st) *prep*, inter *(with acc)*
amiss *adv*, măle; **(to take—)**
 aegre fĕro *(irreg)*
amity ămīcĭtĭa, *f*
ammunition arma, *n.pl*
amnesty vĕnĭa, *f*
among *prep*, inter, ăpud *(with*
 acc)
amorous ămans
amount summa, *f*, finis, *m*
amount to *v.t, use* esse **(to be)**
amphitheatre amphĭthĕātrum, *n*
ample amplus, cōpĭōsus
amplify *v.t*, amplĭfĭco (1), dīlāto
 (1)
amplitude amplĭtūdo, *f*
amply *adv*, amplē
amputate *v.t*, sĕco (1), ampŭto
 (1)
amputation ampŭtātĭo, *f*
amuse *v.t*, dēlecto (1)
amusement dēlectātĭo, *f*
amusing făcētus

anaesthetic *adj*, sŏpōrĭfer
analogy **(comparison)** compărātĭo
analyse *v.t*, discerpo (3), explĭco
 (1)
analysis explĭcātĭo, *f*
anarchical turbŭlentus
anarchy lĭcentĭa, *f*
anathema exsecrātĭo, *f* **(curse)**
anatomy incīsĭo *(f)* corporis
 (incision of the body)
ancestor auctor, *m*; *(in pl)*,
 māiōres, *m.pl*
ancestral proăvītus
ancestry **(descent, origin)** gĕnus, *n*
anchor ancŏra, *f*
anchor *v.i, use phr.* nāvem ad
 ancŏras dēlĭgo (1) **(fasten a ship**
 to the anchors)
anchorage stătĭo, *f*
ancient antīquus, vĕtus
and et, atque, ac; quĕ *(joined to*
 the second of two words, **e.g. I**
 and you: ego tuque) ; **(and ... not)**
 nĕque
anecdote făbella, *f*
anew *adv*, dēnŭo, dē intĕgro
anger īra, *f*, īrācundĭa, *f*
anger *v.t*, irrīto (1), lăcesso (3)
angle angŭlus, *m*
angle *v.i* **(fish)**, piscor (1 *dep*)
angler piscātor, *m*
angrily *adv*, īrācundē, īrātē
angry īrātus; **(irascible)** īrācundus
anguish angor, *m*, dŏlor, *m*,
 ăcerbĭtas, *f*
angular angŭlātus, angŭlāris
animal ănĭmal, *n*, pĕcus, *f*
animal *adj*, ănĭmālis
animate *v.t*, anĭmo, excĭto (1)
animated ănĭmans; **(lively)**
 vĕgĕtus, ălăcer, vĕhĕmens
animation **(liveliness)** vĭgor, *m*
animosity sĭmultas, *f*
ankle tālus, *m*
annalist annālĭum scriptor, *m*
annals annāles, *m.pl*
annex *v.t*, addo (3), iungo (3)
annihilate *v.t*, dēlĕo (2)
annihilation exĭtĭum, *n*,
 exstinctĭo, *f*
anniversary *adj*, anniversārĭus
anniversary *nn*, dĭes
 annĭversārĭus, *m*

annotate *v.t*, annŏto (1)
annotation annŏtātĭo, *f*
announce *v.t*, nuntĭo (1)
announcement prōnuntĭātĭo, *f*
announcer nuntĭus, *m*,
  praeco, *m*
annoy *v.t*, irrīto (1), lăcesso (3)
annoyance mŏlestĭa, *f*,
  vexātĭo, *f*
annual annĭversārĭus
annually *adv*, quŏtannis
annuity annŭa, *n.pl*
annul *v.t*, abrŏgo (1), tollo (3)
annulment ăbŏlĭtĭo, *f*
anoint *v.t*, unguo (3)
anointing *nn*, unctĭo, *f*
anomaly ănōmălĭa, *f*
anon *adv* **(immediately)**, stătim;
  (in a short time) brĕvi tempŏre
anonymously (*adv. phr*) sĭne.
  nōmĭne
another ălĭus; **(the other of two)**,
  alter; **(another's)**, *adj*, ălĭēnus
answer *nn*, responsum, *n*
answer *v.t*, respondĕo (2); **(in
  writing)** rescrībo (3); **(to — for, be
  surety for)** praesto (1)
answerable *use phr*, rătĭōnem
  reddo (3) **(to render an account)**
ant formīca, *f*
antagonism ĭnĭmīcĭtĭa, *f*
antagonist adversārĭus, *m*
antagonistic contrārĭus
antecedent *adj*, antĕcēdens
antechamber ātrĭolum, *n*
anterior prĭor
ante-room ātrĭŏlum, *n*
anticipate *v.t*, occŭpo (1),
  antĕverto (3), praecĭpĭo (3);
  (expect), exspecto (1)
anticipation **(expectation)**
  exspectātĭo, *f*
antics lūdi, *m.pl*
antidote rĕmĕdĭum, *n*,
  antĭdŏtum, *n*
antipathy rĕpugnantĭa, *f* ; **(of
  people)** ŏdĭum, *n*
antipodes antĭpŏdes, *m.pl*
antiquarian *adj*, antīquitatis
  stŭdĭōsus **(keen on antiquity)**
antiquated priscus
antique *adv*, vĕtus, antīquus
antiquity antīquĭtas, *f*, vĕtustas, *f*

antithesis **(opposite)** contrārĭum,
  n; **(in argument)**, contentĭo, *f*
antler rāmus, *m*, cornu, *n*
anvil incūs, *f*
anxiety anxĭĕtas *f*, sollĭcĭtūdo, *f*,
  cūra, *f*; **(alarm)** păvor, *m*
anxious anxĭus, sollĭcĭtus;
  (alarmed) trĕpĭdus
anxiously *adv*, anxĭē
any *adj*, ullus (*after negatives,
  and in questions, and
  comparisons*); quisquam (*pron.
  used like* ullus); qui, quae, quod
  (*after* si, nisi, ne, num)
anyone, anybody *pron*, quis
  (*after* si, nisi, se, num); quisquam
  (*after a negative*)
anything *use neuter of prons.
  given above*
anywhere *adv*, **(in any place)**,
  usquam; **(to any place)**, quō,
  quŏquam; **(in any place)**, ūbĭquĕ
apace *adv*, **(quickly)**, cĕlĕrĭtĕr
apart *adv*, sĕorsum; (*adj*)
  dīversus
apartment conclāve, *n*
apathetic lentus, pĭger
apathy ignāvĭa, *f*, lentĭtūdo, *f*
ape sīmĭa, *f*
aperture fŏrāmen, *n*
apex căcūmen, *n*, ăpex, *m*
aphorism sententĭa, *f*
apiary alvĕārĭum, *n*
apiece *use distributive numeral,
  e.g.* **two each**, bīni
apologize *v.i*, excūso (1), dēfendo
  (3)
apology excūsātĭo, *f*
appal *v.t*, perterrĕo (2)
apparatus appărātus, *m*
apparel vestis, *f*, vestīmentum, *n*
apparent mănĭfestus, ăpertus
apparently *adv*, per spĕcĭem
apparition **(ghost)** spĕcĭes, *f*,
  ĭmāgo, *f*
appeal *v.i*, appello (1), prōvŏco
  (1), **(to —to)** *v.t*, obtestor (1 *dep*)
appeal *nn*, appellātĭo, *f*,
  obsĕcrātĭo, *f*
appear *v.i*, appārĕo (2),
  conspĭcĭor (3 *pass*); **(to seem)**
  vĭdĕor (2 *pass*); **(to come forward)**
  prōdĕo (4)

appearance (looks) spĕcĭes, *f*, aspectus, *m;* (show), spĕcĭes, *f;* (image), sĭmŭlācrum, *n*
appeasable plācābĭlis
appease *v.t*, (people), plāco (1); (feelings), sēdo (1)
appeasement plācātĭo, *f*
appellant appellātor, *m*
append *v.t*, (attach), addo (3)
appendage appendix, *f*
appertain *v.i*, pertĭnĕo (2)
appetite appĕtītus, *m;* (hunger), fămes, *f*
applaud *v.t*, plaudo (3), laudo (1)
applause (clapping) plausus, *m;* (cheers), clāmor, *m*
apple mālum, *n;* (−tree), mālus, *f*
appliance (apparatus) appărātus, *m*
applicable to commŏdus (*with dat*)
applicant pĕtītor, *m*
application (asking) pĕtītĭo, *f;* (mental), stŭdĭum, *n*, dīlĭgentĭa, *f*
apply *v.t*, adhĭbĕo (2), admŏvĕo (2); (to − oneself to) se dēdĕre (3 *with dat*) ; *v.i*, (refer to), pertĭnĕo (2); (−for), flāgĭto (1)
appoint *v.t*, constĭtŭo (3) (people to office, etc), crĕo (1) ; (to appoint to a command) praefĭcĭo (3) (*acc. of person appointed, dat. of person or thing commanded*)
appointment (office) mūnus, *n;* (creation), crĕātĭo, *f* ; (agreed meeting), constĭtūtum, *n*
apportion *v.t*, dīvĭdo (3), distrĭbŭo (3)
apposite aptus
appraise *v.t*, (evaluate), aestĭmo (1)
appraisement aestĭmātĭo, *f*
appreciate *v.t*, (value), aestĭmo (1) magni
appreciation aesĭmātĭo, *f*
apprehend *v.t*, (arrest), comprĕhendo (3) ; (understand), intellĕgo (3), percĭpĭo (3)
apprehension (fear) formīdo, *f;* (arrest) comprĕhensĭo, *f;* (understanding), intellĕgentĭa, *f*

apprehensive (fearful) tĭmĭdus
apprentice tīro, *m*
approach *v.i*, apprŏpinquo (1) (*with* ad *and acc. or dat*), accēdo (3)
approach *nn*, ădĭtus, *m*, adventus, *m*, accessus, *m*
approbation apprŏbātĭo, *f*, laus, *f*
appropriate *adj*, aptus, accommŏdātus (*with dat*)
appropriate *v.t*, sūmo (3)
appropriately *adv*, aptē
approval apprŏbātĭo, *f*
approve (of) *v.t*, apprŏbo (1)
approved spectātus, prŏbātus
approximate proxĭmus
approximate *v.i*, accēdo (3)
April Aprīlis (mensis)
apron ŏpĕrīmentum, *n*
apt aptus, ĭdōnĕus; (inclined), prōnus, prōpensus
aptitude (ability) ingĕnĭum, *n*
aptly *adv*, aptē
aptness *use adj*, aptus (suitable)
aquatic ăquătĭlis
aqueduct ăquae ductus *m*
aquiline ăquilīnus, ăduncus
arable land arvum, *n*
arbiter arbĭter, *m*
arbitrarily *adv*, (according to whim), ad lĭbīdĭnem
arbitrary (capricious) lĭbīdĭnōsus
arbitrate *v.t*, discepto (1)
arbitration arbĭtrĭum, *n*
arbitrator arbĭter, *m*
arbour umbrācŭlum, *n*
arc arcus, *m*
arcade portĭcus, *f*
arch fornix *m*, arcus, *m*
arch *adj*, (playful), lascīvus
archaeology investĭgātĭo, (*f*) rērum antīquārum (search for ancient things)
archaism verbum obsŏlētum, *n*
archer săgittărĭus, *m*
archipelago *use phr*, măre, (*n*) insŭlis consĭtum (sea set with islands)
architect archĭtectus, *m*, ŏpĭfex, *c*
architecture archĭtectūra, *f*
archives tăbŭlae, *f. pl*
arctic septentrĭōnālis
ardent ardens, fervĭdus

ardently *adv,* ardenter, vĕhĕmenter

ardour ardor, *m,* călor, *m,* fervor, *m*

arduous ardŭus

area spătĭum, *n*

arena hărēna, *f,* ărēna, *f*

argue *v.i,* discepto (1), dissĕro (3)

argument (quarrel) rixa, *f,* argūmentum, *n;* **(discussion),** dispŭtātĭo, *f*

arid ārĭdus, siccus

aridity ārĭdĭtas, *f,* siccĭtas, *f*

aright *adv,* rectē

arise *v.i,* surgo (3); **(heavenly bodies),** ŏrĭor (4 *dep*)

aristocracy (aristocratic party) optĭmātes, *c. pl;* **(govt.)** optĭmātĭum dŏmĭnātus, *m*

aristocratic patrĭcĭus

arithmetic ărĭthmētĭca, *n.pl*

ark arca, *f*

arm (fore—) brācchĭum, *n;* **(upper—),** lăcertus, *m;* **(weapon),** telum, *n*

arms (weapons) arma, *n.pl,* tēla, *n.pl;* **(call to —),** ad arma vŏco (1); **(to take —s)** arma căpĭo (3); **(to lay down —s),** arma dēdo (3)

arm *v.t,* armo (1); **(to take —s),** arma căpĭo (3)

armament (forces) cōpĭae, *f.pl;* **(weapon),** tēlum, *n*

armed armātus

armistice indūtĭae *f.pl*

armour arma *n.pl*

armour-bearer armĭger, *m*

armourer făber, *m*

armoury armāmentārĭum, *n*

army exercĭtus, *m;* **(marching —),** agmen, *n;* **(drawn up for battle),** ăcĭes, *f*

around *adv, and prep. with acc,* circā, circum

arouse *v.t,* suscĭto (1), excĭto (1)

arraign *v.t,* accūso (1)

arrange *v.t,* compōno (3), constĭtŭo (3), collŏco (1), instrŭo (3)

arrangement (as an act) collŏcātĭo, *f* **(order),** ordo, *m*

array *nn,* **(clothing)** vestis, *f,* vestĭmenta, *n.pl;* **(battle—),** ăcĭes, *f*

array *v.t,* compōno (3)

arrears rēlīquae pĕcūnĭae, *f.pl* **(money remaining)**

arrest *v.t,* comprĕhendo (3)

arrest *nn,* comprĕhensĭo, *f*

arrival adventus, *m*

arrive *v.i,* advĕnĭo (4), pervĕnĭo (4)

arrogance arrŏgantĭa, *f*

arrogant arrŏgans

arrogate *v.t,* arrŏgo (1) *(with dat)*

arrow săgitta, *f*

arsenal armāmentārĭum, *n*

art ars, *f*

artery vēna, *f*

artful callĭdus, văfer

artfully *adv,* callĭde

artfulness callĭdĭtas, *f*

article (thing) rēs, *f;* **(term of a treaty, etc.),** condĭcĭo, *f*

articulate *adj,* clārus, distinctus

articulate *v.t,* exprĭmo (3)

articulation explānātĭo, *f*

artifice ars, *f*

artificer (craftsman) artĭfex, *m,* ŏpĭfex, *c*

artificial artĭfĭcĭōsus

artificially *adv,* mănu, artĕ

artillery tormenta, *n.pl*

artisa făber, *m,* ŏpĭfex, *c*

artist artĭfex, *m;* **(painter),** pictor, *m*

artistic artĭfĭcĭōsus

artless (person) simplex; **(work),** incomptus

artlessness simplĭcĭtas, *f*

as *conj,* **(because),** quod, cum, quĭa; *(in a comparative phr, e.g.* **as strong as)** tam fortis quam; **(the same as)** īdem atque; **(as ... as possible)** quam *with the superlative, e.g.* **as quickly as possible;** quam cĕlerrime; **(as if)** tamquam, quăsĭ, vĕlut

ascend *v.t,* ascendo (3)

ascendant (to be in the—) *v.i,* praesto (1)

ascendancy praestantĭa, *f*

ascent ascensus, *m*

ascertain *v.t.* **(find out),** cognosco (3), compĕrĭo (4)

ascetic *adj,* abstĭnens

ascribe *v.t*, ascrībo (3), assigno (1), attrĭbuo (3)
ash (tree) fraxĭnus, *f*, *(adj)*, fraxĭnĕus
ashamed (to be —) pŭdet; *impers. with acc. and genit*, *(e.g.* **I am ashamed of my brother)** pŭdet me frātris
ashes cĭnis *m*
ashore *adv*, **(on shore)**, in lītŏre; **(to shore)**, in lītus
aside *use* se, *compounded with verb*, e.g. **to put aside**, sēcerno (3)
ask *v.t*, rŏgo (1) *(with 2 accs)* e.g. **I ask you for a sword**, tē glădĭum rŏgo
askance (to look — at) līmis ŏcŭlis aspĭcĭo (3) **(look with a sidelong glance)**
aslant *adv*, oblīque
asleep (to be —) *v.i*, dormĭo (4); **(to fall—)** obdormĭo (4)
asp aspis, *f*
aspect (appearance) aspectus, *m*, făcĭes, *f*
asperity ăcerbĭtas, *f*
asperse *v.t*, aspergo (3)
aspersion călumnĭa, *f*
asphalt bĭtūmen, *n*
aspirate *nn*, aspīrātĭo, *f*
aspiration (desire) affectātĭo, *f*; **(hope)** spes, f
aspire to affecto (1)
ass ăsĭnus, *m*
assail *v.t*, appĕto (3), oppugno (1)
assailant oppugnātor, *m*
assassin percussor, *m*, sīcārĭus, *m*
assassinate *v.t*, trŭcīdo (1)
assassination caedes, *f*
assault *nn*, impĕtus, *m*, oppugnātĭo, *f*
assault *v.t*, oppugno (1), ădŏrĭor (4 *dep*)
assemble *v.i*, convĕnĭo (4); *v.t*, cōgo (3)
assembly coetus, *m*, conventus, *m*; **(— of the Roman people)**, cŏmĭtĭa, *n.pl*
assent *nn*, assensĭo, *f*
assent to *v.i*, assentĭor (4 *dep*) *(with dat)*

assert *v.t*, affirmo (1), confirmo (1)
assertion affirmātĭo, *f*, dēfensĭo, *f*
assess *v.t* **(evaluate)**, aestĭmo (1)
assessment (valuation) aestĭmātĭo, *f*
assessor censor, *m*
assets bŏna, *n.pl*
assiduity assĭdŭĭtas, *f*, sēdŭlĭtas, *f*
assiduous assĭdŭus, sēdŭlus
assiduously *adv*, assĭdŭe, sēdŭlō
assign *v.t*, assigno (1), trĭbŭo (3)
assignation constĭtūtum, *n*
assimilate *v.t*, sĭmĭlem făcĭo (3)
assist *v.t*, iŭvo (1), auxĭlĭor (1 *dep*), subvĕnĭo (4) *(with dat)*
assistance auxĭlĭum, *n*, ŏpem *(no nomin)*, *f*
assistant adiūtor, *m*
assize (provincial law court) conventus, *m*
associate *nn*, sŏcĭus, *m*
associate *v.t* **(join)**, coniungo (3); *v.i*, ūtor (3 *dep. with abl*)
association sŏcĭetas, *f*, consortĭo, *f*
assort *v.t*. **(arrange)**, dīgĕro *(irreg)*
assortment (heap) ăcervus *m*
assuage *v.t*, lĕvo (1), mītĭgo (1)
assume *v.t*, pōno (3), sūmo (3); **(take on)** suscĭpĭo (3)
assumption (hypothesis) sumptĭo, *f*
assurance (promise) fĭdes, *f*; **(confidence)** fĭdūcĭa, *f*
assure *v.t*, confirmo (1)
assured (certain) explōrātus
assuredly *adv*, **(certainly)** prōfecto
astern *adv*, ā puppi
asthma dyspnoea, *f*
astonish *v.t*, obstŭpĕfăcĭo (3)
astonished stŭpĕfactus; **(to be —)**, *v.i*, obstŭpesco (3)
astonishing mīrĭficus, admīrăbĭlis
astonishingly *adv. phr*, mīrum in mŏdum
astonishment stŭpor *m*
astound *v.t*, obstŭpĕfăcĭo (3)
astray (to go —) *v.i*, erro (1); **(to lead —)**, *v.t*, indūco (3)
astrologer măthēmătĭcus, *m*

astrology astrŏlŏgĭa, *f*
astronomy astrŏlŏgĭa, *f*
astute callĭdus
astuteness callĭdĭtas, *f*
asylum (refuge) perfŭgĭum, *n*
at (*of place*) in (*with abl*), a, ăpŭd
(*with acc*); *with proper names
and* dŏmus *use locative case, e.g.*
at Rome, Rōmae, at home, dŏmi;
(*of time*) *use abl. case, e.g.* at the
third hour, tertĭa hōra; *or
sometimes* ăd *with the acc. case*
atheist ăthĕŏs, *m*
athlete āthlēta, *c*
athletic (strong) fortis
athwart *prep,* (**across**), trans
(*with acc*)
Atlantic Ocĕănus, *m*
atmosphere āēr, *m*
atom ătŏmus, *f,* sēmĭna (*n.pl*)
rērum (**seeds of things**)
atone for *v.t,* expĭo (1)
atonement expĭātĭo, *f*
atrocious nĕfărĭus
atrociousness fĕrĭtas, *f*
atrocity nĕfas, *n*
atrophy tābes, *f*
atrophy *v.i,* tābesco (3)
attach *v.t,* (**fasten**), affigo (3),
applĭco (1); (**connect**) adiungo (3)
attached (fastened) fixus, aptus;
(**fond**) dēvinctus, ămans
attachment (affection) stŭdĭum,
n, ămor, *m*
attack *nn,* impĕtus, *m,*
oppugnātĭo, *f*
attack *v.t,* oppugno (1),
aggrĕdĭor (3 *dep*), ădŏrĭor (4
dep), invādo (3), pĕto (3)
attacker oppugnātŏr, *m*
attain *v.i.* (**reach**), pervĕnĭo (4)
(*with ad and acc*); *v.t.* (**obtain**),
consĕquor (3 *dep*)
attainable impĕtrābĭlis
attainment (obtaining) ădeptĭo, *f;*
(**learning**) ērŭdītĭo, *f*
attempt *nn,* inceptum, *n,*
cōnātum, *n*
attempt *v.i,* cōnor (1 *dep*)
attend *v.i.* (**be present at**),
intersum (*irreg. with dat*); *v.t.*
(**accompany**), cŏmĭtor (1 *dep*),
prōsĕquor, (3 *dep*); (**pay**

attention) ŏpĕram do (1),
ănĭmadverto (3)
attendance (being present) *use
vb.* adsum (*irreg*) (**to be present**);
(**of crowds**), frĕquentĭa, *f;*
(**service**), appārĭtĭo, *f*
attendant *nn,* (**servant**) mĭnister,
m; (**of a nobleman**) sectātor, *m,*
sătellĕs, *c*
attention (concentration) attentĭo
(*f*) ănĭmi; (**to pay —**); ŏpĕram, (*f*)
do (1)
attentive (alert) intentus, attentus;
(**respectful**), observans
attentively *adv,* sēdŭlo
attenuate *v.t,* attĕnŭo (1)
attest *v.t,* testor (1 *dep*)
attestation testĭfĭcātĭo, *f*
attire *nn,* vestis, *f*
attire *v.t,* vestĭo (4)
attitude (of mind) ănĭmus, *m;* (**of
body**), gestus *m,* hăbĭtus, *m*
attract *v.t,* attrăho (3), allĭcĭo (3)
attraction (charms) illĕcĕbrae
(*f.pl*)
attractive blandus, iūcundus
attribute *v.t,* attrĭbŭo (3), assigno
(1)
attune *v.t,* (**adjust**) consŏnum
(aptum) reddo (3) (**make
harmonious (suitable)**)
auburn flāvus
auction auctĭo, *f;* (**to sell by
public —**), sub hastā vendo (3)
(**sell under the spear**)
auctioneer praeco, *m*
audacious audax
audacity audācĭa, *f,* confīdentĭa, *f*
audibly *use phr.* quod audīri
pŏtest (**that can be heard**)
audience (of people) audītōres,
m.pl (**hearing**), ădĭtus, *m*
audit *v.t,* inspĭcĭo (3)
auditorium audĭtorĭum, *n*
augment *v.t,* augĕo (2)
augur *nn,* augur, *c*
augur *v.t,* vātĭcĭnor (1 *dep*)
augury augŭrĭum, *n,* auspĭcĭum, *n*
August Sextīlis or Augustus
(mensis)
august *adj,* augustus
aunt (paternal) ămĭta, *f;*
(**maternal**), mātertĕra, *f*

auspices auspĭcĭum, *n*
auspicious faustus, sĕcundus
auspiciously *adv,* fēlīcĭter
austere (severe) sĕvērus
austerity sĕvērĭtas, *f*
authentic vērus, certus
authentically *adv,* certō
authenticate *v.t,* rĕcognosco (3)
authenticity auctōrĭtas, *f*
author (writer) scriptor, *m*;
  (instigator), auctor, *m*
authoritative grăvis, impĕrĭosus
authority auctōrĭtas, *f,* pŏtestas, *f,*
  impĕrĭum, *n*
authorize (give permission to) *v.i,*
  pŏtestătem (auctōrĭtātem), făcĭo
  (3) (*with dat*)
autocracy tўrannis, *f*
autocrat dŏmĭnus, *m*
autograph mănus, *f*
autumn auctumnus, *m*
autumnal auctumnālis
auxiliary *adj,* auxĭlĭăris,
  auxĭlĭărĭus; *nn* adiŭtor, *m*;
  (—forces) auxĭlĭa, *n.pl*
avail *v.t* **(assist),** prōsusm (*irreg*)
  (*with dat.*); **(make use of),** ūtor (3
  dep. with abl)
available (ready) expĕdītus,
  părātus
avarice ăvārĭtĭa, *f*
avaricious ăvārus
avenge *v.t,* ulciscor (3 *dep*)
avenger ultor, *m*
avenging *adj,* ultrix
avenue xystus, *m*
aver *v.t* **(affirm),** affirmo (1)
average *adj,* mĕdĭus **(middle)**
averse āversus
aversion ŏdĭum, *n*
avert *v.t,* āverto (3), dēpello (3)
aviary ăvĭārĭum, *n*
avid ăvĭdus
avidity ăvĭdĭtas, *f*
avoid *v.t,* vīto (1), fŭgĭo (3)
avoidance vītātĭo, *f,* fŭga, *f*
avow *v.t,* fătĕor (2 *dep*)
avowal confessĭo, *f*
avowed prŏfessus, ăpertus
await *v.t,* exspecto (1)
awake *adj,* vĭgĭlans; **(to be —),**
  v.i, vĭgĭlo (1); **(to awake),** *v.t,*
  excĭto (1)

award *nn,* **(judicial decision)**;
  arbĭtrĭum, *n* **(prize),** palma,*f*
award *v.t,* trĭbŭo (3), adiŭdĭco
  (1)
aware gnārus; **(to be —),** sentĭo
  (4); **(know),** scĭo (4)
away *use* a, ab *compounded*
  with a verb, e.g. (ăbĕo) go
  away (4)
awe formīdo, *f,* mĕtus, *m,*
  rĕvĕrentĭa, *f*
awe (be in —) vĕrĕor (2 *dep*)
awful vĕrendus
awestruck păvĭdus
awhile *adv,* paulisper, părumper
awkward rŭdis, impĕrītus
awkwardness inscītĭa, *f*
awning vēlum, *n*
awry *adj,* perversus; *adj,* perversē
axe sĕcūris, *f*
axiom sententia, *f*
axis, axle axis, *m*
ay, aye *adv,* ĭta, vērō; **(forever)** in
  perpĕtŭum
azure *adj,* caerŭlĕus

B

babble *v.i,* garrĭo (4), blătĕro (1)
babbler, babbling *adj,* garrŭlus
baby infans, *c*
babyhood infantĭa, *f*
bacchanalian bacchānālis
bachelor *adj,* caelebs
back *nn,* tergum, *n,* dorsum, *n*;
  (at the —) a tergo; **(to move**
  something—), rĕtro mŏvĕo (2),
  rēĭcĭo (3); **(to go —)** se rĕcĭpĕre
  (3 *reflex*)
backbite *v.t,* obtrecto (1)
backwards *adj,* **(dull)** pĭger
backwards *adv,* rĕtro
bacon lārĭdum, *n*
bad mălus; **(of health),** aeger; **(of**
  weather), ādversus
badge insigne, *n*
badger mēles, *f*
badly *adv,* mălĕ, prāvē, imprŏbē
badness (worthlessness) nēquĭtĭa, *f*
baffle *v.t,* ēlūdo (3)
bag saccus, *m*
baggage (military) impĕdīmenta,
  n.pl; **(individual packs),** sarcĭnae,

f.pl

bail *nn,* (person), văs, *m;*
(security) vădĭmōnĭum, *n*
bail (to give — for) *v.t,* spondĕo
(2) prō (*with abl*)
bailiff (estate manager) villĭcus,
m; (official), appārĭtor, *m*
bait *nn,* esca, *f*
bait *v.t,* (tease), lăcesso (3),
illūdo (3)
bake *v.t,* torrĕo (2), cŏquo (3)
baker pistor, *m*
bakery pistrīnum, *n*
balance *nn,* (scales), lībra, *f;*
(equilibrium), lībrāmentum, *n*
balance *v.t,* lībro (1), compenso
(1)
balcony maenĭāna, *n.pl*
bald calvus, glăber; (unadorned),
ārĭdus
baldness calvĭtĭum, *n*
bale out *v.t,* (discharge), ēgĕro
(3)
bale (bundle) fascis, *m*
baleful pernĭcĭōsus
balk (beam) trabs, *f*
balk *v.t,* frustror (1 *dep*)
ball (for play) pĭla, *f;* (globe,
sphere), glŏbus, *m*
ballad carmen, *n*
ballad-singer cantātor, *m*
ballast săbura, *f*
ballet *use vb.* salto (1) (dance)
ballista ballista, *f*
ballot suffrāgĭum, *n*
ballot-box cista, *f,* urna, *f*
balm balsāmum, *n,* unguentum, *n*
balmy (soothing) mollis, lēnis
balustrade (railings) cancelli, *m.pl*
bamboo hărundo, *f* (reed)
ban *v.t,* vĕto (1)
band (bond) vincŭlum, *n;* (of
people), mănus, *f,* grex, *m*
band together *v.i,* conĭūro (1)
bandage fascĭa, *f*
bandage *v.t,* lĭgo (1)
bandit lătro, *m*
bandy (to — words) *v.i,* altercor
(1 *dep*)
bandy-legged lōrĭpes
bane (injury) pernĭcĭes, *f;* (poison),
vĕnēnum, *n*
baneful pernĭcĭōsus

bang crĕpĭtus, *m*
bang *v.t.* (beat) tundo (3)
banish *v.t, use phr.* ăquā et igni
interdīco (3) (*with dat*) (forbid on
the use of fire and water), expello
(3)
banishment rĕlēgātĭo, *f,* exsĭlĭum, *n*
bank *nn,* (of earth), tŏrus, *m;* (of
a river) rīpa, *f;* (for money)
argentārĭa tăberna (money shop)
banker argentārĭus, mensārĭus, *m*
bankrupt *nn,* dēcoctor, *m* (to
be —), *v.i,* solvendo non esse
bankruptcy (personal) rŭīna, *f*
(downfall)
banner vexillum, *n*
banquet convīvĭum, *n,* ĕpŭlae,
f.pl
banter *nn,* căvĭllātĭo, *f*
banter *v.i,* căvillor (1 *dep*)
bar (wooden) asser, *m;* (lock),
claustra, *n.pl;* (bolt), sĕra, *f;*
(barrier) rĕpāgŭla, *n.pl*
bar *v.t* (fasten), obsĕro (1);
(— the way), obsto (1) (*with dat*)
barb (hook) uncus, *m*
barbarian barbărus, *m*
barbaric (barbarous) barbărus,
crūdēlis, immānis
barbarity barbărĭa, *f*
barbarously *adv,* (cruelly),
crūdēlĭter
barbed hāmātus
barber tonsor, *m*
bard (poet, etc.) poēta, *m*
bare nūdus; (to make —), *v.t,*
ăpĕrĭo (4), nūdo (1)
barefaced (shameless) impŭdens
barefoot *adv,* nūdo pĕde
barely *adv,* vix
bargain *nn,* pactum, *n*
bargain *v.i,* (make a — with),
paciscor (3 *dep*) (*with cum and
abl. of person*)
barge linter, *f;* (— man), nauta, *m*
bark *nn,* (of trees), cortex, *m;* (of
dogs), lātrātus, *m;* (boat), rătis, *f*
bark *v.i,* lātro (1)
barley hordĕum, *n*
barley-water ptĭsăna, *f*
barn horrĕum, *n*
baron princeps, *m*
barque rătis, *f*

barracks castra *n.pl*
barrel dōlĭum, *n*
barren stĕrĭlis
barrenness stĕrĭlĭtas, *f*
barricade *nn*, agger, *m*
barricade *v.t*, obsaepĭo (4)
barrier impĕdĭmentum, *n*,
  claustra, *n.pl*
barrister pătrōnus, *m*
barrow fercŭlum, *n*
barter *v.t*, **(exchange)**, mūto (1)
barter *nn*, permūtātio, (*f*)
  mercĭum **(exchange of goods)**
base *nn*, băsis, *f*, fundāmentum,
  n
base *adj*, **(worthless)**, turpis;
  (lowborn), hŭmĭlis
baseless *adj*, falsus
basely *adv*, turpĭter
basement băsis, *f*
baseness turpĭtūdo, *f*
bashful vĕrēcundus
bashfulness vĕrēcundĭa, *f*
basin pelvis, *f*
basin băsis, *f*, fundāmentum, *n*
bask *v.i*, ăprīcor (1 *dep*)
basket călăthus, *m*, corbis, *f*,
  quālum, *n*
bass *adj*, grăvis
bastard *adj*, nŏthus
bastion turris, *f*
bat (animal) vespertīlĭo, *m*; **(club,
  stick)**, clāva, *f*
bath *nn*, balnēum, *n*; **(public —)**
  balneae, *f.pl*
bath, bathe *v.i*, lăvor (1 *pass*);
  v.t, lăvo (1)
bathing *nn*, lăvātĭo, *f*
baton scīpĭo, *m*
battalion cŏhors, *f*
batter *v.t*, pulso (1), verbĕro (1)
battering-ram ărĭes, *m*
battery (assault) vĭs, *f*; **(cannon)**,
  tormenta *n.pl*
battle proelĭum, *n*; **(— line)**, ăcĭes,
  f **(— cry)**, clāmor, *m*; **(— field)**,
  lŏcus (*m*) pugnae
battlement pinna, *f*, mūnītĭōnes,
  f.pl
bawd lēna, *f*
bawl *v.i*, clāmĭto (1)
bawling *nn*, clāmor, *m*
bay (of the sea) sĭnus, *m*; **(tree)**

laurus, *f*; **(at bay)** (*adj*) părātus ad
pugnam **(ready for a fight)**
bay *v.i*, lātro (1)
bayonet pŭgĭo, *m*
be *v.i*, sum (*irreg*)
beach lītus, *n*
beacon (fire) ignis, *m*
bead bāca, *f*
beak rōstrum, *n*
beaker pōcŭlum, *n*
beam (of timber) tignum, *n*,
  trabs, *f*; **(cross —)**, transtrum, *n*;
  (ray) rădĭus, *m*
bean făba, *f*
bear *nn*, ursus, *m*, ursa, *f*;
  (constellation), septentrĭōnes,
  m.pl; **(The Great —)**, ursa maior;
  (The Little —) septentrio minor
bear *v.t*, fĕro (*irreg*), gĕro (3);
  (carry), porto (1); **(produce)**,
  părĭo (3); **(— away)** aufĕro
  (*irreg*)
bearable *adj*, tŏlĕrābĭlis
beard barba, *f*; **(bearded)**,
  barbātus
bearer (carrier) bāiŭlus, *m*,
  portĭtor, *m*
bearing (posture) gestus, *m*
beast (wild) bestĭa, *f*, fĕra, *f*;
  (domestic), pĕcus, *f*
beastly (filthy) obscēnus
beat (in music, poetry) ictus, *m*
beat *v.t*, caedo (3), fĕrĭo (4),
  vervĕro (1); **(conquer)**, sŭpĕro
  (1), vinco (3); **(— back)**, rĕpello
  (3); **(— down)** sterno (3); **(be
  beaten)**, *v.i*, vāpŭlo (1)
beating *nn*, verbĕra, *n.pl*
beautiful pulcher
beautifully *adv*, pulchrē
beautify *v.t*, orno (1)
beauty pulchrĭtūdo, *f*, forma, *f*
beaver castor, *m*
becalmed vento dēstĭtūtus
  (deserted by the wind)
because *conj*, quod, quĭa, cum;
  (because of) *prep*, propter, ŏb
  (*with acc*)
beckon *v.t*, innŭo (3) (*with dat*)
become *v.i*, fīo (*irreg*); *v.t* **(to
  suit, adorn)** dĕcet (2 *impers. with
  acc. of person*)
becoming *adj*, dĕcōrus

bed lectus, *m*; **(go to —)**, cŭbĭtum ĕo (4)

bedroom cŭbĭcŭlum, *n*

bedaub *v.t*, lĭno (3)

bedeck *v.t*, orno (1); **(bedecked)**, ornātus

bedew *v.t*, irrōro (1)

bee ăpis, *f*

bee-hive alvĕārĭum, *n*

beech (tree) fāgus, *f*

beef caro būbŭla, *f*, **(ox flesh)**

beer cervisia, *f*

beetle scărăbaeus, *m*

befall *v.i*, accĭdo (3)

befit *v.i* **(suit)**, convĕnĭo (4)

before *prep*, **(time and place)**, antĕ *(with acc)*; **(place)**, prae, prō *(with abl)*; **(in the presence of)**, cōram *(with abl)*

before *adv*, **(time)**, antĕ, prĭus; **(space)** prae; **before** *conj*, antĕquam, prĭusquam

befoul *v.t*, inquĭno (1)

befriend *v.t*, adiŭvo (1)

beg *v.t* **(request)**, pĕto (3), ōro (1); **(be a beggar)**, *v.i*, mendīco (1)

beget *v.t*, gigno (3)

begetter gĕnĭtor, *m*

beggar mendīcus, *m*

begin *v.i*, incĭpĭo (3), coepi (3 *defect*)

beginner (originator) auctor, *m* **(learner)**, tīro, *m*

beginning *nn*, ĭnĭtĭum, *n*, princĭpĭum, *n*, inceptum, *n*

begone! ăpăgĕ!

begrudge *v.t* **(envy)**, invĭdĕo (2) *(with dat)*

beguile *v.t*, fallo (3), dēcĭpĭo (3)

behalf (on — of) *(prep)*, prō *(with abl)*

behave oneself *v. reflex*, se gĕrĕre (3)

behaviour (manners) mōres, *m.pl*

behead *v.t*, sĕcūri fērĭo (4) **(strike with an axe)**

behest (command) iussum, *n*

behind *prep*, post *(with acc)*

behind *adv*, post, ā tergo

behold *v.t*, conspĭcĭo (3)

behold! (exclamation) eccĕ!

being (human —) hŏmo, *c*

belabour *v.t*, verbĕro (1)

belated sērus

belch *v.i, and v.t*, ructo (1)

belch *nn*, ructus, *m*

beleaguer *v.t*, obsĭdĕo (2)

belfry turris, *f*

belie *v.t*, **(conceal)**, dissĭmŭlo (1)

belief fĭdes, *f*; **(impression)**, ŏpīnĭo, *f*, persuāsĭo, *f*

believe *v.t*, crēdo (3) *(with dat. of person)* pŭto (1), arbĭtror (1 *dep)*, censĕo (2)

believer crēdens, *c*

bell tintinnābŭlum, *n*

belligerent bellans, belli cŭpĭdus **(keen on war)**

bellow *v.i*, mūgĭo (4)

bellowing *nn*, mūgītus, *m*

bellows (pair of —) follis, *m*

belly venter, *m*, abdōmen, *n*

belong to *v.i*, use esse *(irreg)* **(to be)** *with genit. of person*

beloved cārus, dīlectus

below *prep*, infrā, subter *(with acc)*, sub *(with abl. or acc)*

below *adv*, infrā, subter

belt baltĕus, *m*

bemoan *v.t*, gĕmo (3)

bench scamnum, *n*; **(for rowers)** transtrum, *n*

bend *v.t*, flecto (3), curvo (1); *v.i*, se flectĕre (3 *pass*)

bend, bending *nn*, flexus, *m*

beneath see **below**

benefactor *phr*, qui bĕnĕfĭcĭa confert **(who confers favours)**

beneficence bĕnĕfĭcentĭa, *f*

beneficent bĕnĕfĭcus

beneficial sălūtāris, ūtĭlis; **(to be —)** *v.i*, prōsum *(irreg) (with dat)*

benefit *v.i* prōsum *(irreg) (with dat)*, adiŭvo (1)

benefit *nn*, bĕnĕfĭcĭum, *n*

benevolence bĕnĕfĭcentĭa, *f*, bĕnĕvŏlentĭa, *f*

benevolent bĕnĕfĭcus, bĕnĕvŏlus

benign bĕnignus

benignity bĕnignĭtas, *f*

bent *adj*, curvus; **(—on)** attentus; **(—back)** rĕsŭpīnus; **(—forward)** prōnus

benumb *v.t*, *phr* torpōre affĭcĭo (3) **(affect with numbness)**

bequeath *v.t,* lēgo (1)
bequest lēgātum, *n*
bereave *v.t,* orbo (1)
bereaved orbus
bereavement orbĭtas, *f,* damnum, *n*
berry bāca, *f*
berth (for a ship) stătĭo, *f*
beseech ōro (1), obsĕcro (1), quaeso (3)
beseem (become) dĕcet (2 *impers. with acc. of person*)
beset *v.t,* obsĭdĕo (2), circumvĕnĭo (4)
beside *prep,* **(near),** prŏpĕ (*with acc*); **(except),** praeter (*with acc*)
besides *adv or conj,* praeterquam
besides *adv,* **(further),** praetĕrĕă, insŭper
besiege *v.t,* obsĭdĕo (2), circum sĕdĕo (2)
besieger obsessor, *m*
besmear *v.t,* illĭno (3)
bespatter *v.t,* aspergo (3)
bespeak *v.t,* **(hire)** condūco (3)
besprinkle *v.t,* aspergo (3)
best *adj,* optĭmus; **(to the best of (one's) ability)** prō (vĭrīli) parte;
best *adv,* optĭmē
bestial *use phr,* bestĭārum mōre **(after the manner of beasts)**
bestir (to — oneself) *v.i,* expergiscor (3 *dep*)
bestow *v.t,* do (1), trĭbŭo (3), confĕro (*irreg*)
bestowal largītĭo, *f*
bet *nn,* pignus, *n*
bet *v.t,* pignŏre contendo (3)
betake *v.t,* conferre (*irreg*)
betimes *adv,* mātūrē
betray *v.t,* prōdo (3)
betrayal prōdĭtĭo, *f*
betrayer prōdĭtor, *m*
betroth *v.t,* spondĕo (2)
betrothal sponsālĭa, *n.pl*
better *adj,* mĕlĭor; **(of health),** sānus; **better** *adv,* mĕlĭus
better *v.t,* **(improve),** corrĭgo (3); ēmendo (1)
between *prep,* inter (*with acc*)
beverage pōtĭo, *f,* pōtus, *m*
bevy căterva, *f*

bewail *v.t,* dēplōro (1), lūgeo (2)
beware *v.i and v.t,* căvĕo (2)
bewilder *v.t,* perturbo (1), distrăho (3)
bewildered turbātus, distractus
bewitch *v.t,* fascĭno (1); **(charm),** căpĭo (3)
beyond *prep,* ultrā, trans, sŭprā, extrā (*with acc*)
beyond *adv,* ultrā, sŭprā
bias inclīnātĭo, *f*
bias *v.t,* inclīno (1)
Bible *use phr.* scripta săcra, *n.pl* **(sacred writings)**
bicker *v.i,* altercor (1 *dep*)
bid *nn,* **(of a price)** lĭcĭtātĭo, *f*
bid *v.t* **(tell, order),** iŭbĕo (2)
bide *v.i* **(stay),** mănĕo (2)
bier fĕrĕtrum, *n,* fercŭlum, *n*
big magnus, vastus, ingens
bigotry obstĭnātĭo, *f*
bile bīlis, *f*
bilge-water sentīna, *f*
bilious bīlĭōsus
bill (written, financial) lĭbellus, *m,* rătĭo, *f,* syngrăpha, *f;* **(proposal in Parliament),** rŏgātĭo, *f;* **(a law),** lex, *f* **(of a bird),** rōstrum, *n*
billet (of wood) lignum, *n;* **(lodging of soldiers),** hospĭtĭum, (*n*) mīlĭtum
billet *v.t* **(soldiers),** per hospĭtĭa dispōno (3) **(distribute through lodgings)**
billow fluctus, *m*
billowy fluctŭosus
bind *v.t,* lĭgo (1), vincĭo (4); **(oblige),** oblĭgo (1); **(— together),** collĭgo (1)
biographer scriptor rērum gestārum **(writer of exploits)**
biography vīta, *f*
birch (tree) betŭla, *f*
bird ăvis, *f;* **(— cage),** căvĕa, *f;* **(— nest),** nīdus, *m*
birth ortus, *m,* gĕnus, *n*
birthday (dĭes) nātālis
birth place sŏlum, (*n*) nātāle
bishop pontĭfex, *m*
bit (bite) offa, *f;* **(small piece of food),** frustum, *n;* **(for a horse),**

frēnum, *n*
bitch cănis, *f*
bite *nn*, morsus, *m*
bite *v.t*, mordĕo (2)
biting *adj*, mordax, asper
bitter ămārus, ăcerbus, asper
bitterness ăcerbĭtas, *f*
bitumen bĭtūmen, *n*
bivouac *nn*, excŭbĭae, *f.pl*
bivouac *v.i*, excŭbo (1)
blab *v.i*, blătĕro (1)
black nĭger; (— art), măgĭce, *f*
blackberry mōrum, *n*, rŭbus, *m*
blackbird mĕrŭla, *f*
blacken *v.t*, nigrum reddo (3)
blackguard nēbŭlo, *m*
Black Sea Pontus Euxĭnus, *m*
blacksmith făber, *m*
bladder vēsīca, *f*
blade (of grass) herba, *f*; (of
   sword, knife), lāmĭna, *f*
blame *nn*, culpa, *f*
blame *v.t*, culpo (1)
blameable culpandus
blameless innŏcens, intĕger
blamelessness innocentĭa, *f*
bland blandus
blandishment blandĭtĭa, *f*,
   blandīmentum, *n*
blank *adj*, (empty), văcŭus;
   (paper), pūrus
blank *nn*, ĭnāne, *n*
blanket lōdix, *f*
blaspheme *v.t*, blasphēmo (1)
blast *nn*, ĭnāne, *n*
blanket lōdix, *f*
blaspheme *v.t*, blasphēmo (1)
blast *nn*, flāmen, *n*, flātus, *m*
blast *v.t*, ūro (3)
blatant *adj*, (manifest), ăpertus
blaze *nn*, flamma, *f*
blaze *v.i*, ardĕo (2), flăgro (1)
bleach candĭdum reddo (3)
bleak algĭdus, frīgĭdus
blear-eyed lippus
bleat, bleating bālātus, *m*
bleat *v.i*, bālo (1)
bleed *v.i*, sangŭĭnem effundo
   (3); *v.t*, sangŭĭnem mitto (3)
bleeding *adj*, (wound), crūdus
bleeding *nn*, *use phr* effūsĭo, (*f*)
   sangŭĭnis (shedding of blood)
blemish *nn*, (physical), vĭtĭum, *n*,

(moral), măcŭla, *f*
blemish *v.t*, măcŭlo (1)
blend *v.t*, miscĕo (2)
bless *v.t*, (favour, make
   successful), sĕcundo (1),
   bĕnĕdīco (3)
blessed beātus; (of the dead),
   pĭus
blessedness bĕātĭtūdo, *f*,
   fēlĭcĭtas, *f*
blessing *nn*, bĕnĕdictĭo, *f*,
   bŏnum, *n*
blight *nn*, rōbīgo, *f*
blight *v.t*, ūro (3); (—of hopes)
   frustror (1 *dep*)
blind *adj*, caecus
blind *v.t*, caeco (1)
blindly (rashly) *adv*, tĕmĕre
blindness caecitas, *f*
blink *v.i*, connĭvĕo (2)
bliss fēlĭcĭtas, *f*
blissful *adj*, fēlix
blister pustŭla, *f*
blithe hĭlăris
blizzard imber, *m*
bloated sufflātus
block *nn*, (of wood), stĭpes, *m*,
   massa, *f*
block *v.t*, obstrŭo (3), obsaepĭo
   (4)
blockade *nn*, obsĭdĭo, *f*
blockade *v.t*, obsĭdĕo (2)
blockhead caudex, *m*
blood sanguis, *m*; (gore), crŭor,
   m
blood-letting *nn*, missĭo, (*f*)
   sangŭĭnis
bloodshed caedes, *f*
bloodshot crŭōre suffusus
   (spread over with blood)
blood-stained crŭentus
bloodthirsty sangŭĭnārĭus
bloody crŭentus, sangŭĭnĕus
bloom *nn*, flōs, *m*
bloom *v.i*, flōrĕo (2)
blooming flōrens
blossom, etc. see bloom
blot *v.t*, măcŭlo (1); (—out,
   obliterate), dēlĕo (2)
blot *nn*, măcŭla, *f*
blow *nn*, (stroke), plāga, *f*, ictus,
   m
blow *v.i. and v.t*, flo (1)

blowing *nn*, flātus, *m*
bludgeon fustis, *m*
blue *adj*, caerŭlĕus
bluff *v.t*, illūdo (3)
blunder *nn*, mendum, *n*, error, *m*
blunder *v.i*, offendo (3), erro (1)
blunt *adj*, hĕbes; **(frank)**, līber
blunt *v.t*, hĕbĕto (1), obtundo (3)
bluntly *adv*, lībĕrē, plāne
blush *nn*, rŭbor, *m*
blush *v.i*, ērŭbesco (3)
bluster *v.i*, dēclāmo (1)
bluster *nn*, dēclāmātĭo, *f*
blusterer iactātor, *m*
boar verres, *m*, ăper, *m*
board *nn*, tăbŭla, *f*; **(council)**, concĭlĭum, *n*
board *v.t* **(ship)**, conscendo (3); **(to — up)**, contăbŭlo (1); **(provide food)**, victum praebĕo (2)
boast *v.i*, glōrĭor (1 *dep*.), se iactare (1 *reflex*)
boasting *nn*, glōrĭātĭo, *f*, iactātĭo, *f*
boat scăpha, *f*, linter, *f*
boatsman nauta, *m*
bode *v.t* **(predict)**, praesāgĭo (4)
bodily *adj*, corpŏrĕus
bodkin ăcus, *f*
body corpus, *n*; **(— of soldiers, etc.)**, mănus, *f*, nŭmĕrus, *m*, multĭtūdo, *f*
bodyguard stĭpātōres, *m.pl*
bog pălus, *f*
boggy păluster
boil *nn*, vŏmĭca, *f*
boil *v.t*, cŏquo (3); *v.i*, fervĕo (2)
boiled *adj*, ēlixus
boiler caldarĭum, *n*
boisterous prŏcellōsus, turbĭdus
bold audax, ănĭmōsus, fortis
boldly *adv*, audacter, anĭmōse, fortĭter
boldness audācĭa, *f*, fĭdentĭa, *f*
bolster cervīcal, *n*, pulvīnus, *m*
bolt *nn*, **(door, etc.)**, ŏbex, *m*, rĕpāgŭla, *n.pl*
bolt *v.t* **(door, etc.)**, obsĕro (1), claudo (3); **(food)**, obsorbĕo (2)

bombastic inflātus
bond vincŭlum, *n*, cătēna, *f*; **(legal)**, syngrāpha, *f*
bondage servĭtus, *f*
bone ŏs, *n*
book līber, *m*, lĭbellus, *m*
bookbinder glūtĭnātor, *m*
bookcase armārĭum, *n*
book-keeper actŭārĭus, *m*
bookseller bĭblĭŏpōla, *m*
boom *v.i*, sŏno (1)
boon (good thing) bŏnum, *n*
boor hŏmo ăgrestis
boorish agrestis
boot calcĕus, *m*; **(heavy —)**, călĭga, *f*
bootless (unsuccessful) *adj*, irrĭtus
booth tăberna, *f*
booty praeda, *f*, spŏlĭa, *n.pl*
booze *v.i. and v.t*, pōto (1)
border margo, *m*, *f*; **(of a country)**, finis, *m*
border *v.i*, attingo (3)
bordering *adj*, fĭnĭtĭmus
bore (person) use, *adj*, importūnus **(rude)**
bore *v.t*, perfŏro (1), tĕrĕbro (1); **(— someone)**, fātĭgo (1)
boredom taedĭum, *n*
born *adj*, nātus; **(to be —)**, *v.i*, nascor (3 *dep*)
borough mūnĭcĭpĭum, *n*
borrow mūtŭor (1 *dep*.)
bosom sĭnus, *m*, pectus, *n*
boss (of a shield) umbo, *m*
botany ars herbārĭa, *f*
botch *v.t*, măle sarcĭo (4), **(patch badly)**
both ambo; **(each of two)** ŭterquĕ; **(both ... and)**, et ... et
bother *nn*, *use adj*, mŏlestus **(troublesome)**
bother *v.t*, lăcesso (3), vexo (1)
bottle ampulla, *f*, lăgēna, *f*
bottom fundus, *m*, *or use adj*, īmus *in agreement with noun*, *e.g.* **at the bottom of the tree**, ad īmam arbŏrem
bottomless (very deep) prŏfundus
bough rāmus, *m*
boulder saxum, *n*
bounce *v.i*, rĕsĭlĭo (4)

bound (limit) fīnis, *m*, mŏdus, *m*;
   (leap), saltus, *m*
bound *v.i*, **(leap)**, sălĭo (4); *v.t*,
   (limit), contĭněo (2)
boundary fīnis, *m*
boundless infīnītus
bountiful largus, běnignus
bounty largĭtas, *f*, běnignĭtas, *f*
bouquet serta, *n.pl*
bout (contest) certāmen, *n*
bow (archery) arcus, *m*; **(of a
   ship)**, prōra, *f*; **(of salutation)**,
   sălūtātĭo, *f*
bow *v.t*, inclīno (1), dēmitto (3);
   v.i, se dēmittěre (3 *reflex*)
bow-legged vătĭus
bowman săgittārĭus, *m*
bowels viscěra, *n.pl*
bower umbrācŭlum, *n*
bowl crātěra, *f*
box arca, *f*, cista, *f*; **(tree)**, buxus,
   f; **(slap)**, cŏlăphus, *m*
box *v.i*, pugnis certo (1), **(fight
   with the fists)**
boxer pŭgil, *m*
boxing *nn*, pŭgĭlātĭo, *f*
boy pŭer, *m*
boyhood pŭěrĭtĭa, *f*
boyish pŭěrīlis
brace (support) fascĭa, *f*; **(in
   architecture)**, fībŭla, *f*
brace *v.t*, lĭgo (1), firmo (1)
bracelet armilla, *f*
bracket mūtŭlus, *m*
brackish ămārus
brag *v.i*, glōrĭor (1 *dep*.)
braggart ĭactātor, *m*
braid *nn*, **(of hair)**, grădus, *m*
braid *v.t*, necto (3)
brain cěrěbrum, *n*
brainless (stupid) sōcors
bramble dūmus, *m*
bran furfur, *m*
branch rāmus, *m*
branch *v.i*, **(separate)**, dīvĭdor (3
   pass)
branching *adj*, rāmōsus
brand (fire —) fax, *f*, torris, *m*;
   (burn-mark), nŏta, *f*; **(stigma)**,
   stigma, *n*
brand *v.t*, ĭnūro (3), nŏto (1)
brandish *v.t*, vibro (1)
brass ŏrĭchalcum, *n*

brave fortis, ănĭmōsus, ācer
bravely *adv*, fortĭter, ănĭmōsē
bravery fortĭtūdo, *f*
brawl *v.i*, rixor (1 *dep*)
brawl *nn*, rixa, *f*
brawny lăcertōsus
bray *v.i*, rŭdo (3)
brazen (made of brass) aēněus,
   aerěus; **(impudent)**, impŭdens
breach rŭīna, *f*, *or use vb*. rumpo
   (3) **(to burst)**; **(— in a treaty, etc.)**
   use vĭŏlo (1) **(to violate)**
bread pānis, *m*
breadth lātĭtūdo, *f*
break *v.t*, frango (3); **(treaty,
   etc.)** vĭŏlo (1); **(— promise)**, fidem
   fallo (3); **(— down)**, *v.t*, rēscindo
   (3); **(— in)**, *v.t*, **(horses)**, dŏmo
   (1); **(— into)**, *v.t*, irrumpo (3);
   (— loose) ērumpo (3)
break (of day) prīma lux, *f*, **(first
   light)**; **(fracture)**, fractūra, *f*
breakfast ientācŭlum, *n*
breakfast *v.i*, iento (1)
breakwater mōles, *f*
breast pectus, *n*, mamma, *f*
breast-plate lōrīca, *f*
breath spīrĭtus, *m*, ănĭma, *f*; **(out
   of —)**, exănĭmātus; **(to hold
   one's —)**, ănĭmam comprĭmo (3)
breathe *v.i*, spīro (1); **(— out)**,
   exspīro (1)
breathing *nn*, aspīrātĭo, *f*
breathless exănĭmātus
breed *v.t*, gěněro (1); *v.i*, nascor
   (3 *dep*.) **(to be born)**
breed *nn*, gěnus, *n*
breeding *nn*, **(giving birth)** partus,
   m; **(manners)**, hūmānĭtas, *f*
breeze aura, *f*
breezy ventōsus
brevity brěvĭtas, *f*
brew *v.t*, cŏquo (3); *v.i*
   (overhang) impenděo (2)
bribe *nn*, praemĭum, *n*
bribe *v.t*, corrumpo (3)
bribery ambĭtus, *m*
brick lăter, *m*; **(made of —)**,
   adj, lătěrīcĭus
bricklayer structor, *m*
bridal nuptĭālis
bride (before marriage) sponsa, *f*
   (after marriage), nupta, *f*

bridegroom (before marriage)
sponsus, *m* **(after marriage)**,
nuptus, *m*, mărītus, *m*
bridge pons, *m*
bridle frēnum, *n*
brief *adj*, brĕvis
briefly *adv*, brĕvĭter
briar dūmus, *m*
brigade lĕgĭo, *f*
bright clārus
brighten *v.t*, illustro (1); *v.i*,
clāresco (3)
brightly *adv*, clāre
brilliance splendor, *m*, nĭtor, *m*
brilliant splendĭdus; **(famous)**,
praeclārus
brim margo, *m*, *f*, labrum, *n*
brimstone sulfur, *n*
brine salsāmentum, *n*
bring, *v.t*, fĕro, affĕro *(irreg)*,
addūco (3) apporto (1);
(— about), confĭcĭo (3); **(— back,
— before),** rĕfĕro *(irreg)*;
(—down), dēfĕro *(irreg)*;
(—forward), prōfĕro *(irreg)*;
(— in), infĕro *(irreg)*; **(— out),**
ĕffĕro *(irreg)*; **(— over),** perdūco
(3); **(—together),** cōgo (3); **(— up)
(children),** ēduco (1)
brink (river, etc.) rīpa, *f*; **(of cliff,
etc.)** *use adj*, summus **(highest)**
brisk ălăcer
briskness ălacrĭtas, *f*
bristle saeta, *f*
bristle *v.i*. horrĕo (2)
brittle frăgĭlis
broach *v.t*, ăpĕrĭo (4), prōfĕro
(irreg)
broad lātus
broadly (widely) *adv*, lātē
broil (quarrel) rixa, *f*
broil *v.t*, torrĕo (2)
broken fractus; **(disabled),**
confectus
broker interpres, *c* **(agent)**
bronze aes, *n*; **(*adj*),** aēnĕus,
aerĕus
brooch fĭbŭla, *f*
brood *v.i*. incŭbo (1)
brood (of young, etc.) fētus, *m*
brook rīvus, *m*
brook (no interference etc) pătĭor
(3 *dep*)

broom scōpae, *f.pl*
broth ius, *n*
brothel gănĕa, *f*
brother frāter, *m*
brotherhood sŏcĭĕtas, *f*
brow (forehead) frons, *f*; **(eyebrow),** sŭpercĭlĭum, *n*; **(of hill),**
căcūmen, *n*
brown fuscus
browse *v.t* **(read),** perlĕgo (3)
bruise *nn*, contūsum, *n*
bruise *v.t*, contundo (3)
brunt (bear the — of) *use* sustĭnĕo
(2) **(to bear)**
brush *nn*, pēnĭcŭlus, *m*
brush *v.t*, dētergĕo
brushwood sarmenta, *n.pl*
brutal fĕrus, ătrox
brutality immānĭtas, *f*
brutally *adv*, immānĭter
brute bestĭa, *f*, fĕra, *f*
bubble bulla, *f*
bubble *v.i*, bullo (1)
buccaneer pīrāta, *m*
buck (male stag) cervus, *m*
bucket sĭtŭla, *f*
buckle fĭbŭla, *f*
buckle *v.t*, fibŭlā necto (3)
(fasten with a buckle)
buckler (shield) scūtum, *n*
bud *nn*, gemma, *f*
bud *v.i*, gemmo (1), germĭno (1)
budge *v.i*, cēdo (3); *v.t*, mŏvĕo (2)
budget rătĭo, *f* **(reckoning,
account)**
buff lŭtĕus
buffet (blow) cŏlăphus, *m*
buffoon scurra, *m*
bug cīmex, *m*
bugbear terrĭcŭla, *n.pl*
bugle būcĭna, *f*
build *v.t*, aedĭfico (1)
builder aedĭfĭcātor, *m*
building (act of —) aedĭfĭcātĭo, *f*,
(structure itself), aedĭfĭcĭum, *n*
bulb bulbus, *m*
bulk magnĭtūdo, *f*, mōles, *f*
bulky ingens, grandis
bull taurus, *m*
bullet glans, *f*
bullion aurum, *n*
bullock iŭvencus, *m*
bulrush iuncus, *m*

bulwark mūnīmentum, *n*
bump *nn*, tūber, *n*, tŭmor, *m*
bump *v.i*, offendo (3)
bumpkin rustĭcus, *m*
bunch ūva, *f*, rācēmus, *m*
bundle fascis, *m*
bung (stopper) obtūrāmentum, *n*
bungle *v.i*, inscītē, ăgo (3) **(do unskilfully)**
bungler *adj*, impĕrītus
buoyancy lĕvĭtas, *f*
buoyant lĕvis
burden ŏnus, *n*
burden *v.t*, ŏnĕro (1)
burdensome grăvis
bureau scrīnĭum, *n*, armārĭum, *n*
burgess cīvis, *c*
burglar fūr, *m*
burglary furtum, *n*
burgle *v.t*, fūror (1 *dep.*) **(steal)**
burial fūnus, *n*, sĕpultūra, *f*
burial-place lŏcus, (*m*) sĕpultūrae
burly lăcertōsus
burn *v.t*, ūro (3), incendo (3); *v.i*, ardĕo (2), flagro (1)
burn *nn*, ambustum, *n*
burning *adj*, ardens
burnish *v.t*, pŏlĭo (4)
burrow cŭnĭcŭlum, *n*
burst *v.t*, rumpo (3); *v.i*, rumpor (3 *pass*)
burst out *v.i*, ērumpo (3)
bursting out *nn*, ēruptĭo (3)
bursting out *nn*, ēruptĭo, *f*
bury *v.t*, sĕpĕlĭo (4), abdo (3)
bush dūmus
bushel mĕdimnum, *n*
bushy frŭtĭcōsus
busily *adv*, sēdŭlō
business nĕgōtĭum, *n*, res, *f*
bust (statue) ĭmāgo, *f*
bustle *nn*, festīnātĭo, *f*
bustle *v.i*, festīno (1)
busy occŭpātus
but *conj*, sed, vērum, at (*first word in clause*) autem, vēro (*second word in clause*); **(except)**, praeter (*with acc*)
butcher lănĭus, *m*
butcher *v.t* **(murder)**, trŭcīdo (1)
butchery trŭcīdātĭo, *f*
butler prōmus, *m*
butt (laughing stock) lūdĭbrĭum, *n*

butt *v.t*, cornū fĕrĭo (4) **(strike with the horn)**
butter būtȳrum, *n*
butterfly pāpĭlĭo, *m*
buttock clūnis, *m*, *f*
buttress antēris, *f*
buxom vĕnustus
buy *v.t*, ĕmo (3)
buyer emptor, *m*
buying *nn*, emptĭo, *f*
by *prep* **(of place, near)**, ad, prŏpe (*with acc*); **(of time)** *often expressed by abl. of noun, e.g.* **by night**, nocte; **(— means of)**, per (*with acc*) **(by an agent,** *e.g.* **by a spear**, *abl. case alone*), hastā; **(—chance)**, *adv*, fortĕ
bygone *adj*, praetrĭtus
bystander spectātor, *m*
byway trāmes, *m*

C

cab raeda, *f*, cĭsĭum, *n*
cabal (faction) factĭo, *f*
cabbage brassĭca, *f*
cabin (hut) căsa, *f*
cabinet (furniture) armārĭum, *n*; **(council)** summum consĭlĭum, *n*
cable (anchor —) ancŏrāle, *n*
cackle, cackling *nn*, strĕpĭtus, *m*
cackle *v.i*, strĕpo (3)
cadaverous cădāvĕrōsus
cadence cursus, *m*
cadet discĭpŭlus, *m*, tīro, *m*
cage căvĕa, *f*
cajole *v.t*, blandĭtor (4 *dep. with dat*)
cajolery blandĭtĭae, *f.pl*
cake *nn*, plăcenta, *f*, lībum, *n*
calamitous exĭtĭōsus
calamity clādes, *f*, mălum, *n*
calculate *v.t*, compŭto (1), aestĭmo (1)
calculation rătĭo, *f*
calendar fasti, *m.pl*
calf vĭtŭlus, *m*; **(of the leg)**, sūra, *f*
call *v.t*, **(name)**, vŏco (1), appello (1); dīco (3); **(— back)**, rĕvŏco (1); **(— to, summon)**, advŏco (1); **(— together)**, convŏco (1); **(— up or out)**, suscĭto (1)

call *nn* (cry), clāmor, *m*; (visit) sălūtătĭo, *f*

caller sălūtător, *m*

calling *nn*, (vocation), ars, *f*, artĭfĭcĭum, *n*

calling *nn*, (vocation), ars, *f*, artĭfĭcĭum, *n*

callous callōsus

callow implūmis

calm *adj*, plăcĭdus, tranquilius

calm *nn*, tranquillĭtas, *f*, mălăcĭa

calm *v.t*, sēdo (1), plāco (1)

calmly *adv*, tranquille, plăcĭde

calumniate *v.t*, crĭmĭnor (1 *dep*)

calumnious crīmĭnōsus

calumny crīmĭnātĭo, *f*

camel cămēlus, *m*

camp castra, *n.pl*; (to pitch —), castra pōno (3); (to move —), castra mŏvĕo (2); (a winter ...), hīberna, *n.pl*

campaign stīpendĭum, *n*

campaign *v.i*, stīpendĭum mĕrĕor (2 *dep*)

can *nn*, urcĕus, *m*

can *v.i*, (to be able), possum (*irreg*)

canal fossa, *f*

cancel *v.t*, dēlĕo (2), abrŏgo (1)

cancer (sign of zodiac) cancer, *m*

candid ăpertus, līber

candidate candĭdātus, *m*

candle candēla, *f*

candlestick candēlābrum, *n*

candour lībertas, *f*

cane hărundo, *f*, băcŭlum, *n*, virga, *f*

cane *v.t*, verbĕro (1)

canister arca, *f*, pyxis, *f*

canker rōbīgo, *f*

canker *v.t*, corrumpo (3)

cannibal anthrōpŏphăgus, *m*

cannon tormentum, *n*

canoe scăpha, *f*

canon (rule) rēgŭla, *f*

canopy vēla, *n.pl*

cant ostentātĭo, *f*

canter *v.i*, lēnĭter curro (3) (run smoothly)

canton pāgus, *m*

canvas vēla, *n.pl*, carbăsus, *f*

canvass *v.i*, ambĭo (4)

canvass *nn*, ambĭtĭo, *f*; (illegal), ambĭtus

cap pillĕus, *m*

capability făcultas, *f*

capable căpax

capacious căpax

capacity căpācĭtas, *f*; (mental —), ingĕnĭum, *n*

cape prōmontŭrĭum, *n*

caper *v.i*, exsulo (1), salĭo (4)

capital *nn*, (city), căput, *n*

capital *adj*, (crime, etc.), căpĭtālis; (chief), princeps

capitulate *v.t*, dēdo (3); *v.i*, se dēdĕre (3 *reflex*)

caprice lĭbīdo, *f*

capricious lĕvis

captain dux, *m*, princeps, *m*; (of a ship), măgister, *m*, nauarchus, *m*

captivate *v.t*, căpĭo (3), dēlēnĭo (4)

captive *adj. and nn*, captīvus, *m*.

captivity captīvĭtas, *f*

capture *nn*, (of city, camp, etc.), expugnātĭo, *f*; (of persons), *use vb*, căpĭo (3) (to capture)

capture *v.t*, căpĭo (3)

car currus, *m*, plaustrum, *n*

caravan (convoy) commĕātus, *m*, (vehicle), raeda, *f*

carbuncle fūruncŭlus, *m*

carcass cădāver, *n*, corpus, *n*

card charta, *f*

cardinal *adj*, prīmus, princeps

care cūra, *f*, sollĭcĭtūdo, *f*

care *v.t* (to — about or for) cūro (1)

career currĭcŭlum, *n*

careful dīlĭgens; (carefully prepared) accūrātus; (cautious) cautus

carefully *adv*, dīlĭgenter

careless neglĕns, indīlĭgens

carelessly *adv*, neglegenter

carelessness neglēgentĭa, *f*

caress blandīmenta *n.pl*, complexus, *m*

caress *v.t*, blandĭor (4 *dep*.) (*with dat*.)

caressing *adj*, blandus

cargo ŏnus, *n*

caricature imāgo, *f*

caricature *v.t*, *use phr*. vultum dĕtorquĕo (2) (distort the

features)
carnage caedes, *f*, strāges, *f*
carnal corpŏrĕus
carnival fērĭae, *f.pl*
carnivorous carnĭvŏrus
carol cantus, *m*
carousal cōmissātĭo, *f*
carouse *v.i*, cōmissor (1 *dep.*)
carp at *v.t*, carpo (3), mordĕo (2)
carpenter făber, *m*
capet strāgŭlum, *n*
carriage (vehicle) raeda, *f*, carpentum, *n*; (transportation), vectūra, *f*; (poise), incessus, *m*
carrier vector, *m*
carrion căro, *f*, cădāver, *n*
carrot pastĭnāca, *f*
carry *v.t*, porto (1), fĕro (*irreg.*), vĕho (3), gĕro (3); (— away or off), aufĕro (*irreg.*); (— back) rēfĕro (*irreg.*); (— in) infĕro (*irreg.*); (— on) gĕro (3); (— over) transporto (1); (— out, perform) exsĕquor (3 *dep*); (— through a law, etc.) perfĕro (*irreg.*)
cart plaustrum, *n*
cart *v.t*, vĕho (3)
cart-horse iūmentum, *n*
cartilage cartĭlāgo, *f*
carve *v.t*, caelo (1), sĕco (1), sculpo (3)
carver sculptor, *m*
carving *nn*, caelātūre, *f*
case (in law) causa, *f* (circumstances), cāsus, *m* (cover), thēca, *f*
casement fĕnestra, *f*
cash nummus, *m*, pĕcūnĭa nŭmĕrāta, *f*
cashier *nn, use phr.* qui nummos dispensat (who dispenses the cash)
cashier *v.t*, (from the army), exauctoro (1)
cask cūpa, *f*
casket arcŭla, *f*
cast *nn*, (throw), iactus, *m*
cast *v.t*, iăcĭo (3), mitto (3); (— down) dēĭcĭo (3); (— off) dēpōno (3); (— out) expello (3)
castaway perdĭtus, *m*
caste ordo, *m*

castigate *v.t*, castīgo (1)
castle castellum, *n*
castor oil cĭcĭnum ŏlĕum, *n*
castrate *v.t*, catro (1)
casual fortŭĭtus
casually *adv*, neglĕgenter
casualty (accident) cāsus, *m*; (killed) *adj*, interfectus
cat fēles, *f*
catalogue index, *c*
catapault cătăpulta, *f*
cataract (waterfall) cătăracta, *f*
catarrh grăvēdo, *f*
catastrophe rŭīna, *f*
catch căpĭo (3), comprĕhendo (3); (a disease), contrăho (3)
categorical (absolute) simplex, plānus
category nŭmĕrus, *m*
cater *v.t*, obsōno (1)
caterpillar ērūca, *f*
catgut chorda, *f*
cattle pĕcus, *n*
cauldron cortīna, *f*
cause *nn*, causa, *f*
cause *v.t*, făcĭo (3), effĭcĭo (3)
causeway agger, *m*
caustic *adj*, mordax (biting)
caution cautĭo, *f*
caution *v.t*, mŏnĕo (2)
cautious cautus
cavalry ĕquĭtātus, *m*, ĕquĭtes, *m.pl*
cave spēlunca, *f*, căverna, *f*, antrum, *n*
caw *v.i*, crōcĭo (4)
cease *v.i*, dēsĭno (3) (*with infin*)
ceaseless perpĕtŭus
cedar cefrus, *f*
ceiling tectum, *n*
celebrate *v.t*, căno (3), cĕlĕbro (1)
celebrated clārus, illustris
celebration cĕlĕbrātĭo, *f*
celebrity fāma, *f*, glōrĭa, *f*; (person), vir praeclārus
celerity cĕlĕrĭtas, *f*
celestial caelstis
celibacy caelĭbātus, *m*
cell, cellar cella, *f*
cement ferrūmen, *n*
cement *v.t*, glūtĭno (1), ferrūmĭno (1)

cemetery sĕpulcrētum, *n*
censor censor, *m*
censure vĭtŭpĕrātĭo, *f*
censure *v.t*, vĭtŭpĕro (1)
 reprĕhendo (3)
census census, *m*
per cent *use nn*, centēsĭma, *f* (one
 hundredth part)
centaur centaurus, *m*
central mĕdĭus
centre (of) mĕdĭus, *in agreement
 with noun, e.g.* in the centre of
 the line, in mĕdĭā ăcĭe
centre on *v.i* (depend on), pendĕo
 (2) (*with* ab *and* abl)
centurion centŭrĭo, *m*
century saecŭlum, *n*
ceremonial rītus, *m*, caerĭmōnĭa, *f*
ceremonious sollemnis
certain certus, explōrātus;
 (a — person) *use pron*, quīdam
certainly *adv*, certo, certē,
 prŏfecto
certainty res certa; *or use adj*,
 certus (certain)
certificate scriptum testĭmōnĭum
 (written proof)
certify *v.i*, rĕcognosco (3),
 confirmo (1)
cessation intermissĭo, *f*
chafe *v.t*, fŏvĕo (2), călĕfăcĭo (3);
 v.i, stŏmăchor (1 *dep.*) (be
 irritated)
chaff pălĕa, *f*
chaffinch fringilla
chagrin stŏmăchus, *m*
chain cătēna, *f*, vincŭlum, *n*
chain *v.t*, cătēnas īnĭcĭo (3) (*with
 dat*)
chair sella, *f*
chairman măgister, *m*
chalk crēta, *f*
chalk out (mark out) *v.t*, dēsigno
 (1)
challenge *nn*, prōcŏcātĭo, *f*
challenge *v.t*, prōvŏco (1)
chamber conclāve, *n*; (bed —),
 cŭbĭcŭlum, *n*
chamberlain cŭbĭcŭlārĭus, *m*
chamois căprĕŏlus, *m*
champ *v.t*, mando (3)
champion victor *m*; (defender),
 prōpugnātor, *m*

chance *nn*, cāsus, *m*, fors, *f*,
 fortūna, *f*
by chance *adv*, (happen), forte,
 cāsu
chance *v.i*, accĭdo (3)
chandelier candēlābrum, *n*
change, changing *nn*, mūtātĭo, *f*,
 permūtātĭo, *f*
change *v.t*, mūto (1), converto
 (3); *v.i*, mūtor (1 *pass*)
changeable mūtābĭlis
channel cănālis, *m*, alvĕus, *m*
chant *v.i and v.t*, canto (1)
chaos pertubātĭo, *f*
chaotic perturbātus
chapel săcellum, *n*
chapter căpŭt, *n*
char *v.t*, ambūro (3)
character mōres, *m.pl*, ingĕnĭum
 n; (reputation), existĭmātĭo, *f*,
 ŏpīnĭo, *f*; (in a play), persōna, *f*
characteristic *adj*, prōprĭus
charcoal carbo, *m*
charge *nn*, (attack), impĕtus, *m*;
 (accusation), crīmen, *n*; (price),
 prētĭum, *n*; (care of), cūra, *f*
charge *v.t*, (attack), impĕtum
 făcĭo (3); signa inferō (*irreg*);
 (accuse), accūso (1); (of price),
 vendo (3) (sell) (3); (put in —),
 praefĭcĭo (3) (*with dat*); (be in —)
 praesum (*irreg.*) (*with dat*)
chariot currus, *m*, essĕdum, *n*
charioteer aurīga, *c*
charitable bĕnignus, mītis
charity ămor, *m*, bĕnĕfĭcentĭa, *f*
charm blandĭmentum, *n*, grātĭa, *f*
 (trinket), bulla, *f*
charm *v.t*, fascĭno (1), dēlēnĭo
 (4), dēlecto (1)
charming vĕnustus, lĕpĭdus
chart tăbŭla, *f*
charter *v.t*, (hire), condūco (3)
chase *nn*, (hunt), vēnātĭo, *f*,
 vēnātus, *m*
chase *v.t*, sector (1 *dep.*), vēnor (1
 dep.)
chasm hĭātus, *m*
chaste castus
chastise *v.t*, castīgo (1), pūnĭo
 (4)
chastisement castīgātĭo, *f*
chastity castĭtas, *f*

chat   *v.i,* făbŭlor (1 *dep.*)
chat   *nn,* sermo, *m*
chatter   *v.i,* garrĭo (4); **(of teeth),**
    crĕpĭto (1)
chatter   *nn,* garrŭlĭtas, *f*
chattering   *adj,* garrŭlus
cheap   vīlis
cheapness   vīlĭtas, *f*
cheat   *nn,* **(person),** fraudātor, *m*
cheat   *v.t,* fraudo (1)
cheating   *nn,* fraudātĭo, *f*
check   *nn,* **(hindrance),**
    impedīmentum, *n,* incommŏdum,
    n; **(set back),** incommŏdum, *n*
check *v.t,* cŏhĭbĕo (2), contĭnĕo
    (2), comprĭmo (3), cŏercĕo (2)
cheek   gĕna, *f*
cheer   *nn,* **(shout),** clāmor, *m*
cheer   *v.i,* **(applaud),** plaudo (3),
    clāmo (1)
cheerful   hĭlăris
cheerfulness   hĭlărĭtas, *f*
cheerless   tristis
cheese   cāsĕus, *m*
cheque   perscriptĭo, *f,* **(written**
    entry)
chequered   vărĭus
cherish   *v.t,* fŏvĕo (2), cŏlo (3)
cherry, cherry tree   cĕrăsus, *f*
chess   latruncŭli, *m.pl*
chest (box)   amārĭum, *n,* cista, *f*;
    (body), pectus, *n,* thorax, *m*
chestnut   glands, *f*; **(— tree),**
    castănĕa, *f*
chew   mando (3)
chicken   pullus, *m*
chide   *v.t,* obiurgo (1), incrĕpĭto
    (1), rĕprĕhendo (3)
chiding   rĕprĕhensĭo, *f*
chief   *nn,* princeps, *m,* prōcer, *m*
chief   *adj,* prīmus, princeps
chieftain   see **chief**
child   pŭer, *m,* infans, *c*; **(pl.)**
    lībĕri, *m.pl*
childbirth   partus, *m*
childhood   pŭĕrĭtĭa, *f*
childish   pŭĕrīlis
childless   orbus
chill, chilly   *adj,* frīgĭdus
chill   *v.t,* rĕfrīgĕro (1)
chime   *nn,* concentus, *m*
chime   *v.i,* **(sound),** căno (3)
chimney   cămīnus, *m*

chin   mentum, *n*
chine   tergum, *n*
chink   rīma, *f*
chip   assŭla, *f*
chirp, chirping   *nn,* pīpātus, *m*
chirp   *v.i,* pīpĭo (4)
chisel   scalprum, *n*
chisel   *v.t,* sculpo (3)
chivalrous   magnănĭmus
chivalry   magnănĭmĭtas, *f*
choice   *nn,* dēlectus, *m*;
    (— between), optĭo, *f*
choice   *adj,* ēlectus
choir   chŏrus, *m*
choke   *v.t,* suffōco (1); *v.i,*
    suffōcor (1 *pass*)
choose   *v.t,* lĕgo (3), ēlĭgo (3)
chop   *v.t,* caedo (3); **(cut off),**
    abscīdo (3)
chord   *use* nervus, *m,* **(string)**
chorus   chŏrus, *m*
Christ   Christus, *m*
Christian   Christĭānus
chronic (long-lasting)   dĭūturnus
chronicle   annāles, *m.pl*
chuckle   *v.i,* căchinno (1)
church   templum, *n*
churchyard   ārĕa, *f*
churl   hŏmo rustĭcus
churlish   rustĭcus
churn   *v.t,* **(stir),** ăgĭto (1)
cinder   cĭnis, *m,* făvilla, *f*
cipher (a nonentity)   nŭmĕrus, *m*;
    (secret writing), nŏta, *f*
circle   orbis, *m*
circuit   circŭĭtus, *m*
circuitous   **(route, etc.),** flexŭōsus
circular   rŏtundus
circulate   *v.t,* spargo (3), dīvulgo
    (1); *v.i,* diffundor (3 *pass*),
    percrēbresco (3)
circulation,   **(to be in —) (of books**
    etc.) in mănibus esse (*irreg*)
circumcise   *v.t,* circumcīdo (3)
circumference   ambĭtus, *m*
circumscribe   *v.t,* circumscrībo (3)
circumstance   res, *f*; *or use neuter*
    of an adj, e.g. adversa **(adverse**
    circumstances)
circumstantial evidence
    coniectūra, *f*
circumvent   *v.t,* circumvĕnĭo (4)
circus   circus, *m*

cistern cisterna, *f*

citadel arx, *f*

cite *v.t*, (quote), prōfĕro (*irreg*)

citizen cīvis, *c*

citizenship cīvĭtas, *f*

city urbs, *f*

civic cīvīlis

civil (polite) urbānus; **(civic)** cīvīlis; **(— war)**, bellum dŏmestĭcum

civilian (opp. military) tŏgātus, *m*

civilization cultus, *m*, hūmānĭtas, *f*

civilize *v.t*, excŏlo (3), expŏlĭo (4)

civilized hūmānus, cultus

claim *v.t*, postŭlo (1), rĕposco (3)

claim *nn*, postŭlātĭo, *f*

claimant pĕtītor, *m*

clammy lentus

clamorous clāmans

clamour *nn*, clāmor, *m*, strĕpĭtus, *m*

clamour *v.i*, vōcĭfĕror (1 *dep*)

clandestine clandestīnus

clang *nn*, clangor, *m*

clang *v.i. and v.t*, strĕpo (3)

clank crĕpĭtus, *m*

clank *v.i*, crĕpo (1)

clap *nn*, **(hands)**, plausus, *m*; **(thunder)**, frăgor, *m*

clap *v.i. and v.t*, plaudo (3)

clash *v.i*, concrĕpo (1), crĕpĭto (1); **(opinions)** rĕpugno (1); **(fight)**, conflīgo (3)

clash *nn*, **(noise)**, crĕpĭtus, *m*; **(collision)**, concursus, *m*

clasp *nn*, **(embrace)**, complexus, *m*; **(fastener)**, fibŭla, *f*

clasp *v.t*, **(fasten)**, fibŭlo (1); **(embrace)**, complector (3 *dep*.)

class classis, *f*, gĕnus, *n*

classic, classical (well-established), prŏbus

classify *v.t*, dēscrībo (3) ordĭne

clatter *nn*, strĕpĭtus, *m*

clatter *v.i*, incrĕpo (1)

clause membrum, *n*, căpŭt, *n*

claw unguis, *m*

clay argilla, *f*, lŭtum, *n*

clean *adj*, mundus, pūrus

clean *v.t*, purgo (1), mundo (1)

cleanliness mundĭtĭa, *f*

cleanse *v.t*, purgo (1)

clear clārus; **(weather)**, sĕrēnus; **(matter)**, mănĭfestus

clear *v.t*, **(open up)**, expĕdĭo (4); **(— oneself)**, sē purgāre (1 *reflex*); *v.i*, **(of the weather)**, dissĕrēnat (1 *impers*)

clearing *nn*, **(open space)**, lŏcus ăpertus

clearly *adv*, clārē, ăpertĕ, plānē

clearness clārĭtas, *f*

cleave *v.t*, **(split)**, findo (3); *v.i* **(stick to)**, adhaerĕo (2)

cleft hĭātus, *m*, rīma, *f*

clemency clēmentĭa, *f*

clement clēmens, lēntis

clench (the fist) *v.t*, comprĭmo (3)

clerk scrība, *m*

clever callĭdus, astūtus

cleverness *f*, callĭdĭtas, *f*

client clĭens, *m*, consultor, *m*

cliff cautes, *f*, scŏpŭlus, *m*, rūpes

climate caelum, *n*

climax grădātĭo, *f*

climb *v.i. and v.t*, ascendo (3), scando (3)

climb *nn*, ascensus, *m*

cling to *v.i*, ădhaerĕo (2) (*with dat*)

clip *v.t*, tondĕo (2)

cloak pallĭum, *n*, lăcerna, *f*

cloak *v.t*, **(hide)**, dissĭmŭlo (1)

clock hŏrŏlŏgĭum, *n*

clod glaeba, *f*

clog (hindrance) impĕdīmentum, *n*; **(shoe)**, sculpōnĕa, *f*

clog *v.t*, **(impede)**, impĕdĭo (4)

close *adj*, **(near)**, vīcīnus; **(packed together)** confertus, densus; **(at close quarters)**, commĭnus, *adv*

close *nn*, **(end)**, fīnis, *m*, termĭnus, *m*

close *adv*, prŏpe, iuxta

close *v.t*, claudo (3); *v.i*, claudor (3 *pass*)

close in on *v.t*, prĕmo (3) **(press)**

closely *adv*, prŏpe; **(accurately)**, exacte

closeness prŏpinquĭtas, *f*

closet cella, *f*

clot (of blood) crŭor, *m*

cloth textum, *n*

clothe *v.t*, vestĭo (4), indŭo (3)

clothes vestis, *f*, vestīmenta, *n.pl*

cloud nūbes, *f*

cloudy nūbĭlus

cloven bĭsulcus
clown scurra, *m*
club (cudgel) clāva, *f*;
  (association), sŏdālĭtas, *f*
cluck *v.i*, singultĭo (4)
clump massa, *f*
clumsy ĭnhăbĭlis, rustĭcus
cluster *nn*, răcēmus, *m*; (people),
  glŏbus, *m*
clutch *v.t*, arrĭpĭo (3)
coach carpentum, *n*, raeda, *f*
coachman raedārĭus, *m*
coagulate *v.i*, concresco (3)
coal carbo, *m*
coalition coniunctĭo, *f*,
  conspīrātĭo, *f*
coarse crassus; (manners),
  incultus
coarseness crassĭtūdo, *f*,
  ĭnhūmānĭtas, *f*
coast ōra, *f*, lītus, *n*
coast *v.i*, praetervĕhor (3 *pass*)
coat tŭnīca, *f*, ămictus, *m*;
  (animal's), pellis, *f*
coat *v.t*, illĭno (3)
coax *v.t*, mulcĕo (2), blandĭor (4
  dep)
cobble *v.t*, sarcĭo (4)
cobbler sūtor, *m*
cock gallus, *m*
code (method, system) rătĭo, *f*
coerce *v.t*, cōgo (3), cŏercĕo (2)
coercion cŏercĭtĭo, *f*
coffin arca, *f*
cog dens, *m*
cogent vălĭdus
cogitate *v.i*, cōgĭto (1)
cognizance cognĭtĭo, *f*
cohabit *v.i*, consŭesco (3)
cohere *v.i*, cŏhaerĕo (2)
coherent cŏhaerens
cohesion cŏhaerentĭa, *f*
cohort cŏhors, *f*
coil *nn*, spīra, *f*
coil *v.t*, glŏmĕro (1)
coin *nn*, nummus, *m*
coin *v.t*, cūdo (3)
coinage nummi, *m.pl*
coincide *v.i*, compĕto (3), concurro
  (3)
coincidence consursātĭo, *f*,
  concursus, *m*
cold *adj*, frīgĭdus, gĕlĭdus

cold (to be —) *v.i*, algĕo (2)
coldness frīgus, *n*
collapse *v.i*, collābor (3 *dep*)
collar torques, *m and f*
collation (comparison) collātĭo, *f*
colleague collēga, *m*
collect *v.t*, collĭgo (3), cōgo (3)
collection (act of —) collātĭo, *f*;
  (heap, etc.), congĕrĭes, *f*
collector (of taxes, etc.) exactor, *m*
college collēgĭum, *n*
collide *v.i*, conflīgo (3), concurro
  (3)
collision concursus, *m*
colloquial (speech) *use* sermo, *m*
collusion collūsĭo, *f*
colon cōlon, *n*
colonel praefectus, *m*
colonist cŏlōnus, *m*
colony cŏlōnĭa, *f*
colonnade portĭcus, *f*
collossal ĭgens
colour cŏlor, *m*; (flag), vexillum,
  n; (— bearer), signĭfer, *m*
colour *v.t*, cŏlōro (1)
coloured pictus
colourful fūcātus
colt equŭlĕus, *m*
column (pillar) columna, *f*;
  (military), agmen, *n*
comb *nn*, pecten, *m*
comb *v.t*, pecto (3)
combat *nn*, proelĭum, *n*
combat *v.i*, pugno (1), luctor (1
  dep)
combat *v.t*, (oppose) obsto (1)
combatant pugnātor, *m*
combination coniunctĭo, *f*
combine *v.t*, coinungo (3)
come *v.i*, vĕnĭo (4); (— about,
  happen), ēvĕnĭo (4); (— across,
  find), *v.t*, invĕnĭo (4); (— back),
  v.i, rĕvĕnĭo (4); (— by, obtain), *v.t*,
  ădĭpiscor (3 *dep*); (— in) incēdo
  (3); (— near) apprŏpinquo (1);
  (— on, advance), prōgrĕdĭor (3
  dep); (— out) exĕo (4); (— to)
  advĕnĭo (4) (regain
  consciousness) ad se rĕdire (4);
  (— together) convĕnĭo (4);
  (—upon), *v.t*, sŭpervĕnĭo (4)
  (attack) incĭdo (3)
comedian cōmoedus, *m*

comedy cōmoedĭa, f
comely pulcher
comet cŏmētes, m
comfort sōlācĭum, n, consōlātĭo, f
comfort v.t, consōlor (1 dep.)
comfortable commŏdus
comforter consōlātor, m
comic, comical cōmĭcus
coming adj, ventūrus
coming nn, adventus, m
command nn, (power), impĕrĭum, n; (an order) iussum, n, mandātus, m; (to be in —) v.i, praesum (with dat)
command v.t. impĕro (1) (with dat.), iŭbĕo (2)
commander dux, m, impĕrātor, m
commemorate v.t, cĕlĕbro (1)
commemoration cĕlĕbrātĭo, f
commence v.i, incĭpĭo (3)
commencement ĭnĭtĭum, n
commend v.t, commendo (1); (praise), laudo (1)
commendable laudābĭlis
comment v.i, dīco (3), sententĭas dīco (3) (declare one's opinion)
comment nn, dicta, n.pl
commentary commentārĭi, m.pl
commerce commercĭum, n
commercial traveller instĭtor, m
commiserate v.i. and v.t, mĭsĕror (1 dep.)
commisariat praefecti (m.pl) rĕi frūmentārĭae (superintendents of corn supply); (provisions), commĕātus, m
commissary prōcūrātor, m, lēgātus, m
commission (task) mandātum, n
commission v.t, (give a task to), mando (1) (dat. of person)
commit v.t, (crime, etc.) admitto (3); (entrust), committo (3), mando (1)
committee dēlecti, m.pl, (selected ones)
commodious (opportune) commŏdus; (capacious), amplus
commodity (thing) res, f
common adj, commūnis; (belonging to the public), pūblĭcus; (ordinary), vulgāris; (common land), ăger pūblĭcus, m (usual), ūsĭtātus
commonplace adj, vulgāris, trītus
commonly adv, (mostly), plērumque
commonwealth respublĭca, f
commotion mōtus, m, tŭmultus, m, commōtĭo, f
communicate v.t, commūnĭco (1); (report), dēfĕro (irreg)
communication commūnĭcātĭo, f; (reporting), nuntĭus, m
communicative lībĕr, lŏquax
communion sŏcĭĕtas, f
community cīvĭtas, f, sŏcĭĕtas, f
commute v.t, mūto (1)
compact adj, confertus, pressus
compact nn, pactum, n, foedus, n
companion sŏcĭus, m, cŏmes, c
companionable făcĭlis
companionship sŏdālĭtas, f
company coetus, m, sŏcĭĕtas, f (military body), mănĭpŭlus, m
comparable confĕrendus
comparative compărātīvus
compare v.t, compăro (1), confĕro (irreg)
comparison compărātĭo, f
compartment lŏcŭlus, m
compass (range) fīnes, m.pl; (pair of compasses), circĭnus, m
compass v.t, complector (3 dep)
compassion mĭsĕrĭcordĭa, f
compassionate mĭsĕrĭcors
compatability congrŭentĭa, f
compatible congrŭens
compatriot cīvis, c
compel v.t, cōgo (3), compello (3)
compensate for v.t, compenso (1)
compensation compensātĭo, f
compete v.i, certo (1) (struggle)
competent căpax; (to be — to), v.i, sufficĭo (3)
competition certāmen, n
competitor compĕtītor, m
complacent sĭbi plăcens (pleasing to oneself)
complain v.i, gĕmo (3); v.t, quĕror (3 dep.)
complaint questus, m, quĕrēla, f; (disease), morbus, m
complement complēmentum, n

complete plēnus, perfectus
complete v.t, complĕo (2), confĭcĭo (3)
completely adv, omnīno
completion perfectĭo, f, confectĭo, f
complex multĭplex
complexion cŏlor, m
compliance obsĕquĭum, n
compliant obsĕquens
complicated invŏlūtus
complication implĭcātĭo, f
compliment nn, (esteem), hŏnor, m; (praise) laus, f; (greeting), sălūtātĭo, f
compliment v.t, (praise), laudo (1)
complimentary hŏnōrĭfĭcus
comply with v.i, concēdo (3) (with dat)
component nn, (part), ĕlĕmentum, n
compose v.t, compōno (3)
composed (calm) sēdātus
composer scriptor, m
composition (act of —) compŏsĭtĭo, f; (a literary —), ŏpus scriptum, n
composure tranquillĭtas, f
compound adj, compŏsĭtus
compound v.t, compōno (3), miscĕo (2)
comprehend v.t, (understand) intellĕgo (3)
comprehension comprĕhensĭo, f
comprehensive use phr, ad omnĭa pertĭnens (extending to everything)
compress v.t, comprĭmo (3)
comprise v.t, contĭnĕo (2)
compromise nn, (agreement), compŏsĭtĭo, f
compromise v.t, compōno (3); (implicate), implĭco (1)
compulsion nĕcessĭtas, f
compunction paenĭtentĭa, f
compute v.t, compŭto (1)
comrade sŏcĭus, m, cŏmes, c
concave căvus
conceal v.t, cēlo (1), abdo (3)
concede v.t, cēdo (3)
conceit arrŏgantĭa, f
conceited arrŏgans
conceive v.t, concĭpĭo (3)

concentrate (mentally) v.i, ălĭmum intendo (3); (bring together), v.t, contrăho (3), cōgo (3)
conception (mental) nōtĭo, f; (physical), conceptĭo, f
concern nn, (affair, circumstance), rēs, f; (worry), sollĭcĭtūdo, f
concern v.t, pertĭnĕo (2); (it concerns), rēfert (irreg. impers)
concerned (to be —) v.i, sollĭcĭtus esse
concerning prep, dē (with abl. of nn. etc)
concern v.t, (plans, etc.), confĕro (irreg), compōno (3)
concession concessĭo, f
conciliate v.t, concĭlĭo (1)
conciliation concĭlĭātĭo, f
conciliatory pācĭfĭcus
concise brĕvis
conciseness brĕvĭtas, f
conclude v.t, (decide), stătŭo (3); (end), perfĭcĭo (3)
conclusion (end) exĭtus, m, fīnis, m (decision), decrētum, n
conclusive certus
concord concordĭa, f
concourse concursus, m
concubine pellex, f
concupiscence lĭbīdo, f
concur v.i, consentĭo (4)
concurrence consensus, m
concurrent use adv, sĭmŭl (at the same time)
concurrently adv, sĭmŭl
condemn v.t, damno (1) (with acc of person and genit. of crime or punishment)
condemnation damnātĭo, f
condense v.t, denso (1), comprĭmo (3)
condensed densus
condescend v.i, dēscendo (3)
condescension cōmĭtas, f, (friendliness)
condition condĭcĭo, f, stătus, m
condole v.i, dŏlĕo (2) cum (with abl)
condone v.t, condōno (1)
conduce v.t, condūco (3)
conductive ūtĭlis (advantageous)

conduct *nn*, (personal, etc.),
mōres, *m.pl*; (administration),
admĭnistrātĭo, *f*
conduct *v.t*, (lead), dūco (3);
(administer), admĭnistro (1);
(— oneself), sē gĕrĕre (3 *reflex*)
conductor dux, *m*
conduit cănālis, *m*
cone cōnus, *m*
confectionery crustum, *n*
confederacy sŏcĭĕtas, *f*
confederate foedĕrātus
confer *v.t*, confĕro (*irreg*);
(—with), collŏquor (3 *dep*);
(—about), ăgo (3) dē
conference collŏquĭum, *n*
confess *v.t*, confĭtĕor (2 *dep*)
confession confessĭo, *f*
confide *v.t*, confīdo (3), fīdo (3),
(*with dat*.)
confidence fīdes, *f*, fĭdūcĭa, *f*
confident fīdens
confidential (trusty) fīdus; (one's
own, special), prŏprĭus; (secret),
arcānus
confine *v.t*, inclūdo (3), contĭnĕo
(2)
confinement inclūsĭo, *f*, custōdĭa,
f; (childbirth), partus, *m*;
pŭerpĕrĭum, *n*
confirm *v.t*, confirmo (1)
confiscate *v.t*, pūblĭco (1), ădĭmo
(3)
confiscation pūblĭcātĭo, *f*
conflagration incendĭum, *n*
conflict *nn*, certāmen, *n*
conflict *v.i*, certo (1); dissentĭo (4)
confluence conflŭens, *m*
conform to *v.i*, obtempĕro (1)
(*with dat*); *v.t*, accommŏdo (1)
conformity convĕnĭentĭa, *f*
confound *v.t*, (disturb), turbo (1);
(amaze), obstŭpĕfăcĭo (3); (bring
to nothing, thwart), frustor (1
dep.)
confront *v.i*, obvĭam ĕo (*irreg*.)
(*with dat*)
confuse *v.t*, turbo (1)
confused perturbātus
confusion perturbātĭo, *f*
congeal *v.i. and v.t*, congĕlo (1)
congenial concors
congested frĕquens

congratulate *v.t*, grātŭlor (1 *dep*)
congratulation grātŭlātĭo, *f*
congregate *v.i*, sē congrĕgare (1
reflex)
congress concĭlĭum, *n*,
conventus, *m*
congruous congrŭens
conjecture *nn*, conĭectūra, *f*
conjecture *v.i*, cōnĭcĭo (3)
conjugate *v.t*, dēclīno (1)
conjunction (grammar)
conĭunctĭo, *f*
conjure *v.i*, (perform tricks),
praestigĭīs ūtor (3 *dep*.); (image)
cōgĭto (1)
conjurer măgus, *m*
connect *v.t*, conĭungo (3)
connected conĭunctus
connection conĭunctĭo, *f*; (by
marriage), affīnĭtas, *f*
connive at *v.i*, connīvĕo (2) in
(*with abl*)
connoisseur *use vb*, stŭdĕo (2) (to
be keen on)
conquer *v.t*, vinco (3), sŭpĕro (1)
conqueror victor, *m*
conquest victōrĭa, *f*
conscience conscĭentĭa, *f*
conscientious rēlĭgĭōsus
conscientiousness fīdes, *f*
conscious conscĭus
consciously *adv, use adj*, scĭens
(knowingly)
consciousness conscĭentĭa, *f*,
sensus, *m*
conscript (recruit) tīro, *m*
consecrate *v.t*, conscĕro (1)
consecrated săcer
consecutive contĭnŭus
consent *nn*, consensus, *m*; (by
the — of), consensu;
consent to *v.i*, assentĭo (4)
consequence (result) exĭtus, *m*;
(importance), mōmentum, *n*; (in
— of), *prep*, propter (*with acc*)
consequent sĕquens
consequently *adv*, ĭgĭtur, ĭtăque
conserve *v.t*, conservo (1)
consider *v.t*, cōgĭto (1), dēlībĕro
(1), existĭmo (1); (—with
respect), respĭcĭo (3)
considerable ălĭquantus
considerate hūmānus

considerateness hūmānĭtas, *f*
consideration consīdĕrātĭo, *f*;
(regard), rătĭo, *f*
considering *conj*, ut
consign *v.t*, mando (1), committo (3)
consignment (of goods) merces, *f.pl*
consist of *v.i*, consisto (3) in (*with abl*)
consistency constantĭa, *f*
consistent (constant) constans; (consistent with), consentānĕus
console *v.t*, consōlor (1 *dep*.)
consolidate *v.t*, firmo (1), sŏlĭdo (1)
consonant consŏnans littĕra
consort (husband) mărītus, *m*; (wife), mărīta, *f*
consort with *v.i*, ūtor (3 *dep*) (*with abl*)
conspicuous mănĭfestus, insignis
conspiracy coniūrātĭo, *f*
conspirator coniūrātus, *m*
conspire *v.i*, coniūro (1)
constable dĕcŭrĭo, *m*, lictor, *m*
constancy fĭdes, *f*; (steadiness), constantĭa, *f*, fĭdēlĭtas, *f*
constant fĭdēlis, constans
constellation sīdus, *n*
consternation păvor, *m*
constituent parts ĕlĕmenta, *n.pl*
constitute *v.t*, constĭtŭo (3), compōno (3), crĕo (1)
constitution (of a state) respūblĭca, *f*; (of a body), hăbĭtus, *m*
constitutional lēgĭtĭmus
constrain *v.t*, cōgo (3), compello (3)
construct *v.t*, făbrĭcor (1 *dep*) exstrŭo (3)
construction *v.t*, făbrĭcor (1 *dep*) exstrŭo (3)
construction (act of —) făbrĭcātĭo, *f*; (method) fĭgūra, *f*, structūra, *f*
construe *v.t*, interprĕtor (1 *dep*)
consul consul, *m*
consulship consŭlātus, *m*
consult *v.t*, consŭlo (3); *v.i*, dēlībĕro (1); (— someone's interests), consŭlo (3) (*with dat*)
consultation collŏquĭum, *n*

consume *v.t*, consumo (3), confĭcĭo (3)
consummate *v.t*, consummo (1), perfĭcĭo (3)
consummate *adj* summus
consummation connsummātĭo, *f*
consumption consumptĭo, *f*
contact tactus, *m*
contagion contāgĭo, *f*
contain *v.t*, contĭnĕo (2)
contaminate *v.t*, contāmĭno (1)
contamination contāgĭo, *f*, măcŭla, *f*
contemplate *v.t*, contemplor (1 *dep*)
contemplation (study) mĕdĭtātĭo, *f*
contemporary aequālis
contempt contemptus, *m*
contemptible contemnendus
contend *v.i*. contendo (3), certo (1), pugno (1); (argue), *v.t*, affirmo (1)
content contentus
content *v.t*, sătisfăcĭo (3) (*with dat*.); *v.i*, (be content) sătis hăbĕo (2)
contentment aequus ănĭmus, *m*
contest *nn*, certāmen, *n*, pugna, *f*
contest *v.t*, certo (1), contendo (3)
contestant pugnātor, *m*, pĕtītor, *m*
contiguous contĭgŭus, confīnis
continent *adj*, contĭnens
continent *nn*, contĭnens, *f*
contingency cāsus, *m*
continual perpĕtŭus, contĭnens
continually *adv*, perpĕtŭo, contĭnenter
continuation perpĕtŭĭtas, *f*
continue *v.t*, prōdūco (3), prōrŏgo (1), *v.i*, mănĕo (2)
continuity perpĕtŭĭtas, *f*
continuous contĭnens
contort *v.t*, torquĕo (2)
contour fĭgūra, *f*
contraband *adj*, vĕtĭtus
contract *nn*, pactum, *n*
contract *v.i*, (grow smaller), sē contrăhĕre (3 *reflex*); *v.t*, contrăho (3)
contraction contractĭo, *f*
contractor conductor, *m*

contradict *v.t,* contrādīco (3)
(*with dat*)
contradiction contrādictĭo, *f*;
(**inconsistency**), rĕpugnantĭa, *f*
contradictory rĕpugnans
contrary *adj,* adversus,
contrārĭus; (**— to**), *prep,* contrā
(*with acc*); **the contrary,** *nn,*
contrārĭum, *n*; (**on the —**), *adv,*
contrā
contrast *v.t,* confĕro (*irreg*); *v.i,*
discrĕpo (1)
contravene *v.t,* vĭŏlo (1)
contribute *v.t,* confĕro (*irreg*)
contribution collātĭo, *f,* trĭbūtum,
n
contrivance (**gadget**) māchĭna, *f*
contrive *v.t,* (**think out**), excōgĭto
(1)
control *v.t,* mŏdĕror (1 *dep*)
(*with dat*); (**guide**), rĕgo (3)
control *nn,* pŏtestas, *f,*
tempĕrantĭa, *f*
controversy contrōversĭa, *f*
contumacious pertĭnax
contumacy pertĭnācĭa, *f*
contumely contŭmēlĭa, *f*
convalescent convălescens
convenience commŏdĭtas, *f,*
opportūnĭtas, *f*
convenient commŏdus,
opportūnus
convention (**meeting**) conventus,
m; (**agreement**), conventĭo, *f*
converge *v.i,* ēōdem vergo (3)
conversation sermo, *m,*
collŏquĭum, *n*
converse *v.i,* collŏquor (3 *dep*)
conversion commūtātĭo, *f*
convert *v.t,* mūto (1), converto
(3)
convex convexus
convey *v.t,* vĕho (3), porto (1)
conveyance (**act of —**) vectūra, *f*;
(**vehicle**), vĕhĭcŭlum, *n*
convict *v.t,* damno (1)
conviction (**belief**) *use phr,*
persuāsum est (*with dat. of*
person) e.g. persuāsum est mĭhi
(**it is my conviction**); (**convicting**),
damnātĭo, *f*
convince *v.t,* persuādĕo (2) (*with*
dat.)

conviviality hĭlărĭtas, *f*
convoke *v.t,* convŏco (1)
convoy *nn,* commĕātus, *m*;
(**escort**), praesĭdĭum, *n*
convulse *v.t,* concŭtĭo (3), ăgĭto
(1)
convulsion tŭmultus, *m,* mōtus,
m; (**medical**), convulsĭo, *f*
cook *nn,* cŏquus, *m*
cook *v.t,* cŏquo (3)
cool frĭgĭdus; (**of mind**), lentus
cool *v.t,* rĕfrīgĕro (1); *v.i,*
rĕfrīgĕror (1 *pass*)
cooly *adv,* frĭgĭde, lentē
coolness frīgus, *n*
co-operate with *v.t,* adiŭvo (1)
co-operation auxĭlĭum, *n,* (**help**)
cope with *v.i.* congrĕdĭor (3 *dep.*)
copious largus, cōpĭōsus
copper aes, *n*
copper *adj,* aēnĕus
coppice dūmētum, *n*
copy exemplum, *n*
copy *v.t,* ĭmĭtor (1 *dep*), dēscrībo
(3)
coral cŏrălĭum, *n*
cord fūnis, *m*
cordial *adj,* bĕnignus
cordiality bĕnignĭtas, *f*
cordon cŏrōna, *f*
core nuclĕus, *m*
cork *nn,* cortex, *m, f*
corn frūmentum, *n*; (**crop**), sĕges,
f; (**on the foot**), clāvus, *m*
corner angŭlus, *m*
cornice cŏrōna, *f*
coronation *use* crĕo (1) (**elect to**
office)
coroner quaesītor, *m*
corporal *adj,* corpŏrĕus
corporal *nn,* dĕcŭrĭo, *m*
corps (**company**) mănus, *f*
corpse cădāver, *n,* corpus, *n*
corpulence ŏbēsĭtas, *f*
corpulent ŏbēsus
correct rectus, pūrus
correct *v.t,* corrĭgo (3), ēmendo
(1)
correction ēmendātĭo, *f*;
(**chastisement**), castĭgātĭo, *f*
correctly *adv,* rectē
correctness vērĭtas, *f*
correspond *v.i,* (**agree with**),

convĕnĭo (4) (*with dat*); **(write)**,
littĕras mitto (3) et accĭpĭo (3)
(send and receive letters)
correspondence missĭo et
acceptĭo ĕpistŏlārum **(sending
and receiving of letters)**
corresponding par, gĕmellus
corroborate *v.t*, confirmo (1)
corrode *v.t*, rōdo (3), ĕdo (3)
corrosive mordax
corrupt *v.t*, corrumpo (3)
corrupt *adj*, corruptus
corruption dēprāvātĭo, *f*
corselet lōrīca, *f*
cost *nn*, prĕtĭum, *n*, sumptus, *m*
cost *v.i*, sto (1) (*with dat. of
person and abl. or genit. of price*)
e.g. **the victory cost the
Carthaginians much bloodshed:**
victōrĭa stĕtit Poenis multo
sanguĭne
costly *adj*, prĕtĭōsus
costume hăbĭtus, *m*
cot lectŭlus, *m*
cottage căsa, *f*
cotton gossypĭum, *n*
couch lectus, *m*
couch *v.i*, subsīdo (3); *v.t*, **(—a
weapon)**, intendo (3)
cough *nn*, tussis, *f*
cough *v.i*, tussĭo (4)
council concĭlĭum, *n*
counsel (advioc) consĭlĭum, *n*;
(lawyer), pătrōnus, *m*
count *v.t*, nŭmĕro (1); **(— upon,
trust)**, confīdo (3) (*with dat*)
countenance *nn*, vultus, *m*
countenance *v.t*, permitto (3),
făvĕo (2), indulgĕo (2)
counter (in shop) mensa, *f*; **(for
counting)** calcŭlus, *m*
counter *adv*, contra
counteract *v.t*, obsisto (3) (*with
dat.*)
counterbalance *v.t*, exaequo (1)
counterfeit *adj*, ădultĕrīnus, fictus
counterfeit *v.t*, sĭmŭlo (1), fingo
(3)
counterpart res gĕmella **(paired,
twin thing)**
countless innŭmĕrābĭlis
country (fatherland) pătrĭă, *f*;
(countryside), rūs, *n*; **(region)**,

rĕgĭo, *f*
country house villa, *f*
countryman (of the same country)
cīvis, *c*; **(living in the countryside)**,
rustĭcus, *m*
couple *nn*, **(pair)**, pār *n*
couple *v.t*, coniungo (3)
courage virtus, *f*, ănĭmus, *m*
courageous fortis, ācer, fĕrox
courier (messenger) nuntĭus, *m*
course (motion) cursus, *m*;
(route), vĭa, *f*, ĭter *n*; **(plan)**, rătĭo,
f; **(race —)**, circus, *m*; **(of —)**, *adv*,
nīmīrum, certē
court (— of justice) iūdĭcĭum, *n*;
(judges themselves), iūdĭces,
m.pl; **(palace)**, aula, *f*, dŏmus, (*f*)
rēgis **(the house of the king)**;
(courtyard), ārĕa, *f*
court *v.t*, cŏlo (3)
court martial *use phr*. in castris
iudĭcare (1) **(to try in camp)**
courteous cōmis, hūmānus
courtesy cōmĭtas, *f*, hūmānĭtas, *f*
courtier aulĭcus, *m*
courtship ămor, *m*
cousin consōrbrīnus, *m* (...a), *f*
covenant pactum, *n*
cover *v.t*, tĕgo (3); **(conceal)**
occulto (1)
cover, covering *nn*, tĕgŭmen, *n*;
(lid), ŏpĕrīmentum, *n*
coverlet strāgŭlum, *n*
covert *nn*, dūmētum, *n*
covet *v.t*, cŭpĭo (3)
covetous ăvārus, ăvĭdus, cŭpĭdus
covetousness ăvārītĭa, *f*,
cŭpĭdĭtas, *f*
cow vacca, *f*
cow *v.t*, terrĕo (2), dŏmo (1)
(tame)
coward ignāvus, *m*
cowardice ignāvĭa, *f*
cowardly *adj*, ignāvus
cowl cŭcullus, *m*
coy (bashful) vĕrēcundus
crab cancer, *m*
crabbed mōrōsus
crack *nn*, **(noise)**, crĕpĭtus, *m*;
(chink), rĭma, *f*
crack *v.t*, findo (3), frango (3);
v.i, **(open up)**, dĕhisco (3);
(sound), crĕpo (1)

cradle cūnae, *f.pl*
craft (deceit) dŏlus, *m*; (skill),
  artĭfĭcĭum, *n*; (boat), rătis, *f*,
  nāvis, *f*
craftsman ŏpĭfex, *m*
crafty callĭdus
crag scŏpŭlus, *m*
cram *v.t*, confercĭo (4)
cramp *v.t*, comprĭmo (3)
crane (bird) grus, *m*, *f*; (machine),
  tollēno, *f*
crank uncus, *m*
cranny rīma, *f*
crash *nn*, frăgor, *m*
crash *v.i*, (noise), strĕpo (3);
  (bring into collision), *v.t*, collīdo
  (3)
crate corbis, *m*
crater crāter, *m*
crave for *v.t*, ōro (1), appĕto (3)
craving *nn*, dēsīdĕrĭum, *n*
crawl *v.i*, rēpo (3)
crayon crēta, *f*
crazy cerrītus, dēmens
creak *v.i*, crēpo (1)
creaking *nn*, strīdor, *m*, crĕpĭtus, *m*
crease *nn*, rūga, *f*
crease *v.t*, rūgo (1)
create *v.t*, crĕo (1)
creation (act of —) crĕātĭo, *f*;
  (making), făbrĭcātĭo, *f*; (universe),
  mundus, *m*
creator auctor, *m*, crĕātor, *m*
creature ănĭmal, *n*
credence (belief) fĭdes, *f*
credible crēdĭbĭlis
credit (belief or commercial credit)
  fĭdes, *f*; (reputation), existĭmātĭo, *f*
credit *v.t*, (believe), crēdo (3);
  (—an account, person, etc.),
  acceptum rĕfĕro (*irreg*) (*with dat.
  of person*)
creditable (honourable) hŏnestus
creditor crēdĭtor, *m*
credulous crēdŭlus, *m*
creek sĭnus, *m*
creep *v.i*, serpo (3), rēpo (3)
crescent lūna, *f*, (crescent moon)
crescent-shaped lūnatus
crest crista, *f*
crested cristātus
crestfallen dēmissus
crevice rīma, *f*

crew nautae, *m.pl*, rēmĭges, *m,pl*
crib (child's bed) lectŭlus, *m*
cricket (insect) cĭcāda, *f*
crime făcĭnus, *n*, scĕlus, *n*
criminal *nn*, hŏmo sons, hŏmo
  nŏcens
criminal *adj*, nĕfārĭus, scĕlestus
crimson *adj*, coccĭnĕus
cringe to *v.i*, ădūlor (1 *dep*)
cripple *nn*, hŏmo claudus
cripple *v.t*, dēbĭlĭto (1); (—a
  person), claudum reddo (3)
crippled dēbĭlis, claudus
crisis discrīmen, *n*
crisp frăgĭlis
critic existĭmātor, *m*, censor, *m*
critical ēlĕgans; (of a crisis, etc.),
  use discrīmen, *n* (crisis)
criticize *v.t*, (find fault)
  rĕprĕhendo (3), iūdĭco (1)
croak *v.i*, căno (3), crōcĭo (4)
crockery fictĭlĭa, *n.pl*
crocodile crŏcŏdīlus, *m*
crocus crŏcus, *m*
crook (shepherd's —) pĕdum, *n*
crooked curvus; (bad, etc.),
  prāvus
crop (of corn) sĕges, *f*, frūges,
  f.pl; (of a bird), inglŭvĭes, *f*
crop *v.t*, tondĕo (2)
cross *nn*, crux, *f*
cross *adj*, transversus; (annoyed),
  īrātus
cross *v.i. and v.t*, transĕo (4
  irreg)
cross-examine *v.t*, interrŏgo (1)
crossing (act of —) transĭtus, *m*;
  (cross-road), compĭtum, *n*
crouch *v.i*, sē dēmittĕre (3 *reflex*)
crow (bird) cornix, *f*
crow *v.i*, (of a cock), căno (3);
  (boast), sē iactare (1 *reflex*)
crowd turba, *f*
crowd together *v.i*, congrĕgor (1
  dep); *v.t*, stīpo (1), frĕquento (1)
crowded confertus, cĕlĕber
crown cŏrōna, *f*; (royal) dĭădēma,
  n; (of head, etc.) vertex, *m*
crown *v.t*, crōno (1)
crucifixion *use phr. with* crux, *f*,
  (cross)
crucify *v.t*, crŭce affĭcĭo (3)
crude rŭdis

cruel   crūdēlis, atrox
cruelty   crūdēlĭtas, *f*
cruet   gutus, *m*
cruise   *nn,* nāvĭgātĭo
cruise   *v.i.* nāvĭgo (1)
crumb   mīca, *f*
crumble   *v.t,* tĕro (3); *v.i,* corrŭo
  (3)
crumple   *v.t,* rūgo (1)
crush   *v.t,* contundo (3), opprĭmo
  (3)
crust   crusta, *f*
crutch   băcŭlum, *n*
cry   *nn,* clāmor, *m,* vox, *f*
cry   *v.i,* clāmo (1); **(weep),** lacrĭmo
  (1)
crystal   *nn,* crystallum, *n*
cub   cătŭlus, *m*
cube   tessĕra, *f*
cubic   cŭbĭcus
cuckoo   cŭcŭlus, *m,* coccyx, *m*
cucumber   cŭcŭmis, *m*
cudgel   fustis, *m*
cudgel   *v.t,* verbĕro (1), mulco (1)
cue   signum, *n*
cuff   *nn,* **(blow),** cŏlăphus, *m,*
  ălăpa
cuff   *v.t,* incŭtĭo (3)
cuirass   lōrīca, *f,* thōrax, *m*
culminate   *use adj,* summus
  (topmost)
culpable   culpandus, nŏcens
culprit   hŏmo nŏcens
cultivate   *v.t,* cŏlo (3)
cultivation   cultus, *m,* cultūra, *f*
cultivator   cultor, *m*
culture   cultus, *m,* cultūra, *f*
cumbersome   inhăbĭlis
cunning   *adj,* callĭdus, dŏlōsus
cunning   *nn,* callĭdĭtas, *f,* dŏlus, *m*
cup   pōcŭlum, *n*
cupboard   armārĭum, *n*
cupidity   cŭpĭdĭtas, *f*
cupola   thŏlus, *m*
curate   săcerdos, *c,* **(priest)**
curator   cūrātor, *m*
curb   *v.t,* frēno (1), cŏhĭbĕo (2)
curdle   *v.t,* cōgo (3), cŏāgŭlo (1);
  v.i, concresco (ī)
cure   *nn,* sānātĭo, *f*
cure   *v.t,* mĕdĕor (2 *dep*) (*with
  dat.*)
curiosity   stŭdĭum, *n*

curious **(inquisitive)** cūrĭōsus; **(rare),**
  rārus
curl   *v.t,* crispo (1)
curl   *nn,* cincinnus, *m*
curly   cincinnātus
currant   ăcĭnus, *m*
currency   mŏnēta, *f,* nummi, *m.pl*
current   *nn,* **(of river),** flūmen, *n*
current   *adj,* **(present),** hic;
  (general), ūsĭtātus
curse   *nn,* imprĕcātĭo, *f,* dīrae, *f.pl*
curse   *v.t,* exsĕcror (1 *dep.*)
cursed   exsĕcrābĭlis
cursorily   *adv,* summātim, brĕvĭter
curt   brĕvis
curtail   *v.t,* arto (1)
curtain   aulaeum, *n*
curve   *nn,* flexus, *m*
curve   *v.t,* flecto (3), curvo (1)
curved   curvātus
cusion   pulvīnar, *n*
custodian   cūrātor, *m*
custody **(keeping)** custōdĭa, *f;*
  (imprisonment), vincŭla, *n.pl*
custom   mos, *m,* consŭētūdo, *f;*
  (— duty), portōrĭum, *n*
customary   ūsĭtātus, sŏlĭtus
customer   emptor, *m*
cut   *nn,* **(incision),** incīsĭo, *f;*
  (blow), ictus, *m,* plāga, *f*
cut   *v.t,* sĕco (1), caedo (3);
  (—away), abscīdo (3); **(— down),**
  succīdo (3); **(— off),** praecīdo (3);
  **(— off from communications,
  supplies, etc.)** interclūdo (3);
  (— out), excīdo (3); **(— short),**
  praecīdo (3); **(— to pieces),**
  concīdo (3), trŭcīdo (1)
cutaneous   *use genit. of* cŭtis
  (skin)
cutlass   glădĭus, *m*
cutlery   cultri *m.pl* **(knives)**
cutter **(boat)** phăsēlus, *m,* cĕlox, *f*
cutting   *adj,* **(biting),** mordax
cuttlefish   sēpĭa, *f*
cycle **(circle)** orbis, *m*
cygnet   pullus, *m*
cylinder   cȳlindrus, *m*
cymbal   cymbălum, *n*
cynic   cȳnĭcus, *m*
cynical   mordax, diffĭcĭlis
cynicism   dūrĭtĭa, *f*
cypress   cupressus, *f*

D

dab *v.t,* illīdo (3)
dabble in *v.t,* attingo (3)
daffodil narcissus, *m*
dagger pŭgĭo, *m*
daily *adj,* quŏtīdĭānus
daily *adv,* quŏtīdĭē
daintiness (of manners)
fastīdĭum, *n*
dainty (things) dēlĭcātus; (people),
fastīdĭōsus
daisy bellis, *f*
dale valles, *f*
dalliance lūsus, *m*
dally *v.i,* (delay) mŏror (1 *dep.*)
dam (breakwater) mōles, *f*
dam *v.t,* obstrŭo (3)
damage *nn,* dētrīmentum, *n,*
damnum, *n*
damage *v.t,* laedo (3), afflīgo (3)
dame dŏmĭna, *f,* mātrōna, *f*
damn *v.t,* damno (1)
damp *adj,* hūmĭdus
damp *v.t,* hūmecto (1);
(enthusiasm, etc.) immĭnŭo (3)
(lessen)
damp *nn,* hūmor, *m*
dance *v.i,* salto (1)
dance *nn,* saltātus, *m*
dancer saltātor, *m* (...trix, *f*)
dandy hŏmo lĕpĭdus, ēlĕgans,
bellus
danger pĕrīcŭlum, *n*
dangerous pĕrīcŭlōsus
dangle *v.i,* pendĕo (2)
dank hūmĭdus, ūvĭdus
dapper (spruce) nĭtĭdus
dappled măcŭlōsus
dare *v.i,* audĕo (2 *semi-dep*)
mŏlĭor (4 *dep*)
daring *adj,* audax
daring *nn,* audācĭa, *f*
dark *adj,* obscūrus tĕnĕbrōsus; **(in**
colour), fuscus
dark, darkness *nn,* tĕnĕbrae, *f.pl*
darken *v.t,* obscūro (1), occaeco
(1)
darling *nn,* dēlĭcĭae, *f.pl; adj,*
mellītus
darn *v.t,* sarcĭo (4)
dart *nn,* tēlum, *n,* iăcŭlum, *n*
dart *v.i,* (rush), *use compound of*

vŏlo (1) **(to fly)**
dash *nn,* **(rush),** *use vb,* vŏlo (1)
(to fly)
dash *v.i,* prōvŏlo (1), rŭo (3); *v.t,*
afflīgo (3), impingo (3)
dashing *adj,* ălăcer
dastardly *adj,* ignāvus
date (fruit) palmŭla, *f;* **(time),**
dĭes, *f*
date *v.t,* **(something),** dĭem
ascrībo (3) in (*with abl.*)
daub *v.t,* oblĭno (3)
daughter fīlĭa, *f;* **(— in-law),** nŭrus
daunt *v.t,* percello (3)
dauntless impăvĭdus
dawdle *v.i,* cesso (1)
dawn prīma lux, aurōra, *f*
dawn *v.i,* dīlūcesco (3)
day dĭes, *m, f;* **(at — break),** *adv.*
phr, prīma lūce; **(by —),** *adv,*
interdĭu; **(every —),** *adv,* quŏtīdĭe;
(late in the —), multo dĭe; **(on**
the — before), prīdĭe; **(on the**
next —), postrīdĭe; **(— time),**
tempus dĭurnum, *n*
daze *v.t,* stŭpĕfăcĭo (3)
dazzle *v.t,* perstringo (3)
dazzling splendĭdus
dead *adj,* mortŭus; **(the dead or**
departed), mānes, *m.pl;* **(a —**
body), corpus, *n*
deaden *v.t,* **(senses, etc.),** hĕbēto
(1)
deadly *adj,* mortĭfer, pernĭcĭōsus,
fūnestus
deaf sturdus
deafen *v.t,* exsurdo (1), obtundo
(3)
deafness surdĭtas, *f*
deal (a good —) ălĭquantum,
(business) nĕgōtĭum, *n*
deal *v.t,* **(distribute),** distrĭbŭo (3);
mētĭor (4 *dep.*); *v.i,* **(deal with),**
ăgo (3) cum (*with abl*)
dealer mercātor, *m*
dealings *nn,* ūsus, *m,*
commercĭum, *n*
dear cārus; **(of price),** prĕtĭōsus
dearly *adv* **(at a high price)** magni
death mors, *f*
deathbed (on his —) *use adj,*
mŏrĭens **(dying)**
deathless immortālis

debar *v.t,* exclūdo (3)
debase *v.t,* dēmitto (3), vĭtĭo (1)
debate contrōversĭa, *f*
debate *v.t,* dispŭto (1), discepto (1)
debater dispŭtātor, *m*
debauch *v.t,* corrumpo (3)
debauchery stŭprum, *n*
debit *nn,* expensum, *n*
debit *v.t,* expensum fĕro (*irreg*) (*with dat*)
debt aes ălĭēnum, *n*
debtor dēbĭtor, *m*
debut ĭnĭtĭum, *n*
decamp *v.i,* castra mŏvĕo (2); discēdo (3)
decant *v.t,* diffundo (3)
decanter lăgēna, *f*
decapitate *v.t,* sēcūri fĕrĭo (4)
decay *nn,* tābes, *f,* dēmĭnūtĭo, *f*
decay *v.i,* dīlābor (3 *dep*), tābesco (3)
decease dēcessus, *m*
deceased *adj,* mortŭus
deceit fraus, *f,* dŏlus, *m*
deceitful fallax
deceive *v.t,* dēcĭpĭo (3), fallo (3)
December Dĕcember (mensis)
decency dĕcōrum, *n,* hŏnestas, *f*
decent dĕcōrus, hŏnestus
deception fraus, *f,* dŏlus, *m*
deceptive fallax
decide *v.t,* constĭtŭo (3), stătŭo (3), dēcerno (3)
decided (persons) firmus; (things), certus
decidedly *adv,* (assuredly), plānē, vēro
decimate *v.t,* dĕcĭmo (1)
decision arbitrĭum, *n,* dēcrētum, *n*
deck pons, *m*
deck *v.t,* orno (1)
declaim *v.t,* dēclāmo (1)
declaration prŏfessĭo, *f* (— of war), dēnuntĭātĭo, *f,* (belli)
declare *v.i,* prŏfĭtĕor (2 *dep*), affirmo (1); *v.t,* dēclāro (1); (— war), dēnuntĭo (1) (bellum)
decline *nn,* dēmĭnūtĭo, *f* (diminution)
decline *v.t,* (refuse), rĕcūso (1); *v.i,* inclīno (1), dēcresco (3)
declivity clīvus, *m*

decompose *v.t,* solvo (3); *v.i,* solvor (3 *pass*)
decomposition sŏlūtĭo, *f*
decorate *v.t,* orno (1), dĕcŏro (1)
decoration (ornament) ornāmentum, *n,* dĕcus, *n*; (badge), insigne, *n*
decorous dĕcōrus
decorum dĕcōrum, *n,* pŭdor, *m*
decoy illex, *m*; (bait), esca, *f*
decrease *nn,* dēmĭnūtĭo, *f*
decrease *v.i,* dēcresco (3); *v.t,* mĭnŭo (3)
decree *nn,* dēcrētum, *n*; (— of the Senate), consultum, *n*
decree *v.t,* dēcerno (3), censĕo (2)
decrepit dēcrĕpĭtus, dēbĭlis
decry *v.t,* vĭtŭpĕro (1), obtrecto (1)
dedicate *v.t,* consĕcro (1)
deduce *v.t,* conclūdo (3)
deduct *v.t,* dēdūco (3)
deduction (taking away) dēductĭo, *f*
deed factum, *n,* făcĭnus, *n*; (legal), tăbŭla, *f*
deem *v.t,* pŭto (1)
deep *nn,* (the sea), altum, *n*
deep altus (of sound), grăvis
deepen *v.t,* altĭōrem reddo (3)
deeply *adv,* altē, pĕnĭtus (deep within)
deer cervus, *m,* cerva, *f*
deface *v.t,* dēformo (1)
defame *v.t,* mălĕdīco (3) (*with dat*)
default *v.i,* dēfĭcĭo (3) (fail to answer bail), vădĭmōnĭum dēsĕro (3)
defeat *nn,* clādes, *f*
defeat *v.t,* vinco (3), sŭpĕro (1)
decect vĭtĭum, *n*
defective vĭtĭōsus
defence (protection) praesĭdĭum, *n*; (legal), dēfensĭo, *f*
defenceless ĭnermis
defend *v.t,* dēfendo (3)
defendant (in a trial) rĕus, *m*
defender dēfensor, *m*; (in court), pătrōnus, *m*
defer *v.t,* (put off), differo (*irreg*); *v.i,* (show deference to), cēdo (3)

deference observantĭa, *f*
defiance prōvŏcātĭo, *f*
defiant fĕrox
deficiency dēfectĭo, *f*
deficient ĭnops, mancus
deficit lăcūna, *f*
defile *v.t*, contămĭno (1)
defile *nn*, augustĭae, *f.pl*
define *v.t*, circumscrĭbo (3)
definite constĭtūtus, certus
definition dēfinītĭo, *f*
deflect *v.t*, dēflecto (3)
deform *v.t*, dēformo (1)
deformity dēformĭtas, *f*
defraud *v.t*, fraudo (1)
defray *v.t*, suppĕdĭto (1) **(supply)**
deft doctus **(skilled)**
defy *v.t*, obsto (1), prōvŏco (1)
degenerate *v.i*, dēgĕnĕro (1)
degenerate *adj*, dēgĕner
degradation ignōmĭnĭa, *f*
degrade *v.t*, mŏvĕo (2), dē *or* ex
   (with abl), **(move down from)**;
   dĕhŏnesto (1)
degree (interval, stage, rank)
   grădus, *m*; **(to such a degree)**,
   adv, ădĕo; **(by degrees)**, *adv*,
   (gradually), grădātim
deify *v.t*, consĕcro (1)
deign *v.t*, dignor (1 *dep*)
deity dĕus, *m*
deject *v.t*, afflīgo (3)
dejected dēmissus, afflictus
dejection maestĭtĭa, *f*
delay *nn*, mŏra, *f*
delay *v.i*, mŏror (1 *dep.*), cunctor
   (1 *dep.*); *v.t*, mŏror (1 *dep.*),
   tardo (1)
delegate *nn*, lēgātus, *m*
delegate *v.t*, **(depute)**, lēgo (1),
   mando (1) *(with acc. of thing and
   dat. of person)*
delegation lēgātĭo, *f*
deliberate *adj*, consīdĕrātus
deliberate *v.t*, consŭlo (3),
   dēlībĕro (1)
deliberately *adv*, consultō
deliberation dēlībĕrātĭo, *f*
delicacy subtīlĭtas, *f*, suāvĭtas, *f*;
   (food), cūpēdĭa, *n.pl*
delicate subtīlis, tĕner; **(of health)**,
   infirmus
delicious suāvis

delight *nn*, **(pleasure)**, vŏluptas, *f*
delight *v.t*, dēlecto (1), *v.i*,
   gaudĕo (2)
delightful iūcundus, ămoenus
delineate *v.t*, dēscrĭbo (3)
delinquency dēlictum, *n*
delinquent *nn*, peccātor, *m*
delirious dēlīrus
delirium dēlīrĭum, *n*
deliver *v.t*, **(set free)**, lībĕro (1);
   (hand over), do (1), trādo (3),
   dēdo (3); **(— a speech)**, hăbĕo
   (2), ōrātĭonem
deliverance **(freeing)** lībĕrātĭo, *f*;
   (childbirth) partus, *m*; **(of a
   speech)**, ēlŏcūtĭo, *f*
delude *v.t*, dēcĭpĭo (3)
deluge dīlŭvĭum, *n*, ĭnundātĭo, *f*
delusion error, *m*; **(trick)**, fallācĭa,
   f, fraus, *f*
delusive (deceitful) fallax;
   (empty), vānus
demagogue plēbĭcŏla, *c*
demand *nn*, postŭlātĭo, *f*
demand *v.t*, posco (3), postŭlo
   (1)
demean oneself dēmittor (3
   pass), sē dēmĭttĕre (3 *reflex*)
demeanour mōres, *m.pl*, hăbĭtus,
   m
demented dēmens
demise *nn*, **(death)**, dēcessus, *m*,
   mors, *f*
democracy cīvĭtas, pŏpŭlāris, *f*
democrat plēbĭcŏla, *c*
demolish *v.t*, dīrŭo (3), dēlĕo (2),
   dēmōlĭor (4 *dep*)
demolition ēversĭo, *f*, rŭīna, *f*
demon daemŏnĭum, *n*
demonstrate *v.t*, dēmonstro (1)
demonstration dēmonstrātĭo, *f*
demur *v.i*, haesĭto (1)
demure *adj*, vĕrēcundus
den lătĭbŭlum, *n*
denial nĕgātĭo, *f*
denominate *v.t*, nōmĭno (1)
denote *v.t*, indĭco (1), signĭfĭco
   (1), nŏto (1)
denounce *v.t*, (nōmen) dēfĕro
   (irreg)
dense densus, confertus
density crassītūdo, *f*
dent nŏta, *f*

dentist dentĭum mĕdĭcus, *m*
denude *v.t*, nūdo (1)
deny *v.t*, nĕgo (1), abnŭo (3)
depart *v.i*, ăbĕo (4), discēdo (3)
departed (dead) mortŭus
**department (of administration,
etc.)** prōvincĭa, *f*; **(part)**, pars, *f*
departure discessus, *m*
depend on *v.i*, pendĕo (2) ex *or*
in (*with abl*); **(rely on)**, confīdo (3
semi-dep) (*with dat*)
dependant *nn*, clĭens, *c*
dependence on clĭentēla, *f*;
(reliance), fīdes, *f*
dependency (subject state)
prōvincĭa, *f*
depict *v.t*, dēscrībo (3), effingo
(3)
deplorable mĭsĕrābĭlis
deplore *v.t*, dēplōro (1)
deploy *v.t*, explĭco (1)
depopulate *v.t*, pŏpŭlor (1 *dep*);
vasto (1)
deport *v.t*, dēporto (1); **(behave
oneself)**, se gĕrĕre (3 *reflex*)
deportment hăbĭtus, *m*
depose *v.t*, mŏvĕo (2) (*with abl*)
deposit *v.t*, dēpōno (3)
deposit *nn*, dēpŏsĭtum, *n*
deprave *v.t*, dēprāvo (1),
corrumpo (3)
depravity prāvĭtas, *f*
deprecate *v.t*, dēprĕcor (1 *dep*)
depreciate *v.t*, dētrăho (3); *v.i*,
mĭnŭor (3 *pass*) **(grow less)**
depreciation (decrease) dēmĭnūtĭo,
f; **(disparagement)** obtrectātĭo, *f*
depredation expīlātĭo, *f*,
praedātĭo, *f*
depress *v.t*, dēprĭmo (3); **(spirits,
etc.)**, infringo (3)
depression (sadness) tristĭtĭa, *f*
deprive *v.t*, prīvo (1) (*with acc. of
person deprived, and abl. of
thing*)
depth altĭtūdo, *f*
deputation lēgātĭo, *f*
depute *v.t*, lēgo (1), mando (1)
(*with dat*)
deputy lēgātus, *m*
deputy-governor prōcūrātor, *m*
derange *v.t*, perturbo (1)
deride *v.t*, dērīdĕo (2)

derision irrīsĭo, *f*, rīsus, *m*
derive (from) *v.t*, **(deduce)** dūco
(3), ab (*and abl*)
derogate from *v.i*, dērŏgo (1) dē
(*with abl*)
derogatory (remark) noxĭus
descend *v.i*, dēscendo (3)
descendant prōgĕnĭes, *f*
descent (lineage) prōgĕnĭes, *f*;
(movement), dēscensus, *m*;
(slope), dēclīve, *n*
describe *v.t*, dēscrībo (3), expōno
(3)
description dēscriptĭo, *f*, narrātĭo,
f
descry *v.t*, conspĭcor (1 *dep*)
desecrate *v.t*, prŏfāno (1)
desert (wilderness) sōlĭtūdo, *f*
desert *v.t*, dēsĕro (3), rĕlinquo (3)
deserted dēsertus
deserter perfŭga, *m*, transfŭga, *m*
deserve *v.t*, mĕrĕor (2 *dep*);
dignus esse (*irreg*) (*with abl*)
deservedly *adv*, mĕrĭto
design dēscriptĭo, *f*; **(plan)**,
consĭlĭum, *n*
design *v.t*, dēscrībo (3); **(intend)**,
in ănĭmo hăbĕo (2)
designate *v.t*, dēsigno (1)
designing *adj*, callĭdus, dŏlōsus
desirable optābĭlis
desire *nn*, dēsīdĕrĭum, *n*,
cŭpĭditas
desire *v.t*, cŭpĭo (3), opto (1)
desirous cŭpĭdus
desist *v.i*, dēsisto (3), dēsĭno (3)
desk scrīnĭum, *n*
desolate dēsertus, sōlus
despair *nn*, dēspērātĭo, *f*
despair *v.i*, dēspēro (1)
despatch *v.t*, mitto (3); **(kill)**,
interfĭcĭo (3)
despatch *nn*, **(sending)**, dīmissĭo,
f; **(letter)**, littĕrae, *f.pl*; **(speed)**,
cĕlĕrĭtas, *f*
desperate dēspērātus; **(situation)**,
extrēmus
desperate desperātĭo, *f*
despicable contemptus
despise *v.t*, dēspĭcĭo (3), sperno
(3)
despite *prep*, contrā (*with acc*)
despoil *v.t*, spŏlĭo (1)

despond *v.i,* ănĭmum dēmitto (3)

despondent *use adv. phr,* ănĭmo dēmisso

despot dŏmĭnus, *m*

despotic tўrannĭcus, *m*

despotism dŏmĭnātus, *m*

dessert mensa sĕcunda **(second table)**

destination *often* quo? **(whither),** *or* ĕo **(to that place)**

destine *v.t,* dēstĭno (1), dēsigno (1)

destiny fātum, *n*

destitute ĭnops

destroy *v.t,* perdo (3), dēlĕo (2), ēverto (3)

destroyer vastātor, *m*

destruction pernĭcĭes, *f,* ēversĭo, *f,* exĭtĭum, *n*

destructive pernĭcĭōsus

desultory inconstans

detach *v.t,* sēiungo (3), sēpăro (1)

detached sēpărātus

detachment (of troops, etc.) mănus

details singŭla, *n.pl*

detail *v.t,* explĭco (1)

detain *v.t,* rĕtĭnĕo (2)

detect *v.t,* dēprĕhendo (3), compĕrĭo (4)

deter *v.t,* dēterrĕo (2), dēpello (3)

deteriorate *v.i,* corrumpor (3 *pass*)

determinate *adj,* certus

determination (resolution) constantĭa, *f*; **(intention),** consĭlĭum, *n*

determine *v.i and v.t,* constĭtŭo (3)

determined (resolute) firmus; **(fixed)** certus

detest *v.t,* ōdi (*v. defect*)

detestable ŏdĭōsus

dethrone *v.t,* regno pello (3) **(expel from sovereignty)**

detour circŭĭtus, *m*

detract from *v.t,* dētrăho (3) dē (*with abl*)

detriment dētrīmentum, *n*

detrimental (to be —) *v.i,* esse (*irreg*) dētrĭmento (*with dat*)

devastate *v.t,* vasto (1)

devestation vastātĭo, *f*

develop *v.t,* explĭco (1), ēdŭco

(1); *v.i,* cresco (3) **(grow)**

development prōlātĭo, *f*; **(unfolding),** explĭcātĭo, *f*

deviate *v.i,* dēclīno (1), discēdo (3)

deviation dēclīnātĭo, *f*

device (contrivance) artĭfĭcium, *n*; **(emblem),** insigne, *n*; **(plan),** dŏlus, *m*

devil daemŏnĭum, *n*

devilish nĕfandus

devious dēvĭus

devise *v.t,* excōgĭto (1), fingo (3)

devoid expers, văcŭus

devolve *v.i,* obvĕnĭo (4); *v.t,* dēfĕro (*irreg*)

devote *v.t,* dēdĭco (1), dēdo (3); **(consecrate),** dēvŏvĕo (2)

devoted dēdĭtus, dēvōtus

devotion stŭdĭum, *n*; **(love),** ămor, *m*

devour *v.t,* dēvŏro (1), consūmo (3)

devouring ĕdax

devout pĭus, vĕnĕrābundus, rēlĭgĭōsus

dew rōs, *m*

dexterity sollertĭa, *f,* callĭdĭtas, *f*

dexterous sollers, callĭdus

diadem dĭădēma, *n*

diagonal *adj,* dĭăgōnālis

diagram forma, *f*

dial sōlārĭum, *n*

dialect dĭălectus, *f*

dialectics dĭălectĭca, *n.pl*

dialogue sermo, *m*; **(written),** dĭălŏgus, *m*

diameter crassĭtūdo, *f*

diamond ădămas, *m*

diaphragm praecordĭa, *n.pl*

diarrhoea prōflŭvĭum, *n*

diary commentārii dĭurni, *m.pl*

dice tāli, *m.pl*; **(the game),** ălĕa, *f*

dictate *v.t,* dicto (1); *v.i,* impĕro (1) (*with dat*)

dictation dictātĭo, *f*

dictator dictātor, *m*

dictatorial impĕrĭōsus

dictatorship dictātūra, *f*

dictionary glossārĭum, *n*

die *v.i,* mŏrĭor (3 *dep*), cădo (3)

diet victus, *m*

differ *v.i,* discrĕpo (1), differo

(*irreg*)
difference discrīmen, *n*,
  dīversĭtas, *f*; (**— of opinion**),
  discrĕpantĭa, *f*
different ălĭus, dīversus
difficult diffĭcĭlis
difficulty diffĭcultas, *f*; (**to be in—**),
  lăbōro (1); (**with —**), *adv,* aegrē
diffidence diffīdentĭa, *f*
diffident diffīdens
diffuse *v.t,* diffundo (3)
dig *v.t,* fŏdĭo (3)
digest *v.t,* concŏquo (3)
digestion concoctĭo, *f*
dignified grăvis
dignify *v.t,* hŏnesto (1)
dignity (of character) grăvĭtas, *f,*
  dignĭtas, *f*
digress *v.i,* dīgrĕdĭor (3 *dep*)
digression dīgressĭo, *f*
dike (ditch) fossa, *f*; (**mound**)
  agger, *m*
dilapidated rŭīnōsus
dilate *v.i,* sē dīlātāre (1 *reflex*);
  v.t, (**— upon**), dīlāto (1)
dilatory ignāvus, lentus
dilemma (difficulty) angustĭae, *f.pl*
diligence dīlĭgentĭa, *f*
dilute *v.t,* dīlŭo (3), miscĕo (2)
dim *adj,* (**light, etc.**), obscūrus;
  (**dull, stupid**), hĕbes
dim *v.t,* obscūro (1)
dimension mŏdus, *m*
diminish *v.t,* mĭnŭo (3); *v.i,*
  mĭnŭor (3 *pass*)
diminution dēmĭnūtĭo, *f*
diminutive parvus, exĭgŭus
dimness obscūrĭtas, *f*
dimple lăcūna, *f*
din strĕpĭtus, *m*
dine *v.i,* cēno (1)
dingy sordĭdus
dining room trīclīnĭum, *n,*
  cēnātĭo, *f*
dinner cēna, *f*
by dint of *prep,* per (*with acc*)
dip *v.t,* mergo (3); *v.i,* mergor (3
  pass)
diploma dĭplōma, *n*
diplomacy (by —) per lēgātos (**by
  means of diplomats**)
diplomat(ist) lēgātus, *m*
direct *adj,* rectus

direct *v.t,* dīrĭgo (3); (**order**),
  praecĭpĭo (3) (*with dat. of
  person*); (**show**), monstro (1)
direction (of motion) cursus, *m*;
  (**pointing out**), monstrātĭo, *f*;
  (**affairs**), admĭnĭstrātĭo, *f*; (**in
  different —s**), (*pl. adj*), dīversi
director cūrātor, *m*
dirt sordes, *f*
dirty sordĭdus, spurcus
dirty *v.t,* inquĭno (1), foedo (1)
disable *v.t,* dēbĭlĭto (1)
disabled inhăbĭlis, confectus
disadvantage incommŏdum, *n*
disadvantageous incommŏdus
disaffected ălĭēnātus
disaffection ănĭmus āversus, *m*
disagree *v.i,* discrĕpo (1),
  dissentĭo (4)
disagreeable (unpleasant)
  iniūcundus
disagreement discrĕpantĭa, *f,*
  dissensĭo, *f*
disappear *v.i,* ēvānesco (3),
  diffŭgĭo (3)
disappearance exĭtus, *m*
disappoint *v.t,* frustror (1 *dep*)
disappointment incommŏdum, *n*
disapproval rĕprĕhensĭo, *f*
disapprove *v.t,* imprŏbo (1)
disarm *v.t,* armis exŭo (3) (**strip
  of arms**)
disaster clādes, *f*
disastrous pernĭcĭōsus
disavow *v.t,* diffĭtĕor (2 *dep*)
disavowal infĭtĭātĭo, *f*
disband *v.t,* dīmitto (3)
disbelieve *v.t,* non crēdo (3),
  diffīdo (3) (*with dat*)
disburse *v.t,* expendo (3)
disc orbis, *m*
discard *v.t.* rĕpŭdĭo (1)
discern *v.t,* cerno (3)
discerning *adj,* perspĭcax
discernment intellĕgentĭa, *f*
discharge *v.t,* (**missiles, etc.**),
  ēmitto (3), iăcŭlor (1 *dep*);
  (**soldiers, etc.**), dīmitto (3);
  (**duties, etc.**), fungor (3 *dep*) (*with
  abl*)
discharge *nn,* ēmissĭo, *f,* dīmissĭo,
  f
disciple discĭpŭlus, *m*

discipline disciplīna, *f*
discipline *v.t*, instĭtŭo (3)
disclaim *v.t*, nĕgo (1), rĕpŭdĭo (1)
disclose *v.t*, ăpĕrĭo (4)
disclosure indĭcĭum, *n*
discolour *v.t*, dēcŏlōro (1)
discomfiture clādes, *f*
discomfort incommŏdum, *n*
disconcert *v.t*, perturbo (1)
disconnect *v.t*, sēiungo (3)
disconsolate maestus
discontented măle contentus
discontinue *v.t*, intermitto (3)
discord (strife) discordĭa, *f*,
  dissensĭo, *f*
discount *nn*, dēcessĭo, *f*
  (decrease)
discourage *v.t*, ănĭmum dēmitto
  (3)
discouragement ănĭmi infractĭo,
  f, or dēmissĭo, *f*
discourse *v.i*, dissĕro (3)
discourse *nn*, sermo, *m*, contĭo, *f*
discover *v.t*, invĕnĭo (4), rĕpĕrio
  (4), cognosco (3)
discovery inventĭo, *f*; **(thing**
  discovered), inventum, *n*
discredit *v.t*, fĭdem abrŏgo (1)
discreditable ĭnhŏnestus
discreet consĭdĕrātus, prūdens
discretion prūdentĭa, *f*
discriminate *v.t*, discerno (3)
discuss *v.t*, discepto (1), dispŭto
  (1)
discussion dispŭtātĭo, *f*
disdain *v.t*, sperno (3), dēspĭcĭo
  (3)
disdain *nn*, fastīdĭum, *n*
disdainful fastīdĭōsus
disease morbus, *m*
diseased aeger
disembark *v.t*, expōno (3); *v.i*,
  ēgrĕdĭor (3 *dep*)
disengage *v.t*, **(release)**, solvo (3)
disengaged (at leisure) ōtĭōsus;
  (free, loose) sŏlūtus
disentangle *v.t*, explĭco (1)
disfigure *v.t*, dēformo (1)
disgrace *nn*, dēdĕcus, *n*,
  ignōmĭnĭa, *f*
disgrace *v.t*, dēdĕcoro (1)
disgraceful turpis, flāgĭtĭōsus
disguise *nn*, persōna, *f*,

intĕgŭmentum, *n*
disguise *v.t*, vestem mūto (1)
  (change the clothes); dissĭmŭlo
  (1) **(pretend, hide)**
disgust *nn*, fastīdĭum, *n*, taedĭum,
  n
disgust *v.t*, taedĭum mŏvĕo (2)
  (with dat)
disgusted (to be —) *use*
  impersonal vb, pĭget (2) **(it**
  disgusts)
disgusting foedus
dish *nn*, pătĭna, *f*
dishearten *v.t*, exănĭmo (1),
  percello (3)
dishonest imprŏbus, perfĭdus
dishonesty *f*, imprŏbĭtas, *f*
dishonour *nn*, dēdĕcus, *n*
dishonour *v.t*, dēdĕcŏro (1)
dishonourable inhŏnestus
disinclination dēclīnātĭo, *f*
disinherit *v.t*, exhērēdo (1)
disintegrate *v.t*, solvo (3); *v.i*,
  solvor (3 *pass*)
disinterested neutri făvens
  (favouring neither side)
disjointed ĭnordĭnātus
disk orbis, *m*
dislike *nn*, ŏdĭum, *n*
dislike *v.t*, ăbhorrĕo (2) ab *(with*
  abl); displĭcĕo (2)
dislocate *v.t*, extorquĕo (2)
dislodge *v.t*, dēĭcĭo (3), pello (3)
disloyal infĭdēlis
dismal āter, maestus
dismantle *v.t*, dīrĭpĭo (3)
dismay *nn*, păvor, *m*
dismay *v.t*, consterno (1),
  pertubo (1)
dismiss *v.t*, dīmitto (3)
dismissal dīmissĭo, *f*
dismount *v.i*, ex ĕquo dēscendo
  (3)
disobedience *use phr. with vb*,
  pārĕo **(obey)**
disobedient măle pārens
disobey *v.t*, măle pārĕo *(with*
  dat)
disoblige *v.t*, offendo (3)
disorder *nn*, perturbātĭo, *f*
disorderly *adv*, turbātus; **(crowd)**,
  turbŭlentus
disown *v.t*, infĭtĭor (1 *dep*)

disparage *v.t,* dētrăho (3), obtrecto (1)

dispatch *v.t,* (see **despatch**)

dispel *v.t,* dēpello (3), discŭtĭo (3)

dispense *v.t,* dispertĭor (4 *dep*) distrĭbŭo (3); (**— with**), dīmitto (3)

dispersal dissĭpātĭo, *f*

disperse *v.t,* dispergo (3), dissĭpo (1), *v.i,* diffŭgĭo (3)

dispirited *use adv. phr,* dēmisso ănĭmo

display *nn,* ostentātĭo, *f*

display *v.t,* ostento (1)

displease *v.t,* displĭcĕo (2) (*with dat*)

displeasing ŏdĭōsus

displeasure offensĭo, *f*

disposal ēmissĭo, *f*; (**power**), arbĭtrĭum, *n*

dispose *v.t,* (**arrange**), constĭtŭo (3), dispōno (3); (**induce**), inclīno (1); (**get rid of**) ēlŭo (3)

disposed inclīnātus

disposition (arrangement) dispŏsĭtĭo, *f*, (**of mind, etc.**), nātūra, *f*, ingĕnĭum, *n*

dispossess *v.t,* dēturbo (1), dētrūdo (3)

disproportion dissĭmĭlĭtūdo, *f*; (**of parts, etc.**) inconcinnĭtas, *f*

disprove *v.t,* rĕfello (3), rĕfūto (1)

dispute *nn,* contrōversĭa, *f*

dispute *v.t,* dispŭto (1)

disqualify *v.t,* (**prevent**), prŏhĭbĕo (2)

disregard *nn,* neglĕgentĭa, *f*

disregard *v.t,* neglĕgo (3)

disreputable infāmis

disrespectful contŭmax, insŏlens

dissatisfaction mŏlestĭa, *f*

dissatisfied (— to be) *use impers. vb,* paenĭtet (*with acc. of subject and genit of object*)

dissect *v.t,* insĕco (1), persĕco (1)

dissemble *v.i,* dissĭmŭlo (1)

dissension discordĭa, *f*, dissensĭo, *f*

dissent *v.i,* dissentĭo (4)

dissimilar dissĭmĭlis

dissipate *v.t,* dissĭpo (1)

dissipated dissŏlūtus, lĭbīdĭnōsus

dissipation lĭcentĭa, *f*

dissolute dissŏlūtus, lĭbīdĭnōsus

dissolve *v.t,* solvo (3), lĭquĕfăcĭo (3), *v.i,* solvor (3 *pass*), lĭquesco (3)

dissuade *v.t,* dissuādĕo (2) (*with dat*)

distaff cŏlus, *f*

distance spătĭum, *n*; (**remoteness**), longinquĭtas, *f*; (**at a —**), *adv,* longē, prŏcul

distant rĕmōtus, distans; (**to be —**), absum (*irreg*)

distaste fastīdĭum, *n*

distasteful iniūcundus

distemper (malady) morbus, *m*

distend *v.t,* tendo (3)

distil *v.t,* stillo (1)

distinct (separate) sēpărātus; (**clear**), clārus, mănĭfestus

distinction (difference) discrīmen, *n*; (**mark of honour**), hŏnor, *m*, dĕcus, *n*

distinctive prŏprĭus

distinguish *v.t,* distinguo (3); *v.i,* (**— oneself**), clāresco (3), ēmĭnĕo (2)

distinguished insignis, clārus

distort *v.t,* dētorquĕo (2)

distortion distortĭo, *f*

distract *v.t,* distrăho (3)

distracted (mentally) āmens, turbātus

distraction (mental) āmentĭa, *f*

distress mĭsĕrĭa, *f*, dŏlor, *m*

distress *v.t* sollĭcĭto (1)

distressed sollĭcĭtus

distribute *v.t,* distrĭbŭo (3), partĭor (4 *dep*)

distributioon partītĭo, *f*

district rĕgĭo, *f*

distrust *nn,* diffĭdentĭa, *f*

distrust *v.t,* diffīdo (3) (*with dat*)

distrustful diffīdens

disturb *v.t,* turbo (1)

disturbance mōtus, *m*, tŭmulus, *m*

disunion discordĭa, *f*

disunite *v.t,* sēiungo (3), dissŏcĭo (1)

disused dēsŭētus

ditch fossa, *f*

ditty carmen, *n*

divan lectŭlus, *m*

dive *v.i,* sē mergĕre (3 *reflex*)

diver ūrīnātor, *m*
diverge *v.i*, discēdo (3)
divergence dēclīnātĭo, *f*
diverse ălĭus, dīversus
diversion dērīvātĭo, *f*; **(of thought, etc.)**, āvŏcātĭo, *f*
divert *v.t*, āverto (3), āvŏco (1); **(amuse)**, oblecto (1), prōlecto (1)
divide *v.t*, dīvĭdo (3); **(share out)**, partĭor (4 *dep*); *v.i*, sē dīvĭdĕre (3 *reflex*)
divine dīvīnus
divine *v.t*, dīvīno (1), augŭror (1 *dep*)
diviner augur, *m*
divinity dīvīnĭtas, *f*
divisible dīvĭdŭus
division (act of —) dīvīsĭo, *f*; **(a section)**, pars, *f*; **(discord)**, discĭdĭum, *n*
divorce dīvortĭum, *n*
divorce *v.i*, dīvortĭum făcĭo (3), cum (*and abl*)
divulge *v.t*, pătĕfăcĭo (3), ăpĕrĭo (4)
dizziness vertīgo, *f*
dizzy vertīgĭnōsus
do *v.t*, făcĭo (3), ăgo (3); **(to be satisfactory)**, *v.i*, sătis esse; **(—away with)** abŏlĕo (2); **(—without)**, cărĕo (2) (*with abl*)
docile făcĭlis, dŏcĭlis
dock nāvālĭa, *n.pl*
doctor mēdĭcus, *m*
doctor *v.t*, cūro (1)
doctrine dogma, *n*, rătĭo, *f*
document tăbŭla, *f*, littĕrae, *f.pl*
dodge dŏlus, *m*
dodge *v.t*, **(elude)**, ēlūdo (3)
doe cerva, *f*
dog cănis, *c*
dog *v.t*, insĕquor (3 *dep*)
dogged (stubborn) pertĭnax, pervĭcax
dogged (by ill-luck, etc.) ăgĭtātus
dogma dogma, *n*
dogmatic arrŏgans
dole (small allowance) dĭurna, *n.pl*
dole out *v.t*, dīvĭdo (3)
doleful tristis, maestus
dolefulness tristĭtĭa, *f*
doll pūpa, *f*

dolphin delphīnus, *m*
dolt caudex, *m*
dome thŏlus, *m*
domestic dŏmestĭcus, fămĭlĭāris; **(animals)** villātĭcus
domestic *nn*, **(servant)**, fămŭlus, *m*
domicile dŏmĭcĭlĭum, *n*
dominant pŏtens
dominate *v.t*, dŏmĭnor (1 *dep*)
domination dŏmĭnātus, *m*
domineering impĕrĭōsus
dominion impĕrĭum, *n*, regnum, *n*
donation dōnum, *n*
donkey ăsĭnus, *m*
doom fātum, *n*
doom *v.t*, damno (1)
door iānŭa, *f*; **(out of —s)** *adv*, fŏrīs
doorkeeper iānĭtor, *m*
doorpost postis, *f*
dormitory cŭbĭcŭlum, *n*
dormouse glīs, *m*
dot *nn*, punctum, *n*
dotage sĕnĭum, *n*
dotard sĕnex, *m*
dote upon *v.i*, dēpĕrĕo (4)
double *adj*, dŭplex, gĕmĭnus
double *v.t*, dŭplĭco (1); *v.i*, dŭplex fīo (*irreg*), ingĕmĭno (1)
double-dealing *nn*, fraus, *f*
double-faced fallax
doubt *v.i*, dŭbĭto (1)
doubt *nn*, dŭbĭum, *n*, dŭbĭtātĭo
doubtful dŭbĭus, incertus
doubtless *adv*, sĭne dŭbĭo, nīmīrum
dough fărīna, *f*
dove cŏlumba, *f*
dove-coloured cŏlumbīnus
dovecot cŏlumbārĭum, *n*
dowager vĭdŭa, *f*
down *prep*, dē (*with abl*); *adv*, use dē *in a coumpound verb, e.g.*
run down dēcurro (3)
down *nn*, **(feathers, etc.)** plūma, *f*
down *v.t*, **(put down)** dēpōno (3)
downcast dēiectus, dēmissus
downfall occāsus, *m*, rūīna, *f*
down-hearted *adv*, dēmisso ănĭmo
downpour imber, *m*
downright dīrectus; **(sheer)**,

mĕrus
downward *adj,* dēclīvis
downwards *adv,* dĕorsum
downy *adj,* plūmĕus
dowry dos, *f*
doze *v.i,* dormīto (1)
dozen (twelve) dŭŏdĕcim
dozing *adj,* somnĭcŭlōsus
drab cĭnĕrĕus **(ash-coloured)**
drag *v.t,* trăho (3)
dragon drăco, *m*
drain *nn,* clŏāca, *f,* fossa, *f*
drain *v.t,* **(land),** sicco (1); **(a
drink),** haurĭo (4)
dram cўăthus, *m*
drama fābŭla, *f,* scēna, *f*
dramatic (theatrical) scēnĭcus
dramatist pŏēta, *m*
drapery vēlāmen, *n*
draught (of air) spīrĭtus, *m*;
(water, etc.) haustus, *m*; **(game of
—s),** lătruncŭli, *m.pl*
draw *v.t,* **(pull)** trăho (3);
(portray), dēscribo (3); **(— a
sword),** glădĭum stringo (3);
(—aside), sēdūco (3); **(— water,
etc.)** haurĭo (4); *v.i* **(— back),**
pĕdem rĕfĕro *(irreg);* **(— lots),**
sortes dūco (3); **(— up troops,
etc.)** *v.t,* instrŭo (3)
drawback, *nn,* incommŏdum, *n*
drawbridge pontĭcŭlus, *m*
drawing (picture) pictūra, *f*
drawl *v.i,* lentē prōnuntĭo (1)
(pronounce slowly)
dray plaustrum, *n*
dread *nn,* formīdo *f,* păvor, *m*
dread *v.t,* tĭmĕo (2), formīdo (1)
dreadful terrĭbĭlis, ătrox
dream *nn,* somnĭum, *n*
dream *v.t,* somnĭo (1)
dreamy somnĭcŭlōsus
dreary tristis
dregs faex, *f*
drench *v.t,* mădĕfăcĭo (3)
dress *nn,* vestis, *f,* hăbĭtus, *m*
dress *v.t,* **(clothe); vestĭo (4); (— a
wound)** cūro (1) **(care for)**
dressing *nn,* **(of wound)**
fōmentum, *n*
drift *nn,* **(heap),** aggĕr, *m*;
(tendency), *use phr. with* quōrsus
(to what end?)

drift *v.i,* dēfĕror *(irreg. pass)*
drill (military) exercĭtātĭo, *f*; **(tool),**
tĕrĕbra, *f*
drill *v.t,* **(pierce),** tĕrĕbro (1);
(train), exercĕo (2)
drill (military) exercĭtātĭo, *f*; **(tool),**
tĕrĕbra, *f*
drill *v.t,* **(pierce),** tĕrĕbro (1);
(train), exercĕo (2)
drink *v.t,* bĭbo (3), pōto (1)
drink *nn,* pōtĭo, *f*
drinker pōtātor, *m*
drinking pōtĭo, *f*; **(— party),**
cōmissātĭo, *f*
drip *v.i,* stillo (1)
dripping *adj,* mădĭdus
drive *nn,* gestatĭo, *f*
drive *v.t,* ăgo (3); **(— away),** fŭgo
(1) pello (3); **(— back),** rĕpello
(3); **(— out),** expello (3)
drive *v.i,* **(on horse-back, etc.)**
vēhor (3 *pass*)
drivel ĭneptĭae, *f.pl*
drivel *v.i,* dēlīro (1)
driver aurīga, *c*
drizzle *v.i,* rōro (1)
droll rīdĭcŭlus, lĕpĭdus
drollery făcētĭae, *f.pl*
dromedary drŏmas, *m*
drone *nn,* **(bee),** fūcus, *m*;
(sound), murmur, *n*
drone *v.i,* murmŭro (1)
droop *v.i,* pendĕo (2), languesco
(3)
drooping *adj,* pendŭlus; **(of
spirits, etc.),** dēmissus
drop *nn,* gutta, *f*
drop *v.t,* dēmitto (3); **(leave off),**
omitto (3); *v.i,* cădo (3)
dropsy hydrops, *m*
drought siccĭtas, *f*
drove (flock) grex, *m*
drown *v.t,* submergo (3); **(of
noise)** obstrĕpo (3)
drowsy somnĭcŭlōsus
drudge *nn,* servus, *m*
drudge *v.i,* servĭo (4); **(weary
oneself)** *v.i,* sē fătīgăre (1 *reflex*)
drudgery lăbor servīlis **(servile
labour)**
drug *nn,* mĕdĭcāmentum, *n*
drug *v.t,* mĕdĭco (1)
drum tympănum, *n*

drunk *adj,* ēbrĭus
drunkenness ēbrĭĕtas, *f*
dry siccus, ārĭdus; **(thirsty)**, sĭtĭens
dry (up) *v.t,* sicco (1); *v.i,* āresco (3)
dryness sĭccĭtas, *f,* ārĭdĭtas, *f*
dubious dŭbĭus
duck *nn,* ănas, *f*
duck *v.t,* mergo (3)
duckling ănătĭcŭla, *f*
duct fŏrāmen, *n*
due *adj,* **(owed)**, dēbĭtus; **(just)**, iustus; **(suitable)**, ĭdōnĕus, aptus
due *nn,* **(a right)**, ius, *n;* **(taxes)**, vectīgal, *n,* portōrĭum, *n*
duel certāmen, *n*
dull (person) hĕbes, obtūsus; **(colour)**, obscūrus; **(blunt)**, hĕbes; **(weather)**, subnūbĭlus
dullness (of mind) tardĭtas, *f*
duly *adv,* **(established by precedent)** rītĕ
dumb mūtus
dumbfound *v.t,* obstŭpĕfăcĭo (3)
dump *v.t,* cŏăcervo (1)
dun fuscus
dunce hŏmo stŭpĭdus
dung stercus, *n*
dungeon carcer, *m*
dupe *nn,* hŏmo crēdŭlus
dupe *v.t,* dēcĭpĭo (3)
duplicate exemplum, *n*
duplicity fallācĭa, *f*
durability firmĭtas, *f*
durable firmus
duration spătĭum, *n;* **(long —)**, dĭŭturnĭtas, *f*
during *prep,* per *(with acc)*
dusk crĕpuscŭlum, *n*
dusky fuscus, nĭger
dust *nn,* pulvis, *m*
dust *v.t,* dētergĕo (2)
duster pēnĭcŭlus, *m*
dusty pulvĕrŭlentus
dutiful pĭus
dutifulness pĭĕtas, *f*
duty (moral) offĭcĭum, *n;* **(given)**, mūnus, *n;* **(tax)** vectīgal, *n;* **(it is my —)** *use vb.* dēbĕo (2) **(ought)**
dwarf pūmĭlĭo, *c*
dwarfish pŭsillus
dwell *v.i,* hăbĭto (1), incŏlo (3); **(— on a theme)**, commŏror (1

dep), haerĕo (2) in *(with abl)*
dweller incŏla, *c*
dwelling (place) dŏmĭcĭlĭum, *n*
dwindle *v.i,* dēcresco (3)
dye *nn,* fūcus, *m*
dye *v.t,* tingo (3), infĭcĭo (3)
dyer infector, *m*
dying *adj,* mŏrĭens
dynasty dŏmus, *f*
dysentry dȳsentĕrĭa, *f*
dyspeptic crūdus

E

each ūnusquisque; **(— of two)**, ŭterque; **(one —)**, *use distributive num,* singŭli, bīnĭ
eager cŭpĭdus, ăvĭdus *(with genit)*
eagerness cŭpĭdĭtas, *f,* ăvĭdĭtas, *f*
eagle ăquĭla, *f*
ear auris, *f;* **(— of corn)**, spīca, *f*
early *adj,* **(in the morning)** mātūtīnus; **(of time, etc.)**, mātūrus
early *adv,* **(in the morning)** māne; **(in time, etc.)**, mātūrē
earn *v.t,* mĕrĕo (2), mĕrĕor (2 *dep)*
earnest intentus, ācer
earnestly *adv,* intentē
earth (land) terra, *f;* **(ground)**, sŏlum, *n;* **(globe)**, orbis *(m)* terrārum
earthenware fictĭlĭa, *n.pl*
earthly *adj* **(terrestrial)** terrestris
earthquake terrae mōtus, *m,* **(movement of the earth)**
earthwork agger, *m*
ease quĭes, *f,* ōtĭum, *n*
ease *v.t,* **(lighten)**, lĕvo (1), exŏnĕro (1)
easily *adv,* făcĭlĕ
easiness făcĭlĭtas, *f*
east *nn,* ŏrĭens, *m*
eastern *use genit.* of ŏrĭens **(east)**
eastward *adv. phr,* ăd ŏrĭentem
easy făcĭlis
eat *v.t,* ĕdo (3); **(— away)**, rōdo (3)
eatable escŭlentus
eating-house pŏpīna, *f*
eaves prōtectum, *n*
eavesdropper auceps, *c*

ebb *v.i*, rĕcēdo (3)
ebb-tide rĕcessus aaestus
  (receding of the tide)
ebony ĕbĕnus, *f*
eccentric (of persons) nŏvus
echo *nn*, ĭmāgo, *f*, ēcho, *f*
echo *v.t*, rĕfĕro (*irreg*), rĕsŏno (1)
echoing *adj*, rĕsŏnus
eclipse *nn*, dēfectĭo, *f*
eclipse *v.t*, obscūro (1)
economical parcus, dīlĭgens
economy parsĭmōnĭa, *f*, (frugality)
ecstasy fŭror, *m*
ecstatic fŭrens
eddy vertex, *m*
edge (of knife etc.) ăcĭes, *f*;
  (margin), margo, *c*, ōra, *f*
edible escŭlentus
edict ēdictum, *n*
edifice aedĭfĭcĭum, *n*
edify *v.t*, instĭtŭo (3)
edit *v.t*, ēdo (3)
edition ēdĭtĭo, *f*
educate *v.t*, ēdŭco (1)
education ēdŭcātĭo, *f*, doctrīna, *f*
eel anguilla, *f*
efface *v.t*, dēlĕo (2)
effect *v.t*, effĭcĭo (3)
effect *nn*, (influence, impression),
  vīs, *f*; (result), effectus, *m*;
  (consequence), ēventus, *m*;
  (without −), (*adv*), nēquīquem
effective (impressive) grăvis; *or use*
  phr. with confĭcĭo (3) (to bring to
  a conclusion)
effectual effĭcax
effeminate effēmĭnātus
effervescence (of spirit, etc.)
  fervor, *m*
efficacy vīs, *f*
efficiency vīs, *f*
efficient hăbĭlis, effĭcĭens
effigy ĭmāgo, *f*
effort ŏpĕra, *f*
effrontery ōs, *n*
effulgent fulgens
effusion effūsĭo, *f*
egg ōvum, *n*
egg on *v.t*, incĭto (1)
egoism ămor (*m*) sŭi (fondness of
  oneself)
egoist ămātor (*m*) sŭi
egregious insignis

egress exĭtus, *m*
eight octo; (− each), octōni;
  (−times), *adv*. octĭens;
  (− hundred) octingenti
eighteen dŭŏdēvīginti
eighteenth dŭŏdēvīcensimus
eight octāvus
eightieth octōgēsĭmus
eighty octōginta
either *pron*, altĕrŭter; *conj*, aut
either ... or aut ... aut, vel ... vel
ejaculate *v.t*, ēmitto (3)
ejaculation (cry) vox, *f*, clāmor, *m*
eject *v.t*, ēĭcĭo (3)
eke out *v.t*, parco (3) (*with dat*)
elaborate *adj*, ēlăbōrātus
elaborate *v.t*, ēlăbōro (1)
elapse *v.i*, (of time), intercēdo (3)
elate *v.t*, effĕro (*irreg*)
elated (joyful) laetus
elbow cŭbĭtum, *n*
elder *adj*, māior nātu (greater by
  birth)
elder tree sambūcus, *f*
elderly *adj*, prōvectus aetāte
  (advanced in age)
elect *v.t*, crĕo (1), dēlĭgo (3)
elect *adj*, dēsignātus
election ēlectĭo, *f*, cŏmĭtĭa, *n.pl*
elector suffrāgātor, *m*
elegance ēlĕgantĭa, *f*, vĕnustas, *f*
elegant ēlĕgans, vĕnustus
elegy ĕlĕgīa, *f*
element ēlĕmentum, *n*, prīncĭpĭa,
  n.pl
elementary prīmus, simplex
elephant ĕlĕphantus, *m*
elevate *v.t*, tollo (3)
elevated ēdĭtus; (mind) ēlātus
elevation altĭtūdo, *f*, ēlātĭo, *f*
eleven undĕcim; (− each), undēni
eleventh undĕcĭmus
elicit *v.t*, ēlĭcĭo (3)
eligible ĭdōnĕus, opportūnus
elk alces, *f*
ell ulna, *f*
elm ulmus, *f*
elocution prōnuntĭātĭo, *f*
elope *v.i*, aufŭgĭo (3) (run away)
eloquence elŏquentĭa, *f*
eloquent ēlŏquens, dĭsertus
else *adj*, ălĭus
else *adv*, ălĭter

elsewhere *adv,* ălĭbī
elude *v.t,* ēlūdo (3)
emaciate *v.t,* attĕnŭo (1)
emaciated măcer
emaciation măcĭes, *f*
emanate *v.i,* ēmāno (1)
emancipate *v.t,* lībĕro (1),
  mănūmitto (3)
embalm *v.t,* condĭo (4)
embankment mōles, *f*
embark *v.t,* in nāvem impōno (3);
  v.i, nāvem conscendo (3)
embarrass *v.t,* **(entangle),**
  impĕdĭo (4); **(confuse),** turbo (1)
embarrassment scrūpŭlus, *m*;
  (difficulty), difficultas, *f*
embassy (delegation) lēgāti, *m.pl,*
  (ambassadors)
embedded sĭtus
embellish *v.t,* orno (1)
embellishment ornāmentum, *n*
embers cĭnis, *m*
embezzle *v.t,* āverto (3), pĕcŭlor
  (1 *dep*)
embezzlement pĕcūlātus, *m*
embezzler āversor (*m*) pĕcūnĭae
embitter *v.t,* exăcerbo (1)
emblem insigne, *n,* indĭcĭum, *n*
embody *v.t,* inclūdo (3)
embolden *v.t,* confirmo (1)
embrace *nn,* amplexus, *m,*
  complexus, *m*
embrace *v.t,* amplector (3 *dep*),
  complector (3 *dep*); **(— an**
  opportunity) arrĭpĭo (3)
embroidered (clothing, etc.)
  pictus
embroil *v.t,* **(entangle),** implĭco (1)
emerald smărăgdus, *c*
emerge *v.i,* ēmergo (3), prōdĕo
  (4)
emergency discrīmen, *n,* tempus,
  n
emigrate *v.i,* mĭgro (1)
emigration mĭgrātĭo, *f*
eminence (high ground) tŭmŭlus,
  m; **(of rank, etc.)** lŏcus
  amplissĭmus
eminent ēgrĕgĭus, insignis
emissary lēgātus, *m*
emit *v.t,* ēmitto (3)
emolument lŭcrum, *n*
emotion mōtus (*m*) ănĭmi

(movement of the mind)
emperor impĕrātor, *m,* princeps,
  m
emphasize *v.t,* prĕmo (3)
emphatic grăvis
empire impĕrĭum, *n*
empirical empīrĭcus
employ *v.t,* ūtor (3 *dep*) (*with*
  abl)
employed (of persons) occŭpātus
employer conductor, *m*
employment (occupation)
  quaestus, *m*; **(business),**
  nĕgōtĭum, *n*; **(using),** ūsurpātĭo, *f*
emporium empŏrĭum, *n*
empower (someone to do ...) *v.i,*
  pŏtestātem făcĭo (3) (*with dat. of*
  person and genit. of gerund(ive))
empty *adj,* văcŭus, ĭnānis
empty *v.t,* exĭnānĭo (4)
emulate *v.t,* aemŭlor (1 *dep*)
emulous aemŭlus
enable *v.t,* făcultātem do (1)
  (*with dat*)
enact *v.t,* **(law)** sancĭo (4),
  constĭtŭo (3)
enactment lex, *f*
enamoured (to be — of someone)
  v.t, ămo (1)
encamp *v.i,* castra pōno (3)
enchant *v.t,* fascĭno (1), dēlecto
  (1)
enchantment (allurement)
  blandīmentum, *n*
encircle *v.t,* circumdo (1)
enclose *v.t,* inclūdo (3), saepĭo
  (4)
enclosure saeptum, *n*
encounter *v.t,* incĭdo (3) in
  (*with acc*); concurro (3), obvĭam
  ĕo (4) (*irreg*) (*with dat*)
encounter *nn,* congressus, *m*
encourage *v.t,* hortor (1 *dep*)
encouragement hortātus, *m,*
  confirmātĭo, *f,* hortātĭo, *f*
encroach upon *v.t,* occŭpo (1)
encumber *v.t,* ŏnĕro (1), impĕdĭo
  (4)
encumbrance impĕdīmentum, *n*
end fĭnis, *m*; *or use* extrēmus,
  adj, agreeing with a noun; e.g. **at**
  the end of the bridge, in extrēmo
  ponte

end *v.t*, confĭcĭo (3), fĭnĭo (4); *v.i,*
use *phr. with* extrēmum, *n,* (end);
(turn out, result) cēdo (3), ēnēnĭo
(4)
endanger *v.t*, in pĕrīcŭlum
addūco (3)
endear *v.t*, dēvincĭo (4)
endeavour *nn*, cōnātus, *m*
endeavour *v.t*, cōnor (1 *dep*)
endless infīnītus, perpĕtŭus
endorse *v.t*, confirmo (1)
endow *v.t*, dōno (1)
endowed praedĭtus
endurable tŏlĕrābĭlis
endurance pătĭentĭa, *f*
endure *v.t*, pătĭor (3 *dep*), fĕro
(*irreg*); *v.i*, dūro (1)
enemy (public) hostis, *c*; (prĭvate),
ĭnĭmīcus, *m*
energetic ācer, strēnŭus, impĭger
energy vīs, *f*, vĭgor, *m*
enervate *v.t*, ēnervo (1)
enervation dēbĭlĭtātĭo, *f*
enfeeble *v.t*, dēbĭlĭto (1)
enforce *v.t*, (carry out) exsĕquor
(3 *dep*)
enfranchise *v.t*, (give the right of
voting) suffrăgĭum do (1) (*with
dat*)
enfranchisement cīvĭtātis
dōnātĭo, *f*, (granting of
citizenship)
engage *v.t*, (join) iungo (3); (hire)
condūco (3); (— in battle); signa
conferre (*irreg*); (enter into),
ingrĕdĭor (3 *dep*)
engaged occŭpātus; (betrothed),
sponsus
engagement (battle) proelĭum, *n*;
(agreement), pactum, *n*;
(promise), sponsĭo, *f*
engender *v.t*, gigno (3), părĭo (3)
engine māchĭna, *f*; (military —),
tormentum, *n*
engineer făber, *m*
England Brĭtannĭa, *f*
English Brĭtannus, Brĭtannĭcus
engrave *v.t*, scalpo (3)
engraver scalptor, *m*
engraving *nn*, scalptūra, *f*
engross *v.t*, occŭpo (1)
enhance *v.t*, augĕo (2), orno (1)
enigma aenigma, *n*, ambāges, *f.pl*

enigmatic ambĭgŭus
enjoin *v.t*, iŭbĕo (2), mando (1)
enjoy *v.t*, frŭor (3 *dep*) (with
abl); (possess), ūtor (3 *dep*) (*with
abl*)
enjoyment (pleasure) gudĭum, *n*,
lĭbīdo, *f*
enlarge *v.t*, augĕo (2), amplĭfĭco
(1)
enlargement prōlātĭo, *f*
enlighten *v.t*, (instruct), dŏcĕo (2)
enlist *v.t*, (troops), conscrībo (3);
(bring over), concĭlĭo (1); *v.i,*
nōmen do (1) (give one's name)
enliven *v.t*, excĭto (1)
enmity ĭnĭmīcĭtĭa, *f*
ennoble *v.t*, (make honourable),
hŏnesto (1)
enormity immānĭtas, *f*; (crime),
scĕlus, *n*
enormous ingens
enough *nn*. and *adv*, sătis; (*foll.
by genit*), e.g. enough water, sătis
ăquae
enquire *v.t*, quaero (3) ab (*with
abl*)
enrage *v.t*, irrīto (1), inflammo
(1)
enrapture *v.t*, oblecto (1)
enrich *v.t*, lŏcŭplēto (1)
enroll *v.t*, scrībo (3)
ensign signum, *n*; (— bearer),
signĭfer, *m*
enslave *v.t*, servĭtūtem iniungo
(3) (*with dat*)
ensue *v.i*, sĕquor (3 *dep*)
entail *v.t*, affĕro (*irreg*)
entangle *v.t*, impĕdĭo (4)
enter *v.i*, *and v.t*, intro (1),
ingrĕdĭor (3 *dep*), ĭnĕo (4 *irreg*);
v.t, (write in), inscrībo (3)
enterprise (undertaking)
inceptum, *n*
enterprising promptus, strēnŭus
entertain *v.t*, (people), excĭpĭo (3)
(receive); (amuse), oblecto (1);
(an idea, etc.) hăbĕo (2)
entertainment (of guests)
hospĭtĭum, *n*
enthusiasm stŭdĭum, *n*, fervor, *m*
enthusiastic fānātĭcus, stŭdĭōsus
entice *v.t*, illĭcĭo (3)
entire tōtus, intĕger

entirely *adv*, omnīno
entitle *v.t*, (give the right to) ius
do (1) (*with dat*); (name),
inscrībo (3)
entitled (to be — to) *v.i*, ius hăbĕo
(2)
entrails viscĕra, *n.pl*
entrance (act of —) ingressĭo, *f*;
(door, etc.) ădĭtus, *m*, ostĭum, *n*
entreat *v.t*, obsĕcro (1), ōro (1)
entreaty obsĕcrātĭo, *f*
entrust *v.t*, crēdo (3) (*with dat*)
committo (3) (*with dat*)
enumerate *v.t*, nŭmĕro (1)
envelop *v.t*, involvo (3)
envelope *nn*, invŏlūcrum, *n*
enviable fortūnātus
envious invĭdus
envoy lēgātus, *m*
envy invĭdĭa, *f*
envy *v.t*, invĭdĕo (2) (*with dat*)
ephemeral brĕvis
epic *adj*, ĕpĭcus
epidemic pestĭlentĭa, *f*
epigram ĕpĭgramma, *n*
epigrammatic ĕpĭgrammătĭcus, a,
um, *adj*
epilepsy morbus cŏmĭtĭālis, *m*
episode (digression) excursus, *m*;
res, *f*
epitaph ĕlŏgĭum, *n*
epoch aetas, *f*
equable aequus
equal *adj*, aequus, pār
equal *nn, use adj*, pār
equal *v.i and v.t*, aequo (1)
equality aequālĭtas, *f*
equanimity aequus ănĭmus, *m*
equator aequĭnoctĭālis circŭlus, *m*
equestrian ĕquester
equilibrium aequĭlībrĭum, *n*
equinox aequĭnoctĭum, *n*
equip *v.t*, orno (1), armo (1)
equipment arma, *n.pl*,
armāmenta, *n.pl*
equitable aequus
equity aequĭtas, *f*; (justice),
iustĭtĭa, *f*
equivalent *adj*, (equal), pār; (to
be —), *v.i, use* vălĕo (2) (to be
worth) tanti
equivocal ambĭgŭus
era tempus, *n*, aetas, *f*

eradicate *v.t*, ēvello (3), exstirpo
(1)
erase *v.t*, dēlĕo (2)
ere (before) *conj*, prĭusquam
erect *v.t*, ērĭgo (3); (build),
exstrŭo (3)
erect *adj*, rectus
erection (act of —) aedĭfĭcātĭo, *f*; (a
building) aedĭfĭcĭum, *n*
err *v.i*, erro (1), pecco (1)
errand mandātum, *n*
erratic văgus
erroneous falsus
error error, *m*
erudite doctus
eruption ēruptĭo, *f*
escape *nn*, fŭga, *f*
escape *v.i, and v.t*, effŭgĭo (3),
ēlābor (3 *dep*)
escarpment praeruptus lŏcus, *m*
escort *nn*, comĭtātus, *m*;
(protective), praesĭdĭum, *n*
escort *v.t*, cŏmĭtor (1 *dep*)
especial praecĭpŭus
especially *adv*, praecĭpŭē
espouse *v.t*, (betroth), spondĕo
(2); (marry) dūco (3), nūbo (3)
essay (attempt) cōnātus, *m*;
(composition), lĭbellus, *m*
essence (nature) nātūra, *f*, vīs, *f*
essential (necessary) nĕcessārĭus
establish *v.t*, constĭtŭo (3),
confirmo (1)
establishment constĭtŭo, *f*
estate (property) rēs, *f*, fundus, *m*
esteem *nn*, existĭmātĭo, *f*
esteem *v.t*, (think) aestĭmo (1),
pŭto (1); (think highly of) magni
aestĭmo (1)
estimable laudātus
estimate *nn*, aestĭmātĭo, *f*
estimate *v.t*, aestĭmo (1)
estimation (opinion) ŏpīnĭo, *f*
estrange *v.t*, ălĭēno (1)
estrangement ălĭēnātĭo, *f*
estuary aestŭārĭum, *n*
eternal aeternus
eternally *adv. phr*, in aeternum
eternity aeternĭtas, *f*
ether aether, *m*
ethereal aethĕrĭus
ethical (moral) mōrālis
eulogy laudātĭo, *f*

evacuate　*v.t,* (**— troops from a place**), dēdūco (3); *v.i,* (**depart from**), excēdo (3), ex (*with abl*)
evade　*v.t,* ēlūdo (3)
evaporate　*v.i,* discŭtĭor (3 *pass*)
evasion　lătĕbra, *f*
evasive　ambĭgŭus
eve (**evening**)　vesper, *m*
even　*adv,* ĕtĭam, *often use emphatic pron, e.g.* even Caesar,　Caesar ipse; (**not —**), nĕ...quĭdem
even　*adj,* (**level, equable**), aequus; (**— number**), pār
even if　*conj,* etsi
evening　vesper, *m* (**in the —**), sub vespĕrum
event (**occurrence**)　rēs, *f*; (**outcome**), exĭtus, *m*
eventually　*adv,* ălĭquando
ever　*adv,* (**at any time**) umquam; (**always**), semper; (**if —**), si quando
evergreen　*adj,* semper vĭrĭdis
everlasting　aeternus
every (**all**)　omnis; (**each**), quisque; (**— day**), *adv,* cottīdĭe; (**— one**), omnes, *m.pl*; (**— thing**), omnĭa, *n.pl*; (**— where**), *adv,* ŭbīque
evict　*v.t,* expello (3)
evidence　testĭmōnĭum, *n*; (**factual**), argūmentum, *n*
evident　mănĭfestus, perspĭcŭus; (**it is —**), appāret (2 *impers*)
evil　*adj,* mălus, prāvus
evil　*nn,* mălum, *n*
evil-doer　hŏmo nĕfārĭus
evoke　*v.t,* ēvŏco (1)
evolve　*v.t,* ēvolvo (3)
ewe　ŏvis, *f*
exact　*adj,* (**number, etc.**), exactus; (**persons**), dīlĭgens
exact　*v.t,* exĭgo (3)
exactness　subtīlĭtas, *f*
exaggerate　*v.t,* augĕo (2)
exaggeration　sŭperlātĭo, *f*
exalt　*v.t,* tollo (3), augĕo (2)
exalted　celsus
examination (**test, etc.**)　prŏbātĭo, *f*; (**enquiry**), investīgātĭo, *f*
examine　*v.t,* investīgo (1), interrŏgo (1); (**test**), prŏbo (1)
example　exemplum *n*; (**for —**),

verbi causā
exasperate　*v.t,* exăcerbo (1)
excavate　*v.t,* căvo (1)
excavation (**cavity**)　căvum, *n*
exceed　*v.t,* sŭpĕro (1), excēdo (3)
exceedingly　*adv,* admŏdum; *or use superlative of adj, e.g.* (**— large**), maxĭmus
excel　*v.t,* praesto (1) (*with dat*)
excellence　praestantĭa, *f*
excellent　praestans, ēgrĕgĭus
except　*prep,* praeter (*with acc*)
except　*v.t,* excĭpĭo (3)
exception (**everyone, without —**)　omnes ad ūnum; (**take — to**) aegre fĕro (*irreg*)
exceptional　rārus, insignis
excess (**over-indulgence**)　intempĕrantĭa, *f*
excessive　nĭmĭus
exchange　*nn,* permūtātĭo, *f*
exchange　*v.t,* permūto (1)
exchequer　aerārĭum, *n*
excitable　fervĭdus, fĕrox
excite　*v.t,* excĭto (1), incendo (3)
excited　commōtus, incensus
excitement　commōtĭo, *f*
exclaim　*v.i,* clāmo (1), conclāmo (1)
exclamation　exclāmātĭo, *f*
exclude　*v.t,* exclūdo (3)
exclusion　exclūsĭo, *f*
exclusive (**one's own**)　prŏprĭus
excrescence　tūber, *n*
excruciating (**pain, etc.**)　ācer
excursion　ĭter, *n*
excusable　excūsābĭlis
excuse　*nn,* excūsātĭo, *f*
excuse　*v.t,* excūso (1); (**pardon**), ignosco (3) (*with dat*)
execrable　nĕfārĭus
execrate　*v.t,* dētestor (1 *dep*)
execute　*v.t,* (**carry out**), exsĕquor (3 *dep*); (**inflict capital punishment**), nĕco (1)
execution (**carrying out**)　*use vb* exsĕquor; (**capital punishment**), supplĭcĭum, *n*
executioner　carnĭfex, *m*
exemplary　ēgrĕgĭus
exempt　*v.t,* excĭpĭo (3)
exempt　*adj* immūnis
exemption　immūnĭtas, *f*

exercise exercĭtātĭo, *f*; **(set task)**, ŏpus, *n*
exercise *v.t*, exercĕo (2)
exert *v.t*, contendo (3), ūtor (3 *dep*) (*with abl*); **(to — oneself)**, *v.i*, nītor (3 *dep*)
exertion contentĭo, *f*, lăbor, *m*
exhale *v.t*, exhālo (1)
exhaust *v.t*, exhaurĭo (4); **(weary)**, confĭcĭo (3), dēfătīgo (1)
exhausted (tired out) confectus
exhaustion vīrĭum dēfectĭo, *f*, **(failing of strength)**
exhibit *v.t*, expōno (3)
exhibition (spectacle) spectācŭlum, *n*
exhilarate *v.t*, hĭlăro (1)
exhilaration hĭlărĭtas, *f*
exhort *v.t*, hortor (1 *dep*)
exhume *v.t*, ērŭo (3)
exile *nn*, **(person)**, exsul, *c*; **(banishment)**, exsĭlĭum, *n*; **(to be in —)**, *v.i*, exsŭlo (1)
exist *v.i*, in exsĭlĭum pello (3) **(drive into exile)**
exist *v.i*, sum (*irreg*), existo (3)
existence (life) vīta, *f*
exit exĭtus, *m*
exonerate *v.t*, lībĕro (1)
exorbitant nĭmĭus
exotic externus
expand *v.t*, extendo (3); *v.i*, extendor (3 *pass*)
expanse spătĭum, *n*
expatiate (on a theme etc.) *v.*, permulta dissĕro (3) dē (*with abl.*)
expatriate *v.t*, ēĭcĭo (3)
expect *v.t*, exspecto (1)
expectation exspectātĭo, *f*
expediency ūtĭlĭtas, *f*
expedient *adj*, ūtĭlis
expedient *nn*, rătĭo, *f*
expedite *v.t*, expĕdĭo (4)
expedition (military, etc.) expĕdītĭo, *f*
expeditious cĕler
expel *v.t*, expello (3)
expend *v.t*, expendo (3)
expenditure ērŏgātĭo, *f*
expense impensa, *f*, sumptus, *m*
expensive sumptŭōsus, prĕtĭōsus
experience ūsus, *m*, pĕrītĭa, *f*

experience *v.t*, expĕrĭor (4 *dep*), pătĭor (3 *dep*)
experienced pĕrītus
experiment expĕrīmentum, *n*
expert *adj*, scĭens
expiate *v.t*, expĭo (1)
expiation expĭātĭo, *f*
expiatory pĭācŭlāris
expiration (breathing out) exspīrātĭo, *f*; **(time)**, *use partic.* confectus **(completed)**
expire *v.i*, **(persons)**, exspīro (1); **(time)**, exĕo (4), confĭcĭo (3)
explain *v.t*, explĭco (1), expōno (3)
explanation explĭcātĭo, *f*
explicit ăpertus
explode *v.i*, dīrumpor (3 *pass*)
explore *v.t*, explōro (1)
export *v.t*, exporto (1)
exports merces, *f*, *pl*
expose *v.t*, expōno (3), dētĕgo (3), nūdo (1); **(— to danger, etc.)**, offĕro (*irreg*)
exposition (statement) expŏsĭtĭo, *f*
expostulate *v.i*, expostŭlo (1)
expound *v.t*, explĭco (1), expōno (3)
express *v.t*, exprĭmo (3); **(— in writing)**, dēscrībo (3)
expression (verbal) vox, *f*, verba, *n.pl*; **(facial)**, vultus, *m*
expressive *use phr*, multam vim hăbens **(having much significance)**
expulsion exactĭo, *f*
expunge *v.t*, dēlĕo (2)
exquisite conquĭsītus
extant (to be —) *v.i*, exsto (1)
extemporary extempŏrālis
extemporize *v.i*, sŭbĭta dīco (3)
extend *v.t*, extendo (3), distendo (3); *v.i*, pătĕo (2); **(— to)**, pertĭnĕo (2) ad (*with acc*)
extension (act of) porrectĭo, *f*; **(of boundaries etc.)** prŏpāgātĭo, *f*
extensive amplus
extent spătĭum, *n*
extenuate *v.t*, lĕvo (1), mītĭgo (1)
exterior *adj*, externus
exterior *nn*, spĕcĭes, *f*
exterminate *v.t*, interfĭcĭo (3), dēlĕo (2)

extermination internĕcĭo, *f*
external externus
extinct exstinctus
extinguish *v.t,* exstinguo (3)
extirpate *v.t,* exstirpo (1), excīdo (3)
extol *v.t,* laudo (1)
extort *v.t,* (by force), extorquĕo (2)
extortion res rĕpĕtundae, *f.pl*
extra *adv,* praetĕrĕă
extract *nn,* (from a book, etc.), exceptĭo, *f*
extract *v.t,* extrăho (3), ēvello (3)
extraction (pulling out) ēvulsĭo, *f*
extraordinary extraordĭnārĭus, insŏlĭtus
extravagance sumptus, *m,* luxŭrĭa, *f,* intempĕrantĭa, *f*
extravagant immŏdĭcus, sumptŭōsus
extreme *adj,* extrēmus, ultĭmus
extremity extrēmum, *n;* (top), căcūmen, *n,* vertex, *m; or use adj,* extrēmus (extreme)
extricate *v.t,* expĕdĭo (4), solvo (3)
exuberance luxŭrĭa, *f*
exuberant luxŭrĭōsus, effūsus
exude *v.i,* māno (1)
exult *v.i,* exsulto (1), laetor (1 *dep*)
exultant laetus, ēlātus
eye ŏcŭlus, *m;* (— lash), palpĕbrae pĭlus, *m;* (— lid), palpĕbra, *f;* (— sight), ăcĭes, *f;* (— witness), arbĭter, *m*

F

fable fābŭla, *f*
fabric (woven) textum, *n;* (building), aedĭfĭcĭum, *n*
fabricate *v.t,* fabrĭcor (1 *dep*)
fabrication mendācĭum, *n*
fabulous fictus, falsus
face făcĭes, *f,* vultus, *m,* ōs, *n*
face *v.t,* (confront), obvĭam ĕo (4) (*with dat*); (look towards), specto (1) ad (*with acc*)
facetious făcētus
facilitate *v.t,* făcĭlĭorem reddo (3) (make easier)

facility (possibility) făcultas, *f;* (dexterity), făcĭlĭtas, *f*
facing *prep,* adversus (*with acc*)
fact rēs, *f;* (in —, truly), *conj,* ĕnim; *adv,* vēro
faction factĭo, *f*
factious factĭōsus
factory offĭcīna, *f*
faculty făcultas, *f,* vīs, *f*
fade *v.i,* pallesco (3)
faggot sarmenta *n.pl*
fail *v.i,* cădo (3), dēfĭcĭo (3), dēsum (*irreg*) (*with dat*)
failing *nn,* (defect) vĭtĭum, *n*
failure (of supplies, strength, etc.), dēfectĭo, *f, otherwise use* irrĭtus (vain, unsuccessful)
faint *v.i,* collābor (3 *dep*), languesco (3)
faint *adj,* (exhausted) dēfessus
faint-hearted tĭmĭdus, imbellis
faintness (of body) languor, *m*
fair *nn,* (market), nundĭnae, *f.pl* (ninth day)
fair *adj,* (beautiful), pulcher; (just), aequus; (colour), candĭdus; (weather), sĕrēnus; (wind, etc.), sĕcundus; (fairly good), mĕdĭŏcris
fairly *adv* (justly), iustē; (moderately), mĕdĭŏcrĭter
fairness (justice) aequĭtas, *f;* (of complexion, etc.) candor, *m*
faith fĭdes, *f;* (to keep —), *v.i,* fĭdem servo (1)
faithful fĭdēlis, fidus
faithfulness fĭdēlĭtas, *f*
faithless infĭdus, perfĭdus
faithlessness perfĭdĭa, *f*
falcon falco, *m*
fall *nn,* cāsus, *m,* rūīna, *f*
fall *v.i,* cădo (3); (— back) rĕcĭdo (3); (retreat), pĕdem rĕfĕro (*irreg*); (— headlong), praecĭpĭto (1); (— in love with) ădămo (1); (— off), dēlābor (3 *dep*); (— out, happen), cădo (3); (— upon, attack), *v.t,* invādo (3)
fallacious fallax, falsus
fallacy vĭtĭum, *n*
falling off *nn,* (revolt), dēfectĭo, *f*
fallow nŏvālis, ĭnărātus
false falsus; (not genuine), fictus; (person), perfĭdus

falsehood mendācĭum, *n*
falsify *v.t,* vĭtĭo (1)
falter *v.i,* haerĕo (2), haesĭto (1)
faltering *adj,* haesĭtans
fame glōrĭa, *f,* fāma, *f*
familiar nōtus, fămĭlĭāris; **(usual),**
 consŭetus, *f*
familiarity fămĭlĭārĭtas, *f*
familiarize *v.t,* consŭesco (3)
family *nn,* fămĭlĭa, *f,* dŏmus, *f,*
 gens, *f*
family *adj,* fămĭlĭāris, gentīlis
famine fămes, *f*
famished făme confectus
 (exhausted from hunger)
famous clārus
fan flābellum, *n*
fan *v.t,* ventīlo (1)
fanatical fānātĭcus
fanaticism sŭperstĭtĭo, *f*
fancied (imaginary) fictus
fancy *nn,* **(notion)** ŏpīnĭo, *f*; **(liking
 for),** lĭbĭdo, *f*
fancy *v.t,* **(imagine),** fingo (3);
 (think), ŏpinor (1 *dep*); **(want)**
 cŭpĭo (3)
fang dens, *m*
far *adv,* **(of distance)** prŏcul,
 longē **(as — as)** *prep; with
 comparatives,* multō, *e.g,* **far
 bigger,** multō māior; **(how —)**
 quātĕnus; **(— and wide),** longē
 lātēque
far-fetched quaesītus
farce mīmus, *m*
farcical mīmĭcus
fare (food) cĭbus, *m*; **(charge),**
 vectūra, *f*
farewell!! ăvē; *(pl)* ăvete; vălē,
 vălēte; **(to bid —),** vălēre iŭbĕo (2)
farm *nn,* fundus, *m*
farm *v.t,* cŏlo (3)
farmer agrĭcŏla, *m,* cŏlōnus, *m*
farming agrĭcultūra, *f*
farther *adj,* ultĕrĭor
farther *adv,* longĭus
farthest *adj,* ultĭmus
farhtest *adv,* longissĭme
fascinate *v.t,* fascīno (1)
fascination fascĭnātĭo, *f*
fashion *nn,* mōs, *m*
fashion *v.t,* fingo (3)
fashionable ēlĕgans

fast *nn,* iēiūnĭum, *n*
fast *v.i,* iēiūnus sum *(irreg)* **(be
 hungry)**
fast *adj,* **(quick)** cĕler; **(firm),**
 firmus; **(make —),** *v.t,* firmo (1),
 dēlĭgo (1)
fast *adv,* **(quickly),** cĕlĕrĭter;
 (firmly), firme
fasten *v.t,* fīgo (3), dēlĭgo (1);
 (doors etc.) obtūro (1)
fastening *nn,* vincŭlum, *n*
fastidious dēlĭcātus
fat *adj,* pinguis
fat *nn,* ădeps, *c*
fatal (deadly) pernĭcĭōsus
fatality cāsus, *m*
fate fātum, *n*
fated fātālis
father păter, *m*; **(-in-law),** sŏcer,
 m
fatherland pătrĭa, *f*
fatherless orbus
fathom *nn,* ulna, *f*
fatigue *nn,* dēfătĭgātĭo, *f*
fatigue *v.t,* fătīgo (1)
fatigued fătīgātus
fatten *v.t,* săgīno (1)
fault culpa *f,* vĭtĭum, *n*
faultless intĕger, perfectus
faulty mendōsus, vĭtĭōsus
favour *nn,* grātĭa, *f,* făvour, *m,*
 stŭdĭum, *n*; **(a benefit),** grātĭa, *f,*
 bĕnĕfĭcĭum, *n*
favour *v.t,* făvĕo (2) *(with dat)*
favourable commŏdus; **(of wind),**
 sĕcundus
favourite *nn,* dēlĭcĭae, *f.pl*
favourite *adj,* grātus
fawn *nn,* hinnŭlĕus, *m*
fawn upon *v.t,* ădūlor (1 *dep*)
fear *nn,* tĭmor, *m,* mĕtus, *m*
fear *v.t,* tĭmĕo (2), mĕtŭo (3),
 vĕrĕor (2 *dep*)
fearful *adj,* **(afraid),** tĭmĭdus;
 (terrible), terrĭbĭlis
fearless intrĕpĭdus
fearlessness audācĭa, *f*
feasible *use phr. with vbs,* posse
 (to be able) *and* effĭcĕre **(to
 bring about)**
feast *nn,* daps, *f,* ĕpŭlae, *f.pl*;
 (— day) dĭes festus, *m*
feast *v.i,* ĕpŭlor (1 *dep*); *v.t,*

pasco (3)
feat făcĭnus, *n*
feather penna, *f*, plūma, *f*
feature (of face, etc.)
līnĕāmentum, *n*; **(peculiarity)** *use*
adj, prŏprĭus **(one's own)**
February Fĕbrŭārĭus (mensis)
fecundity fēcundĭtas, *f*
federal foedĕrātus
fee merces, *f*, hŏnor, *m*
feeble infirmus, imbēcillus
feebleness infirmĭtas, *f*
feed *v.t*, pasco (3), ălo (3); *v.i*,
vescor (3 *dep*.), pascor (3 *dep*)
feel *v.t*, sentĭo (4); **(with the
hands)**, tempto (1)
feeler cornĭcŭlum, *n*
feeling *nn*, **(sensation or
emotion)**, sensus, *m*, tactus, *m*;
(spirit, etc.), ănĭmus, *m*
feign *v.t*, sĭmŭlo (1)
feigned sĭmŭlātus
feint sĭmŭlātĭo, *f*
felicitous fēlix
felicity fēlīcĭtas, *f*
fell *v.t*, excīdo (3), sterno (3)
fellow (companion) cŏmĕs, *c*;
(— citizen), cīvis, *c*; **(— feeling)**,
consensĭo, *f*; **(— soldier)**,
commīlĭto, *m*; **(worthless —)**,
nēbŭlo, *m*
fellowship (companionship),
sŏcĭĕtas, *f*
felt *nn*, cŏactum, *n*
female *nn*, fēmĭna, *f*
female *adj*, mŭlĭĕbris
fen pălus, *f*
fence *nn*, saeptum, *n*, cancelli,
m,pl
fence *v.t*, saepĭo (4); **(with
swords)**, *v.i*, băttŭo
fencing (art of —) ars, (*f*) glădĭi
ferment *nn*, **(excitement)**, aestus,
m
ferment *v.i*, fervĕo (2)
fern fĭlix, *f*
ferocious saevus, fĕrus
ferocity saevĭtĭa, *f*
ferry *nn*, trāiectus, *m*; **(— boat)**,
cymba, *f*
ferry *v.t*, trāĭcĭo (3)
fertile fēcundus, fertĭlis
fertility fēcundĭtas, *f*

fervent ardens, fervĭdus
fervour ardor, *m*, fervor, *m*
festival (holidays) fērĭae, *f.pl*;
(religious —, etc.) sollemne, *n*
festive (gay) hĭlăris
festivity (gaiety) hĭlărĭtas, *f*
fetch *v.t*, peto (3), affĕro (*irreg*)
fetter *nn*, vincŭlum, *n*
fetter *v.t*, vincŭla ĭnĭcĭo (3) **(with
dat)**
feud (quarrel) sĭmultas, *f*
fever fĕbris, *f*
feverish fĕbrĭcŭlōsus; **(excited)**
commōtus
few *adj*, pauci (*pl*)
fewness paucĭtas, *f*
fib mendācĭum, *n*
fibre fibra, *f*
fickle inconstans
fickleness inconstantĭa, *f*
fiction commentum, *n*, făbŭla, *f*
fictitious commentĭcĭus
fiddle (instrument) fĭdes, *f.pl*
fidelity fīdēlĭtas, *f*
fidgety inquĭĕtus
field ăger *m*; **(plain)**, campus, *m*;
(— of battle), lŏcus, (*m*) pugnae;
(scope), lŏcus, *m*
fiendish nēfandus
fierce fĕrox, fĕrus
fierceness fĕrōcĭtas
fiery (of temper, etc.) ardens
fifteen quindĕcim; **(— times)**, *adv*,
quindĕcĭes
fifteenth quintus dĕcĭmus
fifth quintus
fiftieth quinquāgēsĭmus
fifty quinquāginta
fig, fig tree fĭcus, *f*
fight *nn*, pugna, *f*
fight *v.i*, pugno (1)
fighter pugnātor, *m*
figurative translātus
figure fĭgŭra, *f*, forma, *f*
figure *v.t*, **(imagine)**, fingo (3)
figured sĭgillātus
filch *v.t*, surrĭpĭo (3)
file (tool) scŏbīna, *f*; **(rank)**, ordo, *m*
file *v.t*, **(wood, metal)**, līmo (1)
filial (dutiful, respectful) pĭus
fill *v.t*, implĕo (2), complĕo (2); **(a
post, etc.)** fungor (3 *dep*) **(with
abl)**

fillet (for the hair) vitta, *f*
film membrāna, *f*
filter *v.t*, cōlo (1)
filth caenum, *n*
filthy sordĭdus, foedus
fin pinna, *f*
final ultĭmus
finally *adv*, postrēmo, dēnĭque, tandem
finance (of the state) aerārĭum, *n*
find *v.t*, invĕnĭo (4), rĕpĕrĭo (4); (— **out**); cognosco (3), compĕrĭo (4); (— **fault with**), culpo (1); accūso (1)
fine *v.t*, multo (1)
fine *nn*, multa, *f*
fine *adj*, (**of texture**), subtīlis; (**handsome, etc.**) praeclārus; (**weather**), sĕrēnus
finery mundĭtĭa, *f*
finger dĭgĭtus, *m*; (**fore —**), index dĭgitus
finger *v.t*, tango (3)
finish *nn*, (**perfection**), perfectĭo, *f*
finish *v.t*, confĭcĭo (3); (**limit**), fīnĭo (4)
finished (complete, perfect) perfectus
fir, fir tree ăbĭes, *f*
fire ignis, *m*; (**ardour**), vīs, *f*, ardor, *m*; (**to be on —**), *v.i*, ardĕo (2); (**to set on —**) *v.t*, incendo (3)
fire *v.t*, incendo (3); (**missiles**), cōnĭcĭo (3)
firebrand fax, *f*
fireplace fŏcus, *m*
firewood lignum, *n*
firm firmus; (**constant**), constans; (**to make —**), *v.t*, confirmo (1)
first *adj*, prīmus
first *adv*, prīmum, prīmō
fish *nn*, piscis, *m*
fish *v.i*, piscor (1 *dep*)
fisherman piscātor, *m*
fishing *nn*, piscātus, *m*
fishing boat hŏrĭŏla, *f*
fishing net rēte, *n*
fishmonger cētārĭus, *m*
fishpond piscīna, *f*
fissure rīma, *f*
fist pugnus, *m*
fit (violent seizure) accessĭo, *f*, impĕtus, *m*

fit, fitted aptus, ĭdōnĕus, accommŏdātus
fit *v.t*, accommŏdo (1), apto (1); (— **out**), exorno (1)
five quinque; (— **each**), quīni; (— **times**) *adv*, quinquĭes
five hundred quingenti
fix *v.t*, fīgo (3); (**determine**), stătŭo (3), constĭtŭo (3)
fixed certus
flabby flaccĭdus
flag vexillum, *n*
flag *v.i* (**become weak**), languesco (3)
flagrant (clear) mănĭfestus; (**heinous**), nĕfandus
flail pertĭca, *f*
flame *nn*, flamma, *f*
flame *v.i*, flagro (1)
flame-coloured flammĕus
flank (of army, etc.) lătus, *n*; (**of animal**) īlĭa, *n.pl*
flap (of dress, etc.) lăcĭnĭa, *f*
flare *v.i*, flăgro (1)
flash *nn*, fulgor, *m*
flash *v.i*, fulgĕo (2)
flask ampulla, *f*
flat aequus, plānus
flatness plānĭtĭes, *f*
flatter *v.t*, ădūlor (1 *dep*)
flatterer ădūlātor, *m*
flattering ădūlans
flattery ădūlātĭo, *f*
flaunt *v.t*, iacto (1)
flavour săpor, *m*
flaw vĭtĭum, *n*
flawless ēmendātus
flax līnum, *n*
flaxen *adj*, līnĕus
flea pūlex, *m*
flee *v.i* (**flee from,** *v.t.*), fŭgĭo (3)
fleece *nn*, vellus, *n*
fleece *v.t*, (**rob**), spŏlĭo (1)
fleecy lānĭger
fleet *nn*, classis, *f*
fleet *adj*, cĕler
fleeting fŭgax
flexh căro, *f*
flesh-coloured, fleshy carnōsus
flexibility făcĭlĭtas, *f*
flexible flexĭbĭlis
flicker *v.i*, trĕpĭdo (1), cŏrusco (1)

flickering trĕpĭdans, trĕmŭlus
flight (flying) cŏlātus, *m*; **(escape)** fŭga, *f*
flighty mōbĭlis, lĕvis
fling *v.t*, cōnĭcĭo (3)
flint sĭlex, *m*
flippant făcētus
flirt *v.i*, blandĭor (4 *dep*)
flit *v.i*, vŏlĭto (1); **(— in, or upon)**, inno (1) *(with dat)*
float *v.i*, năto (1); **(in the air)**, vŏlĭto (1)
flock grex, *m*, pĕcus, *n*
flock *v.i*, conflŭo (3), concurro (3)
flog *v.t*, verbĕro (1)
flogging verbĕra, *n.pl*
flood dĭlŭvĭes, *f*, *n*
flood *v.t*, ĭnundo (1)
floor sŏlum, *n*; **(upper —)** contăbŭlātĭo, *f*
florid flōrĭdus
flotilla classis, *f*
flounder *v.i*, vŏlūtor (1 *pass*)
flour fărīna, *f*
flourish *v.i*, flōrĕo (2); *v.t*, vĭbro (1)
flourishes (of style) călămistri, *m.pl*
flow *nn*, cursus, *m*, fluxĭo, *f*; **(of the tide)**, accessus, *m*
flow *v.i*, flŭo (3); **(— past)**, praeterflŭo (3); **(— together)**, conflŭo (3); **(trickle)**, māno (1)
flower *nn*, flos, *m*
flower *v.i*, flōrĕo (2)
flowing flŭens; **(hair)**, fūsus
fluctuate *v.i*, iactor (1 *pass*); aestŭo (1)
fluctuation mūtātĭo, *f*
fluency vŏlūbĭlĭtas, *f*
fluent vŏlūbĭlis
fluid *nn*, hūmor, *m*, lĭquor, *m*
fluid *adj*, lĭquĭdus
flurry concĭtātĭo, *f*
flush *nn*, rŭbor, *m*
flush *v.i*, ērŭbesco (3)
fluster *v.i*, ăgĭto (1)
flute tībĭa, *f*; **(— player)**, tībĭcen, *m*
flutter *nn*, trĕpĭdātĭo, *f*
flutter *v.i*, vŏlĭto (1), **(in fear)**, trĕpĭdo (1)
flux (flow) fluctus, *m*, fluxus, *m*

fly *nn*, musca, *f*
fly *v.i*, vŏlo (1)
flying *adj*, vŏlātĭlis, vŏlŭcer
flying *nn*, vŏlātus,
foal ĕquŭlĕus, *m*, pullus, *m*
foam *nn*, spūma, *f*
foam *v.i*, spūmo (1)
foaming, foamy spūmōsus
fodder pābŭlum, *n*
foe hostis, *c*
fog cālīgo, *f*
foggy cālīgĭnōsus
foil (sword) rŭdis, *f*; **(metal leaf)**, lāmĭna, *f*
foil *v.t*, **(parry a blow, delude)**, ēlūdo (3)
fold *nn*, **(of garment, etc.)** sĭnus, *m*
fold *v.t*, plĭco (1)
folding-doors valvae *f.pl*
foliage frons, *f*
folk (people) hŏmĭnes, *c.pl*
follow *v.i. and v.t*, sĕquor (3 *dep*); sector (1 *dep*); **(succeed)**, succēdo (3) *(with dat)*
follower (attendant) assectātor, *m*; or use *adj*, e.g. **(— of Ceasar)** Caesărĭānus
following sĕquens, proxĭmus, sĕcundus
folly stultĭtĭa, *f*
foment *v.t*, fŏvĕo (2); **(— trouble, etc.)** sollĭcĭto (1)
fond ămans *(with genit)*
fondle *v.t*, mulcĕo (2)
fond cĭbus, *m*; **(fodder)**, pābŭlum, *n*
fool hŏmo stultus; **(to act the —)**, *v.i*, dēsĭpĭo
fool *v.t*, lūdo (3)
foolhardy tĕmĕrārĭus
foolish stultus
foot pes, *m*; **(on —)**, *adj*, pĕdester; **(— in length)**, *adj*, pĕdālis; **(bottom of)**, use *adj*, īmus, *in agreement with noun*, e.g. īma quercus **(foot of an oak)**
footing stătus, *m*, or use *vb*, consisto (3), **(to stand)**
footman pĕdĭsĕquus, *m*
footpath sēmĭta, *f*
footprint vestīgĭum, *n*
footsoldier pĕdes, *m*

for *prep* **(on behalf of)**, prō (*with abl*); **(on account of)**, propter, ŏb (*with acc*); **(during a certain time)**, *use acc, e.g.* **for two hours**, dŭas hōras, *or* per (*with acc*); **(expressing purpose)**, *use* ad (*with acc*)

for *conj*, nam, namque; ĕnim (*second word in clause*); **(because)**, quippe, quod

forage *nn*, pābŭlum, *n*

forage *v.i, and v.t*, pābŭlor (1 *dep*)

forbear *v.i, and v.t*, parco (3)

forbearance contĭnentĭa, *f*

forbid *v.t*, vĕto (1)

force *nn*, vīs, *f*; **(military forces)**, cōpĭae, *f.pl*

force *v.t*, **(compel)**, cōgo (3); **(break through)**, perrumpo (3)

forced (unnatural) quaesītus; **(a — march)**, magnum ĭter, *n*

forcible, forcibly *use adv. phr*, per vim

ford *nn*, vădum, *n*

ford *v.i. and v.t*, vădo transĕo (4) **(cross by a ford)**

forearm bracchĭum, *n*

forebode *v.t*, paresāgĭo (4), portendo (3)

foreboding *nn*, praesensĭo, *f*

forecast *v.t*, praevĭdĕo (2)

forefather prŏăvus, *m*; *(pl)* māiōres *m.pl*

forehead frons, *f*

foreign externus, pĕrĕgrīnus

foreigner pĕrĕgrīnus, *m*

foreman qui (servis) praeest **(who is in charge of (slaves))**

foremost prīmus

forensic fŏrensis

forerunner praenuntĭus, *m*

foresee *v.t*, prōvĭdĕo (2)

foresight prōvĭdentĭa, *f*

forest silva, *f*

foretell *v.t*, praedīco (3)

forethought prōvĭdentĭa, *f*

forewarn *v.t*, preaemŏnĕo (2)

forfeit *nn*, poena, *f*

forfeit *v.t*, āmitto (3)

forge *nn*, fornax, *f*

forge *v.t*, făbrĭcor (1 *dep*), excūdo (3); **(strike counterfeit coins)**, nummos ădultĕrīnos cūdo (3); **(documents)**, suppōno (3)

forgery *use phr*. subiectĭo falsārum littĕrāum **(substitution of counterfeit letters)**

forget *v.t*, ovlīviscor (3 *dep*) (*with genit*)

forgetful immĕmor

forgetfulness oblīvĭo, *f*

forgive *v.t*, ignosco (3) (*with dat of person*)

forgiveness vĕnĭa

fork furca, *f*

forked bĭfurcus

forlorn destĭtūtus, perdĭtus

form forma, *f*, fĭgūra, *f*

form *v.t*, **(shape)**, formo (1), fingo (3); **(— a plan)**, ĭnĕo (4), căpĭo (3); **(troops, etc.)** instrŭo (3)

formality rītus, *m*

formally *adv*, rītĕ

formation conformātĭo, *f*

former prĭor, sŭpĕrĭor; **(the — and the latter)**, ille … hic

formerly *adv*, antĕā, ōlim

formidable grăvis, mĕtŭendus

formula formŭla, *f*

forsake *v.t*, rĕlinquo (3), dēsĕro (3)

forswear *v.t*, **(renounce)**, abiūro (1); **(swear falsely)**, periūro (1)

fort castellum, *n*

forth *adv, use compound vb. with* e *or* ex, *e.g.* exĕo, **go forth**; **(of time)**, inde

forthwith, *adv*, stătim, extemplo

fortification mūnītĭo, *f*

fortify *v.t*, mūnĭo (4)

fortitude fortĭtūdo, *f*

fortuitous fortŭĭtus

fortunate fēlix, fortūnātus

fortune fortūna, *f*, **(property, etc.)**, rēs, *f*, ŏpes, *f.pl*

fortune-teller hărĭolŭs, *m*

forty quădrāginta

forum fŏrum, *n*

forward, forwards *adv*, porro, prorsum, ante; *or use compound verb with* pro *e.g.* prōdūco **(lead forward)**

forward *adj*, praecox

forward *v.t*, **(send on)**, perfĕro (*irreg*)

foster *v.t*, nūtrĭo (4)
foster-brother collactĕus, *m*;
(— child), ălumnus, *m*; (— father),
altor, *m*; (— mother), nūtrix, *f*;
(— sister), collactĕa, *f*
foul *adj*, foedus
found *v.t*, condo (3); (metal),
fundo (3)
foundation fundāmenta, *n.pl*
founder condĭtor, *m*
founder *v.i*, submergo (3 *pass*)
fountain fons, *m*
four quattŭor; (— times), *adv*,
quătĕr; (— each), quăterni
fourteen quattŭordĕcim;
(-teenth), quartus dĕcĭmus
fourth quartus; (— part, quarter),
quădrans, *m*
fowl ăvis, *f*, gallīna, *f*
fowler auceps, *c*
fox vulpes, *f*
fraction (part) pars, *f*
fractious difficĭlis
fracture *nn*, fractūra, *f*
fracture *v.t*, frango (3)
fragile frăgĭlis
fragment fragmentum, *n*
fragile frăgĭlis
fragment fragmentum, *n*
fragrance dulcis ŏdōr, *m*,
(pleasant smell)
fragrant dulcis, suāvis
frail frăgĭlis, dēbĭlis
frailty frăgĭlĭtas, *f*, dēbĭlĭtas
frame forma, *f*, compāges, *f*;
(— of mind) ănĭmus, *m*, affectĭo, *f*
frame *v.t*, (shape), făbrĭcor (1
dep), fingo (3); (form), compōno
(3)
franchise (citizenship) cīvĭtas, *f*;
(right of voting), suffrāgĭum, *n*
frank līber, ăpertus
frantic āmens
fraternal frāternus
fraternity (association of men)
sŏdālĭtas, *f*
fratricide (the person) frātrĭcīda,
m; (the crime), fraternum
parrĭcīdĭum, *n*
fraud fraus, *f*, dŏlus, *m*
fraudulent fraudŭlentus, dŏlōsus
fraught opplētus (filled)
fray certāmen, *n*, pugna, *f*

freak (prodigy) prōdĭgĭum, *n*
freckle lentīgo, *f*
free līber; (generous), lībĕrālis; (of
one's will), sŭā sponte (*abl*)
free *v.t*, lībĕro (1), solvo (3)
free-born ingĕnŭus
freedman lībertus, *m*
freedom lībertas, *f*; (— from a
burden, tax, etc.), immūnĭtas, *f*
freehold *nn*, praedĭum lībĕrum, *n*,
(free estate)
freely *adv*, lībĕrē; (generously),
mūnĭfĭcē, largē; (of one's own free
will), sŭā sponte
free-will vŏluntas, *f*
freeze *v.t*, glăcĭo (1); *v.i*, congĕlo
(1)
freight *nn*, ŏnus, *n*
freight *adj*, ŏnustus
French *adj*, Gallĭcus; (The
French), Galli, *pl*
frenzied fŭrens, āmens
frenzy fŭror, *m*, āmentĭa, *f*
frequent *adj*, crēber, frĕquens
frequent *v.t*, cĕlĕbro (1)
frequently *adv*, saepe
fresh (new) rĕcens, nŏvus; (wind),
incrēbresco (3)
freshness vĭrĭdĭtas, *f*
fret *v.i*, dŏlĕo (2)
fretful mōrōsus
fretfulness mōrōsĭtas, *f*
friction trītus, *m*
friend ămīcus, *m*
friendless ĭnops ămīcōrum
(destitute of friends)
friendliness cōmĭtas, *f*
friendly ămīcus, cōmis
friendship ămīcĭtĭa, *f*
fright terror *m*, păvor, *m*; (to
take —), *v.i*, păvesco (3)
frighten *v.t*, terrĕo (2)
frightful terrĭbĭlis, horrĭbĭlis
frigid frīgĭdus
frill segmenta, *n.pl*
fringe fimbrĭae, *f.pl*
frippery nūgae, *f.pl*
frisk *v.i*, lascīvĭo (4)
fritter away *v.t*, dissĭpo (1)
frivolity lĕvĭtas, *f*
frivolous lĕvis; (opinion, etc.)
fūtĭlis
fro (to and —) *adv, phr*, hūc et illūc

frock stŏla, *f*
frog rāna, *f*
frolic *nn*, lūdus, *m*
frolic *v.i*, lūdo (3)
from ā, ab, dē, ē, ex (*all with abl*) (*with expressions of place, time and cause*)
front *nn*, frons, *f*, prĭor pars; (in —) ā fronte, *or use adj*, adversus; (in — of) *prep*, prō (*with abl*)
front *adj*, prĭor
frontage frons, *f*
frontier fīnis, *m*
frost gĕlu, *n*; (— bitten), *adj*, ambustus
frosty gĕlĭdus
froth *nn*, spūma, *f*
froth *v.i*, spūmo (1)
frown *nn*, contractĭo (*f*) frontis (contraction of the forehead)
frown *v.i*, frontem contrăho (3)
frowsy incultus
frozen rĭgĭdus, glăcĭālis
fructify *v.t*, fēcundo (1)
frugal frūgi, *indecl*
frugality parsĭmōnĭa, *f*
fruit fructus, *m*, pōmum, *n*
fruitful fēcundĭtas, *f*
fruition fructus, *m*
fruitless (without result) irrĭtus
fruit tree pōmum, *n*, pōmus, *f*
frustrate *v.t*, (an undertaking, etc.) ad vānum rĕdĭgo (3)
frustrated (to be —) *v.i*, frustrā esse
frustration frustrātĭo, *f*
fry *v.t*, frīgo (3)
frying pan sartāgo, *f*
fuel ligna, *n.pl*
fugitive *nn*, prŏfŭgus, *m*, fŭgĭtīvus, *m*
fugitive *adj*, fŭgĭtīvus
fulfil *v.t*, explĕo (2), exsĕquor (3 *dep*), fungor (3 *dep*) (*with abl*)
full plēnus, replētus; (with people), frĕquens, crēber
full-grown ădultus
fulminate *v.i*, fulmĭno (1), intŏno (1)
fulness (abundance) ūbertas, *f*
fulsome pūtĭdus
fumble *v.t*, (handle), tento (1)
fume *nn*, hālĭtus, *m*
fume *v.i*, (with anger etc.), fŭro (3)

fumigate *v.t*, suffĭo (4)
fun iŏcus, *m*, lūdus, *m*
function offĭcĭum, *n*, mūnus, *n*
fund (of knowledge, etc.) cōpĭa, *f*, with *nn*. in genit.
fundamental prīmus
funeral fūnus, *n*, exsĕquĭae, *f.pl*
funeral, funereal *adj*, fūnĕbris
fungus fungus, *m*
funnel infundĭbŭlum, *n*
funny rīdĭcŭlus
fur pĭlus, *m*
furbish *v.t*, interpŏlo (1)
furious fŭrens, saevus; (to be —), *v.i*, saevĭo (4), fŭro (3)
furl *v.t*, contrăho (3), lĕgo (3), subdūco (3)
furlough commĕātus, *m*
furnace fornax, *f*
furnish *v.t*, suppĕdĭto (1), orno (1)
furniture sŭpellex, *f*
furrow *nn*, sulcus, *m*
furrow *v.t*, sulco (1)
further *adj*, ultĕrĭor; *adv*, ultĕrĭus
further *v.t*, (help), adiŭvo (1)
furthermore *adv*, porro, praetĕrĕa
furthest *adj*, ultĭmus
furtive furtīvus
fury fŭror, *m*
fuse *v.t*, (melt), lĭquĕfăcĭo (3); (— together), miscĕo (2)
fuss *nn*, perturbātĭo, *f*
fussy nĭmis stŭdĭōsus
fusty mūcĭdus
futile vānus, fūtĭlis
futility fūtĭlĭtas, *f*
future *adj*, fŭtūrus
future *nn*, fŭtūra, *n.pl*; (in —), *adv*, in fēlĭquum tempus
futurity tempus fŭtūrum, *n*

G

gabble *v.i*, blătĕro (1)
gabbler blătĕro, *m*
gable fastīgĭum, *n*
gad about *v.i*, văgor (1 *dep*)
gadfly tăbānus, *m*
gag *v.t*, ōs obvolvo (3) (*with dat*) (muffle the mouth)
gage pignus, *n*
gaiety hĭlărĭtas, *f*

gaily   *adv*, hĭlăre
gain   *nn*, lŭcrum, *n*, quaestus, *m*
gain   *v.t*, (profit, etc.) lŭcror (1
   dep); (obtain), consĕquor (3 *dep*),
   pŏtĭor (4 *dep*) (*with abl*); (— a
   victory), victōrĭam rĕporto (1) *or*
   părĭo (3)
gainsay   *v.t*, contrā dīco (3)
gait   incessus, *m*
gaiters   ŏcrĕae, *f.pl*
galaxy   *use* vĭa lactĕa, *f*. (milky
   way)
gale   ventus, *m*, prŏcella, *f*
gall   *nn*, fel, *n*
gall   *v.t*, (chafe), ūro (3); (annoy),
   sollĭcĭto (1); *or* pĭget (2 *impers*) (it
   irks)
gallant   fortis
gallant   *nn*, (lover), ămātor, *m*
gallantry   virtus, *f*
gallery   portĭcus, *f*
galley (ship)   nāvis, *f*
galling   mordax
gallon   congĭus, *m*
gallop   *v.i*, ĕquo cĭtāto vĕhi (3
   pass) (to be carried by a swift
   horse)
gallows   furca, *f*, crux, *f*
gamble   *v.i*, ālĕa lūdo (3) (play
   with dice)
gambler   ālĕātor, *m*
gambling   *nn*, ālĕa, *f*
gambol   *v.i*, lascīvĭo (4)
game   lūdus, *m*; (wild beasts),
   fĕrae, *f.pl*
gamester   ālĕātor, *m*
gammon   perna, *f*
gander   anser, *m*
gang   grex, *m*, căterva, *f*
gangrene   gangraena, *f*
gangway   fŏrus, *m*
gaol   carcer, *m*
gaoler   custos, *m*
gap   lăcūna, *f*, hĭātus, *m*
gape   *v.i*, hĭo (1)
gaping   *adj*, hĭans
garb   vestītus, *m*
garbage   quisquĭlĭae, *f.pl*
garden   hortus, *m*
gardening   cūra (*f*) hortōrum
   (care of gardens)
gargle   *v.i*, gargărīzo (1)
garland   serta, *n.pl*

garlic   ālĭum, *n*
garment   vestīmentum, *n*
garner   *v.t*, (store), condo (3)
garnish   *v.t*, dĕcŏro (1)
garret   cēnācŭlum, *n*
garrison   praesĭdĭum, *n*
garrison   *v.t*, praesĭdĭum collŏco
   (1) in (*with abl*)
garrulity   lŏquācĭtas, *f*
garrulous   lŏquax
gas   spīrĭtus, *m*
gash   *nn*, plāga, *f*
gash   *v.t*, percŭtĭo (3)
gasp   *nn*, ănhēlĭtus, *m*
gasp   *v.i*, ănhēlo (1)
gastric   *use genitive* stŏmăchi (of
   the stomach)
gate   porta, *f*, iānŭa, *f*; (— keeper),
   iānĭtor, *m*
gather   *v.t*, lĕgo (3), collĭgo (3);
   (pluck), carpo (3); *v.i*, convĕnĭo
   (4), congrĕgor (1 *dep*)
gathering   coetus, *m*
gaudy   fūcātus
gauge   *v.t*, mētĭor (4 *dep*)
gauge   *nn*, mŏdŭlus, *m*
gaunt   măcer
gay   hĭlăris
gaze at   *v.t*, tŭĕor (2 *dep*)
gaze   *nn*, obtūtus, *m*
gazelle   dorcas, *f*
gazette   acta dĭurna, *n.pl*, (daily
   events)
gear   appărātus, *m*
geld   *v.t*, castro (1)
gelding   cantērĭus, *m*
gem   gemma, *f*
gender   gĕnus, *n*
geneology (lineage)   ŏrīgo, *f*,
   gĕnus, *n*
general   *adj*, (opp. to particular),
   gĕnĕrālis; (common, widespread),
   vulgāris, commūnis
general   *nn*, dux, *m*, impĕrātor, *m*
generality (majority)   plērīque
generally (for the most part)   *adv*,
   plērumque
generalship   ductus, *m*
generate   *v.t*, gĕnĕro (1), gigno (3)
generation   saecŭlum, *n*
generosity   bĕnignĭtas, *f*
generous (with money, etc.)
   lībĕrālis

genial cōmis
geniality cōmĭtas, *f*
genius (ability) ingĕnĭum, *n*;
(guardian spirit), gĕnĭus, *m*
genteel urbānus
gentle (mild) mītis; (of birth),
gĕnĕrōsus
gentleman hŏmo ingĕnŭus
gentlemanly *adj,* lībĕrālis,
hŏnestus
gentleness lēnĭtas, *f*
gently *adv,* lēnĭter
gentry nōbĭles, *m.pl*
genuine sincērus
geography gĕōgraphĭa, *f*
geometry gĕōmĕtrĭa, *f*
germ germen, *n*
German Germānus
germane affinis
germinate *v.i,* germĭno (1)
gesticulate *v.i,* sē iactāre (1
reflex)
gesture gestus, *m*
get *v.t,* (obtain), ădĭpiscor (3
dep), nanciscor (3 *dep*); (a
request), impĕtro (1); (become),
v.i, fīo (*irreg*); (— about, or
spread, etc.), percrēbesco (3); (—
away), effŭgĭo (3); (— back), *v.t,*
rĕcĭpĭo (3); (— the better of),
sŭpĕro (1); (— down), *v.i,*
dēscendo (3); (— out), exĕo (4);
(— ready) *v.t,* păro (1); (— rid
of), āmŏvĕo (2) in *or* ad (*with
acc*); (— up, rise), surgo (3)
ghastly exsanguis
ghost mānes, *m.pl*
giant vir ingenti stătūra (man of
huge stature)
gibbet crux, *f*
giddy vertīgĭnōsus
gift dōnum, *n*
gifted (mentally, etc.) ingĕnĭōsus
gigantic ingens
giggle *v.i,* use rīdĕo (2), (to laugh)
gild *v.t,* ĭnauro (1)
gills (of fish) branchĭae, *f.pl*
gimlet tĕrĕbra, *f*
gin pĕdĭca, *f*
giraffe cămēlŏpardălis, *f*
gird *v.t,* cingo (3); (— oneself), sē
accingĕre (3 *reflex*)
girder trabs, *f*

girdle cingŭlum, *n*
girl pŭella, *f,* virgo, *f*
girlhood aetas, (*f*) pŭellāris
girth ambĭtus, *m*
give *v.t,* do (1), dōno (1);
(render), reddo (3); (— an
opportunity), făcultātem do (1);
(— back), reddo (3); (— in), *v.i,*
cēdo (3); (— up, deliver), trādo
(3); (abandon), dīmitto (3); (— up
hope), *v.i,* dēspĕro (1); (—
orders), iŭbĕo (2)
glad laetus, hĭlăris
gladden *v.t,* hĭlăro (1)
glade nĕmus, *n,* saltus, *m*
gladiator glădĭātor, *m*
gladness laetĭtĭa, *f*
glance at *v.t,* aspĭcĭo (3); (graze)
stringo (3)
glance *nn,* aspectus, *m*
gland glans, *f*
glare *nn,* fulgor, *m*
glare *v.i,* fulgĕo (2); (look with
stern glance) torvis ŏcŭlis tŭĕor
(2 *dep*)
glaring (conspicuous) mănĭfestus
glass *nn,* vĭtrum, *n*; (drinking —),
pōcŭlum, *n*
glass *adj,* vĭtrĕus
gleam *nn,* fulgor, *m*
gleam *v.i,* fulgĕo (2)
glean *v.t,* spīcas collĭgo (3)
(collect ears of corn)
glee laetĭtĭa, *f*
glen valles, *f*
glib (of tongue) vŏlūbĭlis
glide lābor (3 *dep*)
glimmer *v.i,* sublūcĕo (2)
glimmering *adj,* sublustris
glimpse (get a — of) *v.t,* dispĭcĭo
(3)
glitter *v.i,* fulgĕo (2)
glittering *adj,* fulgĭdus, cŏruscus
gloat over *v.t,* gaudens aspĭcĭo (3)
globe glŏbus, *m*; (the earth) orbis,
m
gloom tĕnebrae, *f.pl,* tristĭtĭa, *f*
gloomy tĕnebrōsus, tristis
glorify *v.t,* laudo (1), extollo (3)
glorious praeclārus, illustris
glory glōrĭa, *f,* dĕcus, *n,* laus, *f*
gloss *n,* nĭtor, *m*
gloss over *v.t,* praetĕrĕo (4)

glossy nĭtĭdus
gloves mănĭcae, *f.pl*
glow *nn*, ardor, *m*
glow *v.i*, ardĕo (2), candĕo (2)
glue *nn*, glūten, *n*
glut *nn*, sătĭĕtas, *f*
glut *v.t*, explĕo (2), sătĭo (1)
glutton hellŭo, *m*
gluttonous ĕdax
gluttony ĕdācĭtas, *f*
gnarled nōdōsus
gnash (the teeth) *v.t*, frendĕo (2),
    (dentibus)
gnat cŭlex, *m*
gnaw *v.t*, rōdo (3)
gnawing *adj*, mordax
go *v.i*, ĕo (*irreg*), vādo (3);
    (depart), ăbĕo (4), prŏfĭciscor (3
    dep); (— abroad), pĕrĕgre exĕo (4
    irreg); (— away), ăbĕo (4 *irreg*);
    (— by, past), praetĕrĕo (4 *irreg*);
    (— down), dēscendo (3); (— in)
    ĭnĕo (4 *irreg*); (— over), transĕo
    (4 *irreg*); (— round), circumĕo (4
    irreg); (— through) ŏbĕo (4 *irreg*);
    (— up), ascendo (3); (— without)
    cărĕo (2) (*with abl*)
goad *v.t*, stĭmŭlo (1)
goal mēta, *f*
goat căper, *m*
go-between *nn*, interpres, *c*
goblet pōcŭlum, *n*
god dĕus, *m*
goddess dĕa, *f*
godless impĭus
godlike dīvīnus
godly *adj*, pĭus
gold aurum, *n*
golden aurĕus
goldsmith aurĭfex, *m*
good *adj*, bŏnus, prŏbus,
    hŏnestus, aptus, commŏdus
good *nn*, bŏnum, *n*; (advantage),
    commŏdum, *n*; (goods,
    possessions), bŏna, *n.pl*; (— for
    nothing), *adj*, nēquam; (to do —),
    prōdesse (*irreg*)(*with dat*)
goodbye! vălē! (*pl*, vălete!)
good-humour cōmĭtas, *f*
good-humoured cōmis
good-looking spĕcĭōsus
good-nature cōmĭtas, *f*
good-natured cōmis

goodness (virtue) virtus, *f*,
    prŏbĭtas, *f*; (excellence) bŏnĭtas, *f*
good-tempered mītis
goose anser, *m*
gore *nn*, crŭor, *m*
gorge (throat) guttur, *n*, fauces,
    f.pl; (mountain pass), angustĭae,
    f.pl
gorge oneself *v.i*, sē ingurgĭtāre
    (1 *reflex*)
gorgeous spĕcĭōsus, splendĭdus
gorgeousness magnĭficentĭa, *f*
gory crŭentus
gossip *v.i*, garrĭo (4)
gossip *nn*, (talk), rūmor, *m*;
    (person), garrŭlus, *m*
gouge *v.t*, (— out eyes), ŏcŭlos
    ērŭo (3)
gourd cŭcurbĭta, *f*
gout morbus (*m*) artĭcŭlōrum
    (disease of the joints)
gouty arthrītĭcus
govern *v.t*, gŭberno (1), impĕro
    (1), tempĕro (1), mŏdĕror (1 *dep*)
government (act of —)
    admĭnistrātĭo, *f*, cūra, *f*;
    (persons), *use phr*, ii qui
    summum impĕrĭum hăbent
    (those who hold supreme
    authority)
governor (supreme) gŭbernātor,
    m; (subordinate), prōcūrātor, *m*,
    lēgātus, *m*
gown (woman's) stŏla, *f*; (man's)
    tŏga, *f*
grace grātĭa, *f*; (pardon), vĕnĭa, *f*;
    (charm), vĕnustas, *f*; (to say —),
    grātĭas ăgo (3)
grace *v.t*, (adorn), dĕcŏro (1)
graceful vĕnustus, lĕpĭdus
gracious prŏpĭtĭus, bĕnignus
grade grădus, *m*
gradient clīvus, *m*
gradually *adv*, paulātim
graft *v.t*, insĕro (3)
grain frumentum, *n*
grammar grammătĭca, *f*
granary horrĕum, *n*
grand magnĭficus, grandis
grandchild nĕpos, *m*, *f*
granddaughter neptis, *f*
grandeur magnĭficentĭa, *f*
grandfather ăvus, *m*

grandiloquent grandĭlŏquus
grandmother ăvĭa, *f*
grandson nĕpos, *m*
granite (hard rock) *use,* sĭlex, *m,* (flint stone)
grant, granting *nn,* concessĭo, *f*
grant *v.t,* concēdo (3), do (1)
grape ăcĭnus, *m,* ūva, *f*
graphic expressus
grapple *v.i,* luctor (1 *dep*)
grappling-iron harpăgo, *m*
grasp *nn,* mănus, *f;* **(of the mind),** captus, *m*
grasp *v.t,* prēhendo (3); **(mentally),** intellĕgo (3); **(snatch at, aim at),** capto (1)
grass grāmen, *n,* herba, *f*
grasshopper gryllus, *m*
grassy grāmĭnĕus
grate crātĭcŭla, *f*
grate *v.t,* tĕro (3); *v.i,* strīdĕo (2)
grateful grātus
gratification explētĭo, *f,* vŏluptas, *f*
gratify *v.t,* grātĭfĭcor (1 *dep*) *(with dat)*
grating *nn,* **(noise),** strīdor, *m*
gratitude grātĭa, *f,* grātus ănimus, *m*
gratuitous grātuītus
gratuity congĭārĭum, *n*
grave *nn,* sĕpulcrum, *n*
grave *adj,* grăvis
gravel glārĕa, *f*
gravity grăvĭtas, *f*
gravy iūs, *n*
gray see **grey**
grayness see **grey, greyness**
graze *v.t,* **(animals),** pasco (3); *v.i,* pascor (3 *dep.*); **(touch lightly),** *v.t,* stringo (3)
grease *nn,* ădeps, *c*
grease *v.t,* ungo (3)
greasy unctus
great magnus, grandis, amplus; **(distinguished),** illustris
greatcoat lăcerna, *f*
great-grandfather prŏăvus, *m*
great-grandson prŏnĕpos, *m*
greatness magnĭtūdo, *f*
greaves ŏcrĕae, *f.pl*
Greece Graecĭa, *f*
greed ăvārĭtĭa, *f*

greedy ăvārus
Greek Graecus
green *adj,* vĭrĭdis; **(unripe),** crūdus; **(to become —),** *v.i,* vĭresco (3)
greet *v.t,* sălūto (1)
greeting sălūtātĭo, *f*
gregarious grĕgālis
grey caesĭus, rāvus; **(of hair),** cānus
greyness (of hair) cānĭtĭes, *f*
gridiron crātĭcŭla, *f*
grief dŏlor, *m,* luctus, *m*
grievance quĕrĭmōnĭa, *f*
grieve *v.i, and v.t,* dŏlĕo (2)
grievous grăvis, ăcerbus
grim trux
grin *v.i,* rīdĕo (2)
grind *v.t,* contĕro (3); mŏlo (3) **(— down, oppress),** opprĭmo (3);
grindstone cōs, *f*
grip *nn, use* mănus, *f,* **(hand)**
grip *v.t,* arrĭpĭo (3)
gripes tormĭna, *n.pl*
grisly horrendus
grist fārīna, *f*
gristle cartĭlāgo, *f*
grit glārĕa
groan *nn,* gĕmĭtus, *m*
groan *v.i,* gĕmo (3)
grocer tūrārĭus, *m*
groin inguen, *n*
groom *nn,* ăgāso, *m*
groom *v.t,* **(look after),** cūro (1)
groove cănālis, *m*
grope *v.i,* praetento (1)
gross *adj,* crassus; **(unseemly),** indĕcōrus
grotto antrum, *n*
grotesque monstrŭōsus
ground (earth) hŭmus, *f,* sŏlum, *n,* terra, *f;* **(cause, reason),** causa, *f;* **(to give —),** pĕdem rĕfĕro *(irreg)*
ground *v.i,* **(of ships)** sīdo (3)
groundless vānus
groundwork (basis) fundāmentum, *n*
group glŏbus, *m*
group *v.t,* dispōno (3)
grouse lăgōpūs, *f*
groove lūcus, *m*
grovel *v.i,* serpo (3)
grow *v.i,* cresco (3), augesco (3);

(— up), ădŏlesco (3); (become), fĭo (*irreg*); *v.t,* cŏlo (3)
growl *nn,* frĕmĭtus, *m*
growl *v.i,* frĕmo (3)
growth incrēmentum, *n*
grub *nn,* vermĭcŭlus, *m*
grudge *nn,* sĭmultas, *f*
grudge *v.t,* invĭdĕo (2) (*with dat*)
grudgingly *adv, use adj,* invītus
gruel ptīsāna, *f*
gruff asper
grumble *v.i,* frĕmo (3)
grunt *nn,* grunnītus, *m*
grunt *v.i,* grunnĭo (4)
guarantee *nn,* fĭdes, *f*
guarantee *v.t,* fĭdem do (1) (*with dat*)
guarantor vas, *m*
guard (person) custos, *c;* (defence), custōdĭa, *f,* praesĭdĭum, *n;* (to keep —) *v.i,* custōdĭam ăgo (3)
guard *v.t,* custōdĭo (4)
guarded (cautious) cautus
guardian custos, *c;* (of child), tūtor, *m*
guardianship custōdĭa, *f;* (of child), tūtēla, *f*
guess *nn,* coniectūra, *f*
guess *v.t,* cōnĭcĭo (3), dīvīno (1)
guest hospes, *m,* hospĭta, *f;* (at a party, etc.) convīva, *c*
guidance (advice) consĭlĭum, *n*
guide *nn,* dux, *c*
guide *v.t,* dūco (3)
guild collēgĭum, *n*
guile dŏlus, *m*
guileful dŏlōsus
guileless simplex
guilt culpa, *f*
guiltless innŏcens, insons
guilty sons, nŏcens
guise hăbĭtus, *m,* spĕcĭes, *f*
gulf (bay) sĭnus, *m;* (abyss), gurges, *m,* vŏrāgo, *f*
gullet guttur, *n*
gullible crēdŭlus
gully (channel) cănālis, *m,* fossa, *f*
gulp *v.t,* haurĭo (4)
gum (of the mouth) gingīva, *f;* (of plants etc.) gummi, *n*
gurgle *v.i,* singulto (1)
gush *v.i,* prŏfundor (3 *pass*)

gust flātus, *m*
gut intestīna, *n.pl*
gutter fossa, *f,* clŏāca, *f*
gutteral grăvis
gymnasium gymnăsĭum, *n*
gymnastics pălaestra, *f*

H

haberdasher lintĕo, *m*
habit consŭētūdo, *f,* mōs, *m*
habitable hăbĭtābĭlis
habitation dŏmĭcĭlĭum, *n*
habitual ūsĭtātus
habituate *v.t,* consŭēfăcĭo (3)
hack căballus, *m*
hack *v.t,* concīdo (3)
hackneyed trītus
haft mănūbrĭum, *n*
hag ănus, *f*
haggard măcĭe corruptus (marred by leanness)
haggle *v.i,* dē prĕtĭo căvillor (1 *dep*) (to quibble about price)
hail *nn,* grando, *f*
hail *v.i,* (weather), grandĭnat (*impers.*); *v.t,* (greet), sălūto (1)
hair căpillus, *m,* crīnis, *m,* caesărĭes, *f*
hairdresser tonsor, *m*
hairless (bald) calvus
hairy pĭlōsus
halcyon *adj,* alcỹŏnēus
hale (healthy) vălĭdus
half *nn,* dīmĭdĭum, *n; adj,* dīmĭdĭus; *adv, use prefix* sēmi-, *e.g.* half-asleep, sēmĭsomnus; (half-dead), sēmĭănĭmis, mŏrĭbundus; (— hour) sēmĭhōra, *f;* (— moon), lūna dīmĭdĭāta, *f;* (— yearly), sēmestris
hall (of house) ātrĭum, *n;* (public), concĭlĭābŭlum, *n*
hallo! heus!
hallow *v.t,* consĕcro (1)
hallucination somnĭa, *n.pl*
halo cŏrōna, *f*
halt *nn, use vb,* consisto (3)
halt *v.i,* consisto (3)
halter (horse) căpistrum, *n;* (noose), lăquĕus, *m*
halve *v.t,* ex aequo dīvĭdo (3)
ham perna, *f*

hamlet vīcus, *m*
hammer *nn*, mallĕus, *m*
hammer *v.t*, contudo (3)
hamper quălum, *n*
hamper *v.t*, impĕdĭo (4)
hamstring *v.t*, poplĭtem succīdo
(3) (*with dat*)
hand mănus, *f*; (left —), mănus
sĭnistra; (right —), dextra mănus;
(to shake — s) detras coniungĕre
(3); (— cuffs), mănĭcae, *f.pl*;
(— writing), chīrgrăphum, *n*; (on
the one—, on the other —) et...et,
or quĭdem (*second word in
clause*) ...autem (*second word in
clause*); (— to — fighting, etc.)
commĭnus, *adv*; (at hand),
praesto, *adv*
hand *v.t*, do (1), trādo (3);
(— down or over), trādo (3)
handful (few) *use adj*, pauci
handicraft artĭfĭcĭum, *n*
handiwork ŏpus, *n*
handkerchief sūdārĭum, *n*
handle mănūbrĭum, *n*
handle *v.t*, tracto (1)
handling (treatment) tractātĭo, *f*
handsome spěcĭōsus, pulcher
handy (manageable) hăbĭlis
hang *v.t*, suspendo (3); (— the
head) dēmitto (3); *v.i*, pendĕo (2);
(— back, hesitate), dŭbĭto (1);
(overhang) impendĕo (2)
hanger-on assecla, *c*
hanging (death by —)
suspendĭum, *n*
hangman carnĭfex, *m*
hanker after *v.t*, opto (1)
haphazard *use adv. phr.* nullo
ordĭne (in no order)
happen *v.i*, accĭdo (3), ēvĕnĭo (4)
happiness fēlīcĭtas, *f*
happy fēlix, bĕātus
harangue *nn*, contĭo, *f*
harangue *v.t*, contĭōnor (1 *dep.*)
harass *v.t*, sollĭcĭto (1)
harbour portus, *m*; (— dues),
portōrĭum, *n*
harbour *v.t*, (shelter), excĭpĭo (3)
hard dūrus; (difficult), diffĭcĭlis
hard *adv*, (strenuously), strēnŭē
harden *v.t*, dūro (1); *v.i*, dūresco
(3)

hard-hearted dūrus
hardiness rōbur, *n*
hardly *adv*, vix; (harshly),
crūdēlĭter
hardness dūrĭtĭa, *f*
hardship lăbor, *m*
hardware ferrāmenta, *n.pl*
hardy dūrus
hare lĕpus, *m*
hark! heus!
harlot mĕrĕtrix, *f*
harm *nn*, damnum, *n*
harm *v.t*, nŏcĕo (2) (*with dat*)
harmful noxĭus
harmless innŏcŭus, innŏcens
harmonious concors
harmonize *v.i*, concĭno (3)
harmony concentus, *m*,
consensus, *m*
harness *nn*, ĕquestrĭa arma, *n.pl*,
(horse equipment), frēnum, *n*
harness *v.t*, iungo (3)
harp fĭdes, *f.pl*; (harpist), fĭdĭcen,
m
harrow *nn*, irpex, *m*
harrow *v.t*, occo (1)
harrowing *adj*, horrendus,
terrĭbĭlis
harsh asper, ăcerbus
harshness aspěrĭtas, *f*
hart cervus, *m*
harvest messis, *f*
hasp fĭbŭla, *f*
haste *nn*, festīnātĭo, *f*
hasten *v.i*, prŏpĕro (1), festīno
(1); *v.t*, mātūro (1), accĕlĕro (1)
hastily *adv*, prŏpĕrē
hastiness (of temper) īrācundĭa, *f*
hasty prŏpĕrus; (of temper)
īrācundus
hat pĕtăsus, *m*
hatch *v.t*, (eggs), exclūdo (3);
(plans etc.) ĭnĕo (4)
hatchet sĕcūris, *f*
hate *nn*, ŏdĭum, *n*
hate *v.t*, ōdi (*v. defect*)
hateful ŏdĭōsus
haughtiness sŭperbĭa, *f*
haughty sŭperbus, arrŏgans
haul *v.t*, trăho (3)
haunt *nn*, lătĕbrae, *f.pl*
haunt *v.t*, (visit frequently),
cĕlĕbro (1); (trouble), sollĭcĭto (1)

have   v.t, hăbĕo (2); or use esse
(irreg) with dat. of possessor, e.g.
   I have a brother, est mĭhĭ frāter
haven   portus, m
haversack   saccus, m
havoc   strāges, f, vastātĭo
hawk   nn, accĭpĭter, m, f
hay   faenum, n
hazard   nn, pĕrīcŭlum, n
hazardous   pĕrīcŭlōsus
haze   nĕbŭla, f
hazel   nn, cŏrўlus, f
hazy   nĕbŭlōsus
he   pron, if not emphatic, use 3rd
pers. of verb; otherwise, ille, hic,
is
head   căput, n, vertex, m; (chief),
princeps, m; (to be at the — of)
praesum (irreg) (with dat)
heat   adj, (of wind) adversus
head   v.t, (be in charge), praesum
(irreg) (with dat)
headache   căpĭtĭs dŏlor, m
headband   vitta, f
headland   promontūrĭum, n
headlong   adj, praeceps
headquarters   praetōrĭum, n
headstrong   adj, pervĭcax
heal   v.t, sāno (1), mĕdĕor (2 dep)
(with dat); v.i, consānesco (3)
healing   nn, sānātĭo, f
healing   adj, sālūtāris
health   vălētūdo, f
healthy   sānus, vălĭdus; (of place
or climate), sălūbris
heap   nn, ăcervus, m
heap   v.t, cŭmŭlo (1), congĕro (3)
hear   v.t, audĭo (4); (learn),
cognosco (3)
hearer   audītor, m
hearing   nn, (sense of —), audītus,
m
hearsay   rūmor, m
heart   cor, n; (interior), use adj,
intĭmus (inmost); (feelings, etc.),
pectus, n, mens, f; (courage),
ănĭmus, m; (— ache), sollĭcĭtūdo,
f; (— break), dŏlor, m; (— broken)
adj. phr, ănĭmo afflictus
hearth   fŏcus, m
heartiness   stŭdĭum, n
heartless   dūrus
heartlessness   crūdēlĭtas, f

hearty   ălăcer
heat   nn, călor, m, ardor, m,
aestus, m, fervor, m
heat   v.t, călĕfăcĭo (3); (excite),
incendo (3)
heath   lŏca obsĭta, n.pl, lŏca
inculta, n.pl
heave   v.t, tollo (3); v.i, tŭmesco
(3)
heaven   caelum, n; (— dwelling)
adj, caelĭcōla
heavenly   adj, dīvīnus
heaviness   grăvĭtas, f; (— of mind),
tristĭtĭa, f
heavy   grăvis; (sad), tristis; (air,
etc.) crassus
hectic (agitated, confused)
turbŭlentus
hedge   saepes, f
hedge in   v.t, saepĭo (4)
hedgehog   ĕchīnus, m
heed   v.t, (obey) pārĕo (2) (with
dat); (to take —), v.i, căvĕo (2)
heedless   incautus
heedlessness   neglĕgentĭa, f
heel   calx, f; (take to one's —s)
fŭgĭo (3)
heifer   iŭvenca, f
height   altĭtūdo, f; (high ground)
sŭpĕrĭor lŏcus, m
heighten   v.t, use augĕo (2)
(increase)
heinous   ătrox
heir, heiress   hēres, c
hell   infĕri, m.pl. Orcus, m
hellish   infernus
helm   gŭbernācŭlum, n
helmet   cassis, f, gălĕa, f
helmsman   gŭbernātor, m
help   nn, auxĭlĭum, n
help   v.t, iŭvo (1), subvĕnĭo (4)
(with dat); (I cannot help coming),
non possum făcĕre quīn vĕnĭam
helper   adiūtor, m
helpful   ūtĭlis
helpless   ĭnops
helplessness   ĭnŏpĭa, f
helpmate   consors m, f
hem   nn, limbus, m
hem in   v.t, circumsĕdĕo (2),
saepĭo (4)
hemisphere   hēmisphaerĭum, n
hemp   cannăbis, f

hen gallīna, *f*; (— **house**),
  gallīnārĭum, *n*
hence *adv*, (**place or cause**), hinc;
  (**time**), posthāc
henceforth *adv*, posthāc
her *pron, adj*, eius; (*if it refers to
  the subject of the sentence*), sŭus,
  a, um
herald praeco, *m*
herb herba, *f*, hŏlus, *n*
herd grex, *m*
herd together *v.i*, congrĕgor (1
  pass)
herdsman pastor, *m*
here hīc; (**hither**), hūc; (**to be —**),
  v.i, adsum (*irreg*)
hereafter *adv*, posthāc
hereby *adv*, ex hōc
hereditary hērēdĭtārĭus
heredity gĕnus, *n*
heretical prāvus
hereupon *adv*, hīc
heritage hērēdĭtas, *f*
hermit hŏmo sōlĭtārĭus
hernia hernĭa, *f*
hero vir fortissĭmus
heroic (brave) fortis
heroine fēmĭna fortis, *f*
heroism virtus, *f*
heron ardĕa, *f*
hers see **her**
herself *pron. reflexive*, sē; (*pron.
  emphatic*) ipsa
hesitancy, hesitation haesĭtātĭo, *f*
hesitate *v.i*, dŭbĭto (1), haesĭto
  (1)
hew *v.t*, caedo (3)
heyday (youth) iŭventus, *f*
hibernate *v.i*, condor (3 *pass*)
hiccough singultus, *m*
hidden occultus
hide *nn*, (**skin**), cŏrĭum, *n*, pellis, *f*
hide *v.t*, abodo (3), cēlo (1)
hideous foedus
hideousness foedĭtas, *f*
hiding-place lătĕbrae, *f.pl*
high altus, celsus; (**of rank**),
  amplus; (**of price**), magnus,
  magni; (— **born**), gĕnĕrōsus;
  (— **handed**), impĕrĭōsus;
  (— **lands**), montes, *m.pl*; (—
  landers), montāni, *m.pl*;
  (— **spirited**), ănĭmōsus;

(— **treason**), măiestas, *f*; (— **way**),
  vĭa, *f*; (— **wayman**) lătro, *m*
hilarity hĭlărĭtas, *f*
hill collis, *m*
hillock tŭmŭlus, *m*
hilly montŭōsus
hilt căpŭlus, *m*
himself *pron, reflexive*, sē; *pron.
  emphatic*, ipse
hind *adj*, postĕrĭor
hinder *v.t*, impĕdĭo (4), obsto (1)
  (*with dat*)
hindrance impĕdīmentum, *n*
hinge *nn*, cardo, *m*
hinge on *v.i*, vertor (3 *dep*),
  versor (1 *dep*) in (*with abl*)
hint *nn*, signĭfĭcātĭo, *f*
hint at *v.t*, signĭfĭco (1)
hip coxendix, *f*
hippopotamus hippŏpŏtămus, *m*
hire (wages) merces, *f*
hire *v.t*, condūco (3)
hired conductus
his *pron*, ēius, hūius, illĭus; *or*
  sŭus (*referring to the subject of
  the sentence*)
hiss *nn*, sībĭlus, *m*
hiss *v.i. and v.t*, sībĭlo (1)
historian scriptor (*m*) rērum
historic(al) *use nn*, historĭa, *f*,
  (**history**)
history histŏrĭa, *f*, rēs gestae, *f.pl*
hit *nn*, (**blow**) plāga, *f*
hit *v.t*, (**strike**) fĕrĭo (4); (— **upon**),
  incĭdo (3)
hitch impĕdīmentum, *n*
hitch *v.t*, necto (3)
hither *adv*, hūc; (— **and thither**),
  hūc illūc
hitherto *adv*, ădhūc
hive alvĕārĭum, *n*
hoard *nn*, ăcervus, *m*
hoard *v.t*, collĭgo (3), condo (3)
hoarfrost prŭīna, *f*
hoarse raucus
hoary cānus
hoax *nn*, lūdus, *m*
hoax *v.t*, lūdĭfĭcor (1 *dep*), lūdo
  (3)
hobble *v.i*, claudĭco (1)
hobby stŭdĭum, *n*
hobnail clāvus, *m*
hoe *nn*, sarcŭlum, *n*

hoe　*v.t*, sarrĭo (4)
hog　porcus, *m*
hogshead　dōlĭum, *n*
hoist　*v.t*, tollo (3)
hold　*nn*, (grasp) *use*
　comprĕhendo (3), *or* mănus, *f*
hold　*v.t*, tĕnĕo (2), obtĭnĕo (2),
　hăbĕo (2); (— an office), obtĭnĕo
　(2), fungor (3 *dep*); (— elections,
　etc.), hăbĕo (2); (— back), *v.i*,
　cunctor (1 *dep*), *v.t*, rĕtĭnĕo (2);
　(— fast), rĕtĭnĕo (2); (— out), *v.t*,
　porrĭgo (3); (endure), sustĭnĕo (2),
　perfĕro (*irreg*); (— up, lift), tollo
　(3)
hold-fast　*nn*, fībŭla, *f*
hole　fŏrāmen, *n*, căvum, *n*
holiday　fērĭae, *f.pl*
holiness　sanctĭtas, *f*
hollow　*nn*, căvum, *n*, lăcūna, *f*;
　(— of the hand), căva mănus, *f*
hollow　*adj*, căvus; (false), vānus
hollow　*v.t*, căvo (1)
holm-oak　īlex, *f*
holy　săcer
homage (respect)　observantĭa, *f*
home　*adj*, dŏmestĭcus; (homely),
　rustĭcus
home　dŏmus, *f*; (at —), dŏmi;
　(homewards), dŏmum; (from —),
　dŏmo (— less), cărens tecto
　(lacking shelter)
homicide (deed)　caedes, *f*;
　(person), hŏmĭcīda, *c*
honest　prŏbus
honesty　prŏbĭtas, *f*, intĕgrītas, *f*
honey　mel, *n*
honeycomb　făvus, *m*
honorary　hŏnōrārĭus
honour　hŏnos, *m*; (glory), dĕcus,
　n; (integrity), hŏnestas, *f*,
　intĕgrĭtas, *f*; (repute), fāma, *f*
honour　*v.t*, cŏlo (3), hŏnesto (1)
honourable　hŏnōrātus, hŏnestus
hood　cŭcullus, *m*
hoof　ungŭla, *f*
hook　hāmus, *m*
hook　*v.t*, hāmo căpĭo (3) (catch
　by a hook)
hooked　hāmātus
hoop　circŭlus, *m*
hoot　*nn*, cantus, *m*
hoot　*v.i*, căno (3); *v.t*, (hoot at),

　explōdo (3)
hop　*v.i*, sălĭo (4)
hope　*nn*, spes, *f*
hope　*v.i. and v.t*, spēro (1)
hopeful (promising)　*use genit*.
　phr, bŏnae spĕi
hopefully　*adj, phr*, multa spērans
hopeless (desperate)　dēspērātus
hopelessness　dēspērātĭo, *f*
horizon　orbis (*m*) fīnĭens (limiting
　circle)
horizontal　lībrātus
horn　cornu, *n*; (made of —), *adj*,
　cornĕus
hornet　crābro, *m*
horrible　horrĭbĭlis, horrendus,
　ătrox, foedus
horrid　horrĭbĭlis, horrendus,
　ătrox, foedus
horrify　*v.t*, (dismay), percello (3),
　terrĕo (2)
horror　horror, *m*
horse　ĕquus, *m*
horseback (to ride on —)　in ĕquo
　vĕhor (3 *pass*); (to fight on —), ex
　ĕquo pugno (1)
horsefly　tăbānus, *m*
horserace　certāmen ĕquestre, *n*
horseshoe　sŏlĕa, *f*
horsewhip　flăgellum, *n*
horticulture　hortōrum cultus, *m*
hospitable　hospĭtālis
hospital　vălētūdĭnārĭum, *n*
hospitality　hospĭtĭum, *n*
host (one who entertains)　hospes,
　m; (innkeeper), caupo, *m*; (large
　number), multĭtūdo, *f*
hostage　obses, *c*
hostess　hospĭta, *f*
hostile　hostīlis, infestus
hostility　ĭnĭmīcĭtĭa, *f*; (hostilities,
　war), bellum, *n*
hot　călĭdus, fervens; (of temper),
　ācer; (to be —), *v.i*, călĕo (2),
　fervĕo (2); (to become —), *v.i*,
　călesco (3); (— headed), *adj*,
　fervĭdus, fervens; (hotly), *adv*,
　ardenter
hotel　hospĭtĭum, *n*
hound　cănis, *m, f*
hound on　*v.t*, (goad on), instīgo
　(1), ăgĭto (1)
hour　hōra, *f*

hourly *adv*, in hōras
hourglass hōrārĭum, *n*
house dŏmus, *f*, aedes, *f.pl*;
(family), gens, *f*; (— hold) dŏmus,
f, fămĭlĭa, *f*; (— keeper), prōmus,
m; (— maid), ancĭlla, *f*; (— wife),
māterfămĭlĭas, *f*
house *v.t*, (store) condo (3),
rĕpōno, (3)
hovel tŭgŭrĭum, *n*, căsa, *f*
hover *v.i*, vŏlĭto (1), impendĕo (2)
how (in what way?) quōmŏdŏ?;
with adj. or adv, quam?;
(— many), quot?; (— often),
quŏtĭes?; (— great or big),
quantus?
however *conj*, tămen; *adv*,
quamvis; (how big or great),
quantumvis
howl *nn*, ŭlŭlātus, *m*
howl *v.i*, ŭlŭlo (1)
hubbub tŭmulus, *m*
huddle *v.i*, (— together),
congrĕgor (1 *dep*), confĕror
(*irreg. pass*)
hue (colour) cŏlor, *m*
huff (to be in a — about) *v.t*,
aegrē fĕro (*irreg*)
hug *nn*, complexus, *m*
hug *v.t*, amplector (3 *dep*)
huge ingens, immānis
hull (of a ship) alvĕus, *m*
hum *nn*, frĕmĭtus, *m*
hum *v.i*, frĕmo (3), strĕpo (3)
human *adj*, hūmānus; (— being),
hŏmo, *c*
humane (compassionate)
mĭsĕrĭcors
humanity hūmānĭtas, *f*; (human
race) hŏmĭnes, *c.pl*;
(compassion), mĭsĕrĭcordĭa, *f*
humble hŭmĭlis, vĕrēcundus
humble *v.t*, dēprĭmo (3); (— in
war), dēbello (1); (— oneself), sē
summittĕre (3 *refles*)
humdrum *adj*, mĕdĭŏcris, tardus
humid hūmĭdus
humidity hūmor, *m*
humiliate *v.t*, dēprĭmo (3)
humility mŏdestĭa, *f*
humorous rīdĭcŭlus
humour făcētĭae, *f.pl*;
(disposition), ingĕnĭum, *n*. lĭbĭdo,

f; (to be in the — to), *use* lĭbet (*v.
2 impers*) (*with dat. of person*)
humour *v.t*, obsĕquor (3 *dep*)
(*with dat. of person*)
hump gibber, *m*
humpbacked *adj*, gibber
hunch, hunchbacked see
humpbacked
hundred *adj*, centum; (— times),
adv, centies; (— fold), *adj*,
centŭplex
hundredth centēsĭmus
hundredweight centumpondĭum,
n
hunger fămes, *f*
hunger *v.i*, ēsŭrĭo (4)
hungry ēsŭrĭens, ăvĭdus (cĭbi)
hunt *v.t*, vēnor (1 *dep*)
hunt, hunting *nn*, vēnātĭo, *f*
hunter vēnātor, *m*
huntress vēnātrix, *f*
hurdle crātes, *f.pl*
hurl *v.t*, iăcŭlor (1 *dep*), cōnĭcĭo
(3)
hurricane tempestas, *f*, prŏcella, *f*
hurried praeceps
hurriedly *adv*, raptim
hurry *v.i*, festīno (1), prŏpĕro (1);
v.t, răpĭo (3); (an action, etc.),
mātūro (1)
hurt *nn*, (wound) vulnus, *n*
hurt *v.t*, laedo (3), nŏcĕo (2)
(*with dat*)
hurt *adj*, (wounded), saucĭus
hurtful nŏcens, noxĭus
husband vir, *m*, mărītus, *m*
husbandry agrĭcultūra, *f*
hush! tăcē; *pl*, tăcētĕ (*from* tăcĕo)
hush up *v.t*, (conceal), tĕgo (3),
cēlo (1)
husk follĭcŭlus, *m*
husky fuscus, raucus
hustle *v.t*, pulso (1), trūdo (3)
hut căsa, *f*, tūgŭrĭum, *n*
hutch căvĕa, *f*
hyacinth hўăcinthus, *m*
hybrid hybrĭda, ae, *c*
hymn carmen, *n*
hyperbole hўperbŏlē, *f*
hyperchondriac mĕlanchŏlĭcus
hypocrisy sĭmŭlātĭo, *f*
hypocrite sĭmŭlātor, *m*
hypocritical sĭmŭlātus

hypothesis coniectūra, *f*,
condĭcĭo, *f*
hysteria āmentĭa, *f*, perturbātĭo, *f*

I

I *pron*, (*emphatic*), ĕgo; *otherwise
use* 1st *pers. sing. of verb, e.g.*
I love, *ămo*
iambic *adj*, ĭambĕus
ice glăcĭes, *f*
icicle stīrĭa, *f*
icy gĕlĭdus, glăcĭālis
idea nōtĭo, *f*, imāgo, *f*, sententĭa,
f; (**to form an —**) *v.i*, cōgĭtātĭōne
fingo (3)
ideal *adj*, (**perfect**) perfectus,
summus, optĭmus
ideal *nn*, exemplar, *n*
identical īdem (**the same**)
identify *v.t*, agnosco (3)
identity (**to find the — of**)
cognosco (3) quis sit ...
ides īdūs, *f.pl*
idiocy fătŭĭtas, *f*
idiom prŏprĭĕtas, *f*. (linguae)
(**peculiarity of language**)
idiot fătŭus, *m*
idiotic fătŭus
idle (**unemployed**) ōtĭōsus; (**lazy**),
ignāvus; (**useless**), vānus; (**to be
—**), *v.i*, cesso (1)
idleness ignāvĭa, *f*, cessātĭo, *f*
idler cessātor, *m*, cessātrix, *f*
idol (**statue**) sĭmŭlācrum, *n*;
(**something loved**) dēlĭcĭae, *f.pl*
idolatry vĕnĕrātĭo, (*f*)
sĭmŭlācrōrum (**worship of
images**)
idolize *v.t*, cŏlo (3)
idyl īdyllĭum, *n*
if *conj*, sī; (**— not**), sīn; *after a vb.
of asking* (**— whether**) num,
ŭtrum; (**whether ... or if**) sīve ...
sīve; (**— only**), dummŏdo
ignite *v.i*, ardesco (3); *v.t*,
accendo (3)
ignoble (**of birth**) ignōbĭlis;
(**dishonourable**) tupis
ignominious turpis
ignominy ignōmĭnĭa, *f*, infāmĭa, *f*
ignorance inscĭentĭa, *f*
ignorant ignārus, inscĭus

ignore *v.t*, praetĕrĕo
ill *adj*, aeger; (**evil**), mălus; (**to
be —**), *v.i*, asgrōto (1); (**to fall —**),
v.i, in morbum incĭdo (3)
ill *adv*, mălĕ
ill *nn*, (**evil**) mălum, *n*
ill-advised (**reckless**) temĕrārĭus
ill-bred inhūmānus
ill-disposed mălĕvŏlus
illegal illĭcĭtus
illegitimate non lēgĭtĭmus
ill-favoured dēformis, turpis
ill-health vălētŭdo, *f*
illicit illĭcĭtus
illiterate illittĕrātus
ill-natured mălĕvŏlus
ill-omened dīrus
ill-starred infēlix
ill-temper īrācundĭa
illness morbus, *m*
illogical absurdus, rĕpugnans
illuminate *v.t*, illustro (1)
illusion error, *m*
illusive vānus
illustrate *v.t*, illustro (1)
illustration exemplum, *n*
illustrious clārus, *lustris*
image ĭmāgo, *f*, effĭgĭes, *f*
imaginable *use phr*, quod concĭpi
pŏtest (**that can be imagined**)
imaginary commentĭcĭus
imagination cōgĭtātĭo, *f*
imagine *v.t*, ănĭmo concĭpĭo (3)
or fingo (3)
imbecile fătŭus
imbecility imbēcillĭtas (*f*) ănĭmi
imbibe *v.t*, bĭbo (3), haurĭo (4)
imbue *v.t*, infĭcĭo (3)
imitate *v.t*, ĭmĭtor (1 *dep*)
imitation ĭmĭtātĭo, *f*; (**likeness**),
effĭgĭes, *f*
imitator ĭmĭtātor, *m*
immaculate intĕger
immaterial (**unimportant**) *use phr*,
nullo mōmento
immature immātūrus
immeasurable immensus
immediate praesens, proxĭmus
immediately *adv*, stătim,
confestim
immemorial (**from time —**), ex
hŏmĭnum mĕmōrĭa
immense immensus, ingens

immensity immensĭtas, *f*
immerse *v.t,* immergo (3)
immigrant advēna, *m. f*
immigrate *v.i,* immĭgro (1)
imminent praesens; **(to be —)** *v.i,*
 immĭnĕo (2)
immobility immōbĭlĭtas, *f*
immoderate immŏdĕrātus,
 immŏdĭcus
immodest impŭdīcus
immodesty impŭdīcĭtĭa, *f*
immolate *v.t,* immŏlo (1)
immoral prāvus, turpis
immorality mōres māli, *m.pl*
immortal immortālis, aeternus
immortality immortālĭtas, *f*
immovable immōbĭlis
immunity immūnĭtas, *f,* văcātĭo, *f*
immutable immūtābĭlis
impair *v.t,* mĭnŭo (3)
impale *v.t,* transfigo (3)
impart *v.t,* impertĭo (4)
impartial aequus, iustus
impartiality aequĭtas, *f*
impassable insŭpĕrābĭlis
impassioned concĭtātus, fervens
impassive pătĭens
impatience (haste) impătĭentĭa, *f,*
 festīnātĭo, *f*
impatient ăvĭdus
impeach *v.t,* accūso (1)
impeachment accūsātĭo, *f*
impeccable impeccābĭlis
impede *v.t,* impĕdĭo (4)
impediment impĕdīmentum, *n*;
 (of speech), haesĭtantĭa, *f*
impel *v.t,* impello (3), incĭto (1)
impend *v.i,* impendĕo (2),
 immĭnĕo (2)
impending fŭtūrus
impenetrable impĕnĕtrābĭlis
imperfect imperfectus
imperfection (defect) vĭtĭum, *n*
imperial (kingly) rēgĭus *or use*
 genit. of impĕrĭum, *n,* **(empire),**
 or impĕrātor, *m,* **(emperor)**
imperil *v.t,* in pĕrīcŭlum addūco
 (3)
imperious impĕrĭōsus
impermeable impervĭus
impersonate *v.t,* partes sustĭnĕo
 (2) **(keep up a part)**
impertinence insŏlentĭa, *f*

impertinent insŏlens
imperturbable immōtus,
 immōbĭlis
impetuosity vīs, *f*
impetuous vĕhĕmens
impetus vīs, *f,* impĕtus, *m*
impious impĭus
implacable implācābĭlis
implant *v.t,* insĕro (3)
implement instrūmentum, *n*
implicate *v.t,* implĭco (1)
implicit *adj,* tăcĭtus; **(absolute),**
 omnis, tōtus
implore *v.t,* implōro (1), ōro (1)
imply *v.t,* signĭfĭco (1); **(involve),**
 hăbĕo (2)
impolite ĭnurbānus
import *nn,* **(meaning),** signĭfĭcātĭo,
 f
import *v.t,* importo (1)
importance mōmentum, *n*; **(of**
 position) amplĭtūdo, *f*
important grăvis; **(people),**
 amplus
importunate mŏlestus
importune *v.t,* flāgĭto (1)
impose *v.t,* impōno (3)
imposition (fraud) fraus, *f*
impossible *use phr,* quod fĭĕri
 nōn pŏtest **(which cannot be**
 done)
imposter fraudātor, *m*
impotence imbēcillĭtas, *f*
impotent imbēcillus, infirmus
impoverish *v.t,* in paupertātem
 rēdĭgo (3)
impoverishment paupertas, *f*
imprecation exsēcrātĭo, *f*
impregnable ĭnexpugnābĭlis
impregnate *v.t,* īnĭcĭo (3)
impress *v.t,* imprĭmo (3); **(the**
 mind), mŏvĕo (2)
impression (mental) mōtus, *(m)*
 ănĭmi; **(idea, thought)** ŏpīnĭo, *f,*
 ŏpīnātĭo, *f*; **(mark),** vestīgĭum, *n*
impressive grăvis
imprint *nn,* signum, *n*; **(of a foot),**
 vestīgĭum, *n*
imprison *v.t,* in vincŭla cōnĭcĭo
 (3) **(throw into chains)**
imprisonment vincŭla, *n.pl*
improbable nōn vērĭsĭmĭlis **(not**
 likely)

improper indĕcōrus
improve *v.t*, mēlĭōrem făcĭo (3) *or*
  reddo; *v.i*, mēlĭor fīo (*irreg*)
improvement ēmendātĭo, *f*
improvident neglĕgens,
  imprōvĭdus
imprudence imprūdentĭa, *f*
imprudent inconsultus,
  imprūdens
impudence impŭdentĭa, *f*
impudent impŭdens
impulse impĕtus, *m*, impulsus, *m*
impulsive vĕhĕmens
impunity (with —) *adv*, impūnĕ
impure impūrus, foedus
impurity impūrĭtas, *f*, incestus, *m*
impute *v.t*, attrĭbŭo (3)
in *prep*, (place), in (*with abl.*) *or*
  use locative case if available, e.g.
  Londīnĭi, in London; (time), *use*
  abl. or in (*with abl.*)
inability (weakness) imbēcillĭtas, *f*
inaccessible ĭnaccessus
inaccuracy (fault) error, *m*
inaccurate (things) falsus
inactive ĭners
inactivity cessātĭo, *f*, ĭnertĭa, *f*
inadequate impar
inadmissible *use phr*, quod nōn
  lĭcet (which is not allowed)
inadvertent imprūdens
inane ĭnānis
inanimate ĭnănĭmus
inappropriate nōn aptus (not
  suitable)
inasmuch as *conj*, quŏnĭam,
  quandōquĭdem
inattention neglĕgentĭa, *f*
inattentive neglĕgens
inaudible *use phr*, quod audīri
  nōn pŏtest (which cannot be
  heard)
inaugurate *v.t*, ĭnaugŭro (1)
inauguration consĕcrātĭo, *f*
inauspicious infēlix
inborn insĭtus
incalculable *use phr*, quod
  aestĭmāri nōn pŏtest (which
  cannot be estimated)
incapable inhăbĭlis
incarcerate *v.t*, in vincŭla cōnĭcĭo
  (3) (throw into chains)
incarnate spĕcĭe hūmānā indūtus

(clothed with human form)
incautious incautus
incendiary incendĭārĭus, *m*
incense *nn*, tūs, *n*
incense *v.t*, ad īram mŏvĕo (2)
  (arouse to anger)
incentive stĭmŭlus, *m*
incessant perpĕtŭus, assĭdŭus
incest incestum, *n*
inch uncĭa, *f*
incident rēs, *f*
incidental (casual) fortŭĭtus
incipient *use vb.* incĭpĭo (begin)
incision incīsūra, *f*
incisive mordax, ācer
incite *v.t*, incĭto (1)
inclemency aspĕrĭtas, *f*, sĕvērĭtas,
  f
inclement asper, sc̆vērus
inclination (desire) stŭdĭum, *n*,
  vŏluntas, *f*; (leaning, bias)
  inclīnātĭo, *f*
incline *v.t*, inclīno (1); *v.i*, inclīnor
  (1 *pass*)
incline *nn*, (slope) acclīvĭtas, *f*
inclined (disposed) prōpensus
include *v.t*, rĕfĕro (*irreg*),
  comprĕhendo (3)
including (together with) cum
  (*with abl*)
incoherent *use vb. phr. with* nōn
  and cŏhaerĕo (2) (to hold
  together)
income fructus, *m*, stīpendĭum, *n*
incomparable singŭlāris
incompatibility rĕpugnantĭa, *f*
incompatible rĕpugnans
incompetent ĭnhăbĭlis
incomplete imperfectus
incomprehensible *use phr*, quod
  intellĕgi nōn pŏtest
inconceivable *use phr*, quod
  ănĭmo fingi nōn pŏtest (that
  cannot be conceived)
inconclusive (weak) infirmus
incongruous rĕpugnans
inconsiderable parvus
inconsiderate inconsīdĕrātus
inconsistency inconstantĭa, *f*
inconsistent inconstans; (to be —),
  v.i, rĕpugno (1)
inconsolable inconsōlābĭlis
inconspicuous obscūrus

inconstancy inconstantĭa, *f*
inconstant inconstans
inconvenience incommŏdum, *n*
inconvenient incommŏdus
incorporate *v.t,* constĭtŭo (3),
  iungo (3)
incorrect falsus
incorrigible perdĭtus
incorruptible incorruptus
increase *nn,* incrēmentum, *n*
increase *v.t,* augĕo (2), *v.i,* cresco
  (1)
incredible incrēdĭbĭlis
incredulous incrēdŭlus
incriminate *v.t,* implĭco (1)
inculcate *v.t,* inculco (1)
incumbent upon (it is —) ŏportet
  (*v.* 2 *impers. with acc. of person*)
incur *v.t,* sŭbĕo (4)
incurable insānābĭlis
indebted obnoxĭus
indecency turpĭtūdo, *f*
indecent turpis, obscēnus
indecisive dŭbĭus, anceps
indeed *adv, emphatic,* prŏfecto;
  (yes —), vēro; *concessive;* quĭdem
indefatigible assĭdŭus
indefensible *use phr,* quod nōn
  pŏtest făcĭlē dēfendi **(that cannot**
  be defended easily)
indefinite incertus
indemnify *v.t,* damnum rēstĭtŭo
  (3) **(restore a loss)**
indentation lăcuna, *f*
independence lībertas, *f*
independent līber
indescribable ĭnēnarrābĭlis
indestructible (unfailing) pĕrennis
indeterminate incertus
index index, *m*
indicate *v.t,* indĭco (1), signĭfĭco
  (1)
indication indĭcĭum, *n*
indict *v.t,* accūso (1)
indictment accūsātĭo, *f*
indifference lentĭtūdo, *f*
indifferent neglĕgens; **(middling)**
  mĕdĭŏcris
indifferently *adv* **(moderately)**
  mĕdĭŏcrĭter
indigenous *adj,* indĭgĕna
indigestible *adv,* grăvis
indigestion crūdĭtas, *f*

indignant īrātus; **(to be —),** *v.i,*
  indignor (1 *dep*), ĭrātus ess
indignation indignātĭo, *f,* īra, *f*
indignity contŭmēlĭa, *f*
indirect oblīquus **(path, etc.)**
  dēvĭus
indiscreet inconsultus
indiscriminate prōmiscŭus
indispensable nĕcessārĭus
indispose *v.t,* ălĭēno (1)
indisposed (not inclined) āversus;
  (ill), aegrōtus
indisposition (unwillingness)
  ănĭmus āversus; **(sickness),**
  vălētūdo, *f*
indisputable certus
indistinct obscūrus
individual *nn,* hŏmo, *c*
individual *adj,* prŏprĭus
indivisible indīvĭdŭus
indolence ignāvĭa, *f*
indolent ignāvus
indomitable indŏmĭtus
indoor *adj,* umbrātĭlis **(in the**
  shade)
indoors (motion) in tectum
indubitable certus
induce *v.t,* addūco (3)
inducement praemĭum, *n*
indulge *v.i and v.t,* indulgĕo (2)
indulgence indulgentĭa, *f*
indulgent indulgens
industrious industrĭus, dīlĭgens
industry (diligence) industrĭa, *f,*
  dīlĭgentĭa, *f*
inebriated ēbrĭus
ineffective ĭnūtĭlis
inefficient *use phr,* qui rem
  cĕlĕrĭter conficĕre nōn pŏtest
  (who cannot complete a matter
  quickly)
inelegant ĭnēlĕgans
inept ĭneptus
inequality dissĭmĭlĭtūdo, *f*
inert ĭners, segnis
inertly *adv,* segnĭter
inestimable ĭnaestĭmābĭlis
inevitable nēcessārĭus
inexcusable *use phr,* quod
  praetermitti nōn pŏtest **(that**
  cannot be overlooked)
inexhaustible infinītus, sĭne fine
inexorable ĭnexōrābĭlis

inexperience impĕrītĭa, *f*,
  inscĭentĭa, *f*
inexperienced impĕrītus
inexplicable ĭnexplĭcābĭlis
inexpressible ĭnēnarrābĭlis, *or*
  phr, quod exprĭmi nōn pŏtest
  (that cannot be expressed)
infallible qui falli nōn pŏtest **(who
  cannot be mistaken)**
infamous infāmis
infamy infāmĭa, *f*
infancy infantĭa, *f*
infant *adj, and nn*, infans
infantry pĕdĭtātus, *m*
infatuate *v.t*, infătŭo (1)
infatuated dēmens
infect *v.t*, infĭcĭo (3)
infection contāgĭo, *f*
infer *v.t*, collĭgo (3)
inference coniectūra, *f*
inferior *adj*, infĕrĭor, dētĕrĭor
infernal infernus
infested infestus
infidelity perfĭdĭa, *f*
infinite infīnĭtus
infinity infīnĭtas, *f*
infirm invălĭdus, infirmus
infirmity infirmĭtas, *f*
inflame *v.t*, accendo (3)
inflammable *use phr*, quod făcĭlē
  incendi pŏtest **(that can be set on
  fire easily)**
inflammation inflammātĭo, *f*
inflate *v.t*, inflo (1)
inflexible rĭgĭdus
inflict *v.t*, inflīgo (3); **(war, etc.),**
  infĕro *(irreg) (with dat of person)*
infliction mălum, *n*, **(trouble)**
influence *nn*, vīs, *f*, mōmentum,
  n; **(authority),** auctōrĭtas, *f*; **(to
  have —)** *v.i*, vălĕo (2)
influence *v.t*, mŏvĕo (2)
influential grăvis
inform *v.t*, certĭōrem făcĭo (3);
  (— against someone), nōmen
  dēfĕro *(irreg) (with genit)*
information (news) nuntĭus, *m*
informer dēlātor, *m*
infrequency rārĭtas, *f*
infrequent rārus
infringe *v.t*, vĭŏla, (1)
infringement vĭŏlātĭo, *f*
infuriate *v.t*, effĕro (1)

infuriated īrā incensus
infuse *v.t*, infudo (3), inĭcĭo (3)
ingenious subtīlis
ingenuity *f*, ars, *f*, callĭdĭtas, *f*
ingenuous ingĕnŭus
inglorious inglōrĭus
ingot lăter, *m*
ingrained insĭtus
ingratiate oneself with *v.t*,
  conncĭlĭo (1), sē grātum reddere
  (with dat)
ingratitude ănĭmus ĭngrātus, *m*
ingredient pars, *f*
inhabit *v.t*, incŏlo (3), hăbĭto (1)
inhabitant incŏla, *c*
inhale *v.t*, (spīrĭtum) haurĭo (4)
inherent insĭtus
inherit *v.t, use phr. with*, hēres
  (heir), *and* accĭpĭo **(to receive)**
inheritance hērēdĭtas, *f*
inherited hērēdĭtārĭus
inhibit *v.t*, interdīco (1)
inhospitable ĭnhospĭtālis
inhuman immānis, crūdēlis
inhumanity immānĭtas, *f*,
  crūdēlĭtas, *f*
inimitable nōn ĭmĭtābĭlis
iniquitous ĭnīquus, imprŏbus
iniquity imprŏbĭtas, *f*
initial *adj*, prīmus
initiate *v.t*, ĭnĭtĭo (1)
initiative (take the —) *v.i*, occŭpo
  (1)
inject *v.t*, inĭcĭo (3)
injudicious inconsultus
injure *v.t*, nŏcĕo (2) *(with dat)*
injurious noxĭus, nŏcens
injury (of the body) vulnus, *n*;
  (disadvantage), dētrīmentum, *n*,
  iniūrĭa, *f*
injustice ĭnīquĭtas, *f*, iniūrĭa, *f*
ink ātrāmentum, *n*
inland mĕdĭterrānĕus
inlay *v.t*, insĕro (3)
inlet aestŭārĭum, *n*
inn dēversōrĭum, *n*, caupōna, *f*;
  (—keeper) caupo, *m*
innate insĭtus, innātus
inner intĕrĭor
innocence innŏcentĭa, *f*
innocent innŏcens, insons
innocuous innŏcŭus
innovate *v.t*, nŏvo (1)

innumerable innŭmĕrābĭlis
inobservant nōn perspĭcax
inoffensive innŏcens
inopportune ĭnopportūnus
inordinate immŏdĕrātus
inquest quaestĭo, *f*
inquire *v.i,* quaero (3) ab *(with abl)* or dē *(with abl)*
inquiry interrŏgātĭo, *f*; **(official),** quaestĭo, *f*
inquisitive cūrĭōsus
inquisitor quaesītor, *m*
inroad incursĭo, *f*
insane insānus, dēmens
insanity insānĭa, *f,* dēmentĭa, *f*
insatiable insătĭābĭlis
inscribe *v.t,* inscrībo (3) in *(with abl)*
inscription inscriptĭo, *f*
inscrutable obscūrus
insect bestĭŏla, *f*
insecure intūtus **(unsafe)**
insecurity *use adj,* intūtus
insensible (unfeeling) dūrus
inseparable *use phr,* quod sēpărāri nōn pŏtest **(that cannot be separated)**
insert *v.t,* insĕro (3)
inside *prep,* intrā *(with acc)*
inside *adv,* intus
inside *nn,* interĭor pars *f*
insidious insĭdĭōsus
insight (understanding) intellĕgentĭa, *f*
insignia insignĭa, *n.pl*
insignificant exĭgŭus, nullĭus mōmenti
insincere sĭmŭlātus
insincerity fallācĭa, *f,* sĭmŭlātĭo, *f*
insinuate *v.t,* insĭnŭo (1); **(hint),** signĭfĭco (1)
insinuating (smooth) blandus
insipid insulsus
insist *v.i,* insto (1); *v.t,* **(— on, demand)** posco (3), flāgĭto (1)
insolence contŭmācĭa, *f,* insŏlentĭa, *f*
insolent contŭmax, insŏlens
insoluble *use phr,* quod explĭcāri non pŏtest **(that cannot be explained)**
insolvent (to be —) *v.i,* nōn esse solvendo

inspect *v.t,* inspĭcĭo (3)
inspection *use vb,* inspĭcĭo (3), *or* lustro (1)
inspector (superintendent) cūrātor, *m*
inspiration (divine, poetic, etc) instinctus, *m,* afflātus, *m*
inspire *v.t,* inĭcĭo (3) *(with acc. of thing inspired and dat. of person);* **(rouse),** accendo (3)
inspired (of persons) incensus
instal *v.t,* ĭnaugŭro (1)
instalment pensĭo, *f*
instance (example) exemplum, *n*; **(for—),** verbi grātĭā
instant *adj,* praesens
instant *nn,* mōmentum, *n*
instantly (at once) *adv,* stătim
instantaneous praesens
instead *adv,* măgis **(rather)**
instead of *prep,* prō *(with abl);* *with a clause, use* tantum ăbĕrat (ăbest) ut … ut
instigate *v.t,* instīgo (1)
instill *v.t,* instillo (1), inĭtĭo (3)
instinct nātūra, *f*
instinctive nātūrālis
institute *v.t,* instĭtŭo (3)
institute, institution collēgĭum, *n*; instĭtūtum, *n*
instruct *v.t,* dŏcĕo (2), ērŭdĭo (4); **(order),** praecĭpĭo (3)
instruction dĭscĭplīna, *f,* institutio, *f*; **(command),** mandātum, *n*
instructor măgister, *m*
instrument instrūmentum, *n*
instrumental (in doing something) ūtĭlis
inssubordinate sēdĭtĭōsus
insufferable intŏlĕrābĭlis
insufficiency ĭnŏpĭa, *f*
insufficient haud sătis *(with genit)* **(not enough …)**
insult *nn,* contŭmēlĭa, *f*
insult *v.t,* contŭmēlĭam impōno (3) *(with dat)*
insulting contŭmēlĭōsus
insuperable *use phr,* quod sŭpĕrāri nōn pŏtest **(that cannot be overcome)**
insure against *v.t,* praecăvĕo (2)
insurgent rĕbellis, *m*
insurrection mōtus, *m*

intact intĕger
integral nĕcessārĭus **(necessary)**
integrity intĕgrĭtas, *f*
intellect mens, *f*, ingĕnĭum, *n*
intellectual ingĕnĭōsus
intelligence ingĕnĭum, *n*; **(news)**,
 nuntĭus, *m*
intelligent săpĭens, intellĕgens
intelligible perspĭcŭus
intemperate intempĕrans
intend *v.t*, in ănĭmo hăbĕo (2)
 (with infinitive)
intense ācer
intensify *v.t*, augĕo (2), incendo
 (3) **(inflame, rouse)**
intensify vīs, *f*
intent *adj*, intentus; **(to be — on)**,
 ănĭmum intendo (3) in *(with acc)*
intention consĭlĭum, *n*,
 prōpŏsĭtum, *n*
intentionally *adv*, consultō
inter *v.t*, sĕpĕlĭo (4)
intercede **(on behalf of)** dēprĕcor
 (1 *dep*) pro *(with abl)*
intercept *v.t*, **(catch)** excĭpĭo (3);
 (cut off), interclūdo (3)
intercession dēprĕcātĭo, *f*
interchange *nn*, permūtātĭo, *f*
interchange *v.t*, permūto (1)
intercourse commercĭum, *n*, ūsus,
 m
interest *nn*, **(zeal)**, stŭdĭum, *n*; **(it
 is in the — of)**, intĕrest *(v.impers.
 with genit)*; **(financial)**, fēnus, *n*,
 ūsūra, *f*
interest *v.t*, tĕnĕo (2), plăcĕo (2);
 (— oneself in), stŭdĕo (2) *(with
 dat)*
interested attentus
interesting *use vb*. to interest
interfere *v.i*, sē interpōnĕre (3
 reflex)
interim *adv*, **(in the —)** intĕrim
interior *adj*, intĕrĭor; *nn*, pars
 intĕrĭor, *f*
interject *v.t*, intĕrĭcĭo (3)
interlude embŏlĭum, *n*
intermarriage connūbĭum, *n*
intermediate mĕdĭus
interminable infinītus
intermingle *v.t*, miscĕo (2); *v.i*, sē
 miscĕre (2 *reflex*)
intermission intermissĭo, *f*

internal intestīnus
international *use genit*, gentĭum
 (of nations)
internecine internĕcīnus
interpose *v.t*, interpōno (3)
interpret *v.t*, interprĕtor (1 *dep*)
interpretation interprĕtātĭo, *f*
interpreter interpres, *c*
interregnum interregnum, *n*
interrogate *v.t*, interrŏgo (1)
interrupt *v.t*, interpello (1),
 interrumpo (3)
interruption interpellātĭo, *f*
intersect *v.t*, sĕco (1) **(cut)**
interval intervallum, *n*, spătĭum, *n*
intervene *v.i*, intercēdo (3), sē
 interpōnĕre (3 *reflex*) *(both with
 dat)*
intervention intercessĭo, *f*
interview collŏquĭum, *n*
interview *v.t*, collŏquor (3 *dep*)
 cum *(with abl)* **(speak with)**
interweave *v.t*, intertexo (3),
 implĭco (1)
intestines intestīna, *n.pl*
intimacy consŭētūdo, *f*,
 fămĭlĭārĭtas, *f*
intimate *adj*, fămĭlĭāris
intimate *v.t*, signĭfĭco (1)
intimidate *v.t*, dēterrĕo (2)
intimidation terror, *m*, mĭnae, *f.pl*
into *prep*, in *(with acc)*
intolerable intŏlĕrābĭlis
intolerance sŭperbĭa, *f*
intolerant sŭperbus
intone *v.t*, căno (3)
intoxicate *v.t*, ēbrĭum reddo (3)
 (make drunk)
intoxicate ēbrĭus
intoxication ēbrĭĕtas, *f*
intractable difficĭlis
intrepid intrĕpĭdus
intricacy **(difficulty)** difficultas
intricate difficĭlis
intrigue dŏlus, *m*
intrigue *v.i*, dŏlīs ūtor (3 *dep*)
introduce *v.t*, intrōduco (3)
introduction intrōductĭo, *f*; **(letter
 of —)** littĕrae commendātīcĭae,
 f.pl
intrude *v.i*, sē inculcāre (1 *reflex*)
intrusive *use phr*, qui interpellāre
 sŏlet **(who usually disturbs)**

intuition cognĭtio, *f*

inundate *v.t,* ĭnundo (1)

inundation ĭnundātĭo, *f*

inure *v.t,* assuēfācĭo (3)

invade *v.t,* bellum infĕro (*irreg*) (*with dat*), invādo (3) in (*with acc*)

invader hostis, *c*

invalid *nn,* aeger, *m*

invalid *adj,* (of no avail), irrĭtus, infirmus

invalidate *v.t,* infirmo (1)

invariable constans

invasion incursĭo, *f*

invective convīcĭum, *n*

inveigh against *v.i,* invĕhor (3 *dep*) in (*with acc.*)

inveigle *v.t,* illĭcĭo (3)

invent *v.t,* invĕnĭo (4)

invention (faculty) inventĭo, *f*; **(thing invented)**, inventum, *n*

inventor inventor, *m*

inverse inversus

invert *v.t,* inverto (3)

invest *v.t,* **(money)**, collŏco (1); **(besiege)** obsĭdĕo (2); **(— someone with an office)** măgistrātum committo (3) (*with dat*)

investigate *v.t,* exquīro (3), cognosco (3)

investigation investĭgātĭo, *f,* cognĭtĭo, *f*

investiture consĕcrātĭo, *f*

inveterate invĕtĕrātus

invidious (envious, hateful) invĭdĭōsus

invigorate *v.t,* vīres rĕfĭcĭo (3)

invincible invictus

inviolability sanctĭtas, *f* **(sacredness)**

inviolable invĭŏlātus

invisible caecus

invitation invĭtātĭo, *f*; **(at your —)**, tŭo invītātu

invite *v.t,* invīto (1)

inviting blandus

invoke *v.t,* invŏco (1)

involuntary nōn vŏluntārĭus

involve *v.t,* involvo (3), illĭgo (1), hăbĕo (2)

invulnerable *use phr,* quod vulnĕrāri nōn pŏtest **(that cannot be wounded)**

inward *adj,* intĕrĭor

inwardly, inwards *adv,* intus

irascibility īrācundĭa, *f*

irascible īrācundus

iris īris, *f*

irk (it —s) pĭget (*v.* 2 *impers.*) (*with acc. of person*)

irksome grăvis, mŏlestus

iron *nn,* ferrum, *n*

iron *adj,* ferrĕus

ironical *use nn,* īrōnĭa, *f,* **(irony)**

ironmongery ferrāmenta, *n.pl*

irony īrōnĭa, *f,* dissĭmŭlātĭo, *f*

irradiate *v.t,* illustro (1)

irrational rătĭōnis expers **(devoid of reason)**

irreconcilable rĕpugnans

irrefutable firmus

irregular (out of the ordinary) ĭnūsĭtātus, extrăordĭnārĭus; **(not well regulated)** nōn ordĭnātus

irregularity vĭtĭum, *n*; *otherwise use adjs. above*

irrelevant ălĭēnus

irreligious ĭmpĭus

irremediable insānābĭlis

irreparable *use phr,* quod rĕfĭci nōn pŏtest **(that cannot be repaired)**

irreproachable intĕger, invictus

irresistible invicus

irresolute dubĭus

irretrievable irrĕpĕrābĭlis

irreverance impĭĕtas, *f*

irreverent impĭus

irrevocable irrĕpĕrābĭlis

irrigate *v.t,* irrĭgo (1)

irrigatin irrĭgātĭo, *f*

irritable stŏmăchōsus

irritate *v.t,* irrīto (1); **(make worse)**, pēius reddo (3)

irruption (attack) incursĭo, *f*

island insŭla, *f*

islander insŭlānus, *m*

isolate *v.t,* sēpăro (1)

isolation sōlĭtūdo, *f*

issue *nn,* **(result)**, ēventus, *m*; **(topic)**, rēs, *f*; **(offspring)**, prŏgĕnĭes, *f*

issue *v.i,* **(proceed)**, ēgrĕdĭor (3 *dep*); **(turn out)**, ēvĕnĭo (4); *v.t* **(give out)**, ēdo (3); **(edicts, etc.)**

ēdīco (3)
isthmus isthmus, *m*
it *pron*, id, hoc, illud; *often*
  expressed by 3rd person sing. of
  verb, e.g. **it is,** est
itch *nn*, prūrītus, *m*; **(disease)**,
  scăbĭes, *f*
itch *v.i*, prūrĭo (4)
item rēs, *f*
itinerant circumfŏrānĕus
itinerary ĭter, *n* **(route)**
itself see **himself**
ivory *nn*, ĕbur, *n*; *adj*, ĕburnĕus
ivy hĕdĕra, *f*

J

jab *v.t*, fŏdĭo (3)
jabber *v.i*, blătĕro (1)
jackass ăsĭnus, *m*
jacket tŭnĭca, *f*
jaded dēfessus
jagged asper
jail carcer, *m*
jailer custos, *c*
janitor iānĭtor, *m*
January Iānŭārĭus (mensis)
jar olla, *f*, amphŏra, *f*, dōlĭum, *n*
jarring dissŏnus
jaunt excursĭo, *f*
javelin pīlum, *n*
jaws faucēs *f.pl*
jealous invĭdus
jealousy invĭdĭa, *f*
jeer at *v.t*, dērīdĕo (2)
jeering *nn*, irrīsĭo, *f*
jejune iēiūnus
jeopardize *v.t*, pērīclĭtor (1 *dep*)
jeopardy pērīcŭlum, *n*
jerk *v.t*, quătĭo (3)
jerkin tŭnĭca, *f*
jest *nn*, iŏcus, *m*
jest *v.i*, iŏcor (1 *dep*)
jester scurra, *m*
jetty mōles, *f*
Jew *nn*, Iūdaeus, *m*
jewel gemma, *f*
jeweller gemmārĭus, *m*
  jibe convĭcĭum, *n*
jilt *v.t*, rĕpŭdĭo (1)
jingle *nn*, tinnītus, *m*
jingle *v.i*, tinnĭo (4)
job ŏpus, *n*

jockey ăgāso, *m*
jocose iŏcōsus
jocular iŏcŭlāris
jocund hĭlăris, iūcundus
jog *v.t*, fŏdīco (1) **(nudge)**
join *v.t*, iungo (3); *v.i*, sē
  coniungĕre (3 *reflex*); **(— battle)**
  committo (3)
joiner lignārĭus, *m*
joint commissūra, *f*
joist tignum transversum, *n*
joke *nn*, iŏcus, *m*
joke *v.i*, iŏcor (1 *dep*)
joker iŏcŭlātor, *m*
jollity hĭlărĭtas, *f*
jolly hĭlăris
jolt *v.t*, concŭtĭo (3)
jostle *v.t*, pulso (1)
jot *v.t*, adnŏto (1)
journal commentārĭi dĭurni, *m.pl*
journey *nn*, ĭter, *n*
journey *v.i*, ĭter făcĭo (3)
journey-man ŏpĭfex, *c*
jovial hĭlăris
jowl gĕnae, *f.pl*
joy (outward) laetĭtĭa, *f*; **(inner)**,
  gaudĭum, *n*
joyful laetus
joyless tristis
jubilant gaudĭo (*or* laetĭtĭā)
  exsultans **(exultant with joy)**
judge *nn*, iūdex, *m*
judge *v.t*, iūdĭco (1), aestĭmo (1)
judgement iūdĭcĭum, *n*
judicature iūdĭces, *m.pl*
judicial iūdĭcĭālis
judicious săpĭens
judiciously săpĭenter
judiciousness prūdentĭa, *f*
jug urcĕus, *m*
juggling tricks praestĭgĭae, *f.pl*
juice sūcus, *m*
juicy sūcōsus
July (before Caesar) Quintīlis
  (mensis); **(after Caesar)**, Iūlĭus
  (mensis)
jumble *nn*, congĕrĭes, *f*
jumble *v.t*, confundo (3)
jump *nn*, saltus, *m*
jump *v.i*, sălĭo (4)
junction coniunctĭo, *f*
juncture tempus, *n*
June Iūnĭus (mensis)

junior mĭnor nātu, iūnĭor
juniper iūnĭpĕrus, f
jurisconsult iūrisconsultus, m
jurisdiction iūrisdictĭo, f
juror iūdex, m
jury iūdĭces, m.pl
just iustus
justice iustĭtĭa, f
justification sătisfactĭo, f
justify v.t, purgo (1), excūso (1)
justly adv, iustē
jut v.i, exsto (1)
juvenile iūvĕnīlis

K

keel cărīna, f
keen ācer; (mentally), perspĭcax
keenness (eagerness) stŭdĭum,
n; (sagacity), săgācĭtas, f;
(sharpness, etc.) ācerbĭtas, f
keep nn, arx, f
keep v.t, (hold), tĕnĕo (2), hăbĕo
(2); (preserve), servo (1); (store),
condo (3); (support, rear), ălo (3);
(– apart), distĭnĕo (2); (– back),
rĕtĭnĕo (2), dētĭnĕo (2); (– off),
arcĕo (2); v.i, (remain), mănĕo (2)
keeper custos, c
keeping (protection) tūtēla, f,
custōdĭa, f
keg dōlĭum, n, amphŏra, f
kennel stăbŭlum, n
kerb (stone) crēpīdo, f
kernel nŭclĕus, m
kettle lĕbes, m
key clāvis, f
kick nn, calcĭtrātus, m
kick v.i, calcĭtro (1)
kid haedus, m
kidnap v.t, surrĭpĭo (3)
kidney rēn, m
kidney bean phăsēlus, m, f
kill v.t, nĕco (1), interfĭcĭo (3)
kiln fornax, f
kind nn, gĕnus, n; (of such a –),
adj, tālis
kind adj, bĕnignus
kindle v.t, accendo (3), excĭto (1)
kindliness bĕnignĭtas, f
kindness bĕnĕfĭcĭum, n; (of
disposition) bĕnignĭtas, f
kindred (relatives) consanguĭnĕi,

m.pl; cognāti, m.pl
king rex, m
kingdom regnum, n
kingfisher alcēdo, f
kinsman nĕcessārĭus, m
kiss nn, oscŭlum, n
kiss v.t, oscŭlor (1 dep)
kitchen cŭlīna, f
kitten fēlis cătŭlus, m (the young
of a cat)
knapsack sarcĭna, f
knave scĕlestus, m
knavery nēquĭtĭa, f, imprŏbĭtas, f
knavish nēquam (indeclinable);
imprŏbus
knead v.t, sŭbĭgo (3)
knee gĕnu, n; (knock-kneed), adj,
vārus
kneecap pătella, f
kneel gĕnu (gĕnĭbus) nītor (3
dep) (rest on the knee(s))
knife cutler, m
knight ĕques, m
knighthood dignĭtas ĕquestris, f
knit v.t, texo (3); (– the forehead)
frontem contrăho (3)
knob bulla, f, nōdus, m
knock v.t, pulso (1); (– against),
offendo (3); (– down), dēpello
(3), dēĭcĭo (3)
knock, knocking pulsus, m,
pulsātĭo, f
knoll tŭmŭlus, m
knot nn, nōdus, m
knot v.t, nōdo (1)
knotty nōdōsus
know v.t, scĭo (4); (get to –),
cognosco (3); (person,
acquaintance), nosco (3); (not
to –), nescĭo (4)
knowing adj, (wise) prūdens
knowingly adv, consultō
knowledge scĭentĭa, f
known nōtus; (to make –),
dēclāro (1)
knuckle artĭcŭlus, m

L

label tĭtŭlus, m, pittăcĭum, n
laborious lăbōrĭōsus
labour lăbor, m, ŏpus, n; (to be
in –) v.i, partŭrĭo (4)

labour *v.i,* lăbōro (1), ēnītor (3 *dep*)
labourer ŏpĕrārĭus, *m*
labyrinth lăbўrinthus, *m*
lace rētĭcŭlāta texta, *n.pl* **(net-like fabric)**
lacerate *v.t,* lăcĕro (1)
laceration lăcĕrātĭo, *f*
lack *nn,* ĭnŏpĭa, *f*
lack *v.i,* ĕgĕo (2), cărĕo (*both with abl*)
lackey pĕdĭsĕquus, *m*
laconic brĕvis
lad pŭer, *m*
ladder scālae, *f.pl*
ladle trulla, *f*
lady mātrōna, *f,* dŏmĭna, *f*
ladylike lībĕrālis **(gracious)**
lag *v.i,* cesso (1)
laggard cessātor, *m*
lagoon lăcus, *m*
lair lătĭbŭlum, *n*
lake lăcus, *m*
lamb agnus, *m*; (agna, *f*)
lame claudus; **(argument, etc.)** lĕvis; **(to be —)** *v.i,* claudĭco (1)
lameness claudĭcātĭo, *f*
lament lāmentātĭo, *f,* complōrātĭo, *f,* ŭlŭlātus, *m*
lament *v.i, and v.t,* lāmentor (1 *dep*), dēplōro (1), lūgĕo (2)
lamentable lāmentābĭlis
lamented dēplōrātus, flēbĭlis
lamp lūcerna, *f*
lampoon carmen rīdĭcŭlum et fāmōsum **(facetious defamatory verse)**
lance lancĕa, *f,* hasta, *f*
lancet scalpellum, *n*
land (earth, etc.) terra, *f*; **(region of country),** rĕgĭo, *f,* fines, *m.pl*; **(native —)** pătrĭa, *f*
land *v.t,* expōno (3); *v.i,* ēgrĕdĭor (3 *dep*)
landing *nn,* ēgressus, *m*
landlord (innkeeper) caupo, *m*; **(owner),** dŏmĭnus, *m*
landmark lăpis, *m*
landslide lapus (*m*) terrae
lane sēmĭta, *f*
language lingua, *f*; **(speech, style),** ōrātĭo, *f*
languid languĭdus, rĕmissus

languish *v.i,* langueo (2), tabesco (3)
languor languor, *m*
lank (hair) prōmissus; **(persons),** prōcerus
lantern lanterna, *f*
lap grĕmĭum, *n,* sĭnus, *m*
lap up *v.t,* lambo (3)
lapse *nn,* **(mistake)** peccātum, *n*; **(of time),** fŭga, *f*
lapse *v.i,* **(err)** pecco (1); **(time),** praetĕrĕo (4)
larceny furtum, *n*
larch lărix, *f*
lard ădeps, *c,* lārĭdum, *n*
larder *use* cella, *f,* **(store-room),** *or* armārĭum, *n* **(food cupboard)**
large magnus
largeness magnĭtūdo, *f*
largess largītĭo, *f*
lark ălauda, *f*
larynx *use* guttur, *n* **(throat)**
lascivious lībĭdĭnōsus
lash (whip) lōrum, *n,* flăgellum, *n*; **(eye —),** pilus, m
lash *v.t,* **(whip),** verbĕro (1); **(bind),** allĭgo (1)
lass pŭella, *f*
last *adj,* ultĭmus, postrēmus, extrēmus; **(most recent),** nŏvissĭmus, proxĭmus; **(at —),** *adv,* tandem
last *v.i,* dūro (1), mănĕo (2)
lasting *adj,* dĭūturnus
lastly *adv,* postrēmo, dēnĭque
latch pessŭlus, *m*
late sērus, tardus; **(dead),** mortŭus; *adv,* sĕro; **(— at night)** (*adv. phr.*), multā nocte
lately *adv,* nūper
latent occultus
lathe tornus, *m*
Latin Lătīnus; **(— language),** lingua Lătīna, *f*
latitude (freedom, scope) lībertas, *f*
latter (the —) hic
lattice cancelli, *m. pl*
laud *v.t,* laudo (1)
laudable laudābĭlis
laugh *nn,* rīsus, *m*; **(loud —),** cāchinnus, *m*
laugh *v.i,* cachinno (1)

laughing-stock lŭdībrĭum, *n*

launch *v.t*, **(a ship)**, dēdūco (3); *v.i*, **(launch out)**, insĕquor (3 *dep*)

laurel laurus; *f*; *adj*, laurĕus

lava massa lĭquĕfacta, *f*, **(molten mass)**

lavish *adj*, prōdĭgus, prŏfūsus

lavish *v.t*, prŏfundo (3)

law (a law) lex, *f*; **(the law)**, iūs, *n*

lawful lēgĭtĭmus

lawless nĕfārĭus

lawn prātum, *n*

lawsuit līs, *f*

lawyer iūrisconsultus, *m*

lax dissŏlūtus

laxness rĕmissĭo, *f*, neglĕntĭa, *f*

laxity rĕmissĭo, *f*, neglĕgentĭa, *f*

lay *v.t*, pōno (3); **(— aside)**, pōno (3); **(— foundations)**, iăcĭo (3); **(— an ambush)**, insĭdĭs collŏco (1); **(— down arms)**, ab armis discēdo (3); **(— eggs)**, ōva părĭo (3)

layer cŏrĭum, *n*, tăbŭlātum, *n*

laziness ignāvĭa, *f*

lazy ignāvus, pĭger

lead *nn*, plumbum, *n*; *adj*, plumbĕus

lead *v.t*, dūco (3); **(— a life, etc.)**, ăgo (3); **(— on, persuade)**, addūco (3)

leader dux, *c*

leadership ductus, *m*; *or use phr. in abl*, e.g. **under the — of Brutus**, Brūto dŭce **(with Brutus leader)**

leading *adj*, princeps

leaf frons, *f*, fŏlĭum, *n*; **(paper)** schĕda, *f*

leafy frondōsus

league foedus, *n*, sŏcĭĕtas, *f*

league together *v.i*, coniūro (1)

leak *nn*, rīma *f*

leak (let in water) ăquam per rīmas accĭpĭo (3)

leaky rīmōsus

lean *adj*, măcer, exīlis

lean *v.i*, innītor (3 *dep*); *v.t*, inclīno (1)

leanness măcĭes, *f*

leap *nn*, saltus, *m*

leap *v.i*, sălĭo (4); **(— down)** dēsĭlĭo (4)

leap year bīsextĭlis annus, *m*

learn *v.t*, disco (3); **(ascertain)** cognosco (3)

learned doctus

learning doctrīna, *f*, ērŭdītĭo, *f*

lease *nn*, conductĭo, *f*

lease *v.t*, condūco (3)

leash cōpŭla, *f*

least *adj*, mĭnĭmus; *adv*, mĭnĭmē; **(at —)**, *adv*, saltem

leather cŏrĭum, *n*

leave *nn*, **(permission)**, pŏtestas, *f*, permissĭo, *f*; **(— of absence)** commĕātus, *m*

leave *v.i*, discēdo (3); *v.t*, rĕlinquo (3), dēsĕro (3)

leave off *v.i. and v.t*, dēsĭno (3)

leavings *nn*, rĕlĭquĭae, *f. pl*

lecture *nn*, audītĭo, *f*, **(hearing)**

lecture *v.i*, schŏlas hăbĕo (2)

lecture-room schŏla, *f*

ledge *use adj*, ēmĭnens **(projecting)** *in agreement with a noun*

ledger cōdex, *m*

leech hĭrūdo, *f*

leek porrum, *n*

leering *adj*, līmus

left *adj*, **(opp. to right)**, sĭnister, laevus; **(remaining)**, rĕlĭquus

leg crus, *n*

legacy lēgātum, *n*

legal lēgĭtĭmus

legalize *v.t*, sancĭo (4)

legate lēgātus, *m*

legation lēgātĭo, *f*

legend făbŭla, *f*

legendary fābŭlōsus

leggings ōcrĕae, *f. pl*

legible *use phr*, făcĭlis ad lĕgendum **(easy for reading)**

legion lĕgĭo, *f*

legislate *v.i*, lēges făcĭo (3) **(make laws)**

legislator lātor, **(*m*)** lēgum **(proposer of laws)**

legitimate lēgĭtĭmus

leisure ōtĭum, *n*; **(to be at —)**, *v.i*, ōtĭor (1 *dep*)

leisurely *adj*, lentus

lend *v.t*, mūtŭum do (1) **(give a loan)**, commŏdo (1)

length longĭtūdo, *f*; **(of time)**, dĭŭturnĭtas, *f*; **(at —)**, *adv*, tandem

lengthen *v.t*, prōdūco (3), longĭōrem reddo (3)
leniency clēmentĭa, *f*
lenient mītis, clēmens
lentil lens, *f*
leper hŏmo lĕprōsus, *m*
leprosy lĕprae, *f. pl*
less *adj*, mĭnor; *adv*, mĭnus
lessen *v.i. and v.t*, mĭnŭo (3)
lesson dŏcŭmentum, *n*
lest *conj*, nē
let *v.t*, sĭno (3) permitto (3) (*with dat of person*); **(lease)**, lŏco (1); **(— go)**, dīmitto (3); **(— in)**, admitto (3); **(— out)**, ēmitto (3)
lethal mortĭfer
lethargic lentus
letter (of the alphabet) littĕra, *f*; **(epistle)**, littĕrae, *f. pl*, ĕpistŏla, *f*
lettering *nn*, littĕrae, *f. pl*
letters (learning) littĕrae, *f. pl*
lettuce lactūca, *f*
level *adj*, plānus; **(— place)**, *nn*, plānĭtĭes, *f*
level *v.t*, aequo (1); **(— to the ground)**, sterno (3)
lever vectis, *m*
levity lĕvĭtas, *f*
levy *nn*, dēlectus, *m*
levy *v.t*, **(troops)**, scrībo (3); **(taxes, etc.)**, impĕro (1), ĕxĭgo (3)
lewd incestus, impŭdīcus
lewdness incestum, *n*
liable obnoxĭus
liar hŏmo mendax
libellous fāmōsus
liberal lībĕrālis, largus
liberality lībĕrālĭtas, *f*, largĭtas, *f*
liberate *v.t*, lībĕro (1)
liberation lībĕrātĭo, *f*
liberty lībertas, *f*
librarian bĭblĭŏthēcārĭus, *m*
library bĭblĭŏthēca, *f*
licence lĭcentĭa, *f*; **(permission)**, pŏtestas, *f*
licentious dissŏlūtus
lick *v.t*, lambo (3)
lid ŏpercŭlum, *n*
lie *nn*, mendācĭum, *n*
lie *v.i*, **(tell a —)**, mentĭor (4 *dep*)
lie *v.i*, iăcĕo (2); **(rest)**, cŭbo (1); **(— ill)**, iăcĕo (2); **(— in wait)**, insĭdĭor (1 *dep*)

lieutenant lēgātus, *m*
life vīta, *f*, ănĭma, *f*; **(vivacity)**, vĭgor, *m*; **(— blood)**, sanguis, *m*
lifeless exănĭmis, exanguis
lifelike *use* sĭmĭlis **(similar)**
lifetime aetas, *f*
lift *v.t*, tollo (3)
ligament lĭgāmentum, *n*
light *nn*, lux, *f*, lŭmen, *n*; **(to bring to —)**, in mĕdĭum prōfĕro (*irreg*)
light *adj* **(not dark)**, illustris; **(in weight)**, lĕvis; **(— armed)**, expĕdītus; **(trivial, of opinions, etc.)**, lĕvis
light *v.t*, **(illuminate)**, illustro (1); **(kindle)**, accendo (3)
lighten *v.t*, **(burden, etc.)**, lĕvo (1); *v.i*, **(of lightning)**, fulgĕo (2)
lighthouse phărus, *f*
lightly *adv*, lĕvĭter
lightning fulmen, *n*
like *v.t*, ămo (1)
like *adj*, sĭmĭlis (*with genit. or dat*), par (*with dat*)
like *adv*, sĭmĭlĭter; **(just as)**, sīcut
likelihood sĭmĭlĭtūdo, (*f*), vĕri
likely sĭmĭlis vĕri; *often use future participle, e.g.* **likely to come**, venturus
liken *v.t*, compăro (1)
likeness sĭmĭlĭtūdo (1)
likewise *adv*, ĭtem
liking *nn*, ămor, *m*, lĭbīdo, *f*
lily lĭlĭum, *n*
limb membrum, *n*, artus, *m. pl*
lime calx, *f*; **(tree)**, tĭlĭa, *f*
limit *nn*, fīnis, *m*, termĭnus, *m*
limit *v.t*, fīnĭo (4)
limitation fīnis, *m*
limited (small) parvus
limitless infīnītus
limp *adj*, **(slack)**, rĕmissus
limp *v.i*, claudĭco (1)
limping *adj*, claudus
limpid limpĭdus
linden tree tĭlĭa, *f*
line līnĕa, *f*; **(boundary —)**, fīnis, *m*; **(of poetry)**, versus, *m*; **(to battle)**, ăcĭes, *f*; **(front —)**, prīma ăcĭes, *f*; **(second —)**, princĭpes, *m. pl*; **(third —)**, trĭārĭi, *m. pl*; **(— of march)**, agmen, *n*

line *v.t*, **(put in —)**, instrŭo (3)
lineage stirps, *f*, gĕnus, *n*
linen *nn*, lintĕum, *n*; *adj*, lintĕus
linger *v.i*, mŏror (1 *dep*); cunctor (1 *dep*)
lingering *nn*, mŏra, *f*
link *nn*, **(of chain)**, ānŭlus, *m*
link *v.t*, coniungo (3)
lint līnāmentum, *n*
lintel līmen sŭpĕrum, *n*
lion lĕo, *m*; **(lioness)**, lĕaena
lip lābrum, *n*
liquefy *v.t*, līquĕfăcĭo (3)
liquid *nn*, līquor, *m*
liquid *adj*, līquĭdus
liquidate *v.t*, solvo (3)
liquor līquor, *m*
lisping *adj*, blaesus
list tăbŭla, *f*
listen (to) *v.t*, audĭo (4)
listener auscultātor, *m*
listless languĭdus
listlessness languor, *m*
literal *use*, prŏprĭus **(its own)**
literally *adv. phr*, ad verbum
literary (person) littĕrātus
literature littĕrae, *f. pl*
lithe flexĭbĭlis, ăgĭlis
litigation līs, *f*
litter (of straw, etc.) strāmentum, *n*; **(sedan)**, lectīca, *f*; **(of young)**, fētus, *m*
little *adj*, parvus, exĭgūus; **(for a — while)**, *adv*, părumper, paulisper
little *adv*, paulum
little *nn*, paulum, *n*, nonnĭhil, *n*; **(too little)**, părum, *n*; *with comparatives*, paulo; *e.g.* **a little bigger**, paulo māior
littleness exĭgŭĭtas, *f*
live *v.i*, vīvo (3); **(— in or at)**, hăbĭto (1), incŏlo (3); **(— on)**, vescor (3 *dep*) *(with abl)*; **(— one's life, etc.)**, vītam ăgo (3)
live *adj*, vīvus
livelihood victus, *m*
liveliness ălăcrĭtas, *f*
lively *adj*, ălăcer
liver iĕcur, *n*
livery vestītus, *m*
livid līvĭdus
living *adj*, vīvus

lizard lăcerta, *f*
load ŏnus, *n*
load *v.t*, ŏnĕro (1)
loaded ŏnustus
loaf pănis, *m*
loam lŭtum, *n*
loan mūtŭum, *n, or use adj*, mūtuus **(borrowed, lent)**
loathe *v.t*, ōdi *(defect)*
loathing *nn*, ŏdĭum, *n*
loathsome tēter
lobby vestĭbŭlum, *n*
local *use genit.* of lŏcus **(place)**
locality lŏcus, *m*
lock (bolt) claustra, *n. pl*; **(hair)**, crīnis, *m*
lock *v.t*, obsēro (1)
locker capsa, *f*, armārĭum, *n*
locust lŏcusta, *f*
lodge *v.i*, dēversor (1 *dep*); **(stick fast)**, adhaerĕo (2) fixus; *v.t* **(accommodate temporarily)**, excĭpĭo (3)
lodger inquīlīnus, *m*
lodgings dēversōrĭum, *n*
loft cēnācŭlum, *n*
loftiness altĭtūdo, *f*
lofty celsus, altus
log tignum, *n*
logic dĭălectĭca, *f*
logical dĭălectĭcus
loin lumbus, *m*
loiter *v.i*, cesso (1), cunctor (1 *dep*)
loiterer cessātor, *m*
loneliness sōlĭtūdo, *f*
lonely *adj*, sōlus
long *adj*, longus *(with acc. of extent of length)*, *e.g.* **three feet long**, longus tres pĕdes; **(a — way)**, *adv*, prŏcul, longē; **(of time)**, dĭūtĭnus, dĭūturnus; **(how — ?)**, quam dĭū? **(for a — time)**, *adv*, dĭū
long *adv*, **(time)**, dĭū
long for *v.t*, dēsĭdĕro (1), cŭpĭo (3)
longevity vīvācĭtas, *f*
longing *nn*, dēsīdĕrĭum, *n*
long-suffering *adj*, pătĭens
look at *v.t*, aspĭcĭo (3); **(— back)**, rēspĭcĭo (3); **(— down (upon))**, dēspĭcĭo (3); **(— for)**, quaero (3);

(— round), circumspĭcĭo (3); *v.i*
(— towards), specto (1); (seem),
vĭdĕor (2 *pass*)
look   *nn*, aspectus, *m*;
(appearance), spěcĭes, *f*;
(expression), vultus, *m*
looking glass   spěcŭlum, *n*
loom   tēla, *f*
loop (winding)   flexus, *m*
loophole   fěnestra, *f*
loose   *adj*, laxus; (at liberty),
sŏlūtus; (hair), passus, prŏmissus;
(dissolute), dissŏlūtus
loose   *v.t*, laxo (1), solvo (3)
loosely   *adv*, sŏlūtē
loot   *nn*, praeda, *f*
loot   *v.t*, praedor (1 *dep*)
lop off   *v.t*, ampŭto (1)
loquacious   lŏquax
loquacity   lŏquācĭtas, *f*
lord   dŏmĭnus, *m*
lordly   *adv*, rēgālis, sŭperbus
lordship (supreme power)
impěrĭum, *n*
lore   doctrīna, *f*
lose   *v.t*, āmitto (3), perdo (3); (—
heart), ănĭmo dēfĭcĭo (3)
loss (act of losing)   āmissĭo, *f*; (the
loss itself), damnum, *n*,
dētrīmentum, *n*; (to be at a —),
v.i, haerĕo (2)
lost   (*adj*) āmissus, perdĭtus
lot (chance)   sors, *f*; (to draw — s),
sortĭor (4 *dep*); (much), multum,
n
loth (unwilling)   invītus
lottery   sortītĭo, *f*
loud   clārus, magnus
loudness   magnĭtūdo, *f*
lounge   *v.i*, (recline), rěcŭbo (1)
louse   pědīcŭlus, *m*
lousy   pědīcŭlōsus
lout   hŏmo agrestis
love   *nn*, ămor, *m*
love   *v.t*, ămo (1), dīlĭgo (3)
loveliness   věnustas, *f*
lovely   věnustus
lover   ămātor, *m*, ămans, *c*
loving   *adj*, ămans
low   hŭmĭlis; (sounds); grăvis; (—
born), hŭmĭli lŏco nātus; (price),
vīlis; (conduct, etc.), sordĭdus; (in
spirits), *adv. phr*, ănĭmo dēmisso

low   *v.i*, mūgĭo (4)
lower   *comp. adj*, infěrĭor
lower   *v.t*, dēmitto (3); (—
oneself), sē ăbĭcĕre (3 *reflex*)
lowering   mĭnax
lowest   infĭmus
lowing   mūgĭtus, *m*
lowlands   lŏca, plāna, *n. pl*
lowness, lowliness   hŭmĭlĭtas, *f*
lowly   hŭmĭlis, obscūrus
loyal   fĭdēlis
loyalty   fĭdes, *f*
lozenge   pastillus, *m*
lubricate   *v.t*, ungo (3)
lucid   lūcĭdus
lucidity   perspĭcŭĭtas, *f*
luck   fortūna, *f*, fors, *f*; (good —),
fēlīcĭtas, *f*; (bad —), infēlīcĭtas
luckily   *adv*, fēlīcĭter
luckless   infēlix
lucky   fēlix, fortūnātus
lucrative   quaestŭōsus
ludicrous   rīdĭcŭlus
lug   *v.t*, trăho (3)
luggage   impědīmenta, *n. pl*
lugubrious   lūgŭbris
lukewarm   těpĭdus
lull   *v.t*, sēdo (1); *v.i*, (of wind),
sēdor (1 *pass*)
lull   *nn, use vb*. intermitto (3)
lumber   scrūta, *n. pl*
luminary   lūmen, *n*
luminous   illustrus, lūcĭdus
lump   massa, *f*
lunacy   insānĭa, *f*, ălĭēnātĭo, *f*
lunar   lūnāris
lunatic   hŏmo insānus
lunch   *nn*, prandĭum, *n*
lunch   *v.i*, prandĕo (2)
lung   pulmo, *m*
lurch   *v.i*, ăgĭtor (1 *pass*) (leave in
the —), rělinquo (3)
lure   *nn*, illex, *c*, illěcěbrae, *f. pl*
lure   *v.t*, allĭcĭo (3)
lurid   lūrĭdus
lurk   *v.i*, lătěo (2)
lurking in wait   *use* insĭdĭor (1
dep) (lie in ambush)
luscious   dulcis
lust   *nn*, lĭbīdo, *f*
lust after   *v.t*, concŭpisco (3)
lustful   lĭbīdĭnōsus
lustiness   vĭgor, *m*

lustre splendor, *m*
lusty vălĭdus
lute cĭthăra, *f*
luxuriance luxŭrĭa, *f*
luxuriant luxŭrĭōsus
luxurious luxŭrĭōsus, lautus
luxury luxus, *m*, luxŭrĭa, *f*
lying *adj*, **(telling lies)**, mendax
lynx lynx, *c*
lyre cĭthăra, *f*, fĭdes, *f. pl*
lyrical lўrĭcus

M

macebearer lictor, *m*
macerate *v.t*, măcĕro (1)
machination dŏlus, *m*
machine māchĭna, *f*
machinery māchĭnātĭo, *f*
mackerel scomber, *m*
mad insānus, vēcors, fŭrĭōsus; **(to be —)**, *v.i*, fŭro (3)
madden *v.t*, mentem ălĭēno (1) *(with dat)*; **(excite)**, accendo (3)
maddening *adj*, fŭrĭōsus
madman hŏmo vēcors
madness insānĭa, *f*
magazine horrĕum, *n*; **(arsenal)**, armāmentārĭum, *n*
maggot vermĭcŭlus, *m*
magic *adj*, măgĭcus
magic *nn*, ars măgĭca, *f*
magician măgus, *m*
magistracy măgistrātus, *m*
magistrate măgistrātus, *m*
magnanimity magnănĭmĭtas, *f*
magnanimous magnănĭmus
magnet lăpis magnes, *m*
magnetic magnētĭcus
magnificence magnĭfĭcentĭa, *f*
magnificent magnĭfĭcus, splendĭdus
magnify *v.t*, amplĭfĭco (1), exaggĕro (1)
magnitude magnĭtūdo, *f*
magpie pīca, *f*
maid, maiden virgo, *f*; **(servant)**, ancilla, *f*
maiden *adj*, virgĭnālis
mail (letters) littĕrae, *f. pl*, ĕpistŏlae, *f. pl*; **(armour)**, lōrĭca, *f*
maim *v.t*, mŭtĭlo (1)
main *adj*, prīmus, praecĭpŭus

mainland contĭnens terra, *f*
maintain *v.t*, servo (1), sustĭnĕo (2); **(with food, etc.)**, ălo (3); **(by argument)**, affirmo (1)
maintenance *use vb*. servo (1) **(to maintain)**
majestic augustus
majesty māiestas, *f*
major *nn*, **(officer)**, praefectus, *m*
major *adj*, māior
majority māior pars, *f*
make *v.t*, făcĭo (3), effĭcĭo (3), fingo (3), reddo (3); **(compel)**, cōgo (3); **(appoint)**, crĕo (1); **(— for, seek)**, pĕto (3); **(— haste)**, *v.i*, festīno (1), accĕlĕro (1); **(— good)**, *v.t*, rĕpăro (1), sarcĭo (1); **(— ready)**, praepăro (1); **(— up, a total, etc.)**, explĕo (2); **(— use of)**, ūtor (3 *dep*) *(with abl)*
maker făbrĭcător, *m*
maladministration măla admĭnistrātĭo, *f*
malady morbus, *m*
malcontent cŭpĭdus nŏvārum rērum **(eager for innovations)**
male *adj*, mascŭlus, mās
male *nn*, mās, *m*
malediction dīrae, *f. pl*, **(curses)**
malefactor hŏmo mălĕfĭcus, nŏcens
malevolence mălĕvŏlentĭa, *f*
malevolent mălĕvŏlus
malice mălĕvŏlentĭa, *f*; **(envy)**, invĭdĭa, *f*
malicious mălĕvŏlus
malignant mălĕvŏlus
maligner obtrectător, *m*
malignity mălĕvŏlentĭa, *f*
malleable ductĭlis
mallet mallĕus, *m*
maltreat *v.t*, vĕxo (1)
maltreatment vexātĭo, *f*
man (human being) hŏmo, *c*; **(opp. to woman, child)**, vĭr, *m*; **(mankind)**, hŏmĭnes, *c. pl*; **(chess, etc.)**, latruncŭlus, *m*; **(fighting —)**, mīles, *c*
man *v.t*, **(ships, etc.)**, complĕo (2)
man-of-war (ship) nāvis longa, *f*
manacle *nn*, mănĭcae, *f. pl*, vincŭla, *n. pl*
manage *v.t*, admĭnistro (1), cūro

(1), gĕro (3)
manageable tractābĭlis, hăbĭlis
management cŭra, f,
  admĭnistrātĭo, f
manager prōcūrātor, m,
  admĭnistrātor, m
mandate impĕrātum, n,
  mandātum, n
mane (of horse) iŭba, f
manful vĭrīlis
manger praesēpe, n
mangle v.t, lăcĕro (1), lănĭo (1)
mangled truncus
mangy scăber
manhood pūbertas, f, tŏga vĭrīlis,
  f **(manly dress)**
mania insānĭa, f
maniac hŏmo vēcors, āmens
manifest v.t, ostendo (3), ăpĕrĭo
  (4)
manifest adj, mănĭfestus, ăpertus
manifestation ostentātĭo, f, or use
  vbs. above
manifold multĭplex
maniple (of a legion) mănĭpŭlus,
  m
manipulate v.t, tracto (1)
mankind hŏmĭnes, c. pl
manliness virtus, f
manly vĭrīlis
manner (way) mŏdus, m, rătĭo, f;
  (custom), mos, m; **(type),** gĕnus,
  n; **(good manners),** dĕcōrum, n
mannerism gestus prŏprĭus
manoeuvre (military) dēcursus, m;
  (trick), dŏlus, m
manoeuvre v.i, dēcurro (3)
manor praedĭum, n
manservant servus, m
mansion dŏmus magna, f
manslaughter hŏmĭcīdĭum, n
mantle palla, f, lăcerna, f
manual adj, use mănus **(hand)**
manual nn, (book), lĭbellus, m
manufacture nn, făbrĭca, f
manufacture v.t, făbrĭcor (1 dep)
manufacturer făbrĭcātor, m
manumission mănūmissĭo, f
manure stercus, n
manuscript lĭber, m
many adj, multi (pl); **(very —),**
  plūrĭmi; **(a good —),** plērīque,
  complūres; **(as — as),** tŏt …

quŏt; **(how — ?),** quŏt?; **(so —),**
  tŏt; **(— times),** adv, saepĕ
map tăbŭla, f
map (to — out) v.t, dēsigno (1)
maple ăcer, n; adj, ăcernus
mar v.t, dēformo (1)
marauder praedātor, m
marble marmor, n; adj,
  marmŏrĕus
March Martĭus (mensis)
march nn, ĭter, n; **(forced —),**
  magnum ĭter; **(on the —),** adv.
  phr, in ĭtĭnĕre
march v.i, ĭter făcĭo (3); **(—
  quickly),** contendo (3); **(advance),**
  prōgrĕdĭor (3 dep)
mare ĕqua, f
margin margo, m, f
marine nn, mīles classĭcus, m
marine adj, mărīnus
mariner nauta, m
maritime mărĭtĭmus
mark nŏta, f, signum, n,
  vestĭgĭum, n; **(characteristic),** use
  genit. case of nn. with esse; e.g. it
  is the — of a wise man, est
  săpĭentis …
mark v.t, nŏto (1); **(indicate),**
  dēsigno (1); **(notice, observe),**
  ănĭmădverto (3)
market fŏrum, n, măcellum, n;
  (cattle —), fŏrum bŏārĭum, n
market v.t, nundĭnor (1 dep)
market-day nundĭnae, f. pl, **(ninth
  day)**
marketing nn, use vb. vendo (3)
  (sell)
marketplace fŏrum, n
marriage conĭŭgĭum, n; **(—
  feast),** nuptĭae, f. pl; **(—
  contract),** pactĭo nuptĭālis, f
marriageable nūbĭlis
marrow mĕdulla, f
marry v.t, **(— a woman),** dūco
  (3); **(— a man),** nūbo (3) (with
  dat)
marsh pălus, f
marshal appārĭtor, m
marshal v.t, **(troops, etc.),**
  dispōno (3)
marshy păluster
martial bellĭcōsus; **(court —),**
  castrense iūdĭcĭum, n

martyr martyr, *c*
martyrdom martўrĭum, *n*
marvel (miracle, etc.) mīrācŭlum, *n*
marvel at *v.t* mīror (1 *dep*)
marvellous mīrus, mīrābĭlis
masculine vĭrīlis
mash *nn*, farrāgo, *f*
mash *v.t* contundo (3)
mask *nn*, persōna, *f*; **(disguise)**, intĕgūmentum, *n*
mask *v.t*, **(oneself)**, persōnam indŭo (3); **(disguise)**, dissĭmŭlo (1)
mason structor, *m*
masonry structūra, *f*
mass mōles, *f*; **(of people)**, multĭtūdo, *f*
mass *v.t*, cŭmŭlo (1), ăcervo (1)
massacre *nn*, caedes, *f*
massacre *v.t*, trŭcīdo (1), caedo (3)
massive sŏlĭdus; **(huge)**, ingens
mast mālus, *m*
master dŏmĭnus, *m*; **(— of the household)**, păterfămĭlĭas, *m*; **(school —)**, măgister, *m*; **(skilled in ...)**, *use adj*, pĕrītus
master *v.t*, **(subdue)**, dŏmo (1); **(knowledge, etc.)**, bĕne scĭo (4), disco (3)
masterful impĕrĭoūsus
masterly *adj*, bŏnus; **(plan, etc.)**, callĭdus
masterpiece ŏpus summā laude dignum **(work worthy of the highest praise)**
masterly (rule) dŏmĭnātus, *m*
masticate *v.t*, mandūco (1)
mastiff cănis Mŏlussus **(Molossian hound)**
mat stŏrĕa, *f*
mat *v.t*, implĭco (1)
match (contest) certāmen, *n*; **(equal)**, *adj*, pār; **(marriage —)**, nuptĭae, *f. pl*
match *v.t*, **(equal)**, aequo (1)
matchless ēgrĕgĭus
matching *adj*, **(equal)** pār
mate sŏcĭus, *m*; **(— in marriage)**, coniunx, *m, f*.
mate *v.i*, coniungor (3 *pass*)
material *nn*, mātĕrĭa, *f*

material *adj*, corpŏrĕus
materially *adv*, **(much)**, multum
maternal maternus
maternity māter, *f*, **(mother)**
mathematician măthēmătĭcus, *m*
mathematics măthēmătĭca, *f*
matter (substance) corpus, *n*, mātĕrĭa, *f*; **(affair)**, res, *f*; **(what is the — ?)**, quid est?; **(it matters, it is important)**, rēfert (*v. impers*)
mattress culcĭta, *f*
mature *adj*, mātūrus, ădultus
mature *v.t*, mātūro (1); *v.i*, mātūresco (3)
maturity mātūrĭtas, *f*
maudlin ĭneptus
maul *v.t*, mulco (1), lănĭo (1)
maw inglŭvĭes, *f*
maxim praeceptum, *n*
maximum *use adj*, maxĭmus **(biggest)**
May Māius (mensis)
may *v. auxiliary*, **(having permission to)**, lĭcet (2 *impers. with dat. of person allowed*), *e.g.* **you may go**, lĭcet tĭbĭ īre; **(having ability to)**, possum (*irreg*); *often expressed by subjunctive mood of verb*
maybe (perhaps) *adv*, fortassĕ
May Day Kălendae Māiae **(first day of May)**
mayor praefectus, *m*
maze *nn*, lăbўrinthus, *m*
meadow prātum, *n*
meagre măcer, iēiūnus
meagreness iēiūnĭtas, *f*
meal (flour) fărīna, *f*; **(food)**, cĭbus, *m*
mean *nn*, mŏdus, *m*
mean *adj*, **(middle, average)**, mĕdĭus; **(of low rank)**, hŭmĭlis; **(miserly)**, sordĭdus
mean *v.t*, signĭfĭco (1); **(intend)**, in ănĭmo hăbĕo (2)
meander *v.i*, **(of a river)**, sĭnŭōso cursu flŭo (3) **(flow on a winding course)**
meaning *nn*, signĭfĭcātĭo, *f*
meanness hŭmĭlĭtas, *f*; **(of disposition)**, sordes, *f. pl*
means (method) mŏdus, *m*; **(opportunity)**, făcultas, *f*;

(resources), ŏpes, *f. pl*; (by no
—), *adv*, haudquāquam, nullo
mŏdo
meantime, meanwhile (in the —)
adv, intĕrĕā, intĕrim
measure mensūra, *f*, mŏdus, *m*;
(plan), consĭlĭum, *n*; (music),
mŏdi, *m. pl*
measure *v.t*, mētĭor (4 *dep*)
measureless immensus
meat căro, *f*
mechanic fǎber, *m*, ŏpĭfex, *c*
mechanical māchĭnālis
mechanism māchĭnātĭo, *f*
medal, medallion phălĕrae, arum,
f. pl
meddle *v.i*, sē interpōnĕre (3
reflex)
mediate *v.i*, sē interpōnĕre (3
reflex), intervĕnĭo (4)
mediator dēprĕcātor, *m*
medical mĕdĭcus
medicine (art of —) ars mĕdĭcīna,
f; (the remedy itself),
mĕdĭcāmentum, *n*
mediocre mĕdĭŏcris
mediocrity mĕdĭŏcrĭtas, *f*
meditate *v.t*, cōgĭto (1)
Mediterranean Sea mărĕ
nostrum, *n*, (our sea)
medium *use adj*, mĕdĭus (middle);
(through the — of) per
medley farrāgo, *f*
meek mītis
meekness ănĭmus summissus, *m*
meet *v.t*, obvĭam fīo (*irreg*) (*with
dat*); (go to — , encounter),
obvĭam ĕo (*irreg*) (*with dat*); *v.i*,
convĕnĭo (4); concurro (3)
meeting *nn*, conventus, *m*
melancholy *nn*, tristĭtĭa, *f*
melancholy *adj*, tristis
mellow mītis
mellow *v.i*, mātūresco (3)
melodious cănōrus
melody mĕlos, *n*
melon mēlo, *m*
melt *v.t*, lĭquĕfăcĭo (3); (people,
etc.), mŏvĕo (2); *v.i*, lĭquesco (3)
member (of a society) sŏcĭus, *m*;
(of the body), membrum, *n*
membrane membrāna, *f*
memoirs commentārii, *m. pl*

memorable mĕmŏrābĭlis
memorandum lĭbellus mĕmŏrĭālis
memorial mŏmŭmentum, *n*
memory mĕmŏrĭa, *f*
menace mĭnae, *f. pl*
menace *v.t*, mĭnor (1 *dep*)
menacing *adj*, mĭnax
mend *v.t*, rĕfĭcĭo (3), sarcĭo (4);
v.i, (in health), mĕlŏr fīo (*irreg*)
(get better)
mendacious mendax
mendicant mendīcus, *m*
menial *adj*, servīlis
mensuration rătĭo (*f*) mētĭendi
(system of measuring)
mental *use genitive of* mens, *or*
ănĭmus (mind)
mention *nn*, mentĭo, *f*
mention *v.t*, mĕmŏro (1), dīco (3)
mercantile mercātōrum (of
merchants)
mercenary *adj*, mercēnārĭus
merchandise merx, *f*
merchant mercātor, *m*
merchant-ship nāvis ŏnĕrĭa, *f*
merciful mĭsĕrĭcors
merciless crūdēlis, inclēmens
mercury (quick silver) argentum
vīvum, *n*; (god), Mercŭrĭus
mercy mĭsĕrĭcordĭa, *f*
mere *adj*, sōlus, *or use
emphathic pron*, ipse
merely *adv*, tantummŏdo
merge *v.i*, miscĕor (2 *pass*)
meridian circŭlus mĕrĭdĭānus, *m*
meridian *adj*, mĕrĭdĭānus
merit *nn*, mĕrĭtum, *n*
merit *v.i*, mĕrĕor (2 *dep*)
meritorious dignus laude (worthy
of praise)
merriment hĭlărĭtas, *f*
merry hĭlăris
mesh măcŭla, *f*
mess (confused state) turba, *f*;
(dirt), squālor, *m*
message nuntĭus, *m*
messenger nuntĭus, *m*
metal mĕtallum, *n*
metallic mĕtallĭcus
metamorphosis *use vb*,
transformo (1) (to change in
shape)
metaphor translātĭo, *f*

metaphorical translātus
meteor fax, *f*
method rătĭo, *f*
methodically ex ordĭne, *or use adv phr*, rătĭōne et vĭā **(by reckoning and method)**
metre nŭmĕrus, *m*
metrical mĕtrĭcus
metropolis căpŭt, *n*
mettle fĕrōcĭtas, *f*
mettlesome ănĭmōsus, fĕrox
mew *v.i*, **(cat)**, quĕror (3 *dep*)
mica phengītes, *m*
mid *adj*, mĕdĭus
midday *nn*, mĕrīdĭes, *m*
midday *adj*, mĕrīdĭānus
middle *adj*, mĕdĭus
middle *nn, use* mĕdĭus *in agreement with noun, e.g.* **the middle of the river**, mĕdĭus flŭvĭus
middling *adj*, mĕdĭŏcris
midnight mĕdĭa nox, *f*
midst *nn, use adj*, mĕdĭus
midsummer mĕdĭa aestas, *f*
midwife obstĕtrix, *f*
might (power) vīs, *f*
mighty fortis, vălĭdus, magnus
migrate *v.t*, ăbĕo (4)
migratory bird advĕna ăvis, *f*
mild mītis, clēmens, lēvis
mildew rōbīgo, *f*
mildness lēnĭtas, *f*
mile mille passus (*or* passŭum) **(a thousand paces)**
milestone mīlĭārĭium, *n*
military *adj*, mīlĭtāris; **(— service)**, stīpendĭa, *n. pl*
militate against *v.t*, făcĭo (3) contrā (*with acc*)
milk lac, *n*
milk *v.t*, mulgĕo (2)
milky lactĕus
mill mŏla, *f*, pistrīnum, *n*
miller mŏlĭtor, *m*
million dĕcĭes centēna mīlĭa
millstone mŏla, *f*
mimic *v.t*, ĭmĭtor (1 *dep*)
mince *v.t*, concīdo (3)
mincemeat mĭnūtal, *n*
mind ănĭmus, *m*, mens, *f*; **(intellect)**, ingĕnĭum, *n*; **(to make up one's —)** constĭtŭo (3)
mind *v.t*, **(I — my own business)**,

nĕgōtĭum mĕum ăgo (3)
mindful mĕmor (*with genit*)
mine *adj*, mĕus
mine *nn*, mĕtallum, *n*, cŭnīcŭlus, *m*
mine *v.i*, fŏdĭo (3)
miner fŏdĭens, *m*
mineral *nn*, mĕtallum, *n*
mineral *adj*, mĕtallĭcus
mingle *v.i*, sē miscēre (2 *reflex*)
miniature *nn*, parva tăbella, *f*
minimum *adj*, mĭnĭmus **(smallest)**
minister mĭnister, *m*, admĭnĭster, *m*
ministry (office) mĭnĭstĕrĭum, *n*
minor *nn*, pūpillus, *m*
minority mĭnor pars, *f*
minstrel tībīcen văgus **(wandering —)**
mint (plant) menta, *f*; **(coinage)**, mŏnēta, *f*
mint *v.t*, cūdo (3)
minute *adj*, exĭgŭus, mĭnūtus
minute *nn*, **(of time)**, mōmentum (*n*) tempŏris
miracle mīrācŭlum, *n*
miraculous mīrus
mire lŭtum, *n*
mirror spĕcŭlum, *n*
mirth hĭlărĭtas, *f*
mirthful hĭlăris
misadventure cāsus, *m*
misanthropy *use phr*. ŏdĭum, (*n*) ergā hŏmĭnes **(hatred towards mankind)**
misapply *v.t*, ăbūtor (3 *dep with abl*)
misbehave *v.i*, mălĕ sē gĕrĕre (3 *reflex*)
miscalculate *v.i*, fallor (3 *pass*), erro (1)
miscalculation error, *m*
miscarriage (childbirth) ăbortus, *m*; **(— of justice)** error, (*m*) iūdĭcum
miscarry *v.i*, **(child)**, ăbortum făcĭo (3); **(fail)** frustrā *or* irrĭtum ēvĕnĭo (4)
miscellaneous vărĭus
mischief (injury, wrong) mălĕfĭcĭum, *n*
mischievous mălĕfĭcus; **(playful)**, lascīvus
misconduct *nn*, dēlictum, *n*
miscreant hŏmŏ scĕlestus
misdeed dēlictum, *n*

misdemeanour dēlictum, *n*, peccātaum, *n*
miser hŏmŏ ăvārus
miserable mĭser, infēlix
miserliness ăvārĭtĭa, *f*
miserly *adj*, ăvārus, sordĭdus
misery mĭsĕrĭa, *f*, angor, *m*
misfortune rēs adversae, *f. pl*
misgiving praesāgĭum, *n*
misgovern v.t, mălĕ rĕgo (3)
misguided (deceived) dēceptus
misinterpret v.t, mălĕ interprĕtor (1 *dep*)
misjudge v.t, mălĕ iūdĭco (1)
mislay v.t, ămitto (3)
mislead v.t, dēpĭcĭo (3)
misplace v.t, ălĭēno lŏco pōno (3) **(put in an unsuitable place)**
misprint *nn*, mendum, *n*
misrepresent v.t, verto (3); **(disparage)**, obtrecto (1)
misrule v.t, mălĕ rĕgo (3)
miss v.i, **(fail to hit or meet)**, ăberro (1), frustrā mittor (3 *pass*); v.t, **(want)**, dēsīdĕro (1)
misshapen dēformis
missile tēlum, *n*
mission (embassy) lēgātĭo, *f*; **(task)**, ŏpus, *n*
misspend v.t, perdo (3)
mist nĕbŭla, *f*
mistake error, *m*; **(make a —)**, v.i, erro (1)
mistake v.t, **(for someone else)** crēdĕre ălĭum esse
mistaken falsus; **(to be —)**, v.i, erro (1)
mistletoe viscum, *n*
mistress (of the house, etc.) dŏmĭna, *f*; **(sweetheart)**, pŭella, *f*, concŭbīna, *f*
mistrust v.t, diffido (3 *semi-dep. with dat*)
misty nĕbŭlōsus
misunderstand v.t, haud rectē, *or* mălĕ, intellĕgo (3)
misunderstanding error, *m*
misuse v.t, ăbūtor (3 *dep. with abl*)
mitigate v.t, mītĭgo (1), lēnĭo (4)
mitigation mītĭgātĭo, *f*
mittens mănĭcae, *f. pl*
mix v.t, miscĕo (2); **(— up**

together), confundo (3); v.i, miscĕor (2 *pass*)
mixed *adj*, mixtus; **(indiscriminate)**, prōmiscŭus
mixture mixtūra, *f*
moan *nn*, gĕmĭtus, *m*
moan v.i, gĕmo (3)
moat fossa, *f*
mob turba, *f*, vulgus, *m*
mobile mōbĭlis
mock v.t, illūdo (3) **(with dat)**; dērīdĕo (2)
mockery irrīsus, *m*, lūdĭbrĭum, *n*
mode mŏdus, *m*, rătĭo, *f*
model exemplum, *n*, exemplar, *n*
model v.t, fingo (3)
moderate mŏdᴇᴙᴀᴛᴜs, mŏdĭcus
moderate v.t, tempĕro (1)
moderation mŏdus, *m*, mŏdĕrātĭo, *f*
modern rĕcens, nŏvus
modest vĕrēcundus
modesty vĕrēcundĭa, *f*, pŭdor, *m*
modify v.t, immūto (1)
modulate v.t, flecto (3)
moist hūmĭdus
moisten v.t, hūmecto (1)
moisture hūmor, *m*
molar dens gĕnŭīnus
mole (animal) talpa, *f*; **(dam, etc.)**, mōles, *f*; **(on the body)**, naevus, *m*
molest v.t, vexo (1), sollĭcĭto (1)
mollify v.t, mollĭo (4)
molten lĭquĕfactus
moment punctum, (*n*) tempŏris; **(in a —)**, *adv*, stătim; **(importance)**, mōmentum, *n*
momentary brĕvis
momentous magni mōmenti **(of great importance)**
momentum impĕtus, *m*
monarch rex, *m*
monarch regnum, *n*
monastery mŏnastērĭum, *n*
money pĕcūnĭa, *f*; **(coin)**, nummus, *m*; **(profit)**, quaestus, *m*
moneybag fiscus, *m*
moneyed pĕcūnĭōsus
moneylender faenĕrātor, *m*
moneymaking quaestus, *m*
mongrel *nn*, hibrĭda, *c*
monkey sīmĭa, *f*
monopolize v.i, use phr. with sōlus **(alone)**, *and* hăbĕo (2)

monopoly mŏnŏpōlĭum, *n*
monotonous *use phr. with*
mŏlestus **(laboured)**, *or* sĭmĭlis **(similar)**
monster monstrum, *n*
monstrous (huge) immuanis; **(shocking)**, infandus
month mensis, *m*
monthly *adj*, menstrŭus
monument mŏnŭmentum, *n*
mood affectĭo (*f*) ănĭmi
moody mōrōsus
moon lūna, *f*
moonlight lūmen (*n*) lūnae; **(by —)**, ad lūnam
moonlit *adj*, illustris lūnā **(lighted up by the moon)**
moor lŏca dēserta, *n. pl*, **(a lonely place)**
moor *v.t*, **(ship, etc.)**, rĕlĭgo (1)
moorhen fŭlĭca, *f*
moot (it is a — point) nondum convĕnit ... **(it is not yet decided ...)**
mop *nn*, pēnĭcŭlus, *m*
mop *v.t*, dētergĕo (2)
moral *adj*, mōrālis; **(of good character)**, hŏnestus
moral *nn*, **(of a story)**, *use phr. wih* signĭfĭco (1) **(to indicate)**, *e.g.* haec fābŭla signĭfĭcat ... **(this story indicates ...)**
morale ănĭmus, *m*
morals, morality mōres, *m. pl*
moralize *v.i*, dē mōrĭbus dissĕro (3) **(discuss conduct)**
morbid aeger, aegrōtus
more *nn*, plus, *n* (*with genit*), *e.g.* **more corn**, plus frūmenti; (*adv. before adjs. or advs*) *use comparative of adj. or adv, e.g.* **more quickly**, cĕlĕrĭus; *otherwise use* măgis **(to a higher degree)** *or* pŏtĭus; **(in addition)**, amplĭus
moreover *adv*, praetĕrĕā
moribund mŏrĭbundus
morning *nn*, tempus mātūtīnum, *n*; **(in the —)**, *adv*, māne
morning *adj*, mātūtīnus
morose tristis
morrow (following day) postĕrus dĭes, *m*
morsel offa, *f*
mortal *adj*, mortālis; **(causing**

death), mortĭfer
mortality mortālĭtas, *f*
mortar mortārĭum, *n*
mortgage pignus, *n*
mortgage *v.t*, oblĭgo (1)
mortification offensĭo, *f*
mortify *v.t*, **(vex)** offendo (3)
mosaic *adj*, tessellātus
mosquito cŭlex, *m*
moss muscus, *m*
mossy muscōsus
most *adj*, plūrĭmus *or* plūrĭmum, *n, with genit, of noun, e.g.* **most importance**, plūrĭmum grăvĭtātis; **(for the — part)**, *adv*, plērumque
most *adv, with adjs. and advs. use superlative*; *e.g.* **most quickly**, cĕlerrĭmē; *with vbs*, maxĭmē
mostly (usually) *adv*, plērumque
moth blatta, *f*
mother māter, *f*; **(-in-law)**, socrus, *f*
motherly *adj*, māternus
motion (movement) mōtus, *m*; **(proposal)**, rŏgātĭo, *f*
motion *v.t*, gestu indĭco (1) **(indicate by a gesture)**
motionless immōtus
motive cause, *f*
mottled măcŭlōsus
motto sententĭa, *f*
mould (soil) sŏlum, *n*; **(shape)**, forma, *f*
mould *v.t*, formo (1)
mouldiness sĭtus, *m*
mouldy mūcĭdus
moult *v.i*, plūmas exŭo (3) **(lay down feathers)**
mound tŭmŭlus, *m*
mount *v.t*, **(horse, ship, etc.)**, conscendo (3); *otherwise*, scando (3)
mounted (on horseback) *adj*, ĕquo vectus
mountain mons, *m*, iŭgum, *n*
mountaineer hŏmŏ montānus
mountainous montŭōsus
mourn *v.t. and v.i*, lūgĕo (2)
mournful luctŭōsus; **(of sounds, etc.)**, lūgŭbris
mourning luctus, *m*, maeror, *n*
mouse mūs, *c*
mousetrap muscĭpŭlum, *n*
mouth ōs, *n*; **(of river)**, ostĭum, *n*

mouthful   bucca, *f*, **(filled out cheek)**
mouth-piece   interpres, *c*, ōrātor, *m*
movable   mōbĭlis
move   *v.t*, mŏvĕo (2); *v.i*, sē mŏvēre
(2 *reflex*)
movement   mōtus, *m*
moving   *adj*, **(of pity, etc.)**,
mĭsĕrābĭlis
mow   *v.t*, sĕco (1)
much   *adj*, multus; **(too —)**, nĭmĭus
much   *adv*, multum; *with*
comparative adj. or adv, multo,
e.g. **much bigger**, multo māior
muck   stercus, *n*
mucous   *adj*, mūcōsus
mud, muddiness   lŭtum, *n*
muddle   *v.t*, confundo (3)
muddle   *nn*, turba, *f*
muddy   lŭtĕus
muffle   *v.t*, obvolvo (3)
mug   pōcŭlum, *n*
muggy   ūmĭdus
mulberry (tree)   mōrus, *f*; **(fruit)**,
mōrum, *n*
mule   mūlus, *m*
mullet   mullus, *m*
multifarious   vărĭus
multiplication   multĭplĭcātĭo
multiply   *v.t*, multĭplĭco (1)
multitude   multĭtūdo, *f*
multitudinous   plūrĭmus, crēber
mumble   *v.i. and v.t*, murmŭro (1)
munch   *v.t*, mandūco (1)
mundane   *use genit. of* mundus
(world)
municipal   mūnĭcĭpālis
municipality   mūnĭcĭpĭum, *n*
munificence   mūnĭfĭcentĭa, *f*
munificent   mūnĭfĭcus
munition   appārātus (*m*) belli **(war-
equipment)**, arma, *n. pl*
murder   *nn*, caedes, *f*
murder   *v.t*, nĕco (1), interfĭcĭo (3)
murderer   hŏmĭcīda, *c*, sīcārĭus, *m*
murky   cālīgĭnōsus
murmur   *nn*, murmur, *n*
murmur   *v.i*, murmŭro (1)
muscle   tŏrus, *m*, lăcertus, *m*
muscular   lăcertōsus
muse   *nn*, mūsa, *f*
muse   *v.i*, mĕdĭtor (1 *dep*)
museum   mūsēum, *n*
mushroom   fungus, *m*

music   mūsĭca, *f*, cantus, *m*
musical   mūsĭcus; **(person)**;
stŭdĭōsus mūsĭcōrum **(keen on
music)**
musician   mūsĭcus, *m*
muslim   byssus, *f*
must   *v.i*, **(obligation)**, *use
gerundive: e.g.* **Carthage must be
destroyed**, Carthāgo dēlenda est;
(duty), ŏportet (2 *impers*) *with acc.
of person and infinitive, e.g.* **we
must go**, nōs ŏportet īre
mustard   sĭnāpi, *n*
muster   *nn*, dēlectus, *m*
muster   *v.t*, convŏco (1), rĕcensĕo
(2); *v.i*, convĕnĭo (4)
musty   mūcĭdus
mutable   mūtābĭlis
mute   *adj*, mūtus, tăcĭtus
mutilate   *v.t*, mŭtĭlo (1), trunco (1)
mutilated   mŭtĭlus, truncātus
mutiny   sēdĭtĭo, *f*
mutiny   *v.i*, sēdĭtĭōnem făcĭo (3)
mutter   *v.i. and v.t*, musso (1)
muttering   *nn*, murmur, *n*
mutton   ŏvilla căro, *f*, **(sheep's
flesh)**
mutual   mūtŭus
muzzle (for the mouth)   fiscella, *f*
my   mĕus
myriad (10,000)   dĕcem mīlĭa (*with
genit*)
myrrh   murra, *f*
myrtle   myrtus, *f*
myself   (*emphatic*), ipse; (*reflexive*)
mē
mysterious   occultus
mystery   rēs abdĭta, *f*; **(religious,
etc.)**, mystērĭa, *n. pl*
mystic   mystĭcus
mystification   ambāges, *f. pl*
mystify   *use adv. phr*, per ambāges
(in an obscure way)
myth   făbŭla, *f*
mythology   făbŭlae, *f. pl*

N

nab   *v.t*, **(catch)**, apprĕhendo (3)
nag   *nn*, căballus, *m*
nag   *v.t*, incrĕpīto (1), obiurgo (1)
nail (finger, toe)   unguis, *m*; **(of
metal)**, clāvus, *m*

nail *v.t*, clāvīs affīgo (3) **(fix on with nails)**

naive simplex

naked nūdus

nakedness *use adj*, nūdus **(naked)**

name nōmen, *n*; **(personal —, equivalent to our Christian name)**, praenōmen, *n*; **(— of a class of things)**, vŏcăbŭlum, *n*; **(reputation)**, existĭmātĭo, *f*

name *v.t*, nōmĭno (1), appello (1)

nameless nōmĭnis expers **(without a name)**

namely (I mean to say) dīco (3)

namesake *use phr*, cui est ĭdem nōmen **(who has the same name)**

nap *v.i*, **(sleep)**, paulisper dormĭo (4)

napkin mappa, *f*

narcissus narcissus, *m*

narcotic miedĭcāmentum somnĭfĕrum, *n*, **(sleep-bringing drug)**

narrate narro (1)

narrative narrātĭo, *f*; *adj, use vb*, narro (1) **(narrate)**

narrator narrātor, *m*

narrow angustus

narrow *v.t*, cŏarto (1); *v.i*, sē cŏartāre (1 *reflex*)

narrowly (nearly, scarcely) *adj*, vix

narrow-minded anĭmi angusti **(of narrow mind)**

narrowness angustĭae, *f. pl*

nasal nārĭum **(of the nose)**

nastiness foedĭtas, *f*

nasty foedus

natal nātālis

nation gens, *f*

national dŏmestĭcus *or use genit. of* gens

nationality pŏpŭlus, *m*, cīvĭtas, *f*

native *adj*, indĭgĕna; **(— land)**, pătrĭa, *f*

native *nn*, indĭgĕna, *c*

nativity (birth) gĕnus, *n*, ortus, *m*

natural nātūrālis; **(inborn)**, nātīvus, innātus; **(genuine)**, sincērus

naturalize *v.t*, cīvĭtātem do (1) **(with dat) (grant citizenship)**

naturally sĕcundum nātūram **(according to nature)**

nature nātūra, *f*; **(character of**

persons), ingĕnĭum, *n*

naught nĭhil, *n*

naughty imprŏbus, lascīvus

nausea nausĕa, *f*

nauseate *v.t*, fastīdĭo (4)

nautical nāvālis, nautĭcus

navel umbĭlĭcus, *m*

navigable nāvĭgābĭlis

navigate *v.i*, nāvĭgo (1)

navigation nāvĭgātĭo, *f*

navy classis, *f*

nay (no) nōn

neaptide mĭnĭmus aestus, *m*

near *adv*, prŏpĕ, iuxtā

near *prep, adv,* prŏpĕ

nearly *adv*, prŏpĕ, fermē

nearness prŏpinquĭtas, *f*, vīcīnĭtas, *f*

neat nĭtĭdus, mundus

neatly *adv*, mundē

neatness mundĭtĭa, *f*

nebulous nēbŭlōsus

necessarily *adv*, nĕcessārĭo

necessary nĕcessārĭus, nĕcesse

necessitate *v.t*, **(compel)**, cōgo (3)

necessity (inevitableness) nĕcessĭtas, *f*; **(something indispensable)**, rēs nĕcessārĭa, *f*

neck collum, *n*, cervix, *f*

necklace mŏnĭle, *n*

need *nn*, ŏpus, *n*, **(with abl. of thing needed or infinitive)**; **(lack)**, ĭnŏpĭa, *f*

need *v.t*, ĕgĕo (2) *(with abl)*

needful nĕcessārĭus, *or use nn*, ŏpus, *n*, **(necessity)**

needle ăcus, *f*

needless nōn nĕcessārĭus

needy ĕgens

nefarious nĕfārĭus

negation nĕgātĭo, *f*

negative *adj, use* nōn **(not)**, *or* nēgo (1) **(to deny)**

neglect *v.t*, neglĕgo (3), praetermitto (3)

neglect *nn*, neglĕgentĭa, *f*

negligent neglĕgens

negotiate *v.t*, ăgo (3) dē *(with abl. of thing)* cum *(with abl. of person)*

negotiation *use vb*, ăgo (3), **(to negotiate)**

negress Aethĭŏpissa, *f*

negro Aethĭops, *m*

neigh *v.i*, hinnĭo (4)

neigh, neighing hinnītus, *m*
neighbour vīcīnus, *m*; (of nations),
  adj, finītimus
neither *pron*, neuter
neither *conj*, nĕque, nĕc; **neither ...**
  nor, neque ... neque, *or* nec ... nec
nephew filĭus, (*m*) frātris (*or*
  sŏrōris)
nerve nervi, *m. pl*
nervous (afraid) tĭmĭdus
nervousness tĭmĭdĭtas, *f*, formīdo, *f*
nest nīdus, *m*
nestle *v.i*, haerĕo (2), ĭacĕo (2)
nestlings nīdi, *m. pl*
net rētĕ, *n*
net *v.t*, plăgīs căpĭo (3) **(catch with
  a net)**
nettle urtīca, *f*
network rētĭcŭlum, *n*
neuter neuter
neutral mĕdĭus; **(to be or remain —),**
  neutri parti făvĕo (2) **(to favour
  neither side)**
neutralize *v.t*, aequo (1), compenso
  (1)
never *adv*, numquam
nevertheless nĭhĭlōmĭnus, tămen
new nŏvus; **(fresh),** rĕcens
newcomer advĕna, *c*
newly *adv*, nūper, mŏdo
newness nŏvĭtas, *f*
news nuntĭus, *m*
newspaper acta dĭurna, *n. pl*
newt lăcertus, *m*
next *adj*, proxĭmus; **(on the —
  day),** *adv*, postrīdĭē
next *adv*, **(of time),** dĕinceps,
  dĕinde; **(of place),** iuxtā, proxĭmē
nibble *v.t*, rōdo (3)
nice (pleasant) dulcis; **(particular),**
  fastīdĭōsus; **(precise),** subtīlis
nicety (subtlety) subtīlĭtas, *f*
niche aedĭcŭla, *f*
in the nick of time in ipso artĭcŭlo
  tempŏris
nickname agnōmen, *n*, **(an
  additional name)**
niece filĭa (*f*) frātris (*or* sŏrōris)
niggardly ăvārus, parcus
night nox, *f*; **(by, at —),** *adv*, noctu,
  nocte; **(at mid —),** mĕdĭā nocte; **(at
  the fall of —),** prīmis tĕnĕbris
nightingale luscĭnĭa, *f*

nimble ăgĭlis
nine nŏvem; **(— times),** *adv*,
  nŏvĭens; **(— each),** nŏvēni; **(—
  hundred),** nongenti
nineteen undēvīginti
ninety nōnāginta
ninth nōnus
nip *v.t*, vellĭco (1); **(with frost),** ūro
  (3)
nipple păpilla, *f*
no *adj*, nullus, nĭhil (*foll. by genit*)
no *adv*, nōn, mĭnĭmē; **(to say —),**
  v.i, nĕgo (1)
nobility (of birth) nōbĭlĭtas, *f*;
  (people of noble birth), nōbĭles, *m.
  pl*
noble (of birth) nōbĭlis; **(of birth or
  character),** gĕnĕrōsus
nobody nēmo, *m*, *f*
nocturnal nocturnus
nod *v.i*, nūto (1); **(assent),** annŭo
  (3)
nod *nn*, nūtus, *m*
noise strĕpĭtus, *m*, sŏnĭtus, *m*; **(of
  shouting),** clāmor, *m*; **(to make a —),**
  v.i, strĕpo (3)
noiseless tăcĭtus
noisily *adv*, cum strĕpĭtu
noisy *use a phr. with* strĕpo **(to
  make a noise)**
nomadic văgus
nominal *use* nōmen **(name)**
nominally *adv*, nōmĭne
nominate *v.t*, nōmĭno (1)
nomination nōmĭnātĭo, *f*
nominee *use vb.* nōmĭno, **(name)**
nonchalant aequo ănĭmo **(with
  un-ruffled mind)**
nondescript non insignis
none nullus
nonentity nĭhil, *n*
nonsense nūgae, *f. pl*, ĭneptĭae, *f.
  pl*
nonsensical ĭneptus, absurdus
nook angŭlus, *m*
noon mĕrīdĭes, *m*; **(at —),** *adv*,
  mĕrīdĭē; *adj.* mĕrīdĭanus
noose lăquĕus, *m*
nor *conj*, nĕc, nĕque
normal (usual) ūsĭtātus
north *nn*, septentrĭōnes, *m. pl*
north, northern, northerly *adj*, septentrĭōnālis

north-east wind ăquĭlo, *m*
North Pole arctos, *f*
northwards versus ad
 septentrĭōnes
north wind ăquĭlo, *m*
nose nāsus, *m*, nāres, *f. pl*
 (nostrils)
not nōn, haud; **(— at all)**, *adv*,
 haudquāquaml **(not even ...)**, nĕ
 ... quĭdem; **(and not)**, nĕc, nĕque;
 (in commands), e.g. do not go,
 nōli īre
notable insignis, mĕmŏrăbĭlis
notary scrība, *m*
notch *nn*, incīsŭra, *f*
notch *v.t*, incīdo (3)
note (explanatory, etc.) adnŏtātĭo,
 f; **(mark)**, nŏta, *f*; **(letter)**, littĕrae,
 f. pl
note v.t, **(notice)**, ănĭmadverto
 (3); **(down)**, ēnŏto (*i*)
notebook commentārĭi, *m. pl*
noted (well-known) insignis
nothing nĭhĭl, *n*; **(good for —)**,
 nēquam
nothingness nĭhĭlum, *n*
notice *v.t*, ănĭmadverto (3)
notice *nn*, **(act of noticing)**,
 ămĭmadversĭo, f; **(written —)**,
 prōscriptĭo, *f*
noticeable insignis
notification dēnuntĭātĭo, *f*
notify *v.t*, dēnuntĭo (1)
notion nŏtĭo, *f*
notoriety infāmĭa, *f*
notorious nōtus, fāmōsus
notwithstanding *adv*,
 nĭbĭlōmĭnus, tămen
nought nĭhil
noun nōmen, *n*, **(name)**
nourish *v.t*, ălo (3)
nourishment ălĭmentum, *n*
novel *nn*, **(story)**, fābūla, *f*
novel *adj*, **(new)**, nŏvus
novelist fābŭlārum, scriptor, *m*,
 (writer of stories)
novelty (strangeness) nŏvĭtas, *f*
November Nŏvember (mensis)
novice tīro, *m*
now (at the present time) *adv*.
 nune; **(at the time of the action)**,
 iam; **(just —)**, mŏdŏ; **(now ...**
 now), mŏdŏ ... mŏdŏ; **(— and**

then)**, ălĭquandŏ
nowadays *adv*, nunc
nowhere *adv*, nusquam
noxious nŏcens
nozzle nāsus, *m*
nude nūdus
nudge *v.t*, fŏdĭco (1)
nuisance incŏmmŏdum, *n*, or use
 adj, mŏlestus **(troublesome)**
null irrĭtus, vānus
nullify *v.t*, irrĭtum făcĭo (3)
numb torpens; **(to be —)**, *v.i*,
 torpĕo (2)
numb *v.t*, torpĕfăcĭo (3)
number *nn*, nŭmĕrus, *m*; **(what —,**
 how many?), quot?; **(a large —)**,
 multĭtūdo, *f*
number *v.t*, nŭmĕro (1)
numbering (in number) ad *(with*
 acc)
numberless innŭmĕrābĭlis
numbness torpor, *m*
numerically *adv*, nŭmĕro
numerous plūrĭmi, crēber
nun mŏnăcha, *f*
nuptial nuptĭālis, iŭgālis
nuptials nuptĭae, *f.pl*
nurse nūtrix, *f*
nurse *v.t*, **(the sick)**, cŭro (1);
 (cherish), fŏvĕo (2)
nursery (for plants) sēmĭnārĭum, *n*
nurture edūcātĭo, *f*
nut, nut tree nux, *f*
nutriment ălĭmentum, *n*
nutrition ălĭmentum, *n*
nutritious vălens
nutshell pŭtāmen, *n*
nymph nympha, *f*

O

o! oh! o! oh!; **(Oh that ...)** ŭtĭnam
 ...
oak quercus, *f*; **(holm —)**, īlex, *f*;
 (oak-wood), rōbur, *n*
oak, oaken *adj*, quernus
oakum stuppa, *f*
oar rēmus, *m*
oarsmen rēmĭges, *m. pl*
oats ăvēna, *f*
oath iusiūrandum; *n*; **(to take an**
 —), *v.i*, iusiūrandum accĭpĭo (3);
 (military —), săcrāmentum, *n*

oatmeal fărīna, ăvēnācĕa, *f*
obdurate obstĭnātus, dūrus
obedience ŏbēdĭentĭa, *f*; *or use*
vb, pārĕo (2) **(to obey, *with dat*)**
obeisance (to make an —) ădōro
(1) **(reverence)**
obelisk ŏbĕliscus, *m*
obese ŏbēsus
obey *v.i. and v.t*, pārĕo (2) (*with
dat*), ŏbēdĭo (4) (*with dat*)
object *nn*, **(thing)**, rēs, *f*; **(aim)**,
consĭlĭum, n. fīnis, m; **(to be an —
of hatred)** ŏdĭo esse (*irreg*)
object *v.t*, rĕcūso (1), nōlo (*irreg*)
objection *use vb*, rĕcūso (1)
(object to)
objectionable ingrātus, *m*
objective *nn*, quod petitur **(that is
sought)**
obligation (moral) offĭcĭum, *n*;
(legal), oblĭgātĭo *f*; **(religious — ,
conscientiousness)**, rĕlĭgĭo, *f*; **(to
put someone under an —)**, *v.t*,
obstringo (3); **(to be under an —)**,
v.i, dēbĕo (2)
obligatory (it is —) ŏportet (2
impers) *or use gerundive of vb*
oblige *v.t*, obstringo (3);
(compel), cōgo (3)
obliging cōmis
oblique (slanting) oblīquus
obliterate *v.t*, dēlĕo (2)
oblivion oblīvĭo, *f*
oblivious immĕmor
oblong *adj*, oblongus
obloquy vĭtŭpĕrātĭo, *f*
obnoxious invīsus, noxĭus
obscene obscēnus
obscenity obscēnĭtas, *f*
obscure obscūrus, caecus,
rĕcondĭtus; **(of birth, etc.)**, hŭmĭlis
obscure *v.t*, obscūro (1)
obscurity obscūrĭtas, *f*
obsequies exsĕquĭae, *f*, *pl*
obsequious obsĕquens, offĭcĭōsus
observance observantĭa, *f*,
conservātĭo *f*; **(practice)**, rītus, *m*
observant attentus, dīlĭgens
observation observātĭo, *f*;
(attention), ănĭmadversĭo, *f*;
(remark), dictum, *n*
observatory spĕcŭla, *f*
observe *v.t*, observo (1),

ănĭmadverto (3); **(remark)**, dīco
(3); **(maintain)**, conservo (1)
observer spectātor, *m*
obsolete obsŏlētus; **(to become —)**,
v.i, obsŏlesco (3), sĕnesco (3)
obstacle impĕdīmentum, *n*
obstinacy pertĭnācĭa, *f*
obstinate pertĭnax
obstreperous (noisy) vōcĭfĕrans
obstruct *v.t*, obstrŭo (3), obsto
(1) (*with dat*)
obstruction impĕdīmentum, *n*
obtain *v.t*, ădĭpiscor (3 *dep*),
nanciscor (3 *dep*), consĕquor (3
dep), **(— possession of)**, pŏtĭor
(4 *dep, with abl*)
obtrude *v.t*, inculco (1)
obtrusive mŏlestus
obtuse hĕbes
obviate *v.t*, **(meet)**, obvĭam ĕo (4
irreg) (*with dat*)
obvious ăpertus, mănĭfestus
occasion (opportunity) occāsĭo, *f*;
(cause), causa, *f*; **(on that —)**, illo
tempŏre
occasion *v.t*, mŏvĕo (2), fĕro
(*irreg*)
occasionally *adv*, interdum, rāro
occult occultus, arcānus
occupancy possessĭo, *f*
occupant possessor, *m*
occupation (act of —) *use vb*,
occŭpo (1); **(employment)**,
quaestus, *m*; nĕgōtĭum, *n*
occupy *v.t*, occŭpo (1), obtĭnĕo
(2); **(to be occupied with
something)**, *v.b*, tĕnĕor (2 *pass*)
occur *v.i*. **(take place)**, accĭdo (3);
(come into the mind), in mentem
vĕnĭo (4), sŭbĕo (4) (*with dat*)
occurrence rēs, *f*
ocean ōcĕănus, *m*
ochre ōchra, *f*
octagon octōgōnum, *n*
October Octōber (mensis)
oculist ŏcŭlārĭus mĕdĭcus, *m*
odd (numbers, etc.) impar;
(strange), nŏvus
odds (to be at — with) *v.i*,
dissĭdĕo (2) ab (*with abl*)
odious ŏdĭōsus, invīsus
odium invĭdĭa, *f*, ŏdĭum, *n*
odorous ŏdōrātus

odour ŏdor, *m*
of *usually the genit. of the noun,*
e.g. the head of the boy, căput
pŭĕri; (made —), ex (*with abl*);
(about, concerning) dē (*with abl*)
off *adv, often expressed by prefix*
ab- *with vb*, e.g. to cut off,
abscīdo (3); (far —), *adv*, prŏcul;
(a little way —), *prep and adv*,
prŏpe
offal (waste) quisquĭlĭae, *f.pl*
offence offensĭo, *f*; (crime, etc.)
dēlictum, *n*; (to take — at), aegrē
fĕro (*irreg.*)
offend *v.t*, offendo (3), laedo (3);
(to be offended), aegrē fĕro (irreg)
(tolerate with displeasure)
offensive *adj*, ŏdĭōsus, grăvis
offensive *nn*, (military), *use phr*,
bellum infĕro (*irreg*) (to inflict
war)
offer *nn*, condĭcĭo, *f*
offer *v.t*, offĕro (*irreg*); (stretch
out), porrĭgo (3); (give), do (1)
offering (gift) dōnum, *n*
office (political power)
măgistrātus m; (duty), officĭum, *n*;
(place of business), fŏrum, *n*
officer (military) praefectus, *m*
official *nn*, măgistrātus, *m*,
mĭnister, *m*
official *adj.* (state), pūblĭcus
officiate *v.i*, (perform), fungor (3
dep)
officious mŏlestus
offing, (in the —) *use* longē (far
off), or prŏpe (near) *acc. to sense*
offshoot surcŭlus, *m*
offspring prōgĕnĭes, *f* lībĕri, *m, pl*
often *adv*, saepĕ; (how — ?),
quŏtĭes?; (so —), *adv*, tŏtĭes
ogle *v.t*, ŏcŭlis līmis intŭĕor (2
dep) (look at with sidelong
glances)
oil ŏlĕum, *n*
oily ŏlĕācĕus
ointment unguentum, *n*
old vĕtus; (of persons), sĕnex; (so
many years — , of persons), nātus
(*with acc. of extent of time*), e.g.
three years old, tres annos nātus;
(— age), sĕnectus, *f*; (— man),
sĕnex, *m*; (— woman), ănus, *f*

olden priscus
oldness vĕtustas, *f*
oligarchy dŏmĭnātĭo, (*f*)
paucōrum (rule of a few)
olive (tree) ŏlĕa, *f*
Olympic *adj*, Olympĭcus; (—
Games), Olympĭa, *n. pl*
omelette lăgănum, *n*
omen omen, *n*
ominous infaustus
omission praetermissĭo, *f*
omit *v.t*, ŏmitto (3), praetermitto
(3)
omnipotent omnĭpotens
on *prep*, in (*with abl*); (in the
direction of, e.g. on the right), ā,
āb (*with abl*); (— everyside), *adv*,
undĭque; (of time), *abl case*, e.g.
on the Ides of March, Īdĭbus
Martĭis; (about a subject) dē
(*with abl*)
once *num. adv*, sĕmel; (— upon a
time), ōlim, ălĭquandŏ; (at — ,
immediately), stătim; (at the same
time), sĭmul
one *num. adj.* ūnus; (in — s,
singly), *adv*, singillātim, *adj*,
singŭli; (at — time), *adv*,
ălĭquandŏ; (one ... another), ălĭus
... ălĭus (one ... the other), alter
... alter; (a certain), quīdam;
(indefinite), *use 2nd pers sing. of
the vb*
onerous grăvis
oneself (*emphatic*) ipse;
(*reflexive*), sē
one-sided ĭnaequālis
onion caepa, *f*
onlooker circumstans, *m*
only *adj*, ūnus, sōlus, ūnĭcus
only *adv*, sōlum, tantum, mŏdŏ;
(not only ...), non mŏdŏ ...
onset impĕtus, *m*
onwards *adv*, porro, *often use
compound vb. with* pro, e.g.
prōcĕdĕre (3) (to go onwards)
ooze *nn*, ūlīgo, *f*
ooze *v.i*, māno (1)
oozy ūlĭgĭnōsus
opal ŏpălus, *m*
opaque caecus
open *v.t*, ăpĕrĭo (4), pătĕfăcĭo (3),
pandi (3); (inaugurate), consĕcro

(1); *v.i*, sē ăpĕrīre (*4 reflex*); **(gape open)**, hisco (3)
open *adj*, ăpertus; **(wide —)**, pătens, hĭans; **(to lie, stand or be —)** pătĕo (2); **(— handed)**, *adj*, līberālis
opening (dedication) consĕcrātĭo, *f*; **(hole)**, fŏrāmen, *n*; **(opportunity)**, occăsĭo, *f*
openly *adv*, pălam
operate *v.t*, **(set in motion)**, mŏvĕo (2); *v.i*, **(in war)**, rem gĕro (3)
operation (task) ŏpus, n; **(military —)**, rēs bellĭca, *f*; **(naval —)**, rēs mărĭtĭma, *f*
operative *adj*, effĭcax
opiate mĕdĭcāmentum somnĭfĕrum, *n*, **(sleep-bringing drug)**
opinion sent- entĭa, *f*, ŏpīnĭo, *f*, existĭmātĭo, *f*
opium ŏpĭum, *n*
opponent adversārĭus, *m*
opportune opportūnus
opportunity occăsĭo, *f*, cŏpĭa, *f*, făcultas, *f*
oppose *v.t*, oppōno (3); **(resist)**, rĕsisto (3 *with dat*), adversor (1 *dep*)
opposite *adj*, adversus, contrārĭus, dīversus
opposite (to) *prep*, contrā (*with acc*)
opposition (from people) *use partic*, adversans *or* rĕsistens; **(from a party)**, *use* factĭo, *f*, **(party)**
oppress *v.t*, opprĭmo (3)
oppression (tyranny) iniūrĭa, *f*
oppressive grăvis, mŏlestus
oppressor tȳrannus, *m*
opprobrious turpis
optical *adj, use genit, case of* ŏcŭlus, *m*, **(eye)**
option optĭo, *f*
opulence ŏpŭlentĭa, *f*, ŏpes, *f, pl*
opulent dīves, lŏcŭples
or aut, vel; **(either ... or)**, aut ... aut, vel ... vel; **(whether ... or)** (*questions*), ŭtrum ... an; **(or not)** (*direct questions*), annon, (*indirect questions*), necne
oracle ōrācŭlum, *n*

oral *use* vox **(voice)**
oration ōrātĭo, *f*
orator ōrātor, *m*
oratory ars ōrātōrĭa, *f*
orb, orbit orbis, *m*
orchard pōmārĭum, *n*
orchid orchis, *f*
ordain *v.t*, ēdīco (3), stătŭo (3)
ordeal discrīmen, *n*
order *nn*, **(arrangement)**, ordo, *m*; **(in —)**, *adv*, ordĭne; **(command, direction)**, iussum, *n*; **(class, rank)**, ordo, *m*; **(in — to)**, ut
order *v.t*, **(command)**, iŭbĕo (2); **(arrange)**, dispōno (3)
orderly *adj*, **(behaviour)**, mŏdestus; **(arrangement)**, ordĭnātus dispŏsĭtus
orderly *nn*, stător, *n*
ordinary ūsĭtātus, mĕdĭŏcris
ordnance tormenta, *n. pl*
ore aes, *n*
organ (of the body) membrum, *n*
organization dispŏsĭtĭo, *f*
organize *v.t*, ordĭno (1)
orgies orgĭa, *n. pl*; **(revelry)**, cōmissātĭo, *f*
orient ŏrĭens, *m*
oriental *use genit. of* ŏrĭens **(orient)**
orifice fŏrāmen, *n*, os, *n*
origin ŏrīgo, *f*, princĭpĭum, *n*
original princĭpālis, antīquus, (one's own), prŏprĭus
originally *adv*, princĭpĭo, ĭnĭtĭo
originate *v.i*, ŏrĭor (*4 dep*)
originator auctor, *m*
ornament *nn*, ornămentum, *n*
ornament *v.t*, orno (1)
ornate *adj*, ornātus, pictus
orphan orbus, *m*
oscillate *v.i*, quătĭor (3 pass)
oscillation *use vb.* quătĭor (*above*) (3 *pass*)
osier *nn*, vīmen, *n*
osier *adj*, vīmĭnĕus
osprey ossĭfrăgus, *m*
ostensible *use adv. below*
ostensibly *adv*, per spĕcĭem
ostentation ostentātĭo, *f*
ostentatious glōrĭōsus
ostler ăgāso, *m*
ostracize *v.t*, vīto (1) **(avoid)**

ostrich strūthĭŏcămēlus, *m*

other *adj*, ălĭus; **(the — of two)**, alter; **(the others, the rest)** cētĕri

others *adj*, **(belonging to —)**, ălĭēnus

otherwise *adv*, **(differently)**, ălĭter; **(in other respects also)**, ălĭoqui

otter lūtra, *f*

ought *v. auxil*, dēbĕo (2), ŏportet (*2 impers, with acc. of person*), e.g. **I ought**, ŏportet mē

ounce uncĭa, *f*

our, ours noster

ourselves (*in apposition to subject*), ipsi; (*reflexive*), nos

out *adv*, **(being out)**, fŏris; **(going out)**, fŏras

out of *prep*, ē, ex, dē (*with abl*); extrā (with acc); **(on account of)**, propter (*with acc*)

outbid *v.t, use phr*, plūs offĕro quam ... **(offer more than ...)**

outbreak use *vb*. ŏrĭor (*4 dep*) (to arise); **(beginning)**, ĭnĭtĭum, *n*

outcast prŏfŭgus, *m*

outcome (result) exĭtus, *m*

outcry clāmor, *m*

outdo *v.t*, sŭpĕro (1)

outdoors *adv*, fŏras

outer *adj*, extĕrĭor

outfit (equipment) appărātus, *m*

outflank *v.i*, circūmĕo (4)

outgrow *v.t, use phr*, magnĭtūdĭne sŭpĕro (1) **(surpass in size)**

outhouse tŭgŭrĭum, *n*

outlast *v.t*, dĭuturnĭtāte sŭpĕro **(surpass in duration)**

outlaw *nn*, prōscriptus, *m*

outlaw *v.t*, prōscrĭbo (3)

outlay *nn*, sumptus, *m*

outlet exĭtus, *m*

outline finis, *m*, ădumbrātĭo, *f*

outlive *v.i*, sŭperstĕs sum (*irreg*) **(to be a survivor)**

outlook (future) fŭtūra, *n.pl*

outnumber *v.t*, plūres nŭmĕro esse quam ... **(to be more in number than ...)**

outpost stătĭo, *f*

outrage *nn*, iniūrĭa, *f*

outrage *v.t*, vĭŏlo (1)

outrageous indignus

outright *adv*, prorsus; **(immediately)**, stătim

outset ĭnĭtĭum, *n*

outside *nn*, extĕrna pars, *f*; **(on the —)**, *adv*, extrinsĕcus; **(appearance)**, spĕcĭes, *f*, frons, *f*

outside *adj*, externus

outside *adv*, extrā

outside of *prep*, extrā (*with acc*)

outskirts *use adj*. sūburbānus **(near the city)**

outspoken (frank) līber

outstretched porrectus

outstrip *v.t*, sŭpĕro (1)

outward *adj*, externus

outwardly *adv*, extrā

outweigh *v.t*, grăvĭtāte sŭpĕro (1) **(surpass in weight)**

outwit *v.t*, dēcĭpĭo (3)

oval *adj*, ōvātus

oven furnus, *m*

over *prep*, (above, across, more than), sŭper (*with acc*)

over *adv*, **(above)**, sŭper, suprā; **(left —)**, *adj*, rĕlĭquus; **(it is — , all up with)**, actum est; **(— and — again)**, *adv*, ĭdentĭdem

overawe *v.t*, percello (3)

overbearing sŭperbus

overboard *adv*, ex nāvi

overcast (sky) nūbĭlus

overcoat lăcerna, *f*

overcome *v.t*, vinco (3), sŭpĕro (1)

overdone *use adv*, nĭmis **(too much)**

overdue *use adv*, dĭūtĭus **(too long)**, *and* diffĕro (*irreg*), **(to put off)**

overflow *v.i*, effundor (3 *pass*); *v.t*, ĭnundo (1)

overgrown obsĭtus

overhang *v.i*, immĭnĕo (2), impendĕo (2) (*both with dat*)

overhanging impendens

overhasty praeceps

overhaul *v.t*, **(repair)**, rĕsarcĭo (4)

overhead *adv*, insŭper

overhear *v.t*, excĭpĭo (3)

overjoyed laetĭtĭā ēlātus **(elated with joy)**

overland *adv*, terrā, per terram

overlap *v.t*, **(overtake)**,

sŭpervĕnĭo (4)
overlay   *v.t,* indūco (3)
overload   *v.t,* grăvo (1)
overlook   *v.t,* prōspĭcĭo (3);
(**forgive**); ignosco (3) (*with dat*);
(**neglect**), praetermitto (3)
overmuch   *adv,* nĭmis
overpower   *v.t,* opprĭmo (3)
overrate   *v.t,* plūris aestĭmo (1)
(**value too highly**)
override   *v.t,* praeverto (3)
overrule   *v.t,* vinco (3)
overrun   *v.t,* pervăgor (1 *dep*)
oversea   *v.t,* cūro (1), inspĭcĭo (3)
overseer   cūrātor, *m*
overshadow   *v.t,* offĭcĭo (3) (*with
dat*)
oversight (**omission**)   error, *m,*
neglĕgentĭa, *f, or use vb,*
praetermitto (3) (**overlook**)
overspread   *v.t,* obdūco (3)
overt   ăpertus, plānus
overtake   *v.t,* consĕquor (3 *dep*)
over tax (**strength etc.**)   v.t, nĭmis
ūtor (3 *dep*) (*with abl*)
overthrow   *nn,* rŭīna, *f*
overthrow   *v.t,* ēverto (3),
opprĭmo (3)
overtop   *v.t,* sŭpĕro (1)
overture (**to make — s**)   *use vb.*
instĭtŭo (3) (**to begin**)
overweening   sŭperbus
overwhelm   *v.t,* opprĭmo (3),
obrŭo (3)
overwork   *v.i,* nĭmis lăbōro (1)
overwriught (**exhausted**)
confectus
owe   *v.t,* dēbĕo (2)
owing to   prep, (**on account of**),
propter, ob (*both with acc*)
owl   būbo, *m,* strix, *f*
own   *adj,* prŏprĭus; *often
expressed by possessive pron, e.g.
my own,* mĕus
own   *v.t,* (**possess**), tĕnĕo (2),
possĭdĕo (2); (**confess**), fătĕor (2
dep)
owner   possessor *m,* dŏmĭnus, *m*
ox   bōs, *c*
oxherd   armentārĭus, *m*
oyster   ostrĕa, *f*

P

pace   *nn,* passus, *m*
pace (**step**)   spătĭor (1 *dep*),
grădĭor (3 *dep*)
pacific   pācĭfĭcus
pacification   pācĭfĭcātĭo, *f*
pacify   *v.t,* plăco (1), sēdo (1)
pack (**bundle**)   sarcĭna, *f*; (**— of
people**), turna, *f*
pack   *v.t,* (**gather together**), collĭgo
(3); (**— close together**), stĭpo (1)
package   sarcĭna, *f*
packet   fascĭcŭlus, *m*
packhorse   iūmentum, *n*
pact   pactum, *n,* foedus, *n*
padding   *nn,* fartūra, *f*
paddle   *nn* (**oar**), rēmus, *m*
paddle   *v.t,* rēmĭgo (1), (**to row**)
paddock   saeptum, *n*
padlock   sĕra, *f*
pagan   pāgānus
page (**book**)   pāgĭna, *f*; (**boy**), pŭer,
m
pageant   spectācŭlum, *n,* pompa,
f
pageantry   spĕcĭes (*f*) atque
pompa *f* (**display and public
procession**)
pail   sĭtŭla, *f*
pain   dŏlor, *m*; (**to be in —**), *v.i,*
dŏlĕo (2)
pain   *v.t,* dŏlōre affĭcĭo (3) (**inflict
pain**)
painful   ăcerbus
painless   *use adv. phr,* sĭne dŏlōre
(**without pain**)
pains (**endeavour**)   ŏpĕra, *f*; (**to
take — over**), ŏpĕram do (1)
(*with dat*)
painstaking   ŏpĕrōsus
paint   *v.t,* pingo (3); (**colour**), fūco
(1)
paint   *nn,* pigmentum, *n*
paintbrush   pēnĭcullus, *m*
painter   pictor, *m*
painting   pictūra, *f*
pair   pār, *m*
pair   *v.t,* iungo (3); *v.i,* iungor (3
pass)
palace   rēgĭa, *f*
palatable   iūcundus
palate   pălātum, *n*

palatial rēgĭus

pale *adj*, pallĭdus; **(to be —)**, *v.i*, pallĕo (2); **(to become —)**, *v.i*, pallesco (3)

pale *nn*, **(stake)**, pālus, *m*

paleness pallor, *m*

palisade vallum, *n*

pall *nn*, pallĭum, *n*

pall *v.i*, **(it —s)**, taedet (2 *impers*)

pallet lectŭlus, *m*

palliate *v.t*, extĕnŭo (1)

palliation *use vb*, extĕnŭo (1) **(palliate)**

palliative lēnĭmentum, *n*

pallid *adj* pallĭdus

pallor pallor, *m*

palm (of hand, tree) palma, *f*

palm (to — off) *v.t*, suppōno (3)

palpable (obvious) mănĭfestus

palpitate *v.t*, palpĭto (1)

palpitation palpĭtatĭo, *f*

palsy părălysis, *f*

paltry vīlis

pamper *v.t*, nĭmĭum indulgĕo (2) (*with dat*) **(to be too kind to ...)**

pamphlet lĭbellus, *m*

pamphleteer scriptor (*m*) lĭbellorum

pan pătĭna, *f*; **(frying —)**, sartāgo, *f*

panacea pănăcēa, *f*

pancake lăgănum, *n*

pander *v.i*, lēnōcĭnor (1 dep)

panegyric laudătĭo, *f*

panel (of door, etc.) tympānum, *n*

panelled lăquĕātus

pang dŏlor, *m*

panic păvor, *m*

panic-stricken păvĭdus

pannier clītellae, *f*, *pl*

panorama prōspectus, *m*

pant *v.i*, ănhēlo (1)

panther panthēra, *f*

panting *nn*, ănhēlĭtus, *m*

pantomime mīmus, *m*

pantry cella pěnaria, *f*

pap (nipple) păpilla, *f*

paper charta, *f*; **(sheet of —)**, schĕda, *f*; **(newspaper)**, acta dīurna, *n.pl*

papyrus păpyrus, *m*, *f*

par (on a — with) *adj*, pār

parable părăbŏla, *f*

parade (military) dēcursus, *m*; **(show)**, appărātus, *m*, pompa, *f*

parade *v.i*, **(of troops)**, dēcurro (3); *v.t* **(display)**, ostento (1)

paradise Ēlysĭum, ĭi, *n*

paragon spěcĭmen, *n*

paragraph căput, *n*

parallel *adj*, părallēlus; **(like)**, sĭmĭlis

paralysis părālysis, *f*, dēbĭlĭtas, *f*

paralyze *v.t*, dēbĭlĭto (1)

paralyzed dēbĭlis

paramount summus

paramour ădulter, *m*, ămātor, *m*

parapet lōrīca, *f*, mūnītĭo, *f*

paraphernalia appărātus, *m*

parasite assecla, *c*

parasol umbella, *f*

parcel fascĭcŭlus, *m*

parcel out *v.t*, partĭor (4 dep)

parch *v.t*, torrĕo (2)

parched (dry) ārĭdus; **(scorched)**, torrĭdus

parchment membrāna, *f*

pardon *nn*, věnĭa, *f*

pardon *v.t*, ignosco (3) (*with dat*)

pardonable *use phr*, cui ignoscendum est **(who should be pardoned)**

pare *v.t*, **(circum)sěco** (1) **(cut around)**

parent părens, *m*, *f*

parentage gĕnus, *n*

parental pătrĭus, *or use genit pl*, părentum **(of parents)**

parenthesis interpŏsĭtĭo, *f*

parish păroecĭa, *f*

park horti, *m*. *pl*

parley collŏquĭum, *n*

parley *v.i*, collŏquor (3 dep)

parliament sěnātus, *m*

parliamentary *use genit. case of* sěnātus

parlour conclāve, *n*

parody versus rīdĭcŭli, *m*, *pl*

parole fĭdes *f* **(promise)**

paroxysm *use* accessus, *m*, **(approach)**

parricide (person) parrĭcīda, *c*; **(act)**, parrĭcīdĭum, *n*

parrot psittăcus, *m*

parry *v.t*, prōpulso (1)

parse *v.t*, *use phr*, verba

singŭlātim percĭpĭo (**understand the words one by one**)
parsimonious parcus
parsimony parsĭmōnĭa, *f*
parsley ăpĭum, *n*
parson (priest) săcerdos, *c*
part pars, *f*; **(in a play)**, persōna, *f*, partes, *f, pl*; **(side, faction)**, partes, *f. pl*; **(duty)**, offĭcĭum, *n*; **(region)**, lŏca, *n.pl*; **(from all — s)**, *adv*, undĭque; **(for the most —)**, *adv*, plērumque; **(to take — in)**, intersum (*irreg*) (*with dat*)
part *v.t*, dīvĭdo (3), sēpăro (1); *v.i*, discēdo (3)
partake of *v.t*, partĭceps sum (*irreg*) (*with genit*); **(food)**, gusto (1)
partaker partĭceps, *adj*
partial (affecting only a part) *use adv. phr*, ex ălĭquā parte; **(unfair)**, ĭnīquus
partiality stŭdĭum, *n*
participate *v.i*, partĭceps sum (*irreg*) (*with genit*)
participation sŏcĭĕtas, *f*
particle partĭcŭla, *f*
particular (characteristic) prŏprĭus; **(special)**, singŭlāris; **(exacting)**, dēlĭcātus
particularly (especially) *adv*, praecĭpŭē
parting *nn*, dīgressus, *m*
partisan fautor, *m*
partition (act of —) partītĭo, *f*; **(wall)**, părĭes, *m*
partly *adv*, partim
partner sŏcĭus, *m* (sŏcĭa, *f*)
partnership sŏcĭĕtas, *f*
partridge perdix, *c*
party (political, etc.) factĭo, *f*; **(of soldiers)**, mănus, *f*; **(for pleasure)**, convīvĭum, *n*
pasha sătrăpes, *m*
pass *nn* **(mountain)**, angustĭae, *f. pl*
pass *v.t.* **(go beyond)**, praetergrĕdĭor (3 dep); **(surpass)**, excēdo (3); **(— on, — down)**, trādo (3); **(of time)**, ăgo (3), tĕro (3); **(— over, omit)**, praetĕrĕo (4); **(— a law)**, sancĭo (4); **(approve)**, prŏbo (1); v.i, praetĕrĕo (4); **(of time)**, transĕo (4); **(give satisfaction)**, sătisfăcĭo (3); **(— over, cross over)**, transĕo (4); **(come to — , happen)**, fīo (*irreg*)
passable (road, etc.) pervĭus
passage (crossing) transĭtus, *m*, trāiectĭo, *f*; **(route, way)**, ĭter, *n*, vīa, *f*; **(in a book)**, lŏcus, *m*
passenger vector, *m*
passion mōtus (*m*) ănĭmi **(impulse of the mind)**; **(love)**, ămor, *m*
passionate fervīdus, ardens, īrācundus
passive pătĭens
passivity pătĭentĭa
passport dĭplōma, *n*
password tessĕra, *f*
past *adj*, praetĕrĭtus; **(just —)**, proxĭmus
past *nn*, praetĕrĭtum tempus, *n*
past *prep*, praeter (*with acc*); **(on the far side of)**, ultrā (*with acc*)
past *adv, use compound vb. with* praeter, e.g. praetĕrĕo (4) **(go past)**
paste fărīna, *f*
paste *v.t*, glūtĭno (1)
pastime oblectāmentum, *n*
pastor pastor, *m*
pastoral pastōrālis
pastry crustum, *n*
pastry-cook crustŭlărĭus, *m*
pasture pascŭum, *n*
pasture *v.t*, pasco (3)
pat *v.t*, **(caress)**, permulcĕo (2)
patch *nn*, pannus, *m*
patch *v.t*, sarcĭo (4)
patent *adj*, ăpertus
paternal păternus
path sēmĭta, *f*, vĭa, *f*
pathetic mĭsĕrandus
pathless invĭus
pathos *f*, affectĭo (*f*) ănĭmi
pathway sēmĭta, *f*
patience pătĭentĭa, *f*
patient *adj*, pătĭens
patient *nn, use* aeger **(ill)**
patiently *adv*, pătĭenter
patrician *nn. and adj*, pătrĭcĭus
patrimony pătrĭmōnĭum, *n*
patriot *use phr*, qui pătrĭam ămat **(who loves his country)**

patriotic ămans pătrĭae
patriotism ămor (*m*) pătrĭae
patrol *nn, use* custŏdes, *m. pl,* (guards)
patrol *v.t*, circŭmĕo (4)
patron pătrōnus, *m*
patronage pătrōcĭnĭum, *n*
patronzie *v.t*, făvĕo (2) (*with dat*)
patter *nn*, crĕpĭtus, *m*
patter *v.i*, crĕpo (1)
pattern exemplum, *n*, exemplar, *n*
paucity paucĭtas, *f*
pauper pauper *c*, ĕgens (needy)
pause *nn*, mŏra, *f*
pause *v.i*, intermitto (3)
pave *v.t*, sterno (3)
pavement păvīmentum, *n*
pavilion *use* praetōrĭum, *n*, (general's tent), *or* tăbernācŭlum, *n*, (tent)
paw *nn*, pes, *m*
paw *v.t*, pĕdĭbus calco (1) (tread with the feet)
pawn (chess) lătruncŭlus, *m*; (security), pignus, *n*
pawn *v.t*, pignĕro (1)
pay *nn*, stĭpendĭum, *n*
pay *v.t*, solvo (3), pendo (3), nŭmĕro (1); *v.i* (— attention), ŏpĕram do (1); (— the penalty), poenas do (1)
paymaster (in army) trĭbūnus aerārius, *m*
payment sŏlūtĭo, *f*
pea pīsum, *n*, cĭcer, *n*
peace pax, *f*, ōtĭum, *n*
peaceable plăcĭdus
peaceful plăcĭdus, pācātus
peacefulness transquillĭtas, *f*
peace offering pĭācŭlum, *n*
peacock păvo, *m*
peak ăpex, *m*; (mountain), căcūmen, *n*
peal (thunder) frăgor, *m*; *otherwise use* sŏnus, *m*, (sound)
peal *v.i*, sŏno (1)
pear pyrum, *n*; (— tree), pyrus, *f*
pearl margărīta, *f*
peasant rustĭcus, *m*, ăgrestis, *m*
peasantry ăgrestes, *m. pl*
pebble lăpillus, *m*
peck (measure) mŏdĭus, *m*

peck *v.t*, vellĭco (1)
peculation pĕcūlātus, *m*
peculiar (to one person, etc.) prŏprĭus; (remarkable), singŭlāris
peculiarity prŏprĭetas, *f*
pecuniary pĕcūnĭārĭus
pedagogue măgister, *m*
pedant hŏmo ĭneptus
pedantic (affected — of style, etc.) pūtĭdus
peddle *v.t*, vendĭto (1)
pedestal băsis, *f*
pedestrian *nn*, pĕdes, *m*
pedestrian *adj* pĕdester
pedigree stemma, *n*
pedlar instĭtor, *m*
peel *nn*, cūtis, *f*
peel *v.i*, cŭtem rĕsĕco (1)
peep *nn*, aspectus, *m*
peep *nn*, aspectus, *m*
peep at *v.t*, inspicio (3); *v.i*, sĕ prōferre (*irreg*)
peer (equal) par, *m*
peer at *v.t*, rīmor (1 *dep*)
peerless ūnĭcus
peevish stŏmăchōsus
peevishness stŏmăchus, *m*
peg clāvus, *m*
pelt *v.t, use* intorquĕo (2) (hurl at); v.i, (of rain, etc.) *use* plŭit (it rains)
pen călămus, *m*; (for cattle), saeptum, *n*
pen *v.t*, (write), scrībo (3)
penal poenālis
penalty poena, *f*, damnum, *n*; (to pay the —), poenas do (1)
penance (do —) *use vb.* expĭo (1) (to make amends)
pencil pēnĭcillum, *n*
pending *prep*, inter, per (*with acc*)
pendulous pendŭlus
penetrate *v.i*, and *v.t*, pĕnĕtro (1) pervādo (3)
penetrating *adj*, ăcūtus, ācer (mentally), săgax
penetration ăcūmen, *n*
peninsula paeninsŭla, *f*
penitence paenitentĭa, *f*
penitent *use vb*, paenĭtet (2 *impers*) (*with acc. of person*), *e.g.*
I am penitent, mē paenĭtet

pennant vexillum, *n*
penny as, *m*
pension annŭa, *n.pl*
pensive multa pŭtans **(thinking many things)**
penthouse vīnĕa, *f*
penultimate paenultĭmus
penurious parcus
penury ĕgestas, *f*, ĭnŏpĭa, *f*
people (community) pŏpŭlus, *m*; **(persons)**, hŏmĭnes, *c. pl*; **(the common —)**, plebs, *f*, vulgus, *n*
people *v.t*, frĕquento (1); **(inhabit)**, incŏlo (3)
pepper pĭper, *n*
perambulate *v.t*, pĕrambŭlo (1)
perceive *v.t*, sentĭo (4), percĭpĭo (3), ănĭmadverto (3), intellĕgo (3)
percentage pars, *f*
perception perspĭcācĭtas, *f*, *or use adj*, perspĭcax **(sharp-sighted)**
perceptive perspĭcax
perch *nn*, pertĭca, *f*; **(fish)**, perca, *f*
perch *v.i*, insīdo (3)
perchance *adv*, fortĕ
percolate *v.i*, permāno (1)
percussion ictus, *m*
perdition exĭtĭum, *n*
peremptory *use vb*. obstringo (3) **(to put under obligation)**
perennial pĕrennis
perfect perfectus, absŏlūtus
perfect *v.t*, perfĭcĭo (3), absolvo (3)
perfection perfectĭo, *f*, absŏlūtĭo, *f*
perfidious perfĭdus
perfidy perfĭdĭa, *f*
perforate *v.t*, perfŏro (1)
perform *v.t*, fungor (3 *dep. with abl*); perăgo (3), praesto (1), exsĕquor (3 *dep*)
performance functĭo, *f*
performer actor, *m*
perfume ŏdor, *m*
perfume *v.t*, ŏdōro (1)
perfunctory neglĕgens
perhaps *adv*, fortĕ, fortassĕ, forsĭtan
peril pĕrīcŭlum, *m*
perilous pĕrīcŭlōsus
period spătĭum, *n*
periodical *adv*, stătus

perish *v.i*, pĕrĕo (4)
perishable frăgĭlis
perjure *v.t*, periūro (1)
perjured periūrus
perjury periūrĭum, *n*
permanence stăbĭlĭtas, *f*
permanent stăbĭlis
permanently *adv*, perpĕtŭo
permeate *v.i*, permāno (1)
permissible (it is —) līcet (2 *impers*)
permission (to give —) permitto (3) *(with dat)*; **(without your —)**, tē invīto
permit *v.t*, sĭno (3), permitto (3)
pernicious pernĭcĭōsus
perpendicular *adj*, dīrectus
perpetrate *v.t*, admitto (3)
perpetual sempĭternus
perpetuate *v.t*, contĭnŭo (1)
perplex *v.t*, distrăho (3), sollĭcĭto (1)
perplexed dŭbĭus
perquisite pĕcūlĭum, *n*
persecute *v.t*, insector (1 *dep*)
persecution insectātĭo, *f*
persecutor insectātor, *m*
perseverance persĕvērantĭa, *f*
persevere *v.i*, persĕvēro (1)
persist *v.i*, persto (1)
persistence pertĭnācĭa, *f*
person hŏmo, *c*; **(body)**, corpus, *n*; **(in person)**, *use pron*, ipse **(self)**
personal (opp. to public) prīvātus
personality ingĕnĭum, *n*
perspicacious perspĭcax
perspicacity perspĭcācĭtas, *f*
perspiration sūdor, *m*
perspire *v.i*, sūdo (1)
persuade *v.t*, persuādĕo (2) *(with dat of person)*
persuasion persuāsĭo, *f*
persuasive suāvĭlŏquens
pert prŏcax
pertain *v.i*, attĭnĕo (2)
pertainacious pertĭnax
pertinacity pertĭnācĭa, *f*
perturb *v.t*, turbo (1)
perusal perlectĭo, *f*
peruse *v.t*, perlĕgo (3)
pervade *v.t*, permāno (1), perfundo (3)
perverse perversus

perversion dēprāvātĭo, *f*
pervert *v.t*, dēprāvo (1)
pervious pervĭus
pest pestis, *f*
pester *v.t*, sollĭcĭto (1)
pestilence pestĭlentĭa, *f*
pestilential pestĭlens
pestle pistillum, *n*
pet *nn*, dēlĭcĭae, *f. pl*
pet *v.t*, dēlĭcĭis hăbĕo (2) **(regard among one's favourites)**, indulgĕo (2)
petition *use vb*. pĕto (3) **(seek)**
petition *v.t*, rŏgo (1)
petitioners pĕtentes, *c.pl*
petrify v.t, **(with fear, etc.)**, terrōrem ĭnĭcĭo (3), (*with dat*)
pettifogging vīlis
petty mĭnūtus
petulance pĕtŭlantĭa, *f*
petulant pĕtŭlans
phantom sĭmŭlācrum, *n*, ĭmāgo, *f*
phases **(alternations)** vĭces, *f. pl*
pheasant āles (*c*) Phāsĭdis **(bird of Phasis)**
phenomenon rēs, *f*; **(remarkable occurrence)**, rēs mīrābĭlis
phial lăguncŭla, *f*
philanthropic hūmānus
philanthropy hūmānĭtas, *f*
philologist phĭlŏlŏgus, *m*
philology phĭlŏlŏgĭa, *f*
philosopher phĭlŏsŏphus, *m*
philosophical phĭlŏsŏphus
philosophy phĭlŏsŏphĭa, *f*
philtre philtrum, *n*
phlegm pītŭīta, *f*; **(of temperament)**, aequus ănĭmus, *m*
phoenix phoenix, *m*
phrase *nn*, lŏcūtĭo, *f*
phraseology *use* verba, *n.pl*, **(words)**
phthisis phthĭsis, *f*
physic mĕdĭcāmentum, *n*
physical **(relating to the body)** *use nn*, corpus, *n*, **(body)**; **(natural)**, *use* nātūra, *f*, **(nature)**
physician mĕdĭcus, *m*
physics phȳsĭca, *n.pl*
physiology phȳsĭŏlŏgĭa, *f*
pick **(axe)** dŏlābra, *f*; **(choice)**, *use adj*, dēlectus **(chosen)**
pick *v.t*, **(pluck)**, lĕgo (3), carpo

(3); **(choose)**, ēlĭgo (3); **(— up, seize)**, răpĭo (3)
picked **(chosen)** dēlectus
picket stătĭo, *f*
pickle mŭrĭa, *f*
pickle *v.t*, condĭo (4)
pickpocket fūr, *c*
picnic *use phr*, fŏrīs ĕpŭlor (1 *dep*) **(to eat out of doors)**
picture tăbūla, *f*
picture *v.t*, expingo (3)
picturesque ămoenus
pie crustum, *n*
piebald bĭcŏlor
piece **(part)** pars, *f*; **(of food)**, frustrum, *n*; **(to pull or tear to — s)**, discerpo (3), dīvello (3); **(to fall to — s)**, dīlābor (3 *pass*)
piecemeal *adv*, membrātim
piece together *v.t*, compōno (3)
pier mōles, *f*
pierce *v.t*, perfŏdĭo (3)
piercing *adj*, ăcūtus
piety pĭĕtas, *f*
pig porcus, *m*, sūs, *c*
pigeon cŏlumba, *f*
pigheaded obstĭnātus, diffĭcĭlis
pigsty hăra, *f*
pike hasta, *f*
pile **(heap)** ăcervus, *m*; **(building)**, mōles, *f*; **(supporting timber)**, sublĭca, *f*
pile *v.t*, ăcervo (1), congĕro (3)
pilfer *v.t*, surrĭpĭo (3)
pilfering *nn*, furtum, *n*
pilgrim pĕrĕgrīnātor, *m*
pilgrimage pĕrĕgrīnātĭo, *f*
pill pĭlŭla, *f*
pillage *nn*, răpīna, *f*, dĭreptĭo, *f*
pillage *v.t*, praedor (1 *dep*) dīrĭpĭo (3)
pillar cŏlumna, *f*
pillory vincŭla, *n.pl*
pillow pulvīnus, *m*
pillow *v.t*, suffulcĭo (4)
pilot gŭbernātor, *m*
pilot *v.t*, gŭberno (1)
pimp lēno, *m*
pimple pustŭla, *f*
pin ăcus, *f*
pin *v.t*, ăcu fīgo (3) **(fix with a pin)**
pincers forceps, *m, f*
pinch *nn*, **(bite)**, morsus, *m*

pine *nn*, pīnus, *f*; *adj*, pīnĕus
pine *v.i*, tābesco (3); *v.t*, (— for),
   dĕsīdĕro (1)
pinion (nail) clāvus, *m*; (bond),
   vincŭla, *n.pl*
pinion *v.t*, rĕvincĭo (4)
pink rŭbor, *m*
pinnace lembus, *m*
pinnacle fastīgĭum, *n*
pint sextārĭus, *m*
pioneer explōrātor, *m*
pious pĭus
pip (seed) sēmen, *n*, grānum, *n*
pipe cănālis, *m*; (musical), fistŭla,
   f
pipe *v.i*, căno (3)
piper tībīcen, *m*
piquant ăcerbus
pique *nn*, offensĭo, *f*
pique *v.t*, laedo (3)
piracy lătrōcĭnĭum, *n*
pirate praedo, *m*, pīrāta, *m*
pit fŏvĕa, *f*; (arm —), āla, *f*;
   (theatre), căvĕa, *f*
pit (— one's wits, etc.) *use* ūtor (3
   dep) (to use)
pitch *nn*, pix, *f*; (in music), sŏnus, *m*
pitch *v.t*, (camp, tent, etc.), pōno
   (3); (throw), cōnĭcĭo (3); (ships),
   use ăgĭtor (1 *pass*) (to be tossed
   about)
pitcher urcĕus, *m*
pitchfork furca, *f*
piteous, pitiable mĭsĕrăbĭlis
pitfall fŏvĕa, *f*
pith mĕdulla, *f*
pitiful mĭser, mĭsĕrĭcors
pitifulness mĭsĕrĭa, *f*
pitiless immĭsĕrĭcors
pittance (small pay) tips, *f*
pity *v.t*, mĭsĕret (2 *impers*) (*with
   acc. of subject and genit. of object,
   e.g.* I pity you); mē mĭsĕret tŭi
pity *nn*, mĭsĕrĭcordĭa, *f*
pivot cardo, *m*
placard inscriptum, *n*
placate *v.t*, plăco (1)
place lŏcus, *m*; (in this —), *adv*,
   hīc; (in that —), illīc, ĭbĭ; (in
   what — ?) ŭbĭ?; (in the same —),
   ĭbīdem; (to this —) hūc; (to that
   —), illūc; (to the same —),
   ĕōdem; (to what — ?), quō; (from

this —). hinc; (from that —),
   inde; (from the same —),
   indĭdem; (from what — ?), unde?
   (in the first —), prīmum; (to take
   — , happen), *v.i*, accĭdo (3)
place *v.t*, pōno (3), lŏco (1);
   (— in command), praefĭcĭo (3);
   (— upon), impōno (3)
placid plăcĭdus, tranquillus
plague *nn*, pestĭlentĭa, *f*, pestis, *f*
plague *v.t*, (trouble), sollĭcĭto (1)
plain *nn*, campus, *m*, plănĭtĭes, *f*
plain *adj*, (clear), clārus, plānus;
   (unadorned), subtīlis, simplex;
   (frank, candid), sincērus
plainness perspĭcŭĭtas, *f*,
   simplĭcĭtas, *f*, sincērĭtas, *f*
plaintiff pĕtītor, *m*
plaintive *adj*, mĭsĕrăbĭlis
plait *v.t*, intexo (3)
plan *nn*, consĭlĭum, *n*; (drawing),
   dēscriptĭo, *f*; (to make a —),
   consĭlĭum căpĭo (3)
plan *v.i*, (intend), in ănĭmo hăbĕo
   (2); v.t, (design), dēscrībo (3)
plane *nn*, (tool), runcīna, *f*; (tree),
   plătănus, *f*
plane *v.t*, runcĭno (1)
planet sīdus (*n*) errans (moving
   constellation)
plank tăbŭla, *f*
plant *nn*, herba, *f*
plant (seeds, etc.) sēro (3);
   (otherwise), pōno (3), stătŭo (3)
plantation plantārĭum, *n*,
   arbustum, *n*
planter sător, *m*
planting *nn*, sătus, *m*
plaster *nn*, tectōrĭum, *n*;
   (medical), emplastrum
plaster *v.t*, gypso (1)
plasterer tector, *m*
plate (dish) cătĭllus, *m*; (thin layer
   of metal), lāmĭna, *f*; (silver, gold),
   argentum, *n*
plate *v.t*, indūco (3)
platform suggestus, *m*
Platonic Plătōnĭcus
platoon dĕcŭrĭa, *f*
plausible spĕcĭōsus
play *nn*, lūdus, *m*, lūsus, *m*;
   (theatre), fābŭla, *f*; (scope),
   camous, *m*

play *v.i*, lūdo (3) (*with abl. of game played*); **(musical)**, căno (3); **(a part in a play)**, partes ăgo (3); **(a trick)**, lūdĭfĭco (1)

player (stage) historĭo, *m*; **(flute —)**, tībīcen, m; **(strings —)**, fĭdĭcen, *m*; **(lute, guitar —)**, cĭthărista, *m*

playful (frolicsome) lascīvus

playfulness lascīvĭa, *f*

playground ārĕa, *f*

playwright făbŭlārum scriptor, *m*

plea (asking) obsĕcrātĭo, *f*; **(excuse)**, excūsātĭo, *f*

plead *v.t*, ōro (1), ăgo (3); **(as an excuse)**, excūso (1); **(beg earnestly)**, obsĕcro (1); **(law)**, dīco (3)

pleader (in law) ōrātor, *m*

pleasing, pleasant iūcundus

pleasantness iūcundĭtas, *f*

please *v.t*, plăcĕo (2) (*with dat*); **(if you —)**, si vis

pleasureable iūcundus

pleasure vŏluptas, *f*; **(will)**, arbĭtrĭum, *n*; **(— gardens)**, horti, *m. pl*

plebeian plēbēius

pledge *nn*, pignus, *n*; **(to make a — , promise)**, sē obstringĕre (3 reflex)

pledge *v.t*, oblĭgo (1), prōmitto (3)

plenipotentiary lēgātus, *m*

plenitude plĕnĭtūdo, *f*

plentiful largus, cōpĭōsus

plenty cōpĭa, *f*; **(enough)**, sătis (*with genit*)

pleurisy pleurītis, *f*

pliable flexĭbĭlis, lentus

plight angustĭae, *f.pl* **(difficulties)**

plight *v.t*, spondĕō (2), oblĭgo (1)

plinth plinthus, *m*, *f*

plod v.i, lentē prōcēdo (3)

plot (of ground) ăgellus, *m*; **(conspiracy)**, coniūrātĭo, *f*; **(story)**, argūmentum, *n*

plot *v.i*, coniūro (1)

plough *nn*, ărātrum, *n*; **(— share)**, vōmer, *m*

plough *v.t*, ăro (1)

ploughman ărātor, *m*, bŭbulcus, *m*

pluck *nn*, fortĭtūdo, *f*, ănĭmus, *m*

pluck *v.t*, carpo (3); **(— up courage)**, ănĭmum rĕvŏco (1)

plug *nn*, obtūrāmentum, *n*

plum prūnum, *n*

plum tree prūnus, *f*

plumage plūmae, *f*, *pl*

plumb line līnĕa, *f*

plume penna, *f*

plump pinguis

plumpness nĭtor, *m*, pinguĭtūdo, *f*

plunder *nn*, praeda, *f*; **(act of plundering)**, răpĭna, *f*, dīreptĭo, *f*

plunder *v.t*, praedor (1 dep), dīrĭpĭo (3)

plunderer praedātor, *m*

plunge *v.i*, sē mergĕre (3 *reflex*); *v.t*, mergo (3)

plural *adj*, plūrālis

plurality multĭtūdo, *f*

ply *v.t*, exercĕo (2)

poach *v.t*, use răpĭo (3), **(to seize)**; **(cook)**, cŏquo (3)

poacher fur, *c*, raptor *m*

pocket sĭnus, *m*

pocket *v.t*, **(money)**, āverto (3)

pocketbook pŭgillāres, *m*, *pl*

pocket money pĕcūlĭum, *n*

pod sĭlĭqua, *f*

poem pŏēma, *n*, carmen, *n*

poet pŏēta, *m*

poetical pŏētĭcus

poetry pŏēsis, *f*, carmĭna, *n. pl*

poignant ăcerbus

point ăcūmen, *n* **(of a sword)**, mūcro, *m*; **(spear)**, cuspis, *f*; **(place)**, lŏcus, *m*; **(issue)**, res, *f*; **(on the — of)**, *use fut. participle of vb, e.g.* on the point of coming; ventūrus

point *v.t* **(make pointed)**, praeăcŭo (3); **(direct)**, dīrĭgo (3)

point out *or* at *v.t*, monstro (1)

pointed praeăcūtus; **(witty)** salsus

pointer index, *m*, *f*

pointless insulsus

poison vĕnēnum, *n*, vīrus, *n*

poison *v.t*, vĕnēno nĕco (1) **(kill by poison)**

poisoning *nn*, vĕnēfĭcĭum, *n*

poisonous vĕnēnātus

poke *v.t*, fŏdĭco (1)

polar septentrĭōnālis

pole (rod, staff) contus, *m*,
  longŭrĭus, *m*; (earth), pŏlus, *m*
polemics contrōversĭae, *f. pl*
police (men) vĭgĭles, *m, pl*
policy rătĭo, *f*
polish *nn*, (brightness), nĭtor, *m*
polish *v.t*, pŏlĭo (4)
polished pŏlītus
polite cōmis, urbānus
politeness cōmĭtas, *f*, urbānĭtas, *f*
politic *adj*, prūdens
political cīvīlis, pūblĭcus
politician qui reĭpūblĭcae stŭdet
  (who pursues state affairs)
politics rēs pūblĭca, *f*
poll (vote) suffrāgĭum, *n*
pollute *v.t*, inquĭno (1)
pollution collŭvĭio, *f*
polytheism *use phr*, crēdĕre
  multos esse dĕos (believe that
  there are many gods)
pomade căpillāre, *n*
pomegranate mālum grānātum, *n*
pommel *v.t*, verbĕro (1)
pomp appărātus, *m*
pompous magnĭfĭcus
pompousness magnĭfĭcentĭa, *f*
pond stagnum, *n*; (fish —),
  piscīna, *f*
ponder *v.t*, rĕpŭto (1)
ponderous gravis
poniard pŭgĭo, *m*
pontiff pontĭfex, *m*
pontoon pons, *m*
pony mannus, *m*
pool lăcūna, *f*
poop puppis, *f*
poor pauper, ĭnops; (worthless),
  vīlĭs; (wretched), mĭser
poorly *adj*, (sick, ill), aeger
poorly *adv*, tĕnŭĭter, mălĕ
pop *v.i*, crĕpo (1)
pope Pontĭfex Maxĭmus, *m*
poplar pōpŭlus, *f*
poppy păpāver, *n*
populace vulgus, *n*, plebs, *f*
popular grātĭōsus; (of the people),
  pŏpŭlāris
popularity făvor (*m*) pŏpŭli
  (goodwill of the people)
population cīves, *c.pl*
populous frĕquens
porch vestĭbŭlum, *n*

porcupine hystrix, *f*
pore fŏrāmen, *n*
pore over *v.i*, ănĭmum intendo
  (3) (direct the mind)
pork porcīna, *f*
porker porcus, *m*
porous rārus
porpoise porcŭlus mărīnus, *m*
porridge puls, *f*
port portus, *m*
portable quod portāri pŏtest (that
  can be carried)
portal porta, *f*, iānŭa, *f*
portcullis cătăracta, *f*
portend *v.t*, portendo (3)
portent portentum, *n*
portentous monstrŭōsus
porter (doorkeeper) iānĭtor, *m*;
  (baggage carrier) baiŭlus, *m*
portfolio lĭbellus, *m*
portico portĭcus, *f*
portion pars, *f*
portion out *v.t*, partĭor (4 *dep*)
portrait ĭmāgo, *f*
portray *v.t*, dēpingo (3)
pose *nn*, stătus, *m*
position lŏcus, *m*; (site), sĭtus, *m*
positive certus
possess *v.t*, hăbĕo (2), possĭdĕo
  (2)
possession possessĭo, *f*; (to take
  — of), pŏtĭor (4 *dep. with abl*);
  (property), *often use possessive
  pron. e.g.* mĕa (my — s), *or* bŏna
  n.pl
possessor possessor, *m*,
  dŏmĭnus, *m*
possibility *use phr. with* posse; (to
  be possible)
possible *use vb*, posse (*irreg*) (to
  be possible); (as ... as possible),
  use quam *with superlative, e.g.* as
  large as possible, quam
  maxĭmus; (as soon as —), quam
  prīmum
post cippus, *m*, pālus, *m*;
  (military), stătĭo, *f*, lŏcus, *m*;
  (letter), tăbellārĭi pūblĭci, *m. pl*
  (state couriers)
post *v.t*, (in position), lŏco (1);
  (letter), tăbellārĭo do (1) (give to a
  courier)
posterior *nn*, nătes, *f. pl*

posterity postĕri, *m. pl*
postern postīcum, *n*
posthumous *use phr*, post mortem (*with genit*) **(after the death of ...)**
postman tăbellārĭus, *m*
postpone *v.t*, diffĕro (*irreg*)
postscript verba subiecta, *n. pl*, **(words appended)**
posture stătus, *m*
pot olla, *f*
potent pŏtens, effĭcax
potentate tўrannus, *m*
potion pōtĭo, *f*
potsherd testa, *f*
potter fĭgŭlus, *m*
pottery (articles) fictĭlĭa, *n. pl*
pouch saccŭlus, *m*
poultice mălagma, *n*
poultry ăves cŏhortāles, *f. pl*
pounce upon v.t, invŏlo (1)
pound *nn*, **(weight)**, lībra, *f*
pound *v.t*, tundo (3), tĕro (3)
pour *v.t*, fundo (3); *v.i*, fundor (3 *pass*)
pouring *adj*. effūsus
pout *v.i*, lăbellum extendo (3) **(stretch a lip)**
poverty paupertas, *f*, ĕgestas, *f*, ĭnŏpĭa, *f*; **(— stricken)**, *adj*, ĭnops
powder *nn*, pulvis, *m*
power vīres, *f. pl*; **(dominion)**, pŏtestas, *f*; **(authority)**, ius, *n*, impĕrĭum, *n*; **(inconstitutional —)**, pŏtentĭa, *f*
powerful pŏtens; **(of body)**, vălĭdus
powerless invălĭdus; **(to be —)**, *v.i*, mĭnĭmum posse (*irreg*)
practicable *use phr*, quod fĭĕri pŏtest **(that can be done)**
practical (person) făbrĭcae pĕrītus **(skilled in practical work)**
practically (almost) *adv*., paene
practice ūsus, *m*; (custom), mos, *m*, consŭĕtūdo, *f*
practise *v.t*, exercĕo (2), factĭto (1)
practitioner (medical) mĕdĭcus, *m*
praetor praetor, *m*
praetorship praetūra, *f*
praise *nn*, laus, *f*
praise *v.t*, laudo (1)

praiseworthy laudābĭlis
prance *v.i*, exsulto (1)
prank *use* lūdĭfĭcor (1 dep) **(to make fun of)**
prattle *v.i*, garrĭo (4)
pray *v.i*, and *v.t*, ōro (1) prĕcor (1 *dep*)
prayer prĕces, *f. pl*
preach *v.t*, contĭōnor (1 *dep*)
preamble exordĭum, *n*
precarious incertus
precaution (to take — s (against)) *v.i*, and *v.t*, praecăvĕo (2)
precede *v.t*, antēcēdo (3), antĕĕo (4)
precedence (to give —) *use vb*, cēdo (3); **(to take —)**, prĭor esse (*irreg*)
precedent exemplum, *n*
preceding *adj*, prĭor, proxĭmus
precept praeceptum, *n*
precious (of great price) magni prĕtĭi; **(dear)**, dīlectus
precipice lŏcus praeceps, *m*
precipitate *adj*, praeceps
precipitate *v.t*, praecĭpĭto (1)
precipitous praeceps
precise subtīlis
precision subtīlĭtas, *f*
preclude *v.t*, prŏhĭbĕo (2)
precocious praecox
preconceived praeiūdĭcātus
precursor praenuntĭus, *m*
predatory praedātōrĭus
predecessor (my —) *use phr*, qui ante me ... **(who before me ...)**
predicament angustĭae, *f. pl*
predict *v.t*, praedīco (3)
prediction praedictĭo, *f*
predilection stŭdĭum, *m*
predisposed inclīnātus
predominant pŏtens
predominate *v.i*, *use phr*, qui in pŏtentĭā sunt **(who are in authority)**
pre-eminent praestans
preface praefātĭo, *f*
preface *v.t*, praefor (1 *dep*)
prefer *v.t*, with infinitive, mālo (*irreg*); **(put one thing before another)**, antĕpōno (3); **(— a charge)**, dēfĕro (*irreg*)
preferable pŏtĭor

preference (desire) vŏluntas, f; (in
—), adv, pŏtĭus
preferment hŏnor, m
pregnant praegnans, grăvĭda
prejudge v.t, praeiūdĭco (1)
prejudice praeiūdĭcāta ŏpīnĭo, f
prejudice v.t, (impair), immĭnŭo
(3)
prejudicial noxĭus; (to be — to),
obsum (irreg) (with dat)
prelate săcerdos, c
preliminary use compound word
with prae, e.g. to make a —
announcement, praenuntĭo (1)
prelude prŏoemĭum, n
premature immātūrus
premeditate v.t, praemĕdĭtor (1
dep)
premeditation praemĕdĭtātĭo, f
premier princeps, m
premise prōpŏsĭtĭo, f
premises (buildings) aedĭficia,
n.pl
premium praemĭum, n
premonition mŏnĭtĭo, f
preoccupy (to be — with) stŭdĕo
(2) (with dat)
preparation compărātĭo, f,
appārātus, m; (to make — s),
compăro (1)
prepare v.t, păro (1), compăro (1)
prepossess v.t, commendo (1)
prepossessing adj, suāvis,
blandus
preposterous praepostĕrus
prerogative iūs, n
presage praesāgĭum, n
presage v.t, portendo (3)
prescribe v.t, praescrībo (3)
presence praesentĭa, f; (in the —
of), prep, cōram (with abl)
present nn (gift), dōnum, n;
(time), praesentĭa, n.pl
present adj, praesens; (to be —),
v.i, adsum (irreg)
present v.t, offĕro (irreg); (give),
dōno (1) (with acc. of person and
abl. of gift)
presentation dōnātĭo, f
presentiment augŭrĭum, n
presently adv, (soon), mox
preservation conservātĭo, f
preserve v.t, servo (1)

preserver servātor, m
preside v.i, praesĭdĕo (with dat)
presidency praefectūra, f
president praefectus, m
press nn, (machine), prēlum, n
press v.t, prĕmo (3); (urge),
urgĕo (2)
pressure nīsus, m
prestige fāma, f, ŏpīnĭo, f
presume v.t, (assume), crēdo (3);
(dare), v.i, audĕo (2)
presumption (conjecture)
coniectūra, f; (conceitedness),
arrŏgantĭa, f
presumptuous arrŏgans
pretence sĭmŭlātĭo, f; (under —
of), per sĭmŭlātĭōnem
pretend v.t, sĭmŭlo (1)
pretended adj, sĭmŭlātus
pretender (claimant) use vb, pĕto
(3) (aspire to)
pretension postŭlātĭo, f
pretext spĕcĭes, f; (on the — of),
use vb. sĭmŭlo (1) (to pretend)
prettily adv, bellē, vēnustē
prettiness concinnĭtas, f,
vĕnustas, f
pretty adj, pulcher
pretty adv, sătis (enough)
prevail v.i, obtĭnĕo (2), sŭpĕrĭor
esse (irreg); (to — upon), v.t,
persuādĕo (2) (with dat)
prevalent vulgātus
prevaricate v.t, tergĭversor (1
dep)
prevent v.t, prŏhĭbĕo (2)
prevention use vb, prŏhĭbĕo
(prevent)
previous prŏxĭmus
previously adv, antĕā
prey nn, praeda, f
prey v.t, praedor (1 dep)
price nn, prĕtĭum, n; (— of corn),
annōna, f
price v.t, prĕtĭum constĭtŭo (3)
(fix the price)
priceless inaestĭmābĭlis
prick nn, punctum, n
prick v.t, pungo (3); (spur),
stĭmŭlo (1)
prickly adj, ăcŭlĕātus
pride sŭperbĭa, f; (honourable —),
spīrĭtus, m

priest săcerdos, *c*
priesthood săcerdōtĭum, *n*
prim mōrōsĭor
primarily *adv*, princĭpĭō
primary prīmus
prime *nn*, (of life, etc.), *use vb*, flōrĕo (2) **(flourish); (best part),** flŏs, *m*
prime *adj*, ēgrĕgĭus
primeval prīmĭgenĭus
primitive prīmĭgenĭus
prince (king) rēgŭlus, *m*; **(king's son),** filĭus (*m*) rēgis
princess (king's daughter) filĭa (*f*) rēgis
principal *adj*, princĭpālis, praecĭpŭus
principal *nn*, măgister, *m*
principality regnum, *n*
principle princĭpĭum, *n*; **(element),** ĕlĕmentum, *n*, prīmordĭa, *n. pl*; **(rule, maxim),** praeceptum, *n*
print *nn*, (mark), nŏta, *f*
print *v.t*, imprĭmo (3)
prior *adj*, prĭor
priority *use adj*, prĭor
prism prisma, *n*
prison carcer, *m*
prisoner captīvus, *m*
privacy sōlĭtūdo, *f*
private prīvātus, sēcrētus
private soldier mīles grĕgārĭus, *m*
privately *adv*, prīvātim, clam
privation ĭnŏpĭa, *f*
privet lĭgustrum, *n*
privilege iūs, *n*
privy *adj*, **(acquainted with),** conscĭus; **(secret),** prīvātus
privy *nn*, fŏrĭca, *f*
privy-council consĭlĭum, *n*
privy-purse fiscus, *m*
prize praemĭum, *n*; **(booty),** praeda, *f*
prize *v.t*, **(value),** magni aestĭmo (1)
probability sĭmĭlĭtūdo (*f*) vēri
probable sĭmĭlis vēri
probation prŏbātĭo, *f*
probe *v.t*, tento (1)
problem quaestĭo, *f*
problematical (doubtful) dŭbĭus
procedure rătĭo, *f*
proceed *v.i*, **(move on),** pergo (3);

(originate) prŏfĭciscor (3 dep);
(take legal action against) lītem intendo (3) (*with dat*)
proceedings (legal) actĭo, *f*; **(doings),** acta, *n.pl*
proceeds fructus, *m*
process rătĭo, *f*; **(in the — of time),** *adv, use phr,* tempŏre praetĕreunte **(with time going by)**
procession pompa, *f*
proclaim *v.t*, praedĭco (1), prōnuntĭo (1)
proclamation prōnuntĭātĭo, *f*, ēdictum, n
proconsul prōconsul, *m*
procrastinate *v.t*, diffĕro (*irreg*)
procrastination tardĭtas, *f*, mŏra, *f*
procreate *v.t*, prōcrĕo (1)
procreation prōcrĕātĭo, *f*, partus, *m*
procure *v.t*, compăro (1)
procurer lēno, *m*
prodigal *adj*, prōdĭgus
prodigality effūsĭo, *f*
prodigious immānis
prodigy prōdĭgĭum, *n*
produce *nn*, fructus, *m*
produce *v.t*, **(into view)** prōfĕro (*irreg*); **(create),** părĭo (3); **(— an effect),** mŏvĕo (2)
productive fĕrax
profanation vĭŏlātĭo, *f*
profane impĭus, prŏfānus
profane *v.t*, vĭŏlo (1)
profanity impĭĕtas, *f*
profess *v.t*, prŏfĭtĕor (2 dep)
profession (occupation) mūnus, n, offĭcĭum, n; **(avowal),** prŏfessĭo, *f*
professor prŏfessor, *m*
proffer *v.t*, pollĭcĕor (2 dep)
proficient (skilled) pĕrītus
profile oblīqua făcĭes, *f*
profit *nn*, ēmŏlŭmentum, *n*, lŭcrum, *n*, quaestus, *m*
profit *v.t*, **(benefit),** prōsum (*irreg. with dat*)
profitable fructŭōsus
profitless ĭnūtĭlis
profligacy nēquĭtĭa, *f*
profligate perdĭtus
profound altus

profuse effūsus
profusion effūsĭo, f
progeny prōgēnĭes, f
prognostic signum, n
programme lĭbellus, m
progress (improvement, etc.)
  prōgressus, m; (to make —),
  prōfĭcĭo (3), prōgrĕdĭor (3 dep)
progress v.i, prōgrĕdĭor (3 dep)
prohibit v.t, vēto (1)
prohibition interdictum, n
project nn, (plan), consĭlĭum, n
project v.t, prōĭcĭo (3); v.i,
  ēmĭnĕo (2)
projectile tēlum, n
projecting ēmĭnens
proleteriat vulgus, n
prolific fēcundus
prolix verbōsus
prologue prŏlŏgus, m
prolong v.t, prōdūco (3); (— a
  command), prōrŏgo (1)
prolongation prōpăgātĭo, f
promenade ambŭlātĭo, f
prominence ēmĭnentĭa, f
prominent ēmĭnens; (person),
  praeclārus
promiscuous prōmiscŭus
promise nn, prōmissum, n, fĭdes,
  f
promise v.i, prōmitto (3),
  pollĭcĕor (2 dep)
promising adj, use adv. phr, bŏnā
  spe (of good hope)
promissory note chīrŏgrăphum, n
promontory prōmontōrĭum, n
promote v.t, prōmŏvĕo (2);
  (favour, assist), iŭvo (1), prōsum
  (irreg) (with dat)
promoter auctor, m
promotion (act of —) use vb.
  prōmŏvĕo (2); (honour), hŏnor, m
prompt adj, promptus
prompt v.t, (assist in speaking),
  sūbĭcĭo (3) (with dat. of person);
  (incite), incĭto (1)
promptitude, promptness
  cĕlĕrĭtas, f
promulgate v.t, prōmulgo (1)
prone prōnus; (inclined to),
  prōpensus
prong dens, m
pronoun prōnōmen, n

pronounce v.t, prōnuntĭo (1)
pronunciation appellātĭo, f
proof argūmentum, n,
  dŏcŭmentum n, prŏbātĭo, f
prop nn, admĭnĭcŭlim, n
prop v.t, fulcĭo (4)
propagate v.t, prōpāgo (1)
propel v.t, prōpello (3)
propensity ănĭmus inclīnātus, m
proper dĕcōrus, vērus, aptus
properly adv, (correctly), rectē
property (possessions) bŏna, n.
  pl, rĕs, f; (characteristic quality),
  prŏprĭētas, f
prophecy praedictĭo, f,
  praedictum, n
prophesy v.t, praedīco (3),
  vātĭcĭnor (1 dep)
prophet vātes, c
prophetic dīvīnus
propitiate v.t, plāco (1)
propitious prŏpĭtĭus, praesens
proportion portĭo, f; (in —),
  prōportĭōne
proportional use adv. phr, prō
  portĭōne
proposal condĭcĭo, f
propose v.t, fĕro (irreg), rŏgo (1)
proposer lātor, m
proposition condĭcĭo, f
proprietor dŏmĭnus, m
propriety (decorum) dĕcōrum, n
prorogation prōrŏgātĭo, f
prosaic (flat) iēiūnus
proscribe v.t, prōscrībo (3)
proscription prōscriptĭo, f
prose ōrātĭo, sŏlūta, f
prosecute v.t, (carry through),
  exsĕquor (3 dep); (take legal
  proceedings) lītem intendo (3)
prosecution exsĕcuutĭo, f; (legal),
  accuusātĭo, f
prosecutor accūsātor, m
prospect (anticipation) spes
  fūtūra, f; (view), prospectus, m
prospective fūtūrus
prosper v.i, flōrĕo (2)
prosperity res sĕcundae, f. pl
prosperous sĕcundus
prostitute nn, mĕrĕtrix, f
prostitute v.t, vulgo (1)
prostitution mĕrĕtrīcĭus quaestus,
  m

prostrate (in spirit, etc.) fractus; (lying on the back), sŭpīnus; (lying on the face), prōnus

prostrate *v.t*, sterno (3), dēĭcĭo (3)

protect *v.t*, tĕgo (3), tŭĕor (2 *dep*), dēfendo (3)

protection tūtēla, *f*, praesĭdĭum, *n*

protector dēfensor, *m*

protest against *v.t*, intercēdo (3)

prototype exemplar, *n*

protract *v.t*, dūco (3)

protrude *v.t*, prōtrūdo (3); *v.i*, ēmĭnĕo (2)

protuberance tūber, *n*

proud sŭperbus

prove v.t, prŏbo (1); (to — oneself) sē praestāre (1 *reflex*); (test), pĕrīclĭtor (1 dep); v.i, (turn out (of things)), fio (*irreg*), ēvĕnĭo (4)

proverb prōverbĭum, *n*

proverbial *use nn*, prōverbĭum, *n*, (proverb)

provide *v.t*, (supply), păro (1), praebĕo (2); v.i, (make provision for), prōvĭdĕo (2); (— against), căvĕo (2) ne (*with vb. in subjunctive*)

provided that *conj*, dum, dummŏdo

providence prōvĭdentĭa, *f*

provident prōvĭdus

province prōvincĭa, f

provincial prōvincĭālis

provision (to make —) prōvĭdĕo (2)

provisional *use adv. phr*, ad tempus (for the time being)

provisions cĭbus, *m*

provocation *use vb*, irrīto (1) (to provoke)

provoke *v.t*, irrīto (1); (stir up), incĭto (1)

prow prōra, *f*

prowess virtus, *f*

prowl *v.i*, văgor (1 *dep*)

proximity prŏpinquĭtas, *f*

proxy prōcūrātor, *m*

prudence prūdentĭa, *f*

prudent prūdens

prune *nn*, prūnum, *n*, (plum)

prune *v.t*, ampŭto (1)

prurient lībĭdĭnōsus

pry *v.t*, rīmor (1 *dep*)

psalm carmen, *n*

psychological *use genit. of* mens, (mind)

puberty pūbertas, *f*

public *adj*, pūblĭcus; (of the state), *use nn*, respublĭca, *f*, (state), *or* pŏpŭlus, *m*, (people)

public *nn*, hŏmĭnes, *c. pl*

publican (innkeeper) caupo, *m*

publication *use* ēdo (3), (publish)

publicity cĕlĕbrĭtas, *f*

publicly *adv*, pălam

publish *v.t*, effĕro (*irreg*), prŏfĕro (*irreg*); (book), ĕdo (3)

pucker *v.t*, corrūgo (1)

puddle lăcūna, *f*

puerile (silly) ĭnseptus

puff *v.i*, (pant), ănhēlo (1); v.t, (inflate) inflo (1); (puffed up), inflātus

pugilist pŭgil, *m*

pull *v.t*, trăho (3); (— down, demolish), dēstrŭo (3)

pulley trochlĕa, *f*

pulp căro, *f*

pulpit suggestus, *m*

pulsate *v.i*, palpĭto (1)

pulse vēnae, *f. pl*. (veins)

pulverize *v.t*, in pulvĕrem contĕro (3) (pound into dust)

pumice pūmex, *m*

pump *nn*, antlĭa, *f*

pump *v.t*, haurĭo (4)

pumpkin pĕpo, *m*

pun făcētĭae, *f. pl*

punch ictus, *m*, pugnus, *m*

punch *v.t*, percŭtĭo (3)

punctilious mōrōsus

punctual, punctuality *use adv. phr*, ad tempus (at the right time)

punctuate *v.t*, distinguo (3)

punctuation interpunctĭo, *f*

puncture *nn*, punctum

puncture *v.t*, pungo (3)

pungency morsus, *m*, ăcerbĭtas, *f*

pungent ācer

punish *v.t*, pūnĭo (4), ănĭmadverto (3) in (*with acc*), poenas sūmo (3); (to be — ed), poenas do (1)

punishment poena, *f*, supplĭcĭum, *n*; (to undergo —), poenam sŭbĕo

(4)
punitive *use vb*, pūnĭo **(punish)**
puny pŭsillus
pup, puppy cătŭlus, *m*
pupil (scholar) discĭpŭlus, *m*; **(of the eye)** pūpilla, *f*
puppet pūpa, *f*
purchase *nn*, emptĭo, *f*
purchase *v.t*, ĕmo (3)
pure pūrus, mĕrus; **(morally)**, intĕger
purgative *use phr. with* mĕdĭcămentum, *n*, **(medicine)**
purge *nn, use vb*, purgo (1)
purge *v.t*, purgo (1)
purification purgātĭo, *f*
purify *v.t*, purgo (1), lustro (1)
purity castĭtas, *f*, intĕgrĭtas, *f*
purloin *v.t*, surrĭpĭo (3)
purple *nn*, purpŭra, *f*
purple *adj*, purpŭrĕus
purport *nn*, **(meaning)**, signĭfĭcātĭo, *f*
purport *v.t*, **(mean)**, signĭfĭco (1)
purpose *nn*, prōpŏsĭtum, *n*, consĭlĭum, *n*; **(for the — of doing something)**, ĕo consĭlĭo ut (*with vb in subjunctive*); **(on —)**, *adv*, consulto; **(to no — , in vain)**, *adv*, frustrā; **(for what — ?)** quāre
purpose *v.t*, **(intend)**, in ănĭmo hăbĕo (2)
purr *v.i*, murmŭro (1)
purse saccŭlus, *m*
in pursuance of ex (*with abl*)
pursue *v.t*, sĕquor (3 *dep*)
pursuit (chase) *use vb*, sĕquor **(to pursue)**; **(desire for)**, stŭdĭum, *n*
purvey *v.t*, obsōno (1)
purveyor obsōnātor, *m*
pus pūs, *n*
push, pushing *nn*, impulsus, *m*, impĕtus, *m*
push *v.t*, pello (3), trūdo (3); **(— back)**, rĕpello (3); **(— forward)**, prōmŏvĕo (2)
pushing *adj*, mŏlestus
pusillanimity ănĭmus, hŭmĭlis, *m*
pusillanimous hŭmĭlis
pustule pustŭla, *f*
put *v.t*, **(place)**, pōno (3), do (1), impōno (3); **(— aside)**, sĕpōno (3); **(— away)**, abdo (3), condo (3); **(— back)**, rĕpōno (3); **(—**

down), dĕpōno (3); **(suppress)**, exstinguo (3); **(— forward)**, praepōno (3), prōfĕro (*irreg*); **(— in)**, immitto (3); **(— into land, port, etc.)**, *v.i*, portum căpĭo (3); **(— off)**, *v.t*, pōno (3); **(delay)**, diffĕro (*irreg*); **(— on)**, impōno (3); **(— clothes)**, indŭo (3); **(— out)**, ēĭcĭo (3); **(quench)**, exstinguo (3); **(— to drive to)**, impello (3); **(— together)**, collĭgo (3), confĕro (*irreg*); **(— under)**, sūbĭcĭo (3); **(— up, erect)**, stătŭo (3); **(offer)**, prōpōno (3); **(put up with, bear)**, fĕro (*irreg*); **(— upon)**, impōno (3); **(— to flight)** fŭgo (1)
putrefy *v.i*, pūtesco (3)
putrid pŭtrĭdus
putty glūten, *m or n*
puzzle *nn*, **(riddle)**, nōdus, *m*; **(difficulty)**, difficultas, *f*, angustĭae, *f, pl*
puzzling *adj*, perplexus; **(in a — way)**, *adv. phr*, per ambāges
pygmy nānus, *m*
pyramid pŷrămis, *f*
pyre rŏgus, *m*
Pyrenees Montes Pŷrēnaei, *m. pl*
python pŷthon, *m*

Q

quack *nn*, **(medicine)**, pharmăcŏpōla, *m*
quadrangle ārĕa, *f*
quadrant quădrans, *m*
quadrilateral quădrĭlătĕrus
quadruped quădrŭpes
quadruple *adj*, quădruplex
quaff *v.t*, haurĭo (4)
quagmire pălus, *f*
quail *nn*, cŏturnix, *f*
quail *v.i*, trĕpĭdo (1)
quaint nŏvus
quake *nn*, trĕmor, *m*
quake *v.i*, trĕmo (3)
qualification iūs, *n*; **(condition)**, condĭcĭo, *f*
qualified (suitable) aptus, ĭdōnĕus
quality *v.t*, **(fit someone for something)**, aptum reddo (3); **(restrict)**, circumscrībo (3), mītĭgo (1)

quality nātūra, *f*
qualm (doubt) dŭbĭtātĭo, f
quantity nŭmĕrus, *m*, magnĭtūdo, *f*; **(a certain —)**, ălĭquantum, *n* **(*nn*)**; **(a large —)** cōpĭa, *f*, multum, *n*; **(what — ?)**, use *adj*, quantus **(how great)**
quarrel iurgĭum, *n*, rixa, *f*
quarrel *v.i*, iurgo (1), rixor (1 *dep*)
quarrelsome lītĭgĭōsus
quarry (stone) lăpĭcīdīnae, *f. pl*; **(prey)**, praeda, *f*
quarry *v.t*, caedo (3)
quart (measure) dŭo sextārĭi, *m. pl*
quarter quarta pars, *f*, quădrans, *m*; **(district)**, rĕgĭo, f; **(surrender)**, dēdĭtĭo, *f*
quarter *v.t*, quădrĭfărĭam dīvĭdo (3), **(divide into four parts)**
quarter-deck puppis, *f*
quartermaster quaestor mīlĭtāris, *m*
quarterly *adj*. trĭmestris
quarters (lodging) hospĭtĭum, *n*; **(at close —)**, *adv*, commĭnus; **(to come to close —)**, signa confĕro **(*irreg*)**
quash *v.t*, opprĭmo (3); **(sentence, verdict)**, rēscindo (3)
quaver *v.i*, trĕpĭdo (1)
quay crēpīdo, *f*
queen rēgīna, *f*
queer rīdĭcŭlus
queerness insŏlentĭa, *f*
quell *v.t*, opprĭmo (3)
quench *v.t*, exstinguo (3)
quenchless ĭnexstinctus
querulous quĕrŭlus
query quaestĭo, *f*
query *v.t*, quaero (3)
quest inquīsītĭo, *f*
question *nn*, rŏgātĭo, *f*, interrŏgātum, *n*, quaestĭo, *f*; *or* use *vb*, rŏgo (1) **(to ask —s)**; **(doubt)**, dŭbĭum, *n*
question *v.t*, rŏgo (1), quaero (3); **(doubt)**, dŭbĭto (1)
questionable incertus
questioner interrŏgātor, *m*
quibble *nn*, captĭo, *f*
quibble *v.i*, căvillor (1 *dep*)

quick *adj*, cĕler; **(sprightly)**, ăgĭlis; **(— witted)**, săgax
quickly *adv*, cĕlĕrĭter, cĭto
quicken *v.t*, accĕlĕro (1), stĭmŭlo (1); v.i, **(move quicker)**, sē incĭtāre (1 *reflex*)
quickness vēlōcĭtas, *f*; **(— of wit)**, săgācĭtas, *f*
quicksilver argentum vīvum, *n*
quick-tempered īrācundus
quiescent quĭescens
quiet *nn*, quĭes, *f*
quiet *adj*, quĭētus, tranquillus
quiet, quieten *v.t*, sēdo (1)
quietly *adv*, quĭētē, tranquillē
quill penna, *f*; **(for writing)**, use stĭlus, *m*, **(pen)**
quilt *nn*, strāgŭlum, *n*
quinquennial quinquennālis
quinsy angīna, *f*
quintessence vīs, *f*, flōs, *m*
quip *nn*, rēsponsum (salsum) **((witty) reply)**
quirk căvillātĭo, *f*
quit *v.t*, rĕlinquo (3)
quite *adv*, admŏdum, prorsus; **(— enough)**, sătis
quiver *nn*, phărĕtra, *f*
quiver *v.i*, trĕmo (3)
quoit discus, *m*
quota răta pars, *f*
quotation prōlātĭo, *f*
quote *v.t*, prōfĕro (*irreg*)
quotidian cottīdĭānus

R

rabbit cŭnīculus, *m*
rabble turba, *f*
rabid răbīdus
race (family) gĕnus, *n*, prōgĕnĭes, *f*; **(running)**, cursus, *m*, certāmen, *n*
race *v.i*, cursu certo (1) **(contend by running)**
racecourse stădĭum, *n*, currĭcŭlum, *n*
racehorse ĕquus cursor, *m*
rack (for torture) ĕquŭlĕus, m
rack *v.t*, **(torture)**, torquĕo (2)
racket (bat) rētĭcŭlum, *n*; **(noise)**, strĕpĭtus, *m*
racy (smart) salsus

radiance fulgor, *m*
radiant clārus, fulgens
radiate *v.i*, fulgĕo (2)
radiation rădĭātĭo, *f*
radical (fundamental) tōtus;
(original), innātus; (keen on
change), cŭpĭdus rērum nŏvārum
radically *adv*, pĕnĭtus, fundĭtus
radish rădix
radius rădĭus, *m*
raffle ālĕa, *f*
raft rătis, *f*
rafter cantērĭus, *m*
rag pannus, *m*
rage fŭror, *m*
rage *v.i*, fŭro (3)
ragged pannōsus
raging *adj*, fŭrens
raid incursĭo, *f*; (to make a —),
invādo (3) in (*with acc.*)
rail longŭrĭus, *m*
rail at (abuse) mălĕdīco (3) (*with
dat.*)
railing cancelli, *m.pl*
raillery căvillātĭo, *f*
raiment vestīmenta, *n.pl*
rain *nn*, plŭvĭa, *f*, imber, *m*
rain *v.i*, (it rains), plŭit (3 impers.)
rainbow arcus, *m*
rainy plŭvĭus
raise v.t, (lift), tollo (3); (forces),
compăro (1); (rouse), ērĭgo (3);
(— a seige), obsĭdĭōnem solvo (3)
raisin ācĭnus passus, *m*, (dried
berry)
rake *nn*, (tool), rastellus, *m*;
(person) nĕpos, *c*
rake *v.t*, rādo (3)
rally *v.t*, (troops) mīlĭtes in
ordĭnes rĕvŏco (1), (call back the
soldiers to their ranks); v.i, se
collĭgĕre (3 reflex)
ram (or battering —) ărĭes m;
(beak of a ship), rostrum, n
ram *v.t*, fistūco (1); (ship) rostro
laedo (3)
ramble *v.i*, erro (1)
rambler erro, *m*
rammer fistūca, *f*
rampart agger, *m*, vallum, *n*
rancid rancĭdus
rancorous infestus
rancour ŏdĭum, *n*

random *adj*, fortŭĭtus; (at —),
adv, fortŭĭto
range ordo, *m*; (— of mountains),
iŭga, *n.pl*; (of a missile), iactus,
m; (scope), campus, *m*
rank *nn*, ordo, *m*
rank *v.i*, sē hăbere (2 *reflex*)
rank *adj*, (smell, etc.), fētĭdus
rankle *v.t*, exulcĕro (1), mordĕo
(2)
ransack *v.t*, dīrĭpĭo (3)
ransom *nn*, rĕdemptĭo, *f*; (—
money), prĕtĭum, *n*
ransom *v.t*, rĕdĭmo (3)
rant *v.t*, dēclāmo (1)
ranting *nn*, sermo tŭmĭdus, *m*,
(bombastic speech)
rap *nn*, pulsātĭo, *f*
rap *v.t*, pulso (1)
rapacious răpax
paracity răpăcĭtas, *f*
rape *nn*, raptus, *m*
rapid răpĭdus, cĕler
rapidity cĕlĕrĭtas, *f*
rapier glādĭus, *m*
rapine răpīna, *f*
rapture laetĭtĭa, *f*
rapturous laetus
rare rārus
rarefy v.t, extĕnŭo (1)
rareness, rarity rārĭtas, *f*
rascal scĕlestus, *m*
rascality scĕlĕra, *n.pl*
rase (to the ground) *v.t*, sŏlo
aequo (1)
rash *adj*, tĕmĕrārĭus
rash *nn*, ēruptĭo, *f*
rashness tĕmĕrĭtas, *f*
rasp *nn*, (file), scŏbīna, *f*
rasp *v.t*, rādo (3)
rat mūs, *c*
rate (price) prĕtĭum, *n*; (tax)
vectĭgal, *n*; (speed), cĕlĕrĭtas, *f*; (at
any —), *adv*, ŭtĭque
rate *v.t*, (value), aestĭmo (1);
(chide), incrĕpo (1); (tax), censĕo
(2)
rather *adv*, (preferably), pŏtĭus;
(somewhat), ălĭquantum; (a little),
with comparatives, e.g. rather
(more quickly), paulo (cĕlĕrĭus)
ratification sanctĭo, *f*
ratify *v.t*, rătum făcĭo (3)

ratio portĭo, *f*

ration *nn*, dēmensum, *n*, cĭbārĭa, *n.pl*

rational (a — being), partĭceps rătĭonis **(participant in reason)**

rationally *adv*, rătĭōne

rattle *nn*, crĕpĭtus, *m*; **(toy)**, crĕpĭtācŭlum, *n*

rattle *v.i*, crĕpo (1)

ravage *v.t*, pŏpŭlor (1 dep.)

ravaging *nn*, pŏpŭlātĭo, *f*

rave *v.i*, fŭro (3)

raven corvus, *m*

ravening, ravenous răpax

ravine fauces, *f.pl*

raving *adj*, fŭrens, insānus

raving *nn*, fŭror, *m*

ravish *v.t*, răpĭo (3), stŭpro (1)

ravishing suāvis

raw crūdus; **(inexperienced, unworked)**, rŭdis

ray rădĭus, *m*

razor nŏvācŭla, *f*

reach *nn*, **(range)**, iactus, *m*; **(space)**, spătĭum, *n*

reach *v.i*, **(extend)**, pertĭnĕo (2), attingo (3); *v.t*, **(come to)**, pervēnĭo (4) ad *(with acc.)*

react *v.t*, **(be influenced)**, afficĭor (3 pass.)

reaction (of feeling) *use vb*, commŏvĕo (2) (to make an impression on)

read *v.t*, lĕgo (3); **(— aloud)**, rĕcĭto (1)

readable făcĭlis lectu

reader lector, *m*

readily *adv*, **(willingly)**, lĭbenter

readiness (preparedness) *use adj*, părātus **(ready); (willingness)**, ănĭmus lĭbens, *m*

reading *nn*, lectĭo, *f*, rĕcĭtātĭo, *f*

reading-room bibliŏthēca, *f*

ready părātus, promptus; **(to be —)**, părātus, praesto esse *(irreg.)*; **(to make, get —)**, păro (1)

real *adj*, vērus

realism vērĭtas, *f*

reality rēs, *f*

realization (getting to know) cognĭtĭo, *f*; **(completion)**, confectĭo, *f*

realize *v.t*, intellĕgo (3); **(a**

project), perfĭcĭo (3), perdūco (3)

really *adv*, rēvērā; **(is it so?)**, ĭtăne est?

realm regnum, *n*

reap *v.t*, mĕto (3); **(gain)**, compăro (1)

reaper messor, *m*

reaping-hook falx, *f*

reappear *v.i*, rĕdĕo *(irreg.)*

rear *nn*, **(of a marching column)**, agmen nŏvissĭmum, n; **(of an army)**, ăcĭes nŏvissĭma, *f*; **(in the —)** *adv*, ā tergo

rear *v.t*, **(bring up)**, ēdŭco (1), ălo (3); v.i, **(of horses)**, sē ērĭgĕre (3 *reflex.*)

reason (faculty of thinking) mens, *f*; **(cause)**, causa, *f*; **(for this —)**, *adv*, ĭdĕo, idcirco; **(for what — , why?)**, cur, quārē; **(without — , heedlessly)**, *adv*, tĕmĕre

reason *v.t*, rătĭōcĭnor (1 dep.); **(— with)**, dissĕro (3), cum *(with abl.)*

reasonable (fair) aequus, iustus; **(in size)**, mŏdĭcus

reasonable (fairness) aequĭtas, *f*

reasoning *nn*, rătĭo, *f*

reassemble *v.t*, cōgo (3), in ūnum lŏcum collĭgo (3), **(collect into one place)**; *v.i*, rĕdĕo (4)

reassert *v.t*, rēstĭtŭo (3)

reassure *v.t*, confirmo (1)

rebel *nn*, sēdĭtĭōsus, *m*

rebel rĕbello (1), dēfĭcĭo (3)

rebellion sēdĭtĭo, *f*

rebellious sēdĭtĭosus

rebound *v.i*, rĕsĭlĭo (4)

rebuff *v.t*, rĕpello (3)

rebuff *nn*, rĕpulsa, *f*

rebuke *nn*, rĕprĕhensĭo, *f*

rebuke *v.t*, rĕprĕhendo (3)

recall *nn*, rĕvŏcātĭo, *f*

recall *v.t*, rĕvōco (1); **(— to mind)**, rĕpĕto (3)

recapitulate *v.t*, ēnŭmĕro (1)

recapitulation ēnŭmĕrātĭo, *f*

recapture *v.t*, rĕcĭpĭo (3)

recede *v.i*, rĕcēdo (3)

receipt (act of receiving) acceptĭo, *f*; **(document)**, ăpŏcha, *f*

receipts (proceeds) rĕdĭtus, *m*

receive *v.t*, accĭpĭo (3), excĭpĭo (3)

receiver (of stolen goods)
rĕceptor, *m*
recent rĕcens
recently *adv*, nūper
receptacle rĕceptăcŭlum, *n*
reception ădĭtus, *m*
receptive dŏcĭlis
recess rĕcessus, *m*; (holidays),
fērĭae, *f. pl*
reciprocal mūtŭus
reciprocate *v.t*, rĕfĕro (*irreg.*)
recital narrătĭo, *f*
recite v.t, rĕcĭto (1), prōnuntĭo
(1)
reckless tĕmĕrărĭus
recklessness tĕmĕrĭtas, *f*
reckon *v.t*, (count), nŭmĕro (1);
(— on, rely on), confīdo (3) (*with*
dat.); (consider), dūco (3)
reckoning rătĭo, *f*
reclaim *v.t*, rĕpĕto (3)
recline *v.i*, rĕcŭbo (1)
recluse hŏmo sōlĭtārĭus
recognizable *use phr*, quod
agnosci pōtest **(that can be**
recognized)
recognize *v.t*, agnosco (3),
cognosco (3); (acknowledge),
confĭtĕor (2 *dep.*)
recognition cognĭtĭo, *f*
recoil *v.i*, rĕsĭlĭo (4)
recollect v.t, rĕmĭniscor (3 *dep.*
with genit)
recollection mĕmŏrĭa, *f*
recommence *v.t*, rĕdintĕgro (1)
recommend *v.t*, commendo (1)
recommendation commendătĭo, *f*
recompense *v.t*, rĕmūnĕror (1
dep)
reconcile *v.t*, rĕconcĭlĭo (1)
reconciliation rĕconcĭlĭātĭo, *f*
reconnoitre *v.t*, explōro (1)
reconsider *v.t*, rĕpŭto (1)
record *v.t*, in tăbŭlas rĕfĕro
(*irreg*)
records tăbŭlae, *f. pl*, fasti, *m. pl*
recount *v.t*, (expound), ēnarro (1)
recourse (to have — to) v.i,
confŭgĭo (3) ad (*with acc*)
recover *v.t*, rĕcŭpĕro (1) rĕcĭpĭo
(3); *v.i*, (from illness, etc.),
rĕvălesco (3), rĕfĭcĭor (3 *pass*), sē
collĭgĕre (3 reflex)

recovery rĕcŭpĕrātĭo, *f*; (from
illness), sălus, *f*
recreate *v.t*, rĕcrĕo (1)
recreation rĕmissĭo, *f*
recruit *nn*, tīro, *m*
recruit *v.t*, (enrol), conscrībo (3)
recruiting *nn*, dēlectus, *m*
rectify *v.t*, corrĭgo (3)
rectitude prŏbĭtas, *f*
recumbent rĕcŭbans
recur *v.i*, rĕdĕo (4)
red rŭber, rūfus; (redhanded), *adj*,
mănĭfestus
redden *v.t*, rŭbĕfăcĭo (3); *v.i.*
rŭbesco (3)
redeem *v.t*, rĕdĭmo (3)
redeemer lībĕrātor, *m*
redemption rĕdemptĭo, *f*
red-lead mĭnĭum, *n*
redness rŭbor, *m*
redouble *v.t*, ingĕmĭno (1)
redound rĕdundo (1)
redress *v.t*, rēstĭtŭo (3)
reduce *v.t*, rĕdĭgo (3)
reduction dēmĭnūtĭo, *f*; (taking by
storm), expugnātĭo, *f*
redundancy rĕdundantĭa, *f*
redundant sŭpervăcŭus
re-echo *v.i*, rĕsŏno (1)
reed ărundo, *f*
reef saxa, *n.pl*
reek *v.i*, fūmo (1)
reel v.i, (totter), văcillo (1)
re-elect *v.t*, rĕcrĕo (1)
re-establish *v.t*, rēstĭtŭo (3)
refectory cēnācŭlum, *n*
refer *v.t*, rĕfĕro *or* dēfĕro (*irreg*)
ad (*with acc*); (to — to),
perstringo (3), specto (1) ad (*with*
acc)
referee arbĭter, *m*
reference rătĭo, *f*
refill *v.t*, rĕplĕo (2)
refine *v.t*, (polish), expŏlĭo (4)
refined pŏlītus, hūmānus
refinement hūmānĭtas, *f*
refinery officīna, *f*
reflect *v.t*, rĕpercŭtĭo (3), reddo
(3); *v.i*, (ponder), rĕpŭto (1)
(ănĭmo) (in the mind)
reflection (image) ĭmāgo, *f*;
(thought), cōgĭtātĭo, *f*
reform ēmendātĭo, *f*

reform *v.t*, rēstǐtǔo (3); **(correct)**, corrǐgo (3); *v.i*, sē corrǐgĕre (3 *reflex*)
reformer ēmendātor, *m*
refract *v.t*, infringo (3)
refractory contǔmax
refrain from *v.i*, sē contǐnēre (2 *reflex*) ad (*with abl*)
refresh *v.t*, rĕcrĕo (1), rĕfǐcǐo (3)
refreshment (food) cǐbus, *m*
refuge perfǔgǐum, *n*; **(to take —)**, *v.i*, confǔgǐo (3) ad (*with acc*)
refugee *adj*, prŏfǔgus
refulgent splendǐdus
refund *v.t*, reddo (3)
refusal rĕcūsātǐo, *f*
refuse *nn*, purgāmentum, *n*
refuse *v.t*, rĕcūso (1); **(to — to do)** nōlo (*irreg*) (*with infi*n); **(say no)**, nĕgo (1)
refute *v.t*, rĕfello (3)
regain *v.t*, rĕcǐpǐo (3)
regal rēgālis
regale *v.t*, excǐpǐo (3)
regalia insignǐa, *n.pl*
regard *nn*, **(esteem)**, studǐum, *n*, hŏnor, *m*; **(consideration)**, rēspectus, *m*
regard v.t, **(look at)**, intǔĕor (2 *dep*); **(consider)**, hăbĕo (2); **(esteem)**, aestǐmo (1)
regardless neglĕgens
regency interregnum
regent interrex, *m*
regicide caedes (*f*) rēgis **(killing of a king)**
regiment lĕgǐo, *f*
region rĕgǐo, *f*, tractus, *m*
register tăbŭlae, *f.pl*
register *v.t*, perscrībo (3)
registrar tăbŭlārǐus, *m*
regret *nn*, dŏlor, *m*
regret *v.t*, **(repent of)**, *use* paenǐtet (2 *impers*) (*with acc. of subject*), *e.g.* **I repent of**, mē paenǐtet (*with genit*)
regular (correctly arranged) ordǐnātus, compŏsǐtus; **(customary)**, sollemnis
regularity ordo, *m*
regularly *adv*, **(in order)**, ordǐne; **(customarily)**, sollemnǐter
regulate *v.t*, ordǐno (1)

regulation (order) iussum, *n*; **(rule)**, praeceptum, *n*
rehabilitate *v.t*, rēstǐtǔo (3)
rehearsal (practice) exercǐtātǐo, *f*
rehearse *v.t*, **(premeditate)**, praemĕdǐtor (1 *dep*)
reign *nn*, regnum, *n*
reign *v.i*, regno (1)
reimburse *v.t*, rĕpendo (3)
rein *nn*, hăbēna, *f*
rein *v.t*, **(curb)**, frēno (1)
reinforce *v.t*, confirmo (1)
reinforcement (help) auxǐlǐum, *n*
reinstate *v.t*, rēstǐtǔo (3)
reiterate *v.t*, ǐtēro (1)
reject *v.t*, rĕǐcǐo (3)
rejection rĕiectǐo, *f*
rejoice *v.i*, gaudĕo (2)
rejoicing *nn*, laetǐtǐa, *f*
rejoin *v.i*, rĕdĕo (4)
relapse *v.i*, rĕcǐdo (3)
relate *v.t*, **(tell)**, narro (1), expōno (3); *v.i*, pertǐnĕo (2)
related (by birth) cognātus; **(by marriage)**, affinis; **(by blood)**, consanguǐnĕus; **(near)**, prŏpinquus
relation (relative) cognātus, *m*, affinis *m*; **(connection)**, rătǐo, *f*
relationship cognātǐo, *f*, affinǐtas, *f*
relative *nn*, cognātus, *m*, affinis, *m*
relative *adj*, compărātus **(compared)**
relax *v.t*, rĕmitto (3); *v.i*, rĕlanguesco (3)
relaxation rĕmissǐo, *f*
relay *v.t*, **(send)**, mitto (3)
relays of horses ĕqui dispŏsǐti, *m.pl* **(horses methodically arranged)**
release *nn*, lībĕrātǐo, *f*
release *v.t*, exsolvo (3) lībĕro (1)
relent *v.t*, rĕmitto (3)
relentless immǐsĕrǐcors
relevant *use vb*, pertǐnĕo (2) **(to concern)**
reliance fīdūcǐa, *f*
relic rĕlǐquǐae, *f, pl*
relief (alleviation) lĕvātǐo, *f*; **(help)**, auxǐlǐum, *n*
relieve *v.t*, lĕvo (1), rĕmitto (3);

(help), subvĕnĭo (4) (*with dat*); (of command, etc.), succĕdo (3) (*followed by in and acc. or by dat*)

religion rĕlĭgĭo, *f*, săcra, *n.pl*

religious rĕlĭgĭōsus, pĭus

relinquish *v.t*, rĕlinquo (3)

relish *nn*, stŭdĭum, *n*, săpor, *m*

relish *v.t*, frŭor (3 *dep. with abl*)

reluctance *use adj*, invītus (unwilling)

reluctant invītus

rely on *v.t*, confido (3) (*with dat. of person or abl. of thing*)

relying on *adj*, frētus (*with abl*)

remain *v.i*, mănĕo (2); (be left over), sūpersum (*irreg*)

remainder rĕlĭquum, *n*

remaining *adj*, rĕlĭquus

remains rĕlĭquĭae, *f*, *pl*

remand *v.t*, amplĭo (1)

remark *nn*, dictum, *n*

remark *v.t*, (say), dīco (3); (observe), observo (1)

remarkable insignis

remedy rĕmĕdĭum, *n*, mĕdĭcāmentum, *n*

remedy *v.t*, sāno (1); (correct); corrĭgo (3)

remember *v.i*, mĕmĭni (*v. defect. with genit*), rĕcordor (1 *dep. with acc*)

remembrance rĕcordātĭo, *f*, mĕmŏrĭa, *f*

remind *v.t*, mŏnĕo (2)

reminiscence rĕcordātĭo, *f*

remiss neglĕgens

remission (forgiveness) vĕnĭa, *f*; (release), sŏlūtĭo, *f*

remit *v.t*, rĕmitto (3)

remittance pĕcūnĭa, *f*

remnant rĕlĭquĭae, *f. pl*

remonstrate *v.i*, rĕclāmo (1) (*with dat*)

remorse conscĭentĭa, *f*

remorseless immĭsĕrĭcors, dūrus

remote rĕmōtus

remoteness longinquĭtas, *f*

removal (driving away) āmōtĭo, *f*; (sending away), rĕlēgātĭo, *f*; (— by force), raptus, *m*

remove *v.t*, rĕmŏvĕo (2); (send away), rĕlēgo (1); *v.i*, migro (1)

remunerate *v.t*, rĕmūnĕror (1 dep)

remuneration rĕmūnĕrātĭo, f

rend *v.t*, scindo (3)

render *v.t*, reddo (3)

rendezvous (to fix a —) lŏcum (et dĭem) constĭtŭo (3), (place (and day))

rending (severing) discĭdĭum, *n*

renegade (deserter) transfŭga, *c*

renew *v.t*, rĕnŏvo (1), rĕdintĕgro (1)

renewal rĕnŏvătĭo, *f*

renounce *v.t*, rĕnuntĭo (1), rĕmitto (3)

renovate *v.t*, rĕnŏvo (1)

renovation rĕstĭtūtĭo, *f*

renown fāma, *f*, glōrĭa, *f*

renowned clārus

rent *nn*, scissūra, *f*; (of houses, etc.), merces, *f*

rent *v.t*, (let), lŏco (1); (hire), condūco (3)

renunciation rĕpŭdĭātĭo, f

repair *v.t*, rĕfĭcĭo (3), sarcĭo (4)

repaired sartus

reparation sătisfactĭo, *f*

repast cībus, *m*

repay *v.t*, (grātĭam) rĕfĕro (*irreg*)

repayment sŏlūtĭo, *f*

repeal *nn*, abrŏgātĭo, *f*

repeal *v.t*, abrŏgo (1), rēscindo (3)

repeat *v.t*, ĭtĕro (1), reddo (3)

repeatedly *adv*, ĭdentĭdem

repel *v.t*, rĕpello (3)

repent *v.i*, paenĭtet (2 *impers*) (*with acc. of person and genit. of cause*), *e.g.* I repent of this deed, mē paenĭtet huius facti

repentance paenĭtentĭa, *f*

repentant paenĭtens

repetition ĭtērātĭo, *f*

replace *v.t*, rĕpōno (3); (substitute), substĭtŭo (3)

replenish *v.t*. rĕplĕo (2)

replete rĕplētus

reply *nn*, rēsponsum, *n*

reply *v.i*, rēspondĕo (2)

report *nn*, nuntĭus, *m*; (rumour), fāma, *f*; (bang), crĕpĭtus, *m*

report *v.t*, rĕfĕro (*irreg*), nuntĭo (1)

repose *nn*, quĭes, *f*
repose *v.i*, (rest) quĭesco (3)
repository rĕceptācŭlum, *n*
reprehend *v.t*, rĕprĕhendo (3)
reprehensible culpandus
represent *v.t*, exprĭmo (3), fingo
(3); (take the place of), persōnam
gĕro (3)
representation ĭmāgo, *f*
representative (deputy)
prōcūrātor, *m*
repress *v.t*, cŏhĭbĕo (2)
reprieve *nn*, (respite), mŏra, *f*
reprieve *v.t*, (put off), diffĕro
(*irreg*)
reprimand *nn*, rĕprĕhensĭo, *f*
reprimand *v.t*, rĕprĕhendo (3)
reprisal *use* poena, *f*,
(punishment)
reproach *nn*, exprŏbrātĭo, *f*,
opprŏbrĭum, *n*
reproach *v.t*, exprŏbro (1), ōbĭcĭo
(3) (*both with acc. of thing and
dat. of person*)
reproachful obiurgātōrĭus
reprobate *nn*, perdĭtus, *m*,
nĕbŭlo, *m*
reproduce *v.t*, rĕcrĕo (1)
reproof rĕprĕhensĭo, *f*, obiurgātĭo,
f, vĭtŭpĕrātĭo, *f*
reprove *v.t*, rĕprĕhendo (3),
obiurgo (1), vĭtŭpĕro (1)
reptile serpens, *f*
republic respublĭca, *f*
republican *adj*, pŏpŭlāris
repudiate *v.t*, rĕpŭdĭo (1)
repudiation rĕpŭdĭatĭo, *f*
repugnance ŏdĭum, *n*
repugnant āversus; (it is — to me,
I hate it), *use phr*, ŏdĭo esse (to be
hateful), *with dat. of person*
repulse *v.t*, rĕpello (3)
repulsive foedus, ŏdĭōsus
reputable hŏnestus
reputation, repute fāma, *f*; (good
—), existĭmātĭo, *f*; (bad —),
infāmĭa, *f*
request nn, rŏgātĭo, *f*
request *v.t*, rŏgo (1), prĕcor (1
dep)
require *v.t*, (demand), postŭlo (1)
(need), ĕgĕo (2) (*with abl*)
requirement (demand) postŭlātĭo,

f; or use adj, nĕcessārĭus
requisite *adj*, nĕcessārĭus
requisition postŭlātĭo, *f*
requite *v.t*, rĕpōno (3)
rescind *v.t*, rēscindo (3)
rescue *v.t*, ērĭpĭo (3)
rescue *nn*, lībĕrātĭo, *f*
research investīgātĭo, *f*
resemblance sĭmĭlĭtūdo, *f*
resemble *v.t*, rĕfĕro (*irreg*), sĭmĭlis
esse (*irreg*) (*with genit. or dat*)
resembling *adj*, sĭmĭlis
resent *v.t*, aegrē fĕro (*irreg*)
(tolerate with displeasure)
resentful īrācundus
resentment īra, *f*
reservation (restriction) exceptĭo,
f
reserve *nn*, (military), subsĭdĭum,
n; (of disposition), grăvĭtas, *f*
reserve *v.t*, servo (1); (put aside),
sēpōno (3)
reserved (of disposition) grăvis
reservoir lăcus, *m*
reside *v.i*, hăbĭto (1)
residence sēdes, *f.pl*, dŏmĭcĭlĭum,
n
resident incŏla, *c*
resign *v.i*, and *v.t*, concēdo (3);
(to — oneself to), sē committĕre
(3 *reflex. with* in *and* acc)
resignation (of office, etc.)
abdĭcātĭo, *f*; (of mind) aequus
ănĭmus, *m*
resin rēsīna, *f*
resist *v.t*, rĕsisto (3) (*with dat*)
resistance rĕpugnantĭa, *f, or use
vb*, rĕsisto (3) (to resist)
resolute firmus, fortis
resolution obstĭnātĭo, *f*,
constantĭa, *f*; (decision), *use vb*,
plăcet (it is resolved)
resolve *v.t*, (determine), stătŭo
(3); (solve), dissolvo (3)
resort to *v.t*, (a place), cĕlĕbro
(1); (have recourse to), confŭgĭo
(3) ad (*with acc*)
resort *nn*, (plan), consĭlĭum, *n*;
(last —), extrēma, *n.pl*
resound *v.i*, rĕsŏno (1)
resource (help) auxĭlĭum, *n*;
(wealth, means) ŏpes, *f, pl*
respect *nn*, (esteem),

observantĭa, *f*; (in all — s),
omnĭbus partĭbus; (in — of), *use*
abl. case, e.g. **stronger in respect
of number**, sŭpērĭor nŭmĕro
respect *v.t*, (esteem), observo (1);
(reverence), sispĭcĭo (3)
respectability hŏnestas, *f*
respectable hŏnestus
respectful observans
respecting *prep*, dē (*with abl*)
respective *use* quisque (each)
with sŭus (his own)
respiration respīrātĭo, *f*
respite (delay) mŏra, *f*
resplendent splendĭdus
respond *v.i*, rēspondĕo (2)
response rēsponsum, *n*
responsibility (duty, function)
officĭum, *n*; *or use imp. vb*,
ŏportet (it behoves)
responsible (to be — for) praesto
(1)
rest *nn*, (repose), quĭes, *f*, ōtĭum,
n; (remainder), *use adj*, rēlĭquus,
e.g. **the — of one's life**, rēlĭqua
vīta, *f*
rest *v.i*, quĭesco (3); (— on,
depend on), nītor (3 *dep*)
resting-place cŭbīle, *n*
restitution (to make —) *v.t*,
rēstĭtŭo (3)
restive *use phr*, qui nōn făcĭle
dŏmāri pŏtest (that cannot easily
be subdued)
restless inquĭētus
restlessness ĭnquĭes, *f*
restoration rēstĭtūtĭo, *f*
restore *v.t*, rēstĭtŭo (3)
restrain *v.t*, cŏercĕo (2), rēprĭmo
(3), cŏhĭbĕo (2)
restraint mŏdĕrātĭo, *f*
restrict *v.t*, circumscrībo (3)
restriction (bound) mŏdus, *m*
result *nn*, ēventus, *m*
result *v.i*, ēvĕnĭo (4)
resume *v.t*, rĕpĕto (3)
resurrection rēsurrectĭo, *f*
resuscitate *v.t*, rĕsuscĭto (1)
retail *v.t*, dīvendo (3)
retailer caupo, *m*
retain *v.l*, rĕtĭnĕo (2)
retainer sătelles, *c*; (*pl*) soldūrĭi,
m. pl

retake *v.t*, rĕcĭpĭo (3)
retaliate *v.t*, ulciscor (3 *dep*)
retaliation ultĭo, *f*
retard *v.t*, mŏror (1 *dep*)
reticent tăcĭturnus
retinue (companions) cŏmĭtes,
c.pl
retire *v.i*, (go away), rĕcēdo (3),
ăbĕo (4); (from a post, etc.),
dēcēdo (3); (retreat), sē rĕcĭpĕre (3
reflex)
retired rĕmōtus
retirement (act of —) rĕcessus, *m*;
(leisure), ōtĭum, *n*
retiring *adj*, vĕrēcundus
retort *v.t*, rĕfero (*irreg*)
retrace *v.t*, rĕpĕto (3)
retract *v.t*, rĕnuntĭo (1)
retreat *nn*, rĕceptus, *m*; (place of
refuge), rĕfŭgĭum, *n*
retreat *v.i*, sē rĕcĭpĕre (3 *reflex*)
retrench *v.t*, mĭnŭo (3)
retribution poena, *f*
retrieve *v.t*, rĕcŭpĕro (1)
retrograde *adj, use comp. adj*,
pēĭor (worse)
retrogression rĕgressus, *m*
retrospect *use vb*, rĕspĭcĭo (3) (to
look back)
return *nn*, (coming back), rĕdĭtus,
m; (giving back), rēstĭtūtĭo, *f*;
(profit), quaestus, *m*
return *v.t*, (give back), reddo (3),
rĕfĕro (*irreg*), v.i, (go back), rĕdĕo
(4)
reunite *v.t*, rĕconcĭlĭo (1)
reveal *v.t*, pătĕfăcĭo (3)
revel *nn*, cōmissātĭo, *f*
revel *v.i*, cōmissor (1 *dep*)
revelation pătĕfactĭo, *f*
revenge *nn*, ultĭo, *f*
revenge oneself on *v.t*, ulciscor (3
dep)
revengeful cŭpĭdus ulciscendi
(keen on revenge)
revenue vectīgal, *n*
reverberate *v.i*, rĕsŏno (1)
revere, reverence *v.t*, vĕnĕror (1
dep)
reverence vĕnĕrātĭo, *f*
revered vĕnĕrābĭlis
reverend vĕnĕrābĭlis
reverent rĕvĕrens

reverse (contrary) *adj*, contrārĭus
(opposite); (defeat), clādes
reverse *v.t*, inverto (3)
revert *v.i*, rĕdĕo (4)
review *nn*, rĕcognĭtĭo, *f*, rĕcensĭo,
f
review *v.t*, rĕcensĕo (2)
revile *v.t*, mălĕdīco (3) (*with dat*)
reviling *nn*, mălĕdictĭo, *f*
revise *v.t*, ēmendo (1)
revision ēmendātĭo, *f*
revisit *v.t*, rĕvīso (3)
revival rĕnŏvātĭo, *f*
revive *v.t*, rĕcrĕo (1), excĭto (1);
v.i, rĕvīvisco (3)
revocable rĕvŏcābĭlis
revoke *v.t*, abrŏgo (1)
revolt *nn*, dēfectĭo, f, sēdĭtĭo, f
revolt *v.i*, dēfĭcĭo (3)
revolting *adj*, (disgusting), foedus
revolution (turning round)
conversĭo, *f*; (political), nŏvae res,
f. pl
revolutionize *v.t*, nŏvo (1)
revolutionary sēdĭtĭŏsus
revolve *v.i*, sē volvĕre (3 *reflex*)
reward *nn*, praemĭum, *n*
reward *v.t*, rĕmunĕror (1 *dep*)
rewrite *v.t*, rēscrībo (3)
rhetoric rhētŏrĭca, *f*
rhetorical rhētŏrĭcus
Rhine Rhēnus, *m*
rhinoceros rhīnŏcĕros, *m*
rhubarb rādix Pontĭca, *f* (Black
Sea root)
rhyme (verse) versus, *m*
rhythm nŭmĕrus, *m*
rhythmical nŭmĕrōsus
rib costa, *f*
ribald obsēnus
ribbon taenĭa, *f*
rice ŏrȳza, *f*
rich dīves, lŏcŭples; (fertile),
pinguis
riches dīvĭtĭae, *f. pl*
richness ūbertas, *f*
rick (heap) ăcervus, *m*
rid *v.t*, lībĕro (1); (to get — of),
dēpōno (3), dēpello (3)
riddle aenigma, *n*; (in — s), per
ambāges
riddle *v.t*, (sift), cerno (3); (—
with holes), confŏdĭo (3)

ride *v.i*, vĕhor (3 *dep*); (— at
anchor), consisto (3)
ride (horseman) ĕquĕs, *m*
ridge (mountain —), iŭgum, *n*
ridicule *nn*, rīdĭcŭlum, *n*
ridicule *v.t*, irrīdĕo (2)
ridiculous rīdĭcŭlus
riding *nn*, ĕquĭtātĭo, *f*
rife frĕquens, crēber
rifle *v.t*, praedor (1 *dep*.)
rift rīma, *f*
rig *v.t*, armo (1)
rigging armāmentum, *n.pl*
right *adj*, (direction), dexter;
(true), rectus, vērus; (correct),
rectus; (fit), ĭdōnĕus; (— hand),
dextra (manus)
right *nn*, (moral), fas, *n*; (legal),
iūs, *n*
rightly adv, rectē, vērē
right *v.t*, rēstĭtŭo (3)
righteous iustus
righteousness prŏbĭtas, *f*
rightful iustus
rigid rĭgĭdus, dūrus
rigorous dūrus
rigour dūrĭtĭa, *f*
rill rīvŭlus, *m*
rim ōra, *f*, lābrum, *n*
rime prŭīna, *f*
rind crusta, *f*
**ring (finger, etc.), ānŭlus, *m*;
(circle), orbis, *m*
ring *v.i*, tinnĭo (4); (surround)
circŭmĕo (4)
ringing *nn*, tinnītus, *m*
ringing *adj*, tinnŭlus
ringleader auctor, *m*
ringlet cincinnus, *m*
rinse *v.t*, collŭo (3)
riot turba, *f*, tŭmultus, *m*; (to
make a —), tŭmultum făcĭo (3)
riotous turbŭlentus; (extravagant),
luxŭrĭōsus
rip *v.t*, scindo (3)
ripe mātūrus
ripen *v.i*, mātūresco (3); *v.t*,
mātūro (1)
ripeness mātūrĭtas, *f*
ripple *v.i*, (tremble), trĕpĭdo (1)
rise *nn*, (of sun, etc., *or* origin),
ortus, *m*
rise *v.i*, surgo (3); (of sun, etc.),

ŏrĭor (4 *dep*); **(in rank)**, cresco
(3); **(in rebellion)**, consurgo (3)
rising *nn*, ortus, *m*; **(in rebellion)**,
mōtus, *m*
rising (ground) *nn*, clīvus, *m*
risk *nn*, pĕrīcŭlum, *n*
risk *v.t*, pĕrīclĭtor (1 *dep*)
ritual rītus, *m*
rival *nn*, aemŭlus, *m*, rīvālis, *c*
ribal *v.t*, aemŭlor (1 *dep*)
rivalry aemŭlātĭo, *f*
river *nn*, flūmen, *n*, flŭvĭus, *m*
riverbank rīpa, *f*
riverbed alvĕus, *m*
rivet clāvus, *m*
rivulet rīvŭlus, *m*
road vĭa, *f*, ĭter, *n*; **(to make a —)**,
vĭam mūnĭo (4)
road-making mūnītĭo, (*f*) vĭārum
roadstead (for ships) stătĭo, *f*
roam *v.i*, văgor (1 *dep*), erro (1)
roaming *adj*, văgus
road *nn*, frĕmĭtus, *m*
road *v.i*, frĕmo (3)
roast *v.t*, torrĕo (2)
roasted assus
rob *v.t*, spŏlĭo (1) (*with acc. of
person robbed, abl. of thing
taken*)
robber lătro, *m*
robbery lătrōcĭnĭum, *n*
robe vestis, *f*, vestīmentum, *n*;
(woman's —), stŏla, *f*; **(— of
state)**, trăbĕa, *f*; **(— of kings)**,
purpŭra, *f*
robe *v.t*, vestĭo (4), indŭo (3)
robust rōbustus
rock rūpes, *f*
rock *v.t*, ăgĭto (1)
rocky scŏpŭlōsus
rod virga, *f*; **(fishing —)**, ărundo, *f*
roe căprĕa, *f*; **(of fish)**, ōva, *n.pl*
(eggs)
rogue scĕlestus, *m*
roguery nēquĭtĭa, *f*
roll *nn*, **(something rolled up)**,
vŏlūmen, *n*; **(names)**, album, *n*
roll *v.t*, volvo (3); *v.i*, volvor (3
pass)
roller cўlindrus, *m*
rolling *adj*, vŏlūbĭlis
Roman Rōmānus
romance (story) fābŭla, *f*

romance *v.i*, fābŭlor (1 *dep*)
romantic (fabulous) commentĭcĭus
Rome Rōma, *f*
romp *v.i*, lūdo (3)
romp *nn*, lūsus, *m*
roof *nn*, tectum, *n*
roof *v.t*, tĕgo (3)
rook (raven) corvus, *m*
room conclāve, *n*; **(space)**,
spătĭum, *n*; **(bed —)**, cŭbĭcŭlum,
n; **(dining —)** trīclīnĭum, *n*
roomy căpax
roost *nn*, pertĭca, *f*
root rādix, *f*; **(to strike — s,
become rooted)**, rādīces ăgo (3);
(— ed to the spot), dēfixus
rope fūnis, *m*, restis, *f*, rŭdens, *m*
rosary (garden) rŏsārĭum, *n*
rose rŏsa, *f*
rosemary ros mărīnus, *m*
rostrum rostra, *n.pl*
rosy rŏsĕus
rot *nn*, tābes, *f*
rot *v.i*, pūtesco (3)
rotate *v.i*, sē volvĕre (3 *reflex*)
rotation turbo, *m*
rotten pŭtrĭdus
rotundity rŏtundĭtas, *f*
rouge *nn*, fūcus, *m*
rouge *v.t*, fūco (1)
rough asper; **(weather)**, ătrox; **(of
sea)**, turbĭdus; **(of manner)**,
incultus
roughness aspĕrĭtas, *f*
round *adj*, rŏtundus
round *adv*, circum
round *prep*, circum (*with acc*)
round *v.t*, **(to make —)**, rŏtundo
(1), curvo (1); **(to — off)**,
conclūdo (3); *v.i*, **(to go —)**,
circŭmăgor (3 *pass*)
roundabout *adj*, dēvĭus
rouse *v.t*, excĭto (1)
rout *nn*, **(flight, defeat)**, fŭga, *f*
rout *v.t*, fŭgo (1)
route ĭter, *n*
routine ūsus, *m*
rove *v.i*, văgor (1 *dep*)
roving *nn*, văgātĭo, *f*
row (line) ordo, *m*; **(quarrel)**, rixa,
f; **(noise)**, strĕpĭtus, *m*
row *v.i*, rēmĭgo (1)
rowing *nn*, rēmĭgĭum, *n*

royal rēgĭus
royalty regnum, *n*
rub *v.t*, tĕro (3), frĭco (1); (— out), dēlĕo (2)
rubbish quisquĭlĭae, *f. pl*
rubicund rŭbĭcundus
ruby *nn*, carbuncŭlus, *m*
ruby *adj*, purpŭrĕus
rudder gŭbernācŭlum, *n*
ruddy rŭbĭcundus
rude (person) asper, ĭnurbānus
rudeness ĭnhūmānĭtas, *f*
rudimentary incŏhātus (incomplete)
rudiments ĕlĕmenta, *n.pl*
rue *nn*, rūta, *f*
rueful maestus
ruff torquis, *m. or f*
ruffian perdĭtus, *m*, lătro, *m*
ruffianly *adj*, scĕlestus
ruffle *v.t*, ăgĭto (1)
rug strāgŭlum, *n*
rugged asper
ruin exĭtĭum, *n*, rŭīna, *f*; (building), părĭĕtĭnae, *f. pl*
ruin *v.t*, perdo (3)
ruinous exĭtĭōsus, damnōsus
rule *nn*, (law), lex, *f*; (precept), praeceptum, *n*; (pattern), norma, *f*; (for measuring), rēgŭla, *f*; (government), impĕrĭum, *n*
rule *v.t*, rĕgo (3); *v.i*, regno (1)
ruler (person) dŏmĭnus, *m*; (measurement), rēgŭla, *f*
rumble *nn*, mumur, *n*
rumble *v.i*, murmŭro (1), mūgĭo (4)
ruminate *v.t*, cōgĭto (1)
rummage *v.t*, rīmor (1 *dep*)
rumour *nn*, rūmor, *m*, fāma, *f*
rump clūnes, *f. pl*
rumple *v.t*, corrūgo (1)
run *v.i*, curro (3); (— about), hūc illūc curro (3); (— after), persĕquor (3 *dep*); (— away), fŭgio (3); (— aground), impingor (3 *pass*), inflīgor (3 *pass*); (— back), rĕcurro (3); (— down), dēcurro (3); (— forward), prōcurro (3); (— into), incurro (3); (— out), excurro (3); (— over, with vehicle, etc.), obtĕro (3); (— through), percurro (3)

runaway *adj*, fŭgĭtīvus
runner cursor, *m*
running *nn*, cursus, *m*
running *adj*, (water), vīvus
rupture (disease) hernĭa, *f*
rupture *v.t*, rumpo (3)
rural rustĭcus
rush *nn*, (plant), iuncus, *m*; (rushing, running), impĕtus, *m*
rush *v.i*, rŭo (3); (— forward), sē prōrĭpĕre (3 *reflex*); (— into), irrŭo (3); (— out), sē effundĕre (3 *reflex*)
rusk crustum, *n*
russet rūfus
rust *nn*, rōbīgo, *f*
rustic *adj*, rustĭcus
rusticate *v.i*, rustĭcor (1 *dep*); *v.t*, rēlēgo (1)
rusticity rustĭcĭtas, *f*
rustle *v.i*, crĕpo (1)
rustle, rustling *nn*, sŭsurrus, *m*
rusty rōbīgĭnōsus
rut orbĭta, *f*
ruthless immītis, sĕvērus
rye sĕcāle, *n*

S

Sabbath sabbăta, *n.pl*
sable *adj*, (black), āter
sabre glădĭus, *m*
sack (bag) saccus, *m*; (pillage), dīreptĭo, *f*
sack *v.t*, (pillage), dīrĭpĭo (3)
sackcloth saccus, *m*
sacrament săcrāmentum, *n*
sacred săcer, sanctus
sacredness sanctĭtas, *f*
sacrifice săcrĭfĭcĭum, *n*; (the victim), hostĭa, *f*
sacrifice *v.i*, săcrĭfĭco (1); *v.t*, immŏlo (1)
sacrificial săcrĭfĭcus
sacrilege săcrĭlĕgĭum, *n*; *or use vb*, dīrĭpĭo (3) **(to plunder)**
sad tristis
sadden *v.t*, tristĭtĭă affĭcĭo (3) **(affect with sadness)**
saddle *nn*, ĕphhippĭum, *n*
saddle *v.t*, sterno (3); (impose), impōno (3)
sadness tristĭtĭă, *f*

safe (free from danger) tūtus;
(having escaped from danger),
incŏlŭmis
safe-conduct fĭdes, f
safeguard (act of —) cautĭo, f;
(defence), prōpugnācŭlum, n
safely adv, tūtō
safety sălus, f
saffron nn, crŏcus, m
saffron adj, crŏcĕus
sagacious prūdens, săgax
sagacity prūdentĭa, f, săgācĭtas, f
sage (wise man) săpĭens, m;
(plant), salvĭa, f
sail nn, vēlum, n; (to set —), vēla
do (1)
sail v.i, nāvĭgo (1), vĕhor (3
pass); (to go by means of sails),
vēla făcĭo (3)
sailing nn, nāvĭgātĭo, f
sailor nauta, m
saint sanctus, m
saintly sanctus
sake (for the — of), prep, causā
(with genit); (on behalf of), prō
(with abl), ŏb, propter (with acc)
salad ăcētārĭa, n.pl
salary merces, f
sale vendĭtĭo, f; (auction), hasta, f
salient adj, primus (first)
saline salsus
saliva sălīva, f
sallow pallĭdus
sally nn, ēruptĭo, f
sally v.i, ēruptĭōnem făcĭo (3)
salmon salmo, m
saloon ātrĭum, n
salt nn, sal, m
salt adj, salsus
salt v.t, sāle condĭo (4) (season
with salt)
saltcellar sălīnum, n
saltmines sălīnae, f. pl
salubrious sălūbris
salutary sălūtāris; (useful), ūtĭlis
salutation sălūtātĭo, f
salute v.t, sălūto (1)
salvation sălus, f
salve unguentum, n
salver scŭtella, f, pătella, f
same prep, īdem; (the same as),
īdem qui, īdem atque; (in the —
place), adv, ĭbīdem (at the —

time), sĭmŭl; (fixed, constant),
constans
sample exemplum, n
sanctification sanctĭfĭcātĭo, f
sanctify v.t, consĕcro (1)
sanction auctōrĭtas, f; (penalty)
poena, f
sanction v.t, fătum făcĭo (3)
sanctity sanctĭtas, f
sanctuary fānum, n, templum, n:
(refuge), rĕfŭgĭum, n
sand hărēna, f
sandal sŏlĕa, f
sandstone tōfus, m
sandy hărēnōsus
sane sānus
sanguinary crŭentus, sanguĭnārĭus
sanguine use spēs, f, (hope)
sanity mens sāna, f
sap nn, sūcus, m
sap v.t, subrŭo (3)
sapient adj, săpĭens
sapless ārĭdus
sapling arbor nŏvella
sappers (military) mūnītōres, m.
pl
sapphire sapphīrus, f
sarcasm căvillātĭo, f, (scoffing)
sarcastic ăcerbus
sarcophagus sarcŏphăgus, m
sash cingŭlum, n
satanic nĕfandus
satchel lŏcŭlus, m
satellite (star) stella, f;
(attendant), sătelles, c
satiate v.t, sătĭo (1)
satiety sătĭĕtas, f
satire sătŭra, f
satirical (bitter) ăcerbus
satirize v.t, perstringo (3)
satirist scriptor sătĭrĭcus, m
satisfaction (inner) vŏluptas, f;
(compensation, punishment),
poena,
satisfactorily adv, ex sententĭā
satisfactory ĭdōnĕus, or sătis
(enough)
satisfied contentus
satisfy v.t, (a need), explĕo (2),
(with dat); (convince), persuādĕo
(2)
satrap sătrăpes, m
saturate v.t, sătŭro (1)

satyr sătȳrus, *m*
sauce condīmentum, *n*
saucepan cācăbus, *m*, cortīna
saucer pătella, *f*
saucy pĕtŭlans
saunter *v.i*, văgor (1 *dep*)
sausage farcīmen, *n*
savage *adj*, fĕrus, ătrox, effĕrātus
savageness, savagery fĕrĭtas, *f*, saevĭtĭa, *f*
save *v.t*, servo (1); **(defend)**, tŭĕor (2 *dep*); **(lay by)**, rĕservo (1)
save *prep*, praeter (*with acc*)
saving *nn*, conservātĭo, *f*
savings pĕcūlĭum, *n*
saviour servātor, *m*
savour *nn*, săpor, *m*
savour *v.t*, săpĭo (3)
savoury *adj*, condītus
saw serra, *f*
saw *v.t*, serrā sĕco (1) **(cut with a saw)**
sawdust scŏbis, *f*
say *v.t*, dīco (3), lŏquor (3 *dep*); **(to — that something will not ...)**, *use* nĕgo (1) **(to deny)**; **(it is said)**, fertur
saying *nn*, dictum, *n*
scab crusta, *f*
scabbard vāgīna, *f*
scabby scăber
scaffold (frame) māchĭna, *f*; **(execution)**, supplĭcĭum, *n*
scald *nn*, ădusta, *n.pl*
scale (pair of —s) lībra, *f*; **(of fish)**, squāma, *f*; **(gradation)**, grădus, *m*
scale *v.t*, **(climb with ladders)**, scālis ascendo (3)
scaling-ladders scālae, *f. pl*
scallop pecten, *m*
scalp cŭtis, *f*, **(skin)**
scalpel scalpellum, *n*
scamp scĕlestus, *m*
scamper *v.i*, fūgĭo (3)
scan *v.t*, contemplor (1 *dep*)
scandal opprŏbrium, *n*; **(disparagement)** obtrectātĭo, *f*
scandalous infāmis
scanty exĭgŭus
scantiness exĭgŭĭtas, *f*
scapegrace nĕbŭlo, *m*
scar cĭcātrix, *f*

scarce rārus
scarcely *adv*, vix, aegrĕ
scarcity (of supplies, etc.) ĭnŏpĭa, *f*
scare *v.t*, terrĕo (2)
scarecrow formīdo, *f*
scarf chlămys, *f*
scarlet *nn*, coccum, *n*
scarlet *adj*, coccĭnĕus
scathing ăcerbus
scatter *v.t*, spargo (3); *v.i*, sē spargĕre (3 *reflex*)
scene (of play) scēna, *f*; **(spectacle)**, spectācŭlum, *n*
scenery (natural —) *use* rĕgĭo, *f*, **(region)**
scent (sense of smell) ŏdōrātus, *m*; **(the smell itself)**, ŏdor, *m*
scent *v.t*, **(discern by smell)**, ŏdōror (1 *dep*)
scented ŏdōrātus
sceptical dŭbĭtans
sceptre sceptrum, *n*
schedule tăbŭla, *f*
scheme *nn*, consĭlĭum, *n*
scheme *v.t*, consĭlĭum căpĭo (3) **(make a plan)**
scholar (pupil) discĭpŭlus, *m*; **(learned man)**, doctus, *m*
scholarly doctus
scholarship littĕrae, *f. pl*
school lūdus, *m*, schŏla
school *v.t*, ērŭdĭo (4)
schoolmaster măgister, *m*
schoolmistress măgistra, *f*
schooner phăsēlus, *m*
sciatica ischĭas, *f*
science scĭentĭa, *f*, discĭplīna, *f*, rătĭo, *f*
scientific *use genit. of nouns above*
scimitar ăcĭnāces, *m*
scintillate *v.i*, scintillo (1)
scion prōles, *f*
scissors forfĭces, *f. pl*
scoff at *v.t*, irrīdĕo (2)
scoffer irrīsor, *m*
scoffing *nn*, irrīsĭo, *f*
scold *v.t*, obiurgo (1), incrĕpo (1)
scoop out *v.t*, căvo (1)
scoop *nn*, trulla, *f*
scope (room) campus, *m*
scorch *v.t*, ambūro (3)

scorched torrĭdus
scorching torrĭdus
score (total) summa, *f*; (account,
  reckoning), rătĭo, *f*; (mark), nŏta,
  f
score *v.t*, (note, mark), nŏto (1);
  (— a victory), victōrĭam rĕporto
  (1)
scorn *nn*, contemptus, *m*
scorn *v.t*, sperno (3), contemno
  (3)
scornful sŭperbus
scorpion scorpĭo, *m*
scoundrel nēbŭlo, *m*
scour *v.t*, (clean), tergĕo (2); (run
  over) percurro (3)
scourge *nn*, (whip), flăgellum, *n*;
  (pest), pestis, *f*, pernĭcĭes, *f*
scourge *v.t*, verbĕro (1)
scourging *nn*, verbĕra, *n.pl*
scout explōrātor, *m*
scout *v.t*, (spy out), spĕcŭlor (1 *dep*)
scowl *nn*, frontis contractĭo, *f*
scowl *v.i*, frontem contrăho (3),
  (contract the brow)
scramble for *v.t*, *use phr*, inter sē
  certāre (struggle among
  themselves)
scrap frustrum, *n*
scrape *v.t*, rādo (3)
scraper strĭgĭlis, *f*
scratch *v.t*, rādo (3), scalpo (3)
scream *nn*, vōcĭfĕrātĭo, *f*
scream *v.i*, vōcĭfĕror (1 *dep*)
screech owl ŭlŭla, *f*
screen tĕgĭmen, *n*
screen *v.t*, tĕgo (3)
screw *nn*, clāvus, *m*
scribble *v.t*, scrībo (3)
scribe scrība, *m*
Scripture Scriptūra, *f*
scroll vŏlūmen, *n*
scrub *v.t*, tergĕo (2)
scruple (religious, etc.) rĕlĭgĭo, *f*
scrupulous rĕlĭgĭōsus, dīlĭgens
scrutinize *v.t*, scrūtor (1 *dep*)
scrutiny scrūtātĭo, *f*
scuffle *nn*, rixa, *f*
scull (oar) rēmus, *m*; (*v.i*, rēmĭgo
  (1))
sculptor sculptor, *m*
sculpture (art of —) sculptūra, *f*;
  (the work itself), ŏpus, *n*

scum spūma, *f*
scurf furfur, *m*
scurrility prŏcācĭtas, *f*
scurrilous scurrīlis, prŏcax
scurvy foedus
scuttle *v.t*, (a ship), *use phr*,
  nāvem ultro dēprĭmo (3) (sink
  the ship of their own accord)
scythe falx, *f*
sea măre, *n*, (to be at —), nāvĭgo
  (1)
sea *adj*, mărĭtĭmus, mărīnus
seacoast ōra mărĭtĭma, *f*
seafaring *adj*, mărĭtĭmus
seafight pugna nāvālis, *f*
seagull lărus, *m*
seal *nn*, (of letter), signum, *n*;
  (animal), phōca, *f*
seal *v.t*, (letter), signo (1); (close
  up), comprĭmo (3)
sealing-wax cēra, *f*
seam sūtūra, *f*
seaman nauta, *m*
sear *v.t*, ădūro (3)
search for *v.t*, quaero (3);
  (explore), rīmor (1 *dep*)
search *nn*, investīgātĭo, *f*
seasick *adj*, nausĕābundus; (to be
  —), *v.i*, nausĕo (1)
seasickness nausĕa, *f*
season tempus, *n*, tempestas, *f*;
  (right time), tempus, *n*
season *v.t*, condĭo (4)
seasonable tempestīvus
seasoned (flavoured) condītus;
  (hardened), dūrātus
seasoning *nn*, condīmentum, *n*
seat sēdes, *f*, sĕdīle, *n*, sella, *f*;
  (home), dŏmĭcĭlĭum, *n*: *v.t*.
  collŏco (1)
seaweed alga, *f*
secede *v.i*, dēcēdo (3)
secession dēfectĭo, *f*
secluded sēcrētus
seclusion sōlĭtūdo, *f*
second *adj*, sĕcundus; (— of two),
  alter; (for the — time), *adv*,
  ĭtĕrum; (— ly), *adv*, de inde
second *nn*, (time), mōmentum, *n*
second *v.t*, adiŭvo (1)
secondary infĕrĭor
second-hand ūsu trītus (worn
  with usage)

secrecy sēcrētum, *n*
secret arcāna, *n.pl*
secret *adj*, occultus, arcānus;
(hidden), clandestīnus; (to keep
something —), *v.t*, cēlo (1)
secretary scrība, *m*
secrete *v.t*, cēlo (1), abdo (3)
secretly *adv*, clam
sect secta, *f*
section pars, *f*
secular (not sacred), prŏfānus
secure *v.t*, mūnĭo (4), firmo (1),
lĭgo (1) (tie up)
secure *adj*, tūtus
security sălus, *f*; (guarantee),
pignus, *n*; (to give —), căvĕo (2)
sedate grăvis
sedative mĕdĭcāmentum
sŏpōrĭfĕrum
sedentary sĕdentārĭus
sedge ulva, *f*
sediment faex, *f*
sedition sēdĭtĭo, *f*
seditious sēdĭtĭōsus
seduce *v.t*, tento (1), sollĭcĭto (1)
seducer corruptor, *m*
seduction corruptēla, *f*
sedulous assĭdŭus
see *v.t* vĭdĕo (2), cerno (3),
aspĭcĭo (3); (to — to it that ...),
cūro (1) ad (*with gerund phr*);
(understand), intellĕgo (3)
seed sēmen, *n* (literal and
metaphorical)
seedling arbor nŏvella, *f*
seedy grānōsus
seeing that *conj*, cum
seek *v.t*, quaero (3), pĕto (3),
affecto (1)
seem *v.i*, vĭdĕor (2 *pass.*)
seeming *nn*, spĕcĭes, *f*
seemly *adj*, dĕcōrus, (it is —),
dĕcet (2 *impers*)
seer vātes, *c*
seethe *v.i*, fervĕo (2)
segment segmentum, *n*
segregate *v.t*, sēcerno (3)
seize *v.t*, răpĭo (3), corrĭpĭo (3),
prendo (3), occŭpo (1); (of
illness, passion, etc.), affĭcĭo (3)
seizure comprĕhensĭo, *f*
seldom *adv*, rārō
select *v.t*, lĕgo (3)

select *adj*, lectus
selection dēlectus, *m*
self *pron*, (emphatic), ipse;
(reflexive), sē
self-confident confīdens
self-satisfied contentus
selfish, selfishness, (to be —) sē
ămāre (1 *reflex*)
sell *v.t*, vendo (3)
seller vendĭtor, *m*
semblance ĭmāgo, *f*
semicircle hēmĭcyclĭum, *n*
senate sĕnātus, *m*
senate house cūrĭa, *f*
senator sĕnātor, *m*
send *v.t*, mitto (3); (— away),
dīmitto (3); (— back), rĕmitto
(3); (— for), arcesso (3); (—
forward), praemitto (3); (— in),
immitto (3)
senile sĕnīlis
senior, (in age) nātu maior
sensation (feeling) sensus, *m*;
mōtus (*m*) ănĭmi (impulse)
sensational nŏtābĭlis
sense (feeling) sensus, *m*;
(understanding), prūdentĭa, *f*;
(meaning), sententĭa, *f*
senseless (unconscious) *use adv.*
phr, sensu ablāto (with feeling
withdrawn); (stupid), sōcors
sensible prūdens
sensitive sensĭlis
sensitiveness mollĭtĭa
sensual lĭbīdĭnōsus
sensuality lĭbīdo, *f*
sentence (criminal) iūdĭcĭum, *n*;
(writing, etc.), sententĭa, *f*
sentence *v.t*, damno (1)
sententious sententĭōsus
sentiment (feeling) sensus, *m*;
(opinion), ŏpīnĭo, *f*
sentimental mollis
sentimentality mollĭtĭa, *f*
sentinel vĭgil, *m*; (to be on —
duty), in stătĭōne esse (*irreg*)
separable dīvĭdŭus
separate *v.t*, sēpăro (), dīvĭdo (3),
sēiungo (3), sēcerno (3)
separate *adj*, sēpărātus, sēcrētus
separately *adv*, sēpărātim
separation sēpărātĭo, *f*
September September (mensis)

sepulchre sĕpulcrum, *n*
sequel (outcome) exĭtus, *m*
sequence ordo, *m*
serene tranquillus
serf servus, *m*
series sĕrĭes, *f*
serious grăvis
seriousness grăvĭtas
sermon ōrātĭo, *f*
serpent serpens, *f*
serried confertus
servant mĭnister, *m*, fămŭlus, *m*,
   servus, *m*
serve *v.t*, servĭo (4), (*with dat*);
   (at table, etc.), mĭnistro (1); (in
   the army), stīpendĭa mĕrĕor (2
   dep); (to — as), esse (*irreg*) (*with*
   prō *and abl*)
service mĭnistĕrĭum, *n*, ŏpĕra,
   (military), mīlĭtĭa, *f*
serviceable ūtĭlis
servile servīlis
servitude servītus, *f*
session (assembly) conventus, *m*
set *nn*, (of people), glŏbus, *m*
set *adj*, stătus
set *v.t*, (place), stătŭo (3), pōno
   (3); *v.i*, (of the sun), occĭdo (3);
   (— about, begin), incĭpĭo (3);
   (— aside), *v.t*, sēpōno (3);
   (— down in writing), nŏto (1);
   (— free), lībĕro (1); (set off *or*
   out), *v.i*, prŏfīciscor (3 *dep*);
   (— up), *v.t*, stătŭo (3)
settee lectŭlus, *m*
setting (of sun) occāsus, *m*
settle *v.t*, constĭtŭo (3); (a
   dispute), compōno (3); (debt),
   solvo (3); *v.i*, (in a home, etc.),
   consīdo (3)
settled certus
settlement (colony) cŏlōnĭa, *f*;
   (— of an affair), compŏsĭtĭo, *f*
settle cŏlōnus, *m*
seven septem; (— hundred),
   septingenti; (— times), *adv*,
   septĭes
seventeen septendĕcim
seventeenth septĭmus dĕcĭmus
seventh septĭmus
seventieth septŭāgēsĭmus
seventy septŭāginta
sever *v.t*, sēpăro (1), sēiungo (3)

several complūres, ălĭquot
severe sĕvērus, dūrus
severity sĕvērĭtas, *f*, ăcerbĭtas, *f*
sew *v.t*, sŭo (3)
sewer (drain) clŏāca, *f*
sex sexus, *m*
sexagenarian sexāgēnārĭus, *m*
sexual *use nn*, sexus, *m*, (sex)
shabbiness sordes, *f. pl*
shabby sordĭdus
shackle *v.t*, vincŭlis constringo
   (3) (bind with chains)
shackle(s) *nn*, vincŭla, *n.pl*
shade *nn*, umbra, *f*; (the —s of
   the dead), mānes, *m. pl*
shade *v.t*, ŏpāco (1)
shadow umbra, *f*
shadowy ŏpācus, ĭnānis
shady ŏpācus
shaft (of a weapon) hastīle, *n*; (an
   arrow), săgitta, *f*; (of a mine),
   pŭtĕus, *m*
shaggy hirtus, hirsūtus
shake *v.t*, quătĭo (3), ăgĭto (1)
   lăbĕfăcĭo (3); *v.i*, trĕmo (3),
   trĕpido (1); (— hands), dextras
   iungo (3) (join right hands)
shaking *nn*, quassātĭo, *f*
shallow *adj*, (sea), vădōsus, brĕvis
shallows *nn*, văda, *n.pl*
sham *adj*, sĭmŭlātus
sham *nn*, sĭmŭlātĭo, *f* (pretence)
sham *v.t*, sĭmŭlo (1)
shamble *use* turba, *f*
shame *nn*, (feeling), pŭdor, *m*;
   (disgrace), dēdĕcus, *n*
shame *v.t*, rŭbōrem incŭtĭo (3)
   (*with dat*)
shamefaced vĕrēcundus
shameful turpis
shamefulness turbĭtūdo, *f*
shameless impŭdens
shamelessness impŭdentĭa, *f*
shamrock trĭfŏlĭum, *n*
shank crus, *n*
shape *nn*, forma, *f*
shape *v.t*, formo (1)
shapeless informis
shapely formōsus
share (part) pars, *f*; (plough —),
   vōmer, *m*
share *v.t*, partĭor (4 *dep*)
sharer partĭceps, *c*

shark pistrix, *f*
sharp ăcūtus, ācer
sharp-sighted perspĭcax
sharp-witted ăcūtus
sharpen *v.t*, ăcŭo (3)
sharply *adv*, ăcūte, ācrĭter
sharpness (of tongue) aspĕrĭtas, *f*;
(mental), ăcūmen, *n*
shatter *v.t*, frango (3)
shave *v.t*, rādo (3)
shawl ămĭcŭlum, *n*
she *pron*, illa, ĕa, haec, ista
sheaf mănĭpŭlus, *m*
shear *v.t*, tondĕo (2)
shearing *nn*, tonsūra, *f*
shears forfex, *f*
sheath vāgīna, *f*
sheathe *v.t*, in vāgīnam rĕcondo
(3) **(put back into the sheath)**
shed *nn*, tŭgŭrĭum, *n*
shed *v.t*, fundo (3)
sheen fulgor, *m*
sheep ŏvis, *f*
sheepfold saeptum, *n*
sheepskin pellis ŏvilla, *f*
sheepish sōcors, *or use adv. phr*,
dēmisso vultu **(with downcast
face)**
sheer (steep) abruptus; **(pure,
absolute)**, mĕrus
sheet (cloth) lintĕum, *n*; **(paper)**,
schĕda, *f*; **(— of a sail)**, pes, *m*
shelf plŭtĕus, *m*
shell concha, *f*, crusta, *f*
shellfish conchȳlĭum, *n*
shelter *nn*, perfŭgĭum, *n*, tectum,
n
shelter *v.t*, tĕgo (3); *v.i, use phr*,
ad perfŭgĭum sē conferre *(irreg)*
(betake oneself to shelter)
shelving *adj*, dēclīvis
shepherd pastor, *m*
shield *nn*, scūtum, *n*
shield *v.t*, tĕgo (3), dēfendo (3)
shift (change) vīcissĭtūdo, *f.*
shift *v.t*, mūto (1); *v.i*, mūtor (1
pass)
shifty versūtus
shin crūs, *n*
shine *v.i*, lūcĕo (2), fulgĕo (2)
ship *nn*, nāvis, *f*; **(war —)**, nāvis
longa, *f*; **(transport —)**, nāvis
ŏnĕrārĭa, *f*

ship *v.t*, **(put on board)**, in nāvem
impōno (3); **(transport)**, nāve
transporto (1)
ship-owner nāvĭcŭlārĭus, *m*
shipping nāvīgĭa, *n.pl*
shipwreck naufrăgĭum, *n*
shipwrecked naufrăgus
shirt sŭbūcŭla, *f*
shiver *v.i*, horrĕo (2)
shivering *nn*, horror, *m*
shoal (water) vădum, *n*; **(fish)**,
exāmen, *n*
shock offensĭo, *f*, ictus, *m*; **(of
battle)**, concursus, *m*
shock *v.t*, offendo (3), percŭtĭo
(3)
shocking *adj*, ătrox
shoe *nn*, calcĕus, *m*
shoe *v.t*, calcĕo (1)
shoemaker sūtor, *m*
shoot *nn*, **(sprout)**, surcŭlus, *m*
shoot *v.t*, **(a missile)**, mitto (3);
v.i, **(— along, across)**, vŏlo (1)
shooting-star fax caelestis, *f*
shop tăberna, *f*
shopkeeper tăbernārĭus, *m* (*pl.
only*)
shore lītus, *n*, ōra, *f*
shore-up *v.t*, fulcĭo (4)
short brĕvis, ĕxĭgŭus; **(— cut)**, via
compendĭārĭa, *f*; **(in —)**, *adv*,
dēnĭque
shortage ĭnŏpĭa, *f* **(lack)**
shortcoming dēlictum, *n*
shorten *v.t*, contrăho (3)
shortly *adv*, **(of time)**, brĕvi;
(briefly), brĕvĭter
shortness brĕvĭtas, *f*
shot (firing) ictus, *m*
shoulder hŭmĕrus, *m*; **(— blade)**,
scăpŭlae, *f. pl*
shoulder *v.t*, fĕro *(irreg)* **(to bear)**
shout *nn*, clāmor, *m*
shout *v.i*, clāmo (1)
shove *v.t*, trūdo (3)
shovel pāla, *f*
show *nn*, **(appearance)**, spĕcĭes, *f*;
(spectacle), spectācŭlum, *n*;
(procession, etc.), pompa, *f*
show *v.t*, monstro (1), praebĕo
(2), ostendo (3); **(— off)**, *v.t*,
ostento (1); *v.i*, sē ostentare (1
reflex)

shower   imber, *m*
shower   *v.t*, fundo (3)
showery   plŭvĭus
showy   spĕcĭōsus
shred   pannus, *m*
shrew   fēmĭna prŏcax
shrewd   ăcūtus, săgax
shrewdness   săgācĭtas, *f*
shriek   *nn*, ŭlŭlātus, *m*
shriek   *v.i* ŭlŭlo (1)
shrill   ăcūtus, ācer
shrine   dēlūbrum, *n*
shrink   *v.t*, contrăho (3); *v.i*,
   (— from), ăbhorrĕo (2)
shrinking   *nn*, contractĭo, *f*
shrivel   *v.t*, corrūgo (1)
shrivelled   rūgōsus
shroud   *use* lintĕum, *n*, (cloth)
shroud   *v.t*, involvo (3)
shrub   frŭtex, *m*
shrubbery   frŭtĭcētum
shudder   *v.i*, horrĕo (2)
shudder   *nn*, horror, *m*
shuffle   *v.t*, miscĕo (2); *v.i, use*
   phr, lentē ambŭlo (1) **(walk
   slowly)**
shun   *v.t*, fŭgĭo (3), vīto (1)
shut   *v.t*, claudo (3); **(— in or up)**,
   inclūdo (3); **(— out)**, exclūdo (3)
shutters   fŏrĭcŭlae, *f. pl*
shuttle   rădĭus, *m*
shy   vĕrēcundus
shy   *v.i*, **(of horses)**, consternor (1
   pass)
shyness   vĕrēcundĭa, *f*
sick   aeger; **(to be —)**, *v.i*, aegrōto
   (1); **(vomit)**, *v.i, and v.t*, vŏmo
   (3)
sicken   *v.t*, fastīdĭum mŏvĕo (2);
   v.i, aeger fio (*irreg*)
sickle   falx, *f*
sickly   infirmus
sickness   morbus, *m*
side   **(of the body)**   lătus, *n*; **(part,
   region)**, pars, *f*; **(party, faction)**,
   pars, *f*; **(from (or on) all —s)**, *adv*,
   undĭque; **(on both —s)**, ŭtrimque;
   (on this —), hinc; **(on that —)**,
   illinc; **(on this — of)**, *prep*, citra
   (*with acc*); **(on that — of)**, ŭltra
side   *adj*, **(sidelong)**, oblīquus
sideboard   ăbăcus, *m*
sideways   *adv*, oblīquē

siege   *nn*, obsĭdĭo, *f*
siege-works   ŏpĕra, *n.pl*
sieve   crībrum, *n*
sift   *v.t*, crībro (1); **(— evidence,
   etc.)**, scrūtor (1 *dep*)
sigh   *nn*, suspīrĭum, *n*
sigh   *v.i*, suspīro (1)
sight **(sense or act)**   vīsus, *m*;
   (view), conspectus, *m*;
   (spectacle), spectācŭlum, *n*
sight   *v.t*, conspĭcor (1 *dep*)
sightly   formōsus, vĕnustus
sign   *nn*, signum, *n*; **(mark)**, nŏta,
   f; **(trace, footprint)**, vestīgĭum, *n*;
   (portent), portentum, *n*
sign   *v.t*, subscrībo (3); **(give a —)**,
   v.i, signum do (1)
signal   signum, *n*
signal   *v.i*, signum do (1)
signature   nōmen, *n*
signet   signum, *n*
significance   signĭfĭcātĭo, *f*
significant   signĭfĭcans
signify   *v.t*, signĭfĭco (1)
silence   sĭlentĭum, *n*
silent   tăcĭtus, **(to be —)**, *v.i*, tăcĕo
   (2), sĭlĕo (2)
silk   *nn*, bombyx, *m*
silk, silken   *adj*, sērĭcus
silkworm   bombyx, *m*
silky   mollis
sill   līmen, *n*
silliness   stultĭtĭa, *f*
silly   stultus
silt   *nn*, līmus, *m*, sentīna, *f*
silver   *nn*, argentum, *n*
silver   *adj*, argentĕus
silver-mine   argentārium metallum
similar   sĭmĭlis (*with genit. or dat*)
similarity   sĭmĭlĭtūdo, *f*
similarly   *adv*, sĭmĭlĭter
simmer   *v.i*, lentē fervĕo (3) **(boil
   slowly)**
simper   *v.i*, subrīdĕo (2)
simple   simplex; **(weak-minded)**,
   ĭneptus
simpleton   stultus, *m*
simplicity   simplĭcĭtas, *f*
simplify   *v.t*, făcĭlem reddo (3)
simulation   sĭmŭlātĭo, *f*
simultaneous   *use adv*, sĭmul **(at
   the same time)**
sin   *nn*, peccātum, *n*

sin *v.i*, pecco (1)
since *conj*, cum (*foll. by vb. in subjunctive*); **(temporal)** postquam
since *adv*, ăbhinc
since *prep*, ē, ex, ā, ăb (*with abl*)
sincere sincērus, simplex
sincerity sincērĭtas, *f*, simplĭcĭtas, *f*
sinew nervus, *m*
sinful impĭus
sinfulness impĭĕtas, *f*
sing *v.i. and v.t*, căno (3)
singe *v.t*, ădūro (3)
singer cantātor, *m*
singing *nn*, cantus, *m*
single *adj*, **(one, sole)**, ūnus, sŏlus; **(unmarried)**, caelebs
single out *v.t*, ēlĭgo (3)
singly *adv*, singŭlātim
singular, **(one)** singŭlaris; **(strange)**, nŏvus
singularly *adv*, ūnĭcē
sinister sĭnister
sink *v.t*, mergo (3); *v.i*, sīdo (3), consīdo (3)
sinner peccātor, *m*
sinuous sĭnŭōsus
sip *v.t*, dēgusto (1), lībo (1)
sir **(respectful address)** bŏne vir
sire păter, *m*
siren sīrēn, *f*
sister sŏror, *f*
sit *v.i*, sĕdĕo (2); **(— down)**, consīdo (3); **(— up, stay awake)**, vĭgĭlo (1)
site sĭtus, *m*
sitting *nn*, sessĭo, *f*
situated sĭtus
situation sĭtus, *m*
six sex; **(— each)**, sēni; **(— times)**, *adv*, sexĭens
sixteen sēdĕcim
sixteenth sextus dĕcĭmus
sixth sextus
sixtieth sexāgēsĭmus
sixty sexāginta
size magnĭtūdo, *f*; **(of great —)**, *adj*, magnus; **(of small —)**, parvus; **(of what — ?)**, quantus?
skeleton ossa, *n.pl*, **(bones)**
sketch *nn*, ădumbrātĭo, *f*
sketch *v.t*, ădumbro (1)
skewer vĕrūcŭlum, *n*

skiff scăpha, *f*
skilful, skilled pĕrītus
skilfulness, skill pĕrītĭa, *f*
skim *v.t*, **(— off)**, dēspūmo (1); **(— over)**, percurro (3)
skin cŭtis, *f*, pellis, *f*
skin *v.t*, pellem dīrĭpĭo (3) **(tear away the skin)**
skip *v.i*, exsulto (1); **(— over)**, *v.i. and v.t*, praetĕrĕo (4)
skipper nauarchus, *m*
skirmish *nn*, lĕve certāmen, *n*
skirmish *v.i*, parvŭlis proelĭis contendo (3) **(fight in small engagements)**
skirmisher vēlĕs, *m*
skirt *nn*, limbus, *m*
skirt *v.t*, **(scrape past)**, rādo (3)
skittish lascīvus
skulk *v.i*, lătĕo (2)
skull calvārĭa, *f*
sky caelum, *n*
sky-blue caerŭlĕus
skylark ălauda, *f*
slab (of stone) ăbăcus, *m*
slack rĕmissus
slacken *v.t*, rĕmitto (3); *v.i*, rĕmittor (3 *pass*)
slackness rĕmissĭo, *f*; **(idleness)**, pĭgrĭtĭa, *f*
slake (thirst) *v.t*, (sĭtim) exstinguo (3)
slander *nn*, călumnĭa, *f*
slander *v.t*, călumnĭor (1 *dep*)
slanderer obtrectātor, *m*
slanderous fāmōsus
slanting *adj*, oblīquus
slap *nn*, ălăpa, *f*
slap *v.t*, fĕrĭo (4)
slash *nn*, **(blow)**, ictus, *m*
slash *v.t*, caedo (3)
slate (roofing) tēgŭlae, *f. pl.*
slate *v.t*, rĕprĕhendo (3)
slaughter *nn*, caedes, *f*, strāges, *f*
slaughter *v.t*, caedo (3)
slaughterhouse *use* lănĭĕna, *f* **(butcher's stall)**
slave servus, *m*
slave-dealer vēnālĭcĭus, *m*
slavery servĭtus, *f*
slave-trade vēnālĭcĭum, *n*
slavish servīlis
slay *v.t*, interfĭcĭo (3)

slayer   interfector, *m*
slaying   *nn*, trŭcīdātĭo, *f*
sledge   trăhĕa, *f*
sleek   nĭtĭdus
sleep   *nn*, somnus, *m*
sleep   *v.i*, dormĭo (4), quĭesco (3);
   (to go to —), obdormisco (3)
sleepless   insomnis
sleeplessness   insomnĭa, *f*
sleepy   somnĭcŭlōsus
sleeve   mănĭcae, *f. pl*
sleigh   trăhĕa, *f*
sleight-of-hand   praestīgĭae, *f. pl*
slender   grăcĭlis
slenderness   grăcĭlĭtas, *f*
slice   segmentum, *n*, frustum, *n*
slice   *v.t*, concīdo (3)
slide   *v.i*, lābor (3 *dep*)
slight   *adj*, lĕvis, exĭgŭus
slight   *v.t*, neglĕgo (3)
slim   grăcĭlis
slime   līmus, *m*
slimy   līmōsus
sling   *nn*, (for throwing), funda, *f*;
   (bandage), mĭtella, *f*
sling   *v.t*, mitto (3)
slinger   fundĭtor, *m*
slip   *v.i*, lābor (3 *dep*); (— away),
   sē subdūcĕre (3 *reflex*); (— out
   from), ēlābor (3 *dep*)
slip   *nn*, lapsus, *m*; (mistake),
   error, *m*
slipper   sŏlĕa, *f*
slippery   lūbrĭcus
slipshod   neglĕgens
slit   *nn*, scissūra, *f*
slit   *v.t*, incīdo (3)
sloop   nāvis longa, *f*
slope   *nn*, clīvus, *m*
slope   *v.i*, sē dēmittĕre (3 *reflex*),
   vergo (3)
sloping   *adj*, (down), dēclīvis; (up),
   acclīvis
sloth   segnĭtĭa, *f*, ignāvĭa, *f*
slothful   segnis
slough (mire)   pălus, *f*
slovenliness   cultus neglectus
   (neglected dress)
slow   tardus, lentus
slowly   *adv*, tardē, lentē
slowness   tardĭtas, *f*
slug   līmax, *f*
sluggish   pĭger, segnis

sluggishness   pigrĭtĭa, *f*
sluice   ductus (*m*) ăquārum
   (bringing of water)
slumber   *nn*, somnus, *m*
slumber   *v.i*, dormĭo (4)
slur   *nn*, măcŭla, *f*
sly   astūtus, callĭdus
smack   *nn*, (blow), ălăpa, *f*;
   (taste), săpor, *m*
smack   *v.t*, (slap), verbĕro (1)
small   parvus, exĭgŭus
smallness   exĭgŭĭtas, *f*
smart   *adj*, ācer; (clothes, etc.),
   nĭtĭdus; (witty), făcētus
smart   *nn*, dŏlor, *m*
smart   *v.i*, dŏlĕo (2), ūror (3 *pass*)
smartness (alertness)   ălăcrĭtas, *f*
smash   *nn*, fractūra, *f*
smash   *v.t*, confringo (3)
smattering   lĕvis cognĭtĭo, *f*, (slight
   knowledge)
smear   *v.t*, līno (3)
smell   *nn*, (sense of —), ŏdōrātus,
   m; (scent), ŏdor, *m*
smell   *v.t*, olfăcĭo (3); *v.i*, ŏlĕo (2)
smelt   *v.t*, cŏquo (3)
smile   *nn*, rīsus, *m*
smile   *v.i*, subrīdĕo (2)
smirk   *nn*, rīsus, *m*
smite   *v.t*, fĕrĭo (4)
smith   făber, *m*
smithy   făbrĭca, *f*
smock   indūsĭum, *n*
smoke   *nn*, fūmus, *m*
smoke   *v.i*, fūmo (1)
smoky   fūmōsus
smooth   lĕvis, (of the sea),
   plăcĭdus; (of temper), aequus
smooth   *v.t*, lēvo (1)
smoothness   lēvĭtas, *f*, lēnĭtas, *f*
smother   *v.t*, suffōco (1), opprĭmo
   (3)
smoulder   *v.i*, fūmo (1)
smudge   *nn*, lābes, *f*
smuggle   *v.t*, furtim importo (1)
   (bring in secretly)
snack   cēnŭla, *f*
snail   cochlĕa, *f*
snake   anguis, *m*, *f*
snaky   vīpĕrĕus
snap   *v.t*, rumpo (3); (— the
   fingers), *v.i*, concrĕpo (1); (— up),
   v.t, corrĭpĭo (3)

snare lăquĕus, *m*
snarl *nn*, gannītus, *m*
snarl *v.i*, gannĭo (4)
snatch *v.t*, răpĭo (3)
sneak *v.i*, corrēpo (3)
sneer *nn*, obtrectātĭo, *f*
sneer at *v.t*, dērīdĕo (2)
sneeze *v.i*, sternŭo (3)
sneezing sternūmentum, *n*
sniff at (smell at) *v.t*, ŏdōror (1 *dep*)
snip *v.t*, (cut off), ampŭto (1)
snob nŏvus hŏmo (upstart)
snore *v.i*, sterto (3)
snore, snoring *nn*, rhonchus, *m*
snort *v.i*, frĕmo (3)
snorting *nn*, frĕmĭtus, *m*
snout rostrum, *n*
snow *nn*, nix, *f*
snow (it —s) ningit (*v. impers*)
snowy nĭvĕus
snub *v.t*, rĕprĕhendo (3)
snub-nosed sīlus
snuff *v.t*, (extinguish), exstinguo (3)
snug commŏdus
so *adv*, (in such a way), sīc, ĭtă; (to such an extent), ădĕo; (*with adj and adv*) tam, *e.g.* so quickly, tam cĕlĕrĭter; (*with a purpose or consecutive clause*, so that ...) ut; (— big, — great), tāntus; (— many), tot; (— much), tantum; (— often), tŏtĭes
soak *v.t*, mădĕfăcĭo (3)
soaking mădens; (of rain), largus
soap *nn*, sāpo, *m*
soar *v.i*, sublīme fĕror (*irreg pass*) (be borne aloft)
sob *nn*, singultus, *m*
sob *v.i*, singulto (1)
sober sōbrĭus
sobriety sōbrĭĕtas, *f*, mŏdĕrātĭo, *f*
sociability făcĭlĭtas, *f*
sociable făcĭlis
social commūnis
society (in general) sŏcĭĕtas, *f*; (companionship), sŏdālĭtas, *f*
sock tībĭāle, *n*
sod caespes, *m*
soda nĭtrum, *n*
sodden mădĭdus
sofa lectŭlus, *m*

soft mollis
soften *v.t*, mollĭo (4); *v.i*, mollĭor (4 *pass*)
softness mollĭtĭa, *f*
soil sŏlum, *n*
soil *v.t*, inquĭno (1)
sojourn *nn*, commŏrātĭo, *f*
sojourn *v.i*, commŏror (1 *dep*)
solace *nn*, sōlātĭum, *n*
solace *v.t*, consōlor (1 *dep*)
solar *use genit. case of* sōl, *m*, (sun)
solder *nn*, ferrūmen, *n*
solder *v.t*, ferrūmĭno (1)
soldier mīles, *c*; (foot —), pĕdes, *m*; (cavalry —), ĕques, *m*; *v.i*, (serve as a —), stīpendĭa mĕrĕor (2 *dep*)
soldierly *adj*, mīlĭtāris
sole *adj*, sōlus
sole *nn*, sŏlum, *n*; (fish), sŏlĕa, *f*
solely *adv*, sōlum
solemn (serious) grăvis; (festivals, etc.), sollemnis
solemnity grăvĭtas, *f*; (religious —), sollemne, *n*
solemnize *v.t*, cĕlĕbro (1)
solicit *v.t*, pĕto (3), osĕcro (1), sollĭcĭto (1)
solicitation flāgĭtātĭo, *f*
solicitor advŏcātus, *m*
solicitude anxĭĕtas, *f*
solid *adj*, sŏlĭdus
solid *nn*, sŏlĭdum, *n*
solidity sŏlĭdĭtas, *f*
soliloquize *v.i*, sēcum lŏquo (3 *dep*) (speak with oneself)
solitary sōlus, sōlĭtārĭus; (places), dēsertus
solitude sōlĭtūdo, *f*
solstice (summer —) solstĭtĭum, *n*; (winter —), brūma, *f*
solution *use vb.* solvo (3) (to solve), *or nn*, explĭcātĭo, *f*
solve *v.t*, explĭco (1)
solvent (to be —) solvendo esse (*irreg*)
sombre obscūrus
some *adj*, ălĭquis, nonnullus; (a certain), quīdam
somebody, someone *pron*, ălĭquis, nonnullus; (a certain one), quīdam; (— or other),

nescĭo quis; **(some . . . others)**, ălĭi . . . ălĭi
somehow *adv*, nescĭo quōmŏdŏ
something *pron*, ălĭquid
sometime *adv*, ălĭquandŏ
sometimes *adv*, ălĭquandŏ, interdum; **(occasionally)**, sŭbinde; **(sometimes ... sometimes ...)**, mŏdŏ ... mŏdŏ ...
somewhat *adv*, ălĭquantum
somewhere *adv*, ălĭcŭbi; **(to —)**, ălĭquo
somnolent sēmĭsomnus
son filĭus, *m*; **(— in-law)**, gĕner, *m*
song carmen, *n*
sonorous sŏnōrus
soon *adv*, mox; **(as — as)**, sĭmul ac, sĭmŭl atque, cum prīmum; **(as — as possible)**, quam prīmum
sooner (earlier) mātūrĭus; **(rather)**, pŏtĭus
soot fulīgo, *f*
soothe *v.t*, mulcĕo (2), lēnĭo (4)
soothing *adj*, lēnis
soothsayer auspex, *c*, hăruspex, *m*
sooty fūlĭgĭnōsus
sop offa, *f*
sophist sŏphistes, *m*
soporific sŏpōrĭfer
sorcerer vĕnēfĭcus, *m*
sorcery vĕnēfĭcĭa, *n.pl*
sordid sordĭdus
sore ăcerbus
sore *nn*, ulcus, *n*
sorrel lăpăthus, *f*
sorrow *nn*, dŏlor, *m*, maeror, *m*
sorrow *v.i*, dŏlĕo (2)
sorrowful maestus, tristis
sorry (to be —) mĭsĕret (2 *impers*) (*with acc. of subject and genit. of object*), e.g. **I am sorry for you**, me mĭsĕret tŭi
sort gĕnus, *n*; **(what — of?)**, quālis?
sort *v.t*, dīgĕro (3)
sot pōtātor, *m*
soul ănĭma, *f*, ănĭmus, *m*, spīrĭtus, *m*
sound *nn*, sŏnus, *m*, sŏnĭtus, *m*
sound *adj*, sānus; **(of sleep)**, artus; **(of arguments)**, firmus

sound *v.i*, sŏno (1); *v.t*, inflo (1); **(— the trumpet)**, būcĭnam inflo (1), căno (3)
soundness sānĭtas, *f*, intgĕrĭtas, *f*
soup iūs, *n*
sour ăcerbus, ācer, ămārus
source fons, *m*, căput, *n*
sourness ăcerbĭtas, *f*
south *nn*, mĕrīdĭes, *m*
south, southern *adj*, mĕrīdĭānus
southwards *adv. phr*, in mĕrīdĭem
sovereign *nn*, princeps, *m*, rex, *m*, tўrannus, *m*
sovereign (independent) *adj, use phr* sŭi iūris **(of one's own authority)**
sovereignty impĕrĭum, *n*
sow *nn*, sūs, *f*
sow *v.t*, sĕro (3)
sower sător, *m*
space spătĭum, *n*; **(— of time)**, spătĭum, (*n*) tempŏris
spacious amplus
spaciousness amplĭtūdo, *f*
spade pāla, *f*
span palmus, *m*
span *v.t*, **(river, etc.)**, *use vb*, iungo (3) **(join)**
spangled distinctus
Spanish Hispānus
spar (of timber) asser, *m*
spare *adj*, exĭlis **(thin)**
spare *v.t*, parco (3) (*with dat*)
sparing *adj*, **(frugal)**, parcus
spark *nn*, scintilla, *f*
sparkle *v.i*, scintillo (1)
sparkling *adj*, scintillans
sparrow passer, *m*
sparse rārus
spasm spasmus, *m*
spatter *v.t*, aspergo (3)
spawn *nn*, ōva, *n.pl*
spawn *v.i*, ōva gigno (3) **(produce eggs)**
speak *v.t*, lŏquor (3 *dep*), dīco (3); **(— out)**, ēlŏquor (3 *dep*); **(— to)**, allŏquor (3 *dep*)
speaker ōrātor, *m*
spear hasta, *f*
special (one in particular) pĕcūlĭāris; **(one's own)**, prŏprĭus; **(outstanding)**, praecĭpŭus

speciality *use adj*, prŏprĭus **(one's own)**
specially *adv*, praecĭpŭē, praesertim
species gĕnus, *n*
specific dīsertus; *or use emphatic pron*, ipse
specify *v.t*, ēnŭmĕro (1)
specimen exemplum, *n*
specious prŏbābĭlis
speck măcŭla, *f*
spectacle spectācŭlum, *n*
spectator spectātor, *m*
spectre ĭmāgo, *f*
spectrum spectrum, *n*
speculate *v.i*, cōgĭto (1); **(guess),** cōnĭcĭo (3)
speculation cōgĭtātĭo, *f*; **(guess),** coniectūra, *f*
speech ōrātĭo, *f*
speechless (literally so) mūtus; **(struck with fear, etc.),** stŭpĕfactus
speed cĕlĕrĭtas, *f*
speed *v.t*, mātūro (1); *v.i*, festīno (1)
speedy cĕler, cĭtus
spell (charm) carmen, *n*
spell *v.t, use phr. with* littĕra, *f*, **(letter)**
spellbound obstŭpĕfactus
spend *v.t*, **(money),** impendo (3), insūmo (3); **(time),** ăgo (3)
spendthrift nĕpos, *m, f*
spew *v.t*, vŏmo (3)
sphere glŏbus, *m*; **(— of responsibility, etc.),** prōvincĭa, *f*
spherical glŏbōsus
sphinx sphinx, *f*
spice condīmentum, *n*
spice *v.t*, condĭo (4)
spicy condītus
spider ărānĕa, *f*
spider's web ărānĕa, *f*
spike clāvus, *m*
spill *v.t*, effundo (3)
spin *v.t*, **(thread, etc.),** nĕo (2); **(turn rapidly),** verso (1); *v.i*, versor (1 *pass*)
spinster virgo, *f*
spiral *nn*, cochlĕa, *f*
spiral *adj*, invŏlūtus
spire turris, *f*

spirit (breath of life) ănĭma, *f*; **(mind, soul),** ănĭmus, *m*; **(disposition),** ingĕnĭum, *n*; **(character),** mōres, *m. pl*; **(courage),** ănĭmus, *m*; **(departed —),** mānes, *m. pl*
spirited ănĭmōsus
spiritual (of the mind) *use* ănĭmus, *m*
spit *nn*, **(for roasting),** vĕru, *n*
spit *v.t*, spŭo (3)
spite mălĕvŏlentĭa, *f*; **(in — of),** *often use abl. phr. with* obstans **(standing in the way)**
spiteful mălignus
spittle spūtum, *n*
splash *v.t*, aspergo (3)
spleen lĭen, *n*; **(vexation),** stŏmăchus, *m*
splendid splendĭdus
splendour splendor, *m*
splint fĕrŭlae, *f. pl*
splinter fragmentum, *n*
split *v.t*, findo (3); *v.i*, findor (3 *pass*)
split *nn*, fissūra, *f*
splutter *v.i*, balbūtĭo (4)
spoil *nn*, praeda, *f*, spŏlĭa, *n.pl*
spoil *v.t*, corrumpo (3), vĭtĭo (1)
spokesman ōrātor, *m*
sponge *nn*, spongĭa, *f*
spongy spongĭōsus
sponsor auctor, *c*
spontaneous *use adv. phr*, sŭā (mĕā), sponte **(of his (my) own accord)**
spoon coclĕar, *n*
sporadic rārus
sport *nn*, lūdus, *m*, lūsus, *m*; **(ridicule),** lūdĭbrĭum, *n*
sport *v.i*, lūdo (3)
sportive (playful) lascīvus
sportsman vēnātor, *m*
spot *nn*, **(stain),** măcŭla, *f*; **(place),** lŏcus, *m*
spot *v.t*, **(look at),** aspĭcĭo (3); **(stain),** măcŭlo (1)
spotless (of character, etc.) intĕger, pūrus
spotted măcŭlōsus
spouse coniunx, *c*
spout *nn*, ōs, *n*
spout *v.i*, ēmĭco (1); *v.t*, **(pour**

out), effundo (3)
sprain *v.t*, intorquĕo (2)
sprawl *v.i*, fundor (3 *pass*)
spray *nn*, aspergo, *f*
spread *v.t*, extendo (3), pando
(3), diffundo (3); **(— about,**
publish), diffĕro (*irreg*) dīvulgo
(1); *v.i*, diffundor (3 *pass*),
incrēbresco (3)
sprightly ălăcer
spring *nn*, **(season)**, vēr, *n*; **(leap)**,
saltus, *m*; **(fountain)**, fons, *m*
spring *adj*, vernus
spring *v.i*, **(leap)**, sălĭo (4); **(—**
from, proceed from), ŏrĭor (4
dep) **(— upon, assault)**, ădŏrĭor
(4 *dep*)
sprinkle *v.t*, spargo (3)
sprout *nn*, surcūlus, *m*
sprout *v.i*, pullŭlo (1)
spruce *adj*, nĭtĭdus
spruce *nn*, **(fir)**, pīnus, *f*
spur *nn*, calcar, *n*
spur *v.t*, concĭto (1)
spurious ădultĕrīnus
spurn *v.t*, aspernor (1 *dep*)
spurt *v.i*, ēmĭco (1)
spy *nn*, explōrător, *m*, dēlātor, *m*
spy *v.t*, spĕcŭlor (1 *dep*)
squabble *nn*, rixa, *f*
squabble *v.i*, rixor (1 *dep*)
squadron (of cavalry) turma, *f*; **(of**
ships), classis, *f*
squalid sordĭdus
squall (storm) prŏcella, *f*
squall *v.i*, **(cry)**, vāgĭo (4)
squalor sordes, *f. pl*
squandor effundo (3)
squanderer nĕpos, *m*, *f*
square *adj*, quădrātus; *nn*,
quădrātum, *n*
square *v.t*, quădro (1); **(accounts,**
etc.), subdūco (3), constĭtŭo (3)
squash *v.t*, contĕro (3)
squat *v.i*, subsīdo (3)
squat *adj*, **(of figure)**, brĕvis
squeak *nn*, strīdor, *m*
squeak *v.i*, strīdĕo (2)
squeamish fastīdĭōsus
squeeze *v.t*, prĕmo (3)
squint *v.i*, străbo esse (*irreg*)
squirrel scĭūrus, *m*
squirt *v.t*, ēĭcĭo (3); *v.i*, ēmĭco (1)

stab *v.t*, fōdĭo (3)
stab *nn*, ictus, *m*
stability stăbĭlĭtas, *f*
stable *adj*, stăbĭlis
stable *nn*, stăbŭlum, *n*
stack *nn*, ăcervus, *m*
stack *v.t*, cŏăcervo (1)
staff băcŭlum, *n*; **(advisers)**,
consĭlĭārĭi, *m. pl*
stag cervus, *m*
stage (theatre) proscaenĭum, *n*;
(step), grădus, *m*
stagger *v.i*, văcillo (1); *v.t*,
concŭtĭo (3), commŏvĕo (2)
stagnant stagnans
stagnate *v.i*, stagno (1)
staid grăvis
stain *nn*, măcŭla, *f*
stain *v.t*, măcŭlo (1)
stainless pūrus, intĕger
stairs scālae, *f. pl*
stake (post, etc.) pālus, *m*, sŭdis,
f, stīpes, *m*; **(pledge, wager)**,
pignus, *n*
stake *v.t*, **(wager)**, dēpōno (3)
stale vĕtus
stalk stirps, *f*
stalk *v.i*, incēdo (3); **(game, etc.)**,
use phr, cautē sĕquor (3 *dep*)
(follow cautiously)
stall (cattle) stăbŭlum, *n*; **(shop,**
etc.**)**, tăberna, *f*
stallion admissārĭus, *m*
stalwart *adj*, fortis
stamina vīres, *f. pl*
stammer *nn*, haesĭtantĭa (*f*)
linguae **(hesitation of speech)**
stammer *v.i*, balbūtĭo (4)
stamp (mark) nŏta, *f*; **(with a ring,**
etc.**)**, signum, *n*
stamp *v.t*, **(mark)**, signo (1); **(—**
with the foot), supplōdo (3)
stand *nn*, **(halt)**, mŏra, *f*; **(to make**
a —) consisto (3) rĕsisto (3),
(*with dat.*); **(platform)**, suggestus,
m; **(stall)**, mensa, *f*
stand *v.i*, sto (1), consisto (3); **(—**
back), rĕcēdo (3), **(— by, help)**,
adsum (*irreg with dat*), **(— for,**
seek a position), *v.t*, pĕto (3);
(endure), pătĭor (3 *dep*); **(— out,**
project) exsto (1); **(— up)**, surgo
(3)

standard signum, *n*; **(of the legion)**, ăquĭla, *f*; **(measure)**, norma, *f*; **(— bearer)**, signĭfer, *m*

standing *nn*, **(position)**, stătus, *m*

staple products merces, *f, pl*

star stella, *f*, sīdus, *n*

starboard *use adj*, dexter **(right)**

starch *nn*, ămўlum, *n*

stare *nn*, obtūtus, *m*

stare *v.t*, **(— at)**, intŭĕor (2 *dep*)

stark (stiff) rĭgĭdus; **(— naked)**, nūdus; **(— mad)**, āmens

starling sturnus, *m*

start *nn*, **(movement)**, trĕmor, *m*; **(beginning)**, ĭnĭtĭum, *n*; **(setting out)**, prŏfectĭo, *f*; **(starting point)**, carcĕres, *m. pl*

start *v.i*, **(make a sudden movement)**, trĕmo (3), horrĕo (2); **(— out)**, prŏfĭciscor (3 *dep*); *v.t*, **(establish)**, instĭtŭo (3)

startle *v.t*, terrĕo (2)

startling *adj*, terrĭbĭlis

starvation fămes, *f*

starve *f.t*, făme nĕco (1) **(kill by starvation)**; *v.i*, făme nĕcor (1 *pass*)

state (condition) stătus, *m*, condĭcĭo, *f*; **(the —)**, respublĭca, *f*, cīvĭtas, *f*

state *v.t*, prŏfĭtĕor (2 *dep*)

stately magnĭfĭcus, cĕlĕber

statement dictum, *n*

statesman *use phr. with* respublĭca **(state)**, *and* admĭnistro (1), **(to manage)**

station (standing) stătus, *m*; **(occupied place)**, stătĭo, *f*

station *v.t*, lŏco (1)

stationary *adj*, immōtus

stationer bibliŏpōla, *m*

statistics census, *m*

statue stătŭa, *f*

stature stătūra, *f*

status stătus, *m*

statute lex, *f*

staunch *adj*, firmus

stave off *v.t*, arcĕo (2)

stay *nn*, **(prop)**, firmāmentum, *n*; **(rest, etc.)**, mansĭo, *f*, commŏrātĭo, *f*

stay *v.i*, mănĕo (2), mŏror (1 *dep*); *v.t*, **(obstruct, stop)**, mŏror

(1 *dep*)

steadfast firmus, stăbĭlis

steady firmus, stăbĭlis

steadfastness stăbĭlĭtas, *f*

steadiness stăbĭlĭtas, *f*

steak offa, *f*

steal *v.t*, fūror (1 *dep*); *v.i*, **(— upon)**, surrēpo (3) **(with dat)**

stealing *nn*, **(theft)**, furtum, *n*

stealth **(by —)**, **(adv)** furtim

stealth furtīvus

steam văpor, *m*

steam *v.i*, exhālo (1)

steed ĕquus, *m*

steel chălybs, *m*; **(iron, sword, etc.)**, ferrum, *n*

steel *v.t*, **(strengthen)**, confirmo (1)

steep praeruptus

steep *v.t*, **(soak)**, mădĕfăcĭo (3)

steeple turris, *f*

steer *nn*, iŭvencus, *m*

steer *v.t*, gŭberno (1)

steersman gŭbernātor, *m*

stem stirps, *f*, **(— literal and metaphorical)**

stem *v.t*, **(check)**, sisto (3), rĕsisto (3) **(with dat)**

stench fētor, *m*

step *nn*, grădus, *m*, passus, *m*; **(foot —)**, vestĭgĭum, *n*; **(— by —)**, pĕdĕtentim; **(steps, stairs)**, scālae, *f.pl*

step *v.i*, grădĭor (3 *dep*); **(— forward)**; prōgrĕdĭor (3 *dep*)

step-brother (father's side) fĭlĭus vĭtrĭci; **(mother's side)**, fĭlĭus nŏvercae; **(— daughter)**, prīvigna, *f*; **(— father)** vĭtrĭcus, *m*; **(— mother)**, nŏverca, *f*; **(— sister)**, fĭlĭa vĭtrĭci *or* nŏvercae; **(— son)**, prīvignus, *m*

sterile stĕrĭlis

sterility stĕrĭlĭtas, *f*

sterling *adj*, **(genuine)**, vērus

stern *nn*, puppis, *f*

stern *adj*, dūrus

sterness sĕvērĭtas, *f*

stew *v.t*, cŏquo (3)

steward vīlĭcus, *m*

stick *nn*, băcŭlum, *n*

stick *v.t*, **(fix)**, fīgo (3); *v.i*, haerĕo (2)

sticky *adj*, tĕnax
stiff rĭgĭdus; **(to be —)**, *v.i*, rĭgĕo (2)
stiffen *v.i*, rĭgĕo (2); *v.t*, rĭgĭdum făcĭo (3)
stiffness rĭgor, *m*
stifle *v.t*, suffŏco (1); **(suppress)**, opprĭmo (3)
stigma stigma, *n*
stigmatize *v.t*, nŏto (1)
still *adj*, immōtus, tranquillus
still *adv*, **(nevertheless)**, tămen; **(up to this time)**, ădhuc; **(even)**, ĕtĭam
still *v.t*, sēdo (1)
stillness quĭes, *f*
stilts grallae, *f. pl*
stimulant (incentive) stĭmŭlus, *m*
stimulus (incentive) stĭmŭlus, *m*
stimulate *v.t*, stĭmŭlo (1)
sting *nn*, ăcūlĕus, *m*
sting *v.t*, pungo (3)
stinging *adj*, mordax
stingy sordĭdus
stink *nn*, fētor, *m*
stink *v.i*, fētĕo (2)
stipend merces, *f*
stipulate *v.i*, stĭpŭlor (1 *dep*)
stir *nn*, mōtus, *m*
stir *v.t*, mŏvĕo (2); *v.i* mŏvĕor (2 *pass*)
stitch *v.t*, sŭo (3)
stock (of tree, family, etc.) stirps, *f*; **(amount)**, vīs, *f*
stock *v.t*, complĕo (2)
stockbroker argentārĭus, *m*
stocking tībĭāle, *n*
stoic *nn. and adj*, stōĭcus
stoical dūrus
stoicism rătĭo Stōĭca, *f*
stolen furtīvus
stomach stŏmăchus, *m*
stomach *v.t*, **(put up with)**, perfĕro (*irreg*)
stone lăpis, *m*; **(precious —)**, gemma, *f*; **(fruit —)**, nūclĕus, *m*
stone *adj*, lăpĭdĕus
stone *v.t*, **(— to death)**, lăpĭdĭbus cŏŏpĕrĭo (4) **(overwhelm with stones)**
stone-quarry lăpĭcīdīnae, *f. pl*
stony lăpĭdōsus; **(of heart)**, asper
stool scăbellum, *n*

stoop *v.i*, sē dēmittĕre (3 *reflex*); **(condescend)**, dēscendo (3)
stop *nn*, intermissĭo, *f*
stop *v.t*, sisto (3); **(— up a hole, etc.)**, obtūro (1); *v.i*, **(pause)**, sisto (3); **(desist)**, dēsĭno (3); **(remain)**, mănĕo (2)
stoppage (hindrance) impĕdīmentum, *n*
stopper obtūrāmentum, *n*
store (supply) cōpĭa, *f*; **(place)**, rĕceptācŭlum, *n*
store *v.t*, condo (3)
storey tăbŭlātum, *n*
stork cĭcōnĭa, *f*
storm *nn*, tempestas, *f*
storm *v.t*, **(attack)**, expugno (1)
storming *nn*, expugnātĭo, *f*
stormy (weather) turbĭdus
story fābŭla, *f*
story-teller narrātor, *m*
stout (fat) pinguis; **(strong)**, vălĭdus; **(— hearted)**, fortis
stove fŏcus, *m*
stow *v.t*, rĕpōno (3)
straddle *v.i*, vārĭco (1)
straggle *v.i*, văgor (1 *dep*)
straight *adj*, rectus
straight *adv*, rectā
straight away *adv*, stătim
straighten *v.t*, corrĭgo (3)
straightforward simplex
strain *nn*, contentĭo, *f*
strain *v.t*, **(stretch)**, tendo (3); **(liquids, etc.)**, cōlo (3); *v.i*, **(strive)**, nītor (3 *dep*)
strait *adj*, angustus
strait *nn*, **(a narrow place or a difficulty)**, angustĭae, *f. pl* **(sea)** frētum, *n*
strand (shore) lītus, *n*
stranded rĕlictus
strange insŏlĭtus, nŏvus
strangeness insŏlentĭa, *f*
stranger hospes, *m*
strangle *v.t*, strangŭlo (1)
strap *nn*, lōrum, *n*
stratagem dŏlus, *m*
strategist *use phr. with* pĕrītus **(skilled in)**, *with phr. below*
strategy ars (*f*) bellandi **(the art of making war)**
straw strāmentum, *n*

strawberry frāgum, *n*
stray *v.i*, erro (1)
stray *adj*, errābundus
streak *nn*, līněa, *f*
streak *v.t*, līněis vărǐo (1),
(variegate with streaks)
streaky virgātus
stream *nn*, flūmen, *n*
stream *v.i*, effundor (3 *pass*)
street vǐa, *f*
strength vīres, *f. pl*, rōbur, *n*
strengthen *v.t*, firmo (1)
strenuous impǐger
stress (importance) mōmentum,
n
stretch *nn*, (extent), spătǐum, *n*
stretch *v.t*, tendo (3); (— out),
extendo (3); *v.i*, sē tenděre (3
reflex)
stretcher lectīca, *f*
strew *v.t*, sterno (3)
strict (severe) dūrus; (careful)
dīlǐgens
strictness sěvērǐtas, *f*
stricture rěprěhensǐo, *f*
stride *nn*, passus, *m*
strife certāmen, *n*, discordǐa, *f*
strike *v.t*, fěrǐo (4), percŭtǐo (3),
pulso (1); (— the mind, occur to),
subvěnǐo (4)
striking *adj*, insignis
string līněa, *f*; (of bow or
instrument), nervus, *m*
stringent sěvērus
strip *v.t*, spŏlǐo (1), nūdo (1)
strip *nn*, (flap, edge), lăcǐnǐa, *f*
stripe līmes, *m*; (blow), verber, *n*
stripling ădŏlescentŭlus, *m*
strive *v.i*, nītor (3 *dep*), contendo
(3)
striving *nn*, contentǐo, *f*
stroke *nn*, verber, *n*, ictus, *m*;
(line), līněa, *f*
stroke *v.t*, mulcěo (2)
stroll *nn*, ambŭlātǐo, *f*
stroll *v.i*, ambŭlo (1)
strong vălǐdus, firmus; (powerful),
fortis; (to be —), *v.i*, vălěo (2)
stronghold arx, *f*
structure (building) aedǐfǐcǐum, *n*
struggle *nn*, certāmen, *n*
struggle *v.i*, luctor (1 *dep*), nītor
(3 *dep*)

strumpet měrětrix, *f*
strut *v.i*, incēdo (3)
stubble stǐpŭla, *f*
stubborn pertǐnax
stucco tectōrǐum, *n*
stud clāvus, *m*; (horses), ěquārǐa,
f
stud *v.t*, insēro (3)
student *use adj*, stŭdǐōsus
(devoted to), *with a suitable
noun*
studied mědǐtātus
studious stŭdǐosus
study *nn*, stŭdǐum, *n*; (room,
library), biblǐŏthēca, *f*
study *v.t*, stŭděo (2) (*with dat*)
stuff (material) mātěrǐa, *f*;
(woven-), textǐle, *n*
stuff *v.t*, farcǐo (4)
stuffing *nn*, fartum, *n*
stumble *nn*, (fall), lapsus, *m*
stumble *v.i*, offendo (3)
stumbling block impědīmentum,
n
stump (post) stīpes, *m*
stun *v.t*, obstŭpěfăcǐo (3)
stupefaction stŭpor, *m*
stupefy *v.t*, obstŭpěfăcǐo (3)
stupendous mīrābǐlis
stupid stŏlǐdus, stultus
stupidity stultǐtǐa, *f*
stupor stŭpor, *m*
sturdiness firmǐtas, *f*
sturdy firmus, vălǐdus
sturgeon ăcǐpenser, *m*
stutter *v.i*, balbūtǐo (4)
sty hăra, *f*; (in the eye),
horděŏlus, *m*
style *nn*, gěnus, *n*
style *v.t*, (name), appello (1)
stylish spěcǐōsus
suave suāvis
subaltern sucentŭrǐo, *m*
subdivide *v.t*, dīvǐdo (1)
subdue *v.t*, sūbǐcǐo (3)
subject *adj*, subiectus
subject *nn*, (of a state, etc.), cīvis,
c; (matter), rēs, *f*
subject *v.t*, sūbǐcǐo (3)
subjection (slavery) servǐtus, *f*
subjoin *v.t*, subiungo (3)
subjugate *v.t*, sŭbǐgo (3)
sublime ēlātus

sublimity ēlātĭo, *f*
submerge *v.t*, submergo (3)
submission (compliance)
  obsĕquĭum, *n*
submissive ŏbēdĭens
submit *v.t*, sŭbĭcĭo (3); **(present)**,
  rĕfĕro (*irreg*); *v.i*, **(yield)**, cēdo (3)
subordinate *adj*, subiectus
subordination (obedience)
  obsĕquĭum, *n*
subscribe *v.t*, **(give money, etc.)**,
  confĕro (*irreg*); **(signature)**,
  subscrībo (3)
subscription (of money, etc.)
  collātĭo, *f*
subsequent sĕquens
subsequently *adv*, postĕā
subservient obsĕquens
subside *v.i*, rĕsīdo (3)
subsidize *v.t*, pĕcūnĭam
  suppĕdĭto (1), **(furnish with**
  money)
subsidy subsĭdĭum, *n*
subsist *v.i*, consto (1)
subsistence victus, *m*
substance (essence) nātūra, *f*;
  (being), rēs, *f*; **(goods)**, bŏna, *n.pl*
substantial (real) vērus;
  (important), grăvis
substitute *nn*, vĭcārĭus, *m*
substitute *v.t*, suppōno (3)
subterfuge lătĕbra, *f*
subterranean subterrānĕus
subtle (crafty) astūtus; **(refined)**,
  subtīlis
subtlety (craftiness) astūtĭa, *f*;
  (fineness), subtīlĭtas, *f*
subtract *v.t*, dēdūco (3)
subtraction detractĭo, *f*
suburb sŭburbĭum, *n*
suburban sŭburbānus
subvert *v.t*, ēverto (3)
succeed *v.t*, **(in, do well)**, bĕnĕ
  effĭcĭo (3); **(of things)**, *v.i*,
  prospĕrē ēvĕnĭo (4); *v.t*, **(follow)**,
  sĕquor (3 *dep*); **(to an office)**,
  succēdo (3)
success res sĕcundae, *f.pl*
successful (persons) fēlix;
  (things), prospĕrus
succession (to an office, etc.)
  successĭo, *f*; **(series)**, contĭnŭātĭo, *f*
successive contĭnŭus

successor successor, *m*
succinct brĕvis
succour *nn*, auxĭlĭum, *n*
succour *v.t*, succurro (3) *(with*
  dat)
succulent sūcōsus
succumb *v.i*, cēdo (3)
such *adj*, tālis, hūius mŏdi **(of this**
  kind)
suck *v.t*, sūgo (3)
sucket planta, *f*
suckle *v.t*, ūbĕra do (1) *(with*
  dat)
suction suctus, *m*
sudden sŭbĭtus
suddenly *adv*, sŭbĭto, rĕpentē
sue *v.t*, **(in law)**, in ius vŏco (1);
  (— for, beg for), rŏgo (1)
suet sēbum, *n*
suffer *v.t*, pătĭor (3 *dep*), fĕro
  (*irreg*); **(permit)**, permitto (3)
  (with dt); *v.i*, affĭcĭor (3 *pass*)
sufferance pătĭentĭa, *f*
sufferer (of illness) aeger, *m*
suffering *nn*, dŏlor, *m*
suffice *v.i*, sătis esse (*irreg*)
sufficiency *use adv*, sătis **(enough)**
sufficient *use* sătis, *adv*, *(with*
  genit. of noun)
suffocate *v.t*, suffŏco (1)
suffrage suffrăgĭum, *n*
sugar sacchăron, *n*
suggest *v.t*, sŭbĭcĭo (3) *(with acc.*
  of thing and dat. of person)
suggestion admŏnĭtus, *m*
suicide mors vŏluntārĭa, *f*; **(to**
  commit —), sĭbĭ mortem
  conscisco (3) **(inflict death upon**
  oneself)
suit (law —) līs, *f*; **(clothes)**,
  vestīmenta, *n.pl*
suit *v.i*, convĕnĭo (4); *or use*
  impers. vb, dĕcet **(it —s)**
suitable aptus, ĭdōnĕus
suite (retinue) cŏmĭtes, *c, pl*
suitor prŏcus, *m*
sulky mōrōsus
sullen torvus
sully *v.t*, inquĭno (1)
sulphur sulfur, *n*
sultry aestŭōsus
sum (total) summa, *f*; **(— of**
  money), pĕcūnĭa, *f*

sum up *v.t*, compŭto (1); **(speak briefly)**, summātim dīco (3)
summarily *adv*, **(immediately)**, sĭne mŏrā
summary *nn*, ĕpĭtŏme, *f*
summary *adj*, **(hasty)**, sŭbĭtus
summer *nn*, aestas, *f*; *adj*, aestīvus
summit căcūmen, *n*, *or use adj*, summus **(top of)**
summon *v.t*, arcesso (3)
summon up *v.t*, excĭto (1)
summons vŏcātĭo, *f*, accītu (*abl. case only*: **at the — of**)
sumptuous sumptŭōsus
sumptuousness appărātus, *m*
sun sōl, *m*
sun *v.i*, **(— oneself)**, ăprīcor (1 *dep*)
sunbeam rădĭus (*m*) sōlis
sunburnt ădustus
sundial sōlārĭum, *n*
sunny aprīcus
sunrise ortus (*m*) sōlis
sunset occāsus (*m*) sōlis
sunshine sōl, *m*
sup *v.i*, cēno (1)
superabound *v.i*, sŭpersum (*irreg*)
superb magnĭfĭcus
supercilious sŭperbus
superficial lĕvis
superfluous sŭpervăcānĕus
superhuman dīvīnus
superintend *v.t*, prōcūro (1)
superintendent cūrātor, *m*, praefectus, *m*
superior sŭpĕrĭor; **(to be —)**, *v.i*, sŭpĕro (1)
superiority *use adj*, sŭpĕrĭor
superlative exĭmĭus
supernatural dīvīnus
supernumerary ascriptīvus
superscription tĭtŭlus, *m*
supersede *v.t*, succēdo (3) (*with dat*)
superstition sŭperstĭtĭo, *f*
superstitious sŭperstĭtĭōsus
supervise *v.t*, prōcūro (1)
supper cēna, *f*
supplant *v.t*, **(surpass)**, praeverto (3)
supple flexĭbĭlis
supplement supplēmentum, *n*

suppliant supplex, *c*
supplication obsēcrātĭo, *f*
supply *nn*, cōpĭa, *f*; **(supplies, esp. military)**, commĕātus, *m*
supply *v.t*, suppĕdĭto (1); affĕro (*irreg*)
support *nn*, **(bearing)**, firmāmentum, *n*; **(military)**, subsĭdĭa, *n.pl*; **(sustenance)**, ălĭmentum, *n*
support *v.t*, sustĭnĕo (2); **(aid)**, adiŭvo (1); **(nourish)**, ălo (3)
supportable tŏlĕrābĭlis
supporter adiūtor, *m*
suppose *v.t*, pŭto (1), ŏpīnor (1 *pass*)
supposition ŏpīnĭo, *f*
suppress *v.t*, opprĭmo (3)
suppurate *v.i*, suppūro (1)
supremacy impĕrĭum, *n*
supreme sŭprēmus
sure ertus; **(reliable)**, fĭdēlis; **(I am —)**, compertum hăbĕo (2)
surely *adv*, prŏfecto; **(no doubt)**, nīmīrum; (*in questions; if an affirmative answer is expected*) nonne; (*if a negative answer*), num
surety vas, *m*, sponsor, *m*
surf fluctus, *m*
surface sŭperfĭcĭes, *f*
surge *v.i*, surgo (3)
surgeon chīrurgus, *m*
surgery chīrurgĭa, *f*
surly mōrōsus
surmise *nn*, coniectūra, *f*
surmise *v.t*, suspĭcor (1 *dep*)
surmount *v.t*, sŭpĕro (1)
surname cognōmen, *n*
surpass *v.t*, sŭpĕro (1)
surplus rĕlĭquum, *n*
surprise *nn*, mīrātĭo, *f*
surprise *v.t*, admīrātĭōnem mŏvĕo (2) (*with dat*); **(to attack)**, ădŏrĭor (4 *dep*)
surrender *nn*, dēdĭtĭo, *f*
surrender *v.t*, dēdo (3), trādo (3); *v.i*, sē dēdĕre (3 *reflex*)
surround *v.t*, cingo (3), circumdo (1)
survey *v.t*, contemplor (1 *dep*); **(land)**, mētĭor (4 *dep*)
surveyor fīnītor, *m*

survive *v.i*, sŭpersum (*irreg*)
survivor sŭperstes, *m, f*
susceptibility mollĭtĭa, *f*
susceptible mollis
suspect *v.t*, suspĭcor (1 *dep*)
suspend *v.t*, suspendo (3);
  (interrupt), intermitto (3);
  (— from office), dēmŏvĕo (2)
suspense dŭbĭtātĭo, *f*
suspension (interruption)
  intermissĭo, *f*
suspicion suspīcĭo, *f*
suspicious suspīcĭōsus
sustain *v.t*, sustĭnĕo (2)
sustenance ălĭmentum, *n*
swaddling clothes incūnābŭla,
  n.pl
swagger *v.i*, sē iactāre (1 *reflex*)
swallow *nn*, hĭrundo, *f*
swallow *v.t*, gluttĭo (4), sorbĕo
  (2)
swamp *nn*, pălus, *f*
swamp *v.t*, opprĭmo (3)
swampy pălūdōsus
swan cycnus, *m*
swarm (people) turba, *f*; (bees),
  exāmen, *n*
swarm *v.i*, glŏmĕror (1 *pass*)
swarthy fuscus
swathe *v.t*, collĭgo (1)
sway *nn*, impĕrĭum, *n*
sway *v.t*, (rule), rĕgo (3); *v.i*,
  (— to and fro), văcillo (1)
swear *v.i*, iūro (1); (— allegiance
  to), iūro in nōmen (*with genit. of
  person*)
sweat *nn*, sūdor, *m*
sweat *v.i*, sūdo (1)
sweep *v.t*, verro (3)
sweet dulcis
sweeten *v.t*, dulcem reddo (3)
  (make sweet)
sweetheart dēlĭcĭae, *f. pl*
sweetness dulcĭtūdo, *f*
swell *nn*, (wave), fluctus, *m*
swell *v.i*, tŭmĕo (2); *v.t*, augĕo (2)
swelling tŭmor, *m*
swerve *v.i*, dēclīno (1)
swift *adj*, cĕler
swiftness cĕlĕrĭtas, *f*
swill *v.t*, (drink), pōto (1)
swim *v.i*, năto (1)
swimmer nătātor, *m*

swimming *nn*, nătātĭo, *f*
swindle *nn*, fraus, *f*
swindle *v.t*, fraudo (1)
swindler fraudātor, *m*
swine sūs, *m, f*
swineherd sŭbulcus, *m*
swing *nn*, oscillātĭo, *f*
swing *v.t*, ăgĭto (1); *v.i*, pendĕo
  (2)
switch (cane) virga, *f*
switch *v.t*, mūto (1)
swollen tŭmĭdus
swoon *v.i*, use *phr*, ănĭmus
  rĕlinquit . . . (sensibility leaves ...)
swoop *nn*, use *vb*, advŏlo (1)
swoop on *v.i*, advŏlo (1)
sword glădĭus, *m*
sword-edge ăcĭes, *f*
swordfish xĭphĭas, *m*
sworn (treaty, etc.) confirmātus
  iūrĕiūrando (confirmed by
  swearing)
sycamore sўcămōrus, *f*
sycophant sўcŏphanta, *m*
syllable syllăba, *f*
symbol signum, *n*
symmetrical congrŭens
symmetry convĕnĭentĭa, *f*
sympathetic mĭsĕrĭcors
sympathize *v.t*, consentĭo (4)
sympathy consensus, *m*
symphony symphōnĭa, *f*
symptom signum, *n*
synagogue sўnăgōga, *f*
syndicate sŏcĭĕtas, *f*
synonym verbum ĭdem signĭficans
  (word expressing the same thing)
synopsis ēpĭtŏma, *f*
syntax syntaxis, *f*
syringe sīpho, *m*
syringe *v.t*, aspergo (3) (sprinkle)
system formŭla, *f*, rătĭo, *f*
systematic ordĭnātus

T

table mensa, *f*, tăbŭla, *f*; (list),
  index, *m*
tablecloth mantēle, *n*
tablet tābŭla, *f*
tacit tăcĭtus
taciturn tăcĭturnus
tack clāvŭlus, *m*

tack *v.t*, **(fix)**, fīgo (3); *v.i*, **(ships)**, rĕcīprŏcor (1 *pass*)
tackle (fittings) armāmenta, *n.pl*
tact dextĕrĭtas, *f*, urbānĭtas, *f*
tactician pĕrītus (*m*) rĕi mīlĭtāris
tactics (military) rătĭo (*f*) bellandi (method of making war)
tadpole rānuncŭlus, *m*
tag *v.t, use* fīgo (3) **(fix)**
tail cauda, *f*
tailor vestītor, *m*
taint *nn*, contāgĭo, *f*
taint *v.t*, infĭcĭo (3)
take *v.t*, căpĭo (3); **(grasp)**, prĕhendo (3); **(receive)**, accĭpĭo (3); **(seize)**, răpĭo (3); **(take possession of)**, occŭpo (1); **(— by storm)**, expugno (1); **(— away)**, aufĕro (*irreg*) ădĭmo (3); **(— in)**, excĭpĭo (3); **(— off)**, dēmo (3); **(— on)**, suscĭpĭo (3); **(— up)**, sūmo (3)
taking (capture of a city) expugnātĭo, *f*
tale fābŭla, *f*
talent (ability) ingĕnĭum, *n*; **(money)**, tălentum, *n*
talk *nn*, sermo, *m*
talk *v.i*, lŏquor (3 *dep*)
talkative lŏquax
tall prōcērus
tallness prōcērĭtas, *f*
tallow sēbum, *n*
tally *v.i*, convĕnĭo (4)
talon unguis, *m*
tamable dŏmābĭlis
tame *v.t*, dŏmo (1), mansŭēfăcĭo (3)
tame *adj*, mansŭēfactus, dŏmĭtus
tameness mansŭētūdo, *f*
tamer dŏmĭtor, *m*
tamper with *v.t*, tempto (1)
tan *v.t*, **(leather, etc.)**, confĭcĭo (3)
tangent *use* līnĕa, *f*, **(line)**
tangible tractābĭlis
tangle *nn*, implĭcātĭo, *f*
tangle *v.t*, implĭco (1)
tank lăcus, *m*
tanner cŏrĭārĭus, *m*
tantalize *v.t*, **(torment)**, fătīgo (1)
tap *nn*, **(blow)**, ictus, *m*
tap *v.t*, **(hit)**, fĕrĭo (4), pulso (1); *with* lĕvĭter **(lightly)**

tape taenĭa, *f*
taper cērĕus, *m*
taper *v.i*, fastīgor (1 *pass*)
tapestry *use* vēlum, *n*, **(curtain)**
tar pix lĭquĭda, *f*
tardiness tardĭtas, *f*
tardy tardus
tare lŏlĭum, *n*
target scŏpus, *m*
tarnish *v.i*, hĕbesco (3); *v.t*, inquĭno (1)
tarry *v.i*, mŏror (1 *dep*)
tart *nn*, crustŭlum, *n*
tart *adj*, ăcĭdus
task ŏpus, *n*
taste *nn*, **(sense of —)**, gustātus, *m*; **(flavour)**, săpor, *m*; **(judgement)**, iūdĭcĭum, *n*
taste *v.t*, gusto (1); *v.i*, **(have a flavour)**, săpĭo (3)
tasteful (elegant) ēlĕgans
tasteless insulsus
tasty săpĭdus
tattered pannōsus
tatters pannus, *m*
tattle *v.i*, garrĭo (4)
taunt *nn*, convīcĭum, *n*
taunt *v.t*, ōbĭcĭo (3) (*dat. of person and acc. of thing*)
taunting *adj*, contŭmēlĭōsus
tavern caupōna, *f*
tavern-keeper caupo, *m*
tawdry fūcōsus
tawny fulvus
tax *nn*, vectīgal, *n*
tax *v.t*, **(impose —)**, vectīgal impōno (3) (*with dat*)
taxable vectīgālis
tax collector exactor, *m*, pūblĭcānus, *m*
teach *v.t*, dŏcĕo (2) (*with acc. of person and acc. of thing*)
teacher doctor, *m*, măgister, *m*
teaching *nn*, doctrīna, *f*
team (— of horses) iŭgum, *n*
tear *nn*, lăcrĭma, *f*; **(to shed —s)**, lăcrĭmas fundo (3); **(rent)**, scissūra, *f*
tear *v.t*, scindo (3); **(— away)**, abscindo (3); **(— down, open)**, rēscindo (3); **(— up, in pieces)**, distrăho (3)
tearful flēbĭlis

tease *v.t*, obtundo (3)
teat mamma, *f*
technical *use phr*, prŏprĭus artis
  (particular to a skill)
tedious lentus
teem with *v.i*, scătĕo (2)
teethe *v.i*, dentĭo (4)
teething *nn*, dentītĭo, *f*
tell *v.t*, (give information), dīco
  (3); narro (1) (*with acc. of thing
  said and dat. of person told*),
  certĭōrem făcĭo (3) (*acc. of
  person told, foll. by* dē *with abl.
  of thing said*); (order), iŭbĕo (2)
teller (counter) nŭmĕrātor, *m*
temerity tĕmĕrĭtas, *f*
temper (of mind) ănĭmus, *m*;
  (bad —), īrācundĭa, *f*
temper *v.t*, tempĕro (1)
temperament nātūra, *f*, ingĕnĭum,
  n
temperance tempĕrantĭa, *f*
temperate tempĕrātus
temperate climate tĕmpĕrĭes, *f*
temperateness mŏdĕrātĭo, *f*
tempest tempestas, *f*
tempestuous prŏcellōsus
temple templum, *n*, aedes, *f*; (of
  the head), tempus, *n*
temporal hūmānus
temporary *use adv. phr*, ad
  tempus (for the time being)
tempt *v.t*, tento (1)
temptation (allurement) illĕcĕbra,
  f
tempter tentātor, *m*
tempting *adj*, illĕcĕbrōsus
ten dĕcem; (— each), dēni;
  (— time), *adv*, dĕcĭes
tenacious tĕnax
tenacity tĕnācĭtas, *f*
tenant inquĭlīnus, *m*
tend *v.t*, (care for), cŏlo (3); *v.i*,
  (go, direct oneself), tendo (3);
  (incline to), inclīno (1); (be
  accustomed), consŭesco (3)
tendency inclīnātĭo, *f*
tender *adj*, tĕner, mollis
tender *v.t*, (offer), dēfĕro (*irreg*)
tenderness mollĭtĭa, *f*,
  indulgentĭa, *f*
tenement conductum, *n*
tenor (course) tĕnor, *m*, cursus,
m

tense *adj*, tentus, intentus
tense *nn*, tempus, *n*
tension intentĭo, *f*
tent tăbernācŭlum, *n*; (general's
  —), praetŏrĭum, *n*
tentacle cornĭcŭlum, *n*
tenth dĕcĭmus
tepid ēgĕlĭdus, tĕpĭdus; (to be —),
  v.i, tĕpĕo (2)
term (period of time) spătĭum, *n*;
  (limit), fīnis, *m*; (word), verbum,
  n; (condition), condĭcĭo, *f*
term *v.t*, vŏco (1)
terminate *v.t*, termĭno (1)
termination fīnis, *m*
terrace sōlārĭum, *n*
terrestrial terrestris
terrible terrĭbĭlis
terrify *v.t*, terrĕo (2)
territory fines, *m. pl*, ăger, *m*
terror terror, *m*, păvor, *m*
terse brĕvis
terseness brĕvĭtas, *f*
test *nn*, expĕrīmentum, *n*
test *v.t*, expĕrĭor (4 *dep*)
testament testāmentum, *n*
testator testātor, *m*
testify *v.t*, testĭfĭcor (1 *dep*)
testimony testĭmōnĭum, *n*
testy stŏmăchōsus
text scriptum, *n*
textile textĭle, *n*
texture textus, *m*
than *conj*, quam
thank *v.t*, grātĭas ăgo (3) (*with
  dat. of person*)
thankfulness grātus ănĭmus, *m*
thankless ingrātus
thanks grātĭas, *f. pl*
thanksgiving actĭo (*f*) grātĭārum
that *demonstrative pron*, ille, is,
  iste
that *relative pron*, qui, quae,
  quod
that *conj*, (*with purpose or
  consecutive clauses*) ut (ne *if
  negative*); (*after vbs introducing
  statements*) *no separate word,
  but rendered by the expression
  itself*: *e.g.* he said that the king
  was coming, rēgem vĕnīre dixit
thatch strāmentum, *n*

thaw *v.t*, solvo (3); *v.i*, sē
  rĕsolvĕre (3 *reflex*)
the *no equivalent in Latin*
theatre thĕātrum, *n*
theatrical thĕātrālis
theft furtum, *n*
their *reflexive*, sŭus; *otherwise*
  ĕōrum, (*f*, ĕārum)
them *use appropriate case of*
  pron, is, ille, iste
theme prōpŏsĭtĭo, *f*
themselves *reflexive pron*, sē;
  (pron. emphatic) ipsi, ae, a
then *adv. of* (time), tum;
  (therefore), ĭgĭtur
thence *adv*, inde, illinc
theologian thĕŏlŏgus, *m*
theology thĕŏlŏgĭa, *f*
theorem thĕōrēma, *n*
theoretical rătĭōnālis
theory rătĭo, *f*
there (in *or* **at that place)**, ĭbĭ; **(to**
  that place), ēŏ; **(— is)**, est;
  (— are), sunt *(from* esse)
thereabouts *adv*, circā
thereafter *adv*, dĕinde
therefore *adv*, ĭgĭtur, ergo
thereupon *adv*, sŭbinde
thesis prōpŏsĭtum, *n*
they *as subject of vb. usually not*
  rendered; otherwise use ĭi, illi,
  isti
thick crassus, densus, confertus
thicken *v.t*, denso (1); *v.i*,
  concresco (3)
thicket dūmētum, *n*
thick-headed crassus
thickness crassĭtūdo, *f*
thick-set (of body) compactus
thick-skinned (indifferent)
  neglĕgens
thief fur, *c*
thieve *v.t*, fūror (1 *dep*)
thieving *nn*, **(theft)**, furtum, *n*
thigh fĕmur, *n*
thin tĕnŭis, grăcĭlis
thin *v.t*, tĕnŭo (1)
thing rēs, *f*
think *v.t*, cōgĭto (1); **(believe,**
  suppose), crēdo (3), arbĭtror (1
  dep), pŭto (1), existĭmo (1)
thinker phĭlŏsŏphus, *m*
thinness tĕnŭĭtas, *f*

third *adj*, tertĭus; **(a — part)**,
  tertĭa pars, *f*; **(thirdly)**, *adv*, tertĭo
thirst *v.i*, sĭtĭo (4)
thirst *nn*, sĭtis, *f*
thirsty sĭtĭens
thirteen trĕdĕcim
thirteenth tertĭus dĕcĭmus
thirtieth trīgēsĭmus
thirty trīginta
this *demonstrative pron*, hīc,
  haec, hōc
thiste cardŭus, *m*
thither *adv*, ĕō, illūc; **(hither and —)**,
  hūc atque illūc
thong lōrum, *n*
thorn sentis, *m*, spīna, *f*
thorn-bush vĕpres, *m*
thorny spīnōsus
thorough perfectus; **(exact)**,
  subtīlis
thoroughbred gĕnĕrōsus
thoroughfare pervĭum, *n*
those *demonstrative pron*, illi
though *conj*, etsi
thought (act or faculty of thinking)
  cōgĭtātĭo, *f*; **(opinion)**, cōgĭtātum,
  n; **(plan, intention)**, consĭlĭum, *n*
thoughtful (careful) prōvĭdus;
  (deep in thought), multa pŭtans
thoughtfulness cūra, *f*, cōgĭtātĭo, *f*
thoughtless tĕmĕrārĭus,
  inconsultus
thoughtlessness nĕglegentĭa, *f*,
  tĕmĕrĭtas, *f*
thousand mille *(indeclinable adj)*;
  in pl, mīlĭa *(n.pl, nn)*
thrash *v.t*, tundo (3); **(corn)**, tĕro
  (3)
thrashing *nn*, trītūra, *f*;
  (chastisement), verbĕrātĭo, *f*
thrashing-floor ārĕa, *f*
thread fīlum, *n*
thread *v.t*, **(— one's way)**, sē
  insĭnŭāre (1 *reflex*)
threadbare obsŏlētus
threat mĭnae, *f. pl*
threaten *v.t*, mĭnor (1 *dep*) *(with*
  acc. of thing and dat. of person);
  v.i, **(impend)**, immĭnĕo (2)
threatening *adj*, mĭnax
three tres; **(— each)**, terni;
  (— times), *adv*, ter
threefold (triple) trĭplex

threehundred trĕcenti
threehundredth trĕcentensĭmus
thresh *v.t*, tĕro (3)
threshold līmen, *n*
thrice *adj*, ter
thrift frūgālĭtas, *f*
thrifty parcus
thrill *v.t*, *use* afficĭo (3) **(affect)**
thrill (of pleasure) hĭlārĭtas, *f*; **(a shock)**, stringor, *m*
thrilling *adj*, *use vb*, afficĭo (3) **(to affect)**
thrive *v.i*, vĭgĕo (2)
throat fauces, *f. pl*
throb *v.i*, palpĭto (1)
throbbing *nn*, palpĭtātĭo, *f*
throne sŏlĭum, *n*; **(regal, imperial power)**, regnum, *n*
throng *nn*, multĭtūdo, *f*
throng *v.t*, cĕlĕbro (1)
throttle *v.t*, strangŭlo (1)
through *prep*, per *(with acc)*; **(on account of)**, propter *(with acc)*
through *adv, often expressed by a compound vb, with* per; e.g. perfĕro **(carry through)**
throughout *prep*, per; *adv*, pĕnĭtus **(entirely, wholly)**
throw *nn*, iactus, *m*
throw *v.t*, iacĭo (3), cōnĭcĭo (3) **(— away)**, ăbĭcĭo (3); **(— back)**, rēĭcĭo (3); **(— down)**, dēĭcĭo (3); **(— oneself at the feet of)**, se prōĭcĕre ad pĕdes *(with genit. of person)*; **(— out)**, ēĭcĭo (3)
thrush turdus, *m*
thrust *nn*, pĕtītĭo, *f*
thrust *v.t*, trūdo (3); **(— forward)**, prōtrūdo (3)
thumb pollex, *m*
thump *nn*, cŏlăphus, *m*
thump *v.t*, tundo (3)
thunder *nn*, tŏnĭtrus, *m*; **(— bolt)**, fulmen, *n*
thunder *v.i*, tŏno (1)
thunderstruck attŏnĭtus
thus *adv*, īta, sīc
thwart *nn*, **(seat)**, transtrum, *n*
thwart *v.t*, obsto (1) *(with dat. of person)*, impĕdĭo (4)
tiara tĭăra, *f*
ticket tessĕra, *f*
tickle *v.t*, tĭtillo (1)

tickling *nn*, tĭtillātĭo, *f*
ticklish lūbrĭcus
tide aestus, *m*
tidiness mundĭtĭa, *f*
tidings nuntĭus, *m*
tidy mundus
tie *nn*, vincŭlum, *n*
tie *v.t*, lĭgo (1), nōdo (1)
tier ordo, *m*
tiger tigris, *c*
tight strictus
tighten *v.t*, stringo (3)
tile tēgūla, *f*
till *prep*, usque ad *(with acc)*
till *conj*, dum, dōnĕc
till *nn*, arca, *f*
till *v.t*, cŏlo (3)
tillage, tilling *nn*, cultus, *m*
tiller (boat) clāvus, *(m)* gŭbernācŭli **(handle of the rudder)**
tilt *v.t*, **(bend)**, dēclīno (1)
timber mātĕria, *f*
time tempus, *n*; **(period, space of —)**, intervallum, *n*, spătĭum, *n*; **(generation, age)**, aetas, *f*; **(— of day)**, hōra, *f*; **(at the right —)**, *adv, phr*, ad tempus; **(at —s)**, *adv*, interdum; **(once upon a —)**, *adv*, ōlim; **(at the same —)**, *adv*, sĭmŭl; **(at that —)**, *adv*, tum
timely *adj*, opportūnus
timid tĭmĭdus
timidity tĭmĭdĭtas, *f*
tin plumbum album, *n*
tincture cŏlor, *m*
tinder fōmes, *m*
tinge *v.t*, tingo (3)
tingle *v.i*, prūrĭo (4)
tinker făber, *m*, **(artificer)**
tinkle *v.i*, tinnĭo (4)
tiny exĭgŭus, parvŭlus
tip căcŭmen, *n*
tip *v.t*, **(put a point on)**, praefīgo (3); **(tip over)**, verto (3)
tire *v.t*, fătīgo (1); *v.i*, dēfătīgor (1 *dep*)
tired fessus
tiresome mŏlestus
tissue textus, *m*
titbits cūpēdĭa, *n.pl*
tithe dĕcŭma, *f*
title tĭtŭlus, *m*

titled (of nobility) nōbĭlis
titter *nn*, rīsus, *m*
to *prep*, (*motion towards a place, and expressions of time*), ad (*with acc*); (*sometimes, e.g. names of towns, acc. of nn. alone*); *often dat. case can be used, e.g. indirect object after vb. to give*; (*before a clause expressing purpose*), ut; (*sometimes indicates the infinitive of a vb*), *e.g.* **to love,** ămāre
toad būfo, *m*
toast *v.t*, torrĕo (2); **(a person's health),** prōpīno (1) (*with dat. of person*)
today *adv*, hŏdĭē
toe dĭgĭtus, *m*
together *adv*, sĭmŭl, ūnā
toil *nn*, lăbor, *m*
toil *v.i*, lăbōro (1)
toilet (care of person, etc.), cultus, *m*
token signum, *n*
tolerable tŏlĕrābĭlis
tolerance tŏlĕrantĭa, *f*
tolerate *v.t*, tŏlĕro (1)
toll *nn*, vectīgal, *n*
tomb sĕpulcrum, *n*, tŭmŭlus, *m*
tombstone lăpis, *m*
tomorrow *adv*, crās
tomorrow *nn*, crastĭnus dĭes, *m*
tone sŏnus, *m*
tongs forceps, *m*
tongue lingua, *f*
tonight *adv*, hŏdĭē nocte
tonsils tonsillae, *f. pl*
too (also) ĕtĭam; (**— little**), părum; (**— much**), nĭmis; *comparative adj. or adv. can be used, e.g.* **too far,** longĭus
tool instrūmentum, *n*
tooth dens, *m*
toothache dŏlor (*m*) dentĭum
toothed dentātus
toothless ēdentŭlus
toothpick dentiscalpĭum, *n*
top *use adj*, summus *in agreement with nn, e.g.* **the top of the rock,** summum saxum, *n*; (**summit**), căcūmen, *n*
top *v.t*, sŭpĕro (1)
topic rēs, *f*

topmost summus
topography *use phr*, nātūra (*f*) lŏci (**nature of the land**)
torch fax, *f*
torment *nn*, crŭcĭātus, *m*
torment *v.t*, crŭcĭo (1)
tornado turbo, *m*
torpid torpens, pĭger
torpor torpor, *m*
torrent torrens, *m*
tortoise testūdo, *f*
tortuous sĭnŭōsus
torture *nn*, crŭcĭātus, *m*
torture *v.t*, crŭcĭo (1)
torturer carnĭfex, *m*
toss *nn*, iactus, *m*
toss *v.t*, iacto (1)
total *nn*, summa, *f*
total *adj*, tōtus
totally *adv*, omnīno
totter *v.i*, lăbo (1)
touch *nn*, tactus, *m*; (**contact**), contāgĭo, *f*
touch *v.t*, tango (3), attingo (3); (**move**), mŏvĕo (2)
touchy stŏmăchōsus
tough *adj*, lentus
toughness dūrĭtĭa, *f*
tour pĕrĕgrīnātĭo, *f*, ĭter, *n*
tourist pĕrĕgrīnātor, *m*
tournament *use* certāmen, *n*, (**contest**)
tow *v.t*, trăho (3)
tow *nn*, (**hemp**), stuppa, *f*
towards *prep*, (**of direction, position**), ad (*with acc*); (**of time**), sub (*with acc*); (**emotions**), ergā, in (*with acc*); (**with names of towns**), versus (*placed after the noun*)
towel mantēle, *n*
tower *nn*, turris, *f*
tower *v.i*, exsto (1)
town urbs, *f*, oppĭdum, *n*
townsman oppĭdānus, *m*
toy (child's rattle) crĕpundĭa, *n.pl*
toy with *v.i*, illūdo (3)
trace *nn*, vestīgĭum, *n*, signum, *n*
trace *v.t*, sĕquendo invĕnĭo (4) (**find by following**)
track *nn*, (**path**), callis, *m*; (**footsteps, etc.**), vestīgĭum, *n*
track *v.t*, (**— down**), investīgo (1);

(pursue), sĕquor (3 *dep*)
trackless āvĭus
tract (region) rĕgĭo, *f*; (booklet),
  lĭbellus, *m*
tractable dŏcĭlis
trade mercātūra, *f*; (a particular —) ,
  ars, *f*
trade *v.i*, mercātūram făcĭo (3)
trade mercātor, *m*
tradition mĕmŏrĭa, *f*
traditional *use phr*, trādĭtus ā
  māiōrĭbus (handed down from
  our ancestors)
traffic (trade, etc.) commercĭum,
  n; (streets, etc.), *use phr. with*
  frĕquento (1) (to crowd)
tragedy trăgoedĭa, *f*
tragic trăgĭcus; (unhappy), tristis
trail (path) callis, *m*
train ordo, *m*; (procession),
  pompa, *f. pl*; (of a dress),
  pēnĭcŭlāmentum, *n*
train *v.t*, instĭtŭo (3), exercĕo (2)
trainer exercĭtor, *m*
training *nn*, disciplīna, *f*
traitor prōdĭtor, *m*
traitorous perfĭdus
tramp *v.i*, ambŭlo (1)
trample on *v.t*, obtĕro (3)
trance (elation, exaltation) ēlātĭo,
  f
tranquil tranquillus, plăcĭdus
transact *v.t*, ăgo (3)
transaction rēs, *f*, nĕgōtĭum, *n*
transcend *v.t*, sŭpĕro (1)
transcribe *v.t*, transcrībo (3)
transfer *nn*, (of property),
  mancĭpĭum, *n*
transfer *v.t*, transfĕro (*irreg*)
transfix *v.t*, transfīgo (3)
transform *v.t*, mūto (1)
transgress *v.t*, vĭŏlo (1); *v.i*,
  pecco (1)
transgression (fault) dēlictum, *n*
transit transĭtus, *m*
transitory cădūcus
translate *v.t*, verto (3)
translation (a work) ŏpus
  translātum, *n*; (act), translātĭo, *f*
translator interpres, *c*
transmigrate *v.i*, transmĭgro (1)
transmit *v.t*, transmitto (3)
transparent perlūcĭdus

transpire *v.i*. (get about), vulgor
  (1 *pass*)
transplant *v.t*, transfĕro (*irreg*)
transport *nn, use vb. below*; (joy),
  laetĭtĭa, *f*, exsultātĭo, *f*
transport *v.t*, transporto (1),
  trāĭcĭo (3)
trap *nn*, insĭdĭae, *f. pl*; (for
  animals), lăquĕus, *m*
trap *v.t, use phr*, illĭcĭo (3) in
  insĭdĭas (entice into a trap)
trappings insignĭa, *n.pl*
trash scrūta, *n.pl*, nūgae, *f. pl*
travel *nn*, ĭter, *n*
travel *v.i*, ĭter făcĭo (3)
traveller vĭātor, *m*
traverse *v.t*, ŏbĕo (4)
travesty (mockery) lūdĭbrĭum, *n*
tray fercŭlum, *n*
treacherous perfĭdus
treachery perfĭdĭa, *f*, fraus, *f*
tread *nn*, grădus, *m*
tread *v.i*, ingrĕdĭor (3 *dep*); *v.t*,
  (— on), calco (1)
treason māiestas, *f*
treasure ŏpes *f. pl*; (hoard,
  treasure-house), thēsaurus, *m*
treasure *v.t*, (regard highly),
  magni aestĭmo (1); (store up),
  rĕcondo (3)
treasurer praefectus (*m*) aerārĭi
  (director of the treasury)
treasury aerārĭum, *n*
treat *nn*, dēlectātĭo, *f*
treat *v.t*, (deal with, behave
  towards), hăbĕo (2);
  (medically), cūro (1); (discuss),
  ăgo (3)
treatise lĭber, *m*
treatment tractātĭo, *f*; (cure),
  cūrātĭo, *f*
treaty foedus, *n*
treble *adj*, trĭplex
treble *v.t*, trĭplĭco (1)
tree arbor, *f*
trellis cancelli, *m. pl*
tremble *v.i*, trĕmo (3)
trembling *nn*, trĕmor, *m*
tremendous ingens
tremulous trĕmŭlus
trench fossa, *f*
trepidation trĕpĭdātĭo, *f*
trespass (crime) dēlictum, *n*

trespass *v.i, use phr. with* ingrēdi (to enter), *and* tē (mē, *etc.*), invīto (without your (my) permission)

tress (hair) grādus, *m*

trial (legal) iūdĭcĭum, *n*; (experiment), expĕrĭentĭa, *f*

triangle trĭangŭlum, *n*

triangular trĭangŭlus

tribe (Roman) trĭbus, *f*; (other), pŏpŭlus, *m*

tribunal iūdĭcĭum, *n*

tribune trĭbūnus, *m*

tributary *adj*, (paying tribute), vectīgālis

tributary *nn*, (river), *use phr*, qui in flūmen inflŭit (which flows into a river)

tribute trĭbūtum, *n*, vectīgal, *n*

trick *nn*, dŏlus, *m*, fraus, *f*

trick *v.t*, dēcĭpĭo (3)

trickery dŏlus, *m*

trickle *v.i*, māno (1)

trickster hŏmo dŏlōsus, fallax

tricky (dangerous) pĕrīcŭlōsus

trident trĭdens, *m*

tried (well —) prŏbātus

trifle *nn*, rēs parva, *f*, nūgae, *f. pl*

trifle *v.i.* lūdo (3)

trifling *adj*, lĕvus

trim *adj*, nĭtĭdus

trim *v.t.* pŭto (1)

trinkets mundus, *m*

trip *nn*, (journey), ĭter, *n*

trip *v.t.* supplanto (1); *v.i.* (stumble), offendo (3), lābor (3 dep)

tripe ŏmāsum, *n*

triple trĭplex

tripod trĭpus, *m*

trite trītus

triumph (Roman celebration of victory) trĭumphus, *m*; (victory), victōrĭa, *f*

triumph *v.i, and v.t*, trĭumpho (1)

triumphant victor

triumvirate trĭumvĭrātus, *m*

trivial lĕvis, vīlis

troop (band) mănus, *f*; (— of cavalry), turma, *f*; (—s), cōpĭae, *f, pl*

troop *v.i*, conflŭo (3)

trooper ĕquĕs, *m*

trophy trŏpaeum, *n*

trot *nn*, lentus cursus, *m*

trot *v.i*, lento cursu ĕo (4); (proceed on a slow course)

trouble *nn*, (disadvantage), incommŏdum, *n*; (exertion), ŏpĕra, *f*; (commotion), tŭmultus, *m*; (annoyance), mŏlestĭa, *f*

trouble *v.t*, (disturb), sollĭcĭto (1); (harass), vexo (1); (— oneself about), cŭro (1)

troublesome mŏlestus

trough alvĕus, *m*

trousers brăcae, *f. pl*

trowel trulla, *f*

truant *nn, use phr*, qui consultō ăbest (who is absent deliberately)

truce indūtĭae, *f. pl*

truck plaustrum, *n*

truculent (grim) trux

trudge *v.i, use phr*, aegrē ambŭlo (1) (walk with difficulty)

true vērus; (faithful), fidus

truffle tŭber, *n*

truly *adv*, vērē, prŏfectō

trumpery scrūta, *n.pl*

trumpet *nn*, tŭba, *f*, būcĭna, *f*

trumpeter tŭbĭcen, *m*

truncheon fustis, *m*

trundle *v.t*, volvo (3)

trunk truncus, *m*; (of elephant) prŏboscis, *f*; (box), arca, *f*

truss fascĭa, *f*

trust *nn*, fides, *f*

trust *v.t*, confido (3 *semi-dep*) (*with dat. of person*), crēdo (3); commit to), commĭtto (3)

trustworthy, trusty certus, fidus

truth vērĭtas, *f*; (true things), vēra, *n.pl*; (in —), *adv*, vēro

truthful vērax

truthfulness vērĭtas, *f*

try *v.i*, (attempt), cōnor (1 *dep*); *v.t*, (put to the test), tento (1); (— in court), iūdĭco (1)

trying *adj*, mŏlestus

tub lābrum, *n*

tube tŭbŭlus, *m*

tuber tŭber, *n*

tubular tŭbŭlātus

tuck up *v.t*, succingo (3)

tuft crīnis, *m*

tug *v.t*, trăho (3)

tuition instĭtuutĭo, *f*
tumble *nn*, cāsus, *m*
tumbler (beaker) pōcŭlum, *n*
tumour tŭmor, *m*
tumult tŭmultus, *m*
tumultuous tŭmultŭōsus
tun (cask) dōlĭum, *n*
tune (melody) cantus, *m*; **(out of —),**
  adj, absŏnus
tune *v.t*, **(stringed instrument),**
  tendo (3)
tuneful cănōrus
tunic tŭnĭca, *f*
tunnel cănālis, *m*, cŭnīcŭlus, *m*
tunny fish thunnus, *m*
turban mĭtra, *f*
turbid turbĭdus
turbot rhombus, *m*
turbulence tŭmultus, *m*
turbulent turbŭlentus
turf caespes, *m*
turgid turgĭdus
turmoil turba, *f*, tŭmultus, *m*
turn (movement) conversĭo, *f*;
  (bending); flexus, *m*; **(change),**
  commūtātĭo, *f*; **(by — s, in —),**
  adv, invīcem, per vĭces; **(a**
  good —), offĭcĭum, *n*
turn *v.t*, verto (3); **(bend)**, flecto
  (3); **(— aside)**, dēflecto (3); *v.i*, sē
  dēclīnāre (1 *reflex*); **(— away),**
  āverto (3); **(— the back)**, *v.i*,
  tergum verto (3); **(change)**, *v.i*,
  mūtor (1 *pass*); **(— back)**, *v.i*,
  rĕvertor (3 *pass*); **(— out)**, *v.t*
  ēĭcĭo (3); *v.i*, ēvĕnĭo (4);
  (— round), *v.t*, circŭmăgo (3); *v.i*,
  circŭmăgor (3 *pass*)
turning *nn*, flexus, *m*
turnip rāpum, *n*
turpitude turpĭtūdo, *f*
turret turris, *f*
turtledove turtur, *m*
tusk dens, *m*
tutelage tūtēla, *f*
tutor māgister, *m*
twang *nn*, sŏnĭtus, *m*
twang *v.i*, sŏno (1)
tweak *v.t*, vellĭco (1)
tweezers volsella, *f*
twelfth dŭŏdĕcĭmus
twelve dŭŏdĕcim; **(— each),**
  duodēni

twentieth vīcēsĭmus
twenty vīginti
twice *adj*, bis
twig rāmŭlus, *m*
twilight crĕpuscŭlum, *n*
twin *nn and adj*, gĕmĭnus
twine *nn*, līnum, *n*
twine *v.t*, circumplĭco (1); *v.i*,
  circumplector (3 *dep*)
twinge *nn*, dŏlor, *m*
twinkle *v.i*, mĭco (1)
twirl *v.t* verso (1)
twist *v.t*, torquĕo (2); *v.i*, sē
  torquēre (2 *reflex*)
twit *v.t*, ōbĭcĭo (3) (*acc. of thing*
  and dat, of person)
twitch *v.t*, vellĭco (1)
twitter *v.i*, **(chirp)**, pīpĭlo (1)
two dŭŏ; **(— each)**, bīni
two-fold dŭplex
two-footed bĭpes
two hundred dŭcenti
type (class, sort) gĕnus, *n*;
  (example), exemplar, *n*
typical *use adj*, ūsĭtātus **(familiar)**
tyrannical tўrannĭcus, sŭperbus
tyrannize *v.i*, dŏmĭnor (1 *dep*)
tyranny dŏmĭnātĭo, *f*
tyrant tўrannus, *m*

U

ubiquitous praesens **(present)**
udder ūber, *n*
ugliness dēformĭtas, *f*
ugly dēformis
ulcer vŏmĭca, *f*
ulcerate *v.i*, suppūro (1)
ulceration ulcĕrātĭo, *f*
ulcerous ulcĕrōsus
ulterior ultĕrĭor
ultimate ultĭmus
ultimatum (to present —) ultĭmam
  condĭcĭōnem ferre (*irreg*)
umbrage (to take — at) *v.t*, aegrē
  fĕro (*irreg*)
umbrella umbella, *f*
umpire arbĭter, *m*
un- *prefix, often* nōn, haud, *can*
  be used
unabashed intrĕpĭdus; **(brazen),**
  impŭdens
unabated immĭnūtus

unable *use vb. phr. with* non
  posse **(to be unable)**
unacceptable ingrātus
unaccompanied incŏmĭtātus
unaccomplished infectus
unaccountable inexplĭcābĭlis
unaccustomed insŏlĭtus
unacquainted ignārus
unadorned ĭnornātus
unadulterated sincērus
unadvisable **(foolhardy)** audax
unadvised inconsĭdĕrātus
unaffected **(natural)** simplex;
  (untouched), intĕger
unaided *use adv. phr,* sĭne
  auxĭlĭo **(without help)**
unalloyed pūrus
unalterable immūtābĭlis
unambitious hŭmĭlis
unanimity ūnănĭmĭtas, *f*
unanimous ūnĭversus **(all
  together)**
unanimously *adv,* ūnā vōce
unanswerable non rĕvincendus
unanswered *use vb.* rēspondĕo
  (2) **(to answer)**
unappeased implācātus
unapproachable nōn ădĕundus
unarmed ĭnermis
unassailable ĭnexpugnābĭlis
unassailed intactus
unassuming mŏdestus
unattainable *use phr. with vb.*
  attīngo (3) **(to reach)**
unattempted ĭnexpertus
unauthorized illĭcĭtus
unavailing fūtĭlis
unavoidable ĭnēvītābĭlis
unaware inscĭus
unawares *adv,* dē imprōvīso
unbar *v.t,* rēsĕro (1)
unbearable intŏlĕrābĭlis
unbecoming indĕcōrus
unbelieving incrēdŭlus
unbend *v.t,* rĕmitto (3)
unbending rĭgĭdus
unbiassed intĕger
unbidden iniussus
unbind *v.t,* solvo (3)
unblemished pūrus
unbound sŏlūtus
unbounded infinītus
unbreakable *use phr,* quod frangi

non pŏtest **(that cannot be
  broken)**
unbridled effrēnātus
unbroken intĕger, perpĕtŭus
unbuckle *v.t,* diffībŭlo (1)
unburden *v.t,* exŏnĕro (1)
unburied ĭnhŭmātus
uncared for neglectus
unceasing perpĕtŭus
uncertain incertus, dŭbĭus; **(to
  be —),** *v.i,* dŭbĭto (1)
uncertainty dŭbĭtātĭo, *f*
unchangeable immūtābĭlis
unchanged constans; **(to
  remain —),** *v.i,* permănĕo (2)
uncharitable inhŭmānus
uncivil ĭnurbānus
uncivilized incultus
uncle **(father's side)** pătrŭus, *m*;
  (mother's side), ăvuncŭlus, *m*
unclean inquĭnātus
unclouded sĕrēnus
uncoil *v.t,* ēvolvo (3); *v.i,* se
  ēvolvĕre **(3** *reflex***)**
uncombed incomptus
uncomfortable mŏlestus
uncommon rārus, insŏlĭtus
uncompleted imperfectus
unconcerned sĕcūrus
unconditional simplex; **(to
  surrender —ly),** mănus do (1)
uncongenial ingrātus
unconnected disiunctus
unconquerable invictus
unconquered invictus
unconscious **(unaware)** inscĭus;
  (insensible); *use phr,* sensu ablāto
  (with feeling withdrawn)
unconstitutional non lēgĭtĭmus
uncontaminated incontāmĭnātus
uncontested *use phr,* quod in
  contentĭōnem non vēnit **(that has
  not come into dispute)**
uncontrollable impŏtens
uncontrolled līber
uncooked incoctus
uncouth incultus
uncover *v.t,* dētĕgo (3)
unction unctĭo, *f*
uncultivated incultus; **(person),**
  ăgrestis
uncut **(hair)** intonsus, prōmissus
undamaged intĕger

undaunted fortis
undeceive *v.t*, errōrem ērĭpĭo (3)
undecided incertus; **(of a battle)**, anceps
undefended nūdus, indēfensus
undeniable certus
under *prep*, sub *(with abl. to denote rest, and acc. to denote motion)*; infra *(with acc)*; **(— the leadership of)**, *use abl. phr, e.g.* tĕ dŭce **(— your leadership)**
underclothes sŭbūcŭla, *f*
undercurrent flŭentum subterlābens, *n*
underestimate *v.t*, mĭnōris aestĭmo (1)
undergo *v.t*, sŭbĕo (3), fĕro *(irreg)*
underground *adj*, subterrānĕus
undergrowth virgulta, *n.pl*
underhand *adj*, clandestīnus
underlying (lying hidden) lătens
undermine *v.t*, subrŭo (3)
undermost *adj*, infĭmus
underneath *adv*, infrā
underrate *v.t*, mĭnōris aestĭmo (1)
understand *v.t*, intellĕgo (3), comprĕhendo (3)
understanding *nn*, mens, *f*; **(agreement)**, conventum, *n*
undertake *v.t*, suscĭpĭo (3); **(put in hand)**, incĭpĭo (3)
undertaker vespillo, *m*
undertaking, *nn*, inceptum, *n*
undervalue *v.t*, mĭnōris aestĭmo (1)
undeserved immĕrĭtus
undeserving indignus
undesirable *use phr. with* nōn *and* cŭpĭo (3) *or* expĕto (3) **(to desire)**
undetected tectus
undeveloped immātūrus
undigested crūdus
undiminished immĭnūtus
undisciplined ĭnexercĭtātus
undisguised non dissĭmŭlātus
undistinguished ignōbĭlis
undisturbed stăbĭlis, immōtus
undo *v.t*, solvo (3); **(render ineffectual)**, irrĭtum făcĭo (3)
undone infectus
undoubted certus

undoubtedly *adv*, sĭne dŭbĭo
undress *v.t*, vestem dētrăho (3) *(with dat. of person)*
undressed *adj*, nūdus
undue nĭmĭus
undulate *v.i*, fluctŭo (1)
unduly *adv*, **(excessively)**, nĭmĭum
undying immortālis
unearth *v.t*, dētĕgo (3)
unearthly *adv, use* terrĭbĭlis **(frightful)**
uneasiness anxĭĕtas, *f*
uneasy anxĭus
uneducated indoctus
unemployed ōtĭōsus
unending aeternus, infīnītus
unenterprising ĭners, ĭnaudax
unequal impar, ĭnīquus
unequalled singŭlāris
unequivocal non dŭbĭus
unerring certus
uneven ĭnaequālis; **(of ground)**, ĭnīquus
unevenness ĭnīquĭtas, *f*
unexampled ĭnaudītus, ūnĭcus
unexpected ĭnŏpīnātus
unexpectedly *adv*, ex *(or* dē*)* imprōvīso
unexplored ĭnexplōrātus
unfailing pĕrennis
unfair ĭnīquus, iniustus
unfairness ĭnīquĭtas, *f*
unfaithful infidēlis, perfĭdus
unfaithfulness infidēlĭtas
unfamiliar insŭētus
unfashionable *use phr. with* extrā consŭētūdĭnem **(outside of custom)**
unfasten *v.t*, solvo (3), rĕfīgo (3)
unfathomable infīnītus
unfavourable ĭnīquus; **(omen)**, sĭnister, infēlix
unfeeling dūrus
unfeigned sincērus, simplex
unfinished imperfectus; **(task)** infectus
unfit incommŏdus
unfitness ĭnūtĭlĭtas, *f*
unfitting indĕcōrus
unfix *v.t*, rĕfīgo (3)
unfold *v.t*, explĭco (1)
unforeseen imprōvīsus

unforgiving implācābĭlis
unforgotten *use phr. with*
mĕmor, *adj*, **(remembering)**
unfortified immūnītus
unfortunate infēlix
unfounded (groundless) vānus
unfriendliness ĭnĭmīcītĭa
unfriendly ĭnĭmīcus
unfulfilled irrĭtus, ĭnānis
unfurl *v.t*, pando (3)
unfurnished nūdus
ungainly rŭdis
ungentlemanly illĭbĕrālis
ungodly incestus
ungovernable impŏtens,
indŏmĭtus
ungraceful ĭnēlĕgans
ungrateful ingrātus
unguarded incustōdītus; **(speech
or action),** incautus
unhappiness mĭsĕrĭa, *f*
unhappy mĭser, infēlix
unharmed incŏlŭmis
unhealthiness vălētūdo, *f*; **(of
place, etc.),** grăvĭtas, *f*
unheard (of) ĭnaudītus
unheeded neglectus
unhesitating cofidens
unhindered expēdītus
unhoped for inspērātus
unhorse *v.t*, ĕquo dēĭcĭo (3)
(throw down from a horse)
unicorn mŏnŏcĕros, *m*
uniform *nn*, **(military —),** hăbĭtus
mīlĭtāris, *m*
uniform *adj*, aequābĭlis
unimaginable *use phr*, quod
mente concĭpi non pŏtest **(that
cannot be conceived in the mind)**
unimpaired intĕger
unimportant lĕvis
uninhabitable ĭnhăbĭtābĭlis
uninhabited dēsertus
uninitiated prŏfānus
uninjured incŏlŭmis
unintelligible obscūrus
unintentional non praemĕdĭtātus
uninteresting (flat, insipid) frīgĭdus
uninterruped contĭnŭus
uninvited invŏcātus
union (act of joining) iunctĭo, *f*;
(— of states), cīvĭtātes foedĕrātae,
f.pl; **(agreement),** consensus, *m*

unique ūnĭcus
unit (one) ūnus
unite *v.t*, coniungo (3), consŏcĭo
(1); *v.i*, sē consŏcĭāre (1 *reflex*), sē
coniungĕre (3 *reflex*)
united consŏcĭātus
unity (one) ūnus; **(agreement),**
concordĭa, *f*
universal ūnĭversus
universe mundus, *m*
university ăcădēmia, *f*
unjust ĭniustus
unjustifiable *use phr*, quod
excūsāri non pōtest **(that cannot
be excused)**
unkind ĭnhūmānus
unkindness ĭnhūmānĭtas, *f*
unknowingly *adj*. imprūdens
unknown ignōtus, incognĭtus
unlawful (forbidden) vĕtĭtus
unlearned indoctus
unless *conj*, nĭsi
unletered indoctus, illittĕrātus
unlike dissĭmĭlis *(foll. by dat. or
genit)*
unlikely non vēri sĭmĭlis **(not like
the truth)**
unlimited infīnītus
unload *v.t*, exōnĕro (1); **(goods,
etc.),** expōno (3)
unlock *v.t*, rĕsĕro (1)
unlooked for ĭnexpectātus
unloose *v.t*, solvo (3)
unlucky infēlix
unmanageable impŏtens;
(things), ĭnhābĭlis
unmanly mollis
unmarried caelebs
unmask *v.t*, **(plans, etc.),** ăpĕrĭo
(4)
unmerciful immĭsĕrĭcors
ummindful immĕmor
unmistakable certus
umitigated mĕrus
unmolested intĕger
unmoved immōtus
unnatural monstrŭōsus;
(far-fetched), arcessītus
unnavigable innāvĭgābĭlis
unnecessary non nĕcessărĭus,
sŭpervăcănĕus
unnoticed *use vb*, lătĕo (2) **(to lie
hidden)**

unnumbered innŭmĕrābĭlis
unoccupied (at leisure) ōtĭōsus;
(of land), ăpertus
unoffending innŏcens
unopposed (militarily) *use phr,*
nullo hoste prŏhĭbente **(with no
enemy impending)**
unpack *v.t,* exŏnĕro (1)
unpaid *use* rĕlĭquus **(remaining)**
unparalleled ūnĭcus
unpitied immĭsĕrābĭlis
unpleasant iniūcundus
unpleasantness (trouble)
mŏlestĭa, *f*
unpolished impŏlītus
unpolluted intactus
unpopular invĭdĭōsus
unpopularity invĭdĭa, *f*
unprecedented nŏvus
unprejudiced intĕger
unpremeditated sŭbĭtus
unprepared impărātus
unpretentious hŭmĭlis
unprincipled (good for nothing)
nēquam (*indeclinable*)
unproductive infēcundus
unprofitable non quaestŭōsus
unprotected indēfensus
unprovoked illăcessītus
unpunished impūnītus
unqualified nōn aptus;
(unlimited), infīnītus
unquestionable certus
unravel *v.t,* rĕtexo (3); **(a problem,
etc.),** explĭco (1)
unreasonable ĭnīquus
unrelenting ĭnexōrābĭlis
unremitting assĭdŭus
unreserved līber
unrestrained effrēnātus
unrewarded ĭnhŏnōrātus
unrighteous iniustus
unripe immātūrus
unrivalled praestantissĭmus
unroll *v.t,* ēvolvo (3)
unruffled immōtus
unruly effrēnātus, impŏtens
unsafe intūtus
unsatisfactory nōn aptus
unscrupulous (wicked) mălus
unseal *v.t,* rĕsigno (1)
unseasonable intempestīvus
unseemly indĕcōrus

unseen invīsus
unselfish (persons) innŏcens;
(actions), grātŭītus
unselfishness innŏcentĭa, *f*
unserviceable ĭnūtĭlis
unsettle *v.t,* turbo (1)
unsettled incertus, dŭbĭus
unshaken immōtus
unshaved intonsus
unsheath *v.t,* stringo (3)
unship *v.t,* expōno (3)
unsightly foedus
unskilful impĕrītus
unskilfulness impĕrītĭa, *f*
unslaked (thirst) nōn explētus
unsociable diffĭcĭlis
unsophisticated simplex
unsound (of health or opinions)
infirmus; (of mind), insānus
unsoundness infirmĭtas, *f*,
insānĭtas, *f*
unsparing (severe) sĕvērus;
(lavish), prōdĭgus; (effort, etc.),
non rĕmissus
unspeakable infandus
unspoiled intĕger
unstained pūrus
unsteadiness mōbĭlĭtas, *f*
unsteady instābĭlis, vărĭus
unstring rĕtendo (3)
unsuccessful irrĭtus; (person),
infaustus
unsuitable incommŏdus
unsuitableness incommŏdĭtas, *f*
unsuspected non suspectus
unsuspecting incautus
untameable impŏtens
untamed indŏmĭtus
untaught indoctus
unteachable indŏcĭlis
untenable (position) *use phr,*
quod tĕnēri non pŏtest **(that
cannot be held)**
unthankful ingrātus
unthinking (inconsiderate)
inconsĭdĕrātus
untie *v.t,* solvo (3)
until *conj,* dum, dōnec
until *prep,* ad, (*with acc*)
untilled incultus
untimely *adj,* immātūrus
untiring assĭdŭus
untold (numbers) innŭmĕrābĭlis

untouched intĕger
untried ĭnexpertus
untroubled sēcūrus
untrue falsus
untruth mendācĭum, *n*
unused (of persons) insŏlĭtus;
 (things) intĕger
unusual insŏlĭtus, ĭnūsĭtātus
unutterable infandus
unveil *v.t*, dētĕgo (3)
unwarily *adv*, incautē
unwarlike imbellis
unwarrantable ĭnīquus
unwary incautus
unwavering constans
unwearied indēfessus
unwelcome ingrātus
unwell aeger
unwholesome grăvis
unwieldy ĭnhăbĭlis
unwilling invītus; (to be —), *v.i*,
 nolle (*irreg*)
unwillingly, unwillingness *use adj*,
 invītus (unwilling)
unwind *v.t*, rĕtexo (3), rĕvolvo
 (3)
unwise stultus, imprūdens
unworthiness indignĭtas, *f*
unworthy indignus, immĕrĭtus
unwrap *v.t*, explĭco (1)
unyielding firmus, inflexĭbĭlis
unyoke *v.t*, disiungo (3)
up *prep*, (— stream or hill),
 adversus (*in agreement with
 noun*); (— to), tĕnus (*with abl*)
up *adv*, sursum; (— and down),
 sursum dĕorsum
upbraid *v.t*, obiugo (1)
upbraiding *nn*, exprŏbrātĭo, *f*
uphill *adv. phr*, adverso colle
uphold *v.t*, sustĭnĕo (2)
uplift *v.t*, tollo (3)
upon *prep*, sŭper (*with acc*); (on),
 in (*with abl*)
upper *adj*, sŭpĕrĭor; (to get the —
 hand), sŭpĕrĭor esse (*irreg*)
uppermost *adj*, summus
upright rectus; (of morals),
 prŏbus
uprightness prŏbĭtas, *f*
uproar clāmor, *m*
uproarious tŭmultŭōsus
uproot ēvello (3)

upset *v.t*, ēverto (3)
upset *adj*, mōtus; (troubled),
 anxĭus
upshot exĭtus, *m*
upside down, (to turn —) *use vb*.
 verto (3) (to overturn) *or* miscĕo
 (2) (throw into confusion)
upstart nŏvus hŏmo
upwards *adv*, sursum; (of
 number, — of), amplĭus quam
urbane urbānus
urbanity urbānĭtas, *f*
urchin pūsĭo, *m*
urge *v.t*, urgĕo (2); (persuade),
 suādĕo (2) (*with dat. of person*)
urgency grăvĭtas, *f*
urgent grăvis
urine ūrīna, *f*
urn urna, *f*
us *obj. pron*, nos
usage mos, *m*
use ūsus, *m*; (advantage),
 commŏdum, *n*
use *v.t*, ūtor (3 *dep. with abl*)
useful ūtĭlis
usefulness ūtĭlĭtas, *f*
useless ĭnūtĭlis
uselessness ĭnūtĭlĭtas, *f*
usher in *v.t*, intrōdūco (3)
usual ūsĭtātus, sŏlĭtus
usually *adv*, plērumque, fĕrē
usurer fēnĕrātor, *m*
usurious fēnĕrātōrĭus
usurp *v.t*, occŭpo (1); (seize),
 răpĭo (3)
usury fēnĕrātĭo, *f*, ūsūra, *f*
utensils vāsa, *n.pl*
utility ūtĭlĭtas, *f*
utilize *v.t*, ūtor (3 *dep. with abl*)
utmost extrēmus, summus
utter *adj*, tōtus
utter *v.t*, dīco (3)
utterance dictum, *n*
utterly *adv*, omnīno

V

vacancy (empty post) lŏcus
 văcŭus, *m*
vacant *adj*, văcŭus, ĭnānis
vacate *v.t*, rĕlinquo (3) (a post),
 ēiūro (1)
vacation fērĭae, *f.pl*

vacillate   *v.i*, văcillo (1)
vacillation   văcillătĭo, *f*
vacuum   ĭnāne, *n*
vagabond   erro, *m*
vagabond   *adj*, văgus
vagary   lĭbīdo, *f*
vagrant   *adj*, văgus
vague   incertus
vagueness   obscūrĭtas, *f*
vain   vānus; (boastful, etc.),
   glŏrĭōsus; (in —), *adv*, frustrā
vainglorious   glōrĭōsus
vainglory   glōrĭa, *f*
vale   valles, *f*
valet   cŭbĭcŭlārĭus, *m*
valetudinarian   vălētūdĭnārĭus, *m*
valiant   fortis
valid   firmus, vălĭdus
validity   grăvĭtas, *f*
valise   capsa, *f*
valley   valles, *f*
valorous   fortis
valour   virtus, *f*
valuable   prētĭōsus
valuation   aestĭmātĭo, *f*
value   *nn*, prētĭum, *n*
value   *v.t*, aestĭmo (1); (— highly),
   magni dūco (3) (— little), parvi
   dūco
valueless   vīlis
valve   ĕpistŏmĭum, *n*
van (vanguard)   prīmum agmen, *n*
vanish   *v.i*, vānesco (3), dīlābor (3
   dep)
vanity   vānĭtas, *f*, iactātĭo, *f*
vanquish   *v.t*, vinco (3)
vanquisher   victor, *m*
vantage-point   lŏcus sŭpĕrĭor, *m*
vapid   văpĭdus
vapour   văpor, *m*
variability   mūtābĭlĭtas, *f*
variable   vărĭus, mūtābĭlis
variance   dissensĭo, *f*; (to be at —
   with), dissĭdĕo (2) ab (*with abl*)
variation   vărĭĕtas, *f*
varicose   vărĭcōsus; (a — vein),
   vărix, *c*
variegated   vărĭus
variety   vărĭĕtas, *f*, dīversĭtas, *f*
various   vărĭus, dīversus
varnish   *nn*, ātrāmentum, *n*
vary   *v.i and v.t*, vărĭo (1)
vase   vās, *n*

vassal   clĭens, *m, f*
vast   vastus, ingens
vastness   immensĭtas, *f*
vat   cūpa, *f*
vault   fornix, *m*
vault   *v.i*, sălĭo (4)
vaunt   *v.t*, iacto (1); *v.i*, glŏrĭor (1
   dep)
vaunting   *nn*, iactātĭo, *f*
veal   vĭtūlīna căro, *f*, (calf's flesh)
veer   *v.i*, sē vertĕre (3 *reflex*)
vegetable   hŏlus, *n*
vehemence   vīs, *f*
vehement   vĕhĕmens, ācer
vehicle   vēhĭcŭlum, *n*
veil   *v.t*, vēlo (1), tĕgo (3)
veil   *nn*, rīca, *f*; (bridal —),
   flammĕum, *n*; (disguise),
   intĕgŭmentum, *n*
vein   vēna, *f*
velocity   vēlōcĭtas, *f*
venal   vēnālis
venality   vēnālĭtas, *f*
vendor   vendĭtor, *m*
veneer   *nn, use* cortex, *m*, (bark,
   shell)
venerable   vĕnĕrābĭlis
venerate   *v.t*, cŏlo (3), vĕnĕror (1
   dep)
veneration   cultus, *m*
venereal   vĕnĕrĕus
vengeance   ultĭo, *f*; (to take —),
   ulciscor (3 *dep*)
venial   *use phr*, cui ignosci pŏtest
   (that can be pardoned)
venison   fĕrīna căro, *f*
venom   vēnēnum, *n*
venomous   vĕnēnātus
vent   *nn*, spīrāmentum, *n*
vent   *v.t*, (pour out), effundo (3)
ventilate   *v.t*, ventĭlo (1); (discuss,
   etc.), *use vb*, prōfĕro (*irreg*) (to
   bring out)
ventilator   spīrāmentum, *n*
ventricle   ventrĭcŭlus, *m*
venture   *nn*, (undertaking), rĕs, *f*,
   inceptum, *n*
venture   *v.t*, pĕrīclĭtor (1 *dep*)
venturous   audax
veracious   vērus
veracity   vērĭtas, *f*
veranda   pŏdĭum, *n*
verb   verbum, *n*

verbal *nn, see adv,* **verbally**
verbally per verba **(by means of words)**
verbatim *adv,* tŏtĭdem verbis **(with the same number of words)**
verbose verbōsus
verdant vĭrĭdis
verdict (of a person or jury) sententĭa, *f;* **(of a court),** iūdĭcĭum, *n*
verdigris aerūgo, *f*
verge *nn,* ōra, *f,* margo, *c;* **(on the — of)** *use phr.* minimum abest quin ... **(it is very little wanting that ...)**
verge *v.i,* vergo (3)
verger appārĭtor, *m*
verification prŏbātĭo, *f*
verify *v.t,* prŏbo (1)
veritable vērus
vermilion mĭnĭum, *n*
versatile vărĭus
versatility ăgĭlĭtas, *f*
verse versus, *m*
versed in *adj,* exercĭtātus
versify *v.i,* versus făcĭo (3)
version *use vb,* converto (3) **(turn)**
vertebra vertĕbra, *f*
vertical rectus
vertigo vertīgo, *f*
very *adj, use emphatic pron,* ipse
very *adv, use superlative of adj.* or *adv, e.g.* — **beautiful,** pulcherrĭmus; — **quickly,** cĕlerrĭme; *otherwise* maxĭmē, valdē, admŏdum
vessel (receptable) vās, *n;* **(ship),** nāvis, *f*
vest *nn,* tūnĭca, *f*
vest *v.t,* **(invest, impart),** do (1)
vestal virgin vestālis virgo, *f*
vestibule vestĭbŭlum, *n*
vestige vestīgĭum, *n;* **(mark),** nŏta, *f,* indĭcĭum, *n*
vestry aedĭcŭla, *f*
veteran *adj,* vĕtĕrānus; **(— soldier),** vĕtĕrānus mīles, *m*
veterinary vĕtĕrīnārĭus
veto *nn,* intercessĭo, *f*
veto *v.i,* intercēdo (3) *(with dat)*
vex *v.t,* vexo (1), sollĭcĭto (1)
vexation indignātĭo, *f,* dŏlor, *m*
vexatious mŏlestus

vial lăgēna, *f*
viands cĭbus, *m*
viaticum vĭātĭcum, *n*
vibrate *v.i. and v.t,* vĭbro (1)
vibration ăgĭtātĭo, *f*
vicarious vĭcārĭus
vice turpĭtūdo, *f*
viceroy lēgātos, *m*
vicinity vīcīnĭtas, *f*
vicious vĭtĭōsus; **(fierce),** fĕrus
vicissitude vĭces, *f.pl,* vĭcissĭtūdo, *f*
victim hostĭa, *f,* victĭma, *f*
victor victor, *m,* victrix, *f*
victorious victor
victory victōrĭa, *f*
victual *v.t, use phr,* rem frūmentārĭam prōvĭdĕo (2) **(to look after the supply of provisions)**
victuals cĭbus, *m*
vie with *v.i,* certo (1) cum *(with abl)*
view *nn,* aspectus, *m,* conspectus, *m;* **(opinion),** sententĭa, *f*
view *v.t,* conspĭcĭo (3); **(consider),** *use* sentĭo (4) **(to feel)**
vigil pervĭgĭlātĭo, *f*
vigilance vĭgĭlantĭa, *f*
vigilant vĭgĭlans
vigorous impĭger
vigour vīs, *f,* vĭgor, *m*
vile turpis
vileness turpĭtūdo, *f*
vilify *v.t,* infāmo (1), dētrăho (3)
villa villa, *f*
village pāgus, *m*
villager pāgānus, *m*
villain hŏmo scĕlĕrātus
villainy prāvĭtas, *f,* scĕlus, *n*
vindicate *v.t,* vindĭco (1); **(justify),** purgo (1)
vindication purgātĭo, *f*
vindictive *use phr,* ăvĭdus iniūrĭae ulciscendae **(eager to avenge a wrong)**
vinegrower cultor, *(m)* vītis
vine vītis, *f*
vinegar ăcētum, *n*
vineyard vīnĕa, *f*
vintage *nn,* vindēmĭa, *f*
vintner vīnārĭus, *m*
violate *v.t,* vĭŏlo (1)

violation vĭŏlātĭo, *f*
violator vĭŏlātor, *m*
violence vīs, *f* vĭŏlentĭa, *f*,
   impĕtus, *m*
violent vĭŏlentus, impŏtens
violet *nn*, vĭŏla, *f*
violet *adj* (— colour), ĭanthĭnus
viper vīpĕra, *f*; *adj*, vīpĕrīnus
virago virāgo, *f*
virgin *nn*, virgo, *f*
virgin *adj*, virgĭnālis
virginity virgĭnĭtas, *f*
virile vĭrīlis
virtually *adv* re ipsā
virtue virtus, *f*, hŏnestas, *f*; (by —
   of), *use abl. case of noun alone,
   or use* per (*with acc*)
virtuous hŏnestus
virulent ăcerbus
viscous lentus
visible (noticeable) mănifestus; *or
   use nn.* conspectus, *m* (**view**)
vision visus, *m*; (**phantom,
   apparition**), ĭmāgo, *f*, spĕcĭes, *f*
visionary vānus
visit *nn*, (**call**), sălūtātĭo, *f*; (**stay**),
   commŏrātĭo, *f*
visit *v.t* vīso (3)
visitor sălūtātor, *m*, hospes, *m*
visor buccŭla, *f*
vista prospectus, *m*
visual *use phr. with* ŏcŭlus, *m*,
   (**eye**)
vital vītālis; (**important**), grăvis
vitality vīs, *f*, vīvācĭtas, *f*
vitiate *v.t*, vĭtĭo (1), corrumpo (3)
vitreous vĭtrĕus
vituperation vĭtŭpĕrātĭo, *f*
vituperate *v.t*, vĭtŭpĕro (1)
vivacious ălăcer
vivacity ălăcrĭtas, *f*
vivid vīvus
vivify *v.t*, ănĭmo (1)
vixen vulpes, *f*
vocabulary verba, *n.pl*
vocal vōcālis
vocation offĭcĭum, *n*
vociferate *v.i*, clāmo (1)
vociferous clāmōsus
vociferously *adv*, magno clāmōre
vogue mos, *m*, (**custom**)
voice *nn*, vox, *f*
voice *v.t*, dīco (3)

void *nn*, ĭnāne, *n*
void *adj*, ĭnānis; (— of), văcŭus
   (*with abl*)
volatile lĕvis
volcano mons qui ēructat
   flammas (**a mountain which emits
   flames**)
volition vŏluntas, *f*; (**of his own —**),
   sŭa sponte
volley (of javelins) tēla missa, *n.pl*
volubility vŏlūbĭlĭtas, *f*
voluble vŏlūbĭlis
volume (book) lĭber, *m*; (**of noise**),
   magnĭtūdo, *f*
voluminous cōpĭōsus
voluntarily *adv*, sponte (**of one's
   own accord**) *with appropriate
   pron*, mĕā, tŭā, sŭā
voluntary vŏluntārĭus
volunteer *nn*, mīles vŏluntārĭus,
   m
volunteer *v.i*, (**of soldiers**), *use
   phr*, ultro nōmen dăre (**enlist
   voluntarily**)
voluptuous vŏluptārĭus
voluptuousness luxŭrĭa, *f*
vomit *nn*, vŏmĭtio, *f*
vomit *v.i. and v.t*, vŏmo (3)
voracious ĕdax, vŏrax
voracity ĕdācĭtas, *f*
vortex vertex, *m*
vote *nn*, suffrāgĭum, *n*, sentenĭa, *f*
vote *v.i*, suffrāgĭum fĕro (*irreg*);
   (**to — in favour of**), in sententĭam
   īre (*irreg*) (*with genit*)
voter suffrāgātor, *m*
voting-tablet (ballot paper) tăbella, *f*
vouch for *v.t*, praesto (1), testor
   (1 *dep*), testĭfĭcor (1 *dep*)
voucher (authority) auctōrĭtas, *f*
vow *nn*, vōtum, *n*; (**promise**), fĭdes, *f*
vow *v.t*, prōmitto (3), vŏvĕo (2)
vowel vōcālis littĕra, *f*
voyage *nn*, nāvĭgātĭo, *f*
voyage *v.i*, nāvĭgo (1)
voyager pĕrĕgrīnātor, *m*
vulgar vulgāris, plēbēius,
   sordĭdus
vulgarity (of manner, etc.) *use
   phr*, mōres sordĭdi, *m.pl*
vulgarize *v.t*, pervulgo (1)
vulnerable ăpertus
vulture vultur, *m*

W

wadding *use* lānūgo, *f*, **(woolly down)**

wade *v.i, use phr*, per văda īre *(irreg)* **(to go through the shallows)**

wafer crustŭlum **(pastry)**

waft *v.t*, fĕro *(irreg)*

wag *nn*, **(jester)**, iŏcŭlātor, *m*

wag *v.t*, quasso (1)

wage (war) *v.t*, gĕro (3) (bellum)

wager *nn*, sponsĭo, *f*

wager *v.i*, sponsĭōnem făcĭo (3)

wages merces, *f*

waggish făcētus

waggon plaustrum, *n*

wagtail mōtācilla, *f*

wail, wailing *nn*, plōrātus, *m*, flētus, *m*

wail *v.i*, plōro (1) flĕo (2)

waist mĕdĭum corpus, *n*

waistcoat sŭbūcŭla, *f*, **(undergarment)**

wait *v.i*, mănĕo (2); *v.t*, **(to — for)**, exspecto (1); **(serve)**, fămŭlor (1 *dep.*); **(— in ambush)**, insĭdĭas făcĭo (3) *(with dat)*

wait *nn*, mŏra, *f*

waiter fămŭlus, *m*

waiting exspectātĭo, *f*, mansĭo, *f*

waive *v.t*, rĕmitto (3)

wake *v.t*, excĭto (1); *v.i*, expergiscor (3 *dep.*)

wakeful vĭgil

wakefulness vĭgĭlantĭa, *f*, insomnĭa, *f*

walk *nn*, ambŭlātĭo, *f*; **(gait)**, incessus, *m*; **(— of life, occupation)**, quaestus, *m*

walk *v.i*, ambŭlo (1), grădĭor (3 *dep.*), incēdo (3)

walker pĕdes, *m*

walking *nn*, ambŭlātĭo, *f*

wall mūrus, *m*; **(ramparts)**, moenĭa, *n.pl*; **(inner —)**, părĭes, *m*

wall *v.t*, mūnĭo (4) **(fortify)**

wallet saccŭlus, *m*

wallow *v.i*, vŏlūtor (1 *pass*)

walnut (tree and nut) iūglans, *f*

wan *adj*, pallĭdus

wand virga, *f*, cādūcĕus, *m*

wander *v.i*, erro (1), văgor (1 *dep.*)

wanderer erro, *m*

wandering *nn*, error, *m*

wane *v.i*, dēcresco (3)

want *nn*, **(lack)**, ĭnŏpĭa, *f*, pēnūrĭa, *f*; **(longing for)**, dēsīdērĭum, *n*; **(failing)**, dēfectĭo, *f*; **(in —)**, *adj*, ĭnops

want *v.i*, **(wish)**, vŏlo *(irreg)*; *v.t*, **(to lack)**, cărĕo (2), ĕgĕo (2) *(with abl)*; **(long for)**, dēsīdĕro (1); **(desire)**, cŭpĭo (3)

wanting (to be — , to fail) *v.i*, dēsum *(irreg)*

wanton *adj*, lascīvus, lĭbīdĭnōsus

wantoness lascīvĭa, *f*

war bellum, *n*; **(civil —)**, bellum cĭvīle, *n*; **(in —)**, *adv*, bello; **(to make — on)**, bellum infĕro *(irreg, with dat)*; **(to declare — on)**, bellum indīco (3) *(with dat)*; **(to wage —)**, bellum gĕro (3)

warble *v.i*, căno (3)

warcry clāmor, *m*

ward pūpillus, *m*, pūpilla, *f*; **(district)**, rĕgĭo, *f*

ward off *v.t*, arcĕo (2)

warden cūrātor, *m*

warder custos, *c*

wardrobe vestĭārĭum, *n*

warehouse horrĕum, *n*

wares merx, *f*

warfare mīlĭtĭa, *f*

warily *adv*, cautē

wariness cautĭo, *f*

warlike *adj*, bellĭcōsus, mīlĭtāris

warm călĭdus; **(to be —)**, *v.i*, călĕo (2)

warm *v.t*, călĕfăcĭo (3)

warmly (eagerly) *adv*, vĕhementer

warmth călor, *m*

warn *v.t*, mŏnĕo (2)

warning *nn*, **(act of —)**, mŏnĭtĭo, *f*; **(the warning itself)**, mŏnĭtum, *n*

warp *nn*, stāmen, *n*

warp *v.t*, **(distort of mind, etc.)**, dēprāvo (1)

warrant *nn*, mandātum, *n*; **(authority)**, auctōrĭtas, *f*

warrant *v.t*, **(guarantee)**, firmo (1), praesto (1)

warranty sătisdătĭo, *f*

warren lĕpŏrārĭum, *n*

warrior mīles, c, bellātor, m
wart verrūca, f
wary prōvĭdus, prūdens
wash v.t, lăvo (1); v.i, lăvor (1 pass)
wash, washing nn, lăvātĭo, f
washbasin ăquālis, c
wasp vespa, f
waspish ăcerbus
waste nn, damnum, n; (careless throwing away), effūsĭo, f; (— land), vastĭtas, f
waste adj, vastus, dĕsertus
waste v.t, consūmo (3), perdo (3); (— time), tempus tĕro (3); v.i, (— away), tābesco (3)
wasteful prŏfūsus
wastefulness prŏfūsĭo, f
watch (a — of the night) vĭgĭlĭa, f; (watching on guard), excŭbĭae, f.pl
watch v.t, (observe), specto (1); (guard), custōdĭo (4); v.i, (not to sleep), excŭbo (1)
watchful vĭgĭlans
watchfulness vĭgĭlantĭa, f
watchman custos, m
watchword tessĕra, f
water ăqua, f; (fresh —), ăqua dulcis, f; (salt —), ăqua salsa, f
water v.t, rĭgo (1), irrĭgo (1)
water-carrier ăquārĭus, m
water closet lātrīna, f
water snake hydrus, m
waterfall ăqua dēsĭlĭens, f, (water leaping down)
watering place ăquātĭo, f; (resort), ăquae, f.pl
waterworks ăquaeductus, m
watery ăquātĭcus
wattle crātis, f
wave nn, unda, f, fluctus, m
wave v.i, undo (1), fluctŭo (1); v.t, ăgĭto (1)
waver v.i, fluctŭo (1) dŭbĭto (1)
wavering adj, dŭbĭus
wavering nn, dŭbĭtātĭo, f
wavy (of hair) crispus
wax nn, cēra, f; adj, cērĕus
wax v.i, cresco (3)
way vĭa, f; (journey), ĭter, n; (pathway), sēmĭta, f; (course), cursus, m; (manner), mŏdus, m;

(habit), mos, m; (system), rătĭo, f; (in the —), adj, obvĭus; (in this —), adv, ĭta, sīc; (out of the —) adj, āvĭus; (to give or to make —), v.i, cēdo (3); (to get one's own —), vinco (3)
wayfarer vĭātor, m
waylay v.t, insĭdĭor (1 dep.) (with dat)
wayward pertĭnax
we pron, nos; often expressed by 1st person plural of vb, e.g we are, sumus
weak infirmus, dēbĭlis; (overcome), confectus; (of arguments, etc.), lĕvis
weaken v.t, infirmo (1), dēbĭlĭto (1); v.t, languesco (3), dēfĭcĭo (3)
weak-hearted pŭsilli ănĭmi (of weak heart)
weakness infirmĭtas, f, dēbĭlĭtas, f, lēvĭtas, f
weal (the common) bŏnum pūblĭcum, n; (on skin), vībex, f
wealth dīvĭtĭae, f.pl, ŏpes, f.pl; (large supply), cōpĭa, f
wealthy dīves, lŏcŭples
wean v.t, lacte dēpello (3) (remove from the milk)
weapon tēlum, n; (pl) arma, n.pl
wear v.t, (rub), tĕro (3); (— out), contĕro (3); (— a garment), gĕro (3); v.i, (last), dūro (1)
weariness lassĭtūdo, f
wearisome lăbōrĭōsus
weary adj, fessus, fătīgātus
weary v.t, fătīgo (1); v.i, (grow —), dēfătīgor (1 pass)
weasel mustēla, f
weather nn, tempestas, f
weather v.t, (endure, bear), perfĕro (irreg)
weave v.t, texo (3)
weaver textor, m
web tēla, f
wed v.t, (of the husband), dūco (3); (of the wife), nūbo (3) (with dat)
wedding nn, nuptĭae, f.pl; (— day), dĭes (m) nuptĭārum
wedge nn, cŭnĕus, m
wedlock mātrĭmōnĭum, n
weed nn, herba ĭnūtĭlis, f (harmful plant)

weed *v.t*, runco (1)
week *use phr*, spătĭum septem dĭērum **(a space of seven days)**
weep *v.i*, lăcrĭmo (1)
weeping *nn*, flētus, *m*
weeping willow sălix, *f*
weevil curcŭlĭo, *m*
weigh *v.t*, pendo (3), penso (1), **(consider)**, pondĕro (1); **(— down)**, grăvo (1)
weight pondus, *n*; **(a —)**, lībrămentum, *n*; **(influence, etc.)**, *use adj*. grăvis **(important)**
weightiness grăvĭtas, *f*
weighty grăvis
weir (dam) mōles, *f*
welcome *adj*, grātus, acceptus
welcome *nn*, sălūtātĭo, *f*
welcome! salve! (*pl*. salvēte!)
welcome *v.t*, excĭpĭo (3)
weld *v.t*, ferrūmĭno (1)
welfare bŏnum, *n*, sălus, *f*
well *adv*, bĕnĕ; **(very —)**, optĭmē
well *nn*, pŭtĕus, *m*
well *adj*, **(safe)**, salvus; **(healthy)**, sānus, vălens; **(to be —)**, *v.i*, vălĕo (2)
wellbeing *nn* sălus, *f*
well-born nōbĭlis
well-disposed bĕnĕvŏlus
well-favoured pulcher
well-known nōtus
well-wisher *use adj*, bĕnĕvŏlus **(well-disposed)**
welter *v.i*, vŏlŭtor (1 *pass*)
wench pŭella, *f*
west *nn*, occĭdens, *m*
west *adj*, occĭdentālis
westward *adv*, ad occĭdentem (sōlem)
wet *adj*, hūmĭdus, mădĭdus
wet *v.t*, mădĕfăcĭo (3)
wether vervex, *m*
wet nurse nūtrix, *f*
whale bālaena, *f*
wharf nāvāle, *n*
what *interrog. pron*, quid? *interrog. adj*, qui, quae, quod; *relative pron*, quod, *pl*, quae; **(— for, wherefore, why)**, quārē; **(— sort)**, quālis?
whatever *pron*, quodcumque; *adj*, quīcumque

wheat trītĭcum, *n*
wheel *nn*, rŏta, *f*
wheel *v.t*, circŭmăgo (3)
wheelbarrow păbo, *m*
wheeling *adj*, circumflectens
whelp *nn*, cătŭlus, *m*
when? *interrog*, quando? (*temporal*), cum (*with vb*, in indicative or subjunctive *mood*), ŭbĭ (*vb. in indicative*)
whence *adv*, undĕ
whenever *adv*, quandōcumque
where? *interrog*, ŭbĭ?; (*relative*), quā; **(— from)**, undĕ; **(— to)**, quō; **(anywhere, everywhere)**, *adv*, ŭbīque
whereas *adv*, quŏnĭam
wherever quācumque
wherefore *adv*, quārē
whereupon *use phr*, quo facto **(with which having been done)**
whet *v.t* **(sharpen)**, ăcŭo (3)
whether *conj*. (*in a single question*), num, nĕ; (*in a double question*, **whether ... or**), ŭtrum ... an; (*in a conditional sentence*), sīve ... sīve
whetstone cōs, *f*
whey sĕrum, *n*
which *interrog*, quis, quid; (*relative*), qui, quae, quod; **(which of two)**, ŭter
while *conj*, dum (*often foll. by vb. in present tense indicative*)
while *nn*, tempus, *n*, spătĭum, *n*; **(for a little —)**, *adv*, părumper; **(in a little —)**, brĕvi (tempŏre)
while away *v.t*, fallo (3), tĕro (3)
whim lībīdo, *f*
whimper *v.i*, vāgĭo (4)
whimsical rīdĭcŭlus
whine *v.i*, vāgĭo (4)
whinny *v.i*, hinnĭo (4)
whip *nn*, flăgellum, *n*
whip *v.t*, verbĕro (1), flăgello (1)
whirl *v.t*, torquĕo (2); *v.i*, torquĕor (2 *pass*)
whirlpool *m*, gurges, *m*
whirlwind turbo, *m*
whirr *nn*, strīdor, *m*
whirr *v.i*, strīdĕo (2)
whiskers *use* barba, *f*, **(beard)**
whisper *nn*, sŭsurrus, *m*

whisper *v.i*, sŭsurro (1)
whispering *adj*, sŭsurrus
whistle, whistling *nn*, sībĭlus, *m*
whistle *v.i*, sībĭlo (1)
white *adj*, albus; (shining —),
candĭdus
white *nn*, album, *n*
whiten *v.t*, dĕalbo (1); *v.i*;
albesco (3)
whiteness candor, *m*
whitewash *nn*, albārĭum, *n*; v.t,
dĕalbo (1)
whither (*interrog. and relative*),
quo
whiz *v.i*, strīdĕo (2)
whiz, whizzing *nn*, strīdor, *m*
who *interrog*, quis? (*relative*),
qui, quae
whoever *pron*, quīncunque
whole *adj*, tōtus; (untouched),
intĕger
whole *nn*, tōtum, *n*, ūnĭversĭtas,
f, or use adj, tōtus, *e.g.* the — of
the army, tōtus exercĭtus, *m*
wholesale trader mercātor, *m*
wholesale trading mercātūra, *f*
wholesome sălūbris
wholly *adv*, omnīno
whoop *nn*, ŭlŭlātus, *m*
whom *acc. case of rel. pron*,
quem, quam; *pl*, quos, quas
whore mĕrĕtrix, *f*
whose *genit. case of rel. pron*,
cūius; *pl*, quōrum, quārum
why *adv*, cur, quārē
wick ellychnĭum, *n*
wicked scĕlestus, mălus,
imprŏbus
wickedness scĕlus, *n*, inprŏbĭtas,
f
wicker vīmĭnĕus
wide lātus; (— open), pătens
widen *v.t*, dīlāto (1); *v.i*, sē
dīlātāre (1 *reflex*)
widow vĭdŭa, *f*
widower vĭdŭus vir, *m*
widowhood vĭdŭĭtas, *f*
width lātĭtūdo, *f*
wield *v.t*, tracto (1)
wife uxor, *f*
wig cāpillāmentum, *n*
wild indŏmĭtus, fĕrus;
(uncultivated), incultus; (mad),

āmens
wilderness dēserta lŏca, *n.pl*
wildness fĕrĭtas, *f*
wile dŏlus, *m*
wilful pervĭcax
wilfully *adv*, pervĭcācĭter;
(deliberately), consultō
wilfulness pervĭcācĭa, *f*
wiliness callĭdĭtas, *f*
will (desire) vŏluntas, *f*; (purpose),
consĭlĭum, *n*; (pleasure), lĭbīdo, *f*;
(decision, authority), arbĭtrĭum, *n*;
(legal), testāmentum, *n*
will *v.t*, (bequeath), lēgo (1)
willing *adj*, lĭbens
willingly *adv*, lĭbenter
willingness vŏluntas, *f*
willow sălix, *f*
wily callĭdus, vāfer
win *v.i*, vinco (3); *v.t*, consĕquor
(3 *dep*), ădĭpiscor (3 *dep*)
wind ventus, *m*; (breeze), aura, *f*
wind *v.t*, volvo (3)
winding *nn*, flexus, *m*
winding *adj*, flexŭōsus
windlass sūcŭla, *f*
window fĕnestra, *f*
windward *use phr*, conversus ad
ventum (turned towards the wind)
windy ventōsus
wine vīnum, *n*
wine cask dōlĭum, *n*
wine cellar ăpŏthēca, *f*
wine cup pōcŭlum, *n*
wine merchant vīnārĭus, *m*
wing āla, *f*; (of army, etc.), cornu,
n
winged pennĭger
wink *nn*, nictātĭo, *f*
wink *v.i*, nicto (1); (overlook),
cōnīvĕo (2)
winner victor, *m*
winning *adj*, (of manner), blandus
winnow *v.t*, ventĭlo (1)
winter *nn*, hĭems, *f*
winter *adj*, hĭĕmālis
winter *v.i*, hĭĕmo (1)
wintry hĭĕmālis
wipe *v.t*, tergĕo (2)
wire fīlum, *n*, (thread)
wisdom săpĭentĭa, *f*, prūdentĭa, *f*
wise *adj*, săpĭens, prūdens
wisely *adv*, săpĭenter, prūdenter

wish   *nn,* **(desire),** vŏluntas, *f;* **(the wish itself),** optātum, *n;* **(longing),** dēsĭdĕrĭum, *n*

wish   *v.t,* vŏlo *(irreg),* cŭpĭo (3), opto (1); **(long for),** dēsīdĕro (1)

wishing   *nn,* optātĭo, *f*

wisp   mănĭpŭlus, *m*

wistful   cŭpĭdus **(longing for); (dejected),** tristis

wit   ingĕnĭum, *n;* **(humour),** făcētĭae, *f.pl;* **(out of one's —s),** *adj,* āmens

witch   sāga, *f*

witchcraft   ars măgĭca, *f*

with   *prep,* cum *(with abl, but when denoting the instrument, use abl. case, alone;* **(among, at the house of),** ăpud *(with acc)*

withdraw   *v.i,* cēdo (3), sē rĕcĭpĕre (3 *reflex*); *v.t,* dēdūco (3), rĕmŏvĕo (2)

withdrawal   regressus, *m*

wither   *v.i,* languesco (3); *v.t,* **(parch),** torrĕo (2)

withered   flaccĭdus

withhold   *v.t,* rĕtĭnĕo (2)

within   *adv,* intus

within   *prep,* **(time and space),** intrā *(with acc);* **(time),** *use abl. case alone, e.g.* **within three days,** trĭbus dĭēbus

without   *prep,* sĭne *(with abl);* **(outside of),** extrā *(with acc); when* without *is followed by a gerund (e.g* **I returned without seeing him)** *use a clause introduced by* nĕque, quīn, ĭta ... ut: *e.g.* rĕgressus sum, nĕque ĕum vīdi

without   *adv,* extrā

withstand   *v.t,* rĕsisto (3) *(with dat)*

witness   *nn,* **(person),** testis, *c;* **(testimony),** testĭmōnĭum, *n*

witness   *v.t,* testor (1 *dep*), testĭfĭcor (1 *dep*); **(to see),** vĭdĕo (2)

witticism   făcētĭe, *f.pl*

witty   făcētus; **(sharp),** salsus

wizard   māgus, *m*

woad   vĭtrum, *n*

woe   dŏlor, *m,* luctus, *m*

woeful   tristis

wolf   lŭpus, *m*

wolfish (greedy, rapacious)   răpax

woman   fēmĭna, *f,* mŭlĭer, *f;* **(young —),** pŭella, *f;* **(old —),** ănus, *f*

womanish, womanly   mŭlĭĕbris

womb   ŭtĕrus, *m*

wonder   mīrātĭo, *f;* **(a marvel)** mīrācŭlum, *n*

wonder   *v.i.* and *v.t,* mīror (1 *dep*)

wonderful   mīrus, mīrābĭlis

wont, wonted   *adj,* sŭētus

wont   *nn,* mos, *m*

woo   *v.t,* pĕto (3), ămo (1)

wood (material)   mātĕrĭa, *f;* **(forest),** silva, *f*

wood-collector   lignātor, *m*

wooded   silvestris

wooden   lignĕus

woodland   silvae, *f.pl*

woodpecker   pīcus, *m*

wooer   prŏcus, *m*

wool   lāna, *f*

woollen   lānĕus

word   verbum, *n;* **(promise),** fĭdes, *f;* **(information),** nuntĭus, *m;* **send word,** *v.t,* nuntĭo (1)

wordy   verbōsus

work   *nn,* ŏpus, *n;* **(labour),** lăbor, *m*

work   *v.i,* ŏpĕror (1 *dep*)

work   *v.t,* exercĕo (2); **(handle, manipulate),** tracto (1); **(bring about),** effĭcĭo (3)

worker   ŏpĭfex, *c,* ŏpĕrārĭus, *m*

workman   ŏpĭfex, *c,* ŏpĕrārĭus, *m*

workmanship   ars, *f*

workshop   offĭcīna, *f*

world   mundus, *m,* orbis *(m)* terrārum; **(people),** hŏmĭnes, *c. pl*

worldliness   *use phr,* stŭdĭum rērum prŏfānārum **(fondness for common matters)**

worm   vermis, *m*

worm-eaten   vermĭnōsus

worm (one's way)   *v.i,* sē insĭnŭāre (1 *reflex*)

wormwood   absinthĭum, *n*

worn (— out)   *adj,* trītus; **(as clothes),** gestus

worry   *nn,* anxĭĕtas, *f*

worry   *v.t,* vexo (1); *v.i,* cūrā affĭci (3 *pass*) **(to be affected by worry)**

worse   *adj*, pēior
worse   *adv*, pēius
worship   *v.t*, věněror (1 *dep*), cŏlo (3)
worship   *nn*, věněrātĭo, *f*, cultus, *m*
worshipper   cultor, *m*
worst   *adj*, pessĭmus
worst   *adv*, pessĭmē
worst   *v.t*, vinco (3)
worth   *nn*, (price), prětĭum, *n*; (valuation), aestĭmātĭo, *f*; (worthiness), virtus, *f*, dignĭtas, *f*; (— nothing), nĭhĭli; (to be — much), *v.i*, multum vălĕo (2); (*adj*) dignus
worthiness   dignĭtas, *f*
worthless   vīlis
worthy   (*with noun*), dignus (*with abl*); (*with phr*) dignus qui (ut) (*with vb. in subjunctive*); (man), prŏbus
wound   *nn*, vulnus, *n*
wound   *v.t*, vulnĕro (1), saucĭo (1)
wounded   vulnĕrātus, saucĭus
wrangle   *v.i*, rixor (1 *dep*)
wrangle, wrangling   *nn*, rixa, *f*
wrap   *v.t*, involvo (3)
wrapper   invŏlūcrum, *n*
wrath   īra, *f*
wrathful   īrātus
wreak vengeance on   *v.t*, ulciscor (3 *dep*)
wreath   *nn*, serta, *n. pl*
wreathe   *v.t*, torquĕo (2)
wreck   *nn*, naufrăgĭum, *n*
wreck   *v.t*, frango (3)
wrecked   naufrăgus
wren   rĕgŭlus, *m*
wrench away, wrest   *v.t*, extorquĕo (2)
wrestle   *v.i*, luctor (1 *dep*)
wrestler   luctātor, *m*
wrestling   *nn*, luctātĭo, *f*
wretch   perdĭtus, *m*
wretched   mĭser
wretchedness   mĭsěrĭa, *f*
wriggle   *v.i*, torquĕor (2 *pass*)
wring   *v.t*, torquĕo (2)
wrinkle   rūga, *f*
wrinkled   rūgōsus
wrist   *use* bracchĭum, *n*, (forearm)
writ (legal —)   mandātum, *n*

write   *v.t*, scrībo (3)
writer   scriptor, *m*; (author), auctor, *c*
writhe   *v.i*, torquĕor (2 *pass*)
writing   scriptĭo, *f*; (something written), scriptum, *n*, ŏpus, *n*
wrong   *adj*, falsus; (improper, bad), prāvus; (to be —), *v.i*, erro (1)
wrong   *nn*, nĕfas, *n*, peccātum *n*; (a —), iniūrĭa, *f*
wrongly   *adv*, (badly), măle; (in error), falso
wrong   *v.t*, fraudo (1), iniūrĭam infĕro (*irreg*) (*with dat*)
wrongful   iniustus
wroth   īrātus
wrought   confectus
wry   distortus

Y

yacht   cĕlox, *f*
yard (measurement)   *often* passus, *m*, (5 ft/1.5 m approx.) (court —), ārĕa, *f*
yarn (thread)   fīlum, *n*; (story), fābŭla, *f*
yawn   *nn*, oscĭtātĭo, *f*
yawn   *v.i*, oscĭto (1)
year   annus, *m*; (a half —), sēmestre spătĭum, *n*; (space of six months)
yearly   *adj*, (throughout a year), annŭus; (every year), *adv*, quŏtannis
yearn for   *v.t*, dēsīdĕro (1)
yearning   dēsīdĕrĭum, *n*
yeast   fermentum, *n*
yell   clāmor, *m*, ŭlŭlātus, *m*
yell   *v.i*, magnā vōce clāmo (1)
yellow   flāvus
yellowish   subflāvus
yelp   *v.i*, grannĭo (4)
yelping   *nn*, gannītus, *m*
yeoman   cŏlōnus, *m*
yes   *adv*, ĭta
yesterday   *adv*, hĕri; *nn*, hesternus dĭes, *m*
yet   *adv*, (nevertheless), tămen; (*with comparatives*) ĕtĭam, *e.g.* yet bigger, ĕtĭam māior; (of time; still), ădhuc

yew taxus, *f*
yield *v.i*, cēdo (3) (*with dat*);
(surrender), sē dēděre (3 *reflex*)
yielding *nn*, concessĭo, *f*
yielding *adj*, (soft), mollis
yoke *nn*, iŭgum, *n*
yoke *v.t*, iungo (3)
yoked iŭgālis; (— pair), ĭugum, *n*
yolk vĭtellus, *m*
yonder *adv*, illic
yore *adv*, ōlim (once, in time
past)
you *pron, often not expressed,*
e.g. you come, vĕnis; *pl*, vĕnĭtis;
otherwise use appropriate case of
tu; *pl*, vos
young *adj*, iŭvĕnis, parvus;
(child), infans; (— person),
ădŏlescens
young *nn*, (offspring), partus, *m*
younger iŭnĭor, mĭnor nātu (less
in age)
young man iŭvĕnis, *m*
youngster iŭvĕnis, *c*
your, yours (*singular*), tŭus; (*of*
more than one), vester
yourself (*emphatic*), *use* ipse in
agreement with pron; (*reflexive*),
te; *pl*, vos
youth (time of —) iŭventus, *f*,
ădŏlescentĭa, *f*; (young man),
ădŏlescens, iŭvĕnis, *c*; (body of
young persons), iŭventus, *f*
youthful iŭvĕnīlis

Z

zeal stŭdĭum, *n*
zealous stŭdĭōsus
zenith *use* summus, *adj*, (top of)
zephyr Zĕphўrus, *m*, Făvŏnĭus, *m*
zero (nothing) nĭhil
zest ălăcrĭtas, *f*
zodiac signĭfer orbis, *m*,
(sign-bearing orb)
zone lŏcus, *m*

teach
yourself

latin
gavin betts

- Are you looking for a comprehensive introduction to Latin?
- Or do you have some previous knowledge of the language?
- Do you want to read and enjoy original Latin texts?

Latin is a comprehensive introduction equally suited to complete beginners or those with some knowledge of the language. Each unit introduces new grammar followed by Latin sentences and passages. The clearly structured course introduces original Latin at an early level and, where appropriate, topics of interest for Latin studies. Review exercises and further reading (including examples of medieval Latin) are available on a free website.